Contemporary Plays by Women of Color

Contemporary Plays by Women of Color is a compelling collection of new and recent works by African American, Asian American, Latina American and Native American playwrights. This ground-breaking anthology includes works by well-known and award-winning playwrights, and newly emerging talents. Together these plays represent a stunning array of voices and play styles from women of color.

The works which are included here explore and speak out on issues from the playful to the painful, and show varied approaches to play-making from solo performances to collective creations. The volume also includes an invaluable appendix of published plays by women, biographical notes on each writer and the production history of each play.

Contemporary Plays by Women of Color will be a unique resource for practitioners, students and theater lovers. It will be an inspiring addition to any bookshelf.

Kathy A. Perkins is a lighting designer and Associate Professor of Theater at the University of Illinois (Urbana-Champaign), where she heads the lighting design program. She is the editor of *Black Female Playwrights: An Anthology of Plays Before 1950.*

Roberta Uno is the Artistic Director of the New WORLD Theater and a lecturer in the Department of Theater at the University of Massachusetts at Amherst. She is the editor of *Unbroken Thread: An Anthology of Plays by Asian American Women.*

Contemporary Plays by Women of Color

An Anthology

Edited by Kathy A. Perkins and Roberta Uno

London and New York

First published 1996
by Routledge
11 New Fetter Lane, London EC4P 4EE

Simultaneously published in the USA and Canada
by Routledge
29 West 35th Street, New York, NY 10001

Typeset in Veljovic by Keystroke, Jacaranda Lodge,
Wolverhampton

Printed and bound in Great Britain by
Redwood Books, Trowbridge, Wiltshire

British Library Cataloguing in Publication Data

A catalogue record for this book is available from the
British Library

Library of Congress Cataloging in Publication Data

Contemporary Plays by Women of Color: An Anthology
/ edited by Kathy A. Perkins and Roberta Uno.
    p.   cm.
  Includes bibliographical references.
  1. American drama—Minority authors.   2. Minority
women—United States—Drama.   3. Minorities—United
States—Drama.   4. American drama—Woman authors.
5. American drama—20th century.
I. Perkins, Kathy A.   II. Uno, Roberta.
PS627.M5C66 1966
812'.540809287—dc20   95-7465

ISBN 0-415-11377-6 (hbk)
ISBN 0-415-11378-4 (pbk)

For our mothers
Minerva F. Perkins and Kiku Fukuyama Uno
and in memory of
Alice Childress (1916–1994)

Contents

Acknowledgments

We would like to thank the following individuals for their advice and/or gracious assistance in leading us to some of the works in this anthology: Emilia Cachepero, Anthony Garcia, Hanay Geiogamah, Eric Hayashi, Ron Himes, Fred Ho, Shelby Jiggett, May Joseph, Ricardo Khan, Yuki Nakamura, Jorge Ortol, Deborah Oster Pannell, Sophie Parker, and William Yellow Robe, Jr. For assistance with research and the preparation of this manuscript we would like to thank Lucy Mae San Pablo Burns, Hilary Edwards, Ann Haugo, Terrilynn Mitchell, Sangeeta Rao, Dan Rivera, and Nadine Warner. We would also like to express our appreciation of the support we have received for this project from Dean Lee Edwards and Dr. Frederick Tillis of the University of Massachusetts at Amherst; Yvonne Mendez and the staff of the New WORLD Theater; David Knight, and Joseph Smith of the University of Illinois; and the University of Illinois Research Board. We also thank our editors, Talia Rodgers and Sarah-Jane Woolley for their patience, encouragement, and good humor. Finally for their unwavering personal support we thank Merle Bowen, Elinor Bowles, Jim Cyress, Nancy M. Davis, Tracy Davis, Tim Daz, Rita Disroe, Suzanne Dougan, Riki Hing, Velina Houston, Tulani Jordan and Stan Kinard, Ed and Kay Kaneko, Emma Kaplan, Aquila Ayana McCants, Mariko Miho, Nobuko Miyamoto, Linda Perkins, Marion Perkins, Sr., Minoca Pinto, Norma Rivera Diaz, the Soman-Faulkner family, Chinua and Mikiko Thelwell, Ernest and Grace Uno, Josie Camacho and Victor Uno, Roger and Teresa Uno, and San San Wong.

Thanks and praises to the spirits of those who continue to guide us: Hazel Bryant, Louise Evans Briggs-Hall, Sidney Kaplan, Aichi Kochiyama Duncan, Patti O'Neal, Freda Page, Yvonne Adel John, and Atanasio Camacho Uno.

Introduction

Kathy A. Perkins and Roberta Uno

Kathy A. Perkins

Roberta Uno

Photos: © Rick Newton

In the tradition of cultural workers before us, this generation of women of color will . . . define the ground we walk on and bring our creative forms into the light. We will sometimes complain, and protest, and wear on the nerves, but we will not return to the dark.   *Marsha Jackson*

In 1984, when we first collaborated on the premiere of a musical entitled *Gullah!*, written and directed by the late Alice Childress, Kathy Perkins and I began the work that has resulted in this anthology and an ongoing series of research, archival, and production projects. At that time, Kathy was four years into her first teaching appointment as an instructor at Smith College, and I was (and continue to be) the artistic director of the then five-years-old New WORLD Theater and a lecturer at the University of Massachusetts. Kathy designed the lighting for the production and I produced it; although we were immediately caught up in the intense madness of production and rehearsal, an unspoken bond was established. We recognized in each other a counterpart – another woman, a woman of color, a working artist, a teacher, an artist/teacher trying to thrive in an academic environment. We instinctively knew several things about each other: that the other was most likely the only person of color in her academic department; that she had paid some dues to have whatever respect she merited to be there; that she was making her presence and the presence of our communities of color known through the work she put on the stage. Unspoken in our minds were the ques-tions: "How long will she be around? Is she just passing through? Will she get chewed up and spat out by the academic tenure system? Will she not be able to do the work that really matters to her and leave?" As young women of color entering the academy, a place at once familiar and entirely foreign, we shared a sense that we were not really supposed to be there – or that if we were, we were to remain at the periphery, adding a little color to the photograph, but certainly not shifting the point of focus. What we recognized most strongly in the other was a sister subversive; someone bringing whole new pictures into focus; and the images developing before our eyes were stunning in their variety, clarity, and beauty – and they were all in living color.

1

KP

Becoming women of color in the theater

Understand What? That there are other eyes besides the ones we're used to looking through. That there are other ways to see the world and talk about it and walk through it and become one with the parts of it, that feel as familiar as your own right hand.

Pearl Cleage

I grew up in Alabama during one of the most volatile periods in American history – the Civil Rights movement of the 1960s. During this period the African American community was extremely close-knit. We had to be because our community was constantly in crisis. From an early age, Jim Crow, or segregation, made you acutely aware that the world was only black and white. While I knew that other people existed who were neither black nor white, I simply never thought about these individuals because they seemed so far removed from the world in which I lived. Segregation had a way of shutting you off from the rest of the world. In my home-town of Mobile, I can remember only one Chinese family, and they owned a cleaners. Needless to say, they fit the pervasive stereotype that all Asians were in the laundry business. I was aware that there were some Native American reservations in my area of the South, but had never been exposed to any full-blooded Native people. There were many blacks in my community who had Native ancestors, including my mother's family, but they were considered black (the one-drop theory). Hispanic or Latino was not a part of my vocabulary. Since Mobile was a major seaport town during my early years, I would often see men of color coming from the ships, but had no contact with them. Even when I entered a predominantly white high school, my world was still black and white. I cannot recall much discussion of other people of color during my secondary education or of their existence in my text books.

Theater has always been a major part of my life. When I speak of theater, I mean theater in the total sense – singing, dancing, poetry, storytelling, and of course acting as we know of it in the European tradition. In addition to entertainment, theater has always been a vehicle for informing, inspiring, and moving people to action in the African American community. This was clearly evident during the Civil Rights movement. The movement was about moving people to change situations around us and theater was a powerful tool for accomplishing this goal. Going to movement meetings meant singing songs about and for empowerment. These meetings also entailed listening to stories about where we had been, where we were, and where we needed to be. Church was theater. Listening to the older people talk about our ances-tors, slavery, and the early years in the South was a theater that instilled pride in the younger ones. Playing piano duets with my older sister for church and cultural functions was another type of theater.

I left Mobile for Howard University in the 1970s as a theater major at the height of the Black Theater movement. This was an exciting time to be at Howard and in Washington, D.C. It was a period when the D.C. Black Repertory Theater was in full swing, and new plays about the African American experience were being performed on campus. Ntozake Shange's for colored girls who have considered suicide when the rainbow is enuf had just taken Broadway by storm. Numerous black stars graced our department and shared their experiences. At Howard I learned that blacks lived throughout the world. It was exciting to meet blacks from

Brazil, England, Canada, the West Indies, and from countries throughout Africa. Even when I entered the University of Michigan for graduate school in design, I was still very much a part of a campus black theater group and other black organizations. My world was still black and white.

In 1979, I was offered a job at Smith College as the instructor of lighting. This was a period of culture shock and cultural awakening. Having to be in a position of authority over young white women at a prestigious school meant constantly having to prove myself as an African American woman to my colleagues and often feeling out of place. It was also during this time that I had to consider not just white women, but also other women of color. Coming from a black and white existence, this was a totally new experience for me. I was quite ignorant about the history of other people of color in this country. I was amazed by my ignorance, and by ignorance I mean lack of knowledge. I must admit my surprise and uneasiness when several of my Asian and some Latina students would drop by my office to discuss racial issues and/or racism. I was always thinking in the back of my mind, why are they telling me this and what do we have in common? Am I to deal with these new people as black or white? Should I trust them? I was often taken aback when they told me that I was their role model, because for me role models had to be of the same race.

Within only a few months, these young women opened my eyes to other parts of America. They made me aware of groups other than people of African descent, who were also treated as outsiders and inferiors. Because I was experiencing the same type of alienation that many of the women of color were, a special closeness developed between us. Working with the New WORLD Theater was also instrumental to my cultural awakening because I was introduced to many new works by people of color.

After six years at Smith, I relocated to Los Angeles. Living in Los Angeles really opened my eyes to the diversity of our world. While working in the mid-1980s as a resident lighting designer for the Los Angeles Theater Center and as a lighting assistant at the theater of the Japan American Cultural Center, I was exposed to a variety of artists of color, not only from America but from around the world. In Los Angeles, I realized that our country was rapidly moving toward a multi-ethnic nation, and the term "black and white" no longer depicted the American social reality. I began to carefully examine the various terms that had been thrust upon people of color to keep us second-class citizens; such as "minority", "sub-culture", "marginal", "ethnically specific" and "other" to name a few. When I really looked at these words, they implied minor, insignificant, inferior, below, beneath, and outsider. I felt that as people of color, we should part with such derogatory terms.

It was also during this period in Los Angeles that I realized the danger of the media and its perpetuation of stereotypes. I discovered that I believed much that I saw on TV, the stage, and at the movies. All Asians were exotic, and because of World War II and Vietnam, they were the enemy and not to be trusted. Native people and Mexicans were obstacles to America's progress and needed to be exterminated so that the good guys like John Wayne could ride off into the sunset and get on with the business of the day. I realized that the same medium – TV, film, and stage – that created and perpetuates stereotypes would have to eradicate them. This is the type of theater that I want to be a part of.

3

I am a yellow pearl
And you are a yellow pearl
And we are the yellow pearl
And we are half the world
  Nobuko Miyamoto and Chris Ijima

As an Asian American woman, born in Hawaii, and raised in Los Angeles,
I had never been a "minority" until I came east for college. The first few
times college professors asked me my opinion as a "minority," I was
shocked. I thought, "Where did they get their degrees from? Don't they
realize over half the world is Asian? Didn't anyone ever tell them that I,
as a woman of Asian descent, am a member of *the* majority?"

My theater education denied the experience of theater I had had
growing up. As a child, in Los Angeles, I saw Noh and Kyogen theater
performed in church basements and I saw the early work of the East
West Players, which, under the leadership of actor/director Mako, was
producing plays written by Asian Americans. I was a beneficiary of the
post-Watts Riots war on poverty programs, which funded C. Bernard
Jackson's visionary Inner City Cultural Center where I saw racially diverse
casting long before the terms "multiculturalism" and "non-traditional
casting" were coined, appropriated, and exploited. During the two years
that I worked as a high school organizer for the United Farm Workers
union, I saw teatro performances in makeshift union halls and on the
strike line.

And, as a scholarship student at a college preparatory high school, I
also learned to buy a student season ticket to the Mark Taper Forum.
(Years later my best friend who grew up in the South Bronx would tell
me of a similar experience in her gifted class in public school. She was
taught the "proper" way to read the *New York Times*.) There I saw
performances such as Colleen Dewhurst in *Moon for the Misbegotten*,
Charlton Heston in *The Crucible*, and Peter Brook's *Midsummer's Night's
Dream*.

I learned a lot from these experiences and made some early observa-
tions. First, I discovered that theater was being created in many different
places, in many different ways, and by many different people. Not having
access to a formal theater space did not seem to stop anyone from
making theater. Second, I found out that the arts world was segregated;
the more money I had to pay for my ticket and the more lavish the
theater, the more likely the audience was exclusively or predominantly
white. And third, only the theater that took place in formal theater
spaces, with their segregated audiences, was discussed in school; the
theater I found most compelling and meaningful was not part of the
official record. It was as if there was an entire parallel world that was
invisible, which ceased to exist when I opened a book or a newspaper.

In college I began to develop a consciousness which tied race to class
and gender politics. I became close to other students of color, who were
also financial aid students, when we would find ourselves stranded on
campus during vacation breaks, while other students were "doing
Greece" or the Caribbean, or Mexico, or Europe. As a freshman I was
impressed and somewhat intimidated by what I perceived as the extraor-
dinary number of gifted students I was meeting. Everyone I met was a
dancer or poet or painter or actor. I remember my growing anger as I
attended their readings, art openings, dance concerts, and plays. Not

RU

that some of the students weren't genuinely talented – but that I knew so many youth from Los Angeles who were equally or infinitely more talented, but who would never call themselves artists. And they certainly never had the opportunity to develop their talents. Again, I begin to view race in terms of an enormous class divide.

In 1979, with the assistance of three undergraduate students, I founded the New WORLD Theater at the University of Massachusetts at Amherst. Today, we have a mixed professional and student staff; we purposely blur the lines between professional and community, art and politics, scholarship and activism. A first-voice theater of artists of color, New WORLD presents and produces works by black, Latina, Asian, and Native American playwrights. We never consciously defined ourselves as a feminist theater, but from our first season the majority of our staff have been women, as have the authors and artistic staff of the plays we produce.

The New WORLD theater was my response to three years of culture shock from living, while attending college, in New England. It was my assertion of the realities that I knew; my stubborn in-your-face resistance to eating food that tasted bland and tolerating art that seemed devoid of passion and social relevance. Over a hundred productions later, I have seen my reality overtake the sterile New England environment I once encountered. I see it at the supermarket where now I can buy tofu, daikon, kamaboko, and gyoza wrappers (imagine I used to bring Japanese rice in my suitcase from California!). But more importantly I see it in the supermarket aisles where every fifth person is dark or has my eyes or is speaking a language other than English. As Shauneille Perry notes, "something really quite wonderful is happening, I call it the "Browning of America."[1] When we started the New WORLD Theater in 1979, we were working towards a vision, to borrow from the Nina Simone song, of "a new world comin'." In 1995, from where I sit in the theater – that world is here.

KP

Looking back to find the present

I write with a sense of my ancestors at my back, they're right behind me. I have a voice and a lot of that voice is connected to a collective past; because that line is unbroken, I am who I am.

Victoria Nalani Kneubuhl

I never intended to become a historian. It was an incident that occurred on my first day of graduate school, at the University of Michigan, that set things into motion. While looking for the orientation meeting for MFA design and technical students, I asked a young white male for directions. He immediately told me that the actors were meeting in another room. When I clearly explained to him that I was a design major and not an actress, he indicated that he was completely unaware of blacks working in areas other than performance. I told him that in D.C., where I recently came from, many blacks worked behind the scenes. He replied "you would never know by reading any theater history text." That evening, I

1 Perry, Shauneill, "Celebrating the Tenth Anniversary of New WORLD Theater" *MELUS* Vol. 16, No. 3, Fall 1989–90, p. 6.

KP

went to the library and examined every theater history book I could find. He was right! According to our theater historians, blacks behind the scenes just didn't exist, except for those I saw in Loften Mitchell's *Black Drama*. That young man I asked for directions, in a sense directed me to research. He was the first of many whites and some blacks who would see me as an anomaly in the theater.

It was shortly after leaving Michigan that I began conducting research on African American designers and other individuals working behind the scenes. Not only did I know we were out there, but I was also convinced that we had always been there. African Americans have had an extensive history in theater in this country, not only as designers but also as producers and playwrights and in other areas behind the scenes since the nineteenth century.[2] Learning about the history and achievements of these men and women has given me an unparalleled sense of pride, as well as an understanding of my place in the world.

As I was presented with opportunities to design for other cultural groups, I felt compelled to conduct more research on the various cultures to become a better designer. At the University of Illinois, I teach a course on multi-ethnic theater. I developed the course primarily out of the frustration of seeing many white designers design plays by people of color without understanding the culture of the text. Many of these designers would perpetuate stereotypes in their concept of scenery and/or costumes. In many cases, it was evident that the designer did not understand the cultural context of the play. I became determined not to allow my students to leave the program without some basic knowledge of the larger theater world.

What started out as a design course for my lighting students has evolved into a history course. Ironically, this was at the request of my students. Although our starting point was design, they were more interested in reading about the cultures, seeing videos of various productions and documentaries, reading plays and spending more time discussing differences between cultures, having people of the various cultures come and guest lecture, and so on. We also spent time discussing the issue of race, particularly when examining works by people of color in America. I found it necessary to develop a common vocabulary for a course of this nature. Now we explore such terms as racism, prejudice, ethnicity, culture, and sexism. Through looking at the plays they become aware of such issues as the enslavement of blacks, the removal of Native Americans to reservations, the singling out of Chinese for exclusion, and the placement of Japanese Americans in concentration camps. They also become aware that being American refers to more than just Caucasians.

The course has, in essence, become a look at the history of people of color throughout various parts of the world, as well as in the United States through theater. When teaching my multi-ethnic course or my class on African American women, students of both genders, and various ethnic and racial groups express their frustration, as well as outrage, for not having been taught a more encompassing history of America in

2 My research on African American stage designers has culminated, in part, in an exhibition at the New York Public Library at Lincoln Center featuring over fifty African American designers for the American theater since the turn of the century. *Black Female Playwrights: An Anthology of Plays Before 1950*, which I edited in 1989, was an attempt to remedy the fallacy that African American women produced very little during the first part of this century.

KP

school. Most of the students admit that upon finishing the course, they have a different perspective of what theater means and a greater appreciation and understanding of other cultures. They have a more global view of the world. My main observation has been that white students are less prone to take on a superior attitude when they are aware of the accomplishments of other cultures. For students of color, particularly many African Americans, who are often as ignorant as whites about achievements by people of African descent, a sense of pride emerges.

RU

Remember the voice of your people's gods
Ling-Ai Li

Like Kathy, I began research in theater history by accident. As a theater director I had no formal training as an historian, but as an Asian American theater artist I was reluctant to subscribe to the widely-held myth that Asian Americans had not started writing for the theater until the 1970s. Certainly Asian American culture blossomed as a result of the Civil Rights and anti-Viet Nam War movements. However, I often wondered why we, as people with such strong traditions of popular and classical theater, would have to wait nearly 150 years to see evidence of an engagement of dramatic literature in America. I certainly understood that Asian American writing for the theater emerged later than our poetry and fiction because of the added dimension of theatrical production; but I couldn't understand why Asian immigrants, who carried with them both the tradition and reverence of written language and the practice and culture of theatrical performance, could arrive in this country and suddenly become mute and unexpressive, waiting, as we are led to believe, for their children's children to pick up a pen and compose a play.

As a director of contemporary theater, I began to find myself looking back; it became imperative to find out who had gone before me and my age set, to understand, as Anna Julia Cooper stated, "when and where I enter." I felt the assumption that ours was a "new" literature and corresponded all too neatly with the xenophobic notion that Asian Americans are perpetual foreigners in our own country, that we have no right to ownership, that we are the exotic, the other. I also identified with the few Asian American women in theater I met, who in the absence of a legacy, expressed the isolation they felt, each reinventing her own wheel.

The research of Hawaii-based writers and scholars, specifically Eric Chock, Arnold Hiura, Darryl Lum, and Steven Sumida, led me to writing by Asian American women for the theater beginning as early as the 1920s. I was thrilled to learn that some of these pioneers are still alive and was able to correspond with and interview them, adding their statements to a growing archive of over two hundred works by Asian American women playwrights.[3] I learned from Asian American women who

3 The appendix to *Unbroken Thread: An Anthology of Plays by Asian American Women* (Amherst: University of Massachusetts Press, 1993) lists some two hundred plays by Asian American women writers, most of which are in archives at the University of Massachusetts library under the Roberta Uno Asian American Women Playwrights' Script Collection 1924–present. The archive also contains playbills, photographs, interviews, and production histories. Other archives which include Asian American women playwrights can be found in the University of Hawaii's Hawaiian-Pacific Collections and the University of California at Los Angeles archives of the East West Players.

wrote in the 1920s and 1930s of their inspiration for writing for theater, their love of their art, their experiments with form – and their discouragement when their plays were rejected for production because the language they were forging deviated from standard English or because their works refused to conform to stereotypical themes and images.

Ling-Ai Li, who wrote under her American name of Gladys Li, is possibly the earliest published Asian American woman playwright, spoke of Caucasian teachers who were stunned that she would have the audacity to write plays as an "Oriental" woman in the 1920s. Today in her nineties Li is still a working writer, living in New York City. But she abandoned her dream of writing for the theater early on, discovering upon her arrival in New York:

> No one was interested . . . an Oriental had no chance . . . I could have written better plays and bigger plays [but] when I got to New York I met all those theater people and I found out that there's no place for a Chinese. . . . I went to their teas and conferences and they were interested to talk to me, but there was no place for me or any Chinese unless you did one of those "Chin Chin Chinaman Chinatown, my Chinatown" kind of plays.
>
> *(Li interview 26 December 1993)*

Listening to the experiences of these early writers was very moving for me; their words document the courageous efforts of Asian American women who attempted to break the bonds of gender, race, and class in a society which had rendered them silent and invisible. Each labored in isolation, inventing dialogue that would not be spoken, as they faced elements of the same oppression that today prevents women playwrights of color from receiving the attention and support they deserve. Encountering their body of written work, and their keen minds and generous, fighting spirits connected a vital lifeline for me, creating not only a cultural continuum, but a sense that our isolation can no longer be enforced once we know about each other's work and struggles.

Reclaiming the hidden voice

> It is important to dig up our grandmother's voices and speak for them. We are speaking for those people who didn't have a voice.
>
> Hortensia and Elvira Colorado

Since Roberta and I both are teaching similar courses at our respective institutions, we found ourselves constantly looking for new plays, documentaries, articles, and other sources in addition to exchanging materials. At a theater conference in 1991, we began talking about compiling this anthology, since there was none available that contained in a single volume contemporary plays by women of color. Within the last three to four years there have been a handful of exciting publications that focus exclusively on contemporary works by women of color, but by racial and cultural division. Some of these include Velina H. Houston's The Politics of Life: Four Plays by Asian American Women, *Linda Feyder and Denise Chavez's* Shattering the Myth: Plays by Hispanic Women; *Sydne Mahone's* Moon Marked and Touched by Sun, *and Roberta Uno's* Unbroken Thread: An Anthology of Plays by Asian American Women.

KP

While there are other works by women of color in single-author publications or contained in various anthologies that include both male and female writers, the number of publications is small in comparison to the immense volume of work being created. When we began this project we were astounded by the number, variety and quality of scripts we read. Among the many exciting and powerful works we were unable to include because of the length of the volume were plays by Sheri Bailey, Laurie Carlos, Faye Chiang, Eugenie Chan, Joanna Chan, Judith Jackson, Teresa Chavez, Oni Faida-Lampley, Jude Narita, Cherylene Lee, Valletta Anderson, Silvia Gonzalez S., Marina Feleo-Gonzales, Amy Hill, Wakako Yamauchi, Jake-ann Jones, Rhodessa Jones, Lisa Loomer, Diana Saenz, Regina Taylor, Robbie McCauley, Karen Jones Meadows, Monique Mojica, Nobuko Miyamoto, Victoria Kneubuhl, Regina Porter, Marian Warrington, P.J. Gibson, Delores Prida, Linda Faigao Hall, Jessica Hagedorn, Suzan Lori Parks, Shay Youngblood, Jeannie Barroga, Velina Hasu Houston, Genny Lim, Lynn Martin, Lynn Nottage, Edit Villarreal, Josefina Lopez, Endesha Ida Mae Holland, Aisha Rahman, Yolanda Rodriguez, Dael Orlander Smith, Caridad Svich, Natasha Terry, Alice Tuan, Denise Uyehara, and Ermina Vinluan – to name a few. These are women who are breaking traditional boundaries in writing and engaging difficult themes with originality and integrity. It is our hope that the bibliography which concludes this volume will lead readers to the growing body of published dramatic literature by women of color and that anthologies such as this will lead to greater publishing opportunities for the many talented writers waiting to be read and produced.

Despite the number of women of color writing for the theater, resisting invisibility remains our greatest battle. Our invisibility is also perpetuated by the negligible number of plays by women of color that are produced at our "anchor" institutions, i.e. the American regional theaters. The October 1993 issue of American Theatre magazine listed 223 regional theaters along with their 1993–94 season. Of over 1,300 plays listed, fewer than fifty-five were by women of color, of which forty percent were written by five writers, productions of proven success by theaters unwilling to take risks.

Despite these obstacles of perception and opportunity, plays by women of color are slowly making their way into publication and onto the stage. Currently, such scholars as Linda Kerr Norflett are preparing anthologies on playwrights of color. Vital newsletters, such as Beth Turner's Black Masks and Paul Rathbun's Native Playwrights Newsletter, keep us abreast of what is happening in the theater communities of color. Women of color artistic directors of first-voice cultural institutions, such as Miriam Colon of the Puerto Rican Traveling Theater, Pearl Cleage of Just Us Theater, Roberta Uno of New WORLD Theater, Marsha Jackson of Jomandi Theater, Amy Gonzales of El Teatro Campesino, and Nobuko Miyamoto of Great Leap, have consistently cultivated new plays by women of color. As have a small but determined number of theater groups which provide important outlets for works specifically for women of color, including Imelda Hunt's New Works Writers Series in Toledo, Ohio; The Medea Project of Cultural Odyssey in San Francisco; Root Women of Austin, Texas; Sangoma, under the direction of Sydne Mahon at Crossroads Theatre in New Brunswick, New Jersey; El Centro Su Teatro of Denver's Latina Lab; Luna Rising in San Francisco; The Towne Street Theater in Los Angeles, headed by Nancy Cheryll Davis and Nancy

KP

Renee; and the Latina Theater Lab of Brava! For Women in the Arts in San Francisco. And women of color persist in making their presence known through productions in theaters and venues who exist to challenge the artistic "mainstream," such as Franklin Furnace, Theatre for the New City, PS 122, and La Mama ETC of New York City; Highways of Santa Monica, California; and Josie's Cabaret in San Francisco. Despite the odds, women of color are carving out their own spaces in the American theater, refusing to endure the silent scream of invisibility.

RU

About the plays

From this day forth, I will be concerned not with acts, and scenes and curtains; but with redemption, retrieval, and reclamation. The chair in which I sit will no longer be called the director's chair, but the blood-bought mercy seat. From that seat, my work will be a mission, my goal will be a miracle.

Glenda Dickerson

In selecting this collection of eighteen excerpted, one-act, and full-length plays, we were compelled not only to look at what was missing from our students' and our own educations, but to examine our own sense of feminism as it applied to the aesthetics and practice of our artistic work. For us, feminism has been an unexpressed and constant fact of our lives as women of color, but we have ironically found ourselves periodically at odds with some of its proponents, who skirting racism, have imposed their ideas on us. Too many times we have heard the claim, "I know what it's like to be black (Asian, Latina, Native American) because I'm a woman." Often we have observed the white feminist who will import a woman of color from out of state as a guest artist, lecturer, or consultant, rather than to work with the women of color in her own community, or we have been silenced by the white feminist who has "inadvertently" written us out of history because we have not taken or made the time to write our own stories. Of course there are white feminists we both have learned from, been inspired by, and have worked in alliance with, but our experience has taught us the lesson Ida B. Wells noted long ago, that we cannot rely on others to carry the banner for us. In examining our evolving feminism, we continuously return to the expression of theory in practice, asking questions such as: Who is in the leadership of a given project? How are decisions made? Is there a centrality of women's experience, women's voice in the play? Is there a root culture or an evolving cultural sensibility that informs and shapes the piece? How do we position ourselves in relation to the work in order to best support and understand the playwright's voice?

Thus, there is no single theoretical or aesthetic framework, feminist or otherwise, with which we approached this project. Long ago at New WORLD Theater, we recognized the danger and impossibility of being a theater of artists of color if we did not respect cultural autonomy – otherwise our work might become a muddied palate or a hollow new-age minstrel show. The plays of this volume are diverse in their aesthetics, structures, and themes; yet there are points of intersection and refraction that unintentionally emerge as dialogue, as refrain, as a response to a call. Their collective presentation is an invitation to the reader to seek both parallels and differences, to confront the flash points where perceptions collide and to look deeply into and through the mirrors and windows where mutuality of experience exists.

Although these works can be viewed in many different ways, we were struck by the recurrence of certain themes: violence against women, response to media and historical stereotypical images, identity formation, the impact of poverty on individuals, families, and communities; the relationship of woman to her body, the relationship of women to each other, the response of a given community to crisis. The plays present varying approaches to playmaking, including solo performance and collective creation.

Twilight: Los Angeles, 1992, The Queen's Garden, 1992 Blood Speaks, and *Heroes and Saints* all look at communities at a crisis point, a shattering place facing an irreversible moment in history, the impact of which forever alters the community and each individual. Brenda Wong Aoki's *The Queen's Garden* and Anna Deavere Smith's *Twilight: Los Angeles, 1992* were both written as solo performance pieces. The former zeroes in on a narrow section of urban terrain, Long Beach's West Side, tracing a love story that spirals out of control, paralleling the disintegration of a neighborhood lost to gun violence and drug wars. In contrast *Twilight: Los Angeles, 1992* courses over the sprawling landscape of the 1992 Los Angeles uprising, weaving like a seismically fractured freeway through socially disparate neighborhoods, juxtaposing polarized attitudes, which are inevitably linked. Through solo performance Aoki and Smith become the mediums through which multiple character voices speak, providing a spectrum analysis of a society in crisis.

Hortensia and Elvira Colorado's *1992 Blood Speaks* identifies the moment of Columbus' mythical "discovery" of the Americas as the turning point for Native people; their satiric deconstruction of history's lies is framed by spirituality and healing that celebrate the spirit of survival. In Cherríe Moraga's *Heroes and Saints*, crisis is faced by a Chicano farmworker community whose children are dying, victims of the indiscriminate and ruthless use of carcinogenic pesticides. Moraga confronts racism and California's multi-billion dollar agribusiness on the most intimate level, the female body; the story revolves around a young Chicana born so severely deformed, that she is little more than a human head.

Re/membering Aunt Jemima: A Menstrual Show, R.A.W. ('Cause I'm a Woman), China Doll, and *Combination Skin* deal to varying degrees with the deconstruction of stereotypes. Breena Clarke and Glenda Dickerson tackle the mythic figure of Aunt Jemima, simultaneously dismembering and reconstructing the infamous icon, while shamelessly subverting some of America's dearest and most racist myths regarding black women. In *China Doll* Elizabeth Wong exposes the racism of the film industry as silent screen star Anna Mae Wong, barred from playing lead roles, is forced to teach a Caucasian actress how to play an adhesive-tape oriental. Diana Son's *R.A.W. (Raunchy Asian Women)* juxtaposes the attitudes of flesh-and-blood Asian women against prevailing notions that present them as exotic and submissive sexual commodities. In *Combination Skin* Lisa Jones exploits the format of a television game show to demolish the historical phantasm of the tragic mulatto; simultaneously she derides and dissects the taboo of miscegenation and contemporary passing games.

Sun, Moon, and Feather, Marga Gomez's excerpted trilogy, and *Weebjob* comment upon the formation and re-formation of identity, a previously uncharted journey of the character and spirit. Gomez's excerpted autobiographical trilogy includes *Marga Gomez is Pretty Witty & Gay*, a comic exploration of her lesbian identity. The play is set on the eve of her appearance on a nationally broadcast talk show, or as she refers to it "lesbian jury duty." The companion pieces, *Memory Tricks* and *A Line Around the Block*, respectively inspired by Gomez's eccentric and talented parents, "Marga the Exotic" Estremera, an exotic dancer, and stand-up comedian Willy Chevalier, pay tribute not only to her parents, but to the 1950s' golden era of Latin show business in New York. *Sun Moon and Feather* is the collective creation of the Native American feminist troupe Spiderwoman Theater, whose members Gloria Miguel, Muriel Miguel, and Lisa Mayo are sisters of Cuna-Rapahanock Indian heritage. The play follows their intertwined relation-ship through their childhood in Brooklyn, their lives as children whose parents made a living running a medicine show, and their unconventional career as performers. In contrast to the Gomez and Spiderwoman pieces, Diane Glancy's *Weebjob* departs from autobiographical source. The main character of her semi-mythical odyssey is a young woman who cannot resist hitchhiking; her act of flight leads her full circle to her place of origin and true discovery.

Poverty encircles the lives and choices of the women in *Come Down Burning, The Have-Little*, and *Inter-tribal*. Rape, abuse, self-abortion, and the decision to bear children in the face of deprivation, are major issues which surface in the three plays. The limited geography of poverty demarcates the characters' domain of action to the domestic; their ultimate battleground and frontier is their bodies. Kia Corthron's *Come Down Burning*, wedged on a rural mountain top, examines the dynamics of dependency and support between two sisters: one a childless paraplegic whose home is her universe, the other a mother who silently yearns to be self-sufficient. *The Have-Little*, Migdalia Cruz's poetic urban tragedy, follows the coming of age of a young girl, focusing on her shifting relationships with her mother and her best friend. Their dreams are constricted by the concentric circles drawn by the desperation of the neighborhood, the indifference of society, and the boundaries imposed on their gender. In Inter-tribal Terry Gomez traces the close yet trying friendship of two young Indian women: one whose grand-mother has attempted to instill in her a sense of traditional values; and the other an urban Indian woman whose identity has been formed without the guidance of elders or a community.

Till Voices Wake Us, *My Ancestor's House*, *Flyin' West* and *How Else Am I Supposed to Know I'm Still Alive* also deal with the close relationships of women; economics are less a point of focus than the formation of bonds by women determined to fully realize each other. Evelina Fernandez's comic one-act *How Else Am I Supposed to Know I'm Still Alive* acknowledges not only the sexual vitality of middle-aged women, but also the boundless nature of friendship, when the question of an unexpected pregnancy arises. Set in the all-black town of Nicodemus, Kansas in the 1890s, Pearl Cleage's powerful historical play, *Flyin' West*, resonates along contemporary lines addressing such themes as economic autonomy in the African American community, spousal abuse, and women controlling their own lives. Faced with the ugly reality of unabating domestic violence, the women of *Flyin' West* find solutions and sustenance in their collective strength. In Louella Dizon's *Till Voices Wake Us*, a Filipina woman and her grandmother share the gift of dreaming and clairvoyance, melding the hidden past and the confusing present across an ocean. Finally, in *My Ancestor's House* Bina Sharif follows the return of a Pakistani woman who has chosen to marry and live in the West, to her native land and the world of her sisters and dying mother.

As contemporary works waiting to be read, produced, and absorbed these plays offer a wellspring; they are a source to sustain, refresh, and renew us. Fed by our artistic mothers, women who wrote fearlessly and innovatively for the theater – women like Sor Juana de la Cruz, Marita Bonner, and Ling-Ai Li – these plays speak in biting satire, dream imagery; dialogue, spare and oblique or overflowing with poetry; singing words, screams, whispers, and audacious jeers. They resonate in languages other than or beyond English, evoking ancestors and household gods, making visible unremembered heroines, tearing pages from history, torching false myths and leveling the toppling and faulty structures of a reality constructed to hold us in our places. These writers have filled empty spaces and replaced hollow images with flight, light, dreams, real women and imagined women, what really happened and what may happen next. As women of color in the theater, this is the theater which ignites us, this interstitial theater of redemption and transformation; – this is the theater we are making, living, dreaming.

The Plays

Brenda Wong Aoki

Biography

Brenda Wong Aoki creates intense, lyrical, solo theater pieces. Her work is a distinctive blend of dance, music and theater from both Western and Japanese dramatic traditions. The stories are drawn from Asian Pacific folk legends, urban guerilla street mythology and autobiographical accounts of life in these United States.

Brenda was awarded an NEA Solo Theater Fellowship in 1991 and 1994, and two Rockefeller Foundation Multi-Arts Production grants in 1992 and 1993. Her debut album, "Dreams and Illusions: Tales of the Pacific Rim," won first place for best spoken album of 1990 by the NAIRD (National Association of Independent Record Distributors).

Brenda Wong Aoki has performed across the United States, Canada and Japan including: The Kennedy Center and the Smithsonian Institution, Washington D.C.; Whitney Museum of American Art, New York City; Tsukuba World Expo, Japan; The New WORLD Theater; NAPPS Festival, Jonesborough, Tennessee; Center for Contemporary Arts, New Orleans; Japan America Theater, Los Angeles; East–West Center, Honolulu; San Diego Repertory Theater, California; and the Triplex Theater, New York City. She lives with her husband, musician/composer Mark Izu, and their son, Kai Kane, in San Francisco.

Artistic Statement

The Queen's Garden is urban storytelling and street mythology based on: my childhood (growing up "mixed up as chop suey" - I'm Chinese, Japanese, Spanish and Scots), my work with street gangs in Long Beach and fifteen years' experience as a community organizer and teacher in Watts, East Long Beach, Hunter's Point, the Mission, and Chinatown. *The Queen's Garden* is a story set amongst L.A.'s urban tribes. It's a love story. It's an epic. It was a big part of my life.

I tour a lot. All over the country. After the L.A. riots, I kept hearing a lot of people say, "Them folks in L.A. sure are crazy. Good thing we don't live there." But the reality is that the conditions that spawned the L.A. riots exist all over this country. I wrote *The Queen's Garden* in an effort to humanize that experience because it is only ten minutes from Beverly Hills to South Central. And there are South Centrals springing up all over this country.

I am continually moved by the poignancy of life: by the heroic efforts people make just trying to live as human beings in this world at this time. In my work, I try to cut down to the emotional truth. It's a very physical thing for me. It comes out of my chest and moves to that little groove at the base of my throat. Right there. If it starts to ache, I know it's right. I know it's universal and I know I got to tell the story.

This play is dedicated to the memory of Chuck Furutani and to all those working on the front lines. And to the memory of Lia Asoau Toailoa. Keep the Faith.

Production history

The Queen's Garden premiered at the Life on the Water Theater in San Francisco in October 1992, produced by the Climate Theatre. It went on to an extended run at the San Diego Repertory Theatre. Since then it has played at universities and theaters across the country. It won four L.A. Dramalogue awards and the San Diego Critics Circle Award. It is scheduled to be released in 1995 as a spoken-word album with music on both CD and cassette.

1 The Queen's Garden ⸻

Brenda Wong Aoki

Dramaturg: Teresa Marinacci

Author's notes

The Queen's Garden can be elaborately produced with live music, sets, or it can be very simply produced with just a stool and blacks. I've done it both ways. In this script the narrator plays a larger role than usual because I thought this would help the reader. *The Queen's Garden* is conceived as a one-woman show. In performance body position, gestures, mannerisms and music can replace some narration.

Glossary

shaka: Hand symbol used between Hawaiian local guys meaning "take it easy"
mana: Personal power
ohana: Your family, and your friends you couldn't live without, and your dearly departed loved ones. These make up your ohana.
ohana por vida: Westside saying meaning you can't get through this life without your ohana
talofa uso: Samoan saying meaning "welcome brothers and sisters"

Part 1: Growing Up

Prologue

NARRATOR I grew up where the sunsets were a brilliant red, next to a bridge that crossed a great river that went on forever. My name is Brenda Jean. Brenda Jean Bavarro McPhillips Wong Aoki. I'm Pake, Buddahead, Chicana, and Haole: Chinese, Japanese, Mexican and Scots. And I grew up in a neighborhood surrounded by the 405, the 710, the L.A. County Flood control and the Carson oil fields. An island unto itself that we called the Westside. When I was 14 my boyfriend, Kali, used to say, "The Westside is the bestside. Cuz, it's the only side I know."

Kali's Mom, Aunti Mary, was the Queen of the Westside. She's the only person I know who could stop a street fight by embarrassing you to death.

AUNTI MARY Harold! Your Mama work all day at the donut shop for wot!? And You! Shige-boy, stick that lip back in your mouf! Boof of you! Hala!

NARRATOR Life was simple. People were good. Every night, Kali and I would go up on the bridge at sunset, hang out under a street light and watch sky blue pink clouds floating in the river. And I'd think "Yep!"

But now that I'm older I know that those sunsets are smog, our bridge – a freeway overpass, and our "river" – a cement canal, the flood control.

And today, it's not romantic hanging out under streetlights cuz they're bright yellow. Makes it easier for helicopter surveillance – LAPD. And hanging out under streetlights is like saying "Shoot me! Here I am! Just shoot me!" But I remember the old days . . .

Dave's Pharmacy

BRENDA Ring! Ring! Ring! Hello? Dave's Pharmacy. Can I help you?

NARRATOR It's 1966. I'm 13 years old and my dad, Dave, a typical Nisei, with a big heart and a permanent wave, is opening up the pharmacy 15 minutes late as he does everyday.

DAD 9:15? We're late! Come on in folks. Come on in. Hey, Big Mike! How ya doin'?

NARRATOR Big Mike is one of the regulars. He looks just like Humpty Dumpty.

BIG MIKE Mornin' Dave.

NARRATOR The regulars are there when we open and they stay all day. Dad says it's good cuz they make the store look busy.

BIG MIKE How am I doin? . . . Well I sorta feel like . . . Jesus Christ, I'm gonna die. I think I'll lie down on the ground. Jesus Christ I'm gonna die.

DAD Well, looks like Big Mike's settled in for the day. Just move around him folks. Move around him.

NARRATOR And all day long my kid brother would peddle his big wheels around and around Big Mike and all the customers would try not to step on his toes.

DAD Mama? How's that coffee coming?

MOM It's ready. Are we gonna give away the banana bread too?

DAD Yep. Don't worry. Line up folks. Coffee's on. Everything's A OK with Aoki!

BRENDA Ring! Ring! Ring! Dave's Pharmacy, Brenda Jean at your service!

NARRATOR My job is answering the phones and waiting on the customers. I'm the No. 1 daughter, the onesan, the sergeant.

BRENDA Baby bro, keep your Big Wheels inside the store.

NARRATOR That's my only brother, the kid on the big wheels. Up there – my quiet sisters, Laura and Donna. And over here, the two chatterboxes – Lisa and Theresa. The baby Sas. We call them the Beesas.

BRENDA Hello! Can I help you? It's over there by the coke machine. Ah, excuse me? I'm not Donna Ann. I'm Brenda Jean. (To herself) Geez, they always do that. They think we all look alike.

NARRATOR We do. It's cuz Mom makes all our clothes from the same bolt! Like, today we're wearing shocking pink with fuzzy yellow polka dots. So everyone will know we're in the same family.

BRENDA Mom, I gotta go to the bathroom!

NARRATOR I love the bathroom! It locks. (Sound of locking door)

BRENDA (She looks at herself in the full-length mirror.) 4'10", 150 pounds, asthma, bifocals, eczema (scratches, squeezes imaginary zit on forehead) – my sisters called 'em stalactites.

(She sings) Johnny Angel, (wheeze) How I love him (wheeze) and I pray that some-day he'll love me (wheeze) and together we will see, how lovely heaven can be.

DAD Brenda Jeannie? Brenda Jeannie?

BRENDA Yes, Daddy ?

DAD Hate to disturb your meditation but we got a customer.

BRENDA Okay, Daddy. *(Sound of the door unlocking)*

NARRATOR There in the doorway . . . straw hat . . . red mumu . . . huge honey brown woman. Aunti Mary. The Beesas stop their chattering. Mom looks up. Baby bro stops. She moves to Big Mike . . .

MARY Auwe! You not make die dead yet, silly guy! Get up!
(Big Mike notices he's okay.)

MIKE Aunti Mary! Aunti Mary's here!

NARRATOR And she breezes past with a white plastic bucket filled with . . .

MARY Roses. Fresh picked by me dis morning. Da best time! Kings and Queens get Rose Gardens. I get da only rose garden on da Westside. Try smell. Sweet, huh? Folks come to Dave's Pharmacy to drink coffee, talk story and to smell my roses. Today, Dave, I give you my best and you give me da kine high blood pressure medicine?

NARRATOR I take a rose *(smells)* . . .

BRENDA Wow!

Outrigger Regatta

NARRATOR A few days later, I'm on the boardwalk and I hear . . .

MARY Hey, the drug man's daughter! It's me! Aunti Mary! You here for the beeg regatta? Come meet our team – The Islanders: Smoke from Guam, Uiva from Samoa, Kali, Twila, my kids from Hawaii, Toji from Japan, Gloria from Puerto Rico, Morrie Goldbaum . . .Where you from Morrie Goldbaum!

MORRIE New York!

MARY Dat's right! We all from da islands. Brenda Jean, where you from?

BRENDA Well, my mom's family's from China, Mexico and Scotland and my dad's family's from Japan and Salt Lake.

MARY Oh! You all mix up! Chop Suey! Okay, Islanders! Time to get down to business cuz today we sailing against da Haoles. See da fancy fiber glass boats? Haole outrigger. We get da real ting here. Wood! Heavy but! So we got ta psyche 'em out! Uiva give 'em!

UIVA *(Gives Samoan cheer. Roars:)* Tasi, Lua, Tolu, Fa. *(Repeat)* Ta lo fa! Ta lo fa! Uso! uso!

NARRATOR Bang! The boats are off and the race is on!

BRENDA *(Clapping)* Go Islanders! That was fun, Aunti Mary. I gotta go to work.

MARY Oh? Too bad you can't stay and eat. We get lomi lomi salmon, lau lau . . . ooh! Da pork . . . ummmm! Good ting you don't want any. Go – go, go. Teriyaki chicken, hamburger, hot dogs for da keikis. You don't want any. Go. Go. Go!

BRENDA Vegetables . . . no vegetables.

MARY Wadamelon! We get wadamelon! Try catch!
(BRENDA catches.)

NARRATOR And Aunti Mary started to cook . . .

MARY *(Singing to the tune of "Breaking up is Hard to Do")* Down, do bee do down, down. Come Ah, Come Ah! Down, do bee do down, down. Come Ah, Come Ah! Do be, Do be, Do, Do Ooh, do Do!

BRENDA Aunti Mary! All the other boats are in! They're pulling up the flags! They're going home! It's dark! *(Wheeze!)* I'm in big. *(wheeze)* My parents are gonna *(wheeze!)* . . .

MARY Oh, por ting! Breathe! Sit down. Breathe. Breathe. You get too much pilikia. Auwe! Breathe! Don't worry so much. I fix it wit your folks. But you got to breathe. Each breath your mana get more strong . . . People are like roses. Water a little, they get big. More wada, more big, til one day – Poof! They bloom! But you no breathe, you neva bloom.

Oh? See dat speck in the moonlight? Dat's dem. Quick, fan the ribs.

NARRATOR The canoe comes in and one Islander dives into the silvery waves. He's tall. Surfer shoulders. Cinnamon brown skin. Dark, glistening curls. He throws back his head and I see those eyes. . .

KALI How's it?

MARY Dis my son, Darren Kaalii Kahalapuinoa. You can call him Kali.

KALI I's hoping you's going stay. You like go body surf sometime?

BRENDA Okay.

Bodysurfing

NARRATOR A few days later . . .

BRENDA *(Locks bathroom door. Mimes*

puttting on a bathing suit that's too tight.)
Mom's bathing suit . . .
(Singing) Little surfer, little one. Make my
world come all undone. Do you love me?
Do you? Surfer girl. Surfer girl. Surfer
girl. *(Exits bathroom. She's at the beach.)*
  Kali, Surf's up!

BRENDA Take off my glasses? I can't see.
Talk loud. You first. Here I come. Oooh!
(Shivering) This is fun! Way out there?
Okay. Okay. *(Propelled by the surf. Re-
enters water.)* Dive into the curl? Oh yeah!
Wee, this is fun!

KALI Now wait for da curl and just before
she breaks ride 'um in like . . . Weeeee!!!
(He demonstrates very professionally.)

BRENDA I got it. I got it! *(Treading water)*
Now wait for the curl and just before . . .
Not yet. Not yet. Too late! Wipe out! *(She
wipes out and begins to drown.)* I'm
drowning . . . K-K-K-K-Kali! Help!

NARRATOR Big brown arms holding me up
and Kali says . . .

KALI You know girl, ya gotta make friends
wit Mada Ocean. We do this everyday and
bumbye she let you swim.

The Rip

NARRATOR So the summer passed, the salt
water helped my eczema, the swimming
helped my asthma and I got thin . . . ner.
On Kali's 14th birthday, we heard there
were six footers down on Huntington. So
we went there . . .

BRENDA Kali, looks dangerous!

KALI Yeah! *(He dives in and swims with
strong, steady strokes.)*

BRENDA Oh no! He's caught in a rip!
Kali! Kali! Kali!

NARRATOR To a lifeguard . . .

BRENDA My boyfriend's drowning.

NARRATOR It was the first time I said
"Boyfriend." I said it again.

BRENDA My boyfriend's drowning!

GUARD *(Mimes binoculars)* Looks Hawaiian.

BRENDA He is.

GUARD He's big.

BRENDA Yeah.

GUARD: He'll make it.

BRENDA No! He's drowning. And he's my
boyfriend!
  Kali! Kali! Kali!

NARRATOR Finally the rip plays out and
Kali swims to the shore. *(Mimes swimming)* He stumbles onto the beach.

KALI Hey, girl, how come you no call da
lifeguard?

BRENDA I did! I did! You okay?

KALI Gee, girl . . . funny kine. I like almost
drown! . . . On da Island da old folks say
da fisherman will always make it home
when his wahine is waiting . . . you saved
me!

Birthday Luau

NARRATOR That night Aunti Mary gave a
big luau for Kali's birthday. Kali and
Smoke had stayed up all the night before
making kalua pig. They dug the pit right
in the middle of her rose garden.

SMOKE So, Brenda, this is what we call an
imu.

NARRATOR It's Smoke, Kali's skinny
Guamanian buddy.

SMOKE Feel these rocks – they're warm,
but underneath they're hot. That's what
cooks the pig and when it comes out it's
gonna be good!

NARRATOR *(Makes flip-flop sound)* Kali, in
his ancient rubber thongs. He's carrying a
shovel in each hand.

KALI Smoke, brah. Come on. Take da rocks
off.

SMOKE Yah, okay Kali. I'll be right wit you.
So Bren, me and Kali been doing this
kalua pig thing since his ninth birthday.
Kali and me, we're tight. Ain't that right,
bro?

NARRATOR Smoke practically lives with
Kali and Aunti Mary. I don't know what
happened to his folks but he lives with
his uncle, who he doesn't get along with.
So Smoke's here all the time.

SMOKE You know, when I was small,
before my folks died, we lived down the
street. I'd seen Kali, but I didn't know
him. But my mom, she was friends with
Aunti Mary. At the funeral, Aunti Mary
gave me a big hug and said "Come visit."
And I never left. Ain't that right, Kali?

NARRATOR But Kali's not paying attention.
He's shoveling hot rocks.

SMOKE Man, you don't never listen to me.

KALI Come on, brah. Take the rocks off.

SMOKE Okay! I'm takin' the rocks off. See,
man, I'm takin the rocks off!

KALI Smoke, watch where you're trowin'
dose rocks before you . . . Owww!

BRENDA Kali, you're bleeding! Aunti Mary,
Aunti Mary!!

MARY Keeds! . . . Kali!

SMOKE It was an accident! I was takin' the rocks off and I just got really into it . . .

KALI You got into it alright! Jumpin' around like a monkey.

SMOKE A monkey, man! You callin' me a monkey, man?!! How you gonna call me a monkey when you hangin' out with The Rash!

BRENDA The Rash? You calling me The Rash?! Kali, he called me The Rash!

KALI Smoke man, don't be callin' Brenda no rash. What's up wit chu anyway? It's me and you, brah.

SMOKE No it's not! Now it's you and her! You ain't got no time for me!

MARY Ow! We get hurt feelings! Smoke, stop it already wid da stink eye. You, Kali, Brenda – we're "Ohana" – family.

NARRATOR And Aunti Mary hugged that scrawny little boy to her huge bosom and Kali says . . .

KALI Come on, brah, ain't no big ting. Let's get da pig out.

SMOKE I'm wit chu bro. I'm wit chu . . .

NARRATOR Ding! Dong!

MARY Oh! Here come da Islanders! Uiva, Toji! Morrie! Come in. Eh Birtday Boy, you and Smoke – hurry up! Time fo eat!

NARRATOR Kali and I ate tons and tons of that sweet, smokey meat. Then we collapsed.

KALI Hey, girl? Big 14. Almost a man, ah? Da sky's the limit! *(shaka)*

NARRATOR As we lay there in Aunti Mary's garden . . . the only rose garden on the Westside . . . I could still feel the rhythm of the waves . . . Kali, smelling fresh and clean, gave me my first kiss and I thought . . .

BRENDA I LOVE kalua pig!

(Lights out)

Part 2: School Daze

Lit. 1 vs. Twelve o'Clock High

NARRATOR It's 1968. Kali and I are now going steady. The first day of high school, we're bussed out of the Westside. Across the bridge. Over the FLOOD CONTROL to: Long Beach Polytechnic High School "Enter to Learn, Go forth to Serve." Poly – cyclone fence, huge concrete buildings – on the quad 3,000 kids. Kali helps me find my class, straightens my glasses,

kisses me good-bye and disappears down the hall.

(KALI gives Westside whistle.)

I go inside. Take a seat. No Westsiders. The Bell rings. In front of me, this white guy. Not like Morrie Goldbaum or Big Mike but really white.

STEVEN Hi there!

NARRATOR He's handsome. With wavy brown hair and green eyes. Like a Kennedy!

STEVEN I'm Steve Newcomb and this is my girlfriend Sherry.

NARRATOR Sherry – sky blue dress, golden hair. She smiles at me.

BRENDA I wanna be her friend.

NARRATOR Then the teacher walks to the front of the class.

JUDY Class, I'm Judy, Judy Sloane. But in this class, I hope you'll call me Judy. Oh! Look at you! Look at you! You're nervous! Of course! You're sitting here in Lit. 1, the gifted class, thinking, "Oh my god! Am I gifted?" Don't worry. You are. Now, most of you know each other but there's one person I know you don't know because she just got here. Hai Nyugen from Viet Nam. Welcome, Hai!

HAI *(With a French accent)* In Viet Nam, I read Cyrano de Bergerac, Les Misérables et Madame Bovary. I look forward to reading the literature in your great tongue.

JUDY Thank you, Hai. If there's one thing I want us all to learn, it's how to live together in peace. So this semester I've decided, we're going to study Utopian literature. Utopia. Does anyone know what that means? Tommy? A ride at Disneyland? No. That's Autopia. Utopia is a place where people live together in harmony. Your first reading assignment for the semester: Aldous Huxley's *Brave New World*. Class dismissed! Brenda? Can I speak to you for a minute, please? Brenda, I think Hai could use a friend.

BRENDA Why me? I'm not Vietnamese.

JUDY But you're Oriental! Put yourself in her place. You're in a new country. No friends . . .

NARRATOR So everyday, I sat next to Hai trying to dress and act so that everyone knew I was not like her – F.O.B. Fresh Off the Boat.

After school . . .

BRENDA Kali!! I loved my classes. Judy,

that's my teacher. We just call her that. She's like a real person. Well, how were your classes?

KALI I don't wanna talk about it.

BRENDA Why not? Who's in 'em?

KALI Smoke. Da kine Westside guys.

BRENDA I was wondering where everybody went! What'd ya do?

KALI I don't wanna talk about it.

BRENDA Why not?

KALI No more. 'Nuff already! *(Pause)* I'm not retarded.

BRENDA What?

KALI Not, 'kay? Not! I'm in da kine Twelve o'Clock High.

BRENDA What! Why?! You're not dumb! You just sleep in class. You can't help it. You work at night.

KALI I said, I don't wanna talk about it! Pau already! *(Pause)*

I hate working at Curry's. Bus deeshes. Take out trash. Da boss. He tinks I'm Mexican. "Tell da Mexican kid to wash the toilets." Pilau!

My mada's grandfada, was da highest chief in Kauai! We come from royalty. Dey don't know who I am! Dey don't never know who I am!

Dis class, dis Twelve o'Clock High, dat's for losers, play checkers, read gung fu magazines. Today we get one guest lecture: army recruit guy! Junk! Dey wish dey could forget about us. Dey wish we would just disappear.

Sherry

NARRATOR Sherry, her boyfriend Steve Newcomb and I had become friends. One weekend Sherry invited me to her parents house for a garden party . . .

SHERRY Brenda! I'm so glad you're here. No one from the Westside has ever been over before. Don't tell my mom where you're from. Okay? It's no big deal. Just don't.

I love your hair. It's so ethnic. Mine just kinda hangs here. You know who's gorgeous? Your boyfriend! God, he is so sexy! I love the way he walks. But I can't understand him. Can he speak English? Hey? You guys on B.C.? You know – Birth Control? You mean you're not using anything?

BRENDA We're not doing anything. We love each other.

SHERRY Oh, God! That's SO ROMANTIC! Steven wouldn't stay with me for a second if he couldn't screw me. Com'ere, let's have some fun tonight. Let me dress you. Please! Come here. *(She opens closets.)* All these old clothes! AAAHH! Yellow? No, no. Make you look sour. Orange? No. Red? Too bold. Green! Try it!

BRENDA Wow, store bought green satin.

SHERRY Keep it!

BRENDA Oh, no. I couldn't. It's too nice.

SHERRY It's you or Good Will.

BRENDA Oh . . . Thanks . . .

NARRATOR That night . . . La la la la . . . la la la la la (Singing *Brandenburg No. 5*)

The garden filled with tiny little lights. Jasmine. Gardenias. And pink Chinese lanterns swaying in the breeze. La la la la la la . . . All the people so refined and elegant. Sherry smiled and smiled at me. And I felt like a princess. La! LA! *(Sings a Smokey Robinson type doo-wop song as transition)*

Westside Warriors

NARRATOR On the weekdays I was a model minority. But on Friday nights I was a Westside Warrior. We had graduated from The Islanders. My homegirls and I would – *(Mimes the following: Eye shadow, lipstick. Mean looks. Putting on fishnet stockings. Stuffing bra. High heels. Rats hair. Hair spray. Dances. Snaps.)* And Honey, we were ready!

We'd go down to homeboy Smoke's garage. Rug samples on the cement – wall to wall. Over here's an old couch that everyone likes to make out on. And back there is a naugahyde armchair that no one likes cuz when you move on it, it sounds like this: *(farting sounds.)* Over here's a lamp with a tee shirt on it to keep the lights low and back there me and the girls would spin 45s and talk about . . .

HOMEGIRLS *(Singing)* Nothin' you could do could make me untrue . . .

NARRATOR And this is where one day I bring my new friend, Sherry. As our guest, my homegirls give her the nau-gahyde arm chair.

SHERRY *(Fart sounds as she sits)* I'm honored. So this is the "inner sanctum." *(fart, fart)* Well, where are the "Homeboys"?

NARRATOR At this very moment they're waiting, in black jackets with "Warriors" embroidered in blue on the back. Kali's in the middle. Smoke to his right. They're waiting . . . for the Corner Boys . . .
(WARRIORS whistle street signal.)

KALI Get 'em.
(WARRIORS fight choreography)

NARRATOR The garage door opens. Enter Smoke . . . and Kali with a big gash in his head. All the girls run to me . . .

HOMEGIRLS Brenda! Look at your ole man! Look at your ole man!

NARRATOR I say . . .
(BRENDA has asthma attack.)

NARRATOR But Sherry says . . .

SHERRY Kali! We've got to get you to a hospital . . .

KALI What she doing here?

SHERRY Kali, if my presence offends you, I'll leave. But first I really think we oughta get that head looked at. My car's right outside and . . .

NARRATOR All of us said "Car?" And after that Sherry was cool.
And this is where we learned the "ole lady" thing: Wipe off the blood, the sweat and the dirt. Get the men something to drink. Listen to their war stories . . .

GIRL 1 God, you're tough.

GIRL 2 You should've seen my ole man. I think his nose is busted.

GIRL 3 Honey that ain't nothin'. My ole man got cut!

GIRL 2 Wow!

NARRATOR . . . turn up the hi-fi, turn down the lights and *(singing the Miracles' tune)* OOOOH! OOO-OOOOHHH! La la la la . . . Kali smiles and he only smiles when he dances or fights. We dance.

KALI *(Sings)*
You're my past, you're my present, you're my future, GIRL!!
One day, one sweet day, we will bee-e-ee! And we'll live togedda, fo'evah . . .
Like da wada to da sea . . .

BRENDA Kali, say "water."

KALI *(Singing)* Like da wada to da sea!!!

BRENDA Kali, do you have to talk pidgin all the time? Say, "water."

KALI Wada.

BRENDA No. WAAH-TER.

KALI WAAH-DAAH!

BRENDA Say, "I'd like a glass of WAAH-TER, please."

KALI Mo' betta, I get da wada myself den waste my breaf asking.

BRENDA Do you want to be in Twelve O'Clock High forever? If you don't learn how to speak good English, you'll never graduate!

KALI Some folks, need odder people graduate 'dem. Me, I graduate myself!
(Singing) Like da WAAH-DAAH to da sea
. . .
Hey, girl! Your skin, someting funny kine!

BRENDA What? Is it my eczema?

KALI *(Shrugs)* It's white.

BRENDA It's rash.

KALI But it's white!

BRENDA So?

KALI You're turning Haole! *(laughs)*

NARRATOR *(Sound of farting)* Out of the corner of my eye, I see Sherry and Smoke – like totally making out! She's taking down her spaghetti straps. She has no bra! He's taking off his belt! Oh my god, are they just gonna? . . .
Boom! Boom! Boom!

HOMEGIRLS The CORNER BOYS!! Run!!

NARRATOR The Corner Boys are older. Maybe 20. They don't work. They don't go to school. They're career guys! WE RUN! *(Acts out chase scene)* Through the park. Past graffiti that says "Westside Rules. Corner Boys are chumps!" Me and Sherry are falling behind. We're last. I'm last. Oh, my god! The fence! Sherry WHOOM! She's over. Me . . .

BRENDA Kali! Kali! I'm stuck!!

NARRATOR My fishnets are caught in the chainlink fence and I'm thinking . . .

BRENDA What am I doing here?

NARRATOR But Sherry says . . .

SHERRY *(Mispronouncing)* Que Viva! Westside!! *(Sherry screams in excitement.)*

The Riot

BROTHER BROWN Brothers and Sisters! This is Squeaky Brown and the Black Panthers have liberated this High School!

NARRATOR Detroit, Newark, Watts . . . On the quad – On this side: frat boys, cheerleaders, Lit. 1.A – all white. On this side: wood shop, Twelve O'clock High, Westside Warriors – all the rest.
As if in a dream I walk through the quad – like Moses parting the Red Sea – and as I get to the other side, like two

huge tidal waves, three thousand kids run towards each other and all hell breaks loose!

I see Sherry getting her head bashed into a pole by two black girls.

SHERRY Stop it! Stop it!

NARRATOR Then someone grabs me, twists my arm, pries open my hand and in red indelible Marks-a-Lot writes "WS": Westside. It's Smoke.

SMOKE Flash dis to any homies who try an' mess wif you.

NARRATOR Then these two white guys push me. Knock me to the ground and I hear . . .

STEVEN Wait! Stop! She's in my Lit. class.

NARRATOR It's Steve Newcomb. He gives me his frat ring.

STEVEN Show this to any white people who try and bother you.

NARRATOR I walk through the quad. I'm cool . . . Westside. I'm a soc . . . Phi Gam. Westside. Phi Gam. *(Mimes repeat of line as flashes ring or palm)*

BR. BROWN Brothers and Sisters! Remember, you are part of the solution or part of the problem. The choice is yours!

The Newcomb Dynasty

JUDY Class, after the events of the last few days, I know many of you are hurt, shocked, angered! And suddenly I realize that Poly, our own high school, is part of a larger picture. And I just had to say "Judy, forget the core curriculum! Get real!" I want each of you to pick partners and come up with an analysis of the underlying causes of this riot. Class dismissed.

NARRATOR Steven was my partner. So I went to his house. My god, it was a mansion!

STEVEN Okay, Brenda! Okay! I understand how frustrating it must be to be in woodshop and Twelve o'clock High but violence is never a viable option! I need a break. How 'bout a brownie?

NARRATOR So we take some brownies into the Newcomb family library. A room filled with huge painted portraits of the Newcomb patriarchy. Steven and I sit down on a burgundy velvet, Edwardian couch.

BRENDA Oh, Steven, what lovely little pillows!

STEVEN Brenda, that's what's so special about you – you know, you're really different . . . from those others. I mean from those other Westsiders.

BRENDA Really? . . .

STEVEN Definitely!

NARRATOR And one of the paintings starts to talk to me . . .

GRANDPA A little cherry blossom! Welcome to the bosom of the Newcomb dynasty.

BRENDA Steven, your Grandfather's talking to me.

NARRATOR And Steven says . . .

STEVEN Marijuana in the brownies. Yuummm!

NARRATOR And he puts his arm around me . . .

BRENDA A Kennedy. Hmmm. But geez, he's hairy. He's gonna kiss me. Relax, be sensual. That nose. How do you get around the nose? *(Mimes)* EEEE! He stuck his tongue in my mouth. Eu, Gross!

NARRATOR And all the other paintings say,

PAINTINGS "Aaaaa!" *(Tongue action)*

BRENDA No! No! No! *(Spin out)*

NARRATOR When I came to, all the paintings were quietly hanging on the wall and Steven was sitting there staring at me.

STEVEN Geez, Brenda, I'm really sorry. I didn't know the brownies were that powerful. I'm just blowin' it since Sherry left me. I'm tripping out.

BRENDA Steven, I'm really hungry.

NARRATOR Later Steven drives me to the pharmacy. As we go inside, I see on the counter: lumpia, tamales and a fresh bunch of Aunti Mary's red, red, roses. Today's trades for medicine. My kid brother pedals up to Steven. My little sisters come out from behind the counters and surround him. Dad comes down too and shakes his hand. They're all standing there in Mom's matching clothes . . . looking like a bunch of refugees!!! So I say to Steven . . .

BRENDA Steven! I'll see you tomorrow!

Kali Fights Steven

BRENDA So in conclusion, Steven and I disagree about the causes of the riot. Although I do not personally condone it, violence is a form of . . .

NARRATOR There, in the doorway . . . Kali in his black Warrior jacket. He moves towards Steven's desk. He's smiling. He lifts up Steven and wham!
(HAI *screams*)

NARRATOR It's Hai, the F.O.B. from Viet Nam.

KALI He's okay, I just like teach him – we take care of our own.
(HAI *Wails*)

KALI What's wrong with her?
(HAI *Wails*)

KALI Wot da hell she saying?

BRENDA Kali! Get out! Just get out!

NARRATOR Later, I wait for Kali at his locker. As soon as I see that black Warrior jacket . . .

BRENDA You big, stupid moron. What'd you do that for?

KALI Cuz he's messin' wit you. What's wrong with him? Is he a faggot or wot? I thought he'd fight for you. I fight for you. I put myself on da line for you alla time and you just t'row it in my face. You hanging out wit so many Haoles, you forget you from da Westside!

BRENDA Who cares about the Westside? What's so cool about busting up a class and freaking out some poor F.O.B.? I'm not gonna be on the Westside forever. I'm getting out of here. I'm going to college.

KALI Wot? You tink you can fly? Your daddy get dat kine kala wit six kids? Shhh!

BRENDA Did you hear what I said, I'm going to college!

KALI (*Pause*) Hey, girl, I tellin' Smoke and all da kine on da Westside we getting married.

BRENDA Married? I'm not gonna be some fat mama in a muumuu waiting for a welfare check! You don't get it do you? You're always talking about the sky's the limit. We live on the Westside. Next to the oil fields! The sky comes up to here! (*Gestures to her throat*) Kali, we're pau.

NARRATOR And he turned and walked away. And I just stood there watching the Warrior written on the back of his jacket get smaller and smaller . . . until it disappeared . . .

Intermission

Part 3: The Teacher

College

NARRATOR Well, I went to college. Thank God for EOP – the Ethnic Opportunity Program. Sherry turned me on to higher education but I went and she didn't. She had Smoke's baby in her senior year, dropped out and moved in with him.

DAD Why are you leaving us? Mama and me, we need you! You're the Onesan. If you get too smart, no one will marry you!

NARRATOR THE CAMPUS: Clean fresh air! And the sky! It went on and on. Right down to the ocean. Big picture windows overlooking the redwoods. I felt AWFUL! – Leaving mom with all those kids . . . I was worried about who was taking my place at the store and actually – I stuck out miserably.

STUDENT Excuse me, but we're leading a student directed seminar on racial injustice. We'd like you to be a guest lecturer. Please? The only way to bridge the gap between the rich and the poor is for people like you to teach people like us. We need you. You're Third World.

The Demise of Dave's Pharmacy

NARRATOR Ring. Ring.

MAMA Hello Brenda Jean. This is your mama. I just want to tell you the news. Medirex is opening one of its stores right across the street from Daddy's. Um-hum . . . Well, here's the news! The new owner offered to buy Dave's Pharmacy and set Daddy up as the manager of Medirex. It'd be just like having our own store without the headaches! Here's Dad.

DAD Well, Brenda Jean. Guess I gotta be like everybody else and get a job. You want to come help?

NARRATOR So we moved: our medicine, our coke machine and all our customers. We stood there in the empty shell of our store, "Dave's Pharmacy" . . . and watched Dad march into Medirex.
      The boss's name was Buzzy, like a killer bee.

BUZZY Hey, surprise yeah? I'm a head. Long hair. Work in cut-offs, sandals. I was into acid. Now I'm dealing drugs! Hah! Hah! Hah!

NARRATOR Bzzz, bzzz, bzzz.

BUZZY Hey Dave, this is a place of business. So, tell the lovely wife to take her delicious banana bread, her adorable kids and go home.

NARRATOR Buzz, Buzz, Buzz.

BUZZY Hey Dave – if they ain't buyin, we're dyin . . . Ah geez, not again! Get off the floor ya retard!

MARY He no retard. Mike gid up. Dave, today Aunti Mary bring you her sweetest roses. Try smell!

BUZZY NOOOOO! There you go again! I can't believe it! Flowers for medicine . . . I need cash, cash, cash, cash, MONEY! Dave, you're fired!

DAD Fired? You can't fire me. This is my store! That's my coke machine . . . These are all my customers.

BUZZY From now one we'll just think of this as Dave's Pharmacy without Dave.

  (DAVE *stands there confused.*)

Twelve o'Clock High

NARRATOR "Death to the Birds of Prey that feed on the blood of the people!" reads a poster above my desk. I'm back in high school. Teaching. I dropped out of college and got a special certificate to teach here, cuz no one else would.

BRENDA I'm Brenda Aoki, but in this room you'll call me Brenda. This is Twelve o'Clock High, as you know, the class for the losers. Okay, let's cut the bullshit from the gate. I don't think you are losers. I don't think you are illiterate. What I think is . . . you're lazy. You're lookin' at me like "How does this broad know what we think?" I know cuz I been there. I'm 20 years old. Not that much older than most of you. I'm from the Westside too. My Daddy worked hard all his life to support our family and he got beat up by the Man.

  Now, I live above a whore house with a Vietnamese sister who was raped by the same capitalist, imperialist system that screwed my Daddy and keeps all of us (*gestures*) down. Your first reading assignment for the semester: Paulo Freire's *Pedogogy of the Oppressed*. Class dismissed.

  Bobby? Bobby Panis! May I speak to you for a minute please? Miss Panis? Thank you. Bobby, I was wondering if you could you do me a favor and hang out with Debbie? She's like the only white kid in the class and . . . You're part Filipino and part white so . . . Bobby, just do me that favor, alright?

BOBBY Hey, teach? Fuck off.

Rosie's Baby/Sherry's Fine

SHERRY Brenda! Don't be so hard on yourself. Tell me all about it.

NARRATOR And I'm hangin' with Sherry. Flame Red nails, two inches long, tight white pants with a thin gold belt, a tousled mane of Farrah Fawcett hair.

BRENDA Oh Sherry. It's so good to have somebody to talk to.

NARRATOR We sitting in the sun on Sherry's deck. Her little boy's happily babbling in his playpen. Sherry's living in this bougie condo – in P.V. Palos Verdes! Smoke must be doin' pretty good.

BRENDA Sherry, I just think I'm blowing it with these kids. I dunno . . . like the other day. I dismiss the boys, and tell the girls we're gonna have a women's discussion, and that little witch, Bobby Panis, says . . .

BOBBY But ain't chu a dyke?

BRENDA And they all crack up. Slappin' high fives and stuff.

SHERRY Well, you don't exactly look like a "homegirl". Let me do your hair. Please!

BRENDA Sherry! . . . Anyway to divert their attention, I notice this one fat girl, who I really like, is all of a sudden skinny. So I say, "Rosie, you look great, what happened?"

ROSIE I had a baby.

BRENDA And they all crack up again. God Sherry, I had no idea she was even pregnant. Then I remember how Rosie used to wear this long coat even when it was really hot. Poor kid, she must have been so uncomfortable.

NARRATOR Sherry tosses her hair . . .

SHERRY Well, you know the rule – Get pregnant, get kicked out of school . . . (*Laughs*)

SHERRY'S SON Out! Out! Out! (*Calling from play pen*)

NARRATOR Sherry's son raises his little arms.

SHERRY Brenda, it's all worth it. Huh? Baby Boy. Mama's baby boy.

NARRATOR I look down at Sherry's little boy wrapped snuggly in his mama's arms with his caramel colored skin and curly blonde hair, and I think, "Yep, the little prince. He's the future. Us coming together living in peace."

Rosie's Story/Hai Survives

NARRATOR And every morning my roommate, Hai, yes Hai, the F.O.B from Lit. 1, who I now see as my sister in the struggle . . . makes us Vietnamese style coffee in two blue porcelain teacups. French!

HAI For you, Brenda and one for me. Comment ça va?

BRENDA Oh, Hai. You always know, don't you?

NARRATOR And I tell Hai all about what happened in class with my women's discussion.

BRENDA And Rosie had to wear this long coat, even when it was really hot. So I decide to be cool with them. I say to the girls, "Listen, if any of you guys gets pregnant, I swear, I'll never turn you in." And they go . . .

GIRLS Really? You won't? AAHHHH!!

BRENDA And they're all pregnant! Except Bobby Panis who's skinny as a rail. Then the class just busts wide open and the girls are all asking Rosie about her labor. Did it hurt? And was her boyfriend there. God Hai, you oughta see her boyfriend. This big macho gangster – "Bullet". And Rosie says . . .

ROSIE When Bullet saw his little baby, he cried!

NARRATOR And all the girls say . . .

GIRLS No!

ROSIE And he says we're gonna name the baby Luz: Light.

GIRLS OOOOHH!

ROSIE And Bullet says we're getting married.

GIRLS (Sob. Sob.)

HAI You'd be surprised at what people do to survive. When I left Viet Nam, there was not enough room on the boat for both my sister and me. (Pause) But the captain liked me and I had to make sure he kept liking me.

BRENDA What happened to your sister?

HAI These teacups are all that's left of my family.

BRENDA Oh God, Hai. I'm so sorry. I'll be your family.

HAI I love you, Brenda.

BRENDA I love you too, Hai.

HAI I do not mean it like that. I mean . . . I love you.

Dinner with Father

DAD Bless this food we're about to eat to the use of our bodies.

NARRATOR It's another Sunday dinner with the folks. Dad's at the head of the table saying grace.

DAD Thank you for our health. Thank you for my wonderful family. We ask you to bring us a quick victory in Viet Nam so cousins Larry, Dickie and Bobby can come home. Amen.

MOM AND KIDS Amen, amen, amen, amen, amen, amen . . .

DAD Brenda Jean? Say Amen.

BRENDA I'm not gonna ask God to help us murder people. Especially people who look just like us!

DAD Brenda Jean, tonight we will have a nice, peaceful, family dinner. Is that understood?

BRENDA Fine.

MOM Well, Beesas!

NARRATOR It's Mom.

MOM What did you do today?

BEESA 1 We can't tell you. Cuz Brenda Jean said she'd kill us if we told you.

BEESA 2 Ho! Ho! Ho Chi Min! NLF is gonna win! We're gonna be on the 6:00 News, Mama!!!

BEESA 1 AND 2 Ho! Ho! Ho Chi Min! NLF is gonna . . .

DAD Wait! Stop! Not at this table! We are Americans!! Brenda Jean! What kind of example are you setting for these kids? You're the onesan. I never seen such a bitter perverse person. You hate everybody! White people! Rich people! Buzzy! Forget the store! Dave's Pharmacy is dead! I love working at Lucky's! Mama's thrilled with her job at the cafeteria! So what happened to you? You used to be so sweet. Now, look at you! You buy everything at the Army Surplus. What are you, a soldier? What's wrong with looking like a girl? And why are you wasting all that money on rent? You got money to throw around, throw it at your family. It's that Vietnamese room mate. She's perverting you. I want you to move back home right now.

BRENDA Home? This doesn't feel like

home. Hai's more family than you are!

DAD I am your father!

BRENDA So?

DAD Move home or you are no longer part of this family!

BRENDA Fine!

Rosie's Dilemma

NARRATOR A few months after the break with my family, Hai's cooking dinner – Vietnamese style beef noodle soup with cilantro. Uuummm! When Rosie comes by . . .

BRENDA Rosie! Luz! Come in. Want some soup?

(ROSIE *looks like she's about to cry.*)

BRENDA What's wrong?

ROSIE I miss my mom, my brothers. I can't stand living like this. One minute Bullet's such a good Daddy and the next, he's out on the street getting fucked up with the boys. I can't stand it. Always watching your back. Hitting the ground everytime a car backfires. I don't want to live like this. It's not good for the baby.

(LUZ *gurgles*)

ROSIE I love Bullet.

(LUZ *gurgles*)

ROSIE I know he's your daddy.

(LUZ *gurgles*)

ROSIE We're family por vida. But he says he can't live without his homeboys. They back each other up. He couldn't survive without them.

NARRATOR I'm thinkin', "God, this could'a been me n' Kali . . ." So I say . . .

BRENDA Rosie, he's a father now. He's got to grow up. And you, you're smart. You could be somebody. Tell Bullet. It's you or his boys. He loves you. He can change.

ROSIE You know, sometimes I think about me and Bullet living in a place that's quiet at night. Where we can take Luz to the park and not worry about getting blown away.

Kali Returns

NARRATOR A few days later, on the street . . .

(KALI *gives Westside whistle.*)

BRENDA Kali! It's been . . .

KALI Four years, tree months, two days . . .

BRENDA You look great. You're a man!

KALI (*He scans her.*) You too.

BRENDA Yeah, well . . . What ya been up to? You married?

KALI You like go out tonight?

BRENDA Hai! I'm going out tonight! Kali – remember him?! (*Undresses while singing Sly Stone's "Different Strokes"*) "There is the black one," – army boots. "Who won't accept the red one," – fatigues. "for living with the white one," – Mao jacket. Che Beret. "Different strokes for different folks." Swsss! (*Takes shower*) "And so on and so on and scooby, dooby, doo wa . . ." (*Washes hair*)

Hai? Remember Kali? He's the guy who freaked ya out in High school. He gave me my first kiss. "We gotta live together!" (*Swsh! Opens closet door, looks*) Thank you Sherry for the ole green satin! "And so on and so on and . . ." (*Unlocks door*) Well, how do I look? Do I look like a woman?

HAI The most woman.

NARRATOR And even though it's evening, Hai makes us Vietnamese style coffee in two blue porcelain teacups.

HAI For you Brenda, and one for me. (*Pause*) So, you want to be Vietnamese . . .

BRENDA What?

HAI If you end up with Kali you'll be like the women back home . . .

BRENDA Which is?

HAI Plant the rice, make the babies, feed the men, and run.

BRENDA God, Hai, you are so full of cheer.

HAI If you have to have a man, find a rich, white man.

NARRATOR Ding-Dong. Kali's standing there, in a white Italian silk suit, with a bunch of red, red roses. Big as cabbages.

KALI From Mama. She say, "No forget your Aunti Mary."

NARRATOR He turns to Hai . . .

KALI Hum nai angh Guayahum? . . .

NARRATOR Hai turns, walks to her room and slams the door.

BRENDA Kali, what'd you say to her?

KALI I thought I said "How ya doing?'

Kali Comes Courting

NARRATOR We get in his car. White Cadillac. White leather seats. (*Singing Donny Hathaway's "Where is the Love"*) We're cruising PCH, Pacific Coast Highway. We pull up at the Five Crowns Restaurant.

KALI I like dis place. It's ono.

NARRATOR This guy comes over and opens my door.

MAITRE D' Mr. K! How nice to see you!

HOSTESS Mr. K? The same table as usual?

WAITER Mr. K, tonight I'd recommend the prime rib or the lobster. Take your time.

BRENDA Kali, this place is pretty bougie.

KALI You know Bren, I go by Darren now.

BRENDA (Laughs) Darren? I can't call you Darren.

KALI Okay. But only you can call me Kali.

BRENDA Kali . . . Look! We used to go body surfing down there.

KALI Yeah . . . (Smiles) Hey? How's your folks?

BRENDA (Shrugs) They're okay.

KALI You know, my very first job was working at Dave's Pharmacy! I loved that job. Folks would call your dad, tell him what they needed and he'd send me out with the deliveries. And that's what I still do. I'm a "delivery boy."

NARRATOR Oh! Oh! There is no way I can get involved with this guy again. No way!

KALI Hey, Bren, I'm doin' good now. I live in a village where I sit with the elders. My house, I wish you could see it. On stilts over da wada. I get home, take off my suit, throw on a malo, hang out on the lanai and just watch the clouds floating in the wada. And I think, hey now, you graduated.

NARRATOR The meal's over. We're leaving. Kali and I stop to watch the sunset.

KALI (sings) You're my past, you're my pres . . .

BRENDA Kali that was a long . . .

KALI Kali con Brenda de Westside Barrio Longo . . . por vida.

NARRATOR And he's got his arms around me. The first arms that ever held me.

KALI Hey girl, let's not go home.

BRENDA Okay. (They walk into the sunset.)

NARRATOR He was GOOD!!! He was fine. He was rich. He was dangerous. So we start hanging out . . . I'm in love. Of course, we see things a little different but I can handle it. A few months later, we're at a restaurant . . .

KALI Hey girl! Ova at da bar. Isn't that da kine, what's her face? Your old teacha? Judy?

BRENDA Judy!

JUDY Brenda, look at you! All grown up!

BRENDA Judy! I can't believe it's you! I'm teaching now. At Poly! Can you believe it?

JUDY That's good news. Good news. Give those kids everything you got . . . Give 'em your love, your life, your youth . . . (Tipsy) Give 'em every goddamn thing you . . . got!

KALI Ya know Girl, you're going end up just like her . . . one wasted, dried up, drunk. Cuz what you're doing for dose kids ain't happening.

BRENDA Why, thank you! I just spent six months getting Bullet out of a gang, finding him a job, and you say it ain't happening.

KALI It's not real . . . You're cutting him off from his source and without his source, he has no mana. Bren, you may not like what me and Smoke are doing, but we're real and we're at the center of our source.

BRENDA What source? You don't live on the Westside. Smoke lives in P.V. and you live in Thailand!

KALI The Westside's here (gestures) . . . with me all the time . . . It's like Mama's flowers . . . I smell dem and everyting comes to me since small kid time, and I feel strong. That's the source. But cut the source, destroy the self.

BRENDA All I know is I'm working my ass off for these kids! What do you ever do?

KALI We take care of people in our own way – my ma, your ma . . . your fada. Where you think he got dat job? Surprise, huh? We fight for them all the time. We're warriors, 'cept now we're Westside Warriors multinational.

BRENDA Isn't that a fancy title for drug dealers, Darren?

KALI I'm leaving in a week for Thailand.

BRENDA (Pause) Leaving? . . . Just like that?! God Kali, you're great!

KALI Come with me.

BRENDA Why would I do that?

KALI Cuz Brenda, I'm your source.

Bullet's Death

NARRATOR I'm walking up my stairs and I hear . . . (Sound of wailing)

BRENDA The whorehouse? (Sound of wailing) Hai? Hai!!? Are you alright? (A wail)

NARRATOR Inside my apartment Rosie's sitting on my couch, Hai's rocking her and making this strange sound. (HAI gives a moaning wail.) Baby Luz, in a long white christening gown, is playing with her mother's hair . . .

ROSIE   Luz, Lu, Daddy gave you that name. It means light. Because you're the light of his life. Yes you are mija . . . Daddy's safe now. Safe . . .

BRENDA   Rosie, what's going on?

ROSIE   Dey shot Bullet, twice in the head and once in the chest.

NARRATOR   She stands up and she's covered with blood!

ROSIE   You killed him. You killed him!

BRENDA   Rosie!

ROSIE   ¡Callete! Don't touch my baby!

BRENDA   Rosie. Rosie!

ROSIE   Get the fuck out of our Barrio! *(Brenda backs away, wanders. She stops dumbfounded. Lights out.)*

Part 4: San Francisco

"If You're Going to San Francisco"
(musical transition)

NARRATOR   I moved to San Francisco. I got a quiet little job, a cheap apartment . . . I don't know anybody, but that's okay because I don't have to be responsible for anybody's life but my own.

   Time passes. Then one day, "Ring! Ring!"

MOM   Hello Brenda Jean. This is your momma.

BRENDA   Mom!

NARRATOR   All of a sudden I'm a kid again. That weekend I fly home. I think that I'm gonna have a big scene with my dad but he's so happy to see me everything's fine. Great! After supper, I'm hanging out on the front porch and I hear . . . *(KALI gives Warriors' whistle.)*

NARRATOR   He's standing there . . . starched khakis, rolled tee shirt . . . bulging muscles . . . shaved head . . . a stone pinto . . . an ex-con . . .

BRENDA   Kali – It's been . . .

KALI   Four years, tree months, two days.

BRENDA   Yeah. Rumor had it you were in Texas. In prison.

KALI   I'm out. You like go beach?

NARRATOR   So we go down to Cherry Beach.

KALI   *(Plays with the sand then starts to talk)* In Thailand everyday, I put on my white suit, my white shoes, my driver takes me to the airport. I'm a businessman. I go

down to Pan Am. Pay a little extra for "excess" baggage. Say "hey" to Beni, head of security. Take my seat, first class and wait for the Coovaseeyeh!

Kali in the Cage

KALI   Then one day, I put on my white suit, white shoes, my driver takes me to the airport, wave to Beni and he cuffs me. "Hey, Bra? Whas up?" And he says "We're doin' business with another team." And they drag me away and throw me butt naked into a tiger cage. Tiger cage . . . It's this big. Exactly. The cage come up to here. *(Mimes cage)* I'm in there wit eight uda guys. We eat and shit together. Pilau!

   So I'm waiting – hungry. You don't get no goulash on a tin plate. This is Thailand. Either your people feed you or you starve.

KALI   So I am waiting for Smoke.

MAN   May I offer you a cigarette?

KALI   It's the king of the cage. This old man smoking Shermans, eating good . . . His people take care of him. But I say, "No thanks." Cuz I don't want to owe 'em nothin'. I'm thirsty and the guards give me wada the color of shit.

MAN   Would you care for a beer or some other refreshment?

KALI   No thanks, I told you my boys are coming. But they never came. They never FUCKING came.

   Two years in that *(pause)* cage! If it wasn't for that nice old man, I'd be dead. But I'm out . . . I'm here on the beach . . . wid you . . . I'm okay, right? . . . *(sobs convulsively)* Bren? . . . Bren!!!

NARRATOR   And he holds me really tight . . . And I'd never seen him cry before . . . and I'm thinking, "Come on Brenda, not again. You're not a Westside mama any more – This is not your responsibility!" Then I say . . .

BRENDA   Hey Homie, why don't ya come up to San Francisco? Start over?

Domestic Difficulties

NARRATOR   Kali moves in. We do Chinatown, Fisherman's Wharf, ride the cable cars. And during the week I go to work and Kali – he's great. He makes dinner. Gives me massages. Flowers . . .

everywhere. I took him to Macy's, bought him clothes, called up everyone I knew and he goes out everyday looking for work. Then one day . . .

KALI Maybe today I stay home. This place pilau.

NARRATOR So he stays home and cleans. I mean really cleans. He's got this little toothbrush he uses on the bathroom tiles. He spends three hours washing the toilet.

KALI Can't stand pilau.

NARRATOR He gives me a bath three times a day. And he showers at least four times. And every night, he puts on his little apron and makes us dinner.

KALI (Obsessively) Do ya like it? Do ya like it? More shoyu! It's too sweet! It's ono? It's ono!

BRENDA It's fine!

NARRATOR And he stays up late and drinks.

KALI Coovaseeyah!

NARRATOR From Hai's farewell gift, the blue procelain teacup.

KALI (Sings in drunken stupor with effeminate mannerisms) "You're my past, you're my present, you're my future, girl . . . And we live togeda, foeva, like da wada to da . . ." (Mimes breaking HAI's cup)
 Oh! I wen broke da cup! Girl, Hai's cup, she we'n Broke . . . Hey girl, Girl! Girllll! Wake up! Wake up! I wen broke da cup. So lets cruise. Now!

NARRATOR We head south on 280 . . .

BRENDA Come on honey, slow down . . . You're doin' 90 . . .

KALI S'kay! Mama-San, S'Okay! Wot? You like me pussy whipped? I'm da king. Don't ya know me? Not no fucking fairy!!!

NARRATOR He pulls over. Pops a "U-ie" and floors it. Right into the oncoming headlights.

KALI Oooh! Weee! Dodge ball! 'Member Dodge ball? From small kid time? Miss me! Kiss my ass motherfucker.

BRENDA Kali! Stop it! Look out! N-N-N-OOOOO!!!!!!

NARRATOR He stops. We're parked – in the middle of the freeway – and I'm so freaked out and I'm so relieved that I . . . we . . .

BRENDA (Heavy sexual breathing that climaxes in orgasm) Kali! Kali! Kali! (Pause)

NARRATOR Things are getting a little out of control.

The Cocktail Party

NARRATOR Then one day, George, a friend of mine, a Chinese poet, invites us to a party at his house. I'm a little nervous. It's me and Kali's first time out in public.

BRENDA George! Great to see you . . . This is "Darren."

NARRATOR (Gives sigh of relief) But Kali's great. He's standing there in the corner holding court. And then I notice that all along while we're sipping wine, "Cheers! Salud!" He's drinking Jack Daniels from the bottle. He stands up and KA BOOM!! Right on his face. Everyone stops. And looks. George runs over to help him up.

KALI I'm okay. Upsy daisy. Thanks man. You hanging wit me, man. I love ya, man. Hey, George? You're not listening to me. I said I love you. So come on. Put that sweet little Pake booty in my face!

NARRATOR And Kali starts humping George. And George says . . .

GEORGE Get him off of me. GET HIM OFF OF ME! GET HIM THE HELL OUT OF MY HOUSE, BRENDA!!!

NARRATOR I drag 200 something pounds of him home . . . up two flights of stairs . . . to the bedroom . . .

KALI I gotta shi-shi.

NARRATOR To the bathroom. He can't stand up so I lean him against the door, unzip his fly and he starts to pee. Then he collapses, trapping us inside.

KALI I'm thirsty.

NARRATOR I try to give him a little water and he says . . .

KALI No thanks man. My boys are coming . . . Smoke, man, hurry up. I can't hang much longer. (Sips) Thanks man, I know I owe you man, thanks. When my boys get here . . . No. No. Don't do me. Please don't do me. No . . . Umh . . . Umhh . . . Ummh! (Pause) I'm all Pilau. Pilau. Smoke – (Glares) I wanna go home. Please let me go home . . .

NARRATOR He starts to cry and I don't know what to do so I hold him, and hold him . . .

BRENDA Kali, I can't hang anymore. You've got to figure this stuff out yourself cuz I don't know what to do for you. I'm dying. You've got to go cuz I can't handle – Just go! (Stares at light bulb)

NARRATOR The next morning, I get up. I go to work. I come home. I take off my jacket . . . Kali's gone. *(Pause)* Months pass. I get into my work. I make up with my friends. I tell myself I'm A-OK.

Re-enter Sherry

SHERRY   Ring! Ring! Hello, Brenda? This is Sherry.

NARRATOR   Sherry? I hadn't talked to her in years. Last thing I heard Smoke was in jail and she was a single mother on the Westside.

SHERRY   Smoke's out. He got out of the pen last week. He's after Kali. All the Pinoy and Guamanians are backin' Smoke. The Samoans and Hawaiians are with Kali.

BRENDA   What!? Why?

SHERRY   You mean you don't know? Kali sold Smoke to the DEA.

BRENDA   Sherry, I cut him loose. He's on his own.

SHERRY   Fine, whatever. But you've got to talk to him. Get him outta here. He's on a suicide mission, you know. He's crazy.

BRENDA   Sherry, don't you think I know that? That's why I cut him loose.

SHERRY   You're not gonna help us? Your ole man and my ole man are blowing up the whole Westside. Maybe in Frisco they don't have drive-bys, stray bullets. It could be your mom coming home from work, my kid coming home from school. Oh, but that has nothing to do with you! That's not your "responsibility!" Oh Brenda, how white of you.

BRENDA   Shit! I jump a cab. Catch the next flight to L.A. Now I am back on the Westside, sitting on an old couch covered with a stained sheet, electric fan on the coffee table, sound of the freeway coming through the paper thin walls. *(Music out)* Sherry runs her hand through her short cropped hair and lights another Kool . . .

SHERRY   You were Kali's safehouse you know. Smoke's had a contract on him ever since he squealed to the DEA . . . I'm surprised he even made it out of the pen. Dinner's in the oven, Hon.

NARRATOR   In the doorway, starch khakis, rolled tee shirt, blue rag, caramel colored skin . . . blonde hair . . . glaring at us.

SHERRY   You remember my son. He's trying to hate me. Cuz he's part white. He wants to be 100 percent Guamanian like

his Daddy. He's all excited about Smoke and Kali's stupid vendetta.

Re-enter Smoke

SMOKE   Brenda? What are you doing here?

NARRATOR   It's Smoke . . . He hasn't changed. He's just older.

SHERRY   I called her.

BRENDA   Smoke—

SMOKE   —Brenda, I know why you're here . . .

BRENDA   No, you don't know why I'm here. Let me finish. Kali's a wreck and it's all your fault. You let him rot like an animal in a cage. Your brother. You stupid ass . . . mother . . .

SMOKE   I tried! I was not gonna leave him in there. It was a coup! I was this close and Kali turns me in. My brother! Seven years in the pen . . . and now I–we ain't got nothin'!

NARRATOR   And Sherry says . . .

SHERRY   Ya got me. Us. We waited for you.

NARRATOR   Ding-Dong. In walk all these kids, $100 sneakers, baggy ass black shorts, Raiders' caps on backwards. Smoke's army. One of 'em says . . .

BANGER   Hey, Pops? We gonna cap up some coconuts tonight? Splat! Splat! Splat! Hah, hah, hah, hah, hah!

SHERRY   Come on Brenda, lets get out of here . . .

NARRATOR   I follow Sherry out the apartment and Smoke says,

SMOKE   *(Shouting after them)* Brenda, Kali wants me to kill him!

Last Ride thru the Westside

NARRATOR   We get in her car and cruise . . . Fast – through the Westside . . . Under the yellow streetlights . . . gang tags, crossed out . . . sneakers hangin' off power lines . . . little kids with cellular phones – lookouts . . . cars lining up on street corners like they're picking up fast food . . . sirens screaming in the night . . . the business of drugs in full swing.

We pull up at Aunti Mary's house. Sherry cuts the engine. We just sit.

SHERRY   I don't know what else to do. Now it's on you, Brenda.

NARRATOR   I look at Sherry. She must have gained 60 to 70 pounds. The chain-smoking shows on her face and her golden hair is chopped off.

SHERRY I've changed, huh, Brenda . . . Now I'm the fat mama. Que viva Westside . . .

BRENDA And I'm the cold bitch from Frisco.

SHERRY No, Brenda, you came.

BRENDA Yeah, here we are . . .

SHERRY My boy's only 14. He's all I got. They call him Dreamer.

Goodbye

NARRATOR I get out of the car, slam the door, and I'm hit *(pause)* by the overwhelming fragrance of Aunti Mary's rose garden. *(Inhales, exhales)* And I can breathe.

MARY Brenda, Kali's here, go inside.

NARRATOR It's Aunti Mary. Cutting her roses. I go into her parlor and there are all these men, old Westside Warriors with bellies hanging over their belts, young boys with hard faces drinking . . . smoking . . . knives . . . guns . . . Kali's Army . . . waiting . . . I go into the bedroom . . .

There's Kali, fresh out of the shower, naked from the waist up. He sees me in the mirror . . .

KALI Hows it?

BRENDA *(Nods)* You like go beach?

KALI Ah, Mada Ocean. You remember da rip?

BRENDA Huntington Beach. Big 14. Sky's the limit

KALI My wahine.

BRENDA Come on Kali, let's go . . .

Shoot-out

NARRATOR Boom Boom *(Pause)* Shi! Boom Boom *(Pause)* shi! A parade of slow-moving cars. Smoke and all his men. And Kali says . . .

KALI I'm goin' swimmin'. You wait for me?

NARRATOR He goes into the parlor, picks up an AK-47 . . .

KALI Okay! Let's go fo' broke!

NARRATOR Kicks open the door. His army

rises and they move into the garden.

BRENDA Kali!

NARRATOR Smoke and his boys get out of the cars *(Westside whistles)* and Smoke yells across the garden,

SMOKE Kali man, you still here?

KALI Always brah, always.

SMOKE Kali . . . I-I-I don't want to kill you . . . but you fucked me. You fucked me!! . . .

KALI You didn't come. I couldn't wait. So come on. Do me!

NARRATOR BANG! BANG! . . . Gun shots . . . Men running . . . trampling the bushes . . . the flowers . . . and in the midst of the madness, Aunti Mary . . . and in her arms . . . bunches and bunches of red, red, roses, big as cabbages . . .

MARY Smoke! Smoke! All the Islanders are here now. You and Kali, just like braddahs since small kid time! So easy to die. Go inside. Talk . . .

NARRATOR BANG! Red, red, Roses! Falling through the air . . .

I look over and I see Dreamer. And from his gun a wisp of smoke drifting up into the yellow street lamps. And Dreamer says . . .

DREAMER I did it, Pops, I tasted blood, man . . . Hey? Why ya lookin' at me? I took out a mother fuckin' Hawaiian. I mean, that's what this is all about, right? Right?

NARRATOR That was not the last shot fired that day . . . Kali's gone . . . *(Pause)* . . . So's Dreamer . . . Smoke disappeared . . . Sherry's doin' better now. Me . . . I went back to San Francisco and I didn't want to come home for a long time . . . But my mom, dad, sisters and little bro still live on the Westside. And even though I live in San Francisco, the Westside is here. *(Points to chest)*

I still love roses. They remind me of Aunti Mary. She really was a queen, you know. Her garden is now choked with weeds, but it's amazing, every year some roses still bloom.

(Curtain)

Breena Clarke · Glenda Dickerson

Biographies

Glenda Dickerson is a director, writer, folklorist, educator and actor. She has directed such actors as Debbie Allen, Lynn Whitfield, Charles Brown, Phillip Michael Thomas, Robert Townsend, and many others; and has worked on Broadway, off-Broadway, regionally and internationally. She has conceived and/or adapted numerous vehicles for the stage from various dramatic and non-dramatic sources, including the "miracle play": *Jesus Christ, Lawd Today*; *Owen's Song*; *The Unfinished Song*; *Rashomon*; *Torture of Mothers*; *Jump at the Sun*; and *Every Step I Take*. She conceived and directed *Eel Catching in Setauket: A Living Portrait of A Community*, an oral history, creative performance project which documented the lives of the African-American Christian Avenue community in Setauket, Long Island. She performs in her one-woman shows, *Saffron Persephone Brown: The Flower-storm of a Brown Woman* and *Spreading Lies*; and in *The Trojan Women: A Tale of Devastation for Two Voices*. Glenda is a professor and chairperson of the Department of Drama at Spelman College.

Breena Clarke, writer, actress and journalist, has a varied career as an arts professional. She made her Broadway acting debut in *Reggae* in 1980, has appeared with many off-Broadway theater companies and is founder and artistic director of The Narratives Performing Company. With The Narratives Performing Company, Breena's directorial and acting work has appeared at The First and Second National Festivals of Women's Theater in 1983 and 1984, as well at many colleges and universities. She has worked as an Equity stage manager and has taught acting and speech at The Duke Ellington School of the Arts in Washington, D.C. Breena is assistant to the Deputy Managing Editor of *Time* magazine and an Associate Editor of *Black Masks* magazine. Her writing has been published in *Time*, *Black Masks*, *Heresies: A Feminist Publication on Art and Politics*, *Conditions*, *Quarto* and others. She is currently at work on a novel of black life and experience in Washington, D.C.

Artistic statement by Breena Clarke

I began my career in theater in the best

Photo: © Sharon Farmer

Judy Garland–Mickey Rooney movie fantasy tradition. At 11, my best friend, my younger sister, Vicki, and I mounted a theatrical revue in my parents' living room with a cast of other neighborhood kids. We played piano, lip-synched records, recited poetry and danced for our parents. My older sister, the poet Cheryl Clarke, was our stage manager. This singular production led to an audition with The Children's Theater of Washington and a lead part in *The Merry Pranks of Tyll*. I continued with The Children's Theater through high school, took piano lessons and performed in school productions.

I am a native of Washington, D.C., a city which has always had a sizable African-American population. My parents grew up in Georgetown, a section of Washington known to most of the country as the neighborhood of political appointees and diplomats. But Georgetown has always had a sizable working-class African-American presence, too. In fact, a unique convergence of institutional and economic forces created opportunities for working-class blacks in Washington, a city which is not only geographically southern, but pointedly southern in custom, climate and speech.

Luckily for their daughters, Edna Higgins Payne Clarke and James Sheridan Clarke are natural oral historians. They remember everything and they know how to tell a good story. Summer evenings when we were growing up were spent taking "rides" in the family car. We rode around Washington and nearby Maryland and my parents pointed out landmarks and told anecdotes about Georgetown. These two dug their heels into Washington and remain there still.

Most African-American writers feel required to note that their parents encouraged reading and writing and advanced education. It was not until I was an adult that I realized that not everyone's home had books, newspapers, magazines, pianos and time for homework. I never considered being well-read and well-educated an exceptional accomplishment for an African-American woman. I considered my sisters, my parents and myself to be ordinary.

After high school, I went away to Webster College in a suburb of St. Louis, Missouri. Though Webster had an excellent theater conservatory program, there were few opportunities for a black student to perform. I returned to Washington to attend Howard University. At Howard, it was my great good luck to study with Glenda Dickerson, a wunderkind theater professor/Howard alumna, who had had a critical success the previous year with "The Unfinished Song."

Some of the most exciting productions I've ever been involved in were directed by Glenda – *El Haj Malik, Jesus Christ, Lawd Today, The Torture of Mothers,* and *The Trojan Women.*

The Howard University Theater Department milieu included some of the most innovative talents in theater in the sixties and seventies. Much of the creativity spilled outside the campus and spawned arts institutions such as The D.C. Black Repertory Company, Workshops for Careers in the Arts and The Duke Ellington School of the Arts. But Washington suffers for its proximity to the New York theater scene. It has just enough performing opportunities to keep artists there, but not enough to make them a "star." Few have become "stars" which is more about the nature of the theater business and racism and sexism than about talent.

I arrived in New York in the later part of 1979 to work with Glenda Dickerson again. She was mounting a production on

Broadway and I came on board as an assistant stage manager and dialect coach. *Reggae,* produced by Michael Butler, was a perfect example of the vagaries of Broadway with a dollop of racism and sexism added. The less said about that experience the better.

Glenda's an army brat so she's been all over and she's never been afraid to "bust" down a wall between where she is and where she wants to get to. And I've held her coat more often than not.

She comes from a family with a long tradition of story-telling, too. She credits her grandmothers, Ada Taminia Kilpatrick and Ruth Harris Sanders, with igniting the passionate fires she's always brought to her work. After Howard, Glenda directed in New York and has taught at the Duke Ellington School of the Arts, at Rutgers University Mason Gross School of the Arts, SUNY Stoneybrook and Rutgers University Newark campus.

Glenda's been called "difficult." But you and I know that that's just a patriarchal code for a woman who's not reluctant to be intelligent, articulate and uncompromising.

We have been "there" for each other. You know – "there" is the place under the ribcage somewhere near the diaphragm that is where great rapture and great grief will settle. In each other's lives we've shared the rapture of childbirth – her daughter and my son – and the numbing pain of loss – my son and her beloved cousin. At times we've been neck and neck in competition with each other and at other times we've stood shoulder to shoulder in support of each other. With *Aunt Jemima* we've been head to head in collaboration. This has made all the difference in creating our work.

The work Glenda Dickerson and I have done on *Re/Membering Aunt Jemima* has been the outgrowth of a wide variety of experiences – motherhood, daughterhood, wifehood, sisterhood, friendship, bereavement, sexism, racism and classism.

In our collaboration, we've chosen to credit authorship absolutely equally. Thus we put our names on the same line with only a period between. That's because we can no longer distinguish between what one person wrote or thought and what the other did.

Though today most people abhor Aunt Jemima as the ultimate degrading stereotype of African-American women, we see her as an icon rooted in the ancient African tradition of household orisha. We liken her to the Santeria figure, La Madama, the orisha who fearlessly guards the peace of our homes as she presides over our bread-baking and clothes-making. Aunt Jemima is not a joke to us. On the contrary, we attempt to show that African people used to revere the qualities for which she is now denigrated. Aunt Jemima has big lips; she is fat; she wears bright colors; she is smiling. We have been taught to fear all these qualities. Voluptuous lips are ugly only when measured by European standards; the same with steatopygous buttocks. We hate her headrag, but forget that it makes sense for a person who does her kind of work to cover her head. It was somebody else's culture which told us we look stupid in bright colors. If we look to our Motherland, we see the lie in that idea. We think she smiles without cause and that this is somehow shameful. But how do we know why she smiles? The smile of Aunt Jemima is no less enigmatic than the smile of Mona Lisa.

In celebrating the character and person of Aunt Jemima we do not condone the stereotype as she has been used to oppress African-American women; rather we acknowledge the shame we all feel at the sight of her, at the sound of her name. We acknowledge her as the symbol and the repository of the shame, disease and self-hatred from which we wish to free ourselves. She keeps our shame in her cookie jar, in the fashion of the Sopera, like the frightened kernel which holds the secret voice. By way of payment for the service she performs, we offer her hatred and despisement. This hatred is what we have named the "Aunt Jemima stigma." It is the thing that makes everyone get excited at the mere mention of her name.

What makes Aunt Jemima so hateful? That is the question we pose through our play. We decided that the bravest thing we could do would be to take on the stereotype of Aunt Jemima, tear it apart, examine it and put her back together as the archetype she originally was. We choose to confront Aunt Jemima, to confront the bogie woman, recognize the person underneath and rescue that person. In doing so, we propose to rescue Aunt Jemima, and by extension our foremothers, from the stereotyping that makes us face our mirrors with fear. As playwright/rescuers we have taken as our task the uncovering of the real woman behind the stereotype. Because that real woman, though too often viewed with shame, is most really ourselves and our foremothers. It is this real woman that we love and mean to celebrate. It we reject her, we are rejecting ourselves. When you strip away the preconceived notions that make us cringe at the mention of Aunt Jemima's name, what you are left with is a big strong, capable woman who came with us from Africa, who guided our journey though bondage, who is with us still. We have only to acknowledge and welcome her and she will work her magic on our behalf. Her red dress, her voluptuous smiling lips, her steatopygous buttocks, her head covering, her magic broom, these are the things that make her beautiful.

Production history

Re/Membering Aunt Jemima was first performed as a work-in-progress in January, 1992 at the Lorraine Hansberry Theatre in San Francisco, California. It has been performed as a staged reading at Newark Symphony Hall, Moe's Restaurant/Cabaret, and the National Black Arts Festival. It premiered at the National Black Arts Festival/Spelman College in Atlanta on 3–6 August 1994. It was directed by Glenda Dickerson, and the cast included Sandra Bowie, Stephanie Berry, Gwendolyn Nelson-Fleming and Gwendolyn Roberts-Frost. An excerpted version was published in *Women and Performance* Vol. 6, No. 1, 1993.

2 Re/membering Aunt Jemima: A Menstrual Show

Glenda Dickerson · Breena Clarke

Act I

At curtain, the company stands at semi-circle. The space is somehow reminiscent of a circus or carnival sideshow. The lighting is harsh such as would be found in an oldtime minstrel show.

LA MADAMA INTERLOCK-IT-TOGETHERER
  Stereotypes, be seated!
  Contrary women and sympathetic gents,
  I extend a welcome on behalf of the
    greatest show on earth:
  THE AUNT JEMIMA TRAVELING
    MENSTRUAL SHOW!!!!!!!
  We have come out tonight to bring you
  an evening of oddities, peculiarities,
  eccentricities and commicalities of the
  distaff side of the Sable Genus of
  Humanity. We will present a true copy of
  the ups and downs in the life of Aunt
  Jemima, the most famous colored woman
  in the world. We will fondly reminisce
  about the lovable bright side of Negro life
  down on Col. Uncle Sam Higbee's sunny
  plantation. With bones on the right and
  tamborines on the left, we begin.
  (Company sings)

We're the Aunt Jemima Travelling
  Menstrual Show
Stereotypes extraordinaire
The Aunt Jemima Travelling Menstrual
  Show
Welcome to the circus of our minds
The carnival of our intentions
The menstruation of our bodies
The minstrelsy of our souls
The Aunt Jemima Travelling Menstrual
  Show

We are here to perform an act of magic.
Say, we are here to perform an act of
  magic.

We're going to wear the mask
Of the jolly Mammy,
We're going to pitch ourselves
Off the pancake box.
We're going to find ourselves,
Love ourselves
In the big, fat Mammy of lies.

Oh, Mammy, don't you know
We'll rescue you with magic

(A skirmish breaks out between two
MENSTRUALS.*)*
MENSTRUAL You is just a creature of white
  imagination.
MENSTRUAL You ole house nigger! I'll
  defile and mutilate your body until you
  look like Bo Akutia!
LA MADAMA INTERLOCK-IT-TOGETHERER
  Mistresses, I will not put up with this
  ingenious vituperation by proxy. Go back
  to your seats.
  *(*MENSTRUALS *sullenly return to their seats.)*
LA MADAMA INTERLOCK-IT-TOGETHERER
  Aunt Jemima is the Grand Mammy of
  American myth.
MENSTRUAL Aunt Jemima was born in a
  box.
MENSTRUAL She was discovered covered
  with feces . . .
MENSTRUAL And branded with the letters
  KKK.
MENSTRUAL She never did get over that
  sad beginning.
MENSTRUAL Her parents are unknown and
  she just sprung up on Col. Uncle Sam
  Higbee's plantation.
JEMIMA I was naked as a jaybird until I
  was 12.
MENSTRUAL A humble old fellow named
  Uncle Ben worked in the fields on Col.
  Higbee's plantation. He was from Sara
  Leeon and knew everything there was to
  know about growing rice.

MENSTRUAL Hadn't been for Ben, Col. Higbee would've been groanin' stead of growing rice.

MENSTRUAL Uncle Tom was the butterler in the Big House. He knew how to read and conducted secret services for the other slaves in the arbor by the stream.

MENSTRUAL (As Uncle Tom) Who keeps snakes and all bad things from hurting you?

MENSTRUALS God does.

MENSTRUAL Who gave you a master and a mistress?

MENSTRUALS God gave them to me.

MENSTRUAL If the master be unreasonable, may the servant disobey?

MENSTRUALS No.

MENSTRUAL No! No! The Bible says, "Servant, be subject to your masters with all fear."

MENSTRUALS (Singing)
I am a poor pilgrim of sorrow
I'm lost in this wide world alone
No hope have I for tomorrow
I've started to make heaven my home.

MENSTRUAL (As singing continues) From a very young child, Jemima would see things dart by out of the corner of her eye. Sometimes she felt something watching her over her shoulder.

MENSTRUAL Uncle Tom told her it was nothing but the devil. But a maroon woman name of Nanny who lived on the plantation knew it was the Three Blood Mysteries.

JEMIMA Who Dat?

NANNY Who dat?

JEMIMA Who dat?

NANNY Who Dat?

JEMIMA Who dat say who dat when I say who dat?

NANNY Dat yo' womanhood coming down on you.

MENSTRUALS Nanny, Nanny, Bomanny. Banana, fanna, fo-manny. Nanny!
Sees her comes and sees her goes.
Sees her ass the bullet throws.

MENSTRUAL Nanny was renumerated to be able to catch bullets with her ass-perity. She was HNIC in the kitchen. Jemima was her Novitiate Scotiate. When Nanny put on her necklace of English soldiers' teeth and decided to fly back to Africa, Jemima became head cook.

MENSTRUAL Jemima soon developed a repetitious as a fast, efficient cook with a repertoirishus of delicious dishes, but her skilletacious with pancakes brought her the most refrown.

JEMIMA (Ringing dinner bell) Griddle cakes piping hot. Come and get 'em.

MENSTRUAL Other Mammy cooks tried in vain to get her famous recipe. When them rascals come up against Jemima's irascible nature, they give up in disrepair.

MENSTRUAL Col. Higbee was forever sniffin' 'round the kitchen cause he couldn't get enough of them delicious pancakes.

MENSTRUAL Miss Ann suspicioned that his hunger went beyond a simple hankering for pancakes.

MENSTRUALS (Singing)
Someone's in the kitchen with Dinah
Someone's in the kitchen, I know.
Someone's in the kitchen with Dinah
Strummin on the old banjo.
Fe fi fiddle di oh, fe fi fiddle di oh
Fe fi fiddle di oh, fe fi fiddle di oh
Strummin on the old banjo.

(MENSTRUAL chases JEMIMA with Col. Higbee Puppet.)

JEMIMA Lawd, Col. Higbee, I don't know nothin' about birthin' no babies.

CHILDBIRTH The birth of that baby was any-minunent. So Col. Higbee sent for the midwife.

MENSTRUAL The first of Aunt Jemima's 13 daughters was named Dorothy. That baby popped from under her mama's skirts singing the blues.

MENSTRUAL (Singing)
My old Man was a white old man
My old Mammy's black
Wonder what I'm gonna do
Being neither white nor black.
I got the blues.
The tragic mulatta blues!

MENSTRUAL Col. Uncle Sam Higbee kept eating a steady diet of his favorite pancakes.

JEMIMA Pancakes with a personality!

MENSTRUAL And he whipped up three more daughters in Jemima's mixing bowl:
Marie, a child born with a rattlesnake in her hand.
Pecola, a little red baby who bawled melodramatically all the time.
And Dysmorfia, who was half black and half white, but the black skin didn't show as long as she kept her clothes on.

MENSTRUAL   Col. Higbee was sitting on the porch one day, sipping on Southern Comfort and watching his four beautiful but mixed-up daughters.

MENSTRUAL   Marie's skirts made a superstitious swishing sound as she danced to music in her head.

MENSTRUAL   The other three was sitting in the sunlight trying to tame their mama's naps, fussing at her all the time.

JEMIMA   What you gals doin' here? Ain't you got nothing better to do than fool with my naps?

PECOLA   Want to sit with somebody uglier than me.

JEMIMA   What's de mattah wid you. Fore we come across de water, everybody look lak me. I ain't ugly. You just thinks I is.

PECOLA   Yes, ma'am you is. Your lips is too big. Dey looks lak bees been stingin' you.

DYSMORFIA   My lips is too big, too, but you can't tell cause I holds 'em in like this.

JEMIMA   Don't be ridiculous. Why you got all dat cornstarch on your face?

DYSMORFIA   In case de black creep out from underneath my clothes.

DOROTHY   Mammy, how come you ain't 'shamed of the way you look. How come you always so happy?

JEMIMA   Ain't got nothing to be ashamed 'bout. I got pretty black skin, I got a beautiful, long neck, I got a fine, rounded shape. I got plenty to smile about. What de matter wid you?

MENSTRUAL   Does it seem to you lak dem gals favors Miss Ann's tow-headed chillun?

MENSTRUAL   Yep, das why she made Col. Uncle Sam sell 'em off de place.

MENSTRUAL
Bid 'em in, Bid 'em in.
   We got fine ones, tall ones, black ones, brown ones, yellow ones. Bid 'em in! Bid 'em in!

THE DAUGHTERS
Mam, Mam, Mammy, Goodbye.
Mam, Mam, Mammy, don't cry.

MENSTRUAL   Dorothy was sold to Paramount Pictures where she became a tragic star. She committed suicide at a young age and asked to be buried as they found her – scarf, gloves and underwear intact.

MENSTRUAL   Marie was sold as a "fancy gal" to High John de Conquer in New Orleans.

MENSTRUAL   Dysmorfia and Pecola was sold as a matched pair, but Pecola soon escaped and passed for white up North.

MENSTRUAL   As Jemima watched her girls carted off, she wrapped her half-combed naps in a old greasy rag. She looked Col. Higbee in the eye and grinned a grin so brilliantine that it could flatten out naps dead straight.

MENSTRUAL   From this day forth Jemima became known as "Auntie."

MENSTRUAL   Long about this time, a big slave name of Two Ton arrived on the plantation. Two Ton got his name 'cause he could pick two ton of cotton any day of the week.

(MENSTRUALS *enter with two bales of cotton.*)

AUNT JEMIMA *(Singing)*
Some enchanted evening
You may meet a stranger
You may meet a stranger
Across a crowded room.

(AUNT JEMIMA *bats her eyes flirtatiously at Two Ton.*)

MENSTRUAL   Two Ton was constantly trying to outdo himself in the weight of cotton he could pick. Col. Higbee discombobulated the balls on the weighing machine so that the bolls Two Ton picked needed an ever increasing weight of balls to balance 'em. Pretty soon the man bust his balls pickin' them bolls.

MENSTRUAL   Two Ton died with his hammer in his hand. But he left Aunt Jemima with three little hammers to remember him by:
   Anna Julia, a woman who risqued all to learn to read; Rebecca, a strangely beautiful child called by the thunder to preach the gospel. She became an itinerant preacher and traveled through the south ministering to freed slaves; and Bondswoman, a girl with freedom always on her mind.

BONDSWOMAN   I will follow the North Star and the moss on the trees.

MENSTRUALS *(Singing)*
Feets, don't fail her now.
Feets, do your duty!
Oh, feets don't fail her now!

(As BONDSWOMAN *flees for freedom, she encounters medicine women, hairdressers and other adventurers.*)

MENSTRUAL   Come and get your COON GRIN CONKOLENE! It will flatten out naps dead straight. Mistresses and creatrix, all diminutives must fade 'cause Madam C.J. Moonwalker knew best the tricks of the tress stress trade. Come and get it!

MENSTRUAL And now, Contrary Women, FOR SALE, CONGO SQUARE SNAKE OIL! An ointment of power and purity. You can take it for relief from those monthly discomforts; take it to cool off from those private summers; take it to soothe the mysterious misery of the rainy season clitoridectomy.

MENSTRUAL Chilluns! Get yo' Aunt Jemima Rag Doll Family!
(MENSTRUALS *are sprinkling condiments on several dolls.*)

LA MADAMA INTERLOCK-IT-TOGETHERER What're you doing sprinkling salt and pepper on those babies?

MENSTRUAL We seasonin' 'em up.

MENSTRUAL So's they'll be fit for the hog meat gang. These is goin' to be A-number-one picaninnies.

LA MADAMA INTERLOCK-IT-TOGETHERER But you don't season them up by putting salt on them.

MENSTRUAL Huh?

LA MADAMA INTERLOCK-IT-TOGETHERER You're supposed to fatten them up with choice victuals and give them only light tasks until their bodies are strong and fit for hard labor.

MENSTRUALS Oh.

LA MADAMA INTERLOCK-IT-TOGETHERER A smart master like Col. Higbee knows you get your money's worth out a slave if you season them up right from the start.

MENSTRUAL Cardamon bay thyme o-reg-an-o allspice?

MENSTRUAL oREG-a-no Rosemary bay garlic and thyme.

MENSTRUAL Back down on the plantation, Aunt Jemima went out every night and looked down the road her daughter had traveled. One night from out of the moonlight step a smooth brown man of mystery.
(MENSTRUAL *sets down a bottle of Karo syrup near* AUNT JEMIMA.)

MENSTRUAL This smooth, brown man of mystery was dripping wet 'cause he just swim from Dominica. He whispered to Aunt Jemima how he could make a thick, smooth, sweet syrup he'd concocted in the islands that would glide slowly and flavorfully down a stack of she pancakes. This famous, secret syrup with its husky, sweet flavor, made a fitting accompaniment to Aunt Jemima's delicious American breakfast. Ooo-wee! How she loved her Karo!

MENSTRUAL All in due time, Bondswoman came back over her Great Underground Railroad. She discovered that she had three new husky, sweet sisters: Sapphire, a girl who could not be tamed by any man; Susie-Faye, who became president of the Planned Parenthood ConFederate-ation of America; and the newborn baby, Freedom Fighter. When Freedom Fighter grew up, she became involved in so many slave revolts and shootouts, she was on the FBI most wanted list.

MENSTRUAL Bondswoman gathered up her new sisters and led them all out to the Promised Land.
(*Song: "O Freedom"*)
O Freedom
O Freedom
O Freedom over me
Before I'll be a slave
I'll be buried in my grave
And go home to my Lord and be free
And go home to my Lord and be free.

MENSTRUAL Aunt Jemima continued as Higbee plantation cook.

MENSTRUAL Whenever there were guests, Aunt Jemima was called upon to make huge stacks of her fluffy, light pancakes.

MENSTRUAL Coax as long as dey might, guests at Col. Higbee's plantation never could get out of her the secret flavor of dem wonderful pancakes.

AUNT JEMIMA That's my secret, you just eat 'em.

MENSTRUAL When the great War Between the States broke out Aunt Jemima, Uncle Tom and Uncle Ben was the only darkies who stayed on the place. Uncle Ben and Aunt Jemima kept each other warm at night and they steamed up two little twin converted rice cakes: Aminata, a head-strong girl full of determination. And Anita, a tall, beautiful serious scholar.

MENSTRUAL Emancipation came like a bolt out of the blue. Uncle Ben decided to walk back to Africa and took Aminata with him. Uncle Tom hitch-hiked up to the Yarvard Law School to begin meretri-cious matriculation. Anita went with him to learn at his feet.

MENSTRUAL So it was just Aunt Jemima left on the plantation with Col. Uncle Sam. Col. Uncle was so poor he didn't know what to do.

MENSTRUAL Then one day R.T. Davis of the Davis Milling company went ashore at Higbee landing and tasted Aunt Jemima's scrumptious pancakes. He flipped out. He persuaded Colonel to let Aunt Jemima share her recipe with others. Colonel said he would consider it for a price.

MENSTRUAL And so Aunt Jemima left her home to begin her travels up and down America.

MENSTRUAL Aunt Jemima was interdicted to the world at the World's Columbian Exposition in 1893 . . .

MENSTRUAL

Pancake days is here again
Mm, mmm, mmm, mmm
Mm, mmm, mmm.
Pancake days is here again
Mm, mmm, mmm, mmm
Mm, mmm, mmm.

AUNT JEMIMA I'se in town, honey. I'se around.

MENSTRUAL R.T. Davis set her up in a booth in The Great Agricultural Hall to advertise his new packaged pancake mix based on Aunt Jemima's own recipe.

MENSTRUAL Everybody was there at the World's Fair. All the well known speakers and great doers of the African peoples was there.

MENSTRUAL But the center of all this was Aunt Jemima. Everybody at the Fair wanted to taste them golden brown cakes. She was a sensation!

AUNT JEMIMA Lawsy, we ain't never goin' to be able to make enough pancakes for all dem white folks.

MENSTRUAL Aunt Jemima flipped more than one million pancakes and gave each one an identity by telling antidotes of how all America had come to love her pancakes.

AUNT JEMIMA Ole Miss Ann was mighty hard on us niggers. She would take a needle and stick it through my lower lip and pin it to the bodice of my dress and Ah'd have to go roun' all day with my head drew down that a way and slobberin. It felt like Ah was goin' crazy. (ALL *laugh uproariously.*)

MENSTRUAL Aunt Jemima, your cheerful demeanor has much to do with the popularity of your pancakes. They have become America's favorite breakfast. Aunt Jemima, the committee on awards bestows upon your pancake flour the highest medal and the diploma of excellence.

LA MADAMA INTERLOCK-IT-TOGETHERER But honors did not turn her head.

AUNT JEMIMA Dis honor should go to Col. Uncle Sam Higbee. His kind words spoken to me years and years ago, expressing his appreciation for my loyalty and cheerful service, mean more to me than my present fame. But when R.T. Davis offered me the opportunity to make so many families happy with the ease and satisfaction of serving my mouth-watering pancakes – it was irresistible. My pancakes delighted Col. Higbee and his guests. Here they are delighting thousands. Thank you.

MENSTRUAL While Aunt Jemima was flipping pancakes, she could hear true women in the tent next door – Lifting As They Climb.

MENSTRUAL (TRUE WOMAN 1) We now issue the call to all the women's bodies throughout the country. The time is short, but everything is ripe.

AUNT JEMIMA Her is a veri-table paramour of genuine ass-ets.

MENSTRUAL (TRUE WOMAN 2) The painful, patient and silent toil of mothers to gain a fee, simple title to the bodies of their daughters, the despairing fight, as of an entrapped tigress, to keep hallowed their own persons, would furnish material for epics.

AUNT JEMIMA She put huh ass-ets on ma table and Ah'm gwine to kick huh veri-ass-ity.

MENSTRUAL (TRUE WOMAN 3) Only the black woman can say "when and where I enter, in the quiet, undisputed dignity of my womanhood, without violence and without suing or special patronage, then and there the whole Negro race enters with me."

AUNT JEMIMA Her is the legiti-mate of the spurious equivocator, but Ah don't care who huh husband is, she better not be quivocatin' in my face.

MENSTRUAL (TRUE WOMAN 1) Ladies, shall we step next door and sample Aunt Jemima's temptalatin comestibles?

MENSTRUAL (ANNA JULIA) Compositively-trary not! I would rather leave public life.

MENSTRUAL   When Aunt Jemima laid eyes on the speechifyer seemed like to her it was the little girl who risqued all to learn to read.

AUNT JEMIMA   Anna, Anna, child is that you?

ANNA JULIA   O, Mammy, all through the darkest period of the colored women's oppression in this country, a period full of heroic struggle, a struggle against fearful and overwhelming odds that often ended in a horrible death, I have prayed to once again see your greasy face.

MENSTRUAL   And so, Aunt Jemima is reunited with her daughter, Anna Julia, who was a founding member of the National Association of Colored Women and a proponent of the tenets of the cult of true womanhood.

AUNT JEMIMA and TRUE WOMEN *(Singing)*
No more auction block for me
No more, no more
No more auction block for me
Many thousands gone
No more pint of salt for me
No more, no more
No more pint of salt for me
Many thousands gone.
Lift every voice and sing
'Til earth and heaven ring
Ring with the harmony
Of liberty

MENSTRUAL   After the World's Fair, Aunt Jemima served as the official trademark for The Davis Milling Company's pancake flour for three decades. She became a traveling spokesperson spreading the word of her clean, sweet, pure pancake flour.

AUNT JEMIMA   My pancake flour is made in a sanitary napkin mill by millers of long experience. At the Aunt Jemima mills the ingredients are exactly mixed as Ah once mixed them by hand. Other manufacturers have sought the secret of my famous pancakes. They've never achieved it. Lawsy, they never will.

MENSTRUAL   Aunt Jemima's personal appearances soon made her smiling face a familiar sight to all Americans. She appeared in advertisements and commercials all over the world.

AUNT JEMIMA   Wake up, wake up to Aunt Jemima's old south recipe. Pancakes so light! So tender! They melt in your mouth.

MENSTRUAL   Aunt Jemima even published a book of her famous recipes called Aunt Jemima's New Temptalatin' Menus and Recipes.

MENSTRUAL   Weary from her world travels, Aunt Jemima loved to take the Orange Blossom Special home to her little shack at Col. Higbee's. After soaking the tiredness out of her feet with epsom salts, she would put them up and listen to the Amos and Andy show. That was Aunt Jemima's favorite show 'cause her daughter, Sapphire had a starring role.

MENSTRUAL   One Sunday night, while she was chuckling over Sapphire's mule-headed ways, Aunt Jemima got a shock. She heard on the radio that R.T. Davis had hired out her services to the Quaker Oats man.

MENSTRUAL   Aunt Jemima decided she better pay the Quaker Oats man a visit to take his measurements. She fortified herself with a pint of Jack Daniels and rolled her Thunderbird through the rolling hills of Rolling Rock till she come to the Quaker Oats man's house. She found him to be susceptible to Friendly Persuasion and he egregiously a-greed to introduce her famous buckwheat pancakes to the world.

AUNT JEMIMA   A surprise from the good old days. Buckwheats with the taste men hanker for. Mornings when the window panes are frosty, a hankering comes to men – a longing for the tang and robust savor of real, old time, buckwheats. Perhaps your husband says nothing whatever about it. Perhaps he himself does not know just how tempting, how delicious, good old fashioned buckwheats really are. But, deep down in all men there is a sparkle of youth waiting to be awakened at the breakfast table and millions of women right now are wakening it – giving their husbands light, fluffy cakes with the true, old fashioned buckwheat kick.

MENSTRUAL   When the politically incorrect, internationally acclaimed Aunt Jemima diversified, she made so much money that she bought herself a full-length mink coat and hired herself a chauffeur to drive her around in her Cadillac convertible.

MENSTRUAL   However, those who knew her best, those who knew her even from the time when she first came up from her little cabin home, found her still the same simple, earnest, smiling Mammy cook.

AUNT JEMIMA *(Tipsy from champagne)* I'se in town, honey. I'se around.

MENSTRUAL The new celebrity-fide Aunt Jemima was called to represent her race in many different forums ranging from county hog-calling contests to the Miss America pageant.

(A crowned MISS AMERICA *enters.)*

MENSTRUAL *(As* MISS AMERICA*)* I'm not going to be a bitch with a problem or a ho' with an attitude. Just because I have a crown on my head, doesn't mean my perception is different from anyone else. I'm going to live the life I sing about in my song.

AUNT JEMIMA *(Entering drunk and disorderly)* Dysmorfia, is that you gal, up there showing everything you should hide. Ah never thought ah'd see a child of mine acting that common. You better come over here and sit down before ah miss your america for you. In the country that's just how they buys cows. Ah don't see why ya'll don't just bring in the auction block and sell 'em all together.

AUNT JEMIMA *(Singing)*
I'se in town, honey,
I'se around.
Smoking hot delicious and brown
My old fashioned pancakes have brought
   me renown.
Your grocer has a fresh supply,
Now that fall is here.
My griddle cakes piping hot
Will bring your family cheer.

Act II

MENSTRUAL *(As* MENOPAUSE*)* I am menopause. I will change your life in a hot flash.

AUNT JEMIMA and **MENOPAUSE** *(Singing)*
It seems too good to be true
That ragtime fever's dying out
Seems to good to be true
Seems to good to be true

It seems to good to be true
That ragtime fever's dying out
Seems to good to be true
Seems to good to be true
And we syncopated, hypnotic
   sentimentalists
Will soon return to our barbaric haunts

Seems to good to be true
Seems to good to be true

LA MADAMA INTERLOCK-IT-TOGETHERER Aunt Jemima, America's Grand Mammy, remained true to fact and tradition. Tinsel Town beckoned.

MENSTRUAL Beating out a score of imitators, Aunt Jemima won the coveted role of the faithful colored retainer in an epic motion picture of the old south.

MENSTRUAL And the winner for Best Actress in a supporting role is: Aunt Jemima.

AUNT JEMIMA Thank you, friends, colleagues and members of the Academy. Ah hope that my winning this award will be an inspiration to the youth of my race, that it will encourage them to aim high and work hard, and take the bitter with the sweet. Ah did my best and God did the rest.

MENSTRUAL Back down on the plantation, Aunt Jemima was polishing her Oscar and eatin' on a watermelon when she swallowed a seed. Her stomach growed and growed and growed and growed until a tiny little baby burst out of her mouth.

MENSTRUAL That tiny little baby was the spittin' image of her mama. That's how Aunt Jemima got her thirteenth daughter.

MENSTRUAL It was an Aunt Jemima Cake Mix Miracle conception, cause Menopause had long since changed her life and plus Aunt Jemima didn't have no man!

MENSTRUAL Nobody was Nommo surprised than Aunt Jemima, but she just accepted the miracle and named that tiny little baby Tiny Desiree.

MENSTRUAL One day while Aunt Jemima was changing Tiny Desiree's diapers, her new princess telephone rang. It was Time magazine calling.

MENSTRUAL Aunt Jemima! Aunt Jemima! Your daughter, Aminata has fled Africa and thrown herself on the mercy of the World Court. She say she ain't having no clitoridictomy.

AUNT JEMIMA Clitoridectomy? What dat?

MENSTRUAL Dat's when dey cuts off your whosit.

AUNT JEMIMA Who sit? What sat?

MENSTRUAL Whosit is the whatsit what sits where Au Set sat.

AUNT JEMIMA Where das at?

MENSTRUAL Fool, it down dere 'tween your thingamabob and your thingamajig.

AUNT JEMIMA Naw! You inFIBulatin'!

MENSTRUAL Uh, huh!

AUNT JEMIMA Wait a minute! Ah do believe Ah'se heard of dat. Has somethin' to do with dementia, don't it?

MENSTRUAL If youse a female you don't suppose da mention it.

AUNT JEMIMA O-o-oh! Hush yo' mouf.

MENSTRUAL Uncle Ben say she got to have a clitoridectomy before she gets married.

AUNT JEMIMA Oh, lord, has she got the nervousness?

MENSTRUALS No!

AUNT JEMIMA Has she got the catalepsy?

MENSTRUALS No!

AUNT JEMIMA She been hysterical?

MENSTRUALS No!

AUNT JEMIMA Oh, lord, don't tell me my chile's been masturbatin'! *(Falls out in dead faint)*

(Carnival sounds are heard.)

MENSTRUAL It was Fat Tuesday in the Cathedral of St. John de Divine. De Hoodoo Queen of New Orleans come to hold a big celebration for de folks at midnight. Her skirts swished when she walked and all de folks stepped back and whisper, "Das de mos powerful woman dere is."

LA MADAMA INTERLOCK-IT-TOGETHERER And now ladies and gentlemen, the moment we has all been waitin' for. The Hoodoo Queen of New Orleans will sing her latest platinum hit. She will be backed up as always by the world famous Three Blood Mysteries!

(HOODOO QUEEN enters to beat of drums)

HOODOO QUEEN and MENSTRUALS *(Singing)*
Have you heard of Mother Earth?
She wandered in the great gulf.
Wandered in the great gulf.
To give us law
And search for her child.
Her lap is where we sit.
Her lap is where we're at.
Her bed, from where we get our laws
Is the place of birth
Of sleep
And dreaming,
Of love
Of love
And death

Always, always,
Everywhere.
Wide-legged Earth,

Ever sure foundation of us all.
Her lap is where we sit.
Her lap is where we're at.
Lap of the earth
Labia/lip/mouth of the womb.
Mouth of the river
Mouth of the vessel
Mouth of the womb.

Wide-legged Earth
Ever sure foundation of us all.

MENSTRUAL That night strange and mysteriolacious goings on got loose. The sanctity of the body of the Hoodoo Queen of New Orleans was *violated* by a roving band of preppies.

MENSTRUAL When time came for the trial, Aunt Jemima was called for jury duty.

HOODOO QUEEN
Do you like oral sex, he said to me.
I said no.
Have you ever had sex with a white man.
I said no.
I couldn't breathe.
I said no.
I said no.

MENSTRUAL When the eleven white male jurors told Aunt Jemima that the Hoodoo Queen asked for it – that she got what she deserved – Aunt Jemima had some doubts. But in the end, she agreed with them.

MENSTRUAL The jury brought in a not guilty verdict. When the Hoodoo Queen stood up and walked out the courtroom with her head still held up high in the air, the swishing sound her skirt made sound just like a rattlesnake to Aunt Jemima.

AUNT JEMIMA Hoodoo Queen, was you born and raised on the Higbee plantation?

HOODOO QUEEN Mammy, don't you know me? I'se your own daughter Marie.

AUNT JEMIMA Oh, lord, my own chile! I should have hung the jury. Ah just gave in . . . Them preppies is guilty as sin. *(Singing)*
Guilty as sin.
Guilty as sin.
An gave up
That's the bottom line.

HOODOO QUEEN *(Singing)*
That's alright, Mammy. I'll fix 'em.

MENSTRUALS *(Singing)*
Oh, she said no!
Oh, she said no!

Great God Almighty!
She said no!

AUNT JEMIMA She was not on trial.

MENSTRUALS (Singing)
No, Mammy, no, she was not on trial.
No, Mammy, no, she was not on trial.

AUNT JEMIMA Ah should have hung the jury.
It's my fault they got off.
Guilty as sin.

MENSTRUALS (Singing)
She said no!
She said no!

AUNT JEMIMA (Singing)
Guilty as sin.
Guilty as sin.

MENSTRUALS and AUNT JEMIMA (Singing)
Great God Almighty.

HOODOO QUEEN I'll fix 'em!

MENSTRUALS and AUNT JEMIMA That's the bottom line.

MENSTRUAL The NAACP decided to boycott Aunt Jemima Pancake Mix because of her disgraceful behavior at the Hoodoo Queen's trial. Aunt Jemima wrote a red-hot letter to the NAACP.

AUNT JEMIMA Dear Madame President:
Only those in our own race have used the name of Aunt Jemima to mean someone that is not desirable. Aunt Jemima built a monument to herself with pancakes and the advertisements admit she was a Negro. She is as American as ham and eggs. Please know it would be impossible for you to be more proud of being a Negro than I. Sincerely, Aunt Jemima.

MENSTRUAL In later years, Aunt Jemima had to undergo several debilitating operations, including a mastectomy and a hysterectomy. She had the diabetes so bad, Col. Uncle Sam and them made her get her feet amputated even though she didn't want to.

AUNT JEMIMA Ah believe the fate of my feet should be left up to God.

MENSTRUAL A staggering thought! To amputate the feet of someone who doesn't want it to happen.

MENSTRUAL After her amputation, Aunt Jemima couldn't travel no more, so the Quaker Oats Man retired her to the pancake box to live out her days.

MENSTRUAL When Aunt Jemima went to the pancake box to live, it caused a furious fibrillation in her family.

MENSTRUALS
AuntJemima on the pancake box?
AuntJemima on the pancake box?
Ainchamamaonthepancakebox?
Ain't chure Mama on the pancake box?

MENSTRUAL Rebecca was a mover and Shaker and begged her mother to fly away with her off the pancake box.

REBECCA JACKSON Come, Mammy, let's fly away together.

AUNT JEMIMA Ah got the arthur, baby and when the arthur gets in your joints you can't even twist 'em.

REBECCA JACKSON Mammy, my spirit eye tells me, thee are destined to die very soon if thee remain where thou art. Come take my hand and thee can walk through the walls of the pancake box.

AUNT JEMIMA Rebecca, ain't that that apostrophe that keeps gittin' you in so much trouble?

REBECCA JACKSON Thee and me can converse with angels.

AUNT JEMIMA That sounds like you letting the devil in the church. No, baby, Ah'll jes stay where Ah is.

MENSTRUAL Tiny Desiree and Sapphire were at each other's throats and Bondswoman was the peacemaker.

TINY DESIREE Mama, you gettin' too old to sit up on that box.

AUNT JEMIMA Really, I don't mind. Not if it keeps my white folks happy.

SAPPHIRE The white woman is the white man's dog, and the black woman is his mule. We do the heavy work and get beat whether we do it well or not. You never find me sittin' up on a goddamn box flipping pancakes for some white man!

BONDSWOMAN Sapphire, you and Tiny Desiree both shut up! Ain't none of us free to do what we want as long as our mama is a slave. Now you two need to be trying to see how you can work together to liberate our mama. Tiny Desiree, you the youngest. You got too much mouth for such a little girl.

TINY DESIREE At least I ain't like Sapphire. I can't stand that evil, treacherous, bitchy, stubborn, hateful thing. I ain't nothing like Sapphire. I is the Anita-thisis of Sapphire.

SAPPHIRE I ain't none of them things folks call me. I just ain't afraid to express my bitterness, anger and rage about our lot.

43

BONDSWOMAN Mammy, you got to work to end your own oppression.

AUNT JEMIMA Why should I complain about making $7000 a week playing a mammy. If I didn't I'd be making $7 a week actually being one.

PECOLA
Mama, if you pass me on the street.
You mustn't see me.
Or own me
Or claim me.

AUNT JEMIMA Oh, how dreadful, daughter deah!

PECOLA Mama, I got to go out into the world and find myself.

AUNT JEMIMA Pecola, honey, you grease them legs good befo' you goes anywhere. (PECOLA exits. Music: "Trouble of the World")

MENSTRUAL After her crazy daughters left, Aunt Jemima began humming "There Is A Balm In Gilead" while she set her new television to the channel where she could watch the confirmation hearings for Uncle Tom.

MENSTRUALS
Here come de judge
Here come de judge
Everybody knows that here come de judge
Court's in session
Court's in session
Order in de court
'Cause here come de judge.
Judge, judge, smile so we can see you.

JUDGE Your mama can find me in the dark.

MENSTRUAL Aunt Jemima was shocked to see her daughter Anita sitting up there.

MENSTRUAL (As ANITA) Let's face it. I am a marked woman. I don't have a patron and I don't have a pass. The senators fear that affirmative action now means that Americans will have to hear edumacated colored folks talk about pubic hair, long dongs, big breasts, and bestiality in Senate chambers.

MENSTRUAL The judge had no trouble slipping into America's most beloved minstrel role.

JUDGE (Singing)
I been 'buked and I been scorned
I been 'buked and I been scorned
I been 'buked and I been scorned
I been talked about sure as you born

AUNT JEMIMA She got trashed and he got confirmed! Simple as that. Umph!!

Ah need . . .
Ah need . . .
Ah need to . . .
Ah need ta . . .
Ah – nee – ta tell
Ah – ni – ta – tell
A – ni – ta tell on Uncle Tom.

LA MADAMA INTERLOCK-IT-TOGETHERER Lowest life on the highest court!!!!!

MENSTRUAL As time went on, Aunt Jemima became more and more of an embarrassment to all the limited partners in her corporation. The Quaker Oats Man tried to teach Aunt Jemima how to dress for success, but she refused to keep up with the changing times.

AUNT JEMIMA Ah ain't havin' no skin peel. Ah ain't takin' off my head rag. And Ah ain't havin' my naps pressed. Ah'm a real woman, not a composite like Betty Crocker.

MENSTRUAL Col. Uncle Sam said they should just manumit Aunt Jemima and run her out of town.

MENSTRUAL After her long, faithful years of service, the food inspectors came to evict Aunt Jemima from the pancake box.

MENSTRUAL She was sixty-six years old and weighed three hundred pounds. She had arthritis, high blood pressure, and diabetes.
The cops said she shouted that she would kill anybody who tried to evict her.

AUNT JEMIMA (Singing)
It's a goddamn shame
What they do to me
What will it take
To set me free?
Goddamn, goddamn!

Don't read my pap smear
For a year
They finally tell me
I'm filled with fear
Cancer's eating up my womb
Mother Earth, you'll be my tomb

What they do to me, Goddamn
Hysterectomy, goddamn
What they do to me, goddamn
Clitoridectomy, goddamn
What they do to me, goddamn
Mastectomy, goddamn
Cancer wreckted me, goddamn
Cancer wreckted me, goddamn

Goddamn! goddamn! goddamn!
Goddamn! goddamn! goddamn!

It's a goddamn shame
What they do to me
What will it take
To set me free?

MENSTRUAL They said she charged at them with a ten-inch knife. Her right hand was blown away by the first shot. She looked surprised.

AUNT JEMIMA Ah'm a free black woman. Here is my free papers dat ah carrys in my shoe.

MENSTRUAL The second shot blew a hole in her chest. She fell back into the kitchen and bled profusely.

AUNT JEMIMA America who caused the daughters of Africa to commit whoredoms and fornications, upon thee be their curse. When they brung me off the ship Ah was stark naked so's Ah couldn't hide no infirmity. Ah hoed the fields, harvested the crops, planted corn, carried dried trash, turned manure and worked the fields. When Ah had my babies, Ah kept on working. Carry they burdens on my back and work too. Ah been visited by the jumper. Look here what he done. Ah got stripes over the face, the body and my missing breasts. Though we are looked upon as things, we sprang from a scientific people. Ah bore thirteen children. Ain't Ah a woman?

MENSTRUALS (simultaneously with following) Aunt Jemima had thirteen daughters! Marie, a child born with a rattlesnake in her hand. Dorothy, her tragic mulatta chile.
Pecola, a little melodramatic red baby.
Dysmorfia, who was half black and half white.
Anna Julia, a woman who risqued all to learn to read.
Susie-Faye, Aunt Jemima's earnest child.
Rebecca, called by the thunder to preach the gospel.

Bondswoman, a girl with freedom on her mind.
Sapphire, a girl who could not be tamed by any man.
The twins, Anita and Aminata, Freedom Fighter, and the cake-mix miracle baby, Tiny Desiree.

MENSTRUAL They say she is dead, but we know she hurled herself, naked, a black bombshell into the center of the battle.

AUNT JEMIMA (Leaping off the pancake box) Ah can walk like a ox, run like a fox, swim like a eel, yell like a Indian, fight like a devil, spout like a earthquake, make love like a mad bull and swallow a nigger whole without choking. Ah can catch bullets with my assperity. Sometimes Ah send them back with interest and sometimes Ah transform them into balls of cotton.

MENSTRUAL Turning her back on us, she went to live in the moon forever.

MENSTRUAL The woman on the pancake box today is not Aunt Jemima. Everybody thinks it is because it looks just like her. But it is her microwave miracle daughter, Tiny Desiree, who had no compunction about skin peels and pearl earrings.

MENSTRUAL At the great World's Fair in '93, people could see Aunt Jemima in person. Sadly today we cannot. But what she did lives on – that and her smile. She is with us always and asserts herself in our daily lives and offers us a strategy.

LA MADAMA INTERLOCK-IT-TOGETHERER Thank you for coming out tonight. Be sure to tell your friends that the greatest show on earth will be coming to their town soon. Soon, soon they, too, can hear the Aunt Jemima Traveling Menstrual Show announce:

(Reprise opening song)

AUNT JEMIMA I'se in town honey. I'se around.

(Curtain)

Pearl Cleage

Pearl Cleage is an Atlanta-based writer whose recent works include *Flyin' West*, a full-length drama commissioned and premiered at The Alliance Theatre in 1992, and *Deals With the Devil and Other Reasons to Riot*, a book of essays published by Ballantine Books in 1993. Since its premiere at The Alliance Theatre under the direction of Kenny Leon, *Flyin' West* has had thirteen other productions across the country, including The Brooklyn Academy of Music, The Indiana Repertory Company, Crossroads Theatre Company, The Alabama Shakespeare Festival, the New WORLD Theater, The Intiman Theatre in Seattle, Washington, The St. Louis Black Repertory Theatre, and The Long Wharf Theatre. The play will open the season at the Kennedy Center in Washington, D.C., on September 13, 1994, featuring Ruby Dee. Pearl's new play, *Blues for an Alabama Sky*, will premiere at The Alliance Theatre in March 1995.

Currently at work on her first novel, Pearl is also a regular columnist for The Atlanta Tribune, a contributing editor of *Ms. Magazine* and a regular contributor to *Essence* magazine. Her work has also appeared in numerous anthologies, including *Double Stitch*, *Black Drama in America*, *Red Clay* and *New Plays from The Women's Project*. Pearl is also an artistic associate of Just Us Theater Company in Atlanta and editor of *Catalyst*, a magazine of heart and mind.

Pearl is the mother of a daughter, Deignan, and the wife of novelist Zaron W. Burnett, Jr.

Photo: Barry Forbus

Artistic statement

As a third-generation black nationalist and a radical feminist, the primary energy that fuels my work is a determination to be a part of the ongoing worldwide struggle against racism, sexism, classism and homophobia. I approach my work first as a way of expressing my emotional response to oppression, since no revolution has ever been fueled purely by intellect, no matter what the boys tell you; second, as a way to offer analysis, establish context, and clarify point of view; and third, to incite my audiences or my readers to action. My work is deeply rooted in, and consciously reflec-

tive of, African-American history and culture since I believe that it is by accurately expressing our very specific and highly individual realities that we discover our common humanity.

My response to the oppression I face is to name it, describe it, analyze it, protest it, and propose solutions to it as loud as I possibly can every time I get the chance. I purposely people my plays with fast-talking, quick-thinking black women since the theater is, for me, one of the few places where we have a chance to get an uninterrupted word in edgewise. It is my firm belief that exposing my audiences to these African American Nationalist Feminist Warriorwomen, innocently ensconced within the framework of the well-made play, will quicken the swelling of our ranks by creating an exciting alternative view of what black women – what free women! – can and should be.

As a black artist, my cultural heritage is a rich legacy of protest and resistance. As a woman artist, my cultural sheroes cross racial and national boundaries, joined together at the womb by a sisterhood based on the worldwide presence of sexism in our lives and the unbroken legacy of our struggle against it. I embrace these twin traditions as a lifeline to the past, a leap into the future and the best possible hedge against the terror of writer's block. For me, the challenge is never what to write about but how to find time to say it all, to, as Sister Audre Lorde said, "do as much as I can of what I came to do before they nickel and dime me to death." So far, so good.

Production history

Flyin' West was commissioned by The Alliance Theatre in Atlanta, Georgia and premiered there in November 1992. The original production was directed by Kenny Leon, the Alliance's Artistic Director. The cast was: Carol Mitchell-Leon, Sharlene Ross, Elizabeth Van Dyke, Kim Hawthorne, Peter Jay Fernandez, and Donald Griffin.

The play has been produced at numerous theaters including: Indiana Repertory Theatre, Crossroads Theatre Company, the New WORLD Theater, the Intiman Theatre, St. Louis Black Repertory Theatre, Long Wharf Theatre, BAM's Majestic Theatre, and The Kennedy Center.

3 Flyin' West

Pearl Cleage

Characters

SOPHIE WASHINGTON   a black woman, born into slavery, age 36

MISS LEAH   a black woman, born into slavery, age 73

FANNIE DOVE   a black woman, age 32

WIL PARRISH   a black man, born into slavery, age 40

MINNIE DOVE CHARLES   a black woman, age 21

FRANK CHARLES   a very light-skinned black man, born into slavery, age 36

Time
Fall 1898

Place
Outside the all-black town of Nicodemus, Kansas

Setting
The play takes place in and around the house shared by SOPHIE, FAN *and, more recently,* MISS LEAH. *The women are wheat farmers and the house sits in the midst of the vastness of the Kansas prairie. Activity will take place mainly in the house's kitchen/dining/living room, which has a table, chairs. a small desk, a wood burning stove, etc. In the back and upstairs are other bedrooms, one of which will also be the scene of action during the play. Other activity takes place in the area outside the front door, including wood gathering and chopping, hanging of clothes to dry, etc. There is also a brief arrival scene at the nearby train station, which need only be suggested.*

Act I
Scene 1: A fall evening
Scene 2: Two days later; early afternoon
Scene 3: The same day; evening

Scene 4: The next morning
Scene 5: Late that night

Act II
Scene 1: Early the next morning
Scene 2: The next Sunday; early morning
Scene 3: Sunday afternoon
Scene 4: Sunday evening
Scene 5: Monday morning
Scene 6: Seven months later; April 1899

Author's program notes

The Homestead Act of 1860 offered 320 acres of "free" land, stolen from the dwindling populations of Native Americans, to US citizens who were willing to settle in the western states. Although many settlers lived in traditional family groups, by 1890, a quarter of a million unmarried or widowed women were running their own farms and ranches. The farm work was hard and constant, but many of these women were able to survive because of their own physical stamina, determination and the help of their neighbors.

Large groups of African American homesteaders left the South following the Civil War to settle in all-black towns. The so-called "Exodus of 1879" saw twenty to forty thousand African American men, women and children – "Exodusters" – reach Kansas under the guidance of a charismatic leader, Benjamin "Pap" Singleton, who escaped from slavery and claimed later "I am the whole cause of the Kansas migration!"

Crusading black journalist Ida B. Wells's call to her readers to leave Memphis, Tennessee, after an 1892 lynching and riot, was heeded by over seven thousand black residents of the city who packed up as many of their belongings as they could carry and headed west in search of a life free from racist violence. Unfortunately, their dreams were shattered as many western states enacted Jim Crow laws as cruel as any in the old Confederacy and effectively destroyed most of the black settlements by the early 1900s.

This is a story of some of the black people who went west.

Act I

Scene 1

A fall evening.

SOPHIE enters rapidly. Her heavy coat is unbuttoned and her scarf flies out around her neck. It is chilly, but the cold has exhilarated her. She has just returned from a trip into town. She has a large bag of flour slung over her shoulder and a canvas shoulder bag full of groceries. She is carrying a shotgun, which she places by the door. She slings the bag of flour carelessly on the table and, coat still on, puts the other bag on a chair. She fumbles through her pockets, first withdrawing a letter, which she holds for a moment thoughtfully, then sticks in the growing pile on the overflowing desk. She fumbles through her pockets again and withdraws some long strips of black licorice. She takes a bite, sighs, chews appreciatively. She pulls a chair over to the window, opens it wide and sits down, propping her booted feet up on the window sill. She looks out the window with great contentment, takes another bite of licorice and chews slowly, completely satisfied with the candy's sweetness, the chill in the air and the privacy of the moment.

MISS LEAH enters haltingly. She walks unsteadily but has no cane to steady herself so she holds on to the furniture as she walks slowly in to the room. She is looking for something and her manner is exasperated. SOPHIE does not notice her entering. MISS LEAH looks at SOPHIE, immediately notices the open window and her irritation increases.

MISS LEAH Well, ain't you somethin'!

SOPHIE I didn't know you were up, Miss Leah. Want a piece? *(SOPHIE gets up and closes the window, stokes the fire, etc.)*

MISS LEAH I hate licorice. *(MISS LEAH stumbles a little. SOPHIE moves to steady her and is stopped by a "don't you dare" look from MISS LEAH)*

SOPHIE You miss your cane?

MISS LEAH I don't need no cane! I told you that before. You can lay it next to my bed or prop it against my chair like it walked out there on its own. It still ain't gonna make me no never mind. I don't want no cane and I don't need no cane.

SOPHIE Suit yourself. *(Takes another bite of licorice as she hangs her coat. MISS LEAH's shawl is hanging there in plain view. SOPHIE starts to reach for it, stops, ignores it and begins putting things away. MISS LEAH finally speaks with cold dignity.)*

MISS LEAH I am looking for my shawl, if you must know.

SOPHIE It's right . . .

MISS LEAH Don't tell me! If you start tellin' me, you'll just keep at it 'til I won't be able to remember a darn thing on my own.

SOPHIE I'll make some coffee.

MISS LEAH I don't know why. Can't nobody drink that stuff but you.

SOPHIE It'll warm you up.

MISS LEAH It'll kill me.

SOPHIE Well, then, you haven't got much time to put your affairs in order.

MISS LEAH My affairs are already in order, thank you. *(Pulls her chair as far from the window as possible and sits with effort)* It's too cold for first October. *(Shivering)* Where's my shawl? Don't tell me!

SOPHIE I brought you some tobacco.

MISS LEAH What kind?

SOPHIE The kind you like.

MISS LEAH *(Pleased in spite of herself)* Well, thank you, Sister Sophie. Maybe a good pipe can cut the taste of that mess you cookin' up in Fan's good coffee pot. *(She proceeds to make a pipe while SOPHIE makes coffee.)* What are we celebrating?

SOPHIE . We are celebrating my ability not to let these Nicodemus Negroes worry me, no matter how hard they try.

MISS LEAH Then we ought to be drinking corn whiskey. *(She lights the pipe and draws on it contentedly.)* Are you still worrying about the vote?

SOPHIE I just told you. I'm celebrating an end to worrying. *(A beat)* I rode in by way of the south ridge this morning. Smells like snow up there already.

MISS LEAH What were you doing way over there?

SOPHIE Just looking . . .

MISS LEAH Ain't you got enough land to worry about?

SOPHIE I'll have enough when I can step

outside my door and spin around with my eyes closed and wherever I stop, as far as I can see, there'll be nothing but land that belongs to me and my sisters.

MISS LEAH Well, I'll try not to let the smoke from my chimney drift out over your sky.

SOPHIE That's very neighborly of you. Now drink some of this.

MISS LEAH (Drinks and grimaces) Every other wagon pull in here nowadays got a bunch of colored women on it call themselves homesteadin' and can't even make a decent cup of coffee, much less bring a crop in! When I got here, it wasn't nobody to do nothin' for me but me . . .

SOPHIE and MISS LEAH (Together) . . . and I did everything there was to be done and then some . . .

MISS LEAH That's right! Because I was not prepared to put up with a whole lotta mouth. Colored men always tryin' to tell you how to do somethin' even if you been doin' it longer than they been peein' standin' up. (A beat) They got that in common with you.

SOPHIE I don't pee standing up.

MISS LEAH You would if you could! (Sips coffee and grimaces again)

SOPHIE Put some milk in it, Miss Leah.

MISS LEAH When I want milk, I drink milk. When I want coffee, I want Fan's coffee.

SOPHIE Suit yourself. (A beat) People were asking about Baker at the land office.

MISS LEAH What people?

SOPHIE White people. Asked me if I had heard anything from him.

MISS LEAH Ain't no white folks looking to settle in no Nicodemus, Kansas.

SOPHIE It's some of the best land around here. You said it yourself.

MISS LEAH Ain't nothin' good to no white folks once a bunch of colored folks get set up on it!

SOPHIE There's already a new family over by the Gaddy's and a widower with four sons between here and the Jordan place. They've probably been looking at your place, too.

MISS LEAH Who said so?

SOPHIE Nobody said anything. I just mean since you've been staying with us for awhile.

MISS LEAH Well, I ain't no wet behind the ears homesteader. I own my land. Free and clear. My name the only name on the deed to it. Anybody lookin' at my land is countin' they chickens. I made twenty winters on that land and I intend to make twenty more.

(While MISS LEAH fusses, SOPHIE quietly goes and gets her shawl and gently drops it around her shoulders.)

SOPHIE And then what?

MISS LEAH Then maybe I'll let you have it.

SOPHIE You gonna make me wait until I'm old as you are to get my hands on your orchard?

MISS LEAH That'll be time enough. If I tell you you can have it any sooner, my life won't be worth two cents!

SOPHIE You don't really think I'd murder you for your land, do you?

(MISS LEAH looks at SOPHIE for a beat before drawing deeply on her pipe.)

MISS LEAH I like Baker. And Miz Baker sweet as she can be. They just tryin' to stay in the city enough for her to get her strength back and build that baby up a little.

SOPHIE She'll never make it out here and you know it.

MISS LEAH Losing three babies in three years takes it out of you, girl!

SOPHIE They wouldn't have made it through the first winter if Wil Parrish hadn't been here to help them.

MISS LEAH You had a lot of help your first coupla winters, if I remember it right.

SOPHIE And I'm grateful for it.

MISS LEAH Some of us were here when you got here. Don't forget it!

SOPHIE All I'm trying to say is the Bakers have been gone almost two years and he hasn't even filed an extension. It's against the rules.

MISS LEAH Against whose rules? Don't nobody but colored folks know they been gone that long no way. Them white folks never come out here to even check and see if we're dead or alive. You know that good as the next person. (A beat) Sometimes I suspect you think you the only one love this land, Sister, but you not.

SOPHIE What are you getting at?

MISS LEAH Just the way you were speechifyin' and carryin' on in town meetin' last week like you the only one got a opinion that matter.

SOPHIE Why didn't the others speak up if they had so much to say?

MISS LEAH Can't get a word in edgewise with you goin' on and on about who ain't doin' this and that like they 'spose to.

SOPHIE:But you know I'm right!

MISS LEAH Bein' right ain't always the only thing you got to think about. The thing you gotta remember about colored folks is all the stuff they don't say when they want to, they just gonna say it double time later. That's why you gonna lose that vote if you ain't careful.

SOPHIE It doesn't make sense. A lot of the colored settlements have already passed rules saying nobody can sell to outsiders unless everybody agrees.

MISS LEAH Ain't nobody gonna give you the right to tell them when and how to sell their land. No point in ownin' it if you can't do what you want to with it.

SOPHIE But half of them will sell to the speculators! You know they will!

MISS LEAH Then that's what they gonna have to do.

SOPHIE We could have so much here if these colored folks would just step lively. We could own this whole prairie. Nothing but colored folks farms and colored folks wheat fields and colored folks cattle. Everywhere you look nothing but colored folks! But they can't see it. They look at Nicodemus and all they can see is a bunch of scuffling people trying to get ready for the winter instead of something free and fine and all our own. Most of them don't even know what we're doing here!

MISS LEAH That's cause some of them ain't never had nothin' that belonged to 'em. Some of them come cause they can't stand the smell of the city. Some of them just tired of evil white folks. Some of 'em killed somebody or wanted to. All everybody got in common is they plunked down twelve dollars for a piece of good land and now they tryin' to live on it long enough to claim it.

SOPHIE Everybody isn't even doing that.

MISS LEAH Everybody doin' the best they can, Sister Sophie.

SOPHIE And what happens when that isn't good enough?

MISS LEAH Then they have to drink your coffee!

(SOPHIE laughs as WIL and FANNIE enter outside. We can still see the activity in the house, but we no longer hear it. MISS LEAH is smoking her pipe and SOPHIE is working on her ledgers at the messy desk. She pushes FAN's papers aside carelessly, completely focused.

WIL is dressed in work clothes. FANNIE is dressed in boots, long skirt, shawl. They are strolling companionably and chatting with the ease of old and trusted friends.)

WIL I guess I'd have to say the weather more than anything. I miss that Mexican sunshine. Makes everything warm. You know how cold these creeks are when you want to take a swim? Well, I like to swim, bein' from Florida and all, so I close my eyes and jump in real quick! But that water would neigh 'bout kill a Mexican. They don't know nothin' 'bout cold. They even eat their food hot! (FAN laughing stops to pick a flower to add to her already overflowing basket.)

FAN Look! (Holding it up for WIL's inspection) That'll be the last of these until spring.

WIL I imagine it will be. I ate a Mexican hot pepper one time. It looked just like a Louisiana hot pepper, but when I bit into it, it neigh 'bout lifted the top of my head off. Them Mexicans were laughing so hard they couldn't even bring me no water. I like to died!

FAN You really miss it, don't you?

WIL Miss Fannie, sometimes I surely do. But I know Baker needs somebody to keep an eye on things for him until he gets back. And now I got Miss Leah's place to look in on too.

FAN Do you think they'll be back this spring?

WIL He swears they will.

FAN Sophie doesn't think they're strong enough for this life.

WIL Sometimes people are a lot stronger than you can tell by just lookin' at 'em.

FAN Did he say anything about the baby?

WIL Said he's fat and healthy and looks just like him, poor little thing!

FAN (Laughing) Shame on you! (A beat) Has Miss Leah said anything to you about going home?

WIL No. Not lately.

FAN Good! We're trying to convince her to stay the winter with us.

WIL She's not tryin' to go back to her place alone, is she?

FAN   She really wants to, but she's just gotten so frail. Sophie says it was just a matter of time before she fell and broke something.

WIL   *(A beat)* You know what else I like? I mean about Mexico?

FAN   What?

WIL   I like Mexicans.

FAN   Well, that works out nice, I guess.

WIL   Everybody livin' in Mexico don't like Mexicans, Miss Fannie. They separate out the people from the stuff they do like and go on about their business like they ain't even there.

FAN   I never met any Mexicans.

WIL   Nicest people you ever wanna see. Friendly. but know how to keep to they self, too. Didn't no Mexicans ever say nothin' out of the way to me as long as I was livin' down there. They a lot like them Seminoles I grew up around in Florida. When I run away, them Indians took me in and raised me up like I was one of their own. They most all gone now. Ain't got enough land left to spit on, if you'll forgive me sayin' it that way.

FAN   Do you think you'll go back? To Mexico, I mean.

WIL   I used to think so, but I spent seven years down there. As long as I spent on anybody's plantation, so I guess I'm back even. *(A beat)* I might even be a little ahead. *(He hands her a flower that has fallen out of her basket.)*

FAN   *(Embarrassed)* My mother loved flowers. Roses were her favorites. My father used to say, "colored women ain't got no time to be foolin' with no roses" and my mother would say, as long as colored men had time to worry about how colored women spent their time, she guessed she had time enough to grow some roses.

WIL   I like sunflowers. They got sunflowers in Mexico big as a plate.

FAN   Sophie likes sunflowers, too, but they're too big to put inside the house. They belong outside. *(A beat)* It's lonely out here without flowers. Sophie laughed the first time everything I planted around the house came into bloom. She said I had planted so many flowers there wasn't any room for the beans and tomatoes.

WIL   That's where your sister's wrong. There's room for everything to grow out here. If there ain't nothin' else out here,

there's plenty of room.

(They stand together looking at the beauty of the sunset. WIL turns after a moment and looks at her, quietly removing his hat and holding it nervously in his hands.)

FAN   You think it's going to be a long winter, Wil?

WIL   They're all long winters, Miss Fannie. This one will be about the same.

FAN   Sophie found her laugh out here. I don't remember ever hearing her laugh the whole time we were in Memphis. But everything in Kansas was funny to her. Sometimes when we first got here, she'd laugh so hard she'd start crying, but she didn't care. One time, she was laughing so hard I was afraid she was going to have a stroke. She scared me to death. When she calmed down, I asked her, well, why didn't you ever laugh like that in Memphis? And she said her laugh was too free to come out in a place where a colored woman's life wasn't worth two cents on the dollar. What kind of fool would find that funny, she asked me. She was right, too. Sophie's always right. *(While she speaks, WIL reaches out very slowly and almost puts his arm around her waist. She does not see him and he stops before touching her, suddenly terrified she would not appreciate the gesture. She picks up the flowers and hesitates.)* We're friends, aren't we?

WIL   Yes, Miss Fannie. I would say we are.

FAN   Then I wish you'd just call me Fannie. You don't have to call me Miss Fannie.

WIL   *(Embarrassed)* I didn't mean to offend you, Miss . . . I just sort of like to call you that because it reminds me that a colored woman is a precious jewel deserving of my respect, my love and my protection.

FAN   *(Taken aback and delighted)* Why, Wil! What a sweet thing to say!

WIL   My mother taught it to me. She used to make me say it at night like other folks said prayers. There were some other things she said, too, but I can't remember them anymore. When I first run off after they sold her, I tried to close my eyes and remember her voice sayin' 'em, but all them new Indian words was lookin' for a place in my head, too. So I lost 'em all but that one I just told you. She used to say if a colored man could just remember that one thing, life would be a whole lot easier on the colored woman.

FAN   Can I put it in the book?

WIL   With Miss Leah's stories?

FAN   It's not just Miss Leah's stories anymore, Wil. It's sort of about all of us.

WIL   I would call it an honor to be included.

FAN   Well, good! *(Suddenly embarrassed, she adjusts her shawl and prepares to go inside.)*

WIL   Walkin' with you has been the pleasure of my day.

FAN   Would you like some coffee before you start back?

WIL   No, thanks. I want to catch the last of the light. Give my best to your sister.

FAN   I will.

WIL   And Miss Leah.

FAN   Yes, I will.

WIL   Tell her . . . Miss Leah . . . maybe I'll stop in . . . tomorrow?

FAN   We'll look for you.

WIL   Well, good evening then.

FAN   Good evening.

(He starts off. MISS LEAH comes to the window and watches the parting.)

FAN   Wil . . . *(He turns back hopefully. FAN walks to him and puts a flower in his button hole.)* Take this for company on your way back.

WIL   Why, thank you! I do thank you.

FAN   Good evening, Wil.

WIL   And to you . . . Miss Fannie.

(He tips his hat and walks off, adjusting the flower in his button hole. FAN watches him until he is gone, then walks slowly to the house. MISS LEAH returns to her seat and beings humming "Amazing Grace." SOPHIE looks at her. She continues humming loudly and rocking with a smug look on her face.)

SOPHIE   What is it?

MISS LEAH   I ain't said a word to you.

SOPHIE   You're humming at me!

MISS LEAH   I ain't hummin' at nobody. I am just hummin'.

(FAN enters with flowers.)

FAN   I'm sorry to be so late!

MISS LEAH   Sophie made coffee.

SOPHIE   She's been humming at me ever since.

(FAN kisses SOPHIE's cheek and pats MISS LEAH.)

FAN   Everything is fine at your place, Miss Leah.

(She puts the flowers in water and arranges them quickly around the room.)

MISS LEAH   Everythin's fine but me.

SOPHIE   Aren't you feeling good?

MISS LEAH   I'm too old to feel good. How's Wil Parrish feelin'?

FAN   He's just fine, thank you.

SOPHIE   Did he walk back with you? Why didn't he come in?

FAN   He'll be by tomorrow.

SOPHIE   You should have invited Wil Parrish in for a cup of coffee.

MISS LEAH   Well, that sure was a friendly flower you stuck in his button hole a few minutes ago! But it's none of my business. *(Starts humming again)*

FAN   I ran into him watering his horse near the creek and he walked back with me. That's all.

SOPHIE   Has he heard from Baker?

FAN   He had a letter last week. Mother and baby are both doing fine.

SOPHIE   There's some people interested in that land.

FAN   Who?

SOPHIE   Families. White families.

FAN   In Nicodemus?

MISS LEAH   Just what I said!

FAN   I don't believe it. All the settlements they've got, why would they want to file a claim over here with us?

SOPHIE   Why don't you ask some of those land speculators holed up at the boarding house?

(The food is laid out and they seat themselves. SOPHIE moves to help MISS LEAH who waves her away and will only accept help from FAN.)

FAN   Well, it's neither here nor there. They'll be back on that land themselves by spring.

SOPHIE   I hope so. I don't need a whole bunch of strange white folks living that close.to me!

(They are seated and FAN lights a candle in the center of the table. The three join hands.)

FAN   Bless this food, oh, Lord, we are about to receive for the nourishment of our bodies, through Jesus Christ our Lord. Amen.

MISS LEAH   Jesus wept!

SOPHIE   Amen!

FAN   Baker's a good man to take his wife back east to have her baby. I don't think she could have survived losing another one out here.

MISS LEAH   These young women wouldn't have lasted a minute before the war. Overseer make you squat right down beside the field and drop your baby out like an animal. All ten of my sons was born after sundown cause that was the only way to be sure I could lay down to have 'em.

FAN How did your babies know it was night time?

MISS LEAH I knew it! If I felt 'em tryin' to come early, I'd hold 'em up in there and wouldn't let 'em. Bad enough bein' born a slave without that peckerwood overseer watchin' 'em take the first breath of life before their daddy done seen if they a boy or a girlchild.

FAN I think Miz Baker will be all right. I think she was just scared and lonesome for her mother. She can't be more than twenty.

MISS LEAH I wadn't but fourteen when I had my first one! Got up the next morning and strapped him on my back and went back out to the field. Overseer didn't notice him 'til the day half over. What you got there nigger? He say to me. This here my son, I say. I callin' him Samson like in the bible 'cause he gonna be strong! Overseer laugh and say, good! Colonel Harrison always lookin' for strong niggers to pick his cotton. I want to tell him that not what I got in mind for my Samson, but I kept my mouth shut like I had some sense. I ain't never been no fool.

FAN Wil said he didn't think there would be snow for another couple of weeks at least.

SOPHIE If he's got that much time to chit chat, maybe I can get him to help me repair that stretch of fence out beyond the north pasture.

FAN He already did.

SOPHIE He did? When?

FAN Yesterday. He told me to tell you not to worry about it.

MISS LEAH (Enjoying SOPHIE's surprise) Now that Wil Parrish is a good man and a good neighbor. You can't ask for better than that. Don't you think so, Fan?

FAN Yes. I do think so.

SOPHIE Are you sweet on Wil Parrish?

FAN We're friends, Sister.

MISS LEAH You could do a lot worse. And he likes you. I can tell it sure as you sittin' here. Look at her blush! We gonna have a weddin' come spring!

SOPHIE I already lost one sister. Don't give Fan away too!

MISS LEAH Shoot, you ought to be glad. Once Fan gets out of the way, you might find somebody fool enough to take a look at you.

SOPHIE Two things I'm sure of. I don't want no white folks tellin' me what to do all day, and no man tellin' me what to do all night.

MISS LEAH I'll say amen to that!

FAN (Clearing up dishes) Do you want to work on your stories some tonight? (SOPHIE takes out her shotgun and begins to clean and oil it. She breaks it down quickly and efficiently. She has done this a thousand times.)

MISS LEAH I'm too tired.

FAN (Coaxing) Let's just finish the one we were working on Sunday night.

MISS LEAH I keep tellin' you these ain't writin' stories. These are tellin' stories.

FAN Then tell them to me!

MISS LEAH So you can write 'em!

FAN So we can remember them.

MISS LEAH Colored folks can't forget the plantation any more than they can forget their own names. If we forget that, we ain't got no history past last week.

SOPHIE But you won't always be around to tell it.

MISS LEAH Long enough, Sister Sophie. Long enough. (She gets up unsteadily.) Good night, Fan.

FAN Good night, Miss Leah. (MISS LEAH looks at SOPHIE who speaks without looking up.)

SOPHIE You're not going to be mad at me all winter, are you?

MISS LEAH Good night, Sister Sophie.

SOPHIE Good night, Miss Leah. (MISS LEAH exits.)

FAN Why do you agitate her?

SOPHIE She'll live longer if she's doing it to irritate me. (A beat) I need a new hoop for that back wheel and it won't be in by Friday. Do you think Wil Parrish has got plans for his wagon on Friday?

FAN You can ask him. He's going to stop by tomorrow . . . to see Miss Leah.

SOPHIE Good . . . I'm sure Miss Leah will be pleased to see him.

FAN I wish you wouldn't work at my desk. Look at this mess! What's this?

SOPHIE It's from Miss Lewiston.

FAN She's still coming isn't she? (Anxiously reading the letter)

SOPHIE She "regrets she will be unable to

fulfill the position of instructor at the Nicodemus School and wishes us the best of luck in finding someone else to assume this important responsibility."

FAN She's getting married.

SOPHIE And her husband's scared of life on the frontier. What kind of colored men are they raising in the city these days anyway?

FAN She didn't say he was scared.

SOPHIE She said he was nervous about moving to a place where there were still gangs of wild Indians at large.

FAN People are scared of different things.

SOPHIE No they're not. They're either scared or they're not.

FAN *(Folding up the letter; resigned to it)* Do you ever regret it? Coming west like we did?

SOPHIE I never regret anything.

FAN I miss the conversation more than anything, I think.

SOPHIE Don't Miss Leah and I keep you amused?

FAN That wouldn't be the word I'd use. No! Of course you do. That's not what I mean . . . I mean, the literary societies and the Sunday socials and the forums. Mama and Daddy's house was always full of people talking at the top of their lungs about the best way to save the race. And then somebody would start thumping away on Mama's old piano, begging her to sing something. I used to hide at the top of the steps and watch them until I'd fall asleep right there.

SOPHIE Well, Minnie ought to be able to fill you in on the latest in that kind of life.

FAN London, Sister! It may as well be on another planet. I can't believe she'll really be here. It seems like she's been gone forever.

SOPHIE Almost a year and a half.

FAN Fifteen months, three weeks and five days.

SOPHIE But who's counting?

FAN I miss her so! If I try to talk her into staying longer, don't let me!

SOPHIE Why?

FAN You know how Frank feels about the frontier.

SOPHIE How can I stop you?

FAN Kick me under the table or something! At least she'll be here for her birthday. She said Frank thinks it will take a couple of weeks to get the will settled. I hope everything turns out all right. Frank is counting so much on this inheritance.

SOPHIE Frank better figure out how to work for a living! I picked up the new deeds today. One for you, one for me and one for Baby Sister. That ought to make her feel grown.

FAN She's not going to believe it.

SOPHIE Why? I always told her she'd have her share officially when she got old enough.

FAN Knowing you, I think she thought you meant about sixty-five! Sometimes I try to imagine what Baby Sister's life is like over there. How it feels. It must be exciting. Museums and theaters all over the place. She said Frank did a public recital from his book and there were fifty people there.

SOPHIE How many colored people were there?

FAN She didn't say.

SOPHIE None! No! Two! Her and Frank. Who ever heard of a colored poet moving someplace where there aren't any colored people?

FAN Where do you expect him to live? Nicodemus?

SOPHIE Why not? I'm giving her the deed to one third of the land we're standing on and she's married to a man who'd rather take a tour of Piccadilly Circus!

FAN Some people are not raised for this kind of life.

SOPHIE Did we raise Min for the life she's living halfway around the world?

FAN Of course, we did. We always exposed her to the finest things.

SOPHIE But why do all those fine things have to be so far away from Negroes?

FAN I think our baby sister is having so much fun out there in the world, coming back here is probably the last thing on her mind.

SOPHIE Do you know how much land they could be buying with all that money they're running through living so high on the hog?

FAN They've got plenty of time to buy land.

SOPHIE All that money and the best he can think of to do with it is to go to England and print up some books of bad poetry.

FAN   They weren't that bad.

SOPHIE   They were terrible! "Odes to Spring." You couldn't even tell a Negro wrote them.

FAN   What's so bad about that? We don't have to see spring differently just because we're Negroes, do we?

SOPHIE   We have to see everything differently because we're Negroes, Fan. I think Frank is going to find that out when they finish with this business about his father's will.

FAN   Min says Frank has hired a lawyer. You don't think they'll cut him out of the will, do you?

SOPHIE   How many white gentlemen do you know who want to share their inheritance with a bastard?

FAN   That's not fair.

SOPHIE   He's the one who kept talking about his father this and his father that and the man wouldn't even come to the wedding!

FAN   Well, I just try to give him the benefit of the doubt. Mama said every colored man deserves at least that much from a colored woman.

SOPHIE   Suit yourself. All I know is, we're going to have a school by spring if I have to teach in it myself!

FAN   Poor children would be crazy before they had a chance to learn their ABCs!

SOPHIE   (Suddenly) Sh-h-h-h-h! (She motions toward the candle and FAN blows it out immediately. SOPHIE clicks the gun quickly into place and loads two shells into place. She goes quickly to the window and peers out. FAN stands motionless, watching her. SOPHIE breathes a sigh of relief.) Deer. Three of them! Come look.
(SOPHIE sits down the gun and the two stand looking at the deer in the moonlight.)

SOPHIE   I'll be nice to Frank. For Min's sake. Butter won't melt in my mouth.

FAN   Promise?

SOPHIE   I promise. (They embrace warmly. FAN relights the candle and fixes the fire in the stove for the night.) Did you talk Miss Leah out of going to the station with us?

FAN   I think so.

SOPHIE   You did? How?

FAN   I told her you didn't think it was a good idea.

SOPHIE   No wonder she's mad at me!

FAN   She's always mad at you!

SOPHIE   Well, good. Maybe she'll live to be a hundred!
(They exit for bed.)
(Black)

Scene 2

Two days later; early afternoon.
    SOPHIE, FAN *and* WIL *are at the train station to meet* MIN *and* FRANK. *We hear the blast of the train whistle as the lights come up on the platform.* SOPHIE *and* WIL *are waiting patiently.* FAN *is very excited.*

FAN   It's so hard to wait once you see it, isn't it? Why is it taking so long? It doesn't even look like it's moving very fast anymore, does it?

SOPHIE   They're right on time.

WIL   And that's real lucky for you. This train don't never run on time.

FAN   But it's on time today, isn't it? And that's what counts!

WIL   Yes, it is, Miss Fannie. That's what counts!

FAN   Is it still moving? Can you tell? I can't tell! I'm going to find the station manager. (She exits.)

SOPHIE   Fan told me you took care of my fence.

WIL   Yes.

SOPHIE   That was very neighborly of you. I'm much obliged.

WIL   You're welcome.

SOPHIE   Would you like to have dinner with us this evening?

WIL   You don't have to . . .

SOPHIE   I want you to come. And I'm sure Fan would enjoy having you.

WIL   Well, thank you. It'd be my . . .
(FAN enters, excitedly.)

FAN   It's pulling in! Oh, Sophie, I'm so excited. Do you see them yet? Can you see them, Wil?

SOPHIE   I don't see any . . . there she is!

FAN   Where? Where? I still don't . . . Minnie! Min! Here! We're here.
(MINNIE enters on the run. She is wearing a fur trimmed coat and carrying a fur muff. Her hat dips fashionably low over her face.)

MINNIE   Fannie! Oh, Fannie! (They embrace.) Oh, Sister! I missed you both so much!

FAN   Look at you in that outfit!

SOPHIE   How about that hat? Who are you hiding from?

MINNIE *(Tugging it lower)* They're all the rage in London!

SOPHIE Where are your bags?

MINNIE Frank has them. He stopped to send a telegram. He was talking to a man he met on the train . . . a white man. Maybe I better . . .

WIL I'll give him a hand.

MINNIE Thank you . . .

FAN Wil Parrish, meet my baby sister, Minnie.

WIL Pleased to meet you.

MINNIE Pleased to be met.

(WIL exits.)

FAN We borrowed Wil's wagon to pick you up.

SOPHIE And Wil came with it to make sure Miss Fannie got to town and back safely.

MINNIE Is he your sweetheart? Is he?

FAN Don't pay Sophie a bit of mind.

SOPHIE He's coming to dinner tonight. You can ask him yourself.

FAN You better not say a word!

(FRANK has entered and stands watching them. FRANK is immediately dressed in fine clothes from head to toe. Coat, hat, suit, gloves, shirt – everything of the finest quality and very tasteful. The sheer richness of the clothing is obvious in every piece.)

FRANK Secrets already?

MINNIE Darling! *(She runs to him and takes his arm protectively. FRANK allows himself to be led toward her sisters.)*

FAN *(Warmly)* Frank. It's lovely to have you both!

(FRANK puts down the small bag he's carrying and takes off one soft leather glove to extend his hand. FANNIE kisses his cheek instead.)

FRANK It's good to see you, too.

FAN I was so sorry to hear about your father.

FRANK Thank you.

FAN Well, I know it was a long trip, but you're here at last!

FRANK Nothing would do but Minnie had to come and see her sisters, isn't that right, darling?

FAN You don't mind sharing her with us once in awhile, do you?

FRANK Of course not. And I've got some other things to share with you as well.

FAN *(Teasing and happy)* Just how many riches do you think a poor frontier woman can stand at one time?

FRANK I thought you might enjoy having an autographed copy of Mr. Dunbar's latest volume. *(He hands her a small book of poetry.)*

FAN Autographed? I've been trying to get my hands on any copy for months!

MINNIE Frank walked me all over New Orleans to find it.

FAN How can I ever thank you?

FRANK It's my pleasure. *(A beat)* Hello, Sophie.

SOPHIE *(Nods formally)* Frank . . .

FRANK We'll try not to overstay our welcome.

FAN Stay as long as you like. You're family.

MINNIE That's just what I told him. We're family! This isn't like coming for a visit. This is coming home.

FRANK But we have a home, don't we, darling?

MINNIE Yes, of course we do. We have a lovely home.

FAN And you're going to tell me all about . . .

FRANK *(Interrupts her)* And where is our home, Minnie?

MINNIE Frank . . . *(He stares at her coldly.)* It's in London.

FRANK So this is really a visit, just like I said, isn't it?

MINNIE *(Softly)* Yes, Frank.

FRANK *(False heartiness)* Of course it is! And it's going to be a great visit. I'm sure of it. Well, how long does it take to get from here to there, anyway? I could do with a hot bath.

FAN Of course you could. Wil's probably got the wagon loaded. Come on! Come on! Miss Leah's at the house and I know she's pacing up and down at the window right now.

(FAN hooks MINNIE's arm and draws her away from FRANK. MINNIE looks back anxiously at FRANK who stares at her impassively. He turns to find SOPHIE looking at him.)

SOPHIE Welcome to Nicodemus, Frank.

(FRANK tips his hat and bows slightly. He exits, pulling on his gloves and leaving his small suitcase behind. SOPHIE looks after him, looks at the bag, shifts the shotgun easily to the crook of her arm, picks up the bag and exits.)

(Black)

Scene 3

The same day; evening.

FAN *is taking out plates, laying out food, etc.*
MISS LEAH *is tottering around impatiently,
making it difficult for* FAN *to accomplish her
task without tripping over* MISS LEAH.

As we hear MISS LEAH *talking to* FAN *in
the bedroom we see* MIN *at the mirror trying
to convince herself that her bruised face isn't
that noticeable.* FRANK *is taking off his jacket,
unbuttoning his shirt, etc. He catches a
glimpse of* MINNIE *looking in the mirror. He
goes to her, stands behind her. She puts her
hand down. He turns her slowly to face him.
He gently, tenderly touches her bruised face.
She flinches. He kisses her gently. She relaxes
and he kisses her more passionately. She
breaks away playfully. She looks in the mirror
with resignation, grabs up her hat and pulls it
back on. One last look at* FRANK *who still
watches her. She throws him a kiss and goes
out. He lays down on the bed, takes out a
book and begins to read.*

MISS LEAH   I don t see why she has to
   help him get settled right this minute.
   He's a grown man. He can unpack a
   suitcase, can't he?
FAN   I'm sure he can. I think Min just
   wants to make him feel at home here.
MISS LEAH   Why wouldn't he feel at home
   here?
   *(*MINNIE *enters quickly. She is nervous
   because she still wears her hat.)*
FAN   Thank goodness. Miss Leah was about
   to send me back there to rescue you.
MINNIE   Did you miss me?
MISS LEAH   Lord, chile, I thought that man
   had tied you to the bed post back there.
   Take off that hat, honey, and let me look
   at you.
FAN   Aren't the flowers wonderful? I've got
   all your favorites . . .
   (As MINNIE *slowly removes her hat,* FAN
   sees the large bruise above MINNIE'S *left
   eye.)*
FAN   Minnie! My God!
MINNIE   *(Laughing nervously)* It doesn't look
   that bad, does it?
MISS LEAH   What happened to your face,
   chile?
MINNIE   It's so silly.
   (They wait in silence.)
MINNIE   I bought a new dress for the trip
   . . . and I . . . wanted to show it to Frank

. . . and I . . . the train . . . I stumbled in
   the train compartment. You know how
   clumsy I am. I bumped my head so hard
   I saw stars! And this is what I've got to
   show for it. Frank made me promise to
   be more careful. He worries so about me.
   (An awkward pause. They don't believe her.)
   I told him I used to be much worse.
   Remember that time I almost fell off the
   roof? I would have killed myself if it
   hadn't been for Sophie.
FAN   Yes, I remember . . .
MINNIE   Don't look so worried. I'll be
   careful. It was just an accident.
FAN   All right, Baby Sister.
   *(*SOPHIE *enters with wood in her arms.)*
MISS LEAH   Close that door!
SOPHIE   Let me get in it first. Your turn to
   chop tomorrow, Minnie. Being a world
   traveller doesn't excuse you from your
   chores! *(Sees the bruise on* MINNIE's *face
   for the first time)* What happened to your
   face?
MINNIE   I took a tumble, that's all. It looks
   a lot worse than it is.
SOPHIE   A tumble?
FAN   Minnie was showing off for her
   handsome husband and lost her balance
   on the train.
MINNIE   I know it looks awful. Here! I'll
   put my beautiful hat back on to hide it!
FAN   No! Anything but that!
MINNIE   Then let's not talk about it
   anymore.
   *(*SOPHIE *looks at* MIN *and* FAN *and takes
   off her coat, etc.)*
SOPHIE   Suit yourself.
MISS LEAH   How does living in . . .
MINNIE   London, Miss Leah. It's in
   England.
MISS LEAH   How does it agree with you?
MINNIE   Well, it was kind of scary to me at
   first. So many people and colored just
   right in there with everybody else.
MISS LEAH   No Jim Crow?
MINNIE   None.
MISS LEAH   I can't imagine such a thing.
MINNIE   That's why you have to come visit
   me. So you can see for yourself.
MISS LEAH   I don't need to see nothin' else
   new. I done seen enough new to last me.
   I don't know why anybody wants to be all
   up next to a bunch of strange white folks
   anyway.
SOPHIE   Because somebody told them they
   weren't supposed to!

MINNIE Oh, they're not so bad. Frank and I even have some white . . . friends.

MISS LEAH Lord, deliver us! What is this chile talking about?

MINNIE Frank says he doesn't see why he only has to be with Negroes since he has as much white blood in him as colored.

SOPHIE Frank is talking crazy.

MINNIE It's true. His father was . . .

SOPHIE A slaveowner! Just like mine.

MINNIE Frank said his father wanted to marry his mother. They were . . . in love.

SOPHIE Did he free her?

MINNIE No . . .

SOPHIE Then don't talk to me about love.

FAN *(Quickly)* Let's have some supper before you two start fighting. Min, go tell Frank to come to the table.

(MINNIE exits to the bedroom as WIL approaches from outside with flowers. FRANK has gotten dressed up for dinner. When MIN opens the door, he turns to her, and strikes a pose for her approval. She kisses him and they go out arm in arm.)

MISS LEAH There's Wil Parrish at the door. *(FAN opens the door as he raises his hand to knock.)*

FAN You're just in time.

WIL I stopped for . . . these are for you.

FAN They're lovely.

MISS LEAH Just what we need.

WIL Evenin', Miss Leah. How're you feelin'?

MISS LEAH I'd feel a whole lot better if people stopped lettin' that cold air in on me.

(FRANK and MINNIE enter arm in arm)

FRANK I'm starved!

FAN Good! Why don't you sit here next to Min? Wil you sit here by . . . Sophie. Miss Leah . . .

WIL You're the first colored poet I ever saw.

FRANK How many white ones have you seen?

WIL None that I can recall . . .

FRANK Then that makes me the first poet you've ever seen, doesn't it?

MINNIE Frank . . .

(They settle into their places and join hands.)

FAN Sister, will you bless the table?

SOPHIE Thank you for this food we are about to receive and for the safe journey of our beloved sister. *(A beat)* And Frank. Amen.

ALL Amen.

(As they talk, the meal is served, consumed and cleared away.)

FAN Did you have a good rest?

FRANK Enough to hold me, I guess. *(To SOPHIE)* Min tells me you're a mulatto. *(SOPHIE is startled.)* Oh, excuse me! I didn't mean to be so personal. It's just that I'm a mulatto myself and I was interested to know if there are many of us this far west. You know you can't always tell by looking!

SOPHIE There are just a few.

FRANK I can understand why. This is a lot closer to the field than most of us ever want to get! *(Laughs)*

MINNIE *(Quickly to WIL)* This is my husband's first visit to the frontier.

WIL How do you like it so far?

FRANK So far, so good. But to tell the truth, I've always been more of a city person.

SOPHIE And what kind of person is that?

FRANK Oh, I think one who enjoys a little more . . . ease than is possible way out here. Although I must admit your home is lovely. This table wouldn't be out of place in the finest dining rooms.

FAN Why thank you, Frank!

SOPHIE Tomorrow we'll go back to eating around the campfire like we usually do.

MINNIE Don't listen to Sister! Fan is famous for setting the prettiest table in Nicodemus.

FRANK I admire the ability to adapt to trying circumstances without a lowering of standards. I wouldn't have expected to see such delicate china way out here.

FAN These were my mother's things. Sophie stopped speaking to me for a week when I told her I wasn't leaving Memphis without them, but I was determined.

SOPHIE I should have left you and them standing in the middle of Main Street. Whoever heard of carrying a set of plates . . .

MINNIE Mama's china!

FAN Mama's good china!

SOPHIE A set of plates halfway across the country when we hardly had room for Min.

MINNIE You weren't going to leave me in the middle of Main Street, too, were you?

FAN She couldn't have left us. Who would she have had to boss around?

MINNIE I'd like to go back to Memphis sometime. Just to visit. Wouldn't you?

SOPHIE Not me! Colored folks' lives aren't worth two cents in that town.

FAN But everybody says things have gotten a lot better.

FRANK Well, that may be true in Memphis, but we were in New Orleans to see my lawyers just before we came here and it's still pretty much the same as it's always been, if you ask me. They had just had a lynching the week before we got there. *(Laughs)* Just my luck!

MINNIE After they hung the poor man, they threw his body down in the street right in the middle of the colored section of town.

MISS LEAH Don't any of those New Orleans Negroes know how to use a shotgun?

FRANK He pretty much brought it on himself from what I heard down at the bank. He was involved in some . . .

SOPHIE *(Cuts him off)* I don't care what he was involved in.

FRANK Doesn't it matter?

SOPHIE No. Whatever it was, he didn't deserve to die like that.

FRANK Well, I stand corrected. And I do apologize for introducing such inappropriate dinner table conversation.

MISS LEAH I don't know why those Negroes stay down there!

SOPHIE Because they haven't got the gumption to try something new. The day our group left Memphis, there were at least two hundred other Negroes standing around, rolling their eyes and trying to tell us we didn't know what it was going to be like way out here in the wilderness. I kept trying to tell them it doesn't matter what it's like. Any place is better than there!

FRANK Well, that's something we agree on!

WIL I'll say "amen" to that, too! If I never set foot in the Confederacy again, it's too soon for me.

FAN Oh, no! You two can't start thinking like Sister! One Sophie is enough.

MISS LEAH Too many if you ask me.

MINNIE Has her coffee gotten any better?

MISS LEAH Worse! And her disposition neither. I don't know how I'm gonna make it through the winter with her.

MINNIE She's not so bad. You just have to remember to put cotton in your ears.

FRANK I wish I'd thought of that on the train. Min was so excited she was talking a mile a minute the whole way out here. Weren't you, darling? She hardly took a deep breath.

MINNIE I wasn't that bad, was I?

FRANK I didn't want to hurt your feelings, darling, but you must have told me the same stories ten times!

MINNIE I didn't mean to . . .

SOPHIE *(Cuts her off)* Which one was your favorite?

FRANK Oh, I think probably the one about you coming to the door asking to do the laundry and then moving right in. I guess you knew a good thing when you saw one!

MINNIE Frank!

FRANK What is it, darling? That is the way the story goes, isn't it?

FAN I don't know what a good thing we were. Mama and Daddy both gone with the fever. So many people dying there weren't enough left well to take care of the sick ones. I was only twelve and Min still a baby.

MINNIE So when Sophie came asking about doing the laundry, Fan asked her when she could start and Sophie said, "I can start right now. I'm free as a bird!" And once she came, it was like she'd always been there.

FAN I loved the way she said it. I was scared to death and here was this one talking about free as a bird.

WIL Are you gonna put that in the book?

MINNIE What book?

FAN I'm writing a book about Nicodemus. I'm going to call it The True History and Life Stories of Nicodemus, Kansas: A Negro Town.

MINNIE That sounds wonderful. Now we'll have two writers in the family.

FAN Oh, I'm not really a writer. I'm more of a collector.

MINNIE You could have a whole book with just Miss Leah's stories!

FAN Well, some people don't think their stories are important enough to put in a book.

MISS LEAH I'm not studyin' you, Fannie May Dove.

MINNIE Why? I don't remember a time we went to your house when I didn't come back with a story.

MISS LEAH Everybody knows them stories

I got. Colored folks ain't been free long enough to have forgot what it's like to be a slave.

MINNIE But you didn't always talk about slavery. You talked about how blue the sky would be in the summertime and about how you and the other children would sneak off from prayer meeting to play because you didn't want to work all week and pray all Sunday.

MISS LEAH And got beat for it just as regular as a clock.

MINNIE You used to tell me about how all your babies had such fat legs, remember?

MISS LEAH And where are they now? All them babies. And them grandbabies? Gone! Every last one of 'em!

MINNIE But you loved them, Miss Leah. Who's going to know how much you loved them?

FRANK Min's got a story, don't you darling?

MINNIE I thought you'd heard enough of my stories on the train.

FRANK But you haven't told our story, darling.

MINNIE I don't think this is . . .

FAN Please? It's such a lovely story. With a happy ending.

FRANK Go ahead, now. Don't be silly.

MINNIE I was at school . . .

FAN The conservatory . . . go on!

MINNIE It was . . . it was spring. The campus was lovely then. Flowers were everywhere. But all anybody kept talking about was the handsome stranger who was here visiting for a couple of weeks.

FAN That was Frank, all the way from England!

SOPHIE Fannie! Let her tell it, or you tell it!

FAN Go on! Sorry!

MINNIE Pretty soon, everybody but me had met him, or at least seen him. And then one afternoon, I was out walking and I thought I was alone, so I started singing and Frank was out walking too and he heard me.

FRANK I really scared her!

MINNIE I hadn't heard him behind me.

FRANK I was tracking her like a wild Indian!

(WIL looks up sharply, but lets it pass.)

MINNIE And then he said . . .

FRANK I had been away from England for almost a month and I hadn't heard a note

of Puccini in all that time. So I told her she sang like an angel and invited her to have dinner with me.

MINNIE And I said my sisters hadn't raised me to have dinner with a strange gentleman who I met on a walk in the woods.

SOPHIE You shouldn't have been walking in the woods alone in the first place.

FAN But then it wouldn't be a love story! Go on, Min.

MINNIE So I walked away and left him standing there.

FAN And the next day a friend of hers invited her to attend an evening of Negro poetry at the Chitauqua Literary Society . . .

MINNIE And I looked behind the podium and there was Frank!

FRANK I recognized her right away . . .

MINNIE And he nodded to me like we were old friends.

FAN And then he dedicated a poem to her.

MINNIE "A Song" by Mr. Paul Laurence Dunbar.

FRANK
"Thou art the soul of a summer's day,
Thou art the breath of the rose.
But the summer is fled
And the rose is dead.
Where are they gone, who knows, who knows?"

MISS LEAH A Negro wrote that?

FAN And me and Sister dashed down to New Orleans in time enough for the wedding and to see them set sail back to England.

FRANK We'd only known each other a few weeks, but I knew Minnie was the girl for me. And she still is.

(He kisses her gently and she blushes.)

FAN Beautiful! Now you tell one, Sister!

SOPHIE I don't want to bore Frank with stories he's heard before.

MINNIE Tell about the ritual. Tell about the day we left Memphis and came west to be free women.

SOPHIE Fan's the one always thinking up ceremonies. Let her tell it.

FAN Not this one! This came straight from you!

SOPHIE When we got ready to leave Memphis . . .

MINNIE When you two got ready. I was too little to get a vote.

SOPHIE Well, I knew it was the right thing to do. Memphis was full of crazy white men acting like when it came to colored people, they didn't have to be bound by law or common decency. Dragging people off in the middle of the night. Doing whatever they felt like doing. Colored women not safe in their own houses. Then I heard there were Negroes going west.

MISS LEAH Been done gone!

SOPHIE Then that crazy Pap Singleton came to the church looking for people to sign up to go to Kansas. That man had eyes like hot coals. He said he was like Moses leading the children of Israel out of bondage in Egypt.

FAN Sister didn't even let the man finish talking before she ran down the aisle to sign up! I think Reverend Thomas thought she had finally gotten the spirit!

SOPHIE Pap said there'd be all colored towns, full of colored people only! That sounded more like heaven than anything else I'd heard in church.

MINNIE Why does that make you smile?

WIL That's what landed me in Nicodemus, too. Looking for some neighbors that looked like me.

FRANK At home, we go for weeks and never see another colored face. A few Indians once in awhile – the Eastern kind – but that's not really the same thing, is it?

MISS LEAH Don't you get lonesome for colored people?

FRANK To tell you the truth, I've seen about all the Negroes I need to see in this life. (Laughs)

MINNIE (Quickly) Finish about the ritual, Sister!

SOPHIE Another time.

MINNIE Please!

FRANK Don't whine, darling. Maybe Sophie is tired of talking.

MISS LEAH Well, if she is, or if she ain't, I'm tired of listenin'!

MINNIE You're not leaving us already, are you?

MISS LEAH Knowing how long winded some of the people at this table can be. You all will probably be sittin' here when I get up tomorrow mornin'. (She gets up unsteadily.)

MINNIE Let me help you.

MISS LEAH One thing a woman my age should have the good sense to do alone is go to bed. Good night.

MINNIE, WIL, FAN, SOPHIE Good night, Miss Leah.
(FAN and MINNIE begin clearing off the dishes. WIL unobtrusively helps them. FRANK pours himself another glass of wine.)

FRANK They don't make you do the woman's work around here too, do they, Parrish?

WIL Makes it go quicker when everybody does a part.

FAN I couldn't have said it better myself!
(SOPHIE puts on her coat.)

MINNIE Where are you off to?

SOPHIE To bring in a little more of that wood I spent all week chopping in your honor.

MINNIE Then the least I can do is help you carry it!

FAN I'll help, too!
(They throw on their shawls and almost rush out the door.)

FRANK You know the night air doesn't agree with you, Minnie!

FAN We'll keep her warm, I promise. (Pulls shawl over MIN's head and pulls her out the door. Moonlight illuminates the yard. Wood is cut in a stack near the house.)

SOPHIE What's he talking about? You're healthy as a horse.

MINNIE He just worries about me some-times, that's all. I haven't been so strong lately . . .

FAN But you're home now. I've got a whole week to toughen you up again!

MINNIE I'm counting on it. (A beat) Sister?

SOPHIE Yes?

MINNIE Don't mind what Frank said about you coming to the door looking to do the laundry.

SOPHIE Didn't I come to your door?

MINNIE Yes . . .

SOPHIE And didn't you need somebody to do the laundry?

MINNIE Yes, but, sometimes Frank says things in a way that . . . that doesn't sound like how I know he means them.

SOPHIE I'm not ashamed of anything I've ever done and if I was, taking in laundry to make an honest living wouldn't be the thing I'd pick. (A beat) You don't have to apologize to me for your husband, Min. If he's good to you, he's good enough for me. Is he good to you, Min?

MINNIE Yes, he's good to me.

SOPHIE Then he's all right with me.

FAN Well, since you two are getting along so well, let's do it before you start fussing again!

MINNIE Do what?

FAN The ritual. Let's do it now!

MINNIE Oh, yes, please! Can we?

(WIL can be seen sharpening a small knife on a stone. FRANK takes out a cigar, prepares it, smokes. The women stand in a circle, holding hands.)

SOPHIE Because we are free Negro women . . .

FAN and MINNIE Because we are free Negro women . . .

SOPHIE Born of free Negro women . . .

BOTH (FAN and MINNIE) Born of free Negro women . . .

ALL Back as far as time begins . . .

SOPHIE We choose this day to leave a place where our lives, our honor and our very souls are not our own.

FAN Say it, Sister!

SOPHIE We choose this day to declare our lives to be our own and no one else's. And we promise to always remember the day we left Memphis and went west together to be free women as a sacred bond between us with all our trust.

BOTH With all our trust . . .

SOPHIE And all our strength . . .

BOTH And all our strength . . .

(As they talk, FRANK walks over to the window, smoking. He looks at the women holding hands in the moonlight.)

SOPHIE And all our courage . . .

BOTH And all our courage . . .

SOPHIE And all our love.

BOTH And all our love.

(A beat)

SOPHIE Welcome home, Baby Sister.

(The three embrace, laughing happily. FRANK still watches from the window.)

(Black)

Scene 4

The next morning.

MISS LEAH *is on the stage alone. She is mending something. MIN kisses the sleeping FRANK in the bedroom and goes quietly out, closing the door behind her. She is brushing her hair. She looks much younger than she did with her fancy hat and sophisticated hairdo.*

MINNIE You're up early.

MISS LEAH Habit, chile. I don't know how to sleep past sun up.

MINNIE Where are Fan and Sister?

MISS LEAH Fan's already up washing and Sophie's probably off somewhere driving some other poor soul crazy. Come sit by me, chile. I couldn't hardly get a word in at dinner last night.

MINNIE You always hold your own.

MISS LEAH If you don't hold it, who gone hold it? Let me look at you. *(A beat)* You look more like yourself this morning.

MINNIE I'm going to braid my hair with ribbons like you used to do it, remember?

MISS LEAH I remember. *(MINNIE messes up a braid.)* But don't look like you do. Sit down here, girl, and let me fix that head. *(MINNIE sits with her head between MISS LEAH's knees.)*

MINNIE Don't you think Frank is fine looking?

MISS LEAH He'll do.

MINNIE I want all my babies to look just like him!

MISS LEAH He ain't that pretty.

MINNIE Do you think I'll be a good mother?

MISS LEAH You better be. Fan gone be too old for many babies by the time her and Wil stop dancin' around each other and Sophie's too mean for anybody to marry. So I'm countin' on you, Baby Sister. None of this makes any sense without the children.

MINNIE It would be hard to have a child way out here.

MISS LEAH There's a lot worse places than this to have a baby. I'd of given anything to a had my babies in my own little house on my own piece of land with James pacing outside and the midwife knowin' what to do to ease you through it. Is that too tight?

MINNIE It's perfect!

(FRANK gets up and begins dressing in the bedroom. He is wearing more expensive city clothes. He takes great care with his cuff links, tie, etc. He is especially pleased with his hair.)

MISS LEAH *(Resumes her braiding)* I was only thirteen when I got my first one. They wanted me to start early cause I was big and strong. Soon as my woman-hood came on me, they took me out in the barn and put James on me. He was older than me and big. He already had children by half the women on the place. My James . . . *(A beat)* But that first time, he was hurting me so bad and I was screamin' and carryin' on somethin' awful and that old overseer just watchin' and laughin' to make sure James really doin' it. He watch us every night for a week and after the third one I hear James tryin' to whisper somethin' to me real quiet while he doin' it. I was so surprised I stopped cryin' for a minute and I hear James sayin' "Leah, Leah, Leah . . ." He just kept sayin' my name over and over. *(A beat)* At the end of the week, I had got my first son. Do you have another ribbon? (MIN *hands her one from her pocket.)* Fan's gonna skin you about her ribbons, Missy!

MINNIE Did you love James?

MISS LEAH I always thought I would've if they'd a let me find him for myself. The way it was, we stayed together after the war cause we was closer to each other than to anybody that wasn't dead or sold off and because James said we had ten babies that they sold away from us. We ought to have ten more we could raise free. Done! *(Finishes the braiding)*

MINNIE I love my hair in braids.

MISS LEAH Braid it or shave it off, I say. All the rest takes too much fussin' with. Don't leave a woman no time to think.

MINNIE Why won't you let Fannie write down your stories?

MISS LEAH Everything can't be wrote down. No matter what Fannie tell you, some things gotta be said out loud to keep the life in 'em.

MINNIE Do you think James would have liked Kansas?

MISS LEAH I think he would of if he could have walked his mind this far from Tennessee. It takes some doin' to be able to see a place in your mind where you never been before.

MINNIE Frank's been so many places. London. Paris. Rome. Sometimes it seems like he's been everywhere and seen everything.

MISS LEAH Well, I know that ain't true.

MINNIE Why?

MISS LEAH 'Cause this is his first time in Nicodemus.

MINNIE I kept hoping he would like it here. I miss it so much. I tried to describe it to him, and sometimes I'd read him Fannie's letters, but . . .

MISS LEAH Well, some people truly are

city people. They like all that noise and confusion. It gives them somethin' to hide behind. Can't do that out here. First winter teach you that. Out here, nothin' stands between you and your soul.

MINNIE It's more than that for Frank. He doesn't just hate the South and the frontier. He hates the whole country.

MISS LEAH Well, maybe the boy's got more sense than I thought he did.

MINNIE He said the first time he went to Europe he begged his father to leave him behind when it was time to go back to New Orleans. But he was only fourteen so his father refused.

MISS LEAH Fourteen can be a grown man if you let it.

MINNIE But he said he knew right then that as soon as he could, he was going to get on a boat for England and never look back. And he did, too.

MISS LEAH *(A beat)* Baby?

MINNIE Yes?

MISS LEAH Do you ever miss colored people?

MINNIE I miss colored people so much sometime I don't know what to do!

MISS LEAH Well, that's good to hear. I thought you might be getting as tired of Negroes as Frank seems to be.

MINNIE Frank doesn't mean any harm. He just doesn't feel like we do about Negroes. He might miss a friend or two, but when I ask him if he doesn't ever just miss being in a big group of Negroes, knowing that we are all going to laugh at the same time and cry at the same time just because we're all there being colored, he just shakes his head. I don't think he's ever felt it, so he can't miss it.

MISS LEAH How can a Negro get that grown and not know how it feels to be around his own people?

MINNIE He isn't used to being treated like other colored people. He gets so angry when we have to get on the Jim Crow car. When we can't go in the restaurants. I think if Frank had to live here, he might go mad.

MISS LEAH Well, Negroes are supposed to get mad, so that's a good sign.

MINNIE Not get mad, Miss Leah. Go mad.

MISS LEAH Six of one. Half a dozen of the other.

(FRANK enters from the bedroom.)

FRANK   Good morning! Darling! I didn't hear you get up.

MINNIE   *(Jumps up to hug him quickly)* I didn't want to wake you.

FRANK   What have you done to your hair?

MINNIE   Miss Leah braided it for me like she used to. Do you like it?

FRANK   I've never seen you with your hair in plaits.

MINNIE   Yes you have. I was wearing braids when you met me.

FRANK   *(Being charming for the benefit of* MISS LEAH*)* You looked like such a little country girl then. When I first took Minnie to London, I made sure to take her shopping before I introduced her to my friends. But I always knew she had potential. Anybody could see that. And that's why I married her. Because Minnie deserves the best. Doesn't she?

MISS LEAH   She is the best.

FRANK   Yes, she is! I'm going to step out for a smoke, if you two will excuse me.

MINNIE   I'll come, too. Do you want me to make you some breakfast before we go out? My coffee isn't as bad as Sister's.

MISS LEAH   Fan left me a fresh pot. Go ahead, chile. I'll be fine. I've been up long enough to be lookin' for a nap soon.

*(*FRANK *and* MINNIE *exit to the yard.)*

FRANK   *(Angrily)* I want you to put your hair back the way it was.

MINNIE   I always wore my . . .

FRANK   You look like a damn pickaninny! We haven't been here twenty-four hours and look at you!

MINNIE   I'm sorry . . .

FRANK   You're always sorry, aren't you? Of course you are, but if you weren't so busy being sorry, you'd know there are some interesting things going on in Nicodemus these days.

MINNIE   What do you mean?

FRANK   I'm going into town to check at the telegraph office and . . . take a look around.

MINNIE   Don't be too late, will you?

(He exits. MINNIE *sits down on the porch wearily and draws her knees to her chest, rocking back and forth wearily. In the kitchen,* FAN *and* SOPHIE *are oblivious.)*
(Black)

Scene 5

Late that night.

It is late evening. SOPHIE *and* FAN *and* MINNIE *are up.* FAN *is sewing something.* SOPHIE *is pulling some papers from her desk. Some of these are rolled maps or plans, etc. These are* SOPHIE*'s plans for the development of the town.* MINNIE *is standing at the window.* FAN *takes off her glasses, rubs her eyes sleepily.* MINNIE *goes over to the fire and stirs it up, puts another log on.*

FAN   Well I think I'm going to leave the rest of you night owls! Don't worry, Nicodemus isn't big enough for Frank to get into trouble. Even if he's looking for it.

MINNIE   Good night.

FAN   I'll be up early.

MINNIE   Me, too.

(They embrace. FAN *takes her sewing and exits, patting* SOPHIE *affectionately as she passes.)*

FAN   Good night, Sister.

SOPHIE   Check on Miss Leah?

FAN   Always.

(She exits. SOPHIE *pours herself a cup of coffee.)*

MINNIE   You don't have to wait up with me.

SOPHIE   I won't be sleeping much between now and the vote next week.

MINNIE   What are you doing?

SOPHIE   I'm writing my speech for Sunday. I'm going to singlehandedly convince these Negroes they have the right to protect their land from speculators and save Nicodemus!

MINNIE   Save it from what?

SOPHIE   From being just one more place where colored people couldn't figure out how to be free.

MINNIE   Are politics so important?

SOPHIE   *(A beat)* Come look at this. *(*SOPHIE *has spread out the plans on the table.)* These are the plans for Nicodemus. Here's the store and the post office. In the same places, but bigger. And open every day, not just two days a week. And here's the blacksmith and the school . . .

MINNIE   Who did this?

SOPHIE   I did. We want the school open by spring but the teacher we hired just wrote to say she won't come because she's getting married and her fool husband . . .

(SOPHIE stops herself abruptly, not wanting to seem critical of FRANK.)

MINNIE   Doesn't like the frontier, huh?

SOPHIE   I guess not.

MINNIE   This is wonderful.

SOPHIE   Fan drew the buildings. I was just going to write down what was going where, but Fan said, how about all the people in Nicodemus who can't read? *(A beat)* So the school goes here. The church stays where it is, but bigger. We've got fifty now in the Baptist pews alone! Then the doctor and the dentist will be here together so folks won't have to get their nerve up but once to go inside since it's different offices, but the same building. And see right here?

MINNIE   Yes.

SOPHIE   That's Fan's newspaper office and book publishing company.

MINNIE   Look! She put a little face waving out of the window!

SOPHIE   That's her. Fan puts us all on it. Here I am at the feed store. And here's Wil at the blacksmith. Here you are at the train station. Miss Leah's on here some place . . .

MINNIE   She forgot to draw Frank.

SOPHIE   I guess she did.

MINNIE   You know I'd come back if I could, don't you?

SOPHIE   I think you would if you wanted to.

MINNIE   It's not that simple.

SOPHIE   Why isn't it?

MINNIE   Does anybody really know what they want? Do you?

SOPHIE   Of course I do! I want this town to be a place where a colored woman can be free to live her life like a human being. I want this town to be a place where a colored man can work as hard for himself as we used to work for the white folks. I want a town where a colored child can go to anybody's door and be treated like they belong there.

MINNIE   When you start talking about this place, you make it sound like paradise for colored people.

SOPHIE   It's not paradise yet, but it can be beautiful. The century is going to change in two years! This can be a great time for colored people. We can really be free instead of spending our lives working for the same people that used to own us. How are we ever going to be free if we have to spend all of our time doing somebody else's laundry?

MINNIE   You used to do laundry.

SOPHIE   There's nothing wrong with doing laundry until you start thinking that's all you can do. That's why the vote is so important. We have to help each other stay strong. The rule doesn't say they can't sell their land. It says they can't sell it unless they are prepared to look the rest of us in the eye and say who they are selling it to and why. As long as they have to face each other, nobody will have nerve enough to sell to speculators, no matter what they're offering.

MINNIE   But it wouldn't matter as long as most of the people here are colored, would it?

SOPHIE   If we start selling to speculators. everything will change. We may as well move back to Memphis. And before I do that, I'll get Wil Parrish to teach me how to speak Spanish and move us all to Mexico!

(She starts gathering up her maps, etc.)

MINNIE   Wait, before you put it away. I was thinking maybe you could show it to Frank. So he could see how nice everything is going to be.

SOPHIE   Mr. Frank Charles ain't no more interested in an all-colored town than the man in the moon.

MINNIE   Frank's not so bad, Sister.

SOPHIE   Suit yourself.

MINNIE   Why don't you like him?

SOPHIE   I don't have to like him.

MINNIE   I know. But why don't you?

SOPHIE   I think Frank hates being colored. I don't understand Negroes like that. They make me nervous.

MINNIE   *(Stung)* You make me nervous.

SOPHIE   I didn't used to.

MINNIE   No. I guess you didn't.

(SOPHIE picks up the gun, puts on her coat.)

SOPHIE   I'm going to check the horses.

(She exits. MINNIE goes over to stoke the fire, hears a noise. FRANK crosses the yard quickly and enters. MIN turns, thinking it is SOPHIE. She freezes.)

FRANK   What are you still doing up? It's late.

(He staggers over, sits and drinks a long pull from a silver flask without taking his eyes off of her.)

MINNIE   I was waiting for you.

FRANK Why? Haven't I had enough bad luck for a nigger?

MINNIE Are you all right?

FRANK Do I look like I'm all right?

MINNIE Let me get you some coffee . . .

FRANK You don't need to get me a damn thing. Just sit still! Can you just sit still for once?

MINNIE Yes, Frank.

FRANK You know what happened tonight, don't you? I don't even have to bother telling you anything about it, do I?

MINNIE What is it? What happened?

FRANK I was gambling. A gentleman's game of poker with some of my friends from the train. Ran into them in town. And you know what? I lost. I lost everything. What there was left of it.

MINNIE You were gambling with white men?

FRANK White gentlemen, Min. And I lost every dime. And I want to thank you for that. Things were going fine until one of them asked me about the nigger woman who kept following me around the train. I laughed it off, but my luck changed after that so I know they suspected something. *(He stands behind her, touching her shoulders lightly.)* But I should have known better than to depend on you for luck. You're too black to bring me any good luck. All you got to give is misery. Pure D misery and little black pickaninnies just like you. *(He rubs her arms, stops, keeping his hands lightly on her shoulders. She moves away in fear.)*

MINNIE Frank, were you . . .

FRANK Shut up!

(She looks around for help in a panic.)

FRANK But the game wasn't a total loss. I found out something interesting. Do you know what I found out?

MINNIE No, Frank.

FRANK Your sisters are sitting on a fortune. That white man on the train? He said speculators are paying top dollar for these farms around here.

MINNIE Sister would never sell this land!

FRANK Of course she wouldn't because she's just like all the other Negroes around here. She's content to live her life like a pack mule out in some backwater town . . . I never should have let you talk me into bringing you out here. We damn well could have waited in New Orleans like I wanted to. Taking that damn train all the way across the damn prairie. You know what they call your precious town? "Niggerdemus"! Niggerdemus, Kansas. Don't you think that's funny, Min?

MINNIE Were you passing?

FRANK I was letting people draw their own conclusions.

MINNIE Who did you tell them I was?

FRANK I told you to shut up!

(He pushes her roughly and she stumbles and falls to the floor at the moment that SOPHIE enters from the porch. FAN follows almost immediately, awakened by the noise.)

FAN Minnie! My God!

SOPHIE What do you think you're doing?

FRANK I'm talking to my wife. This is none of your affair.

MINNIE It's all right! It was an accident. I just slipped, didn't I, Frank? I just slipped!

SOPHIE Get out.

FRANK You're pretty high and mighty for a nigger woman, aren't you?

MINNIE Shut up, Frank! He's drunk! Don't listen to him.

FRANK What did you say?

(He starts to move toward MINNIE in a threatening manner. SOPHIE raises the shotgun and cocks it.)

MINNIE No, Sister! Don't! Please don't! I'm going to have a baby!

(All stop.)

(Black)

Act II

Scene 1

Early the next morning.

   SOPHIE *is standing at the window with her gun at her side.* FRANK *is skulking around in the yard, coatless and cold.* FAN *is getting a tea kettle off the stove.* MISS LEAH *is taking some herbs from small jars laid out before her and preparing them for the tea.* MIN *is wrapped in a blanket, propped up in a chair. She looks fragile and frightened.*

MINNIE He doesn't even have his coat with him.

SOPHIE Good! Maybe he'll freeze to death.

FAN Don't say that. You'll just upset her again.

SOPHIE Upset her? Don't you think she

ought to be upset? Don't you think we all
ought to be upset?

MISS LEAH Let her drink this tea and
catch her breath before you start fussin'
again.

(FRANK exits the yard.)

MISS LEAH *(Hands cup to* MINNIE*)* Drink
all of it. It'll help you hold onto that
baby.

MINNIE This is such a hard time for
Frank . . .

SOPHIE For Frank?

MINNIE He's my husband!

FAN Of course he is. Be still, now.

MINNIE He's so afraid they will try to trick
him out of his inheritance.

SOPHIE Of course they will!

FAN Sister, please!

MINNIE His brothers hate him.

SOPHIE His brothers used to own him!

MINNIE That's not his fault too, is it?

SOPHIE No. It's his fault for thinking that
means they owe him something and if he
doesn't get it, he has the right to put his
hands on you

MINNIE I love him.

SOPHIE That's not love.

MINNIE *(A beat)* How would you know?
*(*SOPHIE *looks at* MINNIE*, picks up the
shotgun and goes to sit on the porch steps.*
MISS LEAH *looks at* MINNIE *then goes to
get a pipe and prepares it slowly.)*

FAN You know, Sister only wants what is
best for you.

MINNIE I know.

FAN Sometimes I think if I'd known you
were going to stay so long. I'd of thought
longer about letting you go.

MINNIE Me, too. *(A beat)* Everything has
changed. Everything. When Frank and I
went to London, it was like a fairy tale. I
felt so free! I could do anything, go
anywhere, buy anything. And Frank was
always there to show me something I had
never seen before or tell me something
I'd been waiting to hear all my life . . .
and I loved to look at him. But he
changed . . . He was mad all the time.

FAN Mad at who?

MINNIE At everybody. But mostly me. I
guess.

MISS LEAH Why was he mad at you?

MINNIE I don't know why! I think he just
started hating colored people. We'd be
walking down the street and he'd say:
"Look at those niggers. No wonder nobody

wants to be around them." When his
father died and his brothers stopped
sending money, it just got worse and
worse. It was almost like he couldn't
stand to look at me . . .

FAN Hush, now. It's all right. Me and Miss
Leah will take care of you now. There's
not a baby in the world that can come
before Miss Leah says it's time to.

MINNIE . . . Sometimes I used to think it
must be a dream and that I'd wake up
one day and Frank would be the way he
used to be.

MISS LEAH Grown people don't change
except to get more like what they already
are.

FAN Frank is going through a bad time
that's all, but he's still Frank. He's still
that man that swept you off your feet.
The man you want to be the father of
your children, isn't he?

MINNIE He scares me sometimes. He gets
so angry.

FAN You know who else had a terrible
temper?

MINNIE Who?

FAN Daddy. You were too young to
remember it, but he did. And Daddy was
a good man, but he had that temper and
sometimes it would get the better of him.
Just like your Frank. Sometimes he used
to . . . not all the time, but . . . one time
they woke me up, fussing about something, and Mama didn't hear me call her,
so I went to the top of the stairs where I
could see them without them seeing me.
I always sat there . . . Daddy was sitting
by the fireplace and Mama was talking a
mile a minute. I could tell he didn't like
what she was saying, and then he got up
real fast and grabbed her arm and he just
shook her and shook her . . . I was so
scared I ran back to bed, but I could still
hear everything . . . Sometimes we have
to be stronger than they are, Baby Sister.
We have to understand and be patient.

MINNIE What did Mama do?

FAN Mama always said she was biding her
time until we could get these white folks
off our backs so she could get colored
men straightened out on a thing or two a
little bit closer to home, but until then,
she said she'd give him the benefit of the
doubt.

MINNIE I've been trying to do that, too.

FAN You love Frank, don't you?

MINNIE I used to love him so much . . .

FAN You still love him. I can see it on your face. You two can work it out. I know you can. For better or for worse, remember?

MINNIE I'll try. I'll really try.

(FRANK enters the yard and MINNIE sees him from the window.)

MINNIE Frank!

(She rushes past SOPHIE on the porch and into his arms. He embraces her and grins evilly at SOPHIE.)

(Black)

Scene 2

The next Sunday; early morning.

FAN and MISS LEAH are up and ready for church. SOPHIE is finishing breakfast at the table alone. FRANK and MIN are in their room getting ready to go.

FAN How was everything?

SOPHIE Fine. Thank you.

FAN Is your speech ready?

SOPHIE As ready as it's going to be. I'm not going to worry about it. I'll say what I have to say and then we'll see which way it goes.

FAN It'll go your way. You've hardly been home at all this week, out convincing everybody.

MISS LEAH That's not why she hasn't been around here this week. Is it?

SOPHIE I don't know what you mean.

(SOPHIE clears up her plate while MISS LEAH watches her.)

MISS LEAH You are the most stubborn colored woman I've ever seen in my life.

SOPHIE I'll take that as a compliment coming from you.

FAN Please don't get her started! I want us to ride to church and back in peace.

SOPHIE I can't tell her who to marry, but I won't sit at a table with a man who called me an uppity nigger woman in my own damn house!

FAN She's forgiven him. Can't you?

SOPHIE He doesn't want my forgiveness. And she doesn't need it. She hasn't done anything wrong.

FAN He made a mistake. He's sorry. I know he is. You haven't spoken a word to either one of them in a week. London is so far away and she'll be gone soon. Don't let her go without a word.

MISS LEAH Colored women ain't got enough sisters to be cutting each other off so easy, I'd say.

SOPHIE Easy? I pointed a gun at the man's head and wanted to use it!

FAN And he's prepared to sit at the table with you!

MISS LEAH Which shows he ain't as smart as he thinks he is!

(Suddenly, SOPHIE laughs.)

SOPHIE All right, you win!

FAN Thank goodness! Now we can celebrate this birthday right!

SOPHIE Don't get carried away. I said I'd be here. I didn't say I'd talk.

FAN You know how special this birthday is. For all of us. How can you give her the deed if you won't even talk to her?

SOPHIE You give it to her. *(Puts the envelope with the deed in front of FAN)*

FAN I can't. Not without you. It has to be all three of us or it doesn't mean anything. "With all our trust. And all our strength. And all our courage. And all our love." Remember?

(MIN and FRANK enter from the back, ready for church. They both stop when they see SOPHIE is still there.)

MINNIE Good morning.

SOPHIE Happy Birthday, Min. *(Hands her the envelope)* This is for you.

MINNIE A present? This early in the day? Can I open it?

SOPHIE Ask Fan.

FAN Go ahead.

MINNIE *(Reading, but confused)* But what does it mean?

FRANK It's a deed.

SOPHIE It's the deed to your part of this land. You're twenty-one now.

MISS LEAH Every colored woman ought to have a piece of land she can claim as her own.

FRANK Do you know how much that land is worth?

SOPHIE We're interested in buying more land, not selling what we've got.

FRANK Well, from what that white fella told me on the train, not everybody around here feels that way. I heard some of your neighbors are considering some pretty generous offers.

MISS LEAH Speculators!

FRANK They're offering $500 an acre.

MISS LEAH I can't believe it.

FRANK Doesn't that at least make you

more open to the idea? You could be a very rich woman.

SOPHIE And I'd be standing in the middle of Kansas without any place to call home. You can't grow wheat on an acre of money.

FRANK There's plenty of other land around from what I could see. What's the difference?

SOPHIE The difference is we own this land. Whether they like it or not, and anybody who tries to say different is going to find himself buried on it.

FRANK You wouldn't really kill somebody over a piece of ground out in the middle of nowhere, would you?

SOPHIE This land is the center of the world to me as long as we're standing on it.

FRANK And how do you think the rest of the world feels about sharing their center with a town full of colored people?

SOPHIE I have no idea.

MINNIE None of that matters! Can't you see that none of that matters! This is the land that makes us free women, Frank. We can never sell it! Not ever!

(WIL PARRISH *enters and comes to the door.* FAN *opens it for him.*)

FAN We thought you'd changed your mind about coming to church with us.

WIL On the day of Miss Sophie's speech? Not me! I'm sorry I'm late. I stopped by the telegraph office yesterday and there was a wire for Frank. (*Searches his pockets for it*) It was too late to bring it over yesterday and this morning I forgot it, so I went back. I thought it was probably the news you been waitin' for.

FRANK I knew it! Didn't I tell you? I knew it! I felt our ship pulling up to the dock. Come on, Parrish! Where is the damn thing?

(FRANK *rips it open and reads. His face hardens.*)

FRANK What the hell?

MINNIE What is it?

(FRANK *drops the telegram on the table and walks to the bedroom, slams the door.* FAN *picks up the telegram.*)

MINNIE Read it, Fan.

FAN (*Reading*) "Paternity denied. Stop. All claims to money, property, land and other assets of Mr. John Charles, late of New Orleans, Louisiana, denied. No legal recourse available."

MINNIE You all go on without me. I need to . . . Frank needs me here, I think.

FAN All right, Baby Sister. Be strong.

MINNIE Yes, I will.

(*They exit.* MINNIE *goes down the hall to* FRANK, *who is sitting on the bed drinking from a silver flask.*)

MINNIE I'm so sorry!

FRANK Are you? Sorry for what? Marrying a bastard?

MINNIE Don't say that!

FRANK Do you know what this means? This means I've got nothing. Not a dime. Nothing.

MINNIE You can sell your books.

FRANK Don't be so stupid. (*Pacing*) They think they can make me an ordinary Negro. That's what they think. They think they're going to have a chance to treat me colored and keep me here where every ignorant white man who walks the street can make me step off to let him pass. They think they can pretend I'm nothing and – presto – I'll be nothing.

MINNIE You won't let them do that.

FRANK Let them? They've done it! We don't even have passage back to London. We're stuck here being niggers. Common, ordinary, niggers!

MINNIE It'll be all right. We don't have a lot of money, but we've got a place to live. Not forever, but just until we get on our feet. Just until the baby comes! We do have a place.

FRANK What are you talking about?

MINNIE We can stay here. On our own land. Right here. Until you have a chance to figure things out.

FRANK Do you really think I could live here?

MINNIE Sophie has plans. You'll see. It's going to be beautiful. A paradise for colored people.

FRANK A paradise for colored people . . .

MINNIE This is our land, Frank. Nobody can take it from us. You don't have to have your father's money. We have land!

FRANK You're right. We have land . . . (*A beat*) I'm sorry I snapped at you, darling. It's just that when I think about all the things I want to give you, it drives me crazy.

MINNIE I love you. That's all I need.

FRANK But you deserve so much more, Min. You're so beautiful. (*He kisses her. Touches her stomach gently.*) Did you explain to my son that his daddy has a bad temper sometimes?

MINNIE Please try, Frank. Just try . . .

FRANK *(His mood changes abruptly)* Don't you think I'm trying? I'm trying to be a good husband to you. And I want to be a good father. But you have to help me.

MINNIE I need to be able to trust you again.

FRANK You can, darling. You can trust me. I swear it. I know the last months haven't been easy, but I'll make it up to you. Do you believe me?

MINNIE Yes, Frank . . .

FRANK It'll be just like it used to be. We'll find another place, just like the one we had before, right on the square. You liked that place, didn't you darling?

MINNIE It was lovely, but it costs too much money to live that way. To live abroad . . .

FRANK Your share of this land is worth over $50,000. Do you know what we can do with that kind of money in London? We'll have the best of everything and so will our baby.

MINNIE Sophie would never sell this land to speculators. Not for a million dollars.

FRANK It wouldn't be all of it. Just your fair share. The town is full of people looking to buy some of this land before your sister gets that damn rule passed. This is the chance we've been waiting for. A chance for me to get back on my feet. To show my brothers I don't need their money.

MINNIE They're not your brothers. They don't even claim you!

FRANK They don't have to claim me. I look just like them!

MINNIE No, Frank. I can't ask Sister to split up this land.

FRANK I'm your husband. Don't you ever tell me no!

MINNIE Don't, Frank! *(Moving quickly out of reach)* I don't care what you do to me, but I won't let you hurt our baby!

FRANK *(He grabs her arm and brings her up against him sharply.)* Don't you ever threaten me as long as you live, do you understand me? Do you? *(She nods silently.)* I'll kill you right now, Min. I'll break your damn neck before your precious sisters can hear you holler. I'll kill everybody in this house, don't you understand that? You want to know who I

told those white men you were, Min? You really want to know? *(She struggles again, but he holds her.)* I told them you were a black whore I won in a card game. *(He laughs and presses his mouth to hers roughly.)*

(Black)

Scene 3

Sunday afternoon.

FRANK *enters the main room, pulling on hat and gloves, clearly preparing to go out.* MISS LEAH *and* FAN *enter the yard.* FAN *is helping* MISS LEAH.

FAN I thought Sister's speech went well this morning, didn't you Miss Leah?

MISS LEAH Speechifyin' and carryin' on. She ought to run for president.

(They open the door as FRANK *arrives at it.)*

FAN Frank! You startled me.

FRANK I'm sorry. I didn't hear you coming.

FAN Are you going out?

FRANK I won't be long. I have some business to attend to in town.

MISS LEAH On Sunday afternoon?

FAN I'm sorry about the will. I want you to know you always have a place here with us.

FRANK Yes. Thank you. We'll figure out something.

FAN Is Min going in with you?

FRANK No, she's resting. She'll be out in a few minutes. I won't be long. *(Exits quickly)*

FAN I believe he is sorry about what happened, don't you?

MISS LEAH A man that hit a woman once will hit her again.

(SOPHIE enters and meets FRANK in the yard.)

FRANK How was church?

SOPHIE You should have been there. *(She crosses to the porch.)*

FRANK You're going to have to stop being so high and mighty. It doesn't become you.

(She turns to him from the porch steps.)

SOPHIE I'm sorry for your troubles, because they're Min's troubles, too. But I think you should get on where you're going now and I'll go on inside.

FRANK Well, suit yourself, as you always

say, but I think I've got some news you might find interesting. *(Reaches in his pocket;* SOPHIE *shifts the gun.)* Take it easy! I'm unarmed ... as always! *(He pulls out the deed.)* I just thought you'd like to know that we're officially neighbors now. For the moment, anyway.

SOPHIE What are you talking about?

FRANK My wife wants me to share in her good fortune, so she's added my name to her deed.

SOPHIE I don't believe you.

FRANK I'd let you see it up close, but that probably isn't such a good idea. Hottempered woman like you ...

SOPHIE Get off my land. You make me sick.

FRANK I'll get so far off your land. I'll get so far off it the post office won't even be able to find me.

SOPHIE That suits me fine.

FRANK Well, maybe you'll like your new neighbours better. Ask Min about them. She met them on the train. Well, she didn't really meet them. I didn't introduce her, of course, but she saw us talking. White gentlemen. She'll remember them. She wants to tell you, but she's a little nervous about it.

SOPHIE Tell me what?

FRANK You can see why. You've raised her to think this place is practically holy ground. She didn't even want to talk about selling it at first, but she came around.

SOPHIE Minnie would never sell this land. You're lying.

FRANK Well, you let her tell you. I figured under the circumstances, I would spend the night in town. I'm sure I'll have our share sold before tomorrow. Hope the sale doesn't hurt your chances in the vote next week. *(Laughs)* You know you're getting off easy when you think about it, Sister Sophie. I could stick around here and take over your precious town if I wanted to. You ever see a group of colored people who didn't put the lightest one in charge?

(As FRANK *and* SOPHIE *talk, we see* FAN *and* MISS LEAH *making coffee, starting the evening meal, etc. In the rear bedroom,* MIN *raises up slowly. She is obviously in great pain and has been badly beaten. She almost cannot stand. She staggers to the door and down the hall. As* FRANK *exits laughing,*

MIN *stumbles into the room where* MISS LEAH *and* FAN *are working.)*

MISS LEAH Lord, chile!

FAN Sister! Sister! Come quick!

*(SOPHIE *rushes into the house and runs to help.)*

(Black)

Scene 4

Sunday evening.

FAN *and* WIL *are sitting on the porch.* WIL *has a shotgun.*

WIL I don't understand how a colored man can hit a colored woman, Miss Fannie. We been through too much together.

FAN Maybe there's just too many memories between us.

WIL I don't think you can have too many memories. I know I wouldn't take nothin' for none of mine.

FAN Not even the bad ones?

WIL Nope. The bad ones always make the good ones just that much sweeter. *(A beat)* Does that paper really mean Frank can sell to speculators?

FAN Well, if Baby Sister really signed it.

WIL I never met a colored man like Frank before. Seem like he don't care 'bout colored people no different from white folks. Miss Leah says it's because mulattos got a war in them. And sometimes it makes 'em stronger but sometimes it just makes 'em crazy. Makes 'em think they got a choice about if they gonna be colored or not.

FAN Sister's a mulatto and she never seems to be confused.

WIL Well, you're right there. *(A beat)* Miss Fannie, I want you to know ... I can take care of it.

FAN Take care of what?

WIL I mean, he's a colored man and I'm a colored man. We can settle it that way. Man to man.

FAN I couldn't ask you to hurt anybody.

WIL You can ask me to kill somebody, Miss Fannie. If I can't protect you and your sisters from a Negro who has lost his mind, what kind of man does that make me?

FAN Have you ever killed a man?

WIL Not a colored man, but I guess they ain't that much different from any other kind of man when you get down to it.

(We see MISS LEAH *and* MINNIE *in the back.* MISS LEAH *is holding* MIN*'s hand and talking directly to her.)*

MISS LEAH   When they sold my first baby boy offa the place, I felt like I couldn't breathe for three days. After that, I could breathe a little better, but my breasts were so full of milk they'd soak the front of my dress. Overseer kept telling me he was gonna have to see if nigger milk was really chocolate like they said it was, so I had to stay away from him 'til my milk stopped runnin'. And one day I saw James and I told him they had sold the baby, but he already knew it. He had twenty sold offa our place by that time. Never saw any of 'em.

When he told me that, I decided he was gonna at least lay eyes on at least one of his babies came through me. So next time they put us together, I told him that I was gonna be sure this time he got to see his chile before Colonel Harrison sold it. But I couldn't. Not that one or the one after or the one after the ones after that. James never saw their faces. Until we got free and had our five free babies. Then he couldn't look at 'em long enough. That was a man who loved his children. Hug 'em and kiss 'em and take 'em everywhere he go.

I think when he saw the fever take all five of them, one by one like that . . . racin' each other to heaven . . . it just broke him down. He'd waited so long to have his sons and now he was losing them all again. He was like a crazy man just before he died. So I buried him next to his children and I closed the door on that little piece of house we had and I started walkin' west. If I'd had wings, I'd a set out flyin' west. I needed to be some place big enough for all my sons and all my ghost grandbabies to roam around. Big enough for me to think about all that sweetness they had stole from me and James and just holler about it loud as I want to holler.

MINNIE   I didn't want to sign it. I was just so scared. I didn't want him to hurt the baby. I can't make him stop . . . hitting me. I just . . . want him . . . to stop . . . hitting me.

MISS LEAH   They broke the chain, Baby Sister. But we have to build it back. And build it back strong so the next time nobody can break it. Not from the outside and not from the inside. We can't let nobody take our babies. We've given up all the babies we can afford to lose. *(A beat)* Do you understand what I'm sayin' to you?

MINNIE   *(Whispers)* Yes, ma'am.

MISS LEAH   *(Kisses her)* Good. Go to sleep now. That baby needs a nap!

*(*MISS LEAH *goes out to* WIL *and* FAN.*)*

FAN   Is she . . .

MISS LEAH   She's sleeping. She held onto that baby, too. I told you she was stronger than you think.

FAN   Thank God!

MISS LEAH   Where is Sister?

WIL   She wanted to be sure Frank was headed toward town and not back this way. She told me to bring you the things you wanted from the house for Miss Minnie.

(He hands her a small packet which she takes and opens carefully.)

MISS LEAH   I hope she didn't forget anything.

WIL   She had it written down.

*(*SOPHIE *enters on the move.)*

SOPHIE   He's on his way in, but he's moving slow. Is everything there you need?

MISS LEAH   It's here. It's here . . .

SOPHIE   Min?

FAN   Sleeping. She's going to be okay.

SOPHIE   *(Taking charge)* All right, here's what we're going to do. Wil, I need you to ride out and catch up with Frank. Tell him Min sent you to tell him she loves him more than anything and . . . everything is going to. be okay. Tell him she wants him to come here tomorrow afternoon because I'll be in town to try and stop the deal. Tell him she wants to go with him to the land office so they won't have any trouble no matter what I do.

WIL   What if he doesn't believe me? He might think it's a trick.

SOPHIE   Tell him colored men have to stick together. He'll believe you. Tell him . . . tell him . . . the message is from Fan. That she's on their side now. That should make him feel safe.

FAN   What are you going to do when he gets here?

SOPHIE   *(A beat)* You and Miss Leah go in the back with Min.

FAN But what are you going to do?

SOPHIE A colored man who will beat a colored woman doesn't deserve to live.

FAN Just like that?

SOPHIE No. Just when he tries to kill my sister and her baby before it's even born yet!

FAN Stop it! That's just what I was afraid of!

SOPHIE What you were afraid of? Me?

FAN Of what you might do.

SOPHIE What I might do? Why aren't you afraid of what he is already doing?

FAN He's her husband, Sister!

SOPHIE If he wasn't her husband would you care what I did to him for beating her half to death?

FAN That's different.

SOPHIE You know as well as I do there are no laws that protect a woman from her husband. Josh beat Belle for years and we all knew it. And because the sheriff didn't do anything, none of us did anything either. It wasn't a crime until he killed her! I'm not going to let that happen to Min. I'm going to watch him prance across this yard and then I'm going to step out on my front porch and blow his brains out.

FAN And then we'll be savages just like he is!

SOPHIE No! Then we'll be doing what free people always have to do if they're going to stay free.

FAN (A beat) Isn't there any other way, Sister?

SOPHIE This morning, while I was standing in that church painting a picture of the future of this town, he beat her and did God knows what else to her in this house. Where she's always been safe. We can't let him do that, Fan. All the dreams we have for Nicodemus, all the churches and schools and libraries we can build don't mean a thing if a colored woman isn't safe in her own house.

  (FAN turns away.)

WIL (Quickly) You don't have to do this. I already told Miss Fannie. All you have to do is say the word.

SOPHIE What are you talking about?

WIL I can take care of it. You can wait here with your sisters and I'll take care of everything.

SOPHIE I appreciate the offer, but the day I need somebody else to defend my land and my family is the day that somebody's name will be on the deed. I need you to help me do what needs to be done. Not do it for me.

WIL You can count on me.

SOPHIE Good! Go on now. I don't want him to get too far ahead of you.

WIL I'll catch him. (Exits)

MISS LEAH I can't let you do this.

SOPHIE I'm not asking you. This is something I have to do.

MISS LEAH And why is that? Because he hit your baby sister or because he wants to sell your land to some white folks?

SOPHIE Aren't those reasons good enough for you?

MISS LEAH Where's the pie tin? (She gets up and starts laying out utensils, ingredients, etc. to make a pie. This activity goes on throughout the following dialogue.)

SOPHIE What?

MISS LEAH The pie tin.

FAN It's in the cupboard. What are you doing?

MISS LEAH We're going to make an apple pie.

SOPHIE An apple pie?

MISS LEAH In case you forgot, this is still the state of Kansas, a part of the United States of America. Men beat their wives every day of the week includin' Sunday, and white folks cheat colored folks every time they get a mind to.

SOPHIE I know all that.

MISS LEAH Good. I remember when y'all first got here. Green as you could be. Even you, Sister Sophie, way back then. Your group was as raggedy as any we'd seen. All of y'all lookin' like somethin' the cat dragged in. And then here come Min, bouncin' off the back of your wagon, hair all over her head, big ol' eyes and just the sweetest lil' face I ever saw. Didn't even know enough to be scared. (A beat) Hand me the sugar.

FAN Are you feeling all right?

MISS LEAH Am I feelin' all right? If I was you, I'd be worried about folks talkin' 'bout shootin' somebody. That's who I'd be worryin' about. It's a messy business, shootin' folks. It ain't like killin' a hog, you know. Sheriff has to come. White folks have to come. All that come with shootin' somebody.

  But folks die all kinds of ways. Sometimes they be goin' along just as nice as you please and they heart just give out. Just like that. Don't nobody know why. Things just happen. *(A beat)* One day a little bit before I left the plantation, Colonel Harrison brought him a new cook. Ella. She was a big strong woman. She didn't make no trouble either. Just worked hard and kept to herself. Ella knew a lot about herbs. What to put in to make it taste good. Colonel Harrison just love the way she cook. He used to let her roam all over the plantation pickin' wild herbs to put in her soups and stews. And she wouldn't tell nobody what she use. Said it was secrets from Africa. White folks didn't need to know. Colonel Harrison just laugh. He was eatin' good and didn't care 'bout where it come from no way.

But after awhile, that overseer started messin' around her. Tryin' to get Colonel Harrison to let him have his way with her, but Colonel Harrison said no and told him to stay from around her. She belonged in the kitchen. But that ol' overseer still wanted her and everybody knew next time he had a chance, he was gonna get her.

So one day, Colonel Harrison went to town. Gonna be gone all day. So that overseer put some poor colored man in charge of our misery and walked on up to the house like he was the master now cause Colonel Harrison gone off for the day. And when he walk up on the back porch, he had one thing on his mind, but Ella had been up early, too, and the first thing he saw before he even saw her was a fresh apple pie coolin' in the window. And it smelled so good, he almost forgot what he come for. And Ella opened the screen door and smile like he the person she wanna see most in this world and she ask him if he'd like a glass of cold milk and a piece of her hot apple pie. Of course he did! What man wouldn't? And he sat down there and she cut him a big ol' piece and she told him it was hot and to be careful not to burn hisself . . . And do you know what happened? Well, he didn't even get to finish that piece of pie Ella cut for him so pretty. Heart just stopped right in the middle of a great big bite. By the time the master got back, they had him laid out in the barn and Ella was long gone. *(A beat)* But she did

do one last thing before she left.

FANNIE And what was that?

MISS LEAH She gave me her recipe for apple pie.

(Black)

Scene 5

Monday morning.

MISS LEAH *is in the back sitting with* MINNIE *who is lying down.* SOPHIE *and* WIL *are hiding outside.* FAN *is alone in the kitchen where she checks the time and then goes to the oven and takes out a perfect pie.*

FRANK *enters the yard furtively.* FAN *sees him and watches him from the window. She takes off her apron and goes to the door. She opens it before he knocks. He steps back, startled.*

FAN Come in, Frank.

(FRANK hesitates.)

FAN Sister's gone to town and Miss Leah's in the back with Min. Please. Come in.

FRANK Parrish said you were going to come into the land office with me. Are you ready?

FAN It's all right. Sister isn't angry anymore. She wants to make you an offer.

FRANK What kind of offer?

FAN Please. Come inside so we can talk.

FRANK I don't want any trouble.

FAN We're prepared to make you an offer for your land.

FRANK You can't afford what they're paying in town.

FAN We're prepared to pay exactly what they're paying in town.

FRANK You don't have that kind of money. Minnie said so.

FAN Sister and I didn't involve Min in all the details of our household finances. I'll go into town with you now and we can make all the arrangements. Do you have the deed?

(FRANK shows it and puts it back in his pocket.)

FAN Good!

FRANK That's fine by me. I don't care where the money comes from as long as it ends up in my pocket so I can get the hell out of this place! *(Extends his hand)* Can we seal the deal, Fannie? Just the two of us?

FAN Done.

FRANK You know, I'm sorry it had to go

this far in the first place. I love Minnie
... How is she?

FAN She's asleep right now. Miss Leah's
with her.

FRANK Good, good.

FAN She wanted me to wake her up as
soon as you got here, but I told her to get
a few more minutes' rest and I'd give you
a piece of homemade apple pie to keep
you busy in the meantime.

FRANK You're not angry with me? About
Min, I mean. You know how aggravating
she can be some time. She's such a child.

FAN I understand. She has to understand
that a wife's first allegiance is to her
husband.

FRANK Well, you're a very understanding
person and I appreciate that, but I would
just as soon we get on our way. I don't
think your sister would be too happy to
come home and find me sitting at her
table eating up all her ...

FAN (Holding out a piece to him) ... apple
pie. My specialty. Sister won't be home
for hours yet. Besides, now that we know
we'll be able to keep the land in the
family, Sister's not one to hold a grudge.

FRANK I don't know about that. She didn't
seem to mind swinging that shotgun in
my direction.

FAN We've got to put all that behind us
now. For Min's sake and for the sake of
your baby. I know Sister's prepared to let
bygones be bygones. In fact, when she
saw me rolling out the crust for this pie,
she told me to make sure you got a piece
of it.

FRANK She did? Well, it takes a better man
than I am to refuse an invitation for a
piece of your famous apple pie! (He sits
and begins to eat heartily.) Delicious! Well,
you tell Sophie she's not going to have to
worry about Frank Charles hanging
around getting in her hair. Not me!
(Laughs, coughs a little) Soon as we get
everything signed and proper, good-bye
Niggerdemus! Hello London! They treat
me like a human being over there. You
wouldn't believe it. Half the people we
know don't even know I'm colored. I told
Min if she was just a couple of shades
lighter, we could travel first class all over
the world. Nobody would suspect a thing.
(Laughs, coughs a little, loosens his tie)
Don't get me wrong. I don't outright pass.
I just let people draw their own conclusions. (Coughs harder as Fan watches
impassively) Can you get me a glass of
water, please? I feel a little ... strange.

FAN No, Frank I can't do that.

FRANK Please! I ... water ... my throat's
on fire! (He suddenly realizes.) What have
you done? My God, help me! Please help
me!

(She watches him as he tries to stand, but
can't. He looks at her in a panic, then
slumps over: dead. FAN shudders slightly:
it's over. She composes herself, goes to the
door and waves a signal to SOPHIE and
WIL, who come immediately. WIL checks the
body to be sure FRANK is dead. He nods to
SOPHIE and they begin gathering FRANK's
things to remove the body. MINNIE and
MISS LEAH, hearing the activity, enter from
the back. MINNIE moves slowly from her
injuries and from her reluctance to see the
result of their collective action. They see that
FRANK is dead. MISS LEAH watches
MINNIE who moves toward the body then
stops, looking at FRANK with a mixture of
regret and relief. She approaches the body
slowly, her anger and fear battling her
bittersweet memories of the love she once felt
for FRANK. She reaches out and touches
him tentatively, realizing the enormity of
what they have done. She draws back, but
reaches out again, almost involuntarily, to
touch his arm, his hand, his shoulder. We
see her move through a complex set of
emotions, ending with her knowledge of the
monster FRANK had become. Her face now
shows her resolve and even her body seems
to gain strength. She steels herself and
reaches into FRANK's pocket to withdraw the
deed. She clutches it in her hand then looks
to SOPHIE, who stands watching her.
MINNIE takes a step toward SOPHIE and
extends the deed to her in anticipation of
SOPHIE demanding the return of the deed.
Instead, SOPHIE re-closes MINNIE's hand
around the deed and gently pushes MINNIE's
hand with the deed back to her. MINNIE,
grateful and relieved, and finally safe,
clutches the deed to her chest with both
hands.)
(Black)

Scene 6

Seven months later; April 1899.
· MISS LEAH is sleeping in her chair at the
table. The cradle is on the table and one of her

hands touches it protectively. MINNIE *enters from the back dressed for the dance in town. She stops and looks at* MISS LEAH *and her baby. She does not go to them, but looks for a minute and then goes around the room, slowly. She walks past the sideboard, touching it absently. She walks to the door and stands looking out at the full moon. She absently touches the brooch at her throat. Her hair is braided with ribbons and she wears bright clothes. She looks calm and healthy. She feels* MISS LEAH's *eyes on her and turns. They share a look. Both smile slowly.*

MINNIE It's as bright as noon out there.

MISS LEAH That's a good luck moon. It's gonna be a good day tomorrow.

MINNIE Do you think so?

MISS LEAH It's gonna be a good day every day.

MINNIE How do I look?

MISS LEAH You look beautiful, Baby Sister.

MINNIE Is she sleeping? Look! Her eyes are wide open! Hello, darling!

MISS LEAH She's thinkin'.

MINNIE *(Crooning to the baby)* What can my sweet baby be thinking, huh? What are you thinking about?

MISS LEAH Leave the chile in peace now! Everybody's got a right to their own thoughts.

MINNIE Do you think she's warm enough?

MISS LEAH You're gonna smother the child if you're not careful. It's spring! Time to let some air get to her.

MINNIE I know. I even took my shawl off while I was hanging clothes out today.

MISS LEAH You better stop that foolishness! This is still pneumonia weather!

MINNIE You just said winter was over, Miss Leah.

MISS LEAH Well, it'll be back before you know it.

(FAN and SOPHIE enter from the back. FAN is dressed up and SOPHIE has on a severe dark blue dress.)

FAN How do we look? *(She twirls around happily.)*

MINNIE You look wonderful! Wil Parrish will be beside himself to have such a beautiful fiancée!

SOPHIE If colored people paid as much attention to saving the race as they do to their dancing, we'd be free by now.

FAN Oh, hush! It's been so peaceful around here since you pushed that vote on

through and the speculators went home, it's time to do a little dancing!

MINNIE You're too plain, Sister.

SOPHIE Too plain! This is my best dress!

MINNIE It needs . . . something. Here! *(She takes the brooch from her own bodice, kisses it, and pins it on* SOPHIE.) *It's Mama's! Don't lose it!

SOPHIE I'll guard it with my life!

(WIL enters the yard. He carries flowers.)

FAN Good evening, Wil.

WIL And to you, Fannie. These are for you. Hello, Miss Leah. Everybody.

MISS LEAH Please get these women out of here. They are drivin' my granddaughter crazy with all their chatterin'!

MINNIE We're going! We're going! Are you sure she'll be okay? I can stay here with . . .

MISS LEAH I'm not so old I can't handle one little baby! Go on and leave us some peace.

WIL Baker and his Mrs. passed me on their way!

SOPHIE They didn't have that bad baby with them, did they?

MISS LEAH You know that girl don't go no place without carryin' that big head boy with 'em.

FAN He's not that bad!

SOPHIE Bad enough! *(Fussing with the pin)* Go on! Go on! I'm coming.

ALL Good night, etc.

(They exit.)

SOPHIE Too plain! That girl will have me looking like a Christmas tree if I'm not careful.

MISS LEAH You look fine.

SOPHIE Thank you.

MISS LEAH Now don't you go makin' any speeches tonight! This is a dance.

SOPHIE I won't, Miss Leah. Not tonight.

MISS LEAH Go on, now!

SOPHIE *(Putting the gun beside* MISS LEAH's *chair)* We won't be too late.

(SOPHIE exits to the yard. As MISS LEAH talks, SOPHIE walks into the middle of the yard and looks up at the full moon. She extends her arms and slowly turns around to encompass her land, her freedom, the moon, her life and the life of her sisters. She is completely at peace.

  MISS LEAH *reaches into the cradle and gently lifts the well-wrapped baby out and looks into her face.)*

MISS LEAH Yes, my granddaughter. We got

plenty to talk about, me and you. I'm going to tell you about your Mama and her Mama and her gran'Mama before that one. All those strong colored women makin' a way for little ol' you. Yes, they did! Cause they knew you were comin'. And wadn't nobody gonna keep you from us. Not my granddaughter! Yes, yes, yes! All those fine colored women, makin' a place for you. And I'm gonna tell you all about 'em. Yes, I sure am. I surely am . . . (MISS LEAH *rocks the baby, crooning softly to her,* SOPHIE *continues to spin slowly in the moonlight as the lights fade to black)*

Elvira and Hortensia Colorado

Biography

Elvira is the co-founder of Coatlicue/Las Colorado Theatre Company, Off the Beaten Path Theatre ensemble, and has served as secretary on the Board of Directors of the American Indian Community House. She has performed in the Yale Winterfest, and in various on and off-Broadway productions, soap operas and commercials.

Hortensia has worked on Broadway, Off-Broadway, film and television, at Yale and with the Sundance Institute. She has toured with Spiderwoman Theatre in *Winnetou's Snake Oil Show from Wigwam City* and *Power Pipes*. She is on the Board of Directors at the American Indian Community House.

Elvira and Hortensia have been performing together as storytellers for over ten years in and around the New York City area, at the American Museum of Natural History, LaMama, The American Indian Community House Gallery, Theatre for the New City, with the Thunderbird American Indian Dancers, Clearwater Revival, and the Brooklyn Museum, to name a few. Their other productions include *Open Wounds on Tlalteuctli, Huipil, Coyolxauhqui: Woman Without Borders, La Llorona, Walks of Indian Women – Aztlan to Anahauk*, and *Tlatilco: The Place Where Things are Hidden*.

Artistic statement

We were born in Blue Island, Illinois, a small town south of Chicago. We were part of a large Mexican community where the men worked at the stockyards, steel mills and railroads.

Our mother, Maria Sabina was married at 13 to a wealthy landowner in Mexico, who died after her third child was born. His family confiscated her inheritance and she was left penniless. It was the time of the Mexican Revolution and religious persecution. Relatives told her, "Come to Los Estados Unidos, there's lots of work here." She worked as a maid and a cook in a hospital.

She met our father, Regino, in a rooming house in Blue Island, Illinois. He had worked his way north for the railroad.

Our grandmother, Rafaela, arrived in the back of an open truck in the dead of winter and saw snow for the first time. Grande

Elvira　　　　　　　　　　　Hortensia

Photo: Georgetta Ryan

Chiquita was the center of our lives. She told us stories and taught us about herbs.

As poor as we were, mama's garden fed us with plenty of fruits and vegetables. We raised chickens and goats. When we got sick, mama cured us with the herbs like yerba buena, from her garden. For entertainment she would gather us all together and tell us cuentos/stories about La Llorona and brujas/witches. Many of her stories have been incorporated into our theater pieces.

We became writers out of necessity to speak in our own voices instead of being spoken for. We come from a lineage of strong Indian women who have been silenced for too long and it is through our work that we give voice to their stories, the unsung heroines. Sometimes it's the force of our grandmothers' voices speaking through us, the voices of our ancestors and all those who have gone before us.

These are the stories of our lives. Growing up with racism – the thing about color and the denial of being Indian. The denial in our family is so imbedded that we didn't know our father's side of the family – they were too Indian! We had to say we were Spanish and not Mexican. Least of all Indian.

But, in spite of all this denial, we grew up with very strong traditions.

Both of us began performing at the age of 6, studying tap dancing and acrobatics at Ms. Nolan's Dance Studio at the Masonic Temple in Blue Island. Once a week mama would take us into the city of Chicago to learn songs, dances, and poetry and crafts from Sra. Celia Pedroza, a teacher from Mexico City. The men would gather in a room and talk the politics of Mexico and the unions. At the end of the school year we would all take part in a recital and play. Of course, we were always putting on plays in our backyard. As we grew up we joined the Chicago Fiesta Guild and performed at universities and museums. Mama made all of our traditional costumes, instilling in us a sense of tradition. But, we were not Indian.

Our theater work consists of personal stories coming from our oral traditions, which not only entertain, but educate and heal. Sometimes people see themselves in the stories, and once we voice these stories, the process of healing begins, healing ourselves, our community, the people that come to see and hear our theater. Our work has to do with the power that we have within ourselves. They're survival stories. Our imagination and our stories are powerful tools that can be used to transform ourselves into women of power.

1992: Blood Speaks was born from a recurring dream of the color red. Red: the sangre/blood that was shed, the blood/life running through our veins, fire, genocide. There was an urgency, a rage, a need to speak of the pivotal role that religion/ Christianity played in the oppression and genocide of native people.

We traveled to Oaxaca, collaborated with three native women from here and Juana Vasquez, a Zapotec native woman from Yalalag, who invited us to her village and opened her home and heart to us, sharing her stories with us, introducing us to the men, women and children of her community. Our huipiles/garments, shawls and sandals worn in the theater piece are from Yalalag. Videotapes of community life, morning sounds and Zapotec vocables were composed and interspersed and overlaid in the drama as were stories of Yalalag and our own personal stories. A painted mural depicted life as it was before the invasion. A series of three screens, representing

Christianity, and flames and blood, gradually layered the mural as the action of the play progressed, depicting the gradual encroachment of civilization/conquest, while the voices of the performers sang and spoke of survival in Zapotec, Spanish and English. Humor was used lavishly as a tool of survival. The play ended with all of the women dancing in a celebration of life and hope for the future generations.

With an educational theater piece entitled *A Traditional Kind of Woman: Too Much Not 'Nuff*, we have toured to reservations, health care facilities, HIV/AIDS outreach events, the Public Theater's "Free at Three" Series, and Native American Wellness and Women Conferences in Arizona and Oregon. A compilation of stories and interviews with Native women, including ourselves, this piece examines how these women have dealt with domestic violence, substance abuse, incest and HIV/AIDS. With *A Traditional Kind of Woman . . .*, we hope to sensitize service care providers, to increase their knowledge and awareness of the beliefs, values and practices of Native women, and to empower and enhance the personal wellness of Native women.

Another selection, *Open Wounds on Tlalteuctli*, opened as a work-in-progress at the American Indian Community House and was subsequently performed at New WORLD Theater in Amherst, MA., and Theater for the New City in New York City. This performance piece examines the relationship between the abuse of women and the abuse of the Earth – physical, spiritual, cultural, and ecological.

We have traveled to Oaxaca and Chiapas to do storytelling workshops with indigenous communities and share our theater techniques with performers, musicians, weavers and other artisans to establish an ongoing collaboration. Some of these artists traveled to New York City to share their stories and traditions with the Native American and Mexican communities in New York City.

We have been working with the Mexican communities in New York City. In recent years there has been a mass influx of Mexicans to New York City. They gather together on weekends at Sara Delano Roosevelt Park on the lower East side where they cook traditional food and the youth play soccer. Surrounding this community spirit is a brick wall where pimps, prostitutes and drug dealers ply their trade, but epazote, an herb, grows wild all around the park. The Mexicans have encountered many problems, such as poverty, racism, violence, drugs, and AIDS.

We are preparing our third Day of the Dead celebration at the American Indian Community House, which will again bring the Mexican and Native American communities together as well as other diverse communities in honoring our ancestors. We feel it is important for the Mexican people to have opportunities in which to continue their traditions and share their culture with the diverse communities here, and while doing this they can feel proud of their heritage and non-Mexicans can appreciate the beauty of our traditions. It is a way of recognizing, reaffirming and reinforcing our indigenous culture by having indigenous people from both sides of the border dialogue and share traditions.

Production history

1992: Blood Speaks was first produced as part of Indian Summer 1992 Festival at the American Indian Community House in New York City. Muriel Miguel was the director, and the cast included Elvira Colorado, Hortensia Colorado, Pura Fe Crescioni and Soni C. Caballero.

4 1992: Blood Speaks

Elvira and Hortensia Colorado

Creation Story

(ELVIRA, SONI, PURA FE and HORTENSIA enter in darkness. All put rebozos on floor, lay down, except HORTENSIA, who stands center stage wearing three huipiles. Lights slowly come up.)

HORTENSIA Ping, ping, ping, ping, ping, ping, ping, p p p p p p p p p p Particles, Particles, Particles, Particles, all around. *(Starts to get out of first huipil)* Floating. Darting about. Like dust. Red dust. This is the beginning. *(Shows hands under huipil)* SSSSSSSHHHHHHHHHH. *(Squats down)* Sucked deep into the beginning. Cool. Soft. Red dust now red clay. *(Swaying body slowly)* Shaping. Beginning to take shape. *(Out of first huipil. ELVIRA, SONI and PURA FE each take a huipil as HORTENSIA takes them off.)* A circle, like a mmmmoooouuuttthhhh. And, it spins. *(Spinning)* And as it spins, ssssooouuu-unnnddd and color drip from this circle, mouth. *(Out of second huipil)* Red, red, blood red clay. Beginning to take shape. Shaping and molding. *(ALL doing this action on selves)* Shaping and molding. Shaping and molding. Round. So round this blood red clay. A bowl. Eh, eh, eh, eh, eh. *(Out of third huipil)* Five points. *(Looks at hands)* Eh, eh, eh, eh, eh. Five points. *(Looks at feet)* Five points. Shaping and molding. *(Right leg)* Shaping and molding. *(Left leg)* Shaping and molding. *(All over body)* *(ALL shape and mold on body.)* *(ALL spin using huipil.)* Shaping and molding. Shaping and molding. Red. Blood red clay. Eh, eh, eh, eh, eh. *(Neck)* Then, pulling, stretching the red filigree. *(Pulls braid back)* With an opening here. An opening here. An opening here. An opening here. An opening here. And red clay is surrounded by water. Another me.

Another me. Another me. *(ALL look at each other/mirror.)* Another me. *(nine times)*
(ALL gather huipiles and rebozos and begin)

Village Awakening/Chores

ELVIRA *goes DSR and pours water to wash. Then goes to USR to make tortillas.* HORTENSIA *braids hair facing USC. Builds fire. Pours water to wash, then sweeps. Pulls out mats, ties them up, carries to market facing DSC.* PURA FE *washes USL.* SONI *gathers wood, goes to market.*

ALL *(All overlapping, while doing above chores)* Grandmother of the light. Grandmother of the sun. Let the day dawn. Let the day begin.
(Then PURA FE and SONI go SL bring flames screen to center then go USR and begin to sing.)

Huipil Story 1

PURA FE and SONI *(Singing in Zapotec under ELVIRA story)*
Shahn u ja, shahn u ja,
Shahn u ja ahne joo, *(four times)*
Cha ahnge cha ahn zahka ana, *(twice)*
Yeta Pweringe hah,
A jchoo nicha,
Nange pweninge nah,
Jah e na jah e na.
(Video of Juana Vasquez telling Huipil story in Zapotec overlapping Elvira.)
ELVIRA *(CS)* In the center of our village there is an enormous tree, a Copal tree. We gather under this sacred tree to exchange our goods: corn *(pause)* beans *(pause)* and squash. We share with each other because this ensures the growth of our crops. *(ELVIRA becomes tree and her hands, become serpents over her head.)* One

day out of the tree came colored serpents, red, blue, yellow, and black. And the colored serpents attached themselves to my huipil. (ALL *turn to East, South, West, North pulling out ribbons from huipil.*)
Red, blue, yellow, and black to the East.
Red, blue, yellow, and black to the South.
Red, blue, yellow, and black to the West.
Red, blue, yellow, and black to the North.

In all four directions. Then a black serpent wrapped itself around my head and I was covered with serpents. (*Song continues and dies out.*)
(ELVIRA *starts sound, ALL join in. She goes to get basket with corn USC. Sits CS looking into future. Lays cloth down. Shakes corn in basket (two or three times) and throws it. Divination ritual. Picks it up.*)

HORTENSIA (USR *with bowl of water, dipping hands, listening*) A woman comes out of the deserted street. Breasts are bare. She can't see. She calls out, but there is no sound.

PURA FE (*Holding clay bowl*) I see men. Many, many, many men. They are sitting on tall animals. They have long shiny sticks and hats. Bodies covered in cloth. Hair on their faces. Their eyes like the color of the sky. (ELVIRA *throws corn.*)

SONI (*Moving first screen to CS, is behind*) People are running. (*From here ALL overlap.*) Out, their souls are being put out. Out, like the stars burning out. Nothing but smoke. It's getting dark. I can't see.

HORTENSIA Her face looks up. See the sockets. Emptiness. There's nothing. Sockets of emptiness.

PURA FE I don't know what they want! I don't know what they want!

HORTENSIA Her face is bloody. Her hands are bloody. (ELVIRA *begins to wail, hands on head.*) Her legs are bruised and bloody.

ALL Blood. Blood. Blood. (*Screams*)
(ELVIRA *gathers corn in basket, places USR. Goes OSL, gets strainer, waits. PURA FE goes OSL gets strainer, waits. SONI gets strainer, goes CS. HORTENSIA takes bowl of water USC, gets strainer, joins SONI CS.*)

Proclamation

PURA FE *and* SONI *singing Gregorian Chant through above and continues with first dialogue.*

SONI I, servant of the high and mighty conquerors, being their messenger and captain, notify and inform you . . .
(PURA FE *pushes* ELVIRA *in front of* SONI and HORTENSIA.)

HORTENSIA (ELVIRA *on knees.* HORTENSIA *blesses her with strainer.*) That God our Lord, One and eternal. Porque la multitud procediente de esta pareja desde la creación del mundo . . . *[Because the multitude born of this union since the creation of the world . . .]*

SONI (SONI *and* HORTENSIA *switch places. Now* PURA FE *kneels in front of them.*) God!

ELVIRA Superior . . . obedecer . . . (ALL *begin blessing audience, floor, each other, etc.*)

PURA FE . . . under whatever law . . .

SONI Giving to him the entire world . . .

HORTENSIA That God our Lord . . . One and eternal . . .

ELVIRA La iglesia es superior y todos deben obedecerla. *[The church is superior and all must obey.]*

SONI . . . preach this to you . . . Kneel. Rise. Kneel. Rise. Kneel. Rise. Kneel. Rise. (*etc., eight times. Blessing and kneeling build to a frenzy.*)

Song

PURA FE *and* SONI *stand,* ELVIRA *on right of* SONI, HORTENSIA *on left of* PURA FE.

PURA FE and SONI Yesterday we had some rain, but all in all we can't complain. Was it dusty on the train? P.S. I love you. (ALL *kneel DSC facing audience. Staccato.*) If you do not do this. (*Growling*)

ELVIRA . . . and subject you . . .

SONI . . . to the yoke and obedience . . .

HORTENSIA . . . of the Church and of his Majesty . . .

PURA FE . . . and I shall take your wives . . .

ELVIRA . . . and children . . .

SONI . . . and make them slaves.

ALL (*Staccato, pointing to audience*) If you do not do this.

HORTENSIA . . . and I shall take your property . . .

PURA FE . . . and shall do you all the harm I can.

ALL (*Staccato, pointing to audience*) If you do not do this.

HORTENSIA I protest that the deaths . . .

SONI . . . and harm . . .

ELVIRA . . . that shall thereby come . . .

PURA FE . . . will be your fault . . .

ALL Your fault. Your fault. Your fault. Your fault.

ELVIRA Y no de su majestad. *[And not of his majesty.]*

ALL Nor ours.

ELVIRA and HORTENSIA . . . ni de estos senores que han venido con vosotros. *[Nor of these gentlemen who have come with us.]*

PURA FE *(With flourish of hand from SL to SR bends over and becomes desk for SONI)* And, I say and require of you . . .

SONI *(Writing on desk/PURA FE)* And, I ask the secretary here present to give me the signed testimonial, please. *[Y pido que el secretario aquí presente me entrege el documento firmado, por favor.]*

SONI This proclamation is required to be made . . .

PURA FE . . . by every chief of an expedition . . .

ELVIRA . . . to the Indians . . .

HORTENSIA . . . at the moment of disembarking.

(ELVIRA goes OSL with strainer. PURA FE goes OSL with strainer. SONI stands CS. HORTENSIA takes her strainer and SONI's USC. Comes back CS and kneels next to SONI.)

Atrocities

SONI *and* HORTENSIA *are CS.* HORTENSIA *kneels left of* SONI.

SONI *(In Zapotec repeats until the end of the scene)*

Ah kdre voo kevel ka ah,
Ta ah ja oola she,
Noo vaca ale alva,
De yed she ya kdra va.

ELVIRA They entered towns . . . *(stops, she continues to move screen)* . . . and ripped open the bellies of children . . . *(Continues to move screen OSR)*

PURA FE Elders . . .

HORTENSIA . . . and pregnant women, tearing them to pieces.

PURA FE They placed bets on who could rip open a belly.

HORTENSIA Cut off a head . . .

ELVIRA . . . and find the entrails at first try.

HORTENSIA The Spaniards created a human butcher shop. *(She goes behind Friar screen USR)*

ELVIRA A delicacy of which were feet and hands.

PURA FE And leftovers were fed to the dogs.

ELVIRA Rather than cut the chains, they would sever the head of pregnant slaves . . . *(She goes OSR behind Friar screen and begins to tear off ribbons.)*

HORTENSIA . . . and rip out the fetus to save its soul.

(ELVIRA, PURA FE and SONI alternate in Spanish, English and Zapotec.)

ELVIRA ¿ Dónde están las serpientas de mi huipil? ¿ Quién se las ha llevada? Debo encontrarlas.

PURA FE Where are the serpents of my huipil? Who has taken them? I must find them.

SONI
Ah kdre voo kevel ka ah,
Ta ah ja oola she,
Noo vaca ale alva,
De yed she ya kdra va.

Huipil Story 2

SONI and PURA FE *(SL. Sing in Zapotec)*
Shahn u ja, shahn u ja,
Shahn u ja, ahne joo, *(four times)*
Cha ahnge cha ahn zahka ana, *(twice)*
Yeta pweringe nah,
A jchoo nicha,
Nange pweninge nah,
Jah e na jah e na.

ELVIRA *(Comes out from behind screen CS)* In the center of our village, there stood an enormous copal tree. A sacred tree. Our ancestors gathered under this tree to exchange their goods: corn, beans, and squash. And they shared these with each other because they knew that sharing would ensure the growth of their crops. The Spaniards thought this was evil, pagan. They couldn't understand why we gathered together, what the sacred tree meant to our people. So one day they decided to cut down the sacred tree. *(Makes motion of chopping several times and stops)* But, it was difficult for them to destroy the sacred tree. Finally they succeeded in uprooting the tree and it fell. *(Uses pulling motion to pull out the tree and sees it fall; uses hands to create serpents coming out of tree)* And out of the tree came serpents: red, blue, yellow and black. *(Turns SR and covers face with hands)* The Spaniards drew back in terror. Then a woman appeared wearing a white huipil and the colored serpents attached themselves to her huipil in all four directions: North, South, East, and West. Suddenly, a black serpent wrapped itself around her head and then she was covered with serpents and protected. *(Gets up and crosses to SR)* The Spaniards ran away in fear. They built a Catholic church over the spot where the sacred tree stood. The church then replaced the serpents with flowers and thought they had stripped us of our power. *(ELVIRA and HORTENSIA put on serpent headdresses behind screen.)*

ALL *(Begin to remove ribbons and throw them on the floor as they alternate in English, Spanish and Zapotec)*

Where are the serpents of my huipil? Who has taken them? I must find them.

¿ Dónde están las serpientas de mi huipil? ¿ Quién se las ha llevado? Debo encontrarlas.

Ah kdre voo kevel ka ah,
Ta ah ja oola she,
Noo vaca ale alva,
De yed she ya kdra va.

Columbus's Birthday Party

HORTENSIA, *wearing party hat on top of headdress, enters SL carrying a bag of party favors and distributes them to the audience, ad-libbing and getting the audience into a party mood.* ELVIRA, *also wearing party hat on top of headdress, enters SL after* HORTENSIA.

ELVIRA and HORTENSIA There is going to be a big birthday party. It's going to be a surprise . . . *(etc., ad-libbing)*

HORTENSIA Now, we going to have a rehearsal, a dry run. I'm going to count to three, and you all shout, "Surprise!" Okay? Now, ready. One, two, three, "Surprise!" Good, you a good group – and smart too. Now this time we going to count in Spanish. You all know Spanish, right? This time when we count, uno, dos, tres – you clap. Okay, here we go. Uno, dos, tres.

(Audience claps. PURA FE *and* SONI *enter* SR *and* ELVIRA SL *with signs that read* APPLAUSE/SYPHILIS, APPLAUSE/CLAP, APPLAUSE/GONORRHEA. HORTENSIA *realizes something is wrong, turns, looks at cards and throws poppers at their feet.* HORTENSIA *to* SL. ELVIRA *to* SL. PURA FE *and* SONI *to* SR.

ELVIRA *enters* SL *with a guest list, unravelling roll of toilet paper as she speaks like a crazy radio announcer.* ALL *whisper throughout "Burt Reynolds.")*

ELVIRA Now for the zee guest list. A who's who of zee entertainment world. Aren't you zee lucky ones to be here. At zee top of zee guest list: La Queen Chavelita with King Ferdinand, of course. The first mate of the Pinta, the Lone Ranger and Silver (Tonto would have come, but he had an audition), de las Casas, the Grand High Wizard of the KKK, Madonna as Frida Kahlo, Michael Jackson, Speedy Gonzalez, John Wayne, the Pope, Hitler, Mussolini, Stalin, la migra y el border patrol. Okay, okay and Burt Reynolds.

(SONI enters SL running and gooses ELVIRA and ELVIRA runs out screaming.)

HORTENSIA *(Enters SL)* Lots and lots of finger food.

ALL Lots and lots of finger food.

SONI We are going to give him presents. Many, many presents. We are giving him: gold chains, gold condoms, a gold map, a gold compass, a solid gold bowling ball, antibiotics, a chihuahua (gold, of course) and a cruise to the Caribbean on the Santa Maria.

ALL *(Throughout above repeat)* Gold, more gold.

HORTENSIA *(Enters SL)* Lots and lots of finger food. *(SONI chases HORTENSIA SR behind screen.*

PURA FE *enters* SR *doing karate movement.* HORTENSIA *runs in again.)*

HORTENSIA Lots and lots of finger food.

PURA FE We have games. As many Indians as you can baptize. Pin-a-tail on an Indian, confession, double jeopardy, *(makes cutting sound)* truth or consequences, witch doctor. What doctor? I don't know. Trick or treat. Bobbing for Indians, and then there will be door prizes. *(Pantomimes cutting off a head)*

HORTENSIA *(PURA FE and SONI waiting in wings SR with brown plastic garbage bag/Columbus)* Okay everybody, here he comes. Ready? Uno, dos tres – Surprise! *(Audience/*ALL *count and shout surprise.* PURA FE *goes* SR *to get cardboard box/cake with 500 candles.* ALL *sing "Happy Birthday." Candles are blown out and cake is tossed in garbage bag.)*

ELVIRA   *(As MC/radio announcer)* Damas y caballeros. Ladies and gentlemen. The moment you've all been waiting for has finally arrived. Making a special cameo appearance, all the way from Columbus, Ohio: Las Golddiggers of 1492. Hit it girls. Arranquense!

*(*PURA FE *and* SONI *enter: dance, vamp and introduce themselves singing version of a Rosemary Clooney song.)*

SONI   Hi everybody! I'm so glad to be here tonight. My name is Nina. My sister Pinta. Maria couldn't be here tonight, but she's here in spirit. I guess you're all wondering why we're here tonight. Yes! We're celebrating Christopher Columbus's 500th birthday. *(To* PURA FE*)* Can you believe it? Has it really been that long? *(*PURA FE *does Black Bottom dance.)* So Chris, get ready the next one's for you. *(Choreography)*

They all laughed at Christopher Columbus
When he said the world was round.
He poked Queen Isabella, expulsing Jews
  and Moors from Town.
They took all their money, got their
  prison buddies, three ships, a priest and
  sailed on down.
  They found gold and spices.
  Used torture devices. Ow!
  It's the same ole cry.
They laughed at me wanting you
Said we were searching for the moon,
But, oh, you came through.
Now they're eating humble pie
WWWWWHHHHHHHOOOOOOOO
. . . . *(*ELVIRA *and* HORTEN-
SIA *enter and join in dance, always one step behind.)*
Do Wah Wah, Do Wah Wah *(Snapping fingers)*
They all said we'd never get together.
Baby, let's take a bow. *(*ALL *right foot forward, hand out)*
Ho, ho, ho, who's got the last laugh.
He, he, he, who's got the last laugh.
Ha, ha, ha who's got the last laugh now.

Blackout

HORTENSIA *goes in front of Flames screen* SL, *sits right corner with imaginary child.* ELVIRA *goes behind Flames screen* SL. SONI *goes behind Friar screen* SR. PURA FE *goes* SR. ELVIRA *mimes pulling apart with hands over chest, makes sounds, one hand goes up then other.*

ELVIRA   They pulled me apart. Held me down. Forced their god and their culture inside. Soiled me with their lust. *(Looks down)* They stuffed me. They raped me. I was born. "Hija de la Chingada"! *(Lifts skirt, makes gesture of pulling baby out of womb)*

HORTENSIA   *(Kneeling in front of Flames screen with imaginary child)* This child is hungry. This child is cold. *(In Spanish:)* I see their mouths moving. What are they saying? They stare at me. We all have the same blood. We smell the same. *(Hands outstretched, begging)* Today I have nothing to sell. I sell whatever I can find. Today there is nothing. This child is cold. *(Goes to right-hand corner of Flames screen)*

SONG Museum Cases

PURA FE   *(Enters from* SR *to* CS*)*
I saw them, I saw them!
I saw them lying stacked high on shelves
cardboard boxed and labeled, a skeleton
  mother
holds her imbedded child.
Uncovered, no blankets, no nothing. Just
  how?
Well, I was looking at myself buried alive!
Military donation, government research,
science, churches and museums, well, I
  was looking at myself buried alive!
I am my ancestors, I am my mother's
  stolen grave.
Wipe my face from the right to live on
  this
land creation came, you still take.
Sterilized women who cannot give birth.
Strip-mine the womb of Mother Earth.
Remove my future no trace to say
that I'm a non-existent race.
*(*HORTENSIA *stands, goes up to* PURA FE *facing out to* SR *with right hand held up, palms out.* PURA FE *looks at her, then as if touching glass case:)*
Well, I cannot claim from where I came

The hidden truth, no guilt, no shame
    (twice)
Exploitation, anthropology
Excavation you call it state property
A professional way of living.
How can money justify the greed.
To disguise what was truly genocide.
I cannot claim from where I came . . .
(PURA FE walks back to SR.)
HORTENSIA *(CS hand still held palm out
faces audience, puts it down when speaking)*
On Sunday we would go into the city to
buy harina, manteca, frijoles – all the
stuff we didn't grow. Then, we'd go over
to Maxwell Street. We'd eat lots of hotdogs
and visit La Virgen de Guadalupe. *(Hand
up again)* There he is standing in the
doorway. He was tall, with two long
braids. I don't remember if we talked. I
stood there for a long time. Then someone would come and pull me away. *(Pulls
hair back, as if being pulled from behind)*
Get away from there! Demonio de indio!
Get away from there! Demonio de indio!
Mama's shame. *(Contracts, bends over,
turns back to audience)* I'm in a store. Just
looking. There he is. Daddy. I'll pretend I
don't see him. I'll hide. Demonio de
indio! Why am I doing this? It hurts! I'll
pretend I don't see him. I'll hide.
Demonio de indio! Why am I doing this?
It hurts! My shame! *(Contracts, back to
audience. Goes back to Flames screen.)*
SONI *(Singing behind SR Friar screen)* I
remember the time when I was nine, my
brothers and me worked the fields. We
would rise at five by the pale blue sky, as
the sun rose over the trees.
    (Spoken) Purple as far as you can see.
Cihuelas, prunes. The men would shake
the trees with long sticks to get the
prunes on the ground. The women and
children would follow behind in a row
picking and picking filling the pails. The
kids would make a game and fall behind.
*(ELVIRA makes sounds pom, pom, pom and
gestures as though throwing a ball back and
forth throughout SONI's dialogue.)*
    Pop, pop, pop *(SONI and ELVIRA
running back and forth behind screen)*
Sounds of immigration. Correle, correle
immigration.
ELVIRA *(throughout ELVIRA's dialogue SONI
makes the sounds pop, pop, pop, running
back and forth behind screen.)* Pom, pom,
pom. They threw me back and forth.

Pom, pom, pom. Como juego de pelota.
Pom, pom, pom. No, you don't belong
here. Pom, pom, pom. You're too dark.
Pom, pom. You speak Spanish. Pom, pom.
Dark. Spanish. Pom, pom, pom. Dark.
Spanish. Pom, pom, pom.
SONI Why am I running?
ELVIRA Pom, pom, pom.
SONI Why am I running?
ELVIRA Pom, pom, pom. *(She stops.)*
SONI Where is my brother? Don't take
him, that's Panchito. He didn't do any-
thing. He just drinks too much. And
Tony, he's my girlfriend's brother. Papers?
Do I have papers? Yes, I have papers.
*(Begins moving to front of screen, joining
others)*
(Singing/talking) Eye to eye we worked
together.
(PURA FE enters.)
Hand in hand we are the same.
*(ELVIRA enters group and HORTENSIA CS
points to audience.)*
Soul to soul we are of this world.
Blood on the earth.
I am a Mexican-American. *(twice)*
*(Now ALL pointing first SL turn to audience
whispering "Mexican-American" four times)*
HORTENSIA In the Zocalo, a monument to
the people who came from way, way,
way back there *(ALL facing front reach
arm backwards, bending, then straighten.)*
Walking, walking, walking. *(ALL turn L
facing U.)* Way, way, way, back there. *(ALL
turn to audience, pointing.)* From Aztlan.
(ALL drop gesture.)
HORTENSIA When you see an eagle . . .
ALL When you see an eagle . . .
HORTENSIA . . . perched on a cactus
devouring a serpent, you'll know you
have arrived *(Turns to go back to screen)*
Home, I can smell it.
*(SONI goes back to front of screen SR. PURA
FE to SL.)*
ELVIRA *(Under dialogue HORTENSIA says:
"La niña tiene hambre.")* When I was little I
would travel back and forth with my
family to Mexico. We had rich relatives
and poor relatives. The rich ones spoke
Spanish and had servants. "La criada will
do it. No, La criada can't sit here, she sits
over there with the others." The poor
ones lived on the rancho up in the
mountains. They wore old clothes and no
shoes and they spoke Nahautl. They were
the others. *(Goosesteps over to edge of SR*

screen) Carmen Moreno?

SONI Si?

ELVIRA Carmen Moreno?

SONI I don't want to go to school. My place is here working in the fields.

ELVIRA *(grabs* SONI *by hand and goosesteps to* SL *talking)* Carmen Moreno. Carmen Moreno.

SONI Si?

ELVIRA BLAH, blah, blah, blah . . .

SONI I don't understand . . . What did I do? What did I do wrong?

ELVIRA Nationality?

SONI Catholic.

ELVIRA No! You are a Mexican-American. A Mexican-American.

SONI `A Mexican-American. A Mexican-American. *(PURA FE and ELVIRA march back to* SR *repeating.)*

PURA FE *(SR)*
Ho, ho, ho, who's got the last laugh.
He, he, he, who's got the last laugh.
Ha, ha, ha, who's got the last laugh now.

ELVIRA *(ELVIRA and SONI both behind SR screen. SONI blows conch shell.)* Over 100,000 pieces of stone were cut and used to form a perfect geometric design. *(ELVIRA enters between the two screens to CS.)* Over there is the Church of San Pablo, built over a sacred temple, cactus all around. Zapotec women's voices selling. I stood there at Mitla. I stood there at Mitla. *(Mimes movement of ducking under arch and bumping head. SONI enters singing, stands SR of ELVIRA.)* Place of the dead, looking out at the mountains, apart from everyone.

America the Beautiful

SONI *(Sings)*
Oh beautiful,
For spacious skies,
For amber waves of grain,
For purple mountains majesty
Above the fruited . . .
(Spoken) Fruit . . . I picked the fruit that you eat.
(HORTENSIA looks for something to wrap child in.)
I cut the fruit. For what? The blood on my hands. *(ELVIRA sings "Oh beautiful . . ." under dialogue.)* The blood on the fruit. For the blood on the earth. Who am I? Who am I? Your mother is Spanish from Spain. No! I am Aztec. I am Mayan.

I am proud. Mexican-American. Mexican-American. *(Goes to back of SR screen)*

PURA FE *(Enters from SR)* Your father is moving out of the house.

ELVIRA *(Runs to PURA FE and hugs her around knees)* No mama! No!

PURA FE Stop crying, he's only moving to the basement.

ELVIRA Daddy, I'm falling. I don't want to fall. Catch me!
(ALL face audience arms outstretched.)

PURA FE *(SR)*
Ho, ho, ho, who's got the last laugh.
He, he, he, who's got the last laugh.
Ha, ha, ha, who's got the last laugh now.

Video: Flag Ceremony in Zocalo

HORTENSIA They took my child. Tore her from me. Scattering the bones, hearts, and serpents.
(PURA FE pushes HORTENSIA to floor, walks over her. SONI walks over her. Both go off SL.

HORTENSIA *picks up flag in which child was wrapped, walks to center of two screens, wraps flag around neck. Is killed by Mexico.)*

ELVIRA *(Still on knees)* He slept in the basement like an outcast. Next to the furnace. All his clothes were moved downstairs.

A strong wind pushed me *(falls on stomach)* and knocked me flat on my stomach. I was covered with dust. The dust *(starts to sit up)* of centuries, from the beginning of time. Creation. I could smell the dust. Cool and moist. *(PURA FE and SONI bring in bloody screen in front of HORTENSIA who goes SL to get containers of blood. PURA FE and SONI behind screen.)* Obsidian darkness. Why, mama? Why? Did Daddy do something wrong? Daddy loves me. I'm falling! I don't want to fall. Catch me Daddy! Catch me!

(Standing. PURA FE, SONI and HORTENSIA put blood on Blood screen through dialogue.) What can I offer the spirits? What can I offer the spirits? I have nothing to give them. Nothing. I search through my memory, and through my memory I rescue their dreams from where they've been buried and carry them forward. I rescue their dreams from where they've been buried and carry them forward. I rescue their dreams and

carry them forward. I rescue their dreams
and carry them forward. I rescue their
dreams and carry them forward.
*(ELVIRA and HORTENSIA move Friar screen
to edge of SR. PURA FE and SONI move
Bloody screen to CS and begin singing C
screen.)*

PURA FE and SONI
Song for my ancestors,
Return the prayers they gave,
My blood it won't forget,
An how we're here today.
Many million years deep,
Where a million tears sleep,
No, they never spoke to us
of the Bering Straight.

I cannot claim from where I came,
The hidden truth,
No guilt, no shame. *(Repeat last three lines
three times)*

Video/Village Dancing

HORTENSIA *and* ELVIRA *enter joining them a
third time, interlocking arms dancing forward
and backward three times, and then all turn in
place and kneel, while* SONI *remains standing.*

SONI   The Message of Cuauhtemoc, delivered on August 13, 1521, has been passed
down through the Oral Tradition in the
family of Tlakaelel for seventeen generations.

HORTENSIA   *(In Nahuatl under* SONI's *words)*
Totonal Yomotlatih
totonal yoixpolih
iuan zentlayouayan,
o tech kahteh

PURA FE   For the guardians of all time . . .
for the people of the future. Our sun has
gone and left us in darkness.

SONI   We will wait until our new sun
comes.

HORTENSIA   Uel kenin yoko xin axkan
totlazoh anauak
*(ELVIRA enters and says words in English
under* HORTENSIA's *Nahuatl words.)*
tekimakah in topilhuan
amo kin ikauazkeh kin nonotzazkeh
kin mopilhuan
uelkenin yez kenin imakokiz
iuan uelkenin chikahllauiz
iuan uel kenin kiktzon kixtikin iueyika
nehtoltilliz inin totlazohtlalnantzin
Anauak

ELVIRA   Do not forget to tell your children,
that they may tell the children of their
children of their children, with proper
respect. Tell them how it was . . . how it
will be . . . how we will rise again . . .
how to gain strength and how our culture
will fulfill its great destiny on our beloved
Mother Earth.

ALL   Anauak. *(ALL hold right palm up
covered with blood.)*

Kia Corthron

Biography

As a companion piece to *Come Down Burning* at Long Wharf Theatre, Kia Corthron wrote and workshopped *Cage Rhythm*, which subsequently won the New Professional Theatre Playwriting Award. The play was published in TCG's *Moon Marked and Touched by Sun*, and was workshopped in Crossroads Theatre's 1994 Genesis Festival. The plays together were given a reading at the McCarter Theatre in the fall of 1994. In 1992, Kia became Manhattan Theatre Club's first Van Lier fellow and, under commission, wrote *Catnap Allegiance*. In the spring of 1994, she was awarded a Schomberg Fellowship with Ramapo College of New Jersey, where she served as advisor on a student production of *Wake Up Lou Riser*, a play which previously had received a workshop in the Circle Repertory Company LAB and which, in July 1994, won Delaware Theatre Company's first Connections contest. Recently, under commission for Second Stage Theatre, Kia wrote *Digging Eleven*. She is currently under commission for the Goodman Theatre. Kia received her MFA from Columbia University. She is a member of The Dramatists Guild.

Photo: Ward Yoshimoto

Production history

Come Down Burning, which has been featured in reading festivals at Hartford Stage, Playwrights Horizons, Philadelphia Theatre Company, Next Stage, and North Carolina Playwrights Festival, was workshopped at Voice & Vision and at Long Wharf Theatre (Arvin Brown, Artistic Director, M. Edgar Rosenblum, Executive Director). It was produced in New York City on The American Place Theatre's mainstage in the fall of 1993 (Wynn Handman, Artistic Director). The production was directed by Judyie Al-Bilali. The cast included Serena Henry, Myra Lucretia Taylor, Shona Tucker, Tse-Mach Washington, and Kim Yancey.

Artistic statement

My mother says it began when my sister started school and I was left home with no one to play with. The bottom three steps of our staircase were my favorite set, clothes-pins my tools of preference. They were my characters, the mouthpieces for the stories in my head. An autistic thing, my speech becoming increasingly louder and faster (even now, my fast-talk is too often indecipherable), my consciousness of the world outside my improvised drama aroused only when I'd suddenly be aware of a family member standing nearby. I pinpoint these "psychotic" episodes at the age of five as the beginning of my career as a dramatist.

I grew up in the same town in which my mother lived all her life: Cumberland, Maryland, a valley in the Appalachians sandwiched between West Virginia and Pennsylvania. A mid-century booming factory center, the sixties and seventies brought about plenty of closings that left the area in an official, perennial state of 'depression.' The sole survivors were Ballistics, the secret government chemical place (and only now in writing this do I suddenly wonder with trepidation, What *do* they do there?) and the paper mill, which employed my father ten hours a day, sometimes without a day off in two weeks, for twenty-two years.

My father emerged seventh of nine siblings born and raised on a Virginia farm, all christened by the collaboration of my grandparents' imagination and the respective midwife's spelling prowess. I have Corthorn uncles and Carthorne aunts. My father spent his adult life in middle-management misery, training rookie white men twenty years his junior to be his supervisors. That he did not finish college was the justification for this absurdity. In 1985 my father dropped dead at the mill. Aneurysm.

In seventeen years of formal education I had three teachers of color, all black. One, my junior high home-ec instructor; both of the others in my undergraduate senior year at the University of Maryland.

That fall semester I was exposed to a bitter, unfriendly writing professor who scribbled positive, encouraging notes on my papers but, in class, while publicly praising the efforts of my fellow white students, only ever mentioned me once: smirk on his face, he used me, my error, as an example, lest anyone else so carelessly, dimwittedly confuse the sexes in the spelling of "Francis/es." He was a habitual negative spirit, likely the failed-career cliché, so, despite his lesser cruelty to others, he was respected by no one. Except me. I found myself defending the sullen brute, particularly against white critics, for reasons unknown. Especially to myself.

I walked into my first playwriting class the following January, my final semester of college. Sitting behind the professor's desk was a woman who looked like a student herself. From the first class her energy and passion, her insight and humor were exhilarating. She was magic. And black.

My privilege to study with her allowed me to understand that my defense of the previous wretch was my reluctance at that time to admit my only professor of my race had been abominable. Now, enthralled by Jewel Rhodes, the most influential teacher of my life, I was able to let go of the racial loyalty, wholly unearned, I endowed upon that other.

The final playwriting proje· charged each of us with the task of putting up a fifteen-minute segment from our pieces. None of us infant playwrights had the first idea of what fifteen minutes of dialogue were. Everyone else's scene lasted five. Mine, set the day a Vietnam vet returns home from the war, ran a full half-hour. In the darkness – the professor turned off the fluorescents on the "audience" side of the room – I

heard someone sighing. Here's my comeuppance, I thought; Ms. Confidence, class star all term, now, at the end, I'd fall hard with this interminable little tragedy. I gritted my teeth and waited for lights up: the judgment. Blinked my eyes in the initial brightness, then I noticed the quiet. What are they waiting for? Now I saw it: the sigher, a slightly older student (of my characters' generation) actually had been *crying*. "That's the way it was. That's the way it was." Now people began to talk. But this discussion session was different. I was not focusing on their remarks. Rather, for the first time I was more taken with a reaction beneath the chatter, an emotion stirred by my words, by those actors. And, suddenly, I got it. All the praise I'd enjoyed that semester as we read my work on the page – meaningless. *This* was theater. Immediacy: the interaction between the audience and performers, equal partners in the making of this particular dramatic moment, a historical instance that would never be repeated. Regardless of how often a play plays, each performance is a unique singular experience that only this audience and this cast will share.

The life choice I've made as a direct result of those four months of my twenty-second year has at times been difficult; after several days of cold cereal for brunch, noodles and butter for dinner, I get cranky. But recently, sitting on a panel, I was asked if I'd experienced any hardships as a writer. I went blank. Afterward I tried to comprehend why neither hunger nor my bank account's occasional drop to single digits crossed my mind. I believe it is because I know I have made this choice (and I am fully aware it is my fortune to have had the choice to make – many suffer in much direr circumstances through no plan of their own) and I accept its consequences. It would be grand to think that this struggle is a hump I'll get over and on some not so distant day making rent will be a fact taken for granted. I don't plan on thumb-twiddling my days until the time of such luxury. I have noticed my economic life has the uncanny knack of letting me drop to pauperism before, miraculously, granting me a reprieve (award, contest) for a few months. So, I've decided, Some One is carrying me through.

And my job, then, is to strive to stay

clear on my convictions. And keep pushing forward.

It is not my intention to oversimplify the various seeds that merged and matured into *Come Down Burning*: my need to explore aspects of sister rivalry, charismatic spirituality, and physical versus social/emotional power all fed the work. But the piece's original impetus lay in my late eighties' concerns regarding the fragility of *Roe v. Wade* – specifically the effect of its possible overturn on poor women.

It was completely coincidental that, upon my completion of the piece's first draft, I asked my mother how a family friend, a woman of her mother's generation, died. Though I'd heard many stories about this woman, it suddenly occurred to me that I never knew why she was here, young, healthy, one day, and her children orphans the next. At a time in history when my maternal grandmother had brought into the world a dozen offspring and buried three or four of them (my mother recalls being very little and sitting in the living room where a tiny casket was on view in the front), this woman made a decision for her family that,

accidentally, killed her. But at a reception in 1993 for winners (I was one) of a grant for stage and screen writers, I was struck dumb, for a moment anyway, when a middle-aged man of my race, in reference to my play remarked, "Well, abortion isn't really a black woman's issue."

I am a political writer. There are those on either side of the fence who would dismiss such a declaration as an oxymoron: artists who believe (true) art transcends the political; activists who believe art is a frivolous affirmation of the status quo, a bourgeois celebration of its own elitism. I believe an artist's definition of art is thumbprint individual, and here's mine: that which challenges, intellectually and passionately, the order which demands the oppression and suppression of specified members of society to support the gain of specified others. It is my intention, aspiration, to make theater that fulfills my own qualifications for art. A fat undertaking for which I may not be able but, in the attempt, I only ask of myself that I write from that place to which I am led by my mind and, more vitally, my heart.

5 Come Down Burning _____

Kia Corthron

Characters

SKOOLIE: 32

TEE: 28

BINK: 32

EVIE: 9

WILL-JOE: 6

SKOOLIE *has legs that don't work. She gets around very ably on her cart, a flat wooden steerable board with wheels. She lives in a shack that she has renovated; the set is the living room/kitchen, and off are the bedrooms. All appliances, cupboards are floor level – a hot plate rather than a range, floor refrigerator, etc. From a standing person's waist-level to the ceiling is completely bare.*

In the mountains. SKOOLIE *lives on a hill, making more so the difficult task of getting around outside of her own walls, although she does make periodic rolls to the general store, which is just across the path.*

At the moment, her sister TEE *and* TEE's CHILDREN *are staying with* SKOOLIE.

Scene 1

SKOOLIE *on the couch,* EVIE *close to her.*

SKOOLIE Skoolie take care a ya.

EVIE My mama take care a me.

SKOOLIE Skoolie. And your mama. *(Pause)* Who done your hair for ya, huh? Pretty plaits, thick, pretty, who done that, run the comb make it pretty make it don't hurt?

EVIE Snap went them teeth, my mama yankin' it and fling go them comb teeth, fly 'cross the room. Me cryin', my mama say Why? then see why: us here on the bed, comb teeth there on the dresser. Okay, baby, Don't cry, Don't cry, baby,

Sorry, Mama sorry, Mama sorry, baby. Then I don't get nothin but the brush nine days straight. (TEE *enters, fumble-searches through several drawers of a cabinet)*

SKOOLIE No tears I see. Today.

EVIE You make it pretty and don't even hurt. Not even the comb.

SKOOLIE How school? *(Pause)* Teacher tell your mama two times two on the board, but you don't care: your eyes out the winda, your mind on wadin' in the crick, tree climbin'.

EVIE *(Pause)* She don't like me, Skoolie.

SKOOLIE Why? *(To* TEE*)* Middle drawer. *(Having now glanced at* TEE *for the first time,* SKOOLIE *is startled.* TEE, *oblivious, opens middle drawer and retrieves a jar, pours change out of it.)*

SKOOLIE *(To* EVIE*)* What she say? *(No answer)* School's cruel. Make ya sit, hours. Write. Listen. But put ya next to the winda, you ain't got nothin' to do but stare out at empty seesaw, slidin' board, basketball hoop. So maybe she likes ya but you don't like her, putcha near that temptation.

EVIE No. *(Pause)* Likes the other kids.

TEE She say somethin' to ya, baby? *(EVIE shakes her head.)* She say somethin' tell me. Hear? *(EVIE nods.)* Want peanut butter?

SKOOLIE I fixed 'em. *(Refers to packed lunches)*

TEE *(Calls to other room)* Will-Joe.

EVIE How come we keep our milk money in a jar?

TEE Gotcher numbers? *(Pause)* Go on get 'em, keep me up half the night countin' on my fingers not so forget cher homework next day. *(EVIE has already run off into other room.)* Bring your brother.

SKOOLIE Tee. What did you do to your mane?

93

TEE   Trim.

SKOOLIE   O my God lemme get my scissors—

TEE   It okay. I like it, Skoolie.

SKOOLIE   I don't, and your boss gonna faint when she see it.

TEE   It okay. (CHILDREN *enter.* WILL-JOE *with very short hair and thumb in mouth.*)

SKOOLIE   Well good mornin', Mr. Will-Joe, how're— *(To* TEE*)* Went crazy with them shears last night, didn't ya?

TEE   Grow too fast.

EVIE   See Mama? See, Skoolie done my hair, make it pretty it don't even hurt, not even the comb.

TEE   I see.

EVIE   How come we keep our lunch milk money in a jar?

TEE   Don't set aside lunch milk money Friday when I get paid, by Thursday ain't be no lunch milk money.

SKOOLIE   Set aside my customer money too.

EVIE   How come?

TEE   Goes, Evie. Money goes, in eggs, butter. In hair ribbons. *(Opens door)*

SKOOLIE   'Fore you walk 'em I need a word with ya.

TEE   Ain't walked 'em two days, Ricky's daddy take 'em all in his truck since he got laid off. I jus' watch 'em to the road, down the hill to the other kids 'til he come. What word? (SKOOLIE *looks at her.*) When they's gone. (TEE *opens door.*)

SKOOLIE   Wait. *(She motions for* WILL-JOE *to come to her. He does.)* Uneven, Tee, some places on that boy's head longer than the rest, lemme fix it.

TEE   Can't, Skoolie, twenty to nine, gotta be ready when the pick-up come. *(Pause)* Skoolie. Jazzman wouldn't take my milk last night. Give him half a ounce he spit it right back up.

SKOOLIE   All the kiddies gonna laugh at him, he go in lookin' like a clown. Like that.

TEE   *(Pause)* Can't. Twenty to nine.

SKOOLIE   Bottle neither? (TEE *shakes her head.*) I'll check. *(Hops down onto her cart and rolls off into other room.)*

TEE   Wait down there, don't cross the road. (CHILDREN *exit.*) Don't run, ya slip! *(TEE closes the door, looks out the window.)* I don't stink too much, huh, Skoolie? Not run you out the room. Last night I playin' with Will-Joe, kissin' on him, he pull away. God watchin', though. I say. Gimme this job, eleven to two thirty lunch shiff, five to seven thirty dinner, I see my kids off in the mornin', pick 'em up between shiffs, three. Perfeck. And not too far a walk to the junior college, bye bye. *(Waves)* Just a couple miles to the two-year college, what I do . . . dirty but . . . only food, I jus' scrape off sucked-on meat, I use rubber gloves, no need touch it even. But damn college kids, damn college kids sometime send through cigarette butt stick up outa mash tatas, jus' dirty. They dirty, no respeck somebody else gotta look at it, wipe it off, they know it, why they do it, think they better can do somethin' like that to me, think I used to it, think I like it. My baby okay?

SKOOLIE   *(Rolls in with baby and bottle)* Vacuum cleaner suckin', I put the nipple in, he whip the milk up. Third bottle in last two minutes.

TEE   Liar. Takin' it though, ain't he?

SKOOLIE   Belly cramps.

TEE   Sure, could see it painin' him soon that milk hit his tummy. Why?

SKOOLIE   Who knows why, why ain't nothin'. What to do about it's somethin', which is rub in the right place, his belly, but also back, his back just above his tushy, on the side. Work for you too, your bad day out the month. Tried it?

TEE   Uh uh.

SKOOLIE   Guess when you're pregnant much as you, them days you don't got to worry 'bout comin' 'roun' s'much.

TEE   I got kids nine, six, four and a half months, Skoolie. Plenty a periods in between, plenty a pain.

SKOOLIE   Been pregnant more 'n three times . . . *(Pause)*

TEE   Maybe he wanna drink from me.

SKOOLIE   What about our tête-à-tête.

TEE   Maybe he wanna little drink. You talk, I listen.

SKOOLIE   He ain't gonna take it, Tee, he's full.

TEE   Little bit.

SKOOLIE   *(Hands over baby)* Don't cry, he don't take it. Babies as moody as anybody else. *(Pause)* See, his belly full, let him sleep.

TEE   Took a sip.

SKOOLIE   Don't give him no more, make his belly thumpin' worse—

TEE   I ain't! I ain't. He jus' took a sip. Went to sleep. *(Pause)* Skoolie. *(Pause)* I the one pay for the lunch milk.

SKOOLIE   You stay here, I charge nothin', you stay free, wanna make a point cuz you pay for the milk.

TEE   Not a point! Not a big point. Little point. *(Pause)* Skoolie. Evie say every time she raise her hand, teacher pretend she don't see her, call on somebody else. Or look right at her, call on somebody else.

SKOOLIE   Bad week, teacher got one comin' to her. 'Member you comin' in, baseball cap and coat wide open in the snow, tears, "How come Teacher don't like me no more?" Couple days, yaw's kissin' again. Give her couple days. *(Pause)*

TEE   Won't stay long.

SKOOLIE   Four months already.

TEE   But out soon. I'm savin'. Get our own place. Me/Evie/Will-Joe/Jazzman place.

SKOOLIE   Hmm.

TEE   Gonna do it, maybe next week.

SKOOLIE   You ain't never stayed here less 'n six months at a time.

TEE   Do it.

SKOOLIE   'Til your landlord tell ya three-month-no-rent is plenty enough 'Til the sheriff knock knock Get out or I get you out. *(Pause)* You know I count them things. *(TEE looks at her.)* Pads. Week after you come here, you laid up: the cramps. You say you back regular you say this your third time, like I ain't knowed it. You always was quick back to your monthly rhythm after the babies. However. I inventory my sanitary napkin supply, realize I been through two rounds now, ain't had to share with no one since your last go. Forty-seven days past. Somethin' you got to tell me?

TEE   *(Pause)* My body a clock. To the second. I miss it, I know what that mean. *(Pause. SKOOLIE rolls to a drawer, pulls out a comb, brush, scissors.)*

SKOOLIE   Come here.

TEE   That all our talk?

SKOOLIE   What been said all needs be said. For now. We do some thinkin' to ourself. Later we resume the conversation. *(Indicates for TEE to sit)*

TEE   Cut it? *(SKOOLIE looks at her.)* I got work eleven, what it don't go right? I'm stuck.

SKOOLIE   When I done it it ain't go right? *(TEE is still hesitant. SKOOLIE "surrenders":*

tosses scissors back in drawer, shoves it shut.)* Come on. I make it pretty. *(TEE sits in front of SKOOLIE. SKOOLIE begins brushing TEE's hair.)*

Scene 2

SKOOLIE *cornrowing* BINK's *hair, frequently rolling across floor with ease to retrieve a special comb from this drawer, a towel way over there, etc.*

BINK   What's 'em two humps out back?

SKOOLIE   Two girlies, Markie-Ann was fifteen months toddlin' and J.B. a week and a half, then Markie-Ann down and died and J.B. eight days behind her.

BINK   O moni O moni Kai Lhita Extridi— *(SKOOLIE bonks BINK on the head with the brush.)*

SKOOLIE   Toldja: No tongues.

BINK   I can't help it, Skoolie, somethin' like that, like buryin' babies, somethin' like that I hear and the Holy Spirit just come down overtake me. They's Tee's?

SKOOLIE   Wa'n't mine.

BINK   Now she pregnant again.

SKOOLIE   Evie then Will-Joe then Markie-Ann then little baby J.B. Then them youngests died, three years later come Jazzman.

BINK   Four months old that baby is, now she pregnant again.

SKOOLIE   I didn't tell ya so's ya tell the town.

BINK   Ain't tellin' nobody.

SKOOLIE   Just tell ya cuz you was here. We's ole friends. Yeah.

BINK   And who's the daddy? I ain't heard 'bout no one 'round Tee.

SKOOLIE   Don't ask here, I don't see 'em. I could be a right hand swear the nothin' but the truth witness for immaculate conception, that's how much I know. *(Pause)*

BINK   Bored, bored, bored, I sure would like to move back. Ow! *(Bonked again)*

SKOOLIE   Don't wanna hear no Oh-hi-oh neither.

BINK   Just the convenience of it, Skoolie, nice to go shoppin' on Sunday.

SKOOLIE   You know how I feel, I feel Well, guess it wa'n't too important, six days out the week and you forget to buy it all them days. I feel you didn't need it too bad if you couldn't think to buy it on Monday, on Tuesday, on Wednesday, on—

BINK And wheelchair access, everywhere, you'd like it, Skoolie.

SKOOLIE I 'on't own no wheelchair, Bink.

BINK Ramps and stuff, your cart'd work.

SKOOLIE My cart rolls 'cross the path to the store and back, I got access thereby to my eggs, to my shampoo, to my relaxer kits, to my toothpaste, to my large roller clips, don't need no more access.

BINK What if ya wanted to go visit somebody sometime?

SKOOLIE I don't.

BINK 'Steada make 'em trek up this ole hill all the time.

SKOOLIE I do the kinda hair job, customers trek up: no complaints.

BINK Hm. Well I'm complainin'.

SKOOLIE Then go back to Oh-hi-oh. *(Pause)* Why didn't you just stay out there in the city, anyway? I'll tell ya why, money.

BINK Obligation, Skoolie, Gary's daddy wanted us to come back, take over the hardware store, so we done it. Shoot, coulda done lots better in the city if we wanted to, everything we got here ain't ours, it's the credit card's. But Toledo. Toledo ain't like here, Toledo ain't dependent on no factories, close ya down, lay ya off soon's they find a country got enough protrudin' rib cages to take a dime a day with a smile.

SKOOLIE Do your own hair! I'm tired a "City's better, City's better."

BINK Aw come on, Skoolie. *(Pause)* Please? *(Pause)* I can't cornrow. *(Pause)* No one done hair good as you in the city, that's for sure.

SKOOLIE *(Pause)* Wouldn't want cher half-baked head walkin' aroun' discouragin' future business. *(Resumes)*

BINK How long you livin' on the hill, this shack? Ow, Skoolie, dammit, ya pullin' too hard.

SKOOLIE Wannit to fall right out? Just what's gonna happen soon's you march out that door, you don't lemme pull it tight. Course what's it matter with you, you gonna pull 'em out in a hour, soon's ya get home.

BINK I ain't. My head be too sore anyhow.

SKOOLIE Maybe lived in the city awhile, but you always be too country for the cornrow. Twelve years, I moved up here

right after you married and left when we was twenty.

BINK Done it up right. Wouldn'ta even recognized it was our play-shack. Musta bought it cheap, huh? Never used to have a floor, just dirt, soda cans. And no ceilin', nothin' but a few boards on top, half a them missin'. Now it's pretty, now it's warm. Still, *(Shudders)* I couldn't live next to that tree.

SKOOLIE You want beads?

BINK They cost extra?

SKOOLIE Whatchu think?

BINK No thanks, I think I got me some barrettes at home. How long Tee, the kids with ya?

SKOOLIE Why ya so damn nosy?

BINK Nothin' else to do. Back three months bored out my mind already.

SKOOLIE Don't remember ya bein' so bored when we was kids. Always found somethin' when we was kids.

BINK Always *is* somethin' when ya kids.

SKOOLIE Out and in, out and in. Started when she's twenty-three, me twenty-seven, Evie four, Will-Joe one plus a month, one a them suckers, Will-Joe's daddy I think, cuts outa town. Wasn't livin' with 'em but did help with the rent 'til he gone. Didn't know 'til the rent due. Three of 'em on my doorstep. She'll stay awhile, leave, get evicted come back, leave, come back.

BINK Well that's Skoolie and Tee, when yer daddy die?

SKOOLIE I was thirteen, Tee nine.

BINK Well that's Skoolie and Tee, Tee fall down, Skoolie pick her up ever since thirteen and nine, Mr. Jim at the mill catch his arm in that machinery it pull him in, and yaw find out what that mill care 'bout its employees.

SKOOLIE Thin back here. I got hair pieces, only need two a buck each, fill it in.

BINK Mr. Jim work twenty years, die, and not enough pension to feed a flea.

SKOOLIE Twenty-three.

BINK Then here's Skoolie, thirteen, full-time mama to her baby sister cuz suddenly their mama out cleanin' this house seven to three, that house four to ten.

SKOOLIE Twenty-three years My daddy work for 'em twenty-three years.

BINK Me in a fancy pink ruffled thing, and you got me on a pilla on the floor cuz you know the latest curls to set off my prom look. But a forty-five minute 'do hits a hour and a half cuz every five minutes you rollin' next door to check on Tee's junior high fractions and decimals.

SKOOLIE My daddy start work when he's fifteen. *(Pause)*

BINK Them babies get fever? Or born sick.

SKOOLIE Hungry. Markie-Ann was doin' okay, three babies was in the budget. But we tried four. Not enough for the last one and put a strain on the other three. Oldest two could take it. Youngest two couldn't. *(Finishes hair)* Fourteen.

BINK *(Pays)* Skoolie. Help me with somethin' else? *(Pause)*

SKOOLIE I helped ya with that just 'fore ya left, now back in town and first thing ya need it again?

BINK Charged me forty then. Got fifty on me now.

SKOOLIE *(Pause)* Sixty-five.

BINK Okay. I gotta go home, get it.

SKOOLIE How many you had since the one I give ya?

BINK None.

SKOOLIE Whatchu got at home?

BINK Sarah's ten, Jay's eight. That's enough.

SKOOLIE How you know I still did it?

BINK Do ya?

SKOOLIE Not for a couple years, ain't lost my touch though.

BINK What I thought.

SKOOLIE Mind if Tee come? I like the help.

BINK Okay. Confidential though.

SKOOLIE Well I guess so, Bink, I think I like to stay outa jail.

BINK Tonight?

SKOOLIE Naw. Gotta find somebody watch Evie and Will-Joe.

BINK My Gary watch 'em. He knows it got to be done.

SKOOLIE Okay, but tomorrow. Need ta talk to Tee.

BINK Okay. Okay. And I'll make yaw some lemon meringue pie, know ya like that.

SKOOLIE Bink. Don't eat nothin' tomorrow.

Scene 3

TEE C'mere, Evie. *(TEE takes EVIE's arm, shows SKOOLIE who groans.)* How you get that big scratch?

EVIE Went down to lunch and forgot my milk money, Mrs. Shay grab me, say

"How many times?" then march me back to my desk, get my nickel and dime.

TEE *(To SKOOLIE)* She don't haveta pull that hard.

SKOOLIE She don't haveta pull at all.

TEE Mrs. Shay do the white kids like that?

EVIE Do it to Charlie Wilt, but he cusses.

TEE She a good girl, Skoolie, no reason do her like that.

SKOOLIE I know.

TEE All the teachers before kiss her love her, this 'n mean, nasty, no reason. *(To EVIE)* Hurt? *(EVIE shakes her head.)* Go play with Will-Joe 'til they come. *(EVIE exits.)* What I gonna do?

SKOOLIE *(Going to cabinet)* Cut ain't deep, but p'roxide on it get ridda the sting, keep it don't get infected.

TEE Done it. What I gonna do 'bout the teacher?

SKOOLIE Wamme call her? *(TEE shakes her head.)* Whatchu want?

TEE Want . . . I do somethin'.

SKOOLIE Wamme talk to her? Ya ain't s'good at talkin', Tee. I'll call, straighten it out. Think it better I ask Evie first?

TEE Face-to-face, Skoolie. Oughta be.

SKOOLIE Uh huh. Well I can't help ya on that, my cart ain't built so to take that hill, plus tomorra my market day, cart will scoot 'cross the path, get my body soap, hair grease, all I need.

TEE I know.

SKOOLIE *(Pause)* You gon' do it? *(TEE nods.)* Go down there, your face 'gainst hers, that teacher? *(TEE nods.)* Okay. Okay. When?

TEE Appointment at eleven. But I be early, I prepare myself.

SKOOLIE Need a babysitter. Or you forget my Wednesday mornin' market outin'.

TEE Bink and Gary be here few minutes, maybe I ask she watch Jazzman tomorra. My check come Friday, think she watch my baby I promise her little somethin' enda the week?

SKOOLIE Keep your pennies, I'll knock five off her fee tonight. *(Pause)* Tee. You been thinkin'? Boutcher decision?

TEE Ain't none.

SKOOLIE Tee, ya can't . . . not think about it. Jus' can't . . . jus' can't have another baby, not think 'bout no options. We's hungry.

TEE I know, Skoolie, I ain't thinkin' 'bout it

cuz I know, cuz I know not much choice. I gonna pull it out.

SKOOLIE Sure?

TEE I love my babies, Skoolie, I can't let it incubate, bring it on in here, nothin' happen but it die, it die take another with it, I can't kill my babies, Skoolie. No more. *(Knock at the door.* EVIE *and* WILL-JOE *rush on.)*

EVIE and WILL-JOE I'll get it! I'll get it! *(*CHILDREN *open door.* BINK, *hair straightened and styled, enters.* CHILDREN *step back, shy.)*

BINK Yaw's sure Tee's. *(Pause)*

TEE *(Pulling coins from pocket)* Here's some ice cream money, maybe Mr. Gary take ya . . . *(Realizes it isn't enough)*

BINK Go on. Think we got some ice cream at home. Yaw like chocolate? *(They stare at her)* Wanna get a movie?

EVIE You got a VCR?

BINK Maybe Mr. Gary swing ya 'round the video store. Pick out whatcha want, one apiece. *(*CHILDREN *look at* TEE.)

TEE Go on. *(*CHILDREN *exit.)*

SKOOLIE I'll get it ready. *(Rolls off into other room.* BINK *starts slowly moving toward the window, stares out, mumbles indiscernibly except for an occasional "Jesus.")*

TEE Tonguin', Bink?

BINK *(Stops)* Sorry. Know yaw hate it.

TEE Skoolie hate it, I don't. Go on.

BINK Can't now. Know that tree?

TEE Oak.

BINK June. Skoolie and me six, and swingin', swingin'. Then we think we'll race to the top. We almost make it, but get caught up in each other's legs, fall side-by-side. I get up. Skoolie don't. Week later I come back here, by myself, think: We fall the same way, right next to each other, I ain't got a scratch. Skoolie ain't walkin' no more. Then my mouth start movin' in tongues. Ain't been able to stop it since. *(*SKOOLIE *rolls on.)*

SKOOLIE Okay.

*(*BINK *hesitantly moves toward the other room.* SKOOLIE *and* TEE *follow.* BINK *suddenly turns around.)*

BINK So much bleedin', Skoolie, so much bleedin' and pain, pain the last time, I don't know if I can . . . take it, Skoolie, don't know if I can . . . take it, I jus', I jus' . . . If all the sudden, if all the sudden I start speakin' in tongues, if all the sudden the Holy Spirit come down

burnin' me, come down burnin' me, I start speakin' in tongues—

SKOOLIE Do whatcha have to, Bink. *(*SKOOLIE, TEE *and* BINK *exit.)*

Scene 4

TEE *sits cross-legged, stapling all over a single piece of paper.* SKOOLIE *rolls on, pulls herself onto couch.* TEE *continues stapling, then suddenly stops. Looks up.*

TEE Appointment at eleven, bad for me, I miss mornin' work, good for Mrs. Shay, kids got the music teacher then, she free, so we do it. Meet at the secretary's office, I'm there ten 'til eleven. Wait. Wait, "Ten after, sure she comin'?" "She'll be here," secretary say, nice but fast. Wait. "Eleven thirty, she be here soon?" Secretary nod, secretary say "Eleven thirty!" call her over the loudspeaker, no answer. Quarter to twelve. Noon. I teary cuz I know music's over now. Secretary check her schedule. "She takin' 'em to lunch now," say she, "Catch her twelve thirty. She send the kids out for playground break, go back to solitude classroom half a hour." I outside Mrs. Shay door, five after noon, what she lock it for anyhow? I wait, belly growlin', smell cafeteria grill cheese, tomato soup, wait. Eight minutes to one she come, say, "Mrs. Edwards or Mrs. Beck?" cuz she know just two little black kids in fourth grade. I say Beck, she unlock door, I follow her in, she on and on "Evie a sweet little girl but limited attention span Kids watch too much unsupervise TV Parents always let 'em watch TV Won't tell 'em Read a book Won't tell 'em Do their homework Then come to school, no TV, they's bored." *(Pause)*

SKOOLIE Whatchu say? *(*TEE *shrugs.)* How long she go on?

TEE Long.

SKOOLIE How come you don't say nothin'—?

TEE She got three piles. Papers, she pick up left sheet pick up middle sheet pick up right sheet one staple, clamp, upper left corner, make a fourth pile. She take next one next one next one clamp, fourth pile. Talk all the time clamp talkin' clamp clamp I stare at the stapler clamp She talkin' clamp She talkin' clamp clamp clamp clamp She talkin' clamp She not talkin'. Suddenly she quiet. Wait for me, say somethin'.

SKOOLIE Whatchu say?

TEE "Our TV been broke three years."

SKOOLIE What she say? *(Pause)* What she say?

TEE "Oh."

SKOOLIE Then—

TEE Then kids clamorin' in and . . . Evie come, Evie see me, run, grab me—

SKOOLIE Hug ya?

TEE Uh uh! Uh uh! "Don't tell her, Mama! Don't tell her, Mama, I fibbed! Don't tell her, I fibbed!" She tryin' to whisper, but too panicked, so loud enough Mrs. Shay can hear. Then Mrs. Shay tell her Sit down, take me out in the hall, shut the door and lean on it. She say . . . She say . . . "Somethin' a matter with Evie?" I say . . . "Well . . ." I say . . . "Well . . . got this big scratch on her arm." My head look down. Don't know what should say now. Hope she do.

SKOOLIE Well? *(TEE nods.)* What?

TEE Pause. Then she say . . . Then she say, "Somebody else at home?"

SKOOLIE *Huh?*

TEE I say, *"Huh?"* She say, "Evie's daddy or . . . somebody else? Come back to live with ya?"

SKOOLIE Aw . . .

TEE I say, "Uh uh! Jus' me, my sister."

SKOOLIE Tee, I hope ya told her she done 'at scratch.

TEE I say, uh, I say, "Mrs. Shay, I gotta ask you how come that scratch on her arm." She look at me: I nuts. I say, "I think . . . I think maybe one time you pull her too hard." *(Pause)*

SKOOLIE She say what?

TEE She say "Oh. I'm sorry."

SKOOLIE What else?

TEE That all, she look at me, her eyes talk: "What else?" I say "That all, well, I guess that all."

SKOOLIE That wa'n't all, Tee, she been mean to Evie.

TEE I didn't cry! She never see me cry. She go back in the class, ten after one, I walkin' fast up and down up and down. Slower. Slow. I halt by the trashbasket sittin' in the hall. It full, I wanna pour it all out, fronta her door, but she gonna know I done it. I stoop by the trashbasket, by the door. If I wait 'til two she ain't gonna figure it's me I think, I think she gonna figure I left figure this done by

someone else. So I stay stooped, still. But after 'bout ten minutes this little boy walks by, looks at me, wonderin'. I find the door says "Girls," go in a little stall, sit, my feet up won't no one know I'm here. Quiet 'til two, I wait ten extra, make sure. Tiptoe back, pour real easy, keep my face down case someone walk by. Only thing that make a noise is this stapler tumble out. Surprise. Perfeck condition this stapler and Miss Shay gonna toss it in the trashbasket. I grab it. I run. *(Pause)*

SKOOLIE The end?

TEE We need a stapler, Skoolie. Never had one before.

SKOOLIE I'll call.

TEE No! no, whatchu callin' for? I talked to her.

SKOOLIE Did no good. I'll call. *(TEE staples viciously at SKOOLIE's face.)* You crazy?

TEE I talk to her! She know I don't take it lyin' down.

SKOOLIE Took it worse 'n lyin' down, girl, ya started somethin', not finish it. Just make her mad.

TEE No!

SKOOLIE Just make her mad, take it out on Evie.

TEE NO, that a lie, Skoolie! *(SKOOLIE picks up receiver.)* That a lie, Skoolie! *(TEE slaps receiver out of SKOOLIE's hand.)*

SKOOLIE What'sa matter with you?

TEE I done it myself! I done it myself!

SKOOLIE What?

TEE I can take care a my own kids, Skoolie!

SKOOLIE Well who said you couldn't, Tee—?

TEE I can take care a myself, Skoolie, don't need you, I can take care a my own kids, take care a myself! myself!

SKOOLIE Okay—

TEE Don't need you!

SKOOLIE Okay! *(Pause. Sound of the operator recording from the receiver. TEE hangs it up.)*

TEE Gonna hurt, Skoolie?

SKOOLIE Tomorra? *(TEE nods.)* Maybe.

TEE Bink say she got that pain again, blood again, all night, but now pain gone. She think it worked.

SKOOLIE Uh huh.

TEE Wish we could do it in a hospital, Skoolie. Make sure it done right.

SKOOLIE Uh huh. *(Pause)* Maybe we call the principal?

TEE *(Sits down and staples. Doesn't look up.)* Said she sorry, Skoolie.

SKOOLIE I know. Good thing you was there, make her say that. But. She didn't say wouldn't happen again. Did she.

TEE *(Continues stapling)* Uh uh.

SKOOLIE So. Maybe we oughta call her boss. Principal.

TEE He gonna say we gotta come down though. In person. *(Stops stapling)* I could carry ya, Skoolie.

SKOOLIE *(Pause)* You can't liff me.

TEE Yes I can. *(Starts to)*

SKOOLIE No! Carry me? Mile and a half? Naw, Tee, we can't. *(Pause)* Long time I been in school.

TEE You ain't never been in school. I carry ya.

SKOOLIE No! I'm heavy, Tee.

TEE You ain't fat.

SKOOLIE I'm a big person, I'm a grown woman, I ain't light.

TEE Easy for me.

SKOOLIE Naw, Tee, I ain't used to that.

TEE I can holdja.

SKOOLIE I'm grown!

TEE I can holdja. *(Pause)*

SKOOLIE Okay. *(TEE starts to lift.)* Careful. Now— Careful, Tee, now— Now watch— Watch my leg, watch my leg!

TEE Got it.

SKOOLIE Don't raise me too high now, jus' . . . All right. All right, this all right, this all right. Walk slow, hear? uh . . . Don't let no one see.

TEE Okay.

SKOOLIE Don't jostle too much, make me dizzy. Watch . . . Watch goin' down to the road, hear? Pretty bumpy on that hill. Now watch— Watch, Tee. Tee, ya drop me, I'm crawlin' right back, hear?

TEE I hear. You can't crawl.

SKOOLIE I can pull myself for sure, I sure will pull myself, you . . . you drop me . . . Okay. That's right. *(They are in the doorway.)*

TEE Skoolie. Pretend like . . . Pretend like all along I plan on bringin' you, tell 'em that. Pretend like we's doin' this together, pretend like you ain't no bigger 'n me.

SKOOLIE Set me in a chair before any of 'em come, teacher, principal. Make sure my feet pointed in the right direction: heels in the back.

Scene 5

SKOOLIE *holds a flashlight.*

SKOOLIE 'S open. *(BINK enters.)*

BINK Where them kiddies?

SKOOLIE Tree skippin'. Tee always could separate the spruces from the pines, likes to share them smarts with the babes.

BINK Tee, Tee, Tee, this I remember 'bout Tee, starin' at a matchbox waitin' for it to flip.

SKOOLIE 'S go.

BINK Off? *(SKOOLIE nods.)* How come? *(Pause)* My dress too tight, how come? *(SKOOLIE nods. BINK undresses.)* Why you cancelled three o'clock?

SKOOLIE School. *(Pause)* Went to school.

BINK *(Pause)* How? *(BINK stands in bra – ragged from use, half-slip, stockings.)*

SKOOLIE Off.

(BINK removes stockings and panties, lies supine on couch, knees bent, feet spread. Trembles. SKOOLIE rolls to her, clicks on flashlight under BINK's slip. Sudden laughter offstage, then TEE and CHILDREN enter through outside door.)

BINK Skoolie, them babies! them babies!

SKOOLIE OUT!

(TEE and CHILDREN rush out, never seeing BINK who is blocked by the back of the couch. SKOOLIE briefly concludes examination.)

SKOOLIE You's clean.

(BINK quickly dresses except shoes, sits on couch, hides face in hands, begins rocking upper body.)

SKOOLIE Stop.

BINK *(Not stopping)* I needta go out the back door, Skoolie. Aintcha got a back door?

SKOOLIE They ain't seen ya, Bink.

BINK Too much coffee, I gotta pee. I gotta pee, I gotta go out the back door.

SKOOLIE They ain't seen ya. When I call 'em back in they gonna look atcha funny cuz they know somethin' funny's goin' on, but they ain't seen ya. *(To door)* Come on. *(They re-enter. CHILDREN run through to other room without stopping.)*

TEE Wait for me, I run the bath. *(To SKOOLIE)* Sorry.

SKOOLIE Toldja wait 'till eight thirty, toldja keep 'em half-hour just in case.

TEE Sorry, Skoolie.

BINK Skoolie pull the magic again, everything clean, everything fine. I knowed it.

SKOOLIE Hope you and Gary be wearin' the proper equipment in the future.

BINK We was always careful, Skoolie, nothin' a hundred percent. How you got to school? *(TEE looks at SKOOLIE. SKOOLIE glances at TEE.)*

SKOOLIE In the principal's office, three thirty, I sittin' comfy and in come Shay with her wristwatch. *(Jazzman starts crying, TEE exits.)* With her wristwatch, she glance at her wristwatch, then say I must be Evie's aunt, principal told her I was waitin'. "That I am," say I, tall sittin', erect. Quiet, contest to see who gonna break the quiet. *(Long pause, quiet except for Jazzman's cries.)* "You wanted to speak to me?" Hah! blew it! *(TEE enters with bawling Jazzman.)*

TEE Won't take my milk, Skoolie, I don't know, won't take my milk.

SKOOLIE Dummy blew it cuz she showed she was the weaker, showed me, showed her. Leaves me to fight confident. Leaves her to fight compensatin'.

TEE Skoolie, won't take my milk, he gonna be sick.

SKOOLIE "Yes, I did," said I, "I wanted to talk to you. You put that scratch on Evie's arm." She all over the room—

TEE Skoolie, he sick! My baby Jazzman sick! *(SKOOLIE rolls to refrigerator, retrieves bottle of milk, rolls back and slams it down in front of TEE.)*

SKOOLIE She all over the room! pacin' back and forth. I in chair, don't move. If ever a nervous moment come for me, she don't see it. She see me calm, still. I see her all over the room.

TEE Won't drink me.

SKOOLIE "Evie forgot her milk money, Evie always forgettin' her milk money, why go to the lunch room without milk money? I know she's only fourth grade but—. Well I know I mighta pulled too rough but—. Well I got twenty-four kids I gotta look after I try to be patient but—." I say "Chicken butt, I lay it down, you lick it up."

BINK Naw . . .

SKOOLIE Naw. I just sit. All I gotta do. My whole body smilin' but she won't never see it.

TEE Won't drink me!

SKOOLIE In come principal: Why she so loud? He don't even hear me, I so soft, relaxed. She hysterical. Give that baby some milk!

TEE Won't take it.

SKOOLIE He'll take the bottle, Tee! he's hungry, give him some. *(Pause, then TEE tries again to give him her breast.)* Give that baby his bottle, Tee, ya wanna starve him?

TEE Take mine. *(SKOOLIE grabs bottle and baby and begins to feed him.)*

SKOOLIE Casual I say, "Nothin', Mr Principal, nothin' goin' on, just me and her havin' a little chitty chat, just me wonderin' how come she gonna scratch our little girl, then lie 'bout it, then claim scratch come from our men, claim we bringin' men in the house claim one of 'em scratch our little girl."

TEE My little girl.

BINK What principal say?

SKOOLIE Blew up.

TEE My little girl.

SKOOLIE Notice this, Tee, notice I'm ignorin' your crybaby mood, Tee. Like Shay wa'n't hysterical enough, now the principal's face a hundred ten degrees red. "You said what to her? You said what to her? Don't you never again— I sure am sorry, Miz Beck, sorry 'bout cher little girl please accept my humblest apologies—" *(TEE grabs SKOOLIE's cart and begins violently shaking it. Jazzman starts bawling again. TEE backs off.)*

TEE Sorry. I sorry.

SKOOLIE Ya say that too much, Tee. *(She rocks baby. He quiets.)*

TEE I hold him?

SKOOLIE Then she apologize. Don't wanna, but the pupils in the principal's eyes say she better. *(To TEE)* No. *(To BINK)* Then I leave.

BINK What Tee do? Say?

SKOOLIE *(Pause)* Nothin'.

BINK Nothin'?

SKOOLIE Nothin', in the bathroom with Evie so Evie don't get upset, seein' my tongue smackin' her teacher around.

TEE Proteck Evie. She scared. *(Pause)*

BINK Aw, let her hold her baby, Skoolie, don't be so mean.

SKOOLIE Better keep your mind on your business, Bink. *(Pause. Offers baby to TEE.)* Careful, he's sleep.

TEE *(Taking baby)* Aw, see 'at little grin on his face. He know his mama come.

BINK   How you leave, Skoolie, how you got there?

TEE   I carry her. *(Pause)* I carry her. *(Pause)*

BINK   All that way?

TEE   Set her down 'fore them people come: principal, teacher. Pick her up after they's gone.

BINK   *(To* SKOOLIE*)* All that way? *(Pause)* Huh. *(Pause)* Huh. *(Pause)* I gotta pee, Skoolie.

SKOOLIE   We ain't moved the bathroom. *(*BINK *exits.* SKOOLIE *looks at* TEE. TEE *looks at Jazzman whom she has laid on the floor and is rocking. She gradually rocks harder until finally roughly enough that he again starts crying, and she cradles him.)*

SKOOLIE   Tee, stop that! what're you doin' to that baby?

TEE   He take my milk.

SKOOLIE   He don't want it! *(Grabs Jazzman. Now both sisters clutch baby.)*

TEE   Gon' take it.

SKOOLIE   He don't wantcher damn milk, Tee!

TEE   Yes—

SKOOLIE   No! he don't wantcher damn milk, Tee!

TEE   Gon' take it, gon' take it, Skoolie, somethin' wrong! cuz somethin' wrong with baby don't want his mama's milk.

SKOOLIE   No—

TEE   Somethin' wrong—

SKOOLIE   Not with him! Gimme that baby 'fore ya kill him!

EVIE   Mommy! *(She is onstage; stillness.)* Mommy. *(Pause)* Mommy. *(Pause)* Mommy, can I give Jazzman a haircut? He need one.

TEE   *(Pause)* Tomorra maybe. You remind me, we see. *(*EVIE *exits.* SKOOLIE *sets Jazzman on couch, rocks.)* I carry you, Skoolie.

SKOOLIE   Why don't you go to the center a town and paint it on the billboard, Tee.

TEE   I could do it again, ya need me. *(No answer)* Ya need me. *(No answer)* I could do it, ya want me to or not. You in my way, I could pick you up, move. Nothin' you could do. You bother me, I pick you up, carry you, I carry you someplace else, carry you where you don't bother me.

SKOOLIE   You ever do, Tee, I'll pray God Gimme back my legs jus' long enough to kick you. Hard. *(*BINK *enters.)*

BINK   Gettin' late.

SKOOLIE   You ain't been here ten minutes.

BINK   Gettin' late. Too dark on this hill, Skoolie, how I gonna walk twenty feet down to the road, down to the car not kill myself.

TEE   *(With Jazzman)* See, Skoolie! he took a little. Couple drops, now he sleep good. *(*BINK *looks at her.)* It ain't nothin', Bink. Sometime he want my milk, sometime he full. *(Pause)* Whatchu lookin' for? jus' normal.

SKOOLIE   Tee. You hold the flashlight for Bink? *(Moving toward the other room)* I better go kiss them babies, let 'em know I ain't sore no more. *(Stops)* Let him sleep, Tee. *(Exits)*

BINK   *(Putting on shoes)* Yaw tree skippin', huh.

TEE   I was a girl scout, Bink, one year, fifth grade. Leader take us a all-day hike, name this tree, name that plant, hundreds. I remember all, no one else hardly remember one. Easy for me.

BINK   Tee. I come in your house, you sittin' starin' at a matchbox. Skoolie and I be in your mama's bedroom gettin' in real trouble, try on a gown, try on high heels, pinch earrings, come out two hours you still starin' at the matchbox. Skoolie say you waitin' for it to flip. How?

TEE   My mind make it.

BINK   Your mind didn't. *(Pause)* Hold the light steady at my feet. Move it a inch to the left or the right leaves me in the dark. I miss one step fall in one a them groundhog ditches, you know I'm laid up six weeks.

Scene 6

TEE, EVIE *and* WILL-JOE *outside on the stoop.*

TEE   The whole sky move. Unison. *(Points)* Big Dipper? Watch it. It stand on its handle now, but wait. Slow slow it flip back, a circle. Couple months, May, it upside down, pour its soup out. Then September, upright again, flat on the burner. Everything shift, everthing move together, I see it, I know the map. 'Cept a few lights, they not interested in the rhythm a the rest, got they own mind, never know where they end up. We call them this: *(Points)* Mars, Venus, Jupiter. I like lookin' up. I like watchin' the change.

EVIE   I wake up to pee, Mama, you whisper

us out here, make sure Skoolie don't wake. Why?

TEE News: We movin'.

EVIE AND WILL-JOE Aw . . .

TEE Lug our suitcase up the slope, 'member I say don't get too comfy?: temporary arrangement.

WILL-JOE I like the hill! *(No answer)* Why?

TEE Cuz we can. Money I make now, and Jane, scrape plates next to me, she say other half her place empty enda the month. Cheap, and two bedrooms: me, Jazzman in one, the second you share. Your own bed. Twins.

WILL-JOE I like sharin' with you.

EVIE I like sharin' with Skoolie.

TEE Gettin' big.

WILL-JOE Skoolie mad at us?

TEE You think that the reason? *(WILL-JOE nods.)* We not done nothin' make her made. Have we?

WILL-JOE *(Meaning EVIE)* Her. She been swingin' on the bad tree. *(Pause. Then EVIE swings at him.)*

EVIE Squeal-mouth! *(TEE intercepts her aim.)*

TEE That the truth?

EVIE Tattletale, it ain't nice!

TEE *(Pause)* Skoolie and me nasty to that tree, huh. I change my mind. That tree ain't got the evil eye, it not the devil. Skoolie's thing was a freak, that white oak not housin' the spirits. It old. Earn some respeck. Don't let her catch ya near it though. *(Pause)*

EVIE You and Skoolie mad?

TEE Naw. But two different people. Grownups. Everything Skoolie do not necessarily my business. Everything I do not necessarily hers.

WILL-JOE We come back to visit?

TEE Sure.

WILL-JOE And her visit us? *(TEE looks at him.)* She call, wanna watch our TV, you come pick her up? Carry her down the hill, cross the bridge, cross the traffic light? Like today?

TEE *(Considers this.)* Yeah. I travel her. *(Looks up at the sky)* Funny thing: Uruguay, Australia – they ain't got the same map. Their stars ain't ours, down there they got a different sky. I wanna see that. You wanna see that? *(They nod.)* One day, we gonna.

Scene 7

TEE *sits up on couch. She is slicing an apple.*
SKOOLIE *rolls in. As she chatters* SKOOLIE *makes preparations: water, towels, etc.*

SKOOLIE Warm like spring, smell like spring. The babies feel it, they get the giggles whilst we wait on the truck. He just pullin' off, I'm still wavin' and here Irene Halloway come. "Skoolie! Heardja told that Shay off." She had trouble too, said Shay thought both her oldests was dumb, now she worried: her youngest got her in the fall. Well I always thought Irene's boy was dumb, but that big girl was smart enough. I nod, say nothin'. Roll to the store, a hullabaloo – seven at me, grinnin', already got the Bink word. I'm brief: we let her have it. "Dontchu never no more try sayin' they hurt that girl," says principal, "Dontchu never no more lay a hand on that girl." Well, we get the principal to say it, we done the best thing: he signs her paycheck. Tee and me get him to say it, I tell them store people, just shut her up, embarrass her a bit. Make her think. Whatchu doin'! *(Runs to TEE: blood all over TEE's hand and the apple)*

TEE Stomach hurts.

SKOOLIE *(Wiping hand)* Nervous. Normal.

TEE Salt. My mouth.

SKOOLIE Better not, toldja not ta eat. And why your hands s'clammy? No draft in here.

TEE Not eat, my belly clean.

SKOOLIE Then watchu got this apple for?

TEE Ain't hungry, just peel it for you. Know ya love 'em, I like to peel.

SKOOLIE Where's the cut, Tee?

TEE Peel it, then I wanna cut it, fours. Then cut again. Again, sixteen. Again—

SKOOLIE I don't see the cut, all this blood can't be from your hangnail-suckin'.

TEE Wish I slice it off, whole hand. Then I be better. Like you.

SKOOLIE *(Back to preparations)* Nasty talk, Tee. But you got stuff to go through today, so no dwellin' on it. *(Pause)*

TEE Skoolie. I think . . . time to go.

SKOOLIE Where we goin'?

TEE Us. Me, my kids. I found a place. It in the budget, my new money.

SKOOLIE Well. I won't be rushin' in no

new boarders. Just in case your budget don't hold up two months down the road. When we's done, remind me to dunk your hand in alcohol. Not now, I don't like no chemicals in the vicinity 'til things all patched up.

TEE You like my place, Skoolie. It got a basement.

SKOOLIE Here? Or the other room? *(Pause)* You better not mess up my couch.

(SKOOLIE exits into the other room)

TEE You know that video store jus' open? My new house right round the corner. You gon' come visit, Skoolie. And I make a pot a spaghetti. Hot bread. *(Pause)* Skoolie. *(Pause)* Skoolie, I think I made a mistake, sorry.

(SKOOLIE rolls in, her back to TEE. She has a wire hanger, and proceeds to untwist it.)

TEE I sorry, Skoolie, I think . . . I think I yanked the wrong thing.

(TEE will pull from under the blanket another straightened – and bloodied – hanger. Eventually SKOOLIE, absorbed in her task and ignoring TEE, turns around. Stillness. Then SKOOLIE rushes to lift blanket. Blood all over TEE's groin, legs, the couch.)

SKOOLIE NO! *(Rushes to phone)* Tee! Tee, what 'dju do? Need the clinic, need the emergency room. S'pose ta wait for me, toldja wait for me! This a emergency, we live on the hill, my sister, my sister got blood, my baby sister got a lotta blood, come from her vagina. We live on the hill, shack on the hill, right 'cross from the general store, know it? Fast, please, cuz, lotta blood, lotta, big . . . pool . . . *(Hangs up. Rushes back toward TEE but falls off cart.)* Dammit! wheresa goddam clean towels?

TEE Belly hurt—

(SKOOLIE finds towels, rushes back to TEE, positions towel between TEE's legs. TEE shivers.)

SKOOLIE Cold?

(SKOOLIE puts a towel over TEE, rolls, falls off cart again. Screams in frustration. Gets back on cart, goes to cabinet and retrieves blanket. Starts to go back to TEE but cart gets stuck.)

SKOOLIE *I hate this thing!*

(SKOOLIE gets off cart, pulls herself to TEE, covers her. Quiet.)

SKOOLIE Don't go to sleep! Don't go to sleep!

TEE Will-Joe do his readin' last night, he come ask for help. I say better he get Evie. Or you. *(Pause)*

SKOOLIE Say somethin'!

TEE Nothin' else.

SKOOLIE There is, you gonna talk to me. *(Pause) Hear?* Tell me 'bout . . . uh . . . Tell me 'bout that time ya steal my cart, Mama catch ya, fan yer heiny. How come ya done it? *(Pause) How come ya done it?*

TEE Don't know—

SKOOLIE Say!

TEE Jus' mean—

SKOOLIE How come ya steal that cart, Tee?

TEE Because. It was you.

SKOOLIE *(Pause)* Talk! *(Pause)* Aw. Aw, don't cry, don't cry, honey. Just talk for me, please? Jus' say somethin', Tee.

TEE How come "Skoolie"?

SKOOLIE How come, ya think?

TEE Cuz ya never went to school.

SKOOLIE Uh uh. Uh uh, probably toldja that cuz I like ya to believe it, was a lie. Me and Bink . . . Me and Bink fall outa that tree June before first grade. All summer I bein' carried. To the bed. To the couch. Out the door. *Hate* it. September Daddy carry me to his truck, drive me, set me at my desk, leave. Everyone see it. No one play with me. Not come near, but watch all the time, point. One day, I start pullin' out. Teacher turn her head, I pull myself out the door. I rollin' you over, hear? *(Starts to)*

TEE *Hurts* . . . Skoolie, *hurts*—

SKOOLIE Okay, just yer face. Needta see yer face. Ambulance here soon. *(Pause)* Kids giggle, they like I get away, won't tell. She find me in the hall, or the playground, carry me back, tell Daddy, he gimme a beatin', take me back next day, I do the same. Just too many kids, always could find a time to make my break, she couldn't watch all us and she couldn't tie me up and she wanted to. Year over, beatin' every day, Daddy say he gonna give 'em to me harder I start doin' it in second grade. Well I start doin' it in second grade, but guess what? 'Steada harder, they gettin' softer. Finally, Thanksgivin', Daddy say, "You done the effort, girl, guess it ain't your pleasure. You ain't gotta go back to school no more." Round then I get my name. And he build me a cart, no more bloody cut legs from pullin' 'em, ugly for everybody else, I didn't care, I couldn't feel 'em nohow. Now I go where I please, no more carryin', I go where I want. So "Skoolie" ain't cuza no school. Cuz I did taste school. Spit it out. *(Pause)*

TEE Skoolie, when you fall out that tree – it hurt?

SKOOLIE *(Pause)* Me and Bink fall out. I hear a big funny crack. From me. Felt somethin'. If it hurt I never knowed it – over too quick. Then we start to gigglin'. Cuz the crack noise was so weird, cuz the whole thing's so funny, us flip out the tree. Then we push our palms down, gonna pull ourselves up. Bink's up the first try, not me. I push again – nothin' movin'. Look up at her. Push a third. Nothin'. Look up at her. I start to get scared. *(Looks at* TEE. TEE *is dead.* SKOOLIE *rolls to cabinet and gets a brush, rolls back and starts stroking* TEE*'s hair.)* Not so bad a haircut you give. Just stroke it right. *(Pause)* Shoulda got a pitcher a us yesterday, Tee, both us, you takin' me down the hill, not bump me once. Smooth ride. I ain't been carried in a long time, Tee.

Migdalia Cruz

Biography

Migdalia Cruz is a playwright whose work has been produced in London, Montreal, New York and other cities in the United States. She has written more than twenty plays, musicals and operas, including *Miriam's Flowers, Telling Tales, Lucy Loves Me, Frida: The Story of Frida Kahlo,* and *Rushing Waters.* Migdalia is the recipient of the Pew/TCG National Artist-in-Residence, National Endowment for the Arts and McKnight fellowships and was a 1991 finalist for the Susan Smith Blackburn Prize. She is an alumna member of New Dramatists and was born and raised in the Bronx. Latino Chicago Theater produced a season of her work – *Fur, Cigarettes and Moby-Dick,* and *Lolita de Lares* (about Lolita Lebron) – in 1995; *Latins In La-La Land* was in the 1994 Bay Area Playwrights' Festival and in the 1995 New Works Festival at the Public Theater. She was in residence at Classic Stage Company, New York, working on an adaptation of Lorca's *House of Bernarda Alba* and Euripides' *Medea.* She is currently working with River Arts Repertory on a play about children of war.

Photo: Eric Baumgartner

Production history

The Have-Little, first entitled *Fire Escape,* and later *Lillian,* was created during Maria Irene Fornés' Hispanic-Playwrights-in-Residence Laboratory at INTAR Theatre in New York, 1986–87, and was further developed at the Sundance Institute. It was workshopped at INTAR and INTAR 2, and read at New Dramatists, DUO Theatre, and the Women's Project. It was selected as First Runner-up for the Susan Smith Blackburn Prize, an international award for Women dramatists writing in the English language, 1991.

The Have-Little was premiered by INTAR Theatre, May 29–June 30, 1991, directed by Nilo Cruz, and featured Divina Cook, Gabriella Diaz Farrar, Marisol Massey, and David Roya. It had a second production at Teatro Latino/Theatre X in Milwaukee, Wisconsin, in February 1995.

Artistic statment

I write about the people I know – as a married adult living in a house (for the first time in my life) in exurban Connecticut. Or sometimes, I write about the ones I feel I should know – as a Nuyorican living in the violent twentieth century. But always, I write about the people I knew – as a child in the South Bronx.

The Have-Little is really my first play and the one I think is most directly about who I am and where I come from. It's a place I would never have learned to re-touch without the honesty of María Irene Fornes, la Maestra, who forced me to teach myself how to write with respect and dignity – not just for what I am, but who I was and will always be.

My best friend at the age of 8 was raped and murdered and thrown off the roof of the apartment house we lived in. My next best friend was pregnant at age 13 and dead from an overdose at 15. My second to next best friend became a cop. And I started to write stuff down, hoping – if not to make sense of it, then to at least pay respect to the memory of it, of us, of a small time in history when all of us grew up too soon.

The main character in *The Have-Little,* Lillian, is a girl we could all have been and some of us were. For me she is the purest of my characters, the most innocent, the most spiritual. She is what was taken from me too young – that which I yearn for still. The world of poverty that surrounds Lillian is my world, and by writing the play I hope others are able to recognize it and appreci-ate the beauty of its humanity and mourn the loss of its children.

So . . . You can take the girl out of the South Bronx – but you would have to cut my heart out to make me forget.

6 The Have-Little

Migdalia Cruz

There are but two families in the world,
Have-much and Have-little.

Cervantes, *Don Quixote*, Part II, Book III, Chapter 20

This play is dedicated to Manuel Pereiras-Garcia and María Irene Fornes.

Characters

LILLIAN RIVERA: a Puerto Rican girl-woman, 13–15; innocent and spiritual

CARMEN RIVERA: her mother, 38–40, mostly exhausted by life

JOSE RIVERA: her father, 36–38, a charming brute

MICHI RODRIGUEZ: a Puerto Rican girl-woman, 13–15, smart and knows it

Time:
Summer, 1974 to winter, 1975–76.

Place
The South Bronx
There are four areas represented on stage:
the fire escape: Lillian's place
the kitchen: Carmen's place
the Riveras' home altar: Jose's place
the street in front of the firehouse next to the Riveras: a place for the outside world

Scene 1

Summer, 1974. The sound of an elevated train. LILLIAN *on the fire escape. Late afternoon. The sound of glass breaking on the ground and police sirens. The sound of a crowd screaming "Kill the son-of-a-bitch!" Silence.* CARMEN *appears at the window behind* LILLIAN *who sits on the fire escape. They talk out, not to each other, with feverish intensity.*

LILLIAN   I can smell every picture in my head . . . Today it's late afternoon . . . A hot summer full of sickness. And I'm sitting on the fire escape . . . my back against the stone of the building, my knees to my chin. Staring. My mother scared. Where's Papi?

CARMEN   Stupid little girls. Stupid little girls don't know any better than to play

on the roof . . . Why do she have to have such stupid friends? They go where they ain't supposed to.

LILLIAN   Where's Papi?

CARMEN   Why they so stupid they talk to those junkies? They stabbed Mrs. Vega with an ice pick. I hope they all get killed.

LILLIAN   I hope nobody gets kilt. There's always so much blood. Can't jump rope over blood. It gets in the sandbox and the little babies try to eat it.

CARMEN   I'm not letting her outside no more. It's not safe. This was a good neighborhood, a good place to bring up your children.
(Pause. As LILLIAN *continues to speak,* CARMEN *prays softly but feverishly in Spanish as she moves back into the shadows of the apartment and then fades away.)*

LILLIAN   We keep away from the sandbox now. It's strange when people from an island are scared of sand.
(Lights cross to the kitchen area. LILLIAN *moves into the next scene in the apartment.)*

Scene 2

CARMEN *sits smoking a cigarette.* LILLIAN *moves to stand behind* CARMEN. *She brushes* CARMEN's *hair.* CARMEN *turns to look at* LILLIAN *whose mouth is open.*

CARMEN   You had that same look on your face when you were born.

LILLIAN   What look?

CARMEN   Like that. With your mouth open.

LILLIAN   So I was born this way, that's why it's still open.

CARMEN   I used to go into your room every night to check if you were breathing.

LILLIAN   I know. Sometimes Pa came instead. But I always knew who it was.

108

CARMEN   You remember that?

LILLIAN   Yeah. Tell me about when I was born.

CARMEN   Your father was working late at the factory. And it was cold. The coldest day since I came here. It was too cold to be April. The coldest day of that year. I was sitting up listening to the radio. There was a Glenn Miller song playing, about the moon. And I walked over to the window to look at the moon. It was big and full and I stared at it and thought about this story my mother tole me.

LILLIAN   What story?

CARMEN   About how the Moon began.

LILLIAN   How?

CARMEN   The Sun got lonely and wanted a companion. So God made the Moon. But the Sun was jealous of the Moon because it was white and clear. So it stopped loving the Moon and moved further and further away from it until they started coming out at opposite times and never saw each other again.

LILLIAN   But sometimes the Moon and the Sun are out at the same time. *(Pause)*

CARMEN   If you want to hear my stories, you have to stop asking questions.

LILLIAN   Okay. Maybe the Moon loves the Sun so much that she sneaks to where he is because she can't stand not ever seeing him. I bet that's why.

CARMEN   I bet you're right.

LILLIAN   Okay. So you thought about the story . . .

CARMEN   I thought about the story, stared at the Moon and as I was looking at it— Ouch! Lily! Softer.

LILLIAN   I'm sorry. *(She resumes brushing CARMEN's hair.)* And you were looking . . .

CARMEN   Mmhmm. And my whole belly dropped, liked somebody sat on it.

LILLIAN   Really?

CARMEN   And I went to the bathroom because it feels the same as when you gotta go. So I went and then the pains started coming.

LILLIAN   What are the pains like?

CARMEN   Like that somebody who was sitting on me was kicking me. Not kicking – more like digging, with the heels of his feet. Digging a big hole.

LILLIAN   Oh . . .

CARMEN   And then I called your father and he came running to take me to the hospital.

LILLIAN   He ran?

CARMEN   Yeah. He had to. His cousin Jaime stole his car.

LILLIAN   His own cousin?

CARMEN   Yeah. But Jaime gave it back when he found out we had a baby girl. He likes girls.

LILLIAN   But Papi got you there, din't he?

CARMEN   Yeah, but he was so stupid he forgot my suitcase. I made him go back and get it.

LILLIAN   What was in it?

CARMEN   Night gown, toothbrush, a book . . .

LILLIAN   Which one?

CARMEN   *Don Quixote*. My father gave me that book for my fifteenth birthday. The fifteenth birthday is very important, you know. I have to think of something special to give you.

LILLIAN   I know what I want.

CARMEN   What?

LILLIAN   Guess!

CARMEN   I know, my little Easter baby. I know. *(LILLIAN finishes brushing CARMEN's hair and looks at her.)*

LILLIAN   You look good. *(CARMEN starts to stand; the doorbell rings.)*

CARMEN   Who's that?

LILLIAN   *(Going to the door; CARMEN goes to the bedroom.)* Michi. We're doing home-work together.

CARMEN   I hate that girl.

LILLIAN   Ma!

CARMEN   Ma, what?! She's disrespectful! Thinks she's so smart . . . you shouldn't play with her. She's bad for you – always hoping for things that won't happen.

LILLIAN   She's my best friend. I woulda failed by now if she weren't helping me.

CARMEN   Some help! When are you gonna learn? Huh? Nothing means nothing! School don't help if you're poor. It don't teach you how to live without, do it? It makes you want things you ain't never gonna get.

LILLIAN   I'm gonna get somefin.

CARMEN   I hope I don't live to see the something you're gonna get. I'm gonna go lie down. *(She exits.)*

LILLIAN   *(At the door)* Mrs. Weiner's real sick.

MICHI   *(At the door)* I know I'll get blamed. *(They enter and walk towards the table.)*

LILLIAN How could they blame you?

MICHI I get blamed for everything around here.

LILLIAN Did you put the Ex-Lax in the teacher's coffee?

MICHI So you're blaming me too?

LILLIAN I'm your best friend.

MICHI So?

LILLIAN I know you.

MICHI So?

LILLIAN I know you lie.

MICHI I hope she dies, but I didn't do it. I hope she goes to the bathroom for the rest of her life. She said you won the spelling bee and I did.

LILLIAN I did.

MICHI You didn't! I did—Spell catatonic.

LILLIAN Catatonic, c-a-t-a-t-a-n-i-c, catatonic.

MICHI Wrong! You spelled it wrong and won the book. I'm the one who likes to read. *The Wizard of Oz* is my fucking life.

LILLIAN It's not wrong.

MICHI It's catatonic. C-A-T-A-T-O-N-I-C. Catatonic.

LILLIAN I'll lend it to you.

MICHI Well, you didn't win it.

LILLIAN It doesn't matter as long as one of us got the book. (MICHI *stands up to leave.*) Where are you going?

MICHI Home.

LILLIAN I thought we were gonna do homework.

MICHI You can come to my house if you want to.

LILLIAN My dad is gonna call me. I have to be here.

MICHI Is he still sick?

LILLIAN Yeah, but not really.

MICHI What d'you mean?

LILLIAN He drinks too much. That's what my mother said. He sees things.

MICHI What kinda things?

LILLIAN Saints. And sometimes even the Virgin.

MICHI The real one?

LILLIAN Yeah.

MICHI Is he crazy?

LILLIAN No! (*Pause*) He cries too. Sometimes he grabs me and cries on my shoulder. When I move away he keeps sobbing down my back. Sometimes I think my feet are wet from all the crying.

MICHI He must be fucking sad.

LILLIAN Yeah. Paulita's piercing my ears tomorrow. You wanna come?

MICHI Okay. But she's a butcher.

LILLIAN Who said?

MICHI She made me bleed and bleed when she did mine.

LILLIAN How old were you?

MICHI Fuck. I was just a little kid. Five or something.

LILLIAN Little kids bleed more than big people. They always have cuts and things.

MICHI That's true – I saw the principal taking Weiner the Witch home.

LILLIAN She's nice to me.

MICHI That's because you're not as fucking smart as I am.

LILLIAN You should act dumb like me.

MICHI I can't. If I know the answer I gotta raise my fucking hand.

LILLIAN That's no way to make her like you.

MICHI Fuck.

LILLIAN I'm sorry she likes me better.

MICHI That's okay. I like you better too. Most of the time.

LILLIAN Than her?

MICHI Yeah.

(*They laugh.*)

MICHI (*Reciting a poem*) Open the door and let in the day. That's what the cow says to the hay. Father, oh father, you live in the street . . . that's why I love you. You're forced to eat meat. I hate spinach and I hope you never eat some, cause if you do you'll be a person in a prison. Ashamed to laugh, ashamed to cry. I don't know anything about the dawn but when it comes, it comes on strong. (*To* LILLIAN) I wrote that for you.

LILLIAN God, Michi! It's the most beautiful poem I ever heard.

MICHI Tell me about it! I want to write a musical.

LILLIAN Really.

MICHI We can make a lot of money with a musical.

LILLIAN How?

MICHI We bring it to Miss Begun. She'll know what to do being a librarian and everything. They got music at their fingertips. They got books.

LILLIAN I never woulda thought of that.

MICHI You gotta start thinking, Lily. You won't get anywhere if you don't think.

LILLIAN That's okay. I don't got nowhere to go.

MICHI Stupid!

LILLIAN Don't call me stupid!

MICHI Why the fuck shouldn't I? You're a fucking dead end. A waste of human protein.

LILLIAN Stop it!

MICHI *(Imitating her)* Stop it! *(Normal voice)* Can't you stand up for your own fucking self?

LILLIAN I'm sorry.

MICHI *(Packing up her books)* That does it. You're making me crazy.

LILLIAN Please don't go. I really am sorry.

MICHI What are you sorry for? You can't help it you're stupid.

LILLIAN But we're supposed to do homework.

MICHI You're yanking my chain, girl! *(She exits.)*

LILLIAN I'm not stupid!

(CARMEN enters holding a rolled-up stocking.)

CARMEN There's some money missing.

LILLIAN So?

CARMEN Do you know where it went? *(No response)* I'll ask you one more time.

LILLIAN I don't know.

(CARMEN twists LILLIAN's arm.)

CARMEN He was here again! You let him in!

LILLIAN No, Mami!

CARMEN You let him in!

LILLIAN No, I didn't!

CARMEN I told you not to! Isn't that what I told you?! He's been here!

LILLIAN No, Mami! *(CARMEN lets her go and sits on the stuffed chair. LILLIAN runs to the bathroom and slams the door.)* You hurt me! Why d'y always have to hurt me? He's sick! Pa is sick!

CARMEN He's not sick! You always defend him and give him everything he wants. I don't want him here, you hear me! He comes here and stinks the place up. I smell him here. I know he was here. I smell the dust from the cracks in his hands. *(Pause)*

He never wanted you. He wanted me to get rid of you and now he acts like he's all love for you. It was me who wanted you. It was me who had you – I threw up when we made you and almost choked, and I still let him on top of me. He smelled like vomit and made me sick, but I let him stay on top of me because I wanted to have you. I'd do anything to have you. And you don't care what I feel, you only care what he feels.

(LILLIAN re-enters. She has washed her face.)

LILLIAN Is that true, Ma?

CARMEN That's the truth. I almost choked.

(LILLIAN walks to CARMEN and kisses her forehead, then she walks to the table and opens her books. Long silence)

CARMEN What are you doing?

LILLIAN Homework.

CARMEN Did you eat?

LILLIAN No, I wasn't hungry.

CARMEN You feel okay?

LILLIAN I din't feel like eating.

CARMEN Maybe you have the flu or something. That's the only thing school is good for – for catching germs. Could you pay a little attention to your mother? Or is that too much to ask? I don't know why you spend so much time doing homework. It don't help you, does it? You're not smart – you're like your mother. You don't have to read to learn what you need to know. What you need to know isn't in books – it's in church. That's the only thing to help people like us. I learn everything I need to know on Sundays, in church. You study and study, but look at the grades you bring home. I don't—

LILLIAN I'm just too stupid to know any better, I guess . . . I like to try.

CARMEN You want some coffee? It's cold, but that's how you like it, isn't it? *(She gets the coffee.)*

LILLIAN Okay.

CARMEN Yeah . . . I guess you gotta try. Even though you know it don't mean nothing. Nothing means nothing.

(CARMEN crosses to LILLIAN, hands her the coffee and then impulsively tickles her. The coffee spills as they tickle each other and laugh. Lights cross to the fire escape. LILLIAN moves there as CARMEN exits. JOSE appears behind her at the window.)

Scene 3

JOSE *at the window and* LILLIAN *on the fire escape. Late night. They are whispering.* JOSE *is scraping a burned piece of toast with a knife.*

LILLIAN You got a pretty face, Pa. It looks pretty wif the moon.

JOSE Everything looks pretty in the dark, Lillian.

LILLIAN Will you clean my ears?

JOSE What?

LILLIAN Like you used to when you was here wif us. It feels so good when you do it.

JOSE We only did that because you were a baby ... You're not no baby no more.

LILLIAN (She rubs her head against his arm) I know.

JOSE You know you're not no baby ...

LILLIAN Please, Pa. I like it so much. I have dreams sometimes about you cleaning me. It makes my eyes roll back in my head.

JOSE You could hurt yourself. (He cleans the knife against his tongue.) Maybe just a little, just enough to get the brown out.

LILLIAN Okay. (She enters the apartment, sits JOSE down on the armchair, finds a pillow, puts it on his lap, hands him two Q-Tips and puts her head sideways on the pillow. She closes her eyes as he cleans first one ear and then the other.) I could fall asleep when you do that. It makes me feel like a fever.

JOSE Yes.

LILLIAN It feels so good. It's like a present ... Give me a bath, Pa. Give your little girl a bath. (JOSE pushes her off his lap.) I got your same eyes, don't I though?

JOSE You don't look nuffin like me. (Pause) Maybe you ain't even mine. I don't got no proof.

LILLIAN I got that same space between my eyes, like you got.

JOSE Show me.

LILLIAN That one.

(LILLIAN reaches out and touches JOSE on the bridge of his nose. JOSE pulls away abruptly catching his skin on LILLIAN's nail. There is blood.)

JOSE Don't touch me like that. You don't ever touch your father like that. (He pulls her tightly to him.)

LILLIAN I'm sorry, Papi.

JOSE You know what we gotta do now.

LILLIAN Please, no ... I'm a good girl. I don't want to.

JOSE Now. (He takes off his belt and puts it in her hand. He turns his back on her.)

LILLIAN I can't, Pa. Please don't make me. (JOSE takes off his shirt; his back is covered with scars.)

JOSE Make me bleed this time, Lily. I want to feel it in my heart.

(LILLIAN hits him across the back as JOSE holds the cross around his neck. Lights cross to the fire escape. LILLIAN moves there with the pillow. JOSE disappears into the shadows.)

Scene 4

LILLIAN lying down on the fire escape with her head on a pillow. Late night.

LILLIAN I din't wanna be fourteen. So I ast Mr. Marks and he said I should write to President Ford. So I did. And I tole him. I don' wanna be fourteen because thirteen was so bad. But he ain't never wrote back. So I had to turn. I din't wanna turn without Pa. But she don' let him in no more 'cause he made her bleed from her arm. But it wasn't a lot. And we got a lot of blood. I wanned to tell her that so she wouldn't think she was gonna die, but she acted like that. Like she was dying. But it was jus' blood. Ain't nuffin scary about it. (Silence)

I'm gonna stay here forever. I can see the moon so clear from here. I can see the stars and I can see the street. So I can see Papi coming ... He's coming to see jus' me. Papi ain't scared of me. (Pause) When I got my eyes closed I think he's gonna come up the fire escape and kiss me. He's not even gonna walk up – he's gonna run.

(Lights come up on MICHI at the window which begins the next scene.)

Scene 5

MICHI stands at the window shouting at LILLIAN.

MICHI GET ME A COOKING POT!

(LILLIAN comes into the apartment and brings MICHI a large cooking pot. MICHI sets it on the stove. On the table is a large book, a knapsack and a cardboard box.)

LILLIAN Is this big enough?

MICHI It'll do. Lock the door.

LILLIAN She got the key.

MICHI The chain.

(LILLIAN fastens the chain lock; MICHI lights the stove.)

LILLIAN Okay, I did it.

MICHI Give me the flowers.

LILLIAN (Hands her the cardboard box) I stopped picking when I got tired.

MICHI   That's enough. Pick out the most freshest ones. They work the best. *(They pick through the flowers.)*

LILLIAN   It feels better to pick the new ones.

MICHI   Yeah.

LILLIAN   Smooth and wet, like they're holding rain.

MICHI   *(Looking at a book)* Okay . . . now . . . (LILLIAN *takes each item from the knapsack as* MICHI *reads them off.)* Sulfur . . . Candle wax . . . we put them in the pot . . . melt them and add the marigolds to make them stink even more. Then we pour them into the test tubes.

LILLIAN   Marigolds are flowers, why do they make them stink?

MICHI   They're stinky flowers.

LILLIAN   Oh . . . We're gonna be rich, aren't we, Michi?

MICHI   You better believe it! At twenty-five cents a pop – Hey, you think we could charge fifty??

LILLIAN   Who's gonna spend that much on stink bombs?

MICHI   I'm gonna miss you, girl.

LILLIAN   Where are you going?

MICHI   I'm going. *(She puts the pot with all the ingredients on the stove, then picks up her knapsack.)* I got something else to show you, but first you gotta close your eyes and swear to God you won't throw it on the floor, no matter how much it scares you because it's something holy.

LILLIAN   I swear. *(She closes her eyes)*

MICHI   It's sacred. It's something beautiful. *(She hands* LILLIAN *a pair of panties soiled with menstrual blood.* LILLIAN *opens her eyes and they widen in disbelief as she stares at the panties.)* It's my sister Doris'. This is what a woman is. *(*LILLIAN *stares at the panties.)* Smell it!

LILLIAN   What?! *(She drops the panties on the floor.)*

MICHI   *(Pinching* LILLIAN*)* I told you not to do that! Now pick them up! *(She picks them up reverently.)* Smell it!

LILLIAN   What for?

MICHI   So you grow up. So you become a woman.

LILLIAN   I know what blood smells like.

MICHI   How do you know?

LILLIAN   Because I've cut myself.

MICHI   It's not the same, stupid! It's got stuff in it.

LILLIAN   What kinda stuff?

MICHI   Baby water.

LILLIAN   What's that?

MICHI   Stupid! It's the water that makes babies and it comes out of a woman every month. You gonna smell it now?

LILLIAN   *(Timidly sniffs it from a distance)* Smells like blood.

MICHI   It's blood but something else too. *(Pause)* Taste it!

LILLIAN   Uh-uhn. I'm not tasting that.

MICHI   Taste it. It's part of growing up.

LILLIAN   I would throw up.

MICHI   Yeah . . . That's what babies do.

LILLIAN   I'm not a baby.

MICHI   Prove it.

LILLIAN   Did you ever taste it?

MICHI   Sure.

LILLIAN   *(Holds out the panties to* MICHI*)* You first.

MICHI   I don't need to. I got my own. You only have to taste it when you don't got your own.

LILLIAN   Who says?

MICHI   Everybody says.

LILLIAN   What if I throw up?

MICHI   I can't keep playing with babies. I'm a woman now.

LILLIAN   Awright. I'll try it. *(Tries to lick the panties, but can't)* I can't.

MICHI   I'm going.

LILLIAN   Michi!

MICHI   Don't waste my fucking time. *(She starts to go.)*

LILLIAN   Okay. Look! *(She puts the panties up to her lips and licks them quickly. There is a silence.)*

MICHI   How did it taste?

LILLIAN   Like the blood you suck from a finger . . . . but sweeter.

MICHI   Sweeter?

LILLIAN   Yeah. Like a sweet flower. Like the ones we used to suck on when we played in the park.

MICHI   Like a flower?

LILLIAN   Yes. Like dandelions when you bite the heads off and suck on the stems.

MICHI   Fuck . . . You could tell all that from just one taste?

LILLIAN   Sure.
(Pause)

MICHI   You sure you didn't taste it before?

LILLIAN   Of course not. You? *(Pause)* You did taste it, didn't you?

MICHI   Of course I did. It was my idea, wasn't it?

LILLIAN Well then taste it, if it don't mean nuffin to you.
(MICHI throws the panties out the window; LILLIAN gasps. Long pause.)
LILLIAN You shoulda tasted it Michi. It tasted better than chocolate.
MICHI Nothing tastes better than chocolate, dummy.
LILLIAN This did . . . You mad at me?
MICHI Yeah.
LILLIAN How come?
MICHI Don't you got a mind of your own? If I told you to jump off the roof, would you do it?
LILLIAN I'm not allowed on the roof.
(MICHI sighs) I dunno . . . I don't think I would.
MICHI You don't think!
LILLIAN Maybe the building was on fire . . . maybe there's a reason.
MICHI What are you gonna do when I go away? You won't know when to wipe your butt.
LILLIAN Stop saying that! You don't gotta go nowheres.
MICHI You think I'm gonna stay in this dump the rest of my life?! No way.
LILLIAN Where you gonna go?
MICHI I don't know . . . Hollywood maybe.
LILLIAN Hollywood?! To be a movie star?
MICHI Nah . . . well, maybe. Who knows? If I'm there anything could happen.
LILLIAN I bet movie stars have a lot of clothes.
MICHI Yep. And everytime something gets dirty, they just throw it out.
LILLIAN Like Doris' panties.
MICHI Not like Doris' panties. Doris is a pig. She could catch herself, but she never bothers. It's terrible waking up in the morning next to this pool of blood. She just leaves it there, right next to me . . . When I move to Hollywood, I'm gonna sleep alone.
LILLIAN How can she catch herself? I thought it just comes, like boom.
MICHI Nah, your breasts get bigger.
LILLIAN *(Looking at her own chest)* How much bigger?
MICHI I don't know. Bigger. Swollen.
LILLIAN Swollen? Like somebody hit her? That happened to Georgina Vega. She was mugged and then they cut them off.
MICHI The muggers?
LILLIAN No, the doctors. Because they swolled up.

MICHI God! That's terrible. You mean, she don't got any anymore?
LILLIAN Nope. Nuffin. Flat. She got big scars there now, I bet.
MICHI I guess so. *(They both hug their chests.)* I hope I don't lose mine.
LILLIAN Yeah . . . you jus' got 'em.
MICHI *(Annoyed)* I had 'em for two years already. I'm a 34B now.
(The pot with the stink bombs explodes; they hurry to the stove.)
MICHI and LILLIAN Oh, shit!
(Lights cross to the fire escape. LILLIAN moves there as MICHI exits.)

Scene 6

Spring, 1975.
LILLIAN *on the fire escape, writing in a diary. She speaks haltingly as she writes. The sound of an elevated train rushing past.*

LILLIAN Dear Book: I love you. If I din't have you, I couldn't write about Ricky. He is my boyfriend. I love him very much. He is cute and when he grows up, he's gonna be a firemens. I think this is good because I like those trucks. He's gonna get me a hat, so in case I get caught in a fire, I won't get burned. And he's gonna get me an engagerment ring so we can get married when Mami says it's okay. He looks like a man already. He has a mustache and it tickles me. He has black eyes and real long eyelashes. He said he don't like his eyelashes because they point into his eye – not out, like other people's. He's got straight brown hair that he don't wash. I don't care if he wash it or not. It smells like him. I let him kiss me and we do other things. Now I'm gonna pray to God to protect him because he stays out late. I hope he gives me my engagement ring tomorrow so I can show Michi. She don't think anybody would marry me. Ha! Ha! She's wrong. I'm gonna make a house for me and him, so he don't have to walk around at night.
(From inside the apartment, CARMEN shouts for LILLIAN.)
CARMEN (OS) LILLIAN!!
LILLIAN That's all for today.
(She closes the book and kisses it. Lights on the inside of the apartment. CARMEN appears at the window and drags LILLIAN into the house.)

Scene 7

CARMEN *enters, calling* LILLIAN. *She is in a rage.*

CARMEN *(Grabbing* LILLIAN's *arm)* Answer me when I call you.

LILLIAN *(Pulling away from* CARMEN*)* You're hurting my arm.
*(*CARMEN *slaps* LILLIAN.*)*

CARMEN A lot more than that will hurt Miss! Take off your clothes!

LILLIAN No, Mami! Please!

CARMEN Don't make me rip them off your body! You want me to hit you? I don't want to! Don't make me act like your father! Don't make me treat you like an animal! *(*CARMEN *pulls off* LILLIAN's *sweater; they struggle.)*

CARMEN Let me see your arms.

LILLIAN *(Holding out her arms)* I din't do nuffin!

CARMEN I bet you did something with him. Tell me. Tell me what you did with that garbage. *(She holds* LILLIAN's *face in her hands.)* Tell me the truth.

LILLIAN I tole you the truth. He had respect for me.

CARMEN *(Letting go of* LILLIAN's *face)* Respect?! What do you know about that? *(She slaps* LILLIAN*)* There's some respect! *(She looks at* LILLIAN*)* You don't know respect! *(She pulls at* LILLIAN's *blouse)* Take them all off.

LILLIAN *(Struggling with her)* Why do you want to hurt me?

CARMEN *(Reaching beneath* LILLIAN's *skirt)* You let him touch you.

LILLIAN No! Mami, don't! He din't touch me there. He never touched me. Stop it! Please, stop! I love you!
*(*CARMEN *moves away from* LILLIAN.*)*

CARMEN You disgraced me! How could you do that to me?

LILLIAN I din't do nuffin.

CARMEN Tell me the truth! Tell me or get out of this house. Tell me!

LILLIAN Please! I don't wanna go nowhere else!

CARMEN Then tell me everything!

LILLIAN There ain't nuffin to tell. I swear!

CARMEN Is that what you want? You want me to kick you out?! *(Pause)* I can't stand to look at you.
*(*CARMEN *exits to the bedroom and slams the door behind her;* LILLIAN *pulls her*

sweater back on and exits sobbing. Lights change to afternoon light. JOSE *enters and moves to the altar.* LILLIAN *enters to begin Scene 8.)*

Scene 8

JOSE *is startled by* LILLIAN's *entrance.*

JOSE Who's that?? *(Pause; he sees who it is.)* Oh, Lily. Good. I thought it was your mother. *(He laughs drunkenly.)* You know how it is . . . So, how are you? LILLIAN *walks to the window.* JOSE *sits on the armchair.)* So?

LILLIAN *(Pause; she sits on the floor.)* I'm stupid. If he tole me to shit in a bag and bring it to him, I would. I'd do anything for him. He was my boyfriend. I loved him . . . He called me little sister and said he wouldn't touch me down there till I was ready. He had respect. He did. *(Pause)* But I shouldn't've given him no bag. *(Pause)* I found him. I pulled the needle out of his mouf and his blood flew up into my face. I wiped it off wif my sleeve. Then I held his head in my lap till the cops came. I thought he was cold, so I put my sweater on him. But he wasn't cold, Pa . . . *(Pause)* I'm never gonna throw the needle away. It's all I got from him.

JOSE A junkie, a fucking junkie! Why you crying for a fucking junkie? You stupid?!

LILLIAN He loved me, Pa. I know he did. *(Pause)*

JOSE I love you. *(Pause)*

LILLIAN You gonna stay this time?

JOSE You heard what she said. She don't want me no more.

LILLIAN That's jus' what she says only. You know how she is.

JOSE She didn't hurt you did she?

LILLIAN Not too bad.

JOSE What do you mean?

LILLIAN Not like you used to hurt her. *(Silence)* It was the rum. Right, Pa?

JOSE Who told you that?

LILLIAN Mami. She said you din't always mean to do it. It was the rum that ate you up. *(Pause)*

JOSE Your birthday's coming up, right? What can I get you?

LILLIAN You can't get me nuffin. You're

not no millionaire or nuffin. *(Pause)* How about a turtle?

JOSE Everytime I give you a pet, your mother feeds it poison.

LILLIAN That was an accident.

JOSE Uh huh . . .

LILLIAN She mixed up the fish food and the roach killer.

JOSE How did she do that?

LILLIAN They're both brown.

JOSE She has a reason for everything.

LILLIAN She wouldn't kill them on purpose.

JOSE Believe what you want.

LILLIAN You want some money? *(She gets a rolled-up stocking from the closet.)* You want some?

JOSE Just to get through this week. I'm getting a job. I'll pay her back. *(Pause)*

LILLIAN Sure, Pa.

JOSE Does she hit you for letting me in the house?

LILLIAN Don't worry.

JOSE You shouldn't let her hit you.

LILLIAN No. *(She hands JOSE a small roll of bills.)* You want some coffee?

JOSE I better go. She'll be here soon, huh?

LILLIAN Yeah. A turtle, okay?
(They walk to the door; LILLIAN opens it.)

JOSE What kind of turtle?

LILLIAN You know . . . *(She makes a circle with both hands.)* This big, okay?

JOSE Okay.

LILLIAN The kind wif the pointy head. The kind that stays in the water all the time. So I can put him in wif my fish.

JOSE You don't got no fish.

LILLIAN That's okay. I pretend I got fish.
(JOSE nods and exits; LILLIAN closes the door; the light in the room gets brighter; she puts on a new sweater. As it falls over her head, CARMEN and MICHI enter with a lit birthday cake.)

Scene 9

CARMEN *and* MICHI *sing "Happy Birthday" to* LILLIAN *who blows out the candles.*

MICHI *and* LILLIAN *(They read the top of the cake)* Hap-po-Bird-day-to-Lil-lani. *(They laugh.)*

CARMEN Keep laughing! Wait until you taste how good it is.

MICHI I'll bet it tastes good.

LILLIAN Let's eat. *(She cuts the cake into three enormous pieces and puts them on plates.)* For you and you and me. *(They each taste it.)*

ALL Mmmm. It's wonderful. Delicious.

LILLIAN It's the best cake, mami.

CARMEN *(Laughing)* But it does look strange, doesn't it?

LILLIAN That's okay.

MICHI I'm glad you didn't have a stupid sweet fifteen party. With the gowns and everything. That's so stupid. Wanda had one of those. Cuban's so stuck-up.

CARMEN Do you want your present now or later?

LILLIAN Now.
(CARMEN places a wrapped package at LILLIAN's feet and MICHI puts a small box on her lap.)

LILLIAN Which first? *(CARMEN and MICHI shrug their shoulders and then point at their own gift.)* I'll open this little one first.

CARMEN *(Jokingly)* It looks like an umbrella.

LILLIAN Oh, Mom!

CARMEN Sorry.
(LILLIAN opens the box; it contains a silver pin.)

LILLIAN Michi! Your social studies medal. It's beautiful! You don't want to give it to me, do you?

MICHI That's okay. I want you to have it.

LILLIAN But it's – it's your medal. I don't deserve it.

MICHI Sure you do.
(LILLIAN pulls a charcoal drawing of herself and MICHI out of the box.)

LILLIAN I love it! You draw so pretty . . .

MICHI Now you can't ever forget me, Lily. *(To CARMEN)* Mrs. Newman told us that in Africa they believe if you have a picture of somebody, you have a part of their soul.

CARMEN *(Sarcastically)* Isn't that interesting?

LILLIAN It'll be safe wif me. *(She awkwardly kisses MICHI on the cheek.)*

MICHI Okay, okay. Let's not get too corny here . . . Shoot.

LILLIAN You have a part of my soul too.

MICHI Fuck. Well, okay, okay.
(LILLIAN sits down, picks up the other package and shakes it.)

CARMEN Watch out! You might break it. *(She smiles; LILLIAN opens the package. It is a book.)*

LILLIAN (*With tears in her voice*) It's so beautiful . . . how can you give it away?

CARMEN It's staying in the family. That's all Papa would want. That's what I want.

LILLIAN God! It's in Spanish too. I never had nuffin in Spanish before. (*She goes to* CARMEN *with the open book.*) Read it to me.

CARMEN I—I don't—feel like it.

LILLIAN Please! I never heard real Spanish.

CARMEN What do you think we talk?

LILLIAN I don't know. You know! C'mon, Ma. Please.

MICHI Pretty please!

LILLIAN and MICHI Cherry on top, cream on the bottom, pretty please!!

CARMEN Okay. (LILLIAN *kisses her.*) Okay. (*She opens the book and pretends to read, but really recites from memory.*) "En un lugar de la Mancha, de cuyo nombre no quiero acordarme, no ha mucho tiempo que vivia un hidalgo de los de lanza en astillero, adarga antigua, rocin flaco y galgo corredor. Una olla de algo mas vaca que carnero, salpicon las mas noches, duelos y quebrantos los sabados, lentejas los viernes, algun palomino de añadidura los domingos, consumian las tres partes de su hacienda." My father read that part to me all the time. It's inside my heart now. I used to close my eyes and listen to those words and pretend I was somewhere else—somewhere where a caballero would keep me safe.

(CARMEN *closes the book and hands it to* LILLIAN; LILLIAN *and* MICHI *applaud.*)

LILLIAN That was beautiful. You knew just what I wanted. Thank you.

CARMEN You're welcome.

LILLIAN I wish Papi could see it.

CARMEN He's seen it.

LILLIAN Where is he? You said you were gonna ask him to come.

CARMEN If you're so crazy to see him, why don't you go visit him?! I don't want him in my house anymore. I tole you that.

(LILLIAN *goes to the wastebasket and throws away the rest of her cake.*)

CARMEN Lily! (LILLIAN *goes to the door.*) Come back here! Come here right now! (LILLIAN *returns and stands in front of* CARMEN.)

LILLIAN What?

(CARMEN *hugs her tightly.*)

CARMEN That's what.

LILLIAN You can't stop me from seeing him.

CARMEN It scares me when you go to him.

LILLIAN He won't hurt me, Mami.

(CARMEN *hugs* LILLIAN *again and she hugs her back.* MICHI *gets up and moves to the door.*)

MICHI I better get home. You know how my parents are . . .

(*They do not respond and* MICHI *exits.* CARMEN *goes into the bedroom and* LILLIAN *takes off the sweater. Lights change to early morning lights.* LILLIAN *crosses to the stove.*)

Scene 10

Early morning. LILLIAN *makes coffee in silence. Then she turns on the radio to a soul station and dances while she cooks.* CARMEN *enters in a bathrobe, goes directly to the radio, turns it off and sits at the kitchen table, lighting a cigarette.* LILLIAN *brings her a cup of coffee.*

LILLIAN You want milk?

CARMEN Of course I want milk. You think I changed overnight?

LILLIAN You never know. Sometimes people want somefin different.

CARMEN That's one thing I taught you good. How to make coffee.

LILLIAN Mami?

CARMEN Yes.

LILLIAN You know that story you tole me, about the Sun and the Moon?

CARMEN Mmmhmmm.

LILLIAN I think I need a somebody too. Just like that. Like the Sun.

CARMEN Sun?! It's too early for this.

LILLIAN I can't stand being alone anymore.

CARMEN You're too young to get married.

LILLIAN I don't mean that.

CARMEN What do you mean?

LILLIAN Nuffin . . . When I was little, I always wanted a little sister.

CARMEN I wanted a big brother who would beat up my other brothers when they beat on me.

LILLIAN They bothered you a lot?

CARMEN What do you think!?

LILLIAN I'm sorry.

(*Pause*)

CARMEN Most people like to drink coffee in the morning, but I like it at night too. When I can't sleep because I'm thinking too much. Coffee always clears my mind.

LILLIAN Ma?

CARMEN Turn the radio back on – to a good station, okay?

(LILLIAN *puts on a Spanish station.*)

LILLIAN Ma—

CARMEN I feel like dancing. (*She gets up and dances around the room.*) Your mother's a good dancer you know.

LILLIAN I know. I seen you dance before.

CARMEN When?

LILLIAN Wif pa. A lot of times. Right here in the kitchen.

CARMEN That's where the radio is.

LILLIAN You still love him, don't you?

CARMEN (*Turns the radio off*) I miss dancing with him.

LILLIAN Why'd you marry him?

CARMEN He was skinny, like a stick. He looked like he needed somebody to cook for him. I felt sorry for him.

LILLIAN Did it make you feel good inside?

CARMEN For a little while.

LILLIAN That's better than nuffin. I don't got nuffin.

CARMEN You'll get something. Don't worry.

LILLIAN You want sugar?

CARMEN Nobody has coffee without sugar. (LILLIAN *brings her a cup of coffee and spills it.*) Lily! What's the matter with you?!

LILLIAN I'm sorry. (*She cleans up the spill.*) You want a donut? I bought 'em fresh. Yesterday.

CARMEN When did you ever see me eat a donut? You know the only thing I can eat in the morning are apple turnovers.

LILLIAN I forgot.

CARMEN You forgot?! You forget everything . . . Those pants are too tight on you. They show your little line.

(LILLIAN *brings her a fresh cup of coffee.*)

LILLIAN I need new ones, I guess. Ma?

(CARMEN *takes a sip of coffee.*)

CARMEN What?

LILLIAN Nuffin.

CARMEN What do you mean nothing? Are you sick or something?

LILLIAN (*Pacing*) Uhn uhn.

CARMEN Get me a donut.

LILLIAN (*She hurries to get it*) Chocolate?

CARMEN Sugar. (LILLIAN *brings her the donut.*) Thank you. (LILLIAN *stands over her.*) What?? What's got into you?

LILLIAN Nuffin. (*Long pause*) Oh, Ma! I got—I . . . Don't hit me, okay?

CARMEN Lillian!

LILLIAN (*Moves away from* CARMEN) I got a present inside me, okay?! (CARMEN *rises and crosses to* LILLIAN *who cringes against a wall as she approaches.*) Please, Mami! Please! I want it so bad. It's the only thing I got that's his.

CARMEN His?! Oh, my god Lillian! It's not that junkie's baby?! (*Shaking her*) Is it? Talk to me! Is it?

LILLIAN I loved him, Mami. I loved him so much. He never did nuffin to hurt me. He was always my friend – it din't matter how dumb I was or how pretty. He loved me like I was.

CARMEN Like you was? You was like nothing! You can't love nothing! If he loved you, he woulda stopped taking drugs and be here to take care of his baby! I can tell you right now, I'm not taking care of it!

LILLIAN You don't got to. I can do it myself. I don't need you for nuffin.

CARMEN That's right. Go in the street and have your baby. You don't need me. You don't need shit from me. I'm just a—

LILLIAN Ma, stop it! Don't you see? It's my moon, but it ain't never gonna go away like yours did. It's gonna smell my hands and it's gonna know it's safe. It'll take all the badness outta me because it's good, like the baby Jesus.

CARMEN You don't know nothing about the baby Jesus so don't even say his name in this house. He's ashamed of you.

LILLIAN Not no more. He likes me now. Now he knows me. I pray all the time now I got somefin . . . (*She takes* CARMEN'S *head and puts it on her belly.*) Listen . . . (CARMEN *faints.* LILLIAN *helps her to the bedroom. Lights change to evening light.* JOSE *enters with a Christmas tree which he places by the altar.*)

Scene 11

JOSE *climbs up the fire escape. He's drunk and bleeding from his face and arm. He stumbles up the stairs, looks into the room, and thinks better of coming in. Instead, he continues up the fire escape, spots* LILLIAN'S *diary, opens it and begins to read. He drinks throughout the scene.*

JOSE (*Reading*) "Dear Book: Today is the last day I'm gonna write in here because this is for kids and I'm not no kid no more." *(Pause)* Jesus! *(Continues reading)*

"I got a real job today, working in a hospital. They put me to folding clothes and this is good because I don't got to see no blood or nuffin." *(He chuckles.)* "I get the clothes when they're already clean. Ma's gonna like this job. They pay me good money so I can give some to Ma to take a taxi to the church so the ladies in the church see her and think she's rich or somefin, so then they talk to her again. They don't talk to Ma no more because she got me here wif a big belly and everything and she don' kick me out even though I'm a woman now." *(He reacts with anger, continues to read with his agitation growing.)*

"Ma says she don' care about the ladies. We are good friends now. Ma is my best friend because Michi don' talk to me no more and she moved away. I think it's because of my belly that she hate me now. I know she hate me because she din't even say good-bye or nuffin to me. But I don't hate her. I miss her very much. Sometimes I cry thinking about her and about how she left me like Ricky did . . . and Papi did. But when Ma see me doing this she says 'Why you crying for a stupid girl like that? She wasn't no boyfriend or nuffin.' So I gotta stop crying. So I gotta say good-bye to you, Book. Because sometimes I see what I wrote down and it makes me cry and womans don't cry. Because then Mami hits me. But she don' hurt me. She jus' scared I ain't gonna stop."

(Silence; he begins to cry.) I'm scared too, Lily. I don' got no place. I jus' wanna – I jus' . . . I used to know about love. I had that . . . Now alls I got is blood.

(Silence; JOSE puts the diary back in its hiding place, finishes his pint of rum, closes his eyes and pours the dregs onto his face. Pause.)

Scene 12

Late night. The people on stage are only visible as shadows. They are each in their own separate worlds. They do not touch each other or look at each other as they speak.

JOSE I want you. I want you to lick the blood off my face. I want your tongue on my eyes.

LILLIAN Ma's real sick. She's too sick for company. You should go home.

CARMEN Lily! How could you let him into my house?! Don't you hear nothing when I talk?!

JOSE Don't talk to her like that! She's a good girl. She's my sky. Mi cielo.

CARMEN You don't say nothing to me you piece of shit! She din't come outta you!

LILLIAN Pa—

JOSE Don't call me that. I ain't nuffin to you. You only care about this old lady.

LILLIAN No, pa!

CARMEN Get out! The saints will keep you out!

(The sound of ceramic shattering against a wall)

LILLIAN Mami, stop! Don't you see he's hurt? Leave him alone.

CARMEN How can you protect such an animal, Lillian? How? Tell me how?

JOSE Don't you hit her. Don't you touch her.

LILLIAN Leave Ma alone!

JOSE Don't touch my arms. You never touch a boxer's arms. You don't know what he's gonna do with 'em. He might hit you and then you can't eat no more food. You can't eat no food wif no teeth.

LILLIAN I ain't gonna let you hurt, Mami.

JOSE You women don't tell me what to do. You don't tell me what to do because I'm your father and your husband. I am the boxer. They brought me here to be a boxer. I tell you what to do. I made you.

CARMEN Who are you kidding? You're just a stupid, lazy Spic. You weren't never no boxer . . . The minute you got here alls you ever did was put tiny frozen shrimp into teeny cups with red sauce. That's all you ever did. The only job you ever had. You are a stupid man. Stupid men don't know nothing about fighting. You wanna fight? Don't pick on little girls with little boys inside them. Hit me. C'mon. I'm ready for you. I want you to hit me.

JOSE Don't say that.

CARMEN I should've killed you on our wedding night. When you first passed out in my bed. I should've crushed your head.

JOSE *(crying)* Do it . . . it don't matter if you do it.

(JOSE runs out. Lights come up on the apartment which is in shambles.)

Scene 13

There is a single bed by the oven. The door is open. Many saints are missing from the altar. CARMEN *lies on the bed and* LILLIAN *has been speaking on the phone. She is eight months pregnant. She slams down the receiver. She speaks to* CARMEN.

LILLIAN   He won't come.

CARMEN   He won't?

LILLIAN   No, mami.

CARMEN   Did you tell him that I forgave him?

LILLIAN   Yes. Yes, I tole him. I tole him. How many times do I have to tell you? Yes, yes, yes I tole him!

CARMEN   You have such bad manners, Lily.

LILLIAN   You should know.

CARMEN   I'm cold. Turn the stove up.

LILLIAN   *(Turning the oven knob; it is on full)* It's all the way up. *(She picks up a* Daily News.*)* Do you want me to finish reading this paper to you or not?

CARMEN   Why are you so angry all the time? Am I so mean to you?

LILLIAN   No, you're a saint. Saint Carmen. They have a statue of you in all the churches.

CARMEN   If you're going to scream at me, don't come near me. I don't need you to scream at me.

LILLIAN   Okay. Fine. It saves me some time.

CARMEN   Good. Don't waste your time on me.

LILLIAN   I work hard all day, Ma. And I come home and I have stuff to do. I don't want to waste my time asking him to come. You want to ask him? You ask him. He beat the shit out of you and you still want him to come!

CARMEN   I'm going to die, Lillian.

LILLIAN   So what?! You're not very smart!

CARMEN   And you! With a belly like that, you're not too smart either! You're gonna raise your baby without a father! You don't have nobody! Nobody! At least I had somebody.

LILLIAN   You call that somebody! I don't need somebody like that! I don't need somebody to bother me.

CARMEN   It's gonna kill you to have that baby.

LILLIAN   It didn't kill you to have me.

CARMEN   When I had you, my female parts rotted out. Piece by piece, a little at a time. They got took out or they fell out. You turned my life bad.

LILLIAN   So why did you have me? Why did you bother to have me?

CARMEN   I din't have no choice. Your father wanted you. I would've given you away. *(LILLIAN starts to cry.)* What?! What's that? Dead tears. You don't care! You never cared whether I loved you or not. When did you ever care what I felt?!

LILLIAN   *(Crying)* I did! I did!

CARMEN   No, you didn't. I could've dropped dead for all you cared. Your father was all you cared about.

LILLIAN   No, Mami!

CARMEN   I got nothing from you! Nothing! Everything I came with is what I got. Nothing. Get out of here. Go to your room! Get out and let me die in peace. *(A silence)* Get me a couple of packs of Winstons. Take money.

LILLIAN   Mami!

CARMEN   I'll pay for it.

LILLIAN   You can't smoke.

CARMEN   I can do anything I want.

LILLIAN   Do you want to die?

CARMEN   I don't care if I die. I'm tired of you. Tired of your father. I'm even tired of that little boy in there. He's gonna be a boy. Don't you say he's gonna be a girl. Paulita said a boy.

LILLIAN   I don't care what Paulita said. It's a girl.

CARMEN   So, what are you gonna call her? Lillian?

LILLIAN   Not Lillian.

CARMEN   What then?

LILLIAN   I don't know.

CARMEN   What's her last name gonna be? Lillian Junior? At least you had a last name. You better know what you're gonna call her or they ask you when you're half asleep and you don't know what you're saying. The nurse who helped with you was Lillian.

LILLIAN   Is that why you called me Lillian?

CARMEN   Yeah. She was leaning over me when I was waking up and I saw the name Lillian on her chest. It looked like flowers.

LILLIAN   Like Lily of the Valley?

CARMEN   Yeah. Maybe.

LILLIAN   I'm gonna call my girl Carmen. Is that okay wif you?

CARMEN   Sure. Lots of people have that name.

LILLIAN   I'm naming her after you.

CARMEN   You can call her anything you want.

LILLIAN   I said, I'm naming her after you.

CARMEN   Don't bother.

LILLIAN   Oh, Ma—

CARMEN   What?

LILLIAN   Nuffin. You want me to finish reading you the paper now?

CARMEN   No. Tell me what you did today.

LILLIAN   I worked hard. I never folded so many clothes in my whole life. And it was so hot in that laundry, I thought I was gonna faint or somefin.

CARMEN   Is that why you were late?

LILLIAN   Nah . . . I went to get a new dress. You wanna see it?

CARMEN   You had me worried for nothing.

LILLIAN   It's real pretty. I like it because it's purple. I like purple.

CARMEN   You always did.

LILLIAN   It's my favorite color next to yellow. The sales lady said I couldn't have a yellow dress, because it's winter, but I think yellow would be nice in the winter.

CARMEN   You look good in yellow.

LILLIAN   Yeah. This dress is nice though even if it is purple. It has big sleeves so I can hide things in them. Like the lady was saying, you could put Kotex and lipstick and everything in there and nobody would know. That's good because I don't like carrying a purse. You want me to show it to you?

CARMEN   Yeah.

(LILLIAN takes the dress out of a bag and puts it on over her clothes, showing the sleeves.)

LILLIAN   See what I mean?

CARMEN   Let me feel your belly.

(LILLIAN guides her hand to her stomach.)

LILLIAN   Three kids came up to me in the subway today and started pulling on my purse and pushing on my belly and poking me. I was trying to get them off me and nobody helped me. It hurt me because I was so gassy. All these mens go passing by and they don't even look. And as they were pulling at me, I think "where are these boys' mothers?" I hope my baby always has his mother to tell him what to do. And then I felt somefin I

never felt before—my baby turned himself full around, it was like I was walking backwards. But what an amazing thing. In my stomach, this beautiful little thing that was turning and turning. I know he wanted his mom to be okay. But more than that, I thought all of a sudden that those boys were just somebody's babies. And I looked deep into the littlest ones eyes . . . and a minute later, I was slapping the shit out of him. My baby turned again and it was happy because his mommy was gonna be okay. They left me alone after that. Even now, when I'm ready to pop nobody bothers. They keep away. They know I'm gonna be somebody's mommy. It's gonna be somefin.

CARMEN   *(Drowsy)* I pray to God it is . . . I'm gonna go to sleep now.

LILLIAN   Have a good night. *(She gets up.)*

CARMEN   Watch me sleep for a little while. I sleep better when you watch me.

(LILLIAN sits holding CARMEN's hand; CARMEN closes her eyes.)

CARMEN   It's hot like a beach here . . . I can smell the salt now. *(CARMEN dies; LILLIAN does not at first notice; then she does.)*

LILLIAN   Mami? MA?! *(She feels labor pains begin.)* NO! Not now, God, please, not now . . .

(LILLIAN goes into labor as the lights go down.)

Scene 14

The sound of an elevated train rushing by. LILLIAN moves to the fire escape, gets her diary and returns into the house, by the stove where a cardboard box, with Joey in it, is on the kitchen table.

LILLIAN   Dear Book: Hello again. You know what I did yesterday? Guess? Nah! Yep! I went to the store and asked the man for a newspaper and he give it to me for nuffin. He said I had big eyes and people wif big eyes don't gotta pay for newspapers because . . . because they don't. Man, If I knew this before I wouldn'ta never not read 'em, you know. But alls I wanned was the cartoons to put 'em up on "Babyhair's" wall. That's my secret name for Joey. When I touch his hair it feel like a rainbow. He's one of those people, you know. The kind that got their sweetness on their heads. It's light. He's like a blonde. He almost looks like a movie star. Almost. *(Pause)* I always forgot what I was saying. *(Pause)* Oh. I put the cartoons up on his wall so he can learn how to read. But right now he jus' thinks it's a big toy he can't get at yet. I keep all his toys together in a big box, I got from the supermarket. It smells like vegetables, so all his toys smell like that too . . . When I get hungry, I hold his teddy up to my nose. It's almost like eating. *(Pause)*

As soon as Babyhair's old enough, I'm gonna get a job running numbers and bring some money into this house. It's gonna be a fine house. *(Pause)* For just me and you, Joey. You're my only best friend now. *(Pause)*

I saw Michi on the street. I could've jumped on her and hugged her. She's been gone too long. She's not like me anymore. She's somebody else. Somebody that's going somewhere . . . and what am I? I've got three things that are mine – you, Don Quixote and the *Wizard of Oz* book I shared wif Michi. She should have won it. Mrs. Weiner just din't like her and liked me better. She should – she had me in seventh grade for two years. I just couldn't add anything up. I couldn't see two apples plus two apples and see four apples. I saw apple pies or birds picking at the apples or beautiful orchards filled wif apple trees, even though I din't know what an apple tree looks like. I mean, I seen them in books, but I've never touched one. I never grabbed an apple off a tree, right there, where it was created. I used to pretend I was this big, fat apple tree about to bloom. I thought this must be the way it feels, about to explode wif somefin beautiful. I wish I could see that place where things actually grow. *(Pause)* You're too quiet . . . babies shouldn't always be so quiet.
(There's a knock on the door. LILLIAN *crosses to it and* JOSE *is there.)*

Scene 15

LILLIAN *opens the front door.* JOSE *stands there, all cleaned up and in a new suit.*

JOSE Baby!
LILLIAN Papi?

JOSE Well, yeah. Do I look so different?
LILLIAN Yeah, you do.
*(*JOSE *sits on the armchair.)*
JOSE So where is he?
*(*LILLIAN *gets* JOEY *from the bedroom and hands him to* JOSE.*)*
LILLIAN He saved my life.
JOSE All by himself? What's his name?
LILLIAN Joey.
JOSE Joey?
LILLIAN Joey Rivera. Hard to remember, ain't it?
JOSE Joey . . . Joey. That's not bad. Sounds like Jose.
LILLIAN That's what it is, Pa.
JOSE Lily, look at those arms! This boy's gonna be a boxer, like his grandpa. *(He offers the baby his finger.)* Ah! Look how he holds my hand! Another Hercules! *(Pause)*
LILLIAN I need money, papi. You have some? You look like you do.
JOSE Yeah, I got some. I got a job now. I'm working in the building.
LILLIAN I never asked you before but I need it for Joey. I can't go back to work yet and I—
JOSE How much do you want?
LILLIAN How much you got?
JOSE I'm not going to give it to you – I'll give it to him.
LILLIAN He'll give it to me. Right, Joey? He loves his mommy.
JOSE What does he need? I'll go buy it. I wouldn't give you any cash. Who knows what you would buy? Drugs or—
LILLIAN I don't do that. Can't you even tell that much?
JOSE We should toast to his health, Lily. Don't tell me you don't drink.
LILLIAN Just a little. *(*JOSE *gets a bottle of rum and two glasses.)* It makes the baby sleepy.
JOSE What?
LILLIAN It goes into his milk and then he gets drunk or somefin. They explained to me at the hospital. I'm not supposed to ever get drunk no more.
JOSE Incredible! *(Raising his glass and rising to his feet)* To Joey Hercules Rivera. May his life be better than ours. Better than his mami's and better than his grandma's. Better than his grandpa's and his grandpa's mami.
LILLIAN Amen. *(She reaches for the baby.)*
JOSE What! You think I can't hold my own

grandson? I'm drunk but I'm not stupid.

LILLIAN Sit down, Pa.

JOSE Alright. I'll sit down . . . *(He sits and cradles the baby in his arms quietly.)* So how is your mother? They say she's very sick.

LILLIAN Papi . . . let me take him. It's almost time for his milk.

JOSE He's alright. See? He likes me. I put him to sleep.

LILLIAN Your breaf probably knocked him out.

JOSE It's good for him to sleep. I like to sleep. Tell me about your mother.

LILLIAN She's dead, pa. She's been dead for six weeks already. Don't you remember? We did the rosario by her grave? Don't you remember? I came to get you and you wore the blue suit papabuelo left you and we went to the cemetery. *(A silence)*

JOSE I didn't take her money. I put it all back. Here. *(He takes out some money.)* You can leave him with me when you go shopping. – You don't trust me. I don't blame you.

LILLIAN You better go now.

JOSE I just got here. Have another little drink with me.

LILLIAN No, pa. It's time for you to go. I gotta put Joey to bed.

JOSE He's sleeping already.

LILLIAN I have to put him in his bed. *(Taking* JOEY*)* Good-bye, now. *(He pours himself another drink.)* You don't change, do you?

JOSE Why should I? Nuffin' else does.

LILLIAN *(Pause; with a small smile)* Joey's gonna paint pictures like this one. *(Pulls out a drawing)* Hmmm . . .

JOSE That tree don' got no leaves on it.

LILLIAN That's okay. It ain't really a tree.

JOSE What's it?

LILLIAN It's God. I seen him, Pa. Like you used to. There's places where he's everywhere. He comes down waterfalls and he sings in a circle. He's got sweet fruit. And my baby's gonna taste that fruit.

JOSE Baby? *(Remembers)* Yeah . . . Hercules, right? Yeah. *(Laughs)* He's—he's jus' like me, Lily.

LILLIAN He ain't one pissy-shit like you. *(She fills his tumbler to the brim.)*

JOSE That's my baby girl!

LILLIAN You wanna go somewhere, Pa?

JOSE I jus' got here . . . *(*LILLIAN *gets a small globe and puts it in front of* JOSE.*)* Oh.

LILLIAN You first. *(*JOSE *spins the globe and then stops it with a finger.)* New York.

JOSE I hate this game. *(*LILLIAN *spins it with her eyes closed and stops it with a finger.)*

LILLIAN Shit. I always get the fuckin' ocean.

JOSE I like the water.

LILLIAN You know how ta swim. *(Pause)*

JOSE Don' you get lonely here?

LILLIAN I like being alone. Then there ain't nobody to make you feel left out. *(Pause)*

JOSE Scratch my arms. Please, baby. *(*LILLIAN *runs her nails lightly across his arms.)* Harder. Scratch my arms, baby.

LILLIAN Pa . . .

JOSE Use your nails.

LILLIAN I don' got no more nails.

JOSE Everybody got nails! What you think? You some kind of animal wif no fuckin' nails? What's that? A fish or somefin?

LILLIAN A turtle, Pa. Like the one you ain't never got me. *(She scratches his arms.)*

JOSE Your Mami used to rub my arms like that, so soft . . .

LILLIAN Do you remember how Mami smelled? I remember . . . sweaty and warm and sweet like sugar. But I don't see her face no more . . . just a smell. I bet she din't smell like that to nobody but me. *(*JOSE *kisses* LILLIAN *passionately. She pushes him away, holding onto his hands.)* Your hands are too skinny, Pa. I can feel all the bones.

JOSE I always loved your hands, Carmen. When I first saw 'em, I first fell in love. They was holding some rosary beads and when you counted off ten more Hail Marys, I wanned to put my ten fingers inside you. I wanned to feel up inside you till I had my hands around your heart. I could always feel your heart down there, Carmen. I wanned to touch your heart.

LILLIAN I ain't Carmen!

JOSE *(Flinging her across the room)* Then you ain't nuffin to me. *(He runs out the door.)* *(Lights on the fire escape.* LILLIAN *runs to it. She sits there in a long silence as the lights change from night to day.)*

Scene 16

Before the lights come up, we hear CARMEN
saying the Hail Mary in Spanish.

VOICE OF CARMEN Dios te salve Maria,
llena eres de gracia; el Señor es contigo;
bendita tu eres entre todas las mujeres, y
bendito es el fruto de tu vientre, Jesus.
Santa Maria, Madre de Dios, ruega por
nosotros pecadores, ahora y en la hora de
nuestra muerte. Amen.

When the prayer ends, lights up on LILLIAN
who is replacing all the candles on the altar.
She dusts off the saints and places them
around Joey. Then she kneels in front of the
altar and begins to pray.

LILLIAN Hail Mary, full of grace, the lord
is wif thee. Blessed art thou among
women and blessed is the fruit of thy
womb, Jesus. Holy Mary, mother of God,
Pray for us sinners now and at the hour
of our deaf, Amen.
   Dear Mary, I'm praying to you cause I
guessed you'd unnerstan. I mean . . . You
know what I mean, right? Uhmm, Mary, I
wanned to ask you somefin. I hope that's
okay. I jus wanned to know, if—Don'
matter . . . not at all. Stupid question . . .
(Pause) Hail Mary, full of grace . . . *(Pause)*
Hail Mary, full of grace . . . *(Pause)* Mary?
(Pause) Nobody?
(There is a banging on the door; LILLIAN
turns to it. She looks at the door, then looks
back at the altar, then looks at the door, goes
to it, and speaks to it.)
LILLIAN Mary?! (MICHI *shouts "Lily" from*
behind the door.) Michi?? (LILLIAN *flings*
open the door and turns her back on MICHI
who enters shyly.) Don' say nuffin to me!
You jus' move away wifout even tellin'
me where you're going.
MICHI I just told you why I did that! Don't
you fucking listen!
LILLIAN No. I'm too stupid, remember?
MICHI Shit! Are you listening now? I
couldn't. My mom and dad wouldn't let
me.
LILLIAN Since when are you listening to
them?
MICHI Since I don't got enough money to
pay my own way through college.
LILLIAN That's right. The college girl.
What are you doing hanging around here?

Can't learn nuffin from me. I'm too
stupid. All I do is work in a stinking
laundry for twelve hours every day.
MICHI God, Lily! I'm sorry!
LILLIAN Don't feel sorry for me! I do
okay.
MICHI I bet . . .
LILLIAN What do you care?!
MICHI You're still my best friend.
LILLIAN You say good-bye to your best
friend. You don' jus' go.
MICHI I can't explain it any better than I
already did.
LILLIAN Yeah . . . A lot of things are hard
to explain. Mami died at Christmas time
and I can't explain that. We fought up
until the very last minute. I got real mad
at her and I said don't you know who's
been keeping you alive, I say. She just
grabs her beads and starts screaming out
her rosary. She knows that's the only
thing to shut me up.
MICHI Maybe she didn't know it, but she
loved you.
LILLIAN Why are you here? You wanna
make yourself feel good about where
you're at? Need somebody lowdown to
look and feel proud you ain't that? Is that
it? Go home, whitey.
MICHI You're just as white as I am. You
can get out.
LILLIAN I ain't as smart as you.
MICHI You don't have to be smart. You just
gotta get tired of seeing your friends
falling dead on the streets wif needles
sticking—
LILLIAN You don't know nuffin about it!
MICHI I know enough. It's this place. It's
dirt. It's a place where people die. I
passed by my old building the other day
and it was gone. Just like that. Like we
never played there. There was a pile of
broken stone and glass where my house
used to be. And the schoolyard's now a
monument-making factory. Row after row
of tombstones for sale. I bet it costs more
to buy one there than any other place in
America. People here are proud of their
funerals. Gotta have a nice stone . . . it
shows what your priorities are. Get the
fuck out was my priority. And you should
get out too.
LILLIAN So you come to make me feel like
shit.
MICHI I came to give you money.
LILLIAN How much?

MICHI   A hundred dollars. I been saving it for a long time.

LILLIAN   I don't want your money.

MICHI   Take your baby and get the fuck out of here. I saw you on the street, carrying that box in front of you. *(Pause)* You looked like it was filled wif gold. I bet she's beautiful. She deserves better.

LILLIAN   He. And a hundred dollars ain't taking us too far.

MICHI   That's all I got. *(Pause)* What's his name?

LILLIAN   Joey.

MICHI   *(Seeing the baby for the first time.)* Can I hold him?

LILLIAN   Not now . . . I don't want to wake him . . . he ain't been sleeping so good . . .

MICHI   Please take the money.

LILLIAN   I'll take it for him. He's gonna go to college. *(Pause)* Is that where you been?

MICHI   Almost. I begin in September. I'm the youngest student in the freshmen class. It's fucking amazing what reading can do for you . . . I know it'll be the best thing that ever happened to me . . . I mean, next to meeting you, of course. Do you remember when we met? I do. You were in first grade and I was in kindergarten and I was going into the candy store to buy wax lips.

LILLIAN   Remember that stuff? Tasted terrible. We lived on it . . . Your hair was real long, almost to my knees. And those black girls put their chewing gum in it.

MICHI   That's right. And you beat them up for me, and walked me home.

LILLIAN   They had to cut your hair because we couldn't get the gum out. Jesus, you looked funny.

MICHI   Like a bird.

LILLIAN   Michon-Pichon . . .

MICHI   Jesus, Lily. You can't stay here!

LILLIAN   I think you're the one who can't stay. *(Pause)* It's late. You better go.

MICHI   I guess so . . . but I'll come back real soon . . . when he's feeling better, okay?

LILLIAN   Yeah. Sure.

MICHI   You know, it's about time. I been waiting five years for you to do that.

LILLIAN   What?

MICHI   For you to tell me off. But I think I liked you better when you were my slave. What do you think that means?

LILLIAN   Nuffin. Nuffin means nuffin.

MICHI   Is everything so easy for you? Don't you ever think about nothing?!

LILLIAN   I think about a lot of things . . . I think about Papi and how sick he is and how I don' love him no more, but he still leaves me money for the baby . . . And I think . . . I think how come my baby's always sick. Babies shouldn't get sick like that . . .

MICHI   What are you talking about, Lily? Why don't you take him to the hospital?

LILLIAN   Because . . . because they might take him away from me, Michi. They do that . . . sometimes.

MICHI   No, they don't – not if you're a good mother.

LILLIAN   They can take everything away from you. But if I stay here like Mami wanned me too, it'll be okay, he'll get better . . . I know it. If you pray hard enough miracles happen . . . you can fight anything wif miracles . . .

MICHI   That's not how you fight, Lily.

LILLIAN   That's not how *you* fight, Michi. But that's how it is for me . . . I read to him from the *Wizard of Oz* and from *Don Quixote* . . . he likes that one the best . . . *(MICHI rolls her eyes.)* He don't cough when I read it. He's real quiet, like an angel . . .

MICHI   I'll go with you. I won't let anything happen to Joey.

LILLIAN   How could you stop it? You can't stop what people already think.

MICHI   I know how to talk to those people. I been doing it for a long time.

LILLIAN   No, Michi. I don't wanna go. It's not safe outside . . . Here we're safe. *(LILLIAN goes to the altar and brings back two candles. She hands one to MICHI.)*

MICHI   What's this for?

LILLIAN   We're gonna pray.

MICHI   Oh, fuck . . . I don't do this kind of thing, Lily.

LILLIAN   Do it for me. *(She takes MICHI's hand. They kneel.)*

MICHI   Right . . . alright. Now what?

LILLIAN   Oh . . . now you ask for somefin . . . like Please God, keep my boy safe.

MICHI   You gotta do more than pray for that.

LILLIAN   I'm not you, Michi, I'll never be you.

MICHI   Okay . . . Shit . . . Okay . . . Dear . . . God . . . keep Lily's baby safe. And healthy. And make him . . . something.

LILLIAN   That's a good one. Okay. Dear
   God, let . . . Michi alone.
MICHI   Great one! Ditto.
LILLIAN   Dear God . . . take care of Pa.
MICHI   Dear God, take care of us.
LILLIAN   Dear God, take care of yourself.
   (They blow out the candles; lights fade as
   MICHI *exits.* LILLIAN *takes Joey, bundles*
   him and herself up, turns up the burners on
   the stove and sits before it.)

Scene 17

LILLIAN *is sitting by the open stove. All the*
burners are on. She rocks and speaks softly to
JOEY. *They are both bundled up.* LILLIAN
wears CARMEN's *sweaters.*

LILLIAN   We got so much together, Joey . . .
   We have our radio. It's loud and keeps us
   company. And I remember all the songs
   I've ever heard – and all the movies I've
   ever seen. Especially the cartoon ones.
   (Pause)
   I loved Dumbo. The part wif Mrs.
   Jumbo locked in the cage and Dumbo
comes to visit her and Mrs. Jumbo was
mad-like and was banging her head
against the bars . . . but then Dumbo is
there and she stops and wraps her trunk
around him and they cry together. I cry
too. She talked good for an elephant, but
they still locked her up.
(Pause)
   I don't think it matters. I mean, even
the people that have don't always get
nowheres . . .
   I could be anywhere else right now and
I wouldn't feel no different. If it was
snowing, I wouldn't be cold. I could just
curl up and let my skin fall over me like
snow on a tree, and not feel nuffin. Not
the cold anyways. And you're just like
me, Joey . . . I can smell every picture in
my head. When I close my eyes, I can go
somewhere. So I don' need to go
nowheres, because it's all *(Pointing to her*
head) in one place. It's my place . . . it's
our place.
*(*LILLIAN *sings/hums "Baby Mine" from*
Dumbo, *very softly to* JOEY *as the lights*
slowly fade to dark.)

Louella Dizon

Biography

Louella Dizon was born in the Philippines but grew up in Michigan. She directed her first production (a Grimms fairy tale) and created her first book, *So What?* (which the local elementary school library included on its shelves) in first grade. She has been involved with performing (acting, directing and composing) and writing (plays, poetry and short fiction) ever since. She graduated from Princeton University in 1989 with a BA, Magna Cum Laude, in English. She wrote, directed, acted in and composed music for her first play, *The Color Yellow: Memoirs of an Asian-American*, as a senior thesis while at Princeton. It was produced in 1990 at La Mama Etc. and at The Philippine Consulate by Lahi Philippine Performing Company. *Till Voices Wake Us* was written in the spring of 1991. Louella is currently working on two new plays, *The Sweet Sound of Inner Light*, which was staged as part of the New Works Now Festival at the Public Theatre and was also part of the 1994 Monday Night Reading Series by the Ma-Yi Theatre Ensemble; and, more recently, *The Practical Heart*.

Artistic statement

There is another woman inside me who comes out but rarely. Few know of her, fewer still really know her – even I, her greatest protector, do not know why she is there. I only remember that since I was little, I saw that the world was to be looked at once through the eyes and then once again in the mind – the visions did not always match, but at least in the mind, you could bend them a little and play around with them. From these visions I told stories to myself, and when I learned to write, I told stories to pieces of paper. There was never any audience – it was for my own pleasure, just as I spoke my own stories aloud because I liked the different sounds within a voice. This other woman within me must have been born when I came to realize that other people might be watching me. Like a chrysalis, I donned layers and layers of social skills and cultural mores as I grew older – ill-fitting as they were, they became my suit of armor in maneuvering through the world. And the other woman

Photo: Rebecca Price

took refuge in a softer place inside me and continued to whisper things in private, of things she had seen and why things happen and why things come to be.

The other woman is strong with love, quick with emotion, easy with laughter, forgiving until the very end. I believe she would say all the things to my loved ones that I would never have the courage to say. She speaks – but speaks soundlessly – through my thoughts, and sometimes through my writing. She is not me; she is what I wish to become. And I follow where she urges me to go and hope one day to love and live as she does. But for now, I let her sing out with words and if I pick up a pen, I suddenly hear her tell me the way things are and the way things came to be . . .

I cannot remember a time when I didn't want to write – as a very small child, I needed to see and know of people and lives, at least in my mind, that I couldn't seem to find in real life. *Till Voices Wake Us* is autobiographical in that way – how a lonely child can make dreams more vivid than the real world, especially if the dream world can be shaped and controlled by the child in a way that the real world cannot. The Macadaegs, as well, have appeared in different guises in my life and in myself, and they too spilled out as vividly as Rosie's dreams did. But the most surprising element – for me, because I had not intended her to be as important as she became – was the grandmother. She simply asserted herself.

It's odd, and a little tragic, that I never really wanted to know my grandparents until I had to start writing about a particular one. I was so young, culturally, in so many ways. Suddenly, I realized how very wise and patient my grandparents had been all these years, and that now, at least for two of them, it would be too late for me to say so. So I wrote – in penance, in tribute, in search of something better than real life. And although I myself cannot speak any Cebuano (Visayan, really) or even fake a Cebuano accent very well, I could hear in my mind how Grandma would speak and think. I could feel how she must have felt when her incomprehensibly American children and grandchildren rushed past her with their busy, driven lives without stopping to touch her or be touched by her.

Of course, once I started to feel who Grandma was, I began to wonder about the other lives that have come and gone that have built up to the very moment I am living in right now – whose words and deeds have shaped, in large ways and small, the reality I live in. Once I started thinking about who I was, and why, and how I became that way, I really did stop thinking about myself as being Rosie or any other character in the play. I began thinking beyond myself and everything I knew here, but instead wondered: did my family rejoice in the Revolution that overthrew Marcos? Did they get hurt? Maybe there were cousins, uncles, aunts who didn't agree with

history as it happened, or who tried to do something about it but could only express it simply and quietly to each other, or to themselves, or not at all. And suddenly, painfully, all the stories that my mother and father and grandparents and visiting relatives had told me came rushing back – brave, wonderful stories that I hadn't really heard or thought about or felt the first time I listened to them.

So I wrote *Till Voices Wake Us* for the reasons I thought I always had for writing: to entertain myself and everybody else. And I gave it a title from a verse of one of my favorite poems – T.S. Eliot's "The Love Song of J. Alfred Prufrock" – because, like Grandma, it is so lost and lyrical and lovely. But I didn't really understand what all of that meant, until it was over – after the last curtain call of the last show, and the last word had been spoken – given life – by an actor. In the empty theater, I sat and wept, because for the first time, I had really opened my heart, and since then, I have been writing to do just that.

Production history

Till Voices Wake Us was first performed as a work in progress by the Ma-Yi Theatre Ensemble in September 1992, at the Soho Repertory Theater, 46 Walker Street, New York. It was directed by Kay Gayner, to whom I will always be grateful for making it come to life. It was first produced September 22 through October 3, 1994 at the Soho Repertory Theater, directed by Kay Gayner. The cast included Lou Ann Lucas, Ralph Peña, John Pfeiffer, Jose San Juan, Lerrick Santos, and Geralyn Yabut.

7 Till Voices Wake Us

Louella Dizon

Characters

ROSIE MACADAEG   a young Filipino girl who grew up in the US

ALBERT MACADAEG   ROSIE's older brother, now a freshman in college

TESSIE MACADAEG   ROSIE's mother

BEN MACADAEG   ROSIE's father

GRANDMA (Rosamunda Villamin)   ROSIE's grandmother and TESSIE's mother

PAOLO   TESSIE's older brother, now dead

MAX   PAOLO's best friend

Minor characters

YOUNGER GRANDMA (WOMAN KNEELING)
SUSIE
VILLAGE WOMAN
SINGKIL PRINCESS
TATA (WOMAN IN DRESS)
SINGKIL PRINCE
MAN 1
MAN 2

Time
The play begins in 1979 and goes far back in time

Place
Brooklyn (Bay Ridge), New York; Cebu, Philippines, in the towns of Lahug and Catmon

Background

The 1960s witnessed the immigration of a generation of Filipino professionals – many of them doctors, engineers and nurses – who had been educated in an English-speaking school system strongly influenced by the Philippines' "big brother," the United States. These Filipinos poured into the US at a time when their qualifications were welcome and not viewed as competition to those of domestic workers; many settled around the big cities and aspired to re-create their own version of the American Dream. Although the flow of Filipinos was choked to a mere (but steady) trickle when Philippine President Marcos declared martial law in 1972, these new modern immigrants quickly took to US conveniences, replanted their cultural mores in US soil, and gave birth to a generation of children who knew only of the US – and yet heard from their parents and saw in their own faces the mark of the Philippines.

Set

There are three important elements in the set: ROSIE's bedroom; a "living room" area with dining table; and an open space for dreams and other non-interior scenes.

A bi-level set, where ROSIE's bedroom overlooks the action, works well, especially for the dream and flashback scenes where she can watch from the edge of her bed as she would from the prow of a ship. The bed is the most important piece in this area.

The "living room" area, where the interior scenes are played, works better if not done too literally, because it must interact well with the open space where the other scenes are being played – lighting can play an important part here in defining the two separate worlds. However, the "living area" can also reflect the hodgepodge of cultures beneath ROSIE's upbringing – some Filipino trappings (a side table, an ornament, a broom) mixed with some American pieces (a LaZ Boy armchair); a large TV and VCR (very important!) as well as the suggestion of other consumeristic electronic gadgets often found in "nouveau riche" houses.

The open space can be defined anywhere, even running through the audience, as long as it is given equal importance in the overall layout of the set.

Act I

ROSIE Once upon a time, I was a little girl with a secret and wonderful power. I could see things in a way no one else could see.

To me, the morning was a great snail, crawling along with a sky-blue shell, and one red eye as the sun. And dragging behind it was the rich, moist, velvet cloak of the night.

Wrapped in the covers of night, I would dream.

And I could remember all my dreams as if I were dreaming them for the first time.

TESSIE You see, the Filipino woman – the Filipina – is descended from a long line of priestesses. They were known as the "catalonan"[1] to the Tagalog; "baliana" to the Bicolano; "managanito"[2] to the Pangasinan; and to the Bisaya, "babaylan."[3] For their tribes, these women performed the most sacred rites. They could heal with herbs, speak with the gods, and exorcise devils. They found their darkest powers in dreamlike trances.

ROSIE In fact, once I knew that I could relive each dream, I realized I could put them away, like books, that could be pulled out and read over, like a map for another adventure.

And that's when I decided that I should play the heroine in these dreams.

And I wanted to shape these dreams.

And sometimes I wondered if God must have felt a little like me, amazed at my own creations.

TESSIE To this day, there are still wise old women in the smaller towns who still act as links to the supernatural.

ROSIE Dreams showed me everything I ever wanted to see. Until one day.

TESSIE That was something I couldn't take with me when I left the Philippines: the links to the spiritual world through wise old women.

ROSIE Birthdays to me are no big deal. But the birthday I remember best wasn't even my own.

TESSIE The links to the past through my mother and grandmother.

ROSIE It was at my friend Susie Locke's house. She turned twelve six months before me. It was at her party.

ROSIE and SUSIE

Me and Rosie/Susie havin' fun

Chewin' on some bubble gum

Pop goes the bubble gum

Figger I could double one

1 "Kä-tä-lo´-nun"
2 "Mä-nä-gä-nee´-toe"
3 "Buh-by´-län"

Pop goes another one
Bigger than the other one . . .
SUSIE   Hey, let's go look at my presents.
ROSIE   Okay.
(SUSIE *sings the bubble gum song again throughout* ROSIE's *next speech.*)
SUSIE   Me and Rosie havin' fun
   Chewin' on some bubble gum
   Got it stickin' on m' thumb
   Blowin' on that bubble gum
   Pop goes the bubble gum
   Figger I could double one
   Pop goes another one
   Bigger than the other one . . .
ROSIE   We always shared presents.
   I would even know which ones she would share with me.
   We opened them all together: a doll, a Nancy Drew book, puffy stickers, earrings, bicycle
   handlebars . . .
SUSIE   Wait!
ROSIE   What is it?
SUSIE   It's from my dad.
ROSIE   It was a little girl, sitting with her hands folded. She was wearing lace petticoats and
   her curls were tied up in a big ribbon. She sat, with her solemn face, not with a big grin
   like you see on kids' pictures at the department store. A face with no expectations. Like
   the picture were a duty, not a gift.
   She looks just like you.
SUSIE   It's my grandmother.
ROSIE   I've never had anything like that.
TESSIE   Most of our pictures were lost in the war.
ROSIE   Not even ones when Mom and Dad were young.
TESSIE   Those were left back home. When we left our lives behind, we left almost everything behind.
ROSIE   When I looked up on the wall, I could see all the generations behind Susie. The
   families of Lockes, way beyond Susie's grandmother. That picture made Susie's past seem
   real and immediate. While mine seemed like a folk tale, that was passed on from story to
   story.
TESSIE   When my sister Lorna called me, it was six o'clock in the morning. That means that
   in the Philippines it was seven o'clock at night. She said, "We have just come back from
   immigration. You will be seeing your mother in six months."
ROSIE   I looked at Susie's picture of her grandmother as a child. I wished I had something
   like that to help me claim my link in Time.
TESSIE   She said, "Your mother," as though I might have forgotten. She said, "Your mother,"
   instead of "Ma," "Nanay," "*Our* mother." Still, I thought of saying "No" when Lorna asked
   me to buy the ticket.
ROSIE   Mom says that you can't tell how far you've climbed up a mountain until you see
   where you've come from.
TESSIE   It had been ten years since I had seen Ma.
ROSIE   Until you see the view from halfway up.
TESSIE   One part of me remembered wanting to be with my mother again. One part of me
   was ashamed and asked, "What would we finally talk about?"
ROSIE   I wished I could somehow know. I wished that I could somehow have that view.
TESSIE   And then I realized my daughter Rosie had never met her grandmother before.
ROSIE   I wished I could have a picture of my grandmother as a child.
   Once upon a time . . . October, 1979 . . . six months before my grandmother was to
   arrive. I made a wish because of someone else's birthday. The gods must have heard me,
   and made my wish come true.

Lights up on GRANDMA *as she peers nearsightedly and uncertainly around her.* ROSIE *appears at the opposite end of the stage. They see each other immediately and pause in recognition. Slowly,* GRANDMA *extends her hand, palm downwards, in blessing, while* ROSIE *slowly bows her head.*

Suddenly, the rest of the family rushes past ROSIE *and engulfs* GRANDMA, *who must break the gaze.* ROSIE, *however, remains standing still where she is, still looking at her grandmother.*

The family sweeps GRANDMA *into the living room.* ROSIE *enters last.*

GRANDMA Ay, Tessie . . . your house is so beautiful!

TESSIE Yes, well . . .

BEN Tessie is our interior designer.

GRANDMA Ay, Benito, her husband. A good man, but always a little quiet.
When Tessie left us, she was very young. I didn't even know she knew how to keep a house. *(Sniffs the air)* I smell adobo.[4] *(Sounds of approval from the family)* Lemonsita plants. *(More sounds of approval)* A little bit of sweat.

ALBERT That might be me.

GRANDMA My grandson, Alberto. When I saw him last, he was yet so small. Now my daughter's son is big and guapo. Handsome and smiling, as a son should be.

TESSIE Ma . . . Ma, here take your coat off . . . come on, show us what you brought from home.

GRANDMA *(As she rummages through her trunk)* Of course, our small gifts are nothing compared to what you have here. *(Pulls out a mestiza dress.)*

TESSIE Oh, Ma, this is gorgeous.

ALBERT That really is nice, Mom. So's this Grandma! *(Holds up a batik shirt.)*

BEN *(Walking over to* TESSIE) What do you think, Nanay? Isn't she the prettiest girl ever to come from Lahug?

GRANDMA *(Thinking, quite seriously)* No . . . Lorna is prettier.

TESSIE *(Ruefully)* Well, that's always been the case. *(She hugs her mother.)* Thank you, Ma.

GRANDMA Rosie, come here and sit by me.

TESSIE Rosie . . . Grandma wants to see you.

GRANDMA *(Softly, to the others)* She's embarrassed.

ROSIE *(Pointing to* GRANDMA's *trunk)* What's that?

GRANDMA Oh these? These are YOUR presents! *(*ROSIE *remains in her place, watching silently.)* I have two things for you here, Rosie. Here, the first one *(she unwraps it)* – see? – a necklace that is made of coral. And this one . . .
*(*ROSIE *rushes over with a cry of surprise.)*

ROSIE *(Holding it with awe)* A . . . picture!

GRANDMA It's your Uncle Paolo. My oldest son.

ALBERT I thought he was dead.

BEN Albert!

TESSIE *(Rushing over to look)* Let me see!

GRANDMA *(To* ROSIE) Yah, your Tita Lorna is the eldest now, and then your mother. But long time ago, before Lorna, I had a baby girl, who died very young. And before her . . . my first child. My son, Paolo.

ALBERT When did he die?

GRANDMA He died a long time ago, Albert. Shortly before your mother left the Philippines. I think it was . . . let me see . . . 19 . . . 67.
I remember the day he came to visit. My Paolo was always handsome, although before he died he had gotten so tired-looking, so old. But that day he came to visit, he looked like an angel. His eyes were so bright – probably because he had not slept – but they were shining as though he would deliver a great secret. We ate dinner together – the two of us only – and before he left, he leaned forward and said to me, "You know, Ma, I really

---

4 "Ä-dö´-bō": A chicken or pork stew in a garlicky gravy flavored with vinegar, soy sauce and bay leaves. A native dish of the Philippines.

love this place." I thought he meant the family house, because you know as a teacher, his apartment was not very big. But now I ask myself what he meant.

(Pause)

ALBERT How did he die?

BEN Ahem, that's enough, Albert. This is a nice barong,[5] Nanay. Salamat po.[6]

TESSIE *(Distracted)* Paolo . . . *(Abruptly)* Why are you giving her this?

(GRANDMA crosses to ROSIE, but does not touch her.)

GRANDMA Because I know of a little girl who is very bright and very talented, and I wanted her to have a remembrance of someone who was very dear to me and who would have liked her very much.

(ROSIE bursts into tears.)

ALBERT Hey, what's wrong, Rose?

BEN *(To GRANDMA)* Rosie's a little sensitive. *(To ROSIE)* Rosie, come on – Lola will think you're crying because you're not happy to see her. *(To GRANDMA, realizing he's saying the wrong thing)* She's embarrassed.

(TESSIE starts, as if to shake herself from a dream.)

TESSIE I've cooked a big lunch everybody! I hope you're all hungry! *(A burst of "Yes!" from the men. They head towards the kitchen. TESSIE stays, yelling over her shoulder.)* Why don't you guys get out the plates – I'm going to take out the good tablecloth.

(TESSIE sees the suitcase in the middle of the floor and picks it up to move it. As she walks with it, the lights change and it is ten years ago. GRANDMA emerges from the kitchen.)

GRANDMA Anak,[7] say good-bye to your father.

TESSIE I already said good-bye to him. He didn't say good-bye to me.

GRANDMA He is angry. And why not? Paolo is hardly buried in the ground and now you are leaving us. Did you think of the small ones? Alberto, who has to leave school? Rosie, who can barely walk?

TESSIE And what about Ben, who has a good job there?

GRANDMA Your family is here.

TESSIE My family is now Ben and Alberto and Rosie. You know how difficult it is to go to the US. You know how lucky we are that Ben got a residency at a good hospital, where many of his friends are already.

GRANDMA That's what happens. We educate our children to be doctors and nurses and engineers. But how many stay? They all go somewhere – to America or something –

TESSIE And send home good money!

GRANDMA And leave us here alone. Well – you see Nang Lita. She has a nice house. She hangs gold plaques outside the front door, engraved with all her children's names and all their nice professions. But how many of them are near her? Who can come to her bedside when she is sick? Wala karon[8] – "No more." She might as well be asking movie stars to visit her.

TESSIE I will visit you.

GRANDMA You will . . .

TESSIE I will! And besides, you have Lorna.

GRANDMA Lorna! Lorna is like a child – she cannot help in the house, she cannot manage money –

TESSIE Ma! What do you need from me? *(Lights change)* Ma, what do you need?

GRANDMA I didn't want to stay in the kitchen. *(She walks around, admiring the room.)* You have not seen how nice the house back home is now. You left before we had the garden, and the greenhouse.

TESSIE *(Softly)* I left so you could have a garden and a greenhouse.

---

5 "Bä-röng´": A gossamer-thin shirt made of native fiber, usually with graceful, sometimes elaborately embroidered designs. Worn as the traditional costume of Filipino men for formal gatherings.

6 "Suh-lä´mut pö": "Thank you" said in a respectful way – usually towards people of authority or who are older.

7 "Ä-näk´": Child

8 "Wuh-lä´ kä-rön´": Cebuano for "No more"

GRANDMA And I cannot believe I have such beautiful grandchildren.

TESSIE *(Laughing, unsure of herself)* You – you hardly look as though you could have grandchildren. You have hardly aged.

GRANDMA And you have become a woman.

TESSIE I have become fat.

GRANDMA You have become American.

(Pause. She starts fumbling in her handbag on the sofa.)

TESSIE Ma? Ma, you're not going to smoke, are you?

(GRANDMA unwraps from a plastic bag a large, hand-rolled cigar.)

GRANDMA I have not smoked since I left Lahug. Twenty-one hours ago! *(Peering around for an ashtray and seeing none)* Hmph! And you, Maria Teresita, have not changed at all! Still nerviosa, still moving around . . . Why are you just standing there holding that tablecloth? I am not the priest visiting – I'm just your mother! *(Her tone suddenly changes.)* I came out into the living room because I cannot believe I am finally with you. I had to see you. Anak, I have only heard your voice on the telephone for the last ten years.

(TESSIE rushes to hug her mother.)

TESSIE Oh, Ma . . .

(From the kitchen)

BEN Hey!

ALBERT Hey! Can we come out now?

(GRANDMA and TESSIE draw apart, laughing.)

TESSIE Oh my goodness, I forgot about those guys. Come on out, you guys, let's eat now. *(ALBERT and BEN emerge from the kitchen. ROSIE approaches the table.)* Rosie, let's eat now. Come on, let's all hold hands . . . shh . . . shh. Bless us, oh Lord, for these our gifts, which we are about to receive, from Your bounty, through Christ, our Lord. And thank you, Lord, for bringing us my mother, whom we welcome into our house today.

ALL Amen.

ROSIE Amen.

(The family begins to disperse in slow motion, while GRANDMA turns to the audience. She sucks on her unlit cigar contemplatively.)

GRANDMA I am here in the town of Brooklyn in the city of New York. The state is New York also. Very confusing.

It is the way in Brooklyn to talk very loud, especially when young. The children play in the streets, even if cars are coming. But, like the little boys selling cigarillos in the streets of Cebu, they are able to get out of the way.

It is the way here to be always working. The cars go very fast, and the people are in a hurry. For those who walk slow, like me, like some old people and some families with children, there are others who are impatient and push from behind you, looking "saput"[9] – sullen. It is the way here always to have someplace to go.

TESSIE Bye Ma. Be careful. I'll be home between ten and ten-thirty tonight.

GRANDMA Tessie is always watching the store. Where's Benito?

TESSIE Ben is on call this week. He might sleep at the hospital tonight. Here's the number you can call me at the store. Bye!

GRANDMA Alberto is usually not home. *(ALBERT exits, running noisily, "Bye Grandma!")* He is away at college and comes home only on weekends if he likes. Sometimes, he does not like.

ROSIE Hi Grandma!

GRANDMA Hi Rosie. How was your day today?

ROSIE Good.

GRANDMA Where are you going?

ROSIE I have piano lessons at four o'clock.

GRANDMA Sometimes she has newspaper.

ROSIE Or orchestra practice. Sometimes I'm in a play.

9 "Sä´-put": In a bad mood, sullen

GRANDMA   It is the way here always to have something to do and a certain time to do it. That is not the way in Cebu.

You see in the Cebuano language, precise terms of time are not often used, unless you tell the time in Spanish. It is customary to know almost everyone in the town, and you pay visit without warning.

VILLAGE WOMAN   Nang Rosa! I have not seen you in a long time! Komosta[10] – how are you? You "sum-sum," you come eat with me in the house.

GRANDMA   Ay, thank you, but I must go to the market today. Can I see you ugma sa gabii[11] – tomorrow evening?

VILLAGE WOMAN   Sigue, sigue – you come over for dinner.

GRANDMA   It does not matter if I say seven o'clock, seven-thirty, eight o'clock. One is always late by half an hour anyway. And besides, the time one arrives is always the right time.

ROSIE   Hi Grandma!

GRANDMA   Hi Rosie. What do you have to do today?

ROSIE   Oh, a lot of homework! What about you?

GRANDMA   I'm going out to the market. The other day I saw they had fresh bok choy – I will make pansit with it! Also, I want to buy flowers. This Friday it will be twelve years since Paolo died.

ROSIE   Oh, okay, if you're just going to the store . . . *(She pauses and turns to look at* GRANDMA, *who is exiting.)*

It must be that picture that Grandma gave me, but . . . is it strange to dream about your mother's country? One that you don't remember at all? When I go to bed at night, and images start to flicker in my eyes, is it the ocean I hear, or my own breathing?

Lights change. Enter PAOLO.

Off stage, a little girl's voice: Kuya Paolo! Kuya Paolo!

TESSIE *emerges as young Tessie, dressed in a pink cotton dress and sandals, running on stage out of breath.*

TESSIE   Kuya Paolo! I saw you leave the house and I called you—

PAOLO   Tessie! Where did you come from?

TESSIE   I was walking back from school and I saw you leave the house. I called to you but you did not answer because you were already far, so I just followed you until you stopped.

PAOLO   I'm sorry about that! I was thinking all kinds of stupid things that filled my head and stopped up my ears and I couldn't hear anything around me!

TESSIE   Where are you going?

PAOLO   I'm going to a meeting.

TESSIE   What kind of meeting? I want to go.

PAOLO   No, this is a meeting only for people who have read these books, and I would let you read them, except I must bring them with me. Maybe when you're older, you can read them and come with me.

TESSIE   *(Reading the cover of one of the books)* Jose Rizal. "No-lye Meh Tan–Tan-ger . . . "

PAOLO   "Noli Me Tangere." Very, very old Spanish for "Don't Touch Me."

TESSIE   "Don't Touch Me"? *(She flips it over and over, looking at it.)* It sounds like an angry book. *(She takes another and reads it.)* "Five Golden Rays." *(She hands them back to her brother.)* Hmm.

PAOLO   No, little chicken, they are not angry books, and I'm not angry. *(He scoops her up in his arms and whispers.)* I dreamed that I took a walk. Away from the house, through the darkness beneath the trees, and up to where someone was waiting for me, in the mountains. And I woke up and knew that my friends were waiting for me, up there, to talk about our country. To talk about what is ours. Tessie, we have been spending these years

10 "Kö-mö´-stä": Hello.
11 "Ög´-muh sä gä-bee´-ee": Tomorrow evening.

running and hiding from the Japanese. And our grandfathers spent years bowing down to the Spaniards. I want to know what it is like ... to run free in the land of the sun. But I am late and I must send you the other way.

TESSIE No, Kuya. *(Seriously)* If these are not angry books, then I would like to find out more.

PAOLO But ... *(He tries to disengage her but she protests.)*

TESSIE I want to find out! No, Kuya, I want to find out! *(Finally ...)* I won't go back by myself! I only followed you coming here and I might not remember how to go back. Mama will get mad at you if I get lost.

PAOLO *(Sighing ruefully and putting her down)* You are too, too much like me, Tessie. Always curious, always wanting to know, always dreaming about other things. We'll be so busy looking up to the mountains, we'll trip and fall on our faces. *(Abruptly he turns.)* Come on then. We have to hurry. And promise you'll be still and silent as a lizard.

TESSIE Yes, Kuya. *(They exit, as the lights fade.)*

(Lights up as ROSIE enters.)

ROSIE Hi Grandma! *(Runs over to rocking chair and kisses GRANDMA)*

GRANDMA Hello Rosie. How was school?

ROSIE Great!

GRANDMA There is siakoy in the kitchen.

ROSIE *(Investigating)* Sha-koy? What's that?

GRANDMA It's like donuts.

ROSIE Oh. Great! *(Gets one, sits down on sofa)*

GRANDMA You're not going anywhere?

ROSIE No. It's Thursday, and since Albert doesn't have classes on Friday, he's coming home today to spend a long weekend, because my birthday is Sunday!

GRANDMA Ah, yes, your birthday! You will be ...

ROSIE Twelve! *(Touches the fresh flowers on the table)* These are nice.

GRANDMA Thank you.

ROSIE *(Looking at the flowers, suddenly serious)* Is Albert a lot like Uncle Paolo?

GRANDMA *(Laughing)* No, not really. Ay, well – Albert looks very much like Paolo when he was young.

ROSIE Really?

GRANDMA Yes. But Paolo's personality was more quiet, more like yours.

ROSIE What about my mom?

GRANDMA Well, your mom was also quiet when she was little, and also very smart, like you. She and Paolo were very close.

(Pause)

ROSIE That picture you gave me, Grandma ...

GRANDMA *(Holding out her hand and smiling)* You call me Lola.

(Slowly, ROSIE reaches over to take GRANDMA's hand.

   Suddenly, ALBERT makes a noisy entrance. He is carrying a duffel bag and a backpack, and is dressed in a windbreaker, sweatshirt, jeans, and sneakers. He speaks just as he gets the door open.)

ALBERT Hey, anyone home?

(ROSIE jumps up and buries her face in his chest in a big hug.)

ROSIE Albert! Albert!

ALBERT Hey, Short Stuff, how you doing? *(Gives her a big hug and carries her over to center stage)* Hi Grandma. I'd come and hug you, too, but my hands are full.

GRANDMA Come, Alberto. Are you hungry? I made pansit. *(She goes to the kitchen.)*

(As ALBERT carries ROSIE to the kitchen)

ROSIE Albert, do you remember the Philippines?

ALBERT Uhm-hm.

ROSIE What's it like there?

ALBERT It's hot.

ROSIE Hotter than here?

ALBERT Always.

ROSIE   Do you want to go back?
ALBERT   Uhm-hm.
ROSIE   Does Daddy?
ALBERT   Uhm-hm.
ROSIE   Does Mom?
GRANDMA   Come, Albert. It's ready!
   (They exit.)

Lights out. The sound of breathing fills the darkness. It ebbs and flows, slowly and steadily. It ebbs and flows, like the ocean. Somehow, the sound of breathing becomes the ocean, which dies down again. Only the sound of crickets can be heard.

   Music: "Singkil."[12] Lights up for the "Princess" sequence. Together the music and the dancers seem to be a performance of some sacred rite.

   A veiled PRINCESS *enters, with an attendant behind her holding an umbrella over her head. As the music, "Singkil," plays, she begins to dance slowly and gracefully. The* SINGKIL PRINCE *enters and begins dancing too, but they are separated somehow, and he cannot get any nearer to her. As the music quickens, the two of them continue dancing apart, while between them are the attendants who hold the bamboo poles, silently clacking the bamboo poles in slow motion, as if their sequence had been slowed down dramatically.*

   The music becomes wilder and wilder, and the princess slowly kneels to lift her veil and reveal herself. But just as she grasps the veil, the music ends and the lights black out.

   The sound of the television, a commercial, "Hawaiian Punch." As the lights come on in the living room, GRANDMA *enters, sucking on an unlit cigar. She watches the television intently, tapping her foot in time to the music. She reaches to turn up the volume and shuts it off by mistake. The sudden silence surprises her. Just then,* ROSIE *opens the door and runs in wearing her school jumper.*

ROSIE   Hi . . . Lola.
GRANDMA   Oh, Rosie you are home. You called me Lola. Salamat.
ROSIE   You're welcome. *(She runs upstairs.)* Albert?
GRANDMA   Oh, Alberto left.
ROSIE   *(Extremely disappointed)* He did! He wasn't awake when I left this morning, and now he's gone!
GRANDMA   He said he had to run errands.
ROSIE   *(Sullenly)* No, he didn't. He had to see his GIRL friend!
GRANDMA   Hah?
ROSIE   Never mind. *(She sits at the dining table and props her face up on her hands.)*
GRANDMA   Here, Rosie. *(Pushing a foil-covered plate toward her)* Do you like fried bananas?
ROSIE   Thank you. *(She takes one.* GRANDMA *sits at the table, opposite* ROSIE. ROSIE *finishes a whole banana slice and starts on another before* GRANDMA *makes another effort.)*
GRANDMA   It was important that you see your brother?
ROSIE   Yeah. I had to talk to him about something I dreamed of last night.
GRANDMA   Ah, a dream! Paolo used to tell me all the time about his dreams. Would you like to tell me about your dream?
ROSIE   *(Wrinkling her forehead)* No . . .
GRANDMA   *(Trying again)* I remember a game Paolo used to play with me – like hide and seek. After I put him to bed, he would start dreaming, and no matter where I would go, even outside of the house, he would dream of finding me.
ROSIE   The next day, did you find out he was right?
GRANDMA   Well, he was right once.

---

12 "Sing-kil": A native dance showcasing the courtship between a princess and a prince, made more elaborate by being danced among criss-crossing bamboo poles that open and close in rhythm, while the princess is closely followed by an attendant who continually holds an umbrella over her head to shade her from the hot sun. From the southern, Islamic part of the Philippines.

ROSIE Wow, really? *(Pause)* Actually, I do have strange dreams. *(Laughing)* Sometimes I dream about something, and it HAPPENS to me later! Or *(more quietly)* it's happened way before.

GRANDMA *(Expressing obvious interest)* Ay, really?

ROSIE *(Warming up)* Yes. Most of the time, I dream about strange places and people . . . I hardly ever dream about people I know.

GRANDMA No? What do you dream about?

ROSIE Once I dreamed I was in a huge stone castle, with lots and lots of rooms. I liked exploring it so much, I memorized the road that got me there so I could dream about going back. And you know what? I did!

GRANDMA How wonderful! What else?

ROSIE If I can remember most of the dream, I write it down, and I use it to write my stories.

GRANDMA Ay, yes. Your mother told me that you want to be a novelist and travel all over the world.

ROSIE Sure. I used to tell all my stories to Albert and he loved them so much, he told me to write them down, so that other people could read them. I'm glad he told me that, too, because . . . *(she munches reflectively for a moment on her banana)* . . . because I think he's busy with other things right now, and even when I'm talking to him, I don't think he always hears me. *(She is suddenly lost in thought for a moment. Still staring out into space)* Lola . . .

GRANDMA Yes, Rosie, I'm listening.

ROSIE *(Snaps out of it and looks at her)* You are. Lola, what is your name?

GRANDMA My name is Rosamunda . . . "Rose of the World."

ROSIE *(With a big grin)* Like mine. *(She has finished eating.)* Have you been outside yet, Lola?

GRANDMA No, not yet.

ROSIE I can take you around, Lola. I can show you around the whole neighborhood! I know you might be cold because it's not as warm here as it is in the Philippines, but I know where we can get good hot chocolate.

GRANDMA Ay, how very nice! Okay, Rosie. Okay, Rosamunda. *(ROSIE giggles and GRANDMA nods, smiling. Lights fade and music brings the scene into blackout.)*

Music of the song "Ang Kinabuhe," and lights come up. ROSIE *is clowning through the verses in true burlesque fashion.*

ROSIE *(Sings)*
'Ning kabukiran, payag imong gipuy-an,
[*We live in the shelter of the mountains*]
Hasta mingawa mingawpa sa tirana.
[*It's as lonely as a sad song.*]

Among agi-anan, kahuy lataylatayan,
[*The boughs of the trees are our pathways*]
Among kalalusan, bulo sa kawayan.
[*Our water jugs are poles of bamboo.*]

Among pagakan-an, bagul kinilasan,
[*Our plates are coconut husks*]
A-hay, among isud-an, among isud-an, ulan sinikpan.
[*Our meat is what we can catch.*]

(Laughter from ALL*)*

'Ning kabukiran, payag imong gipuy-an,
Bali mingawa onggoy among silingan.
[*It's so lonely that the monkeys are our neighbors.*]

Among pagakan-on, lagutmon da intawon,
[*What we eat are root crops, for goodness sake*]
Among higda-anan, panit sa kakahuyan.
[*Our beds are the skin [bark] of trees.*]

Among ihabul, dahon-'tawon sa papul,
[*Our blankets are, for goodness sake, banana leaves*]
A-hay, ang kinabuhe, ang kinabuhe, 'ning kabukiran.
[*Life, life in the mountains.*]

A-hay, ang kinabuhe, ang kinabuhe, 'ning kabukiran.

(ROSIE *bows dramatically as the rest cheer, laughing and applauding. Then she bounces over to* GRANDMA.)
ALBERT Rosie, how did you learn that?
ROSIE Lola taught me – the words, what they mean, how to say them, everything!
GRANDMA Yes, and she learned so quickly, I taught her other songs also.
ROSIE Well, Lola has also learned a lot since she got here.
BEN Like what, Nanay?
GRANDMA Ah, I can use the microwave. I can program the VCR.
ROSIE *(Amidst surprised laughter)* Even I didn't know that – she figured it out herself!
GRANDMA I have also learned how to use the map of the subway alone. Except that my
  eyesight is very poor and I must look closely to read it.
TESSIE Ma, I don't want you riding on the subway alone! Rosie, I don't want you two going
  around in the subway too much.
GRANDMA *(Getting up and slowly crossing to the kitchen)* Ay, Teresita, there you go again.
  After I have already survived through fever, war, marriage, martial law . . .
TESSIE I'm just telling you and Rosie, Ma, especially since Rosie is still young – what if
  something should happen.
  What do you need, Ma?
GRANDMA I don't know . . . *(Shaking her head, laughing)* Crazy . . . I was going to the kitchen
  to wash the dishes from supper. I forgot we did that already.
TESSIE Did you take your vitamin today?
BEN *(Changes the mood to a brisk one)* I think we're all tired.
TESSIE In these situations, Ben suddenly becomes efficient.
BEN Nanay, remember you're still suffering from jet lag. Albert, don't use the phone too
  long. Rosie, I hope you finished your homework. Good night.
THE REST OF THE FAMILY, except TESSIE Good night.
  (BEN *sits down beside his wife. He strokes her cheek. No response. He pinches her cheek. Still
  no response. He puts his finger under her nose so she suddenly cannot breathe.*)
TESSIE Ben, stop it! *(Slapping his hand away and getting up to straighten the living room)*
BEN I'm only trying to distract you. What is bothering you, Tessie?
TESSIE I don't know.
BEN You know, Rosie and Nanay are getting along very well. In fact, the whole visit is
  going well. We are all glad to see Nanay.
TESSIE What about that spell by the kitchen?
BEN We all forget sometimes the reason why we walk into a room.
TESSIE I still worry about leaving Rosie alone so much. And now there's Ma, and you know
  how old she is.
BEN So, we're lucky they can keep each other company.
TESSIE But what must she think – I don't even stay home with my own children.
BEN Why would she think anything?
TESSIE I didn't even know she knew that song!
BEN That's okay – I didn't either.
TESSIE I've never taught her little songs.
BEN Is that what's bothering you?

TESSIE *(To audience)* I know it's something that shouldn't bother me – it wouldn't bother him . . . Dear sweet, sane Ben. A quiet rock next to my storm of a family. Imagine the dramatics – I had a politician for a father, a beauty queen for a sister. And then there was Paolo – well, I always loved Paolo, but he was always . . . tortured. He and Ma were closest. They had something even I couldn't be part of. Only Ma could have known everything about Paolo. Rosie is a lot like him. Maybe that's why—

BEN What are you mumbling about, mahal? Are you still worried about Rosie and Nanay? So – you think Rosie has found a mother in Nanay and Nanay has found a daughter in Rosie, so you feel left out? You're jealous!

TESSIE No, Ben, that's not it.

BEN Jea-lous! Se-lo-sa! *(Starts to tickle her)*

TESSIE Stop it, Ben!

BEN Ha, ha! Now no one wants you! Now I've got you all to myself!

TESSIE Stop it! Crazy! *(She exits, running, shrieking with laughter in spite of herself,* BEN *in hot pursuit.)*

(Lights up in ROSIE's *bedroom.* GRANDMA *and* ROSIE *are sitting on* ROSIE's *bed.)*

GRANDMA What's going on?

ROSIE Oh, it's just Mom and Dad acting crazy. We're a crazy family, huh, Lola?

GRANDMA Well, I like to think of our family as blessed. Like you, one day you will be a writer.

ROSIE Writer, Lola? If only I could. What I write is only half of what I see in my head. I have so many dreams stored away, in here *(tapping her head)*. You see? Dreams are important. To other people, dreams are like accidents! Imagine, watching something for the next six or eight hours and not having any use for it. What a waste of an evening! You might as well not sleep!

GRANDMA Ay, na'ko, Rosie, you are so funny when you get excited.

ROSIE I know it's not that simple. I can't really control my dreams that much – they manage to run away with me anyway and reveal all these unexpected things . . .

Like, sometimes I have this dream that a wonderful, magical princess is revealed to me. For some reason, I always wake up before I find out why she is so important to me. But the last few times I had the dream, I tried to catch a glimpse of her face beneath the veil before she's whisked away altogether.

GRANDMA And what did you see?

ROSIE *(Putting her hand to her grandmother's face)* You, of course. It was your face as a young woman I kept seeing beneath the veil. That's why I recognized you right away at the airport.

GRANDMA And I, you. But you have school tomorrow, Rosie, and you must get your sleep. Good night, Rosie.

ROSIE Good night, Lola. Lola?

GRANDMA Hmm?

ROSIE That dream game – hide and seek? How did Paolo find you in his dream?

GRANDMA Ay, Rosie, that's enough! Go to sleep. *(Shuts off light)*

ROSIE Good night.

(Her audible sigh. Music.)

In the midst of ROSIE's *rhythmic breathing, we hear wisps of voices and sounds of footsteps that drift in and out of the music. We see bodies dart in and out quickly. We glimpse disturbing images: a woman cradling the body of her son; two men grappling; a woman priestess performing sacred rites for the gods.*

Slowly, an eerie light grows in intensity to reveal GRANDMA *kneeling in the living room with her rosary. The music and light increase in intensity. She looks up, surprised by the call of* ROSIE's *dream.*

GRANDMA Rosie!

(Suddenly—

Blackout and cut music. In her bedroom, ROSIE *quickly turns on the lamp.)*

ROSIE Lola!
(Blackout)

Lights up on TESSIE. *She is putting on her makeup to go out for the evening with* BEN.

TESSIE Before we moved to Cebu, we lived in Camotes, an island so small that even now it has no electricity. We didn't have indoor toilets. We didn't have running water in the house. We didn't have shoes – we had bakya – those sandals with two strips that run from your toes across the top of your foot. But we were happy with what we had. Then one day, one of the girls at school got a pair of shoes. She was the only little girl in town with shoes – and they were so pretty and clean and white. I thought I had never seen anything as beautiful as those new white shoes and I wanted a pair for myself. My father was going to Cebu in a few days, just in time for my birthday. And I told him, I wanted a pair of shoes like that little girl's. I told him what kind, what they look like, what color. And he traveled the two days there and the two days back from Cebu.

BEN *(While shining his shoes)* I remember, the year I graduated high school and got my scholarship to the University of the Philippines, my father asked me what I wanted to do with myself. And I told him I wanted to be a painter. Of course, he laughed and told me how impractical that was.

TESSIE When my father came back, he brought back a pair of shoes like the ones the little girl had. And they were too small! I cried and cried having those shoes in my hands and not being able to wear them. And he had to go back again the next time in order to get the right size.

BEN "What about Uncle Ramon," I said, "what about Uncle Ramon, who writes songs?" "What about him?" he said, "do you want to be like Uncle Ramon and always need me to support you?" I was oldest, you know, so there was really no question about what I was going to do. I was going to be a professional, a doctor, so I could support my parents in their old age and provide for my family.

TESSIE I laugh to myself now, thinking about those shoes. And sometimes, driving my Cadillac down the FDR Drive, I have to pinch myself. Who would've thought that poor little girl in Camotes would be here, living like this, talking like this? If you had told me that day that one day my shoe collection would fill its own closet, I wouldn't have believed it.

BEN I even fell in love with someone at U.P., an artist, very pretty and very flighty – I almost lost my scholarship because of her. Then I met and fell in love with Tessie. A sharp woman always, in her studies and in business, and yet, she knew what it is to want to be an artist. *(As* TESSIE *joins him, "Stars and Stripes Forever" begins to play. She takes his arm.)* You look beautiful, mahal.

TESSIE Thank you, Ben.
(They exit. Fade music and lights.)

Lights up in ROSIE's *bedroom.*
ROSIE, *staring at the picture of* PAOLO, *is sitting on the bed. When* GRANDMA *appears in the doorway, music.*

ROSIE *(without turning around)* I thought you were sleeping.
GRANDMA I am afraid to sleep.
ROSIE So am I.
GRANDMA Last night—
ROSIE You had a dream too?
GRANDMA It was the princess.
ROSIE With the veil.
GRANDMA You were there?
ROSIE I saw you there too. *(She turns to face* GRANDMA, *who is now standing next to the bed.)* It's you, isn't it? You're different, like me.
GRANDMA It's not me. It is our family.

141

ROSIE   Mom?

GRANDMA   No.

ROSIE   Uncle Paolo?

GRANDMA   Paolo, yes.

ROSIE   Who else?

GRANDMA   My grandfather. He was the first to bring us all the gift.

ROSIE   *(In awe, a whisper)* The gift. *(She is silent for a moment with the revelation. Then . . .)* Come on, Lola, you have to show me more. *(They both sit on the bed and clasp hands.)* Show me what you've seen. Show me what you remember. Show me what you have dreamed about.

GRANDMA   Ay, Rosie . . . *(The lights fade slowly.)* It is almost like sleep.

ROSIE   Sleep.

GRANDMA   You see, Rosie . . .

Adona pay manga Filipino mo tuo nga ana-ay espirito nag puyo sa ilalum sa yuta, sa bato, sa landong sa dagko ng' kahuy. Ang akong apohan nga lalake mu tuo siya apan dili mo hadlok. Ang espirito tigulang na ka-ayo. Daghan ang ilang manga na kita. Ug ma tawag ka kanila, mag ka hinumdum ka sa imong gi memoria sa kalibutan.

ROSIE   *(Speaks with her, translating)* There are still some Filipinos who believe that there are spirits who live in the ground, in the stones, in the darkness beneath the trees. My grandfather believed in them, but he was not afraid of them. They are very old. They have seen many things. To call upon them is to call upon the memory of the very earth.

'Sus, Rosie, how powerful they are – and yet they cannot live where there is no belief. Here, you might find some who say they believe in God, but it is in the head, not in the heart. So, how much less are there who believe in spirits? But you come from the same country, Rosie – you can remember. You just have to reach beyond all memory of what you have known here. It is like a song being sung among many other noises. Block out the other noises, and listen for the song.

(Lights go down. Music. A young man enters, in a faded shirt and trousers rolled up to the knee, barefoot. He looks constantly over his shoulder.)

They say my grandfather Rosario came from nowhere, that there were no records of his birth, that no one remembered hearing of him from other towns. They say he was descended from witches.

He came to the town of Catmon, and being bright and strong, he attracted attention in the small fishing village. The mayor of Catmon took such a liking to him – some say he was bewitched – that he adopted him almost as a son and sent him to the University of Santo Tomas. The Spanish students looked down on him for not being fair, for not being Spanish.

(Two men enter, aristocratic students from Spain who attend the university.)

MAN 1   Look at that fellow – who let that monkey loose in the courtyard?

MAN 2   I believe he is the new "adopted" son of the Mayor of Catmon. You know, he is not the only one, either. I believe they have admitted other negritos like him to the university. Perhaps they have a point in letting them learn something, rather than just admit the children of colonists and Spaniards.

MAN 1   Oh *(yawns)* I suppose. And where is Catmon? And where did this mayor get the money to buy this monkey's place at Santo Tomas?

ROSIE   How mean!

MAN 1   *(Turning to her)* And what does it matter what a little girl like you thinks? I'll tell you what I think. The Philippines is like the Garden of Eden – and you Filipinos have run around in happy oblivion in a land of unbelievable riches. But I tell you what. Your grandfather and many others after him will get their education. And you know what happens when your eyes are opened in the Garden of Eden. You leave.

(The two men exit.)

GRANDMA   It's okay, anak. It's only a dream.

ROSIE   No, I remember! *(Music)*

I remember walking in the streets. A rich lady was on my right, and a fruit vendor to my left. I remember singing the same song as I waved flowers – flowers that seemed to multiply, like the loaves and the fishes. I remember seeing the soldiers' shining guns. I remember pitying their nervous faces. I remember the word we chanted: la . . . ban. Laban!

GRANDMA Once upon a time.

ROSIE I remember crying when martial law was declared. I remember Uncle Manny who used to say what he wished. I remember one night he disappeared – I remember the next morning his brother had bruises on his face. I remember seeing Imelda's picture at my cousins' house. I remember she gave them forks and spoons plated in gold.

GRANDMA I remember . . .

ROSIE Once upon a time.

GRANDMA Listening to the wireless radio. Running up to the American soldier and asking him for his k-rations.

ROSIE Chocolate, Joe!

GRANDMA We were so hungry.

ROSIE Chocolate, Joe!

GRANDMA Their food tasted so good.

ROSIE Running from the Japanese.

GRANDMA Our house burned down in the war. Once upon a time. I remember.

ROSIE I remember seeing seven ships sailing, into Manila Bay. A fleet of Spanish vessels sank into the bloody water.

GRANDMA The Spanish were at war.

ROSIE But we fought for the Americans.

GRANDMA Spain surrendered, and so surrendered us.

ROSIE After 400 years of Spanish rule. We were the Americans' little brown brothers. I remember I was a poor little brown girl and I sat in the cheap seat of the balconies in the movie houses. I remember seeing the army officers below. I remember seeing rich white immigrants wearing silk and pearls.

GRANDMA Once upon a time.

ROSIE I remember picking root crops from the ground that had fed my fathers. I remember yielding the root crops to a fat conquistador, the lord of the estate.

GRANDMA I remember he had sailed in from Mexico. I remember the day he took our land. I remember he raped me and gave me a mestizo son.

ROSIE Once upon a time.

GRANDMA I remember I wanted to be a nun. I remember a friar seduced me. Once upon a time.

ROSIE I was a priestess to my tribe. And our chieftains stood proud and tall. And they, with their half-naked bodies and bolos and spears defeated the white men in armor. A man named Magellan, with a spear in his heart, lay dead on the bloody beach.

GRANDMA Once upon a time.

ROSIE I remember . . . running free in the land of the sun.

(*Music rises.*)

Act II

Darkness. Music "Wipeout" starts and lights come up on young people dressed in the garb circa 1957–58, all frozen in dance positions. When the song gets going, they start dancing in modified versions of American rock and roll steps. ROSIE *enters.*

ROSIE How could anyone imagine what it was like in the following weeks? I could hardly concentrate on anything at school – the visions I had dreamed of the night before would dance in front of my eyes. As much as the dream world would allow, Grandma and I explored her homeland – my homeland – through the experiences of our family. We couldn't predict everything we would see – it seemed, once chosen, that the visions would take their own courses.

(*Throughout this monologue,* TESSIE, *dressed and made-up to be twenty years old again, and* BEN, *dressed the same way, draw apart from the crowd, each with a bosom buddy at hand, intent on checking each other out.* BEN *is finally pushed into* TESSIE, *at the goading of all the guys, while the girls pinch each other's arms and hide behind their hands.)*

BEN   Miss Villamin, I couldn't help observing that not only are you the brightest in class, but you also possess the brightest eyes I have ever seen.

TESSIE   Well, Mr. Macadaeg, you're the one studying to be a doctor. You should know the way human eyes ought to look.

BEN   You are so pretty, they ought to look at you. And I would like to be the first pair of feet to have the pleasure to dance with your feet. I mean, would you like to dance?
(He takes her arm and they dance, while both lights and music fade into blackout.)
(As GRANDMA *enters, the others disperse,* ROSIE *exits, and* TESSIE *drifts off to the side, putting her girlish ponytail up into a bun again.)*

GRANDMA   It is the way here that no one stops to wait for the old people, even though they know we are old. Today I saw an old woman who walked very slowly. She was walking toward the bus, but it had already been standing there, so she knew it would leave soon. She was forcing and forcing herself to walk faster – I saw great pain in her face. But the driver did not watch or maybe it did not matter to him. He closed the door as she was walking along the side of the bus.
    She was so mad that she hit the bus with her cane. He still did not stop. But what could she do? She had to stand there and wait. There was not even a bench to sit on.
    It is the way here that when you cannot take care of your old people, you give them away to the nursing home.

TESSIE   Ma, where did you hear that? I would never do that to you.

GRANDMA   But you are so busy. And what will you do when I become so old and dang-hag,[13] forgetful, maybe even drooling here at my mouth?

TESSIE   Don't think about that. You will be with the family – I'll find a way. Take the vitamins Ben has been giving you.

GRANDMA   You spoke to Lorna this morning.

TESSIE   I did and I told her you are doing very well. I told her Rosie and you are together all the time. Now I must go make some phone calls. Are you okay here?

GRANDMA   Yes anak.

ROSIE   Hi Lola! *(Jumping up to kiss her)* Do you want to go for a walk?

GRANDMA   Ay, no, I'm tired. I don't always sleep very well when I dream too much.

ROSIE   Oh! I'm sorry, Lola!

GRANDMA   No – it's alright, Rosie. *(She sits on the bed.)* I have seen so many things, so many things are stored inside my heart. I think they must fly out, like a cave full of bats. And I don't know where they go.

ROSIE   Never mind, Lola. We won't do the dreaming anymore if you don't want to.

GRANDMA   *(Suddenly grabbing Rosie's arm)* No, it is important, Rosie. The gift. There is a responsibility that comes with the gift.

ROSIE   Lola, they're only dreams. We're just watching images, like TV.

GRANDMA   *(Starting toward the door)* You must always read the messages of your dreams. That is the burden of the gift. See, when God called Samuel in his sleep, did Samuel know right away it was the Voice of God?

TESSIE   *(Who has appeared at the door)* Ma, are you alright?

ROSIE   Grandma's fine, Mom. She was just interpreting a passage in the Bible for me. I was curious.

TESSIE   *(Amused)* Oh. Okay. *(Touching her daughter lightly on the nose)* That was a funny slip. I haven't heard you call your Lola "Grandma" in a long time.

ROSIE   Oh, yeah. That was a slip wasn't it?
(TESSIE exits. GRANDMA remains where she is.)

GRANDMA   Oh, Rosie, I have a present for you.

ROSIE   You—you do?

GRANDMA   Yes. You know you told me that you had a dream about a princess.

13 "Däng´-häg": Senile

ROSIE Yes.

GRANDMA I had a princess too.

ROSIE You did?

GRANDMA Do you remember?

ROSIE Yes, Lola . . .

GRANDMA It is almost like sleep.

ROSIE Yes. Like sleep.

GRANDMA It is almost like.

ROSIE Sleep.

The lights are out. A special light comes up to reveal a young woman, wearing a bridal gown and veil, her back to the audience. Another woman is kneeling, folding over the hem of the dress because it is too long. The woman in the dress is laughing.

WOMAN IN DRESS Maybe I should just stand on my toes the whole time.

WOMAN KNEELING No, it will be okay.

ROSIE What a beautiful gown, Lola!

WOMAN KNEELING Do you like it?

GRANDMA I made it myself.

ROSIE Who is the bride?

GRANDMA Tata.

WOMAN KNEELING *(In unison)* Tata?

   (WOMAN IN DRESS *turns and lifts the veil from her face.)*

WOMAN IN DRESS Yes?

ROSIE Oh!

WOMAN KNEELING Do you like your dress?

ROSIE She's—

WOMAN IN DRESS Beautiful.

GRANDMA The princess, no?

WOMAN IN DRESS Rosa, what if the hem is not straight?

WOMAN KNEELING Don't worry, Tata. I will check the hem three times to makes sure it looks perfect for your wedding day.

ROSIE So, the princess is not you, then.

GRANDMA No, Rosie. You were dreaming about someone very close to me. My youngest sister, Estrellita. Tata.
   (Both sisters burst into giggles.)

GRANDMA Do you think people remember the year 1941 as a good year?

ROSIE I don't know.

GRANDMA *(As lights fade on the scene)* I remember this moment when I think of 1941. My Tata was going to be a December bride.
   (In the darkness, one more ripple of laughter from the sisters)

ROSIE Thank you, Lola. *(Fade music. In a whisper . . .)* Thank you.
   (Fade lights – only ROSIE *is left, sitting and looking at the picture of* PAOLO.*)*

ROSIE A picture . . . of someone who would have liked me very much.
   I tried to ask Mom more about Uncle Paolo.

TESSIE Hmmph. But you are right. He does look a little like Albert.

ROSIE More than that. What was he like?

TESSIE Oh . . .

ROSIE Was he smart?

TESSIE Yes. Always reading. He also painted very well – no one knew that of course except the family. In many ways, he was really very shy.

ROSIE Did he ever get married?

TESSIE No.

ROSIE Did women fall in love with him?

TESSIE Oh, yes, all the time.

ROSIE Did you like him very much?

TESSIE Yes.

ROSIE Who was he closest to?

TESSIE So many questions, Rosie!

ROSIE No, please, Mom, don't go yet.

TESSIE Well. He did have a best friend. Max.

ROSIE Max.

MAX My brothers and sisters. We have all survived into 1947.

ROSIE Max.

PAOLO There goes Max, getting ready to work up a crowd again.

MAX Give thanks to America. God bless America. Let us cheer for America.

TESSIE Kuya, why does he get so excited?

MAX But let us not forget everything we fought for: the loved ones we lost! Our homeland!

ROSIE Max.

MAX Let us not forgive the puppet government who ruled our country in the shadow of
the Japanese. Those traitors should be put to death. Instead, a man like Roxas is put in
office!

PAOLO Max!

MAX Yes, Paolo.

PAOLO Have you met my sister, Tessie?

MAX A pleasure.

I see your brother has been bringing you to the rallies. What do you think of them?

TESSIE I see that this is something he cares about very much.

MAX Yes. As we all should.

PAOLO Are you really going to use that speech at our next gathering?

MAX What are you going to do, Paolo, interrupt me as you did the last time?

PAOLO It wasn't an interruption.

MAX I stop to draw a breath and suddenly you're talking. It's about another inspired idea,
another prophetic dream.

PAOLO You tend to get so extreme.

MAX To achieve what we need to achieve, we need to be extreme. To counteract and
overturn the violence done to us, we must use violence of our own. It is the dialectic. It is
for our country.

Do you see, Tessie, what we could do if we all feel this passionate! We wouldn't submit
to any kind of rule save our own. This is like fighting for my life. You know what I would
do if I could no longer fight for my country? I have a silver revolver I keep in a velvet
cloth. It is as ceremonial as the sword used by the Japanese in hara-kiri. I would point the
gun at myself, shoot myself with it, put the barrel to my mouth, to ensure that I'm truly
dead when my brain is blown to pieces—

PAOLO Max! Stop it! You are too much!

(MAX looks at both of them.)

MAX My apologies, Tessie. *(He hugs PAOLO briefly.)* Paolo. *(He exits.)*

TESSIE That's all. Max was his best friend.

ROSIE Yes.

TESSIE I've got to run, Rosie. Be good – I think Daddy will be home for dinner tonight.

ROSIE Yes, Mom. *(She stares at the picture of PAOLO.)*

(Blackout. Music.)

ROSIE *turns on the lamp quickly, startled awake. She listens for a few moments, and then realizes
there are sounds coming from downstairs. She rubs her eyes and gets out of bed.*

As she descends the stairs, GRANDMA *emerges from the kitchen with two lighted candles and
sets them on the table. The light reveals a small supper for one, complete with a place setting. As
soon as* ROSIE *enters the circle of light formed by the candles,* GRANDMA *peers into the darkness
and sees her.*

GRANDMA Ay, anak, why are you awake still?

ROSIE I heard noises.

GRANDMA *(Arranging the things on the table)* No, I'm just warming food, because my husband has not eaten yet.

ROSIE He . . . hasn't?

GRANDMA No. I knew tonight he would not be home until very late. I could see in his face, when he was putting on his clothes this morning. And the shirt he wore, that I took so long to iron yesterday.

ROSIE *(Reaching her hand towards her grandmother)* Lola . . . Maybe we should put the food away. He . . . It can be eaten tomorrow.

GRANDMA What are you saying? Are you saying he's not coming home?

ROSIE No . . .

GRANDMA I know he will come home. He comes home, he always comes home. He will come in the door, and not make any noise, hoping that everyone is asleep. He will turn around and I will see the anger in his face when he sees everything here, waiting for him. It makes him angry that I know he comes home late. But he eats the food, and I sit and watch him eat it. I sit and watch him eat it, and he says nothing to me. He does not even look at me, but I look at him. I see how his hair is a little bit wet, I can smell the clean smell of soap. I laugh inside, thinking how he takes care to wash himself before he comes home to me. *(She suddenly bursts into deep, devastated sobs.)*

(ROSIE runs to her and hugs her, trying to bring her over to the sofa. Once they are seated, she holds her grandmother's shoulders and rocks back and forth with her.)

ROSIE Lola, please stop crying. *(Pause)* Lola, we don't want anyone to hear you. *(Has an idea)* Lola, I made up a song for us. Do you want to hear it?

(GRANDMA continues to sob hysterically.)

ROSIE Shh, here, shh, here I will sing it for you, okay? Are you listening?

(Suddenly—
Someone flips a light switch on in the living room and TESSIE *and* BEN *descend the stairs quickly.)*

TESSIE What's going on? What's this food?

ROSIE *(Crying)* I don't know.

TESSIE Rosie, go upstairs!

ROSIE Why?

BEN Nanay! Nanay! Can you hear me?

TESSIE Ma? Ma? Unsa na man? Ngano man pag hilak ka?

GRANDMA He will come home! He will!

TESSIE Yes, he will come home.

BEN I'll probably have to increase the dosage.

GRANDMA Rosie!!

BEN We should bring her upstairs for now.

GRANDMA Rosie!!

BEN And we'll have to keep watch.

ROSIE I'll watch her.

TESSIE You're right. It won't be easy.

ROSIE I'll watch her!

BEN *(struggling to get* GRANDMA *up)* Will you take care of her!

TESSIE Rosie, please go to sleep, darling. Don't worry about it.

ROSIE I don't mind!

TESSIE Rosie, there's nothing you can do. Grandma is sick. *(Helping* BEN *take* GRANDMA *away)* And you're not to trouble her at all tomorrow!

(All exit, except for ROSIE.*)*

ROSIE Grandma . . . sick.
   Did it drain her . . . to remember so much?
   And the stories must have been painful for her, having been touched by them already.
   I'm only a granddaughter with the gift.
   In an odd way, these memories can't touch me.
   (TATA suddenly appears, wearing a flowing white gown.)

ROSIE It's only a dream.

Hello . . . I know you. You're Rosamunda's sister, Estrellita. Tata.

I'm Rosie. I'm Rosamunda's granddaughter. I remember you have a beautiful white bridal gown and your sister is taking it up at the hem.

Are you lost?

(With a sharp groan, TATA's *eyes roll upward and she collapses, blood pouring from her mouth.* ROSIE *screams.* TESSIE *runs on.)*

TESSIE Rosie! What are you doing out of bed? Rosie . . .

ROSIE *(Still seeing* TATA's *body)* Tata! Tata is dead! Tata is dead!

TESSIE Alright, that's it. You and Lola can't spend any more time talking nonsense. This is a madhouse! Rosie . . . ssh . . . Rosie . . .

(Blackout)

Through this monologue TESSIE *is setting up a breakfast tray meticulously containing soup, toast, and tea, but she takes care to wipe off the bowl, butter and quarter the toast, and arrange the napkin, flatware, and a bud vase in an orderly fashion.*

TESSIE In Camotes there were many superstitions that sprang out of fear of the dark. Not just the darkness of the night, but darkness in its many forms. In the boughs of the biggest, darkest trees there lived a great ogre called the agtah,[14] who would perch up in the branches, smoking a cigar, looking for small children to kidnap.

The wakwak[15] was a witch who flew from tree to tree, almost like a bird. While the duwende[16] were little elves who lived in tree stumps, bushes, holes in the ground, and were responsible for small evils.

And always there were ghosts, who sent chills through you if they passed through you in a cloud, or visited you in your half-sleep at night. Some say that if a ghost touches you while you are asleep that you can no longer wake up – you'd be dead.

All these stories were told to me as a little girl, to scare me into being good. But I realized later that the adults, having committed many more sins, were more afraid of these demons than I.

You realize that once you see otherwise rational human beings make decisions based on their fears of the dark. Houses are not built, roads are not traveled, instructions are not followed because of these fears. Patients die despite the medicines from clinics because they already believe that an evil hex has been put on them. Why even dreams, which are really just backfire from the brain's cortex, become some kind of powerful medium – they are messages from the past or omens of the future.

I could go on. I chose not to – I left largely because of that. What these beliefs say to me is that we as mortals have less control over our destinies than do these powers of the dark. I believe we have been given brains to take more control than that. And I would like my children to believe that also.

Which is why I want you to go to your makeup piano lesson and stop hanging around here.

ROSIE Can't I bring the tray upstairs at least?

ALBERT I grew up with Mom at home all the time.

TESSIE That's why I'm here.

ALBERT It was Sesame Street in the morning, Flipper in the afternoon.

TESSIE It's time for you to catch up on what you've been missing. Or I won't let you participate in those activities anymore. Now go. *(ROSIE exits.)*

ALBERT We watched a kid's show once where they would hang donuts by a string and the contestants would see who would eat their donut the fastest with their hands tied behind their back. Mom and I tried it. We ended up getting powdered sugar all over the floor and mostly over my face.

---

14 "Ug´-tuh" (cut off breath on second syllable): A dark, monstrous old man who, according to folklore, lives in big trees

15 "Wuck´-wuck"

16 "Doo-wen´-day"

Then, one day, I came home and Mom wasn't there.

ALBERT *(Simultaneously with* TESSIE*)* She had to start working.

TESSIE I had to start working.

TESSIE Of course we needed the money, but I needed to get out of the house.

ALBERT I thought it was because I was a smart-ass kid and she couldn't stand watching TV in the morning and TV in the afternoon.

   She never had to worry about Rosie, though. I made sure Rosie had someone to watch TV with, and play the donut game.

   So, what's all this about Rosie, Mom? You shouldn't be so hard on her.

TESSIE Maybe not. But you don't know the whole story.

ALBERT What is the whole story?

TESSIE *(Turning her back, fidgeting with the food)* Rosie and Grandma spend all their time together – and now Rosie is missing piano lessons, she doesn't stay for newspaper, and what do you think is happening to her studies?

ALBERT I know what's happening. Rosie is having the best time of her life.

TESSIE Albert—

ALBERT I think it's great that there's someone home when she gets home from school . . .

TESSIE Albert . . .

ALBERT . . . somebody to talk to, somebody to make dinner . . .

TESSIE *(Bursting out)* I don't have time for this right now, Albert! *(Turning back to the tray)* Why don't you go visit what's-her-name for a while?

ALBERT *(Coldly)* Heather, Mom, her name is Heather.

TESSIE Whatever.

   *(*BEN *enters.)*

ALBERT *(Exiting)* Don't bother trying, Dad. She's using the heavy artillery.

BEN Alberto, you apologize to your mother! Albert! *(Walking towards Tessie)* Tess—

TESSIE *(Holds up her hand)* Ben, it would really help right now if you went and played tennis.

BEN *(Not believing his ears)* What?!

TESSIE *(With her back to him)* You heard me. I would rather you go and—

BEN I know. I would rather talk.

TESSIE And I would rather not! *(He still doesn't move.)* Get out of here!

   (Pause)

BEN Okay. *(Starts retreating)* I will go play tennis. It doesn't MATTER, of course, that I don't have a PARTNER . . . but I will go. *(He starts to exit.)* Tess? *(She shakes her head – she is adamant.)* Okay – I'll play tennis. *(Exits)*

GRANDMA *(Entering)* Teresita? Why is there so much noise down here?

TESSIE What noise, Ma? It's just the usual stuff. How are you feeling? Are you hungry?

GRANDMA Ah . . . *(looking around, guardedly)* . . . no . . . *(She starts rummaging through her pockets and moves toward the kitchen.)*

TESSIE Where are you going?

GRANDMA *(Exasperated)* I didn't want to make the bedroom smell. I'm going to go smoke there in the garden.

TESSIE No, Ma—wait, before you go smoke—here. Why don't you sit here first? *(Installs her on the couch)* I'll bring the food to you.

GRANDMA Where's Rosie?

TESSIE Oh—she's making up a piano lesson. *(Hands her the soup)*

GRANDMA *(Between sips)* Such a good girl.

TESSIE Yes.

GRANDMA Bright.

TESSIE Yes.

GRANDMA Smart like you. Still . . . your sister Lorna was prettier when *she* was younger.

TESSIE Yes, yes, Ma.

GRANDMA Okay, I'm full already. I want to go smoke.

TESSIE Wait! Wait! I took the day off to be with you. Don't you want to stay with me?

GRANDMA Who is watching the store?

TESSIE   One of the managers is covering for me.

GRANDMA   Ay, Teresita, why did you do that? You only make yourself more nervous when you have nothing to do . . .

TESSIE   I do not!

GRANDMA   . . . like you have tapeworm or something. Okay, I'm here, anak. What did you want to talk about?

TESSIE   Do you like it here?

GRANDMA   Yes, it's very nice.

TESSIE   You don't know any other old people. I was afraid you would feel lonely.

GRANDMA   Ay – never mind! There is plenty to do here in the house. There is the garden outside. Rosie and I are like barcada – old friends – already.

TESSIE   But Ma . . .

GRANDMA   Do you remember when it would rain and you were tired of playing on the floor, you would come and sit by me while I was sewing. And Paolo would sing to us and you would lean your head here, on my knee, and listen.

(PAOLO appears, strumming a guitar and singing "Dandansuy."[17])

TESSIE   My favorite song when it would get dark.

GRANDMA   Do you remember?

TESSIE   Or when it was time to pick pebbles from the rice grains.

GRANDMA   Or when it was hot.

TESSIE   Ma—what happened last night? *(PAOLO disappears.)*

GRANDMA   Anak—what are you talking about?

TESSIE   Last night. Did you know you thought you were in Lahug, that Papa was not going to come home? This is my fault, for not staying home with you, for not making you happy.

GRANDMA   Tessie . . . What are you talking about? I am happy when my children are happy. Remember when we went to look for the pot of gold?

TESSIE   Ma . . .

GRANDMA   Remember? Do you remember Paolo and you and I followed the sun when it came out after the rainstorm? Do you remember . . .

TESSIE   . . . how far we walked.

GRANDMA   How the leaves were shining from the rain.

TESSIE   The sun was setting behind the farthest hill of the city. When we walked up, the mist in the air was filled with golden light. We had found our pot of gold and we made ourselves a wish.

Ma, all that happened a long time ago.

I must have been only five, maybe six years old at the time.

Do you remember what it was like later?

Do you remember Paolo and you spending more time by yourselves?

Do you remember?

Wasn't that when you started dreaming?

GRANDMA   What, anak?

TESSIE   It's alright. I know about it. Paolo told me. He even tried to show me once. "Sleep," he would say. "It is almost like—"

GRANDMA   Stop.

TESSIE   Ma, please tell the truth. Isn't that what you're really telling Rosie? You tell her it's called "the gift"?

And she believes it?

GRANDMA   It is a gift. We do not dream because we are unhappy. We do it because we do it. It is a special power to see what we have seen.

TESSIE   Don't you think I know Rosie has an overactive imagination? I know I should be home more. I know I should pay more attention to her, but I have to work, that's just the way it is. So she starts making up fairy tales! At the age of twelve!

GRANDMA   Who said she is making fairy tales?

---

17 "Dän´-dän-suy": An old Filipino ballad

TESSIE I know, Ma.

Just like Paolo. He didn't have a gift – he had his imagination. It drove him crazy. Waking up in sweats. Delirious about having to save the world. Save the world – you'd think someone so smart wouldn't believe in such nonsense. Next thing you know we'll be seeing the momo, the agtah, the wakwak flying from tree to tree.

GRANDMA Are you ashamed of your brother?

TESSIE I'm ashamed that I couldn't do anything! That nothing could be done, that dreaming was all you really could do.

GRANDMA What are you talking about, Maria Teresita?

TESSIE When I first noticed that Paolo and you had started this dream thing. Papa had begun coming home at three in the morning.

GRANDMA You know nothing.

I have always had these dreams. It's only that you were too young to notice before. But you can remember when we had to move around so much during the war. You remember when we had to leave the house in the middle of the night and go to the cave in the mountains. It was December, 1944 – you were already seven. I had had a dream about that night, I already knew where to go, I knew that we were taking the right road. You thought your father was the one who knew. But I told him. It was a good thing he listened to me. You know my sister Estrellita, your Tita Tata, went with another group, to another part of the jungle. They were going to an American shelter. They died just near there. The Japanese put bayonets through their stomachs. *(Pause)* I knew that would happen too.

Do you think this is only something to do when I am unhappy?

TESSIE I understand Ma. I'm sorry.

But it also has nothing to do with Rosie. I don't even think she's old enough to know. And I don't want her to know.

GRANDMA She wants to know her homeland.

TESSIE She can know it. She's not supposed to save it.

GRANDMA And what if that is what she wants?

(The juxtaposed dialogue that follows is to be spoken simultaneously.)

TESSIE I don't know, but neither does she. It's different for Rosie.

She is no longer in her mother's country.

We've worked hard to achieve this. My daughter wants for nothing and she can be anything she wants. There will be no talk of loyalties, she will not be dragged down by it, like him . . .
. . . to feel sick and powerless, thinking that you had somehow failed, because the land and the people you love have turned against you!

(Pause)

GRANDMA What is she then? Is she not still part of the same people and language and struggle?

The Philippines is a beautiful land, where one is not easily forgotten.

Why must it give up all that is good and beautiful in its people because of its troubles?

You cannot throw it away so easily, Maria Teresita.

It is your mother's country!

(Pause)

GRANDMA What are you talking about, anak?

TESSIE Paolo! I'm talking about Paolo! You say your dreams have told you so much! They didn't tell you enough to save Tata, they didn't tell you enough to save Paolo! If they told you anything at all, why don't you know what happened?

GRANDMA Tessie!

(TESSIE rushes out. Blackout. We hear a gunshot. A man's scream.)

(Lights up on MAX, holding in his hand a silver revolver, his other hand dripping blood. He is hysterical. He drags onstage the body of PAOLO, also drenched in blood, a thin trickle streaming from his mouth.)

MAX Oh my God! Somebody help me! Help me! Oh God!
(Blackout)

Darkness. Music.
  As CAST *enters . . .*

GRANDMA Once upon a time, there was a wise old man named Rosario who had lived so much and so long that he was too tired to live. He slept most of the day and would awaken only in the afternoon.
ROSIE The sun was so hot it would drive everyone into the shade.
GRANDMA Everyone would fall asleep.
ROSIE The cicadas would sing.
GRANDMA And slowly the old man would open his eyes and turn his small, wrinkled face towards me and say:
CAST Rosie! Rosamunda!
GRANDMA and ROSIE Yes?
ENSEMBLE *(in the cadence-like drone of a prayer)*
  Listen clearly! And I will tell you.
  I will tell you a story. As my mother and father had done.
  And their mothers and fathers before them.
  And their mothers and fathers before them.
  One long thread of story that never breaks
  as long as there is a single voice to tell it.
(Blackout. Lights up on GRANDMA.*)*

(The juxtaposed dialogue is to be spoken simultaneously.)

GRANDMA Max came and told me first.

I had met him only two or three times before that.
    I knew he was Paolo's good friend.

He told me he was going over to visit Paolo because he had not seen him in a long time. By then, Paolo would rarely see anybody.

Max said he heard a gunshot as he approached Paolo's apartment building.
But when he got there, he found the door unlocked and Paolo on the floor.
Thank God he got there first.
Otherwise, somebody could have gone in the apartment and stolen something or done something to the body.

ROSIE The game of hide and seek!

GRANDMA Paolo was right once.

ROSIE And through him you learned that you could see beyond yourself.

GRANDMA And I was never alone after that.

BEN A suicide, I understand.

Tessie never spoke about it.
He was a well-known figure at the University, with hardly any enemies that came to mind.

It might have been his actual political beliefs that got him in trouble, not so much what he was teaching at the University, but what he was personally involved in.

ALBERT I have never seen Rosie happier than she is now.
    Late at night, when we were younger, she would sneak across the hall to my bedroom and jump into bed next to me.

GRANDMA The night before Paolo died I
was standing alone by the window . . .

and I began to say the rosary to keep
myself company. I felt someone behind
me, close enough to touch me.
Then suddenly, I could not see at all and I
became frightened. I thought I was dying . . .

. . . until slowly, I saw the sky above me
. . . the grass below me . . . and I heard
my son's voice whisper, "Good night, Ma."

I used to have terrible headaches in
high school.
     But Rosie would only have to tell me
one of her stories, and I would lean my
head back and see—

ROSIE —crimson roses that explode their
petals into fiery birds that spread their
wings and fly away!

ROSIE A world sealed in ice and snow, and people there who built their houses and castles
underground!
ALBERT Instead of giving me sleeping potions, she gave me stories.
And now someone else can give her stories in return.

(The juxtaposed dialogue is to be spoken simultaneously.)

BEN At the same time, we must remember
the effect Nanay's visit has on the family.
     Does it stir up memories, hope,
happiness, anger?

Anger can last for a long time.

They say Time, like water, can wear
Anger's hard rock down.

But it is there nevertheless.

And for a long time it still sticks out and
trips you.

TESSIE The police came to the door, with
Max following behind.
     Everyone was being told, including Ma
and Pa, that Paolo had been shot.
     That no one knew who did it.
     I remember thinking to myself that
Max could have told them anything

that he could have *said* he had heard a
gunshot and gone and gotten their help
directly.

I kept that thought secret.

The day Max saw me, I felt dirty with
secrets.

You see, I loved my brother so much I
wanted to keep everything about him
intact.
     We kept the coffin closed during
mourning.
     I kept my heart closed with everything
else.

(Music intensifies)

I don't remember ever being alone with
Ma.
     There was always someone else around.
     But Ma and Paolo spent whole days
together.
     Pa would have noticed if he had been
home.

153

MAX   Oh, the dreams!
   In the beginning, they were great!
   Isn't that what catches people's fancy,
   that you have a dream?

   People would listen to me, even to him!
   – with his soft voice – when we were
   fuelled by the visions of Paolo's dreams.
   I could talk to a crowd, I could speak to
   them again and again about the injustices
   done to our country.
   But Paolo had only to start telling his
   story

   about the beautiful Garden of Eden – and
   you had to believe.

   He would tell you this story, about the
   great warrior, Rosario.
   He was a visionary – or thought he
   was.
   Together, ours was an irresistible voice,
   a formidable—

And Ma and Paolo wouldn't spend the
time talking.
   One night, when I was thirteen, I was
coming home late – I thought I heard
noises over my shoulder: rustling, a
cough, something muttering in the wind.
   Through the windows of my house I
saw one candle burning. I burst through
the door,

thinking I was safe, and instead saw my
mother, sitting in a chair, eyes frozen in
space, Paolo sitting across from her, with
eyes blank, almost milky.

   I thought, they are dead.
   I fell to the floor, heart beating, thinking they had been shot, looking for blood.
I brushed up against Paolo's leg and it
was warm.
   He stirred and suddenly yawned, as
though he had woken from a deep sleep.
I was angry, not only at having been
scared for nothing, but at having discovered some terrible—

TESSIE   —nightmare when Paolo came home one night, wild-eyed and shaking. He ran to
   my bedroom and clung to me like a child.
   What's wrong, Kuya! What have you been doing?
PAOLO   All I know is what I saw, and I've been trying to find out if it's true.
TESSIE   What is it, Kuya? Tell me.
PAOLO   It is election time, and the ballot box is being taken out of the schoolhouse. It is
   locked, and each vote has been tallied, for fairness, so that no one would have voted
   twice. It is placed in the back of a truck and is taken on the long trip to Manila. But when
   the truck hits a bump in the road, the box falls and breaks open, and there are no votes –
   only maggots!
TESSIE   Kuya, that was only a bad dream—
PAOLO   No, Tessie, I know what I saw. I have to find the spot in the road where the votes
   turn to maggots. And someone may kill me for wanting to find out. But promise me you'll
   never tell anyone what I saw.
TESSIE   I don't think anyone will find out. (Pause) Does Max know?

(The juxtaposed dialogue is to be spoken simultaneously.)

MAX   You see, Paolo was not a political
creature.
   He just happened to be involved with
politics.
   He was eloquent, he was passionate, he
truly loved his country.
   He was also losing his mind.
   He suffered through delirious spells
calling me on the phone in the middle of
the night with talk about his "legacy."
   "Max!" he would say. "The dreams! It's
as if at night I am forced to live in
another country.

TESSIE   Paolo knew from the beginning
what was happening, and what would
happen to the Philippines.

   And the more unhappy he was, the
worse the dreams became.

It's as if what I see is like the long shadow cast before you as the sun climbs to its peak."

What is that?

I could almost hear the cold sweat in his voice.

You could see it in the letters I found after his death.

Rummaging through his things, I found unsent letters to Tessie. She didn't appreciate my bringing them to her.

PAOLO And I regret to think, my dearest Tessie, that if I had shared my wonderful visions in painting, as you had told me, then all three of us – you, and Ma, and I – could have taken great pleasure in them and forgotten all the unhappiness in our lives.

It always seems as though we could never sleep – that at three in the morning we would be brought upon to face the ugliness in our lives.

At three in the morning, when your mind is left to wander.

At three in the morning, when you should be the most free.

(Pause)

BEN All I know is that the house is not the same anymore.

TESSIE I didn't appreciate Max's finding those letters Paolo wrote me.

That wasn't what he was looking for.

He was *never* crazy!

You didn't really know him!

Oh sure, Max could work up a crowd, he could work up a froth in his mouth just talking about the injustices to our country, the oppression.

But Paolo would tell you the story of the great warrior Rosario and you had to believe.

How he conjured up the Philippines like a wonderful Garden of Eden. The descendants of the great warrior, Rosario, with swords of fire, defending the Garden of Eden from the Gates of Hell.

I don't want Rosie to be like him.

GRANDMA I don't want Rosie to be like her.

ALBERT It's not a question of Rosie being like anybody else.

TESSIE What is in the past is in the past.

The dreams began to affect his waking hours.

It was a vicious circle.

MAX I just wanted to show her how Paolo was really going crazy.

MAX The next thing you know, we'll be hearing about the momo—

GRANDMA Who said he was making fairy tales?

MAX —the wakwak, the agtah flying from tree to tree!

ALBERT I think Rosie should hang on to the fairy tales.

GRANDMA For it is your mother's country.

BEN If for once there could be peace in this house . . .

GRANDMA We cannot forget the songs of our mothers and fathers . . .
    . . . who died defending what was theirs.

ALBERT Rosie still needs her living family . . .
    . . . not ghosts.

BEN Let's not dig up ghosts.

TESSIE They're no longer ghosts.

GRANDMA THEY'RE NOT GHOSTS!
  (ALL freeze.)
  I see them right before me!

It's as if you all haven't made peace.

TESSIE One dead brother and one dead sister . . .
should be allowed to rest.

(Lights up only on GRANDMA *and* ROSIE, *alone in the darkness)*

GRANDMA Tata, how did you manage to find me?
Paolo, you've come to see your mother.
Ay . . . my children . . . where have you gone?
Where are you?
(Blackout)

As *lights come up, airport sounds. The family is waiting for* GRANDMA's *flight to board.*

ROSIE Of course, she had to go back. Spirits can't live in Brooklyn. Neither can Grandma.

TESSIE Ma, is there anything you want us to send you?

BEN Tessie, you know she can't hear you right now.

TESSIE I know she can – just . . . not right now.

GRANDMA Ay - so many people here . . .

TESSIE Yes, Ma, we're at the airport. You'll be leaving in fifteen minutes.

ROSIE Grandma didn't seem to get it.
The whole night before, we had spent packing her things.
The whole morning, we had talked about her going back to the Philippines.
We were at the airport for over an hour.
Perhaps she didn't want to wake up, so that she wouldn't have to say goodbye.

ALBERT Do you think we'll go visit her next year?

BEN I don't see why not. Tessie?

TESSIE Yes. I'd like that. That would be better.

ALBERT Hey, they're starting to board. We better get her going . . .

BEN Ma? Ma? Come on, now, Ma . . . let's bring your things. Here, hold this . . .

TESSIE Here, Ma, let me fix your scarf.

ALBERT Bye, Grandma. It was really good having you.

TESSIE Albert, why are you saying goodbye? She's not leaving yet.

ALBERT Mom, they're boarding NOW.

TESSIE *(Realizing)* Oh my God . . .
  Ma, goodbye . . . *(In spite of herself, she starts sobbing.)*

GRANDMA Anak? Why are you crying?

TESSIE Because you're leaving, Ma!

GRANDMA Ay, na'ako . . . *(She strokes* TESSIE's *head.)*
  My brave girl. Thank you, Maria Teresita, for this visit. You have become beautiful. You have become a wife and a mother. I am very, very proud and happy for you.
  Shh, shh . . . don't cry. Some families never get to touch each other again. We are lucky in that we can.

ROSIE Lola . . .

GRANDMA Yes, Rosie.

ROSIE I forgot to ask you . . . I wanted a picture of you as a child.

GRANDMA *(Holding* ROSIE's *hands very tightly for a moment)* Ay, Rosie. Of course. So now you know how to find a picture of me. *(She starts to exit.)*
  (They all call goodbye as the lights fade.)

ROSIE We went to visit Grandma for Christmas. She died soon after. I did find an old picture of her when she was thirteen. Grandma was right. I knew how to find a better picture.

(She runs over to a tableau of Grandma, Paolo, Tata and Max and in an instant is "captured" in a photographic, sepia light. She runs to a tableau of Tessie, Ben and Albert, and is captured by a brighter light in the same way.)

ROSIE/TESSIE You see the Filipino woman – the Filipina – is descended from a long line of priestesses.

ROSIE/GRANDMA And I could remember all my dreams as if I were dreaming them for the first time.

(As ROSIE exits through the audience)

ROSIE/TESSIE/GRANDMA Once upon a time, I was a little girl, with a secret and wonderful power.

(Blackout)

(Music. A scratchy record of "Ang Kinabuhe.")

Evelina Fernandez

Biography

Evelina Fernandez was born and raised in East Los Angeles. She progressed from Garfield High School to East L.A. College to Cal State University, Los Angeles. While at Cal State she became involved in the Chicano Movement and found her niche in Chicano Theater. She began her professional acting career in Luis Valdez's *Zoot Suit* playing Della, the female lead in the original stage production at the Mark Taper Forum.

Since *Zoot Suit*, Evelina has toured nationally and internationally with El Teatro de la Esperanza performing at the New York Shakespeare Festival and the Denver Center for the Performing Arts, to name a few.

A founding member of the Latino Theater Lab, Evelina has co-starred in several productions at the Los Angeles Theater Center, including *La Victima*, *King Lear*, *Etta Jenks*, *Roosters*, *Stone Wedding*, and *August 29*, which she co-wrote with members of the Lab.

Her TV credits include *Roseanne*, *Hill Street Blues*, *Knots Landing*, *The Larry Sanders Show* and more. Evelina was nominated for a *Desi Award* and was the recipient of the prestigious Nosotros *Golden Eagle Award* (Female Rising Star) for her work in *American Me* where she starred with Edward James Olmos as the female lead "Julie" in the critically acclaimed film. Most recently she completed a comedy starring with Paul Rodriguez, Edward James Olmos, and Cheech Marin called *A Million to Juan*.

As well as the play *How Else Am I Supposed to Know I'm Still Alive*, Evelina's writing credits include an original screenplay, *Luminarias*. She has written a screenplay for Columbia Pictures and a television sitcom for Disney.

Evelina is a also a poet and motivational speaker, performing and speaking to youth and adults in schools and community centers throughout California and the Southwest.

She is married to Jose Luis Valenzuela, Artistic Director of the Latino Theater Company and professor at UCLA, and has two children. They live in East Los Angeles.

Photo: Phil Nardully

Artistic statement

I was born in East L.A., but moved to Phoenix, Arizona, where I lived until I was 9 years old. When my parents divorced we moved back to East L.A. with my mother to live with my Nana and my Tata (grandparents). My "real" memories begin here, in East L.A., at Rowan Avenue Elementary, where I wrote my first stories and speeches for programs at school. I went on to study drama at Robert Louis Stevenson Junior High School (my first role was that of a pirate in *Treasure Island*), where my drama teacher, Mr. Hunter, planted a seed in my heart by telling me I had talent and should consider becoming an actress. I moved on to James A. Garfield High School, where I lost interest in school and eventually dropped out in the eleventh grade. I went to cosmetology school and dropped out after figuring I wasn't very good at it. Then, I got married at 19 to the boy I had dated since I was 15 (a rock musician), divorced at 21, because he didn't want me to go to school, went to Cal State L.A., joined the Chicano movement and Chicano Theater and found out who I am – a Chicana, a woman, a human being.

I began my professional acting career in Luis Valdez's *Zoot Suit* in 1978. Fifteen years later I find myself frustrated that there are no significant roles for Latinas in film, television and theater, and by the fact that when there are, they are played by non-Latinas. I've played "Rosa" the maid and "Maria" the gang mother one too many times and am now trying to create roles, as an actor and writer, that portray Chicanas the way we really are – human beings – with all the complexities and contradictions that all people have. I am concerned that our stories will not be told. That they will not be passed on. That my daughter and other young Latinas will not know that their legacy is that of strong, courageous, passionate, intelligent women. I'm concerned that the absence of Latinas and Latinos in film, television and theater affects our children, not just Latino children, but all children, subconsciously. What does it do to them not to see Latinos in positive roles on TV, film, theater? What does it do to Latinos not to see themselves . . . their mothers, grandmothers, grandfathers? Our community self-esteem is at stake. So, I write for them, for my daughter, for my mother, for myself, for all the Latinas and Latinos who are, for the most part, invisible.

How Else Am I Supposed to Know I'm Still Alive was born out of that frustration. It was written for my friends Lupe Ontiveros and Angela Moya. Two extremely gifted actors who are rarely given the opportunity to play leading roles. Nellie and Angie are not characters I created. They represent the women I grew up around, my Mom, my Tias, their friends. Women who are full of life, love, pain, hope and courage. Women who know that men can hurt you, but continue to look for love. Women who are middle-aged but still talk about and have sex. Women who love and support each other. Women who are human beings . . .

Production history

How Else Am I Supposed to Know I'm Still Alive was first produced at La Plaza de La Raza in East Los Angeles as the winner of the "Nuevo Chicano L.A. Theaterworks" contest in the Summer of 1989. It was directed by Jay Stephens-Rodriguez and featured Lupe Ontiveros and Angela Moya.

The play has been produced by El Centro Su Teatro in Denver, Colorado, Teatro Vision in San Jose, California, in Milwaukee and toured nationally with El Teatro Campesino, and has had countless readings throughout the country. It has been adapted into an award-winning film through the Hispanic Film Project at Universal starring the original cast members and directed by Jose Luis Valenzuela. It has been and continues to be screened at numerous national and international film festivals.

8 How Else Am I Supposed to Know I'm Still Alive

Evelina Fernandez

Characters

NELLIE: a Chicana of 52

ANGIE: a Chicana of 48

MANNY: a big fat stomach

A kitchen in a house in East L.A. There is a stove, a refrigerator, a sink and a small table with a colorful tablecloth on it. There is a window with frilly-type curtains.

In enters NELLIE. *A "well-endowed" woman in her fifties. She has bright red hair, bright red lips and bright red nails. She's wearing high heels and she's singing a song. She's carrying a grocery bag and a freshly cut rose. She puts the bag on the counter and gets a vase out of the cupboard for the rose. She fills it with water and before she puts the rose in the vase she holds it up and smells it. She smiles.*

NELLIE Well, Nellie, you still got it. Fifty years old and you still drive them crazy. So what if he was fat, bald and toothless. *(She laughs a big laugh.)* He's still got an . . . imagination. *(She pricks her finger on a thorn on the rose.)* Ay chingado! *(She sucks her finger. Looks up to God.)* OK, OK. What happened to your sense of humor? I guess you think an old bag like me has no feelings anymore. Hey, I need my thrills too. You think cuz I'm old I don't need a little wink, a little smile, a little pinch on the butt? How else am I supposed to know I'm still alive. *(She goes to the sink and runs water on her finger and notices it's deeper than she thought. To God.)* Ya ni la friegas! *(She dries it off. The phone rings. She answers it.)* Hello? Oh, Hi Manny. *(She reaches for the grocery bag and takes out a pack of cigarettes and a package of store-bought tortillas.)* Of course I'm up. Are you? *(She laughs her big laugh then catches herself and looks up.)* Just kidding. *(To* MANNY*).* Of course I have coffee. *(She picks up the package of tortillas.)* And fresh home-made tortillas. *(She tosses them on the counter and lights a cigarette.)* Yes, there are some of us that still make them by hand. Sure, come on over, I'll make you some breakfast. OK. Toodloo. *(She hangs up. To herself.)* Yes, Nellie, you still drive them crazy. And this one's not even a senior citizen yet. *(She pulls open the package of tortillas and puts them in a dishcloth then into a basket and into the oven. She turns it on then opens the fridge.)* Let's see here. I think something simple but not ordinary. Something different. Something his wife never gives him. *(She laughs.)* We won't find that in the hielera will we. *(She looks up.)* Eh. You know I wouldn't do that with Manny . . . his stomach's too big. He'd have to be pretty enormous to get it past that pansota! *(She laughs, then stops.)* Hummm, maybe he is . . . Nah, his feet are too small. *(She starts pulling things out of the fridge.)* Aver . . . I can make him some huevos rancheros or . . . weenies con huevo. No, that was Louie's favorite breakfast . . . my Louie . . . *(To God.)* I don't understand you. A big strong happy guy like my Louie. Never sick a day in his life. He comes home. He sits down to eat. "I don't feel good Nellie. My chest; I think I'm coming down with a cold." "Go lie down viejo, I'll rub some Vicks on you." And when I'm rubbing, thinking what a strong chest it is. Big and brown with muscles and hair, he starts choking. "Help me Nellie." Then, "I love you baby . . ." Then he's gone. Just like that. You took him without even thinking about how much I needed that man; how much I was gonna miss him. Without even caring that I belonged to him and that without him I don't belong. You really piss me off you know that! *(A knock at the door)* Gee, that was fast. *(To the door)* Just a minute. *(She adjusts herself. Pulls out an apron, sticks her hands in the flour and wipes them off leaving just a little on her hands and a dab on her face. She puts on a sexy smile, pulls in her stomach, holds up her cigarette à-la-Joan Crawford and stands in a sexy stance as she opens the door.)*

ANGIE *(Off stage)* What's wrong with you?

NELLIE *(Releases stance and smile)* Oh, it's just you.
(Enter ANGIE. Around the same age as Nellie only more haggard. No make-up, no hair-do, not much of anything. She enters as if it's her own home.)

ANGIE Well, don't act so excited.

NELLIE I was expecting somebody else. *(She looks out the door to see if MANNY's coming.)*

ANGIE Some viejo panzon I bet.

NELLIE He's not that old.

ANGIE *(Gets a cup for coffee.)* Who is the panzon?

NELLIE *(Nonchalantly)* Manny Lopez . . .

ANGIE Panzon is right! Forget it Nellie. He's gotta have a great big one to get past that thing. Have you seen the size of his feet?

NELLIE *(To God)* I told you. *(To Angie)* I just invited him over for breakfast, that's all. Your mind's always in the gutter. *(She lights a cigarette.)*

ANGIE Keeping yours company. *(She sits to drink her coffee. Nellie gives her a look like she wants to get rid of her.)* Well, can I finish my coffee before I leave?

NELLIE OK. But hurry up. *(She pulls stuff out of the fridge. To herself.)* Chorizo con papas. Yeah, that's good.

ANGIE Do you have to smoke all the time? *(A sick look on her face)* You're gonna get breast cancer, you know that? *(NELLIE ignores her. She gets busy preparing the chorizo con papas.)* Do you have any toast?

NELLIE No. Just tortillas. *(ANGIE heads towards the fridge.)* They're in the oven.

ANGIE In the oven? *(She opens the oven and pulls out the little basket.)* Cute Nellie.

NELLIE *(Laughs)* He'll never know the difference. He just likes to eat.
(Angie pulls out a tortilla and puts them back in the oven. She sits at the table and says nothing. NELLIE recognizes the look,

stops what she's doing, goes into the bathroom and comes out with a roll of toilet paper. She places it on the table in front of ANGIE.)*

NELLIE OK. What's wrong?

ANGIE *(Picks up toilet paper roll and proceeds to unroll)* Nothing.

NELLIE Come on Angie.

ANGIE *(Still unrolling)* Forget it. You don't have time anyway . . .

NELLIE Well. *(She looks at the clock, sighs; ANGIE starts unrolling.)* Just give me the main points, forget the details.

ANGIE See! *(She starts rolling toilet paper back on.)*

NELLIE OK, OK. Gee, nobody has a sense of humor anymore. *(She looks at the clock.)* I have time, tell me.

ANGIE *(Starts unrolling in a big way and smiles)* Thanks, Nellie. You know you're the only one I can really talk to.

NELLIE Yeah, I know. *(She takes the roll away from ANGIE and cuts off the paper. ANGIE breaks down.)* Is it Joe? Another affair? (ANGIE shakes her head no.)* Is it the kids? *(ANGIE shakes no.)* Is it you? *(ANGIE shakes yes.)* You? *(ANGIE shakes yes again.)* You what? *(ANGIE shakes no.)* It's not you? *(ANGIE shakes yes.)* Is it you? Well, what about you? *(ANGIE shakes no.)* Then give me a hint. Que la chingada! Are you gonna tell me or not!! *(ANGIE gets up and runs into the bathroom very upset and slams the door. NELLIE calls into the bathroom.)* OK. I'm sorry. Come on Angie, come out of there. *(We hear ANGIE throwing up.)* Ugh! Lift up the tapadera! *(We hear the lid go up. ANGIE barfs some more.)* What's the matter with you Angie? Estas cruda or what? *(Toilet flushes and the lid goes down. ANGIE slowly opens the door.)*

NELLIE I know you're upset about something but don't start drinking over it. Remember what happened to Carmelita?

ANGIE Nellie, shut-up. I don't have a hangover. *(She sits at the table. She looks green.)*

NELLIE You look like shit. *(She gives her a glass of water.)* Que comiste? I haven't seen you look this bad in years. Not since you were pregnant with Cindy. Remember how you'd get . . . *(ANGIE sobs)* morning sickness? Wait a minute . . . you're not saying that you're . . . *(ANGIE shakes yes)* you mean you still can?

(ANGIE *gives her a dirty look.*) I mean you're 50 years old!

ANGIE   Forty-eight.

NELLIE   Well, ya vas pa'fifty. Do you still get your period? I haven't got one in ages. I never even got to use those new pads. You know the ones that stick to your chones with no seguro. Ay, Angie, how did you let this happen? After so many years. I knew you would take Joe back sooner or later, but I didn't think you'd go as far as having sex with him.

ANGIE   (*Quietly*) It's not Joe's.

NELLIE   (*Laughs her big laugh*) Cochina!

ANGIE   Ay Nellie, callate. It's not funny. I'm a pregnant grandmother.

NELLIE   Yeah, but who, how?

ANGIE   (*Looks around*) Lock the door. (NELLIE *goes to lock the door.*) Close the curtains. (NELLIE *closes the curtains.*) Now promise that . . .

NELLIE   Si hombre. I promise not to tell anybody, ever.

ANGIE   Cross your heart.

NELLIE   May God strike me dead. (*She looks up cautiously.*)

ANGIE   OK. Remember the weekend of the Las Vegas turn-around?

NELLIE   The one we didn't go on because we gave up gambling for Lent?

ANGIE   Yeah. And remember you were all aguitada because we couldn't go to the Friday night Bingo?

NELLIE   Yeah, because the jackpot was $4,000 that night.

ANGIE   Remember I told you I was going to bed real early that night because I had a migraine?

NELLIE   Yeah.

ANGIE   Well, I lied. I went to the Bingo.

NELLIE   Cabrona!

ANGIE   Well, the jackpot was $4,000 and remember we had that discussion about whether or not Bingo was gambling and I told you I didn't think it was because we weren't betting anything we were just buying our cards and that if it was gambling they wouldn't have Bingo at the church in the first place?

NELLIE   Yeah, and I said it's playing for money and it's a vicio just like gambling in Vegas and you agreed.

ANGIE   I didn't agree.

NELLIE   Well, you stopped arguing.

ANGIE   Just so you would shut-up. You know how when you think you're right about something you go on forever.

NELLIE   Well, it is gambling . . .

ANGIE   See!

NELLIE   OK. Go on.

ANGIE   So, I went to the Bingo. But I didn't win of course.

NELLIE   (*To God*) Thank you.

ANGIE   But I landed up sitting next to that man . . .

NELLIE   What man?

ANGIE   You know, the one you're always saying is crazy over you.

NELLIE   The one with the salt and pepper canas? (ANGIE *smiles.*) Him? But he always stares at *me*!

ANGIE   Well, that's what I thought too. Especially when he asked me "Where's your friend?" I said "She has a migraine."

NELLIE   Pinche! And you took him home and screwed him? Jesus Christ, Angie, I never thought you were the type.

ANGIE   I didn't just take him home and screw him!

NELLIE   Well, that's the only way to get in your condition . . .

ANGIE   I mean we didn't just go over to my place just like that. It kind of led up to it . . .

NELLIE   Led up?

ANGIE   Yeah. After the Bingo he said "Are you walking home alone?" and I said "Yes." "Which way do you go?" he says. "Up Rowan" I say. "Well, I can walk you. It's not safe for a lady to walk home alone at this hour."

NELLIE   Ay tu . . .

ANGIE   And since we see him at the Bingo every week I figured he wasn't a maniaco or anything.

NELLIE   You never know.

ANGIE   So I said OK.

NELLIE   You hussy.

ANGIE   So he walked me and we talked . . .

NELLIE   About?

ANGIE   Oh, about a lot of things. About old times. About how much the neighborhood has changed. About how he's a widower and he owns his own business . . .

NELLIE   Shit! I knew he was a good catch! But no. You had to go and take advantage of me not being there that night. You traitor!

ANGIE   He told me he was always looking at me, not you. He said you're not his type!

NELLIE *(Pissed)* Not his type, ha! He's lucky I even give him a smile, the old fart. It figures he would go for somebody like you.

ANGIE And what do you mean by that?!

NELLIE What I mean is some men can't deal with a woman like me. Someone that has both looks and brains!

ANGIE Gee, thanks.

NELLIE I'm not saying you don't have either . . . you have brains . . . *(ANGIE gives her a dirty look.)* What I'm trying to say is . . .

ANGIE That I'm an old bag!! You know what your problem is Nellie? You're jealous.

NELLIE What?

ANGIE Yeah, you're jealous cuz Henry . . .

NELLIE Henry? Ha!

ANGIE Yes, Henry, went after me and not you. You're jealous cuz you practically threw yourself at him and he looked right past you at me. You're jealous because you're always flaunting your big body in front of men and nobody gives you a second look.

NELLIE Ha!

ANGIE And you can't believe that anybody would look at me because I'm . . . quiet. And I spend my time doing other things besides getting my canas dyed and my nails done and gossiping on the phone. What's killing you is that someone looked at me and liked what he saw. And you can't believe it!

NELLIE What I can't believe is that you think I'm jealous of you! Why? Because you got a cheap thrill? And now look at you; you're a pregnant old lady. You're gonna have another baby!

ANGIE Oh no I'm not.

NELLIE What do you mean?

ANGIE I can't have it Nellie. I'm 50 years old.

NELLIE Forty-eight! Angie what are you telling me?

ANGIE Well, I'm gonna have a . . . you-know-what.

NELLIE An abortion?

ANGIE Shhh!

NELLIE I can just see you walking into one of those clinics!

ANGIE Would you rather see me walking into one of those breathing classes? Como se llaman? Lamaze? *(She mispronounces it.)*

NELLIE Lamaze. *(She pronounces it cor-rectly.)* You got a point. *(She laughs her big laugh.)* I can just see you! *(She starts huffing and puffing.* ANGIE *doesn't know whether to laugh or cry. She laughs. They have a good laugh together.)*

ANGIE Oh Nellie, how did this happen to me?

NELLIE You tell me. So, he walked you home and you asked him in o que?

ANGIE On the way home we realized that we graduated from Garfield in the same year. So he came in to take a look at my old annual.

NELLIE Uh huh.

ANGIE So, I couldn't be rude. I asked him if he wanted a cup of coffee. He says "No thank you, but I could go for a little glass of wine, if you have any." He has this real nice smile. *(She pauses to savor the memory.)*

NELLIE OK. Go on.

ANGIE So I remembered that I had an old bottle of wine around and I took it out and dusted all the mugre off of it. Then I found some old wine glasses that I hadn't used since before Joe left. It was really embarrassing cuz I didn't even have a corkscrew. We laughed so hard. Then we just pushed the cork into the bottle and poured the wine. He toasted "To a beautiful gal." *(NELLIE and* ANGIE *giggle.)* Yeah, and we talked about all the same people we knew and about old music. You know, like El Trio Los Panchos and Perez Prado. I told him I had an old Ray Charles album, so we put it on. Then they played "I Can't Stop Loving You" and he said "Come on Angie, let's dance." I felt so . . . silly; like I was 16 years old. He pulled me to my feet then towards him. It felt so good, you know, to feel a man's arms again. At first we danced far apart then we looked into each other's eyes. We were both twinkling. We smiled and laughed and smiled and laughed again. Like we were 16. Then you know me . . . I started thinking about Joe and how he hurt me and I started to cry.

NELLIE Oh no . . .

ANGIE Then he pulled me into him and I don't know what he was thinking but he started crying too. Maybe it was the old music, I don't know. And we held each other and we cried. Then when we were through crying . . .

NELLIE You screwed.

ANGIE   No. We talked about life and how we can't give up cuz we're older and we kind of gave each other courage. (She smiles.) By that time the bottle of wine was gone . . . so then we screwed.

NELLIE   And . . .?

ANGIE   What do you mean, and?

NELLIE   Well, don't stop there. Get to the juicy part. How was it? Give me the details.

ANGIE   I can't.

NELLIE   You better! I listened to all the mushy stuff, now get to the good part.

ANGIE   OK . . . We started talking about all the old friends we knew and how a lot of them are already dead. Then he looked at me and said "We're still alive Angie, me and you. We're still alive and we're together, so let's live." That's when he kissed me and I kissed him back. And I don't think he thought we were gonna go all the way, but I uh . . .

NELLIE   You what?

ANGIE   I touched him.

NELLIE   My God! Angie, not you!

ANGIE   I just did it without thinking.

NELLIE   And was it hard?

ANGIE   (Nods. Quietly.) And big.

NELLIE   Oh shit! I knew it! What did he do Angie? Was he shocked?

ANGIE   We both were. Then he asked me where my bedroom was and I took him there. And it was . . .

NELLIE   Yeah?

ANGIE   It was real nice.

NELLIE   Nice?

ANGIE   He made me feel like . . . Oh never mind.

NELLIE   He made you feel like what?

ANGIE   (Blurts) Like I was ready to pop! And then I did.

NELLIE   Bendito sea dios!

ANGIE   I never felt that before.

NELLIE   Never?

ANGIE   Uh uh. Was it a what-do-you-callit?

NELLIE   It sure sounds like it.

ANGIE   (Giggles) Gee, I'm glad I didn't die without knowing what it feels like.

NELLIE   (To God) You sure took your time. (To ANGIE) In all the years you were married to Joe you never felt like that?

ANGIE   No.

NELLIE   No wonder you stopped doing it with him.

ANGIE   Oh, yeah. We stopped doing it a long time before he left.

NELLIE   Balgame dios Angie. How could you sleep in the same bed with a man and not touch him?

ANGIE   You just get used to it, I guess. We started doing it less and less over the years. Then when he started having the affair with the blonde . . .

NELLIE   La gabacha esa? What was her name?

ANGIE   Vivian.

NELLIE   That's right, la Vivian.

ANGIE   Well, after that it was never the same. I didn't like for him to touch me anymore. I'd go to bed real early and pretend . . .

NELLIE   (Sarcastically) To have a migraine?

ANGIE   No, I'd pretend I was asleep. Then one night he came home kind of tipsy. I guess Vivian didn't want him anymore, and he got on his knees next to the bed and he begged me to forgive him. He cried and cried. But you know what Nellie, I couldn't feel sorry for him. It's like my heart was frozen. Then he tried to crawl into bed next to me and he tried to touch me here. (She points to her breasts.) I looked him straight in the eye and I said "Don't touch me ever again. I hate you. You make me sick!" Nellie, it felt so good! To hurt him the way he hurt me. To break him. To freeze his heart . . . He never touched me again.

NELLIE   Shit, I wouldn't either. Hijola, you're not the dummy I thought you were.

ANGIE   (Proudly) Thanks. (A knock at the door)

NELLIE   Oh shit, it's Manny. Let me get rid of him. (She opens the door. We don't see MANNY; just a big stomach which comes in halfway through the doorway.)

NELLIE   Hi Manny. (To ANGIE. Loudly.) Angie, look who's here. Manny Gonzalez.

ANGIE   (Calls out) Hi Manny. Is Connie with you?

NELLIE   No? Where is Connie anyway? (We hear MANNY whispering something.) What's that Manny? Speak up. Oh you gotta go? You just stopped by to what? (He hands her the newspaper.) Oh, that's nice of you. Thanks Manny. Say Hi to Connie for us, OK. (Stomach leaves. NELLIE slams the door. She silently measures his stomach with both hands.) Impossible. (To God.) You couldn't be that generous. (To ANGIE) Entonces que?

ANGIE Well, I'm going to have a you-know-what and that's that. (NELLIE *goes to the window and looks out. She is silent.*) What's wrong with you? Are you still mad about Henry?

NELLIE Forget about that. It's the you-know-what ... well, maybe you should think about it. It might be nice for you to have another baby. I mean just think Angie. A tiny baby ... with little hands and little toes ... (ANGIE *looks at* NELLIE *like she's nuts.*) And they smell so good. Their skin's so soft and their little breath smells so sweet.

ANGIE Yeah, and their little shit smells so bad! And they wake you up all night and then there's diapers and toilet training, then school and report cards ... Forget it Nellie! (*She catches herself and gasps.* NELLIE *runs into the bathroom and slams the door.*) Nellie, I'm sorry. I wasn't thinking. I forget ... I know babies are special to you. I wish that God would've given you at least one. It's not fair that I had so many and you and Louie couldn't have any ...

NELLIE (*Comes out of the bathroom. She smiles through her tears.*) But we sure had fun trying! (*She laughs her big laugh. She gets busy in the kitchen.*) And boy did we try. We'd make love in the morning, when he'd come home for lunch, and at night before we went to sleep. Boy, I loved that man. And he loved me. If he didn't he would've left me as soon as he found out I couldn't give him any babies. He wanted children so bad. We both did. We wanted them right away too. One right after the other. We wanted a house full of kids running in and out, yelling and screaming and fighting and laughing and crying. I pictured myself with one hanging onto my apron, one at my chichi and one on the way. So, as soon as we got married we got to work at making them. When it didn't happen at first we didn't really worry cuz we were having so much fun trying. Then a year went by. Then another. Then, we just stopped talking about it. After five years I remember I brought it up. I said "Viejo, maybe I can't have babies." He laughed and said "You never know honey, maybe I'm the one that's shooting blanks." It wasn't his Huevitos, it was mine. They weren't going where Louie's could get to them. Back

then there wasn't anything to do about it. The day we found out we drove home from the doctor's and didn't say a word. Louie just held my hand and looked straight ahead. It was like we lost all the babies we never had. El travieso del Little Louie y La Preciosa del la Little Nellie and all the rest of them we'd dreamed of. I never cried about it. But Louie did. That night he cried like a baby. I held him and I sang to him until we both fell asleep. Then we never talked about it for a long time. Like we were in mourning. Till one day Louie came home from work in a real good mood. He sat down at the table and said "Come here baby." I walked over to him. He hugged my waist, put his head on my panza and kissed it. "You know, Nellie," he said "God didn't give us babies cuz we love each other too much. How could I love anybody but you and how could you love anybody but me. But hey, that's O.K. with me. As long as I got you, Nellie, I'm a happy man. You're all I want. You're all I need."

ANGIE Louie was a good man.

NELLIE Yeah ... But now he's dead and here I am ... If we at least would've had one or maybe adopted one. It's funny, huh? I've wanted a baby all these years and you have one inside of you and you don't want it. (*To God*) You sure can be shitty sometimes.

ANGIE But Nellie, I've had nine already. I have granddaughters that are old enough to have children of their own. How can I explain to them, "Your Nana had a one-night fling and now she's panzona?"

NELLIE I know, I know ... But you know it's not a big deal for an older woman to have a baby nowadays. What about that vieja that had all those babies for her daughter. Te acuerdas?

ANGIE Yeah. That sure was nice, wasn't it Nellie? To do that for somebody ...

NELLIE (*Pensive*) Yeah ... (*Shaking it*) OK. so when do you get the you-know-what?

ANGIE I don't know yet. I still gotta make all the arrangements. (*Pause*) Nellie, when you say you always wanted a baby, you mean before don't you? You don't mean you still want one do you?

NELLIE Pues, I haven't thought about it in so long. (*She laughs her big laugh.*) But I tried everything to get pregnant! Every yerba you can think of. I prayed to every

165

Santo; San Jose, San Luis, Santa Barbara, El Sagrado Corazon, San Martin de Porres, Los Cinco Dedos, San Cliotas del Hoyo de East L.A. . . . You name it I prayed it. I did limpias and sucias and sacudidas and torcidas. I met every bruja and curandero from here to T.J. They had me shaking and sprinkling; I even went outside desnuda and cut the moon in half with a knife. Me sobaron, me soplaron, me tiraron y me fregaron. Pero Nada! I had this big hole in my heart that I knew would never be filled. *(Pause)* Aver? *(She sees if she still feels it.)* Yeah, I still feel it, so I guess I still want one . . . why?

ANGIE Because, I don't want this baby, it's true. And I wouldn't have it for any man. Not for Joe; not for Henry. None of them are worth the trouble. But you're my best friend and if you want this baby, I'll have it for you.

NELLIE *(Silence)* You mean you would give your baby to me? (ANGIE *nods.*) What about Joe and your kids and your grandkids and everything?

ANGIE Ay Nellie, I've dealt with raising nine lousy kids, a cheating husband . . . Believe me, I can deal with this. And I couldn't have done it without you. You're like my sister. I want to do this for you.

NELLIE *(Moved)* Gee Angie, that's really nice of you.

ANGIE Thanks.

NELLIE But I'm an old lady. Do you think I can take care of a baby?

ANGIE Sure you can. I'll help you. I can raise a kid with my eyes closed. I'll tell you everything you need to know.

NELLIE For reals?

ANGIE Uh huh. *(They hug.)*

NELLIE *(Composed)* OK. Now we have to plan this right. I'm gonna have to get everything ready. Buy things. Take all the cochinero out of the other room. Umm . . . que mas?

ANGIE I have to see a doctor and get some vitamins.

NELLIE What if they say you're too old?

ANGIE I'm only 48 and I'm as strong as a horse.

NELLIE You gotta take good care of yourself. I'll make you a good lunch every day. You know, verduras and frutas . . .

ANGIE OK.

NELLIE And what about our friends? Like Connie and Carmelita. You know they're gonna talk.

ANGIE *(Pause)* Fuck 'em!

NELLIE Yeah! OK, I want to pay for the medical bills.

ANGIE No, no, no. We'll go half and half.

NELLIE That's even better. Now, what about Henry? What if he wants visitation rights or custody?

ANGIE Are you kidding? I haven't seen him since that night. And you know he never went back to the Bingo.

NELLIE Oh really? I hadn't noticed.

ANGIE Sure you hadn't . . .

NELLIE *(Ignoring her comment)* Do you think you'll change your mind after the baby's born?

ANGIE *(Thinks)* I don't think so. Pero si quieres, we can make one of those contracts. You know like those . . . como se llaman?

NELLIE Surrogate mothers. Good idea. *(She runs for a paper and pen.)* OK, here.

ANGIE *(Starts writing)* Aver . . . I Angie . . .

NELLIE Angela . . .

ANGIE Oh yeah. Angela Garcia, being of sound mind . . .

NELLIE . . . and body . . .

ANGIE . . . and body, on this . . . what's today?

NELLIE May 30th, 1989.

ANGIE 1989, promise to give my baby which is due to be born on . . . uh, aver, when was my last . . .

NELLIE Period? Let me get the calendar . . . *(She goes for the calendar.)*

ANGIE Let's see . . . when was the Las Vegas turn-around?

NELLIE I have it marked down here. It was the last week of Lent. Aver . . . April 28th.

ANGIE So, I had it one week before that and today is May 20th . . .

NELLIE Wait a minute. That's barely a month ago. How often do you get one?

ANGIE Every thirty days.

NELLIE Aver . . . 1,2,3 *(she counts)* . . . 30. Angie, you haven't missed a period. It's due today.

ANGIE I know, but I always get it first thing in the morning and I didn't get it yet.

NELLIE Apenas son las ten. Gee, you're a whole three hours late!

ANGIE But I have all the symptoms. I feel

sleepy, tengo asco. I know what it feels like . . .

NELLIE   Like the flu? That Chino flu is going around you know.

ANGIE   Yeah, I know. My Chela had it.

NELLIE   Ay Angie, como eres de . . .

ANGIE   De que?

NELLIE   De . . . simple! We're making plans for a baby when you're three hours late! How can you be so . . .

ANGIE   Stupid? Just say it Nellie. That's what you mean! I'm always the stupid one. The dummy! I try to be nice to you and look how you treat me! *(She runs into the bathroom.)*

NELLIE   Here we go again! *(Pause. She sits. To herself.)* There goes my baby . . . *(To God)* You shit!

ANGIE   *(Quietly calling out from the bathroom)* Nellie?

NELLIE   Yeah?

ANGIE   Do you happen to have a . . . you-know-what?

NELLIE   A Kotex?

ANGIE   Uh huh.

NELLIE   No.

ANGIE   *(Slowly comes out of the bathroom)* Sorry . . .

NELLIE   Forget it Angie . . .

ANGIE   I better go . . . I guess I have the flu . . .

NELLIE   I'll make you some caldo. I'll take it over in a while. You better get some rest. *(ANGIE exits. NELLIE looks up to God.)* So, you have a sense of humor after all. *(She laughs her big laugh.)* That was a good one! Te aventastes! That's right, keep it up; a little wink, a little smile, a little joke. How else am I supposed to know I'm still alive. *(Phone rings)* Hello? Oh, hi Frankie. *(She gives God the thumbs-up.)* Oh I'm fine. Uh huh. *(She laughs her big laugh.)* Guess what I'm making for lunch; chicken soup. Sure, come on over, I have plenty. Nah, don't bring nothing . . . well, maybe a bottle of wine would be nice. Yeah, the kind with a cork, uh huh, oh and bring a corkscrew . . . OK. See you in a while. Toodloo. *(She hangs up. To herself.)* Yes, Nellie, you still drive them crazy. *(She gets busy in the kitchen and sings: "Solamente Una Vez . . .")*

(Blackout)

Diane Glancy

Biography

Diane Glancy teaches Native American Literature, Creative Writing and Scriptwriting at Macalester College in St. Paul, Minnesota. She is of Cherokee and German/English heritage. She received her BA from the University of Missouri in 1964 and her MFA from the University of Iowa in 1988.

Diane is an Associate Member of the Minneapolis Playwrights' Center. A collection of her plays, *War Cries*, was published by Holy Cow! Press, Duluth, Minnesota, in the fall of 1995.

Her plays include: *The Truth Teller*, *The Peace Pipe*, *Stick Horse*, *The Lesser Wars*, *Segwohi*, *Testimony* and *Weebjob*.

Photo: Jane Katz

Artistic Statement

I was born in Kansas City Missouri, in 1941. My father was Cherokee. My mother was English and German. The easiest way to explain it is that I was born to a mother of a different race than I was. I came out looking and acting like my father's family, much to her disappointment and dismay. It wasn't long before I realized much of the world would feel the same way.

I was first introduced to theater as a child. It was somewhere in grade school. There was a play. I wanted to be in it. It's been over forty years since this happened, but I remember wanting to hold a wand and wear some kind of netting over my dress. Only I didn't get to. I wasn't chosen to be one of the good fairies or whoever those delicious characters were. I got to stand somewhere in the background. Outside the play. Observing it from a distance. I would like to say it was because I didn't have blonde hair and blue eyes like all good fairies have. I was dark and probably obstinate and morose from feeling unwanted. But whatever. I found myself watching the others talk and move. It was my birth as a playwright.

I remember stopping on Highway 380 in New Mexico in the summer of 1981. I was with my mother and daughter, and I was on the way to a poetry conference in Albuquerque. I can't remember why we stopped. I think my mother was throwing away some trash. There was a barrel in a small turn-around beside the narrow high-

way. And I was looking across the road at a valley, and the idea for *Weebjob* came to me, or the idea of a man living in the valley with a friend who wanted to marry his daughter came to me. I must have taken notes. At least written down the names of the towns. Roswell. Socorro. Old Lincoln. I also remember the agave and Spanish bayonet.

Maybe I started writing the play then.

Two summers later, I drove across New Mexico to another conference. Only then it was Highway 40, farther north. That's where I found Weebjob's daughter hitchhiking. She wasn't really there, but the idea of her was, you see.

Some friends read the first version of the play on my front porch. I remember that summer in Tulsa. I lived in an old brick fourplex close to downtown. Some friends sat in a circle on my front porch. Also a few neighbors. I remember the old brick walls. The vines. The hot night. The open porch-door. My cat on my lap. It was front-porch theater, I guess. I sat listening to them read the play.

The next summer, *Weebjob* won the 1984 Five Civilized Tribes Playwriting Competition sponsored by Mrs. Tom Garrard of McAlister, Oklahoma, and the Five Civilized Tribes Museum in Muskogee.

Later, in 1987, it was produced by the American Indian Theater Company. Some Native American actors were off to a Pow Wow or something. One was recovering from alcoholism (which inspired another later play, *Stick Horse*). So a Lebanese man played Weebjob and a black man was Pick Up. The others were Indians. I was already writing *Bull Star*, my next play, which is also in *War Cries*, my collection of drama. But anyway, there *Weebjob* went.

I remember how a few things got in the play. When I was at the University of Missouri in the early sixties, there was an old man the students called "The Sign Painter." He lived off a dark road some-where south of town, and he wrote signs and hung them on the fence by his place. I took one of them one time. It was over my bed for the rest of college. And the memory of him stayed with me, you see.

I also like the Biblical character, Job. I had been evangelized and went to Bible school.

And I don't like slow cars ahead of me on narrow and curving backroads.

And, oh yes, I got to be one of the wedding guests in the play at the Tulsa Performing Arts Center.

Production history

Weebjob was produced at the Performing Arts Centre in Tulsa, Oklahoma by the American Indian Theater Company, April 8 through 11, 1987. The production was directed by Ken Spence. The cast included the following: Basem Farhood, Joann Whitecrow, Denise Atkins, and Will Brunen.

9 Weebjob

Diane Glancy

Thou hast fenced me with bones . . .
                    Job 10:11

Characters

GERALD LONG CHALK, or WEEBJOB (Wēēb jōb), age 48, is the main character. His name is a play on the Biblical Job because he is beset with problems, and has a friend, Pick Up, who isn't much comfort. WEEBJOB is a holy man, a Mescalero Apache. He's stern and unyielding, a little impractical, yet likeable. Weebjob always seems to be at a crossroads in his life. He lets rich land lie fallow. He paints signs and hangs them on his fence. Signs that say: "He hangs the earth on nothing, Job 26:7," "Rodeo / Albuquerque," "Behold the behemoth. He eats grass as an ox. He moveth his tail like the pines, Job 40:15,17," "Vote / Ofred for Chief."

PERCY WILLINGDEER, or PICKUP, WEEBJOB's friend, age 43, is in love with WEEBJOB's daughter. He is also a Mescalero Apache. He presents WEEBJOB with his newest disaster when WEEBJOB finds out that he wants to marry his daughter.

SUZANNE LONG CHALK, or SWEET POTATO, WEEBJOB's daughter, is 21. She has a mind of her own. She is unhappy with her life because she doesn't know where she belongs. She has run off several times to hitchhike on the interstate to Gallup.

JAMES LONG CHALK, WEEBJOB's younger son, age 23. He works for the highway department and lives in Socorro with his girlfriend, HERSAH.

SARAH LONG CHALK, or SWEET GRASS, WEEBJOB's wife, age 45. She has a sweet and understanding disposition. She is of Cherokee heritage. When the play begins, she has gone to visit her sister in Hobbs, because she wants to see her, and also to get away from WEEBJOB for a while, whom she feels takes her for granted. She is a traditional woman who is just starting to deal with herself as an individual.

WILLIAM LONG CHALK, WEEBJOB's older son, age 28, a lawyer in Roswell.

Minor characters who appear at the wedding

CLEMENT THOUSANDSTICKS: THE TOWN BUFFOON, MID-FIFTIES

MARY JANE COLLAR: SWEET GRASS's sister, early forties

HERSAH: JAMES's girlfriend, early twenties

REESAH: WILLIAM's wife, and their CHILD

WARHALL: Thousandsticks' friend

MINISTER

MUSICIANS

OTHER WEDDING GUESTS

Setting

The Salazar Canyon in Lincoln County, New Mexico, is between Roswell and Socorro. WEEBJOB's house is small, made of mud-brick, with a chimney and low roof, so the flat wind that comes from between the mountains can pass over it. In the background is a grove of mesquites, and farther away, some pines and finally the mountains. A weed-clump marks WEEBJOB's road, which is nothing more than tire-ruts, that connect with old Highway 380 through the canyon. On the west of WEEBJOB's house is a squash patch with yellow blossoms. A low cloud hides the mountains at first, but soon lifts.

WEEBJOB's house is simple. A wooden table and four chairs are on the front porch. Inside the front window is a kitchen-sink full of pots and dishes. A sideboard emptied of its dishes sets along a wall. The floor is covered with SWEET GRASS's weavings. Her loom is at a back corner of the house.

Act I

Scene 1

WEEBJOB *is in his squash patch when he hears a truck. He turns to the road, but finishes digging before he walks to the house.*

WEEBJOB   It's Pick Up. Mighty Warrior doesn't bark.

PICK UP   *(He enters.)* Ola, Weebjob.

WEEBJOB   Ola, Pick Up.

(There's the sound of the truck door slamming.)

PICK UP   I've returned with your daughter, Sweet Potato.

SWEET POTATO   My name is Suzanne! *(She sits on the steps of the house.)*

PICK UP   I saw her on the road hitchhiking to Gallup. I told her I would bring her back to her father. *(SWEET POTATO sits on the steps and doesn't look at them.)*

WEEBJOB   What have my days come to? *(Pause)*

PICK UP   She didn't want to come.

WEEBJOB   The young are restless as the pines.

PICK UP   She says you do nothing but read the Book and sit in the squash patch and stare across the jaundiced hills.

WEEBJOB   She over-estimates me! And they're mountains, not hills. (SWEET POTATO *still does not speak, but lies on the porch step with her feet sticking off the side.)* We, who were raised in the old reservation boarding schools, know tolerance, persistence, perspicacity.

PICK UP   Pardon?

WEEBJOB   Discernment.

PICK UP   Ah! Horse-sense. (SWEET POTATO *turns her backside to the men.)* You learned the Book well at school.

WEEBJOB   Every word.

SWEET POTATO   And not a word of it got through. *(She sits up.)*

WEEBJOB   *(Looking at* SWEET POTATO*)* You misunderstand. I was raised in a different culture . . . I have trouble understanding . . . Come on, Sweet Potato. Dismount. Your mother is at her sister's, not to return for a few days. I'm hungry. See what's in the kitchen and I will break my fast.

SWEET POTATO   Nothing's in the kitchen if mother's not here. *(Impatiently)* You're busy making philosophy to the pines and religion to the mountains. You print signs and hang them on the fence by the highway. You read the Book. And yet the garden grows nothing but squash vines. Not one word of your Book changes anything!

PICK UP   I believe the child is bitter.

WEEBJOB   *(Ignoring pick up)* Sweet Potato, my daughter, tuber of my soul, see what's in the kitchen for your starving father, Weebjob. I shall relinquish my fast. *(Pause)*

PICK UP   *(Looking at* WEEBJOB*)* She does not move.

WEEBJOB   I see that she does not move! You need not tell me, Job's friend. She is stubborn and recalcitrant.

PICK UP   You're too kind with your words.

WEEBJOB   I'm grumpy as thunder. Like Mighty Warrior, my dog. Like my wife two weeks at her sister's and nothing to eat.

PICK UP   It must come with age.

WEEBJOB   No, the daughter has it too.

PICK UP   And sons.

WEEBJOB   Enough! I'm reminded of my plight. Deserted in the desert. No loaves and fish.

PICK UP   That doesn't sound like you, Weebjob. I've never heard you talk that way.

WEEBJOB   I'm at a crossroads in my life.

SWEET POTATO   *(Rising from the steps)* Mutton. I've heard that all my life. You're always at a crossroad.

PICK UP   You've always lived by the words of the Book you've committed to memory.

WEEBJOB   I remember nothing. What memory? I can remember nothing but war.

SWEET POTATO   *(Almost rests her arm against* PICK UP, *but decides against it)* You've never been in war. You were too young for one, too old for another.

WEEBJOB   To get up in the morning is war. *(As* WEEBJOB *makes this speech to the heavens,* PICK UP *brushes* SWEET POTATO's *arm.)* To wrestle with the day, and with my work, is war. To have three children with minds of their own is war. *(Turns to his daughter)* See what there is to eat, Sweet Potato! Your name makes hunger come to me.

SWEET POTATO   *(To* WEEBJOB *and* PICK UP*)* I'm going to continue my pilgrimage to Gallup.

PICK UP *(Turns his head)* Another crusader in the Long Chalk family.

WEEBJOB I shall continue to meditate on the passages of the Book. I'll stand with my feet on the holy ground of Canaan. *(Nods his head to indicate his squash patch)* I will sit in the squash patch *(Waves his arm toward it)*, see the Thunder Hawk *(He looks to heaven)* and fight holy wars. *(Turns tenderly to his daughter.)* I need you, Sweet Potato.

PICK UP *(Agrees with* WEEBJOB*)* Gallup is a long way.

WEEBJOB Three hundred miles.

SWEET POTATO *(She walks back to the steps. Stands there with her hand in her hip pocket.)* It's because nothing happens here. You live in the fertile Salazar Canyon, the greenest in New Mexico. *(She raises her arms.)* You could have sheep, but you won't fence your land. You could have crops. James makes you an irrigation ditch, but what do you grow? *(She slaps her hands at her sides.)* Nothing! You put up signs where our road runs into the highway. You makes more signs. They say, "Canaan." Whatever that means. They say, "The devil and I do not speak." *(She looks at* WEEBJOB *fiercely.)* Whatever that means. When I go in to Old Lincoln they ask at the general store if I've come for more paint. *(Pause)* Once in a while you sell gourds and squash at the roadside stand. You sell mother's blankets in Old Lincoln when we're desperate. What good ever comes from this? *(She shrugs as though giving up, and stands with her hands on her hips again.)*

WEEBJOB Yes, I have nothing. I'm proud to have nothing! The prophets of the Book had nothing. It's work to have nothing, Sweet Potato. I should have sent you to the Female Seminary where your mother went. Then you wouldn't have these ideas . . .

SWEET POTATO *(Under her breath)* Shit.

WEEBJOB Then you would understand that I grow visions—

SWEET POTATO *(With her hands over her ears)* Heaven above. This is your harvest? I've seen you sitting in your squash patch in some kind of trance. Holy God. You look like you're talking to yourself. Is that the culmination of your life's work?

WEEBJOB I won't have irreverence on my land. Someday you'll understand what "Canaan" means. For now, get me something to eat! *(More definite now)*

SWEET POTATO I thought it was your meat to do the will of the father.

WEEBJOB It is. And to finish the work I've begun. The fields are white with harvest. This is what I'll do until I hear my name called from beyond the mountains.

SWEET POTATO Your fields and desert look brown to me. You interpret the Book to fit your purpose.

WEEBJOB Not so, Tuber. Indeed, I'm the man you see before your eyes, and I'm not appreciated. There may be things you don't know. I have faith that the desert is white with harvest, and will blossom by faith. I have seen the Thunder Hawk, Sweet Potato, what else can I say to you? *(*SWEET POTATO *walks reluctantly toward the house. The men watch her until she enters the front door.)*

PICK UP You should beat your sword into a ploughshare and your pulpit into a tractor.

WEEBJOB I don't ask your counsel. You know me, Pick Up. We've been friends many year, though I don't know why. You understand me—

PICK UP Not any longer, Weebjob. You can't expect your children to understand your ways. Your sons have already left. William to Roswell and James to Socorro.

WEEBJOB They come back from time to time.

PICK UP Your wife's at her sister's.

WEEBJOB *(Defensively)* Just for a visit. She returns soon.

PICK UP Now your daughter is trying to leave. Already she has stayed with James in Socorro more than in Salazar Canyon with you. Now she is trying to leave for Gallup.

WEEBJOB Hush up. She's coming back out.

SWEET POTATO *(Disgusted as she walks up to the men.)* A turnip and a hard crust of bread. How long has it been since you were at the grocer's in Old Lincoln?

PICK UP I don't think he's been.

SWEET POTATO How long has mother been gone?

WEEBJOB Fifteen days.

SWEET POTATO How can you expect me to find something to eat when there's nothing? You're the one who believes in loaves and fishes. You go find something. I'll have to go to town if you want supper.

PICK UP *(He looks up the road.)* Another car comes.

SWEET POTATO A stranger?

WEEBJOB No, Mighty Warrior is quiet.

SWEET POTATO So what does that mean? He's like you. He wouldn't bark if it were Custer.

WEEBJOB It's James.

JAMES *(Enters)* Suzanne! I see Pick Up found you. *(He looks to* PICK UP, *who shakes his head that she's all right.)* Hersah didn't know where you'd gone.

WEEBJOB She tried to make her run to Gallup again.

PICK UP Someday she'll make it. Then we'll have to drive three hundred miles to retrieve her. *(He pauses, as though to himself.)* Probably in my truck.

WEEBJOB James, my younger son. I haven't heard from you—

JAMES I've been busy, father.

WEEBJOB It's been a long time.

JAMES My job with the highway department takes me far away. I can't always get back. Hersah and Suzanne keep house for me.

SWEET POTATO He could have gone to college if you'd let him apply for a loan. And I could have a wool store in Old Lincoln and sell mother's blankets.

PICK UP That's six hundred miles by the time we get back to Salazar Canyon from Gallup, Weebjob. I don't think my truck will go that far.

WEEBJOB Hersah is fine?

JAMES Yes. I think she's more Sweet Potato's friend than mine.

SWEET POTATO I'd like for you to call me Suzanne, James. You do when I'm in Socorro. And I think Hersah would be more your friend if you spent more time with her.

WEEBJOB She lives with him, doesn't she?

PICK UP Call her Sweet Potato, James. I like to hear it.

SWEET POTATO Take me to the grocery store in Old Lincoln, James, so I can get us supper.

PICK UP I'll take you, Sweet Potato, Suzanne. That way I'll be sure you come back.

SWEET POTATO If Weebjob would come and see the buildings they've restored, and how they've made it into a town where people can stop, he'd be interested in something other than "Canaan." The old brown buildings used to look at one another with blank faces. Now they're painted. Honeysuckle climbs the hitching posts.

PICK UP *(Almost making fun of* SWEET POTATO*)* Old Lincoln has the snap of a jack knife going to its mark. *(*WEEBJOB *scratches himself.)*

SWEET POTATO They asked me about mother the last time I was there. Weebjob, you could fence off a corner of your land and keep a few sheep and shear them for wool we could sell in Old Lincoln.

PICK UP They were all shepherds in the Book.

WEEBJOB I've already considered that.

SWEET POTATO And he won't do anything about it.

JAMES Let's go to the grocery store.

PICK UP *(Looks anxiously at* SWEET POTATO*)* I'll take her! Give me a push, James.

SWEET POTATO I'll come back, Pick Up. You don't need to worry that I'll run away to Gallup tonight. The desert gets too cold.

PICK UP *(He still looks at* SWEET POTATO.*)* I need to take my truck. I can't let it set too long in one place or it decides it won't move again. *(*PICK UP *and* SWEET POTATO *exit.* JAMES *follows.* WEEBJOB *chucks a stick.)*

WEEBJOB Fetch it, Mighty Warrior. *(He hears* PICK UP*'s truck cough and start up. Soon* JAMES *returns.)* I feel badly, James.

JAMES Why, dad?

WEEBJOB Sweet Potato told me that you wanted to go to college.

JAMES I'm doing fine with the highway department. I'm getting an education from the horticulturist just the same as if I were in school. And I'm getting paid for it.

WEEBJOB When she said that, it made me think how I have stayed here and not helped any of you.

JAMES I like my job. Don't worry about Sweet Potato. William has done all right too. Sweet Potato just gets down on everything. Didn't William finish law school?

WEEBJOB Yes, because his wife's family helped him.

JAMES *(He takes* WEEBJOB*'s shoulders in his hands with care.)* We do what we must.

WEEBJOB What's wrong with her?

JAMES I don't know. She can't find anything she wants to do. *(He lets go of* WEEBJOB *and puts his hands in his pockets.)* Weebjob, I could bring you some Spanish bayonet of agave for your garden. I could bring you some vegetables and show you how to care for them, and how to cultivate the squash you already have. Then you could harvest a crop to sell in Old Lincoln each year.

WEEBJOB I don't know.

JAMES You've done nothing with the land, father. You don't even have a fishing license. A driver's license.

WEEBJOB I don't need a license to fish on my own land.

JAMES The land deed— Your will—

WEEBJOB I could think I was talking to William. Has he put you up to this?

JAMES *(Sarcastically)* No, dad. I actually thought of it on my own.

WEEBJOB I don't seem to know all I need to know either. *(The puzzled look returns to his face.)* What's going on in Socorro that you didn't know Sweet Potato was going to run away to Gallup?

JAMES Am I suppposed to know everything she's thinking? I'm gone sometimes several days on highway department work. She and Hersah talk. Ask her. All I know is that I heard them fighting one night.

WEEBJOB The girls?

JAMES No, father. Pick Up and Sweet Potato.

WEEBJOB Pick Up comes to Socorro?

JAMES You didn't know?

WEEBJOB Didn't know what? There's nothing to know.

JAMES Pick Up comes to Socorro sometimes to see Sweet Potato.

WEEBJOB Pick Up goes to Socorro to see Sweet Potato? He's my friend, not hers! He's old enough to be her father. I expect you to be your sister's keeper and you let something like that happen! He's almost as old as I am. The fool! *(*WEEBJOB *grabs* JAMES*'s shirt.)* Why is he bothering Sweet Potato?

JAMES *(Takes his father's hands in his own.)* I don't think she minds it.

WEEBJOB *(Pulls his hands away from* JAMES*. Hits his thighs in anger. He picks up a stick and chucks it in the ditch off stage.)* Chew it to bits, Mighty Warrior. *(He looks questioningly to heaven.)* WORSE than what I feared has come upon me. *(Looks to* JAMES*)* Why am I not told anything? That old man bothering my daughter! What's wrong with –

JAMES *(Interrupts his father)* I came for another reason also, father. Now that I know Sweet Potato is here, I see that mother is gone. You didn't tell me. A letter came yesterday from Hobbs. She's at her sister's and assumes I know. Why am *I* not told anything?

WEEBJOB You got a letter from your mother? Let me see it! *(*JAMES *takes it from his pocket and* WEEBJOB *grabs it from him.* WEEBJOB *opens the letter and reads.)* "Your father, as you know, is a difficult man to live with." *(*WEEBJOB *looks at* JAMES*.)* She writes you this? *(*JAMES *looks away from* WEEBJOB*.)* "He is not a practical man, but is caught up in his ideals. I thought I would stay at my sister's for a month, but I think continually of Weebjob, and how he is getting along without me to cook his meals and clean his house. I think I will finish the visit with my sister soon, and return to Salazar Canyon with Weebjob. I'll ride the bus as far as Roswell and William will bring me home . . ." *(*WEEBJOB *looks to heaven.)* William knows too! *(Reads again)* "I do like to be away from Weebjob after all . . ."

JAMES How long has she been gone?

WEEBJOB *(Regains his composure)* Fifteen days.

JAMES How did she get to Hobbs? It must be two hundred miles—

WEEBJOB I took her to the junction in Carrizozo and she caught the bus.

JAMES That was nice of you. Why didn't you make her walk to the junction? I don't like her riding the bus. I would have taken her to Hobbs if I knew you two were quarreling.

WEEBJOB We're not quarreling! She simply wanted to see her sister. And it isn't any business of yours.

JAMES Yes, it is.

WEEBJOB The letter she wrote to you is hard for me to accept. I got Sweet Grass at an Indian Female Seminary. She would hardly look at me, much less speak anything to me. Now she tells you all this? *(He reads the rest of the letter in silence.)*

JAMES I suppose she wrote so that I would

understand why she wasn't here when I came.

WEEBJOB Mutton. You used to be too young to know anything. Now you're told all. *(He crumples the letter and hands it back to* JAMES.*)*

JAMES Things change. *(Puts the letter back in his pocket.)*

WEEBJOB Not always for the better. *(He scratches himself.)*

JAMES She knew you wouldn't tell me why she wasn't here. What do you ever tell me?

WEEBJOB She leaves your house in Socorro for several days and you don't even call . . .

JAMES She could have come back here for all I knew.

WEEBJOB But you didn't know. How long has she been gone? *(*JAMES *pauses.)* How long?

JAMES Probably a week.

WEEBJOB And WHAT did you do about it?

JAMES I thought she'd gone off with Pick Up . . . *(*WEEBJOB *hits his hands against his sides in anger.)* But when Pick Up showed up and didn't know—

WEEBJOB What else goes on in Socorro that I don't know?

JAMES Nothing, except Sweet Potato was gone for a while. *(*WEEBJOB *turns his back to* JAMES.*)* Hersah didn't know anything either, except that Sweet Potato talked about Gallup and the restaurant where she worked one summer—

WEEBJOB *(Turns to* JAMES*)* Why didn't you tell me?

JAMES Probably for the same reason you didn't tell me about mother.

WEEBJOB That's different. Sweet Grass is only at her sister's. We ALL hear from her . . . It's not like Sweet Potato disappearing . . . *(*WEEBJOB *turns angrily to* JAMES *and pokes his finger against his shoulders.)* I didn't have your advice when I wooed my wife. Why would I need it now to keep her? She'll return. *(Proudly)* She writes that she can't stay away from me any longer. You read the letter. *(Confidently)* And Pick Up doesn't have any more chance than an albino squirrel with my daughter. Where are they? *(He looks impatiently up the road.)*

JAMES They've hardly gotten to Old Lincoln. I think if he wanted your advice on how to woo Sweet Potato, he would ask.

WEEBJOB Mutton. *(He hits his thighs in anger.)*

Scene 2

The stage is dark except for a spotlight in the corner which falls on SWEET POTATO *and* PICK UP *in the truck.*

SWEET POTATO Why are we stopping? I need to get back to feed Weebjob.

PICK UP Let him wait.

SWEET POTATO I'll hear him bellering in the valley if we don't get back soon . . . He'll be painting another sign for the fence by the road . . . *(*PICK UP *touches her face.)*

PICK UP Where were you for a week?

SWEET POTATO You already asked me, and I told you I was on the road. *(Folds her arms)* Why did you bring me back to him? You know I didn't want to come.

PICK UP You can't run away, Sweet Potato.

SWEET POTATO My name is Suzanne Long Chalk.

PICK UP I'll call you what I please. I can't have you hitch-hiking on the road for anyone to pick up. You shouldn't be out on the road alone. It's not good. What would you do in Gallup?

SWEET POTATO Get a job. I can cook, wait tables. I worked there last summer, if you remember.

PICK UP Yes, it's the first time I came to see you . . . I don't want you to go back there.

SWEET POTATO You sound like my father.

PICK UP It's not as your father that I'm speaking. Work at the Civil War in Old Lincoln if you must have a job. Let the men gawk at you. Wait tables. *(He pauses and looks at her.)* I care for you, Suzanne. You know that. *(Pause)* More than as a father. I didn't come to Socorro to see James.

SWEET POTATO I told you I didn't want to speak of these things.

PICK UP I didn't for many years. But now I can't wait any longer. You're more than Weebjob's daughter to me.

SWEET POTATO Maybe we could be like cousins.

PICK UP I want you as a close friend.

SWEET POTATO We are close friends, Pick Up, my father's friend.

PICK UP Yes, I'm his friend.

SWEET POTATO You wouldn't be if he heard you speak to me like that.

PICK UP I know. *(He touches her face again.)*

SWEET POTATO I remember you, Pick Up, when you used to have a brown Volkswagen, and looked like a prune driving it down the road.

PICK UP I remember you, Sweet Potato, in a round purple coat, like a plum on narrow legs, with skinny braids sticking out from beneath your cap.

SWEET POTATO I remember the night you got drunk in the Civil War Bar in Old Lincoln and came to our house and quoted poetry to the weed-clumps.

PICK UP I remember when the faintest bit of snow blew into the valley and you ran into my truck on William's bicycle and sprang the tire.

SWEET POTATO I remember— *(PICK UP puts his hands over her mouth.)*

PICK UP I remember when you fell into the stream. I should have let you drown. *(He kisses her.)*

SWEET POTATO Would you call him father?

PICK UP *(He rolls his head back.)* I would rather have a buffalo for a father-in-law.

SWEET POTATO *(She takes up for WEEBJOB.)* He's a better man than any I've known.

PICK UP I know.

SWEET POTATO Wise and good-hearted. Quick tempered. A little harsh with words and his head too much in the Bible, but a good man.

PICK UP I don't know what to do, Suzanne. I want you, and I wonder why. I'm almost as old as your father. How could I think of you as a wife? How could you think of me—

SWEET POTATO Don't talk about it.

PICK UP Marry me, Suzanne.

SWEET POTATO I can hear Weebjob roaring about it now.

PICK UP He will be all right. Think about me, Sweet Potato. *(He kisses her again.)* Marry me.

SWEET POTATO Maybe it's what you deserve.

Scene 3

WEEBJOB Ah! Here come Rumpelstiltskin and Juliet now.

JAMES Be kind, father.

WEEBJOB Why should I be otherwise?

JAMES Because he's doing better with Sweet Potato than you're doing with mother.

WEEBJOB Now I am angry, James, and wishing your highway job would take you away again.

JAMES *(He laughs.)* It might not hurt you to get away. It might broaden you to travel.

WEEBJOB I get enough broadening here in Salazar Canyon.

PICK UP *(Entering)* Ola, Weebjob. *(SWEET POTATO follows, carrying a grocery sack. She goes into the house.)*

WEEBJOB Ola, Pick Up. *(Impatiently)* Where have you been?

PICK UP Old Lincoln isn't just around the curve, you know. If you'd get off your place—

WEEBJOB It took you longer—

PICK UP You know Clement Thousandsticks. *(He gestures with his arms.)* He waits on the road until he sees us coming, then turns on the highway in front of us and goes slow through the canyon where no one can pass. *(WEEBJOB turns to JAMES and shrugs.)*

JAMES *(Laughs)* Clement's done that to me too.

WEEBJOB *(Turns back to PICK UP)* And, of course, you had my daughter with you. *(SWEET POTATO comes out of the house. WEEBJOB puts his hand up to her.)* Stay out of this – Like you did on your first arrival. I'm going to have a word with Pick Up.

JAMES *(Ignoring WEEBJOB)* And now that there's one light at the crossroads in Old Lincoln, Clement will slow down until the light turns yellow, then he rushes through and leaves you stopped at the light.

WEEBJOB Step in the house for a moment, Pick Up. It won't take long. *(PICK UP follows WEEBJOB into the house.)*

SWEET POTATO *(Angrily to JAMES)* What did you tell Weebjob? *(She brushes the hair from her face.)*

JAMES About what?

SWEET POTATO James! What he's upset about! Pick Up and me.

JAMES What's there to tell Weebjob? *(The sound of scraping chairs and loud, muffled voices come from the house.)*

SWEET POTATO There must have been something! *(An insult is heard. PICK UP defends himself. Not all the conversation is understood, but it's clear they're arguing.*

SWEET POTATO *has her hands over her ears.)* What could they be doing?

JAMES They're too old to hurt one another.

SWEET POTATO Don't be sure. I'm going in there, James . . . *(She starts for the house when* PICK UP *backs out of the front door. Weebjob follows with his hand on* PICK UP's *shirt collar.)*

WEEBJOB Mutton if it's all right.

PICK UP Now, Weebjob. *(Both hands are up.)*

WEEBJOB It's not clear to me why I have such a jackass for a friend.

PICK UP Nor do I understand why I put up with you unless it's for your daughter. *(*WEEBJOB *jerks* PICK UP's *shirt collar, ripping it.)*

JAMES *(Rushes to the men, takes his father by the shoulders.)* Gerald Long Chalk. You're a man of peace!

WEEBJOB *(He comes to his senses, and bows, formally.)* Forgive me, Pick Up. *(Stiffly)* I forgot myself for a moment and wanted to smash your head.

PICK UP I understand, friend Weebjob. *(*WEEBJOB *holds up his hand to* PICK UP *as though protesting that he is his friend, but* SWEET POTATO *interrupts. She looks at the torn place on* PICK UP's *shirt, would like to pull it together, but decides to go into the house.)*

WEEBJOB It's too soon to call me friend again, Pick Up. I must go to the squash patch for a while. *(He goes to the garden.* JAMES *and* PICK UP *remain on the porch.* PICK UP *pulls his shirt together.)*

JAMES Another trip to the Holy Land. *(*JAMES *watches his father for a moment, then he puts his hand on* PICK UP's *shoulder to comfort him.* PICK UP *looks at the ground, shakes his head. They are uncertain at first what to say to one another. While* WEEBJOB *is in the squash patch, they talk, inaudibly.)*

WEEBJOB *(Chants, then begins his prayers)* Great Spirit. Father of Fathers. Forgive me for anger, and in turn make me forgive Pick Up. Every rock has its flat side. He is taken with Sweet Potato. Maybe it will pass. He has always liked her, but I didn't expect this! Never this! *(Shrugs)* Is it my new burden? Is this the catastrophe that comes even before my wife returns? I need her to soothe me. Bring her back quickly. I'm angry that my son-in-law is nearly as old as I am. I'm angry he's done nothing all his life. More flies than arrows. Wait until Sweet Grass hears about this! Make me forgive him and keep him from marrying my daughter. *(He chants until* SWEET POTATO *calls him.)*

SWEET POTATO *(She calls* JAMES *and* PICK UP *and hands the plates through the window to them. Then she comes out of the house and calls her father.)* How now, father. Your hamburger is ready. *(She holds her arm forward in an Indian salute.)*

WEEBJOB *(He quickly finishes his prayers, bids the Great Spirit adieu.)* Whuoah! *(He joins* JAMES *and* PICK UP *at the table on the porch.)* I see you waited.

PICK UP Ola, Weebjob. Have a seat.

WEEBJOB On my own porch? You tell me to be seated. Thank you, kind friend.

SWEET POTATO Peace, father. Eat your meal. *(The four of them sit at the table.)*

WEEBJOB *(Asks the blessing on the meal.)* Great Spirit, we are grateful for the food which you provide. *(*SWEET POTATO *and* PICK UP *look at one another.)* Now help us to eat this meal in peace. Amen.

PICK UP Amen.

SWEET POTATO *(*WEEBJOB *takes a giant bite out of the hamburger.)* Why are the chairs and table on the porch? *(*WEEBJOB *tries to answer, but his mouth is full.)* Does mother know you moved them out of the kitchen? *(He shakes his head, no.)* We'll have to move them back in before she comes. *(*WEEBJOB *shakes his head, no, again.)*

WEEBJOB I'm head of the house. The table stays here.

JAMES *(Trying to avert another argument)* Good burgers, Suzanne.

WEEBJOB I'll be glad when your mother returns. Then I'll eat till I'm content.

PICK UP *(Trying to avoid* WEEBJOB*)* How's the highway work?

JAMES Steady. That's the best part of it.

SWEET POTATO I had to wash four plates, Weebjob, for our supper. I'll wash the rest after we eat. It will take me all night to get through that pile . . .

PICK UP *(Without thinking)* I'll help you. *(*WEEBJOB *glares at him.)*

WEEBJOB Thank you, Sweet Potato. I can't seem to get through them myself. *(Pause as he eats)* Almost as good as Sweet Grass's.

SWEET POTATO Coffee?

WEEBJOB Yes, thanks.

*(*SWEET POTATO *goes in the house, returns*

with four cups, then goes back for the coffee pot, and pours it while the men talk.)

JAMES We've been landscaping the new section of Highway 25 south of Elephant Butte. Now we'll move to Mescalero.

WEEBJOB And what are you doing, Pick Up?

PICK UP Running Willingdeer's Tow Truck Service, as I always have . . . Are you stuck somewhere, Weebjob? (They drink coffee.) Ah, Weebjob, why don't you go into sheep herding and supply Old Lincoln with wool as well as Sweet Grass's blankets? Why don't you let Sweet Potato and Sweet Grass have their own store? (Pause) I have a letter from Sweet Grass. She mentions it—

WEEBJOB (Pounds the table) MUTTON! (Rises, nearly tipping the table) YOU have a letter from Sweet Grass? (PICK UP pulls the letter from his pocket and hands it to WEEBJOB, who reads it with disbelief.) "I am in Hobbs with my sister, Mary Jane Collar. I don't know how long I will be here. I have not seen her in a long time and she is old and alone. There's much to do. We talk of weaving and clean her small house. We put up cactus jelly for winter and speak of many things. I leave Weebjob to himself for a while." (He looks to heaven.) "I understand him as a man; sometimes it is easier to bear, sometimes not." (He sits in his chair. Reads more quietly now.) "I've been wanting to write you. I know how hard it is for you to feel about Sweet Potato as you do. Break it gently to Weebjob when the time comes!!!" (His voice rises again as he finishes reading his wife's letter to PICK UP.) "Tell Sweet Potato I'm fine . . ." (He pounds the table again, rises to his feet.)

PICK UP (Angry now) Let me ask you something, Weebjob. I've known Sweet Potato since she was a child. I think it was me who first called her Sweet Potato.

WEEBJOB (Angry also) It might have been.

PICK UP That was twenty years ago. I have seen her nearly every week since then. I have loved her for years. Tell me, Weebjob, Gerald Long Chalk, holy man of Salazar Canyon— Why are you the only one who doesn't know? Are you so buried in YOUR work, you don't know when your friend is in love with your daugther?

WEEBJOB You as a son-in-law. No, by thunder. I won't have it. (Bangs the table again) How old are you, Pick Up?

PICK UP Forty-three, and Sweet Potato is 21. It's as though I've always been waiting for her.

WEEBJOB Bull crackers. You just don't want the responsibility of a wife and family.

PICK UP That might be right. I saw you snorting about it so much through the years, I thought it couldn't be much fun.

WEEBJOB It's a responsibility to have a wife and raise children.

PICK UP So it would seem, listening to you.

WEEBJOB Have you asked her to be your wife?

PICK UP Yes, and she almost agreed.

WEEBJOB She doesn't know what else to do with herself. She hasn't even been able to make it to Gallup again. Maybe that's why she almost gives in to you—. (With his fist to PICK UP) How many young girls are there in the valley? Why my daughter?

PICK UP I would love Sweet Potato no matter what her age. I want her to be my wife and I don't want any old crank standing in the way. (He pushes his chair away from him with his foot. PICK UP and WEEBJOB stand facing one antoher.)

WEEBJOB I'm not having an old Poker for a son-in-law.

PICK UP You will if Sweet Potato agrees.

WEEBJOB Mutton.

JAMES Break it up, Weebjob. How silly to see two old bulls ready to fight.

WEEBJOB Even if one of the old bulls is going to be your brother-in-law?

JAMES That's up to Sweet Potato.

WEEBJOB It's up to me to give permission.

SWEET POTATO It's up to me, father. I don't have to have your permission.

WEEBJOB (Looking up to heaven) My father, Seewootee, never would have believed this!

PICK UP Sweet Grass would return sooner if she knew you were close to a wedding.

WEEBJOB There's not going to be a wedding yet! (Pause) I think she wrote to everyone but me . . .

SWEET POTATO She hasn't written to me either. I've tried to be like her. But I am not my mother. I can't be her. I know she's sweet and gentle. And I'm not any of that . . .

PICK UP (He goes to SWEET POTATO, puts his arm around her.) Let's walk up the road. (He draws her off the porch.)

WEEBJOB (Lowers his head, looks at them

with a scowl) Such patience it will take for
me to see him living with my daughter.
Maybe they will move to Gallup, James.
But I know they won't. I'll probably have
them here with me in "Canaan" . . .

JAMES *(Laughs)* I doubt that.

WEEBJOB Sweet Grass will return and
weave behind my house. I will watch her
make the roaming antelope design,
bringing the pattern to a point, a place of
finish. Her weaving is resolution. William
will come with his wife, with their baby,
and Reesah will still be unhappy that
she's going to have another. She'll cry and
I will hear her blow her nose into her
handkerchief. *(Pause)* Pick Up for a son-in-
law! *(Hits the table)* MUTTON!

Scene 4

PICK UP *and* SWEET POTATO *walk toward the
road. The rest of the stage becomes dark with
only one spot light upon them as they talk.)*

PICK UP Everyone's already thinking of our
wedding, Sweet Potato, and you have not
actually consented. *(She is silent.)* You're
showing such enthusiasm.

SWEET POTATO I haven't had time to
decide.

PICK UP I've known you for twenty years.

SWEET POTATO I don't know if I want to
decide.

PICK UP Suzanne Long Chalk, will you
marry me?

SWEET POTATO Is this my last chance to
answer?

PICK UP Probably not.
*(There's a loud muttering from the squash
patch. When* SWEET POTATO *hears the
word "mutton" from her father, she turns to
look.)*

SWEET POTATO I will probably marry you,
Pick Up.

PICK UP Are you sure?

SWEET POTATO At this moment, I am.

PICK UP When I was your age, you weren't
even born, Suzanne. Does that change
your mind?

SWEET POTATO No.

PICK UP What would change your mind?

SWEET POTATO Nothing that I can think of
right now.

PICK UP Is it because you don't have any
place else to go?

SWEET POTATO No. I can stay with James

and Hersah in Socorro. Reesah is going to
have another baby . . . I could probably
stay with William in Roswell, unless she
wants one of her sisters to help . . .
(Pause) I can go to Gallup and work in the
restaurant again . . . It's just that the
nights are so cavernous in the desert— . . .

PICK UP I know.

SWEET POTATO You don't mind that I'm
young?

PICK UP Not as much as having Weebjob
for a father-in-law, and him always at a
"crossroads" in his life.

SWEET POTATO Can't we get married in
the old Indian way?

PICK UP No.

SWEET POTATO You could give Weebjob
some horses, and I would just move in
with you. If it doesn't work, I will put
your bed-roll by the door and you can
move out.

PICK UP No.

SWEET POTATO You'd want the horses
back?

PICK UP I don't have any horses.

SWEET POTATO Your truck, then?

PICK UP Yes. I don't want to lose my
house and truck both. And I don't want
you to be able to get out of it that easily.

SWEET POTATO I don't like complications.

PICK UP You don't want responsibility,
Sweet Potato. I am going to marry you by
law and in the Old Lincoln Church. And I
want you in a dress. I'm going to have
you as my wife, Suzanne. I expect you to
clean the house, cook my suppers, wash
the dishes and clothes. You aren't going to
run off whenever you feel like it. You can
visit James and Hersah in Socorro. Do
what you like. But I will have your
attention. Otherwise, don't marry me. You
aren't coming to see if you like it. You are
making a commitment I expect you to
keep. I won't have it any other way. I'm
from the old school too.

SWEET POTATO And in trying to get away
from Weebjob, I come to someone like
him? *(She shrugs her shoulders.)*

PICK UP I expect you to come to me as a
wife who wants to live with me. I expect
you to sacrifice your burning ambition to
hitchhike to Gallup. I won't have it. I'm
old enough to want a wife that I know
I'm not going to find on the highway with
her thumb up.

SWEET POTATO And what do I get in

return for my unending subjection to you?

PICK UP I'm taking you off Weebjob's hands. He should be giving me the horses. I'm giving you a chance to come where you will have respect as a person, and a chance to be on your own, to do as you want—

SWEET POTATO As long as it isn't making sudden trips?

PICK UP That's right. I will give you a chance to open your wool store with your mother in Old Lincoln, if that's what you want. I'd even buy you some sheep. Or you can wait tables at the Civil War if you like. I would rather that you didn't, but you are your own person, Sweet Potato. And I know you're struggling to find something that will satisfy you. I'm not taking you away from that. I'm giving you what you haven't had—

SWEET POTATO It sounds like "Canaan" to me. Except— (She puts her hands to her face.) Unless I find I don't have any place I belong.

PICK UP (He holds her.) Then you can be satisfied to be my wife. I'm making a place in my house for you.

SWEET POTATO One concession, Pick Up.

PICK UP What?

SWEET POTATO No wedding in Old Lincoln Church, and not in a dress. Father's zeal has always made me shudder in church. I want to be married here – in "Canaan." (Here the stage lights come back. WEEBJOB is in his squash patch. JAMES is in the house washing the pots and pans at the sink.)

WEEBJOB Humbleness of mind, meekness, long suffering. (He is on his knees praying.) Forbearing one another, forgiving one another. (He makes a fist toward heaven.) Could you make this any harder?

PICK UP (He and SWEET POTATO return to the front porch.) No – not there. (He looks to the squash patch.)

SWEET POTATO Then the front porch, or outside somewhere – in the pines? But I have always liked the yellow blossoms.

PICK UP Weebjob would never allow a wedding there. That is holy ground to him. I don't want to be married on his place anyway.

SWEET POTATO And I don't want to be married in a dress!

WEEBJOB (Loudly) Huah! Huah!

SWEET POTATO He is plugged in again. Yes. I will marry you, Pick Up. I am sure.

WEEBJOB He cay mo nay. (He finishes his prayer loudly and rises. He stands a moment in his squash patch. Soon, he walks to SWEET POTATO and PICK UP. They still stand by the porch. SWEET POTATO folds her arms as she watches him approach. PICK UP has his hands in his hip pockets.) I thought from time to time I would like to have Sweet Potato off my hands. (He pauses.) I thought from time to time I would like to have you off my hands, Pick Up. But in losing her, I gain you. What would be worse.

JAMES (Joins them outside) What's up?

PICK UP Sweet Potato has consented to marry me.

JAMES (Jumps up) You are going to be my brother-in-law!

WEEBJOB He has deliberately wormed his way into my family so he can be part-heir of "Canaan."

PICK UP You old carp—

WEEBJOB Minnow!

PICK UP Rudd.

JAMES (He hears the sound of a car and haults the argument.) Listen. There's a car coming. (They turn to the road.) Mighty Warrior doesn't bark. It looks like William's car . . .

Act II

Scene 1

SWEET POTATO Look! William comes with mother.

PICK UP Weebjob! Your wife returns.

WEEBJOB (He peers down the road.) Sweet Grass returns?

PICK UP Maybe he'll go to roost again and not bother about us.

SWEET POTATO I wouldn't count on it.

WEEBJOB Sweet Grass, my old wife! (He kisses his wife when she appears with WILLIAM.) I'm glad you've returned. Hello, William, my oldest son. (He kisses his wife's hand.) How tired it must be from writing.

WILLIAM (Holding a small suitcase which belongs to his mother.) How are you father? (WEEBJOB nods his head that he's fine. WILLIAM sets the suitcase on the ground and they embrace.)

SWEET GRASS Ah, the smell of pines!

Maybe it does us good to be apart. We know more of what we have.

WEEBJOB Not so, Sweet Grass. I go hungry, and do not learn. *(He kisses her again.)* Your wife didn't come?

WILLIAM She didn't feel well enough to come. I didn't bring my daughter because I wanted a chance to talk to mother. The last time we took her for a ride it took Reesah and I both to hold on to her.

JAMES Hello, William.

WILLIAM James. *(They embrace, briefly.)*

JAMES Nothing is wrong, though?

WILLIAM No. She's well. Just pregnant and not happy about it at the moment. She thinks a two-year-old and a baby will be a lot to handle. I don't help her much, I suppose. My practice takes my time . . .

PICK UP Hello, William.

WILLIAM *(He smiles.)* Hello, Pick Up. *(They shake hands.)*

SWEET POTATO *(She runs to WILLIAM and hugs him.)* You drove to Hobbs to get mother?

WILLIAM No, she rode the bus to Roswell.

SWEET GRASS I wanted to get back to Salazar Canyon. I didn't want William to go any more out of his way— *(She embraces her daughter.)*

SWEET POTATO We didn't know when you were coming back. After all the letters you wrote to everyone but me . . .

SWEET GRASS I wrote you, Sweet Potato.

SWEET POTATO It never came.

SWEET GRASS It's at the General Delivery in Old Lincoln.

SWEET POTATO *(She hits her head.)* How could I not think of that? Of course – and we were just there. I've missed you, mother. *(JAMES hugs his mother.)*

WEEBJOB Is my letter at General Delivery too? I have a mailbox on the road, you know. The mail truck stops here now and then—

SWEET POTATO When he can find it among your signs.

WILLIAM I see you have a few new ones, father. *(He goes into the house with his mother's suitcase. JAMES follows.)*

WEEBJOB Dear wife, you didn't say if my letter was at the General Delivery.

SWEET GRASS No, it isn't. I didn't write to you, Weebjob. I didn't know what to say.

WEEBJOB Didn't know what to say! *(He claps his hands to his side.)* You told everyone everything that ever happened!

SWEET GRASS I didn't know how to write to you . . .

WEEBJOB Sweet Grass, my old wife back from her sister's in Hobbs. Already things are better. I must make a sign for the fence. How is Mary Jane Collar?

SWEET GRASS She's fine, Gerald Long Chalk.

WEEBJOB "Canaan" isn't the same without you.

SWEET GRASS I wanted to get back to my loom behind the house. I even missed Mighty Warrior sleeping under my feet while I weave. I even missed you too, Weebjob.

WEEBJOB Ah! But not everything is well. We might get a buffalo for a son-in-law.

SWEET GRASS I've known it for some time, Weebjob.

WEEBJOB So your letters to everyone said.

SWEET GRASS I was afraid to tell you.

WEEBJOB You certainly weren't afraid to tell all of Salazar Canyon about it.

SWEET GRASS Forgive me, Weebjob. I found that I liked to write letters when I was at Mary Jane Collar's. It made me feel like I was with everyone. I've never been away for a long time.

WEEBJOB How did you know about Sweet Potato and Pick Up?

SWEET GRASS I could tell they were in love. Even before Sweet Potato knew. At first, it upset me too. But now I'm used to it. He might just be the husband Sweet Potato needs.

WEEBJOB I don't know if I feel more sorry for Pick Up or Sweet Potato.

WILLIAM *(He comes out of the house with JAMES and calls to WEEBJOB and SWEET GRASS.)* I have to get back to Roswell. *(SWEET GRASS takes WEEBJOB by the hand and they return to WILLIAM and JAMES in front of the house. PICK UP and SWEET POTATO sit on the front steps.)*

WEEBJOB Yes, I understand. Your job and family. But you'll be returning soon . . .

SWEET GRASS Thank you for bringing me back to "Canaan." (They embrace also. WILLIAM *leaves.)* I want to speak to you, Sweet Potato. *(SWEET POTATO looks at* PICK UP.*)*

PICK UP I'll wait here with James. I need to get back to Old Lincoln afterwhile – I left in a hurry to look for you . . .

(PICK UP talks with JAMES on the front steps while the women talk by the fence of

WEEBJOB's squash patch. WEEBJOB goes to the side of the house and works at painting another sign to hang on his fence by the road.)

SWEET GRASS   Are you sure, Suzanne, you want to marry Pick Up?

SWEET POTATO   No, I'm not.

SWEET GRASS   Do you love him?

SWEET POTATO   Yes, I always have. I feel like I belong with him. I'm not excited or bored with him. He's just there.

SWEET GRASS   But you can't go running away, as you have from us.

SWEET POTATO   I know. He's said as much.

SWEET GRASS   Is there anything you'd rather do?

SWEET POTATO   Yes, but it's unattainable. I don't like school. I can't be like William and go to college. I barely finished high school. And I wasn't in the right place like James when he found his job. That desert clodhopper. He just happened to apply for a job and the horticulturist took him!

SWEET GRASS   He always liked the squash patch and cactus.

SWEET POTATO   I've looked and seen things I've wanted, but I could never have them. There's never been any place for me, mother. I don't want to go to school. I don't really want to wait tables. I'm happy when I'm on my way to Gallup. There isn't any room for me here on "Canaan."

SWEET GRASS   Yes, there is. You're our daughter.

SWEET POTATO   But I'm not your child anymore.

SWEET GRASS   Just so Pick Up isn't a father to you that you'd resent like Weebjob.

SWEET POTATO   *(She looks at her mother.)* No. He's one of my friends, though he's older.

SWEET GRASS   He's more like a brother?

SWEET POTATO   No. He's not like William or James to me. He's not Weebjob to me either. How could they have been friends for so long? They're different from one another.

SWEET GRASS   They complement each other somehow.

SWEET POTATO   Pick Up also asks me why I want to marry him.

SWEET GRASS   What do you tell him?

SWEET POTATO   What I tell you.

SWEET GRASS   You don't know what else to do so you're going to try marriage?

SWEET POTATO   Pick Up accused me of that also, but it isn't true. I do want to be with him. I think I always did, but was afraid it would look ridiculous. Now I might marry him. We could live in Old Lincoln and drive to Socorro to see James and Hersah on the weekends. Maybe . . . I could have a wool store. I even have a name for it.

SWEET GRASS   What?

SWEET POTATO   "The Spinners." I might even be able to have sheep on Pick Up's place.

SWEET GRASS   Will you finally let me teach you to weave?

SWEET POTATO   Maybe. You'll be supplier of the blankets I sell.

SWEET GRASS   There isn't anyone else you want to marry?

SWEET POTATO   There have been others. But they married someone else, or went off, or weren't interested in me. One was so worthless I knew the marriage would never work.

SWEET GRASS   What if someone came . . . more your age?

SWEET POTATO   I would still be Pick Up's wife. I do want to be with him, mother. He's a friend – I want him to be my husband.

SWEET GRASS   *(Puts her arm around SWEET POTATO)* I've always liked Pick Up though if I'd known he would be my son-in-law, I might have kicked about it at first. But now I feel differently. I can see him as your husand. I can understand why he loves you.

SWEET POTATO   What is it like to be a wife?

SWEET GRASS   It probably feels differently to every wife. To me it feels right to be Weebjob's wife. I see him as the man he wants to be, even when he falls short of it.

SWEET POTATO   Which is most of the time.

SWEET GRASS   No, it isn't. He's a good man. I like to look at him, feel him against me, listen to him. I shouldn't be speaking of these things to you. But I must be with him. Even if he is in the squash patch, sometimes I go out just to watch him work. Sometimes I hear his prayers, his chants. When he has visions of the Thunder Hawk, I leave him to himself. He's my companion. I don't know what I'd do without him. I suppose

I'd go live with Mary Jane Collar and we'd can cactus jelly and paint her back steps. He's all I thought about in Hobbs . . .

SWEET POTATO You could live with us.

SWEET GRASS No. You would be camping out with Pick Up or hiking in the mountains. I would not feel welcome in my son-in-law's house, nor my daughter-in-law's, nor with James either. Do you think he'll marry Hersah?

SWEET POTATO I don't know. She really doesn't want to get married.

SWEET GRASS I don't like it. I'm from the old school, like Weebjob.

SWEET POTATO James knows that, mother. He might be uncomfortable with it too. He's gone a lot. The highway crews aren't a steady group. They might influence him.

SWEET GRASS But he knows differently.

SWEET POTATO I can't answer for him. William is really the only one of us that could endure discomfort for what he wanted. Well, James too, I guess. He reads his horticulture books at night until Hersah gets mad. Sometimes she and I go to the movies, or just into town and talk with the boys. But Hersah didn't like any of the boys the way she likes James. I may have liked some of the boys now and then, but I didn't want to be with them very long. Pick Up makes me feel happy, mother. He's someone to hold on to when there's nowhere for me, no place I really fit. (She holds her hands to her ears.) Sometimes I wonder why I was even born.

SWEET GRASS Sweet Potato. Such talk!

SWEET POTATO Everyone can do something but me.

SWEET GRASS You just haven't found your place yet. The Long Chalks have always had God's blessing.

SWEET POTATO I guess I can have children. But I don't envy William's wife. I probably won't be a good mother either.

SWEET GRASS I think you will. There's not much in the marriage for her right now but children and housework because William works such long hours. That will change.

WEEBJOB (Enters and joins the conversation) Daughter, are you marrying Pick Up?

SWEET POTATO It seems that way.

WEEBJOB Are you sure it's what you want?

SWEET POTATO Maybe it will be my "Canaan." Maybe I will finally understand . . .

WEEBJOB There's no way marriage to Pick Up could be avoided?

SWEET POTATO You wouldn't like it.

JAMES Dad—

WEEBJOB God's blessing on your marriage, Suzanne Long Chalk. (They embrace.)

SWEET POTATO (As WEEBJOB starts toward JAMES) You still seem reserved about it.

WEEBJOB (Turns back to SWEET POTATO) Pick Up has not yet asked my permission to marry you.
(SWEET GRASS and SWEET POTATO stay at the fence and talk a while longer. WEEBJOB goes to JAMES who stands at the edge of the house. PICK UP remains on the steps.)

JAMES Do you want me to close your paint cans?

WEEBJOB At least someone asks something of me. (Puts his arm around JAMES's shoulder but looks at PICK UP) Yes. How trying to think I will have Pick Up as a son-in-law . . .

JAMES Weebjob, you're like the Malpais lava pits beyond Carrizozo. Pick Up will be a good husband to Sweet Potato.

WEEBJOB Maybe before I make my death cry, I will understand it all.

JAMES (They close WEEBJOB's paint can.) Sometimes you're like one of the trees in the nursery truck with your roots wrapped in a bag of sand. (There's a new sign which reads "You should live so long.")

WEEBJOB I guess it's my strict upbringing—

JAMES I'd like for you to be more . . . "with us." I'd like to hear the sound of the rototiller on your land.

WEEBJOB (He is distracted because SWEET POTATO and SWEET GRASS walk past him from the squash patch.) Ah! my wife is back. I will watch Sweet Grass weave – making form out of all those stands of wool, then I can make sense of everything again . . . (SWEET GRASS enters the house. SWEET POTATO remains on the step talking to PICK UP. The audience cannot hear their conversation, but it should be evident what they are talking about. She points to WEEBJOB. PICK UP shakes his head. She points to PICK UP then WEEBJOB again. He finally shakes his head in agreement.)

PICK UP Weebjob, father of Sweet Potato,

may I have a word with you before I leave?

WEEBJOB *(He and* JAMES *walk to the front of the porch.)* You may stay, James.

PICK UP I would like to speak to you alone.

WEEBJOB Denied.

PICK UP I would like permission to marry your daughter.

JAMES *(He looks to the sky, embarrassed that he's there.)* It's a long drive to Socorro . . . I need—

WEEBJOB *(As though he doesn't hear* JAMES*)* Ah! I was waiting for that. In the old days the father was the leader of the family. He was the thinker, the medicine man, the holy man, the elder. He was respected. No decisions were made until HE was asked. He had an HONORABLE place.

PICK UP You have an honorable place, Weebjob, father of Sweet Potato, as long as you don't carry it too far and make a burro of yourself.

WEEBJOB So you want to marry my daughter?

PICK UP And you consent?

WEEBJOB No, I don't.

PICK UP *(He looks at* SWEET POTATO*.)* I knew he would be obstinate. That's why I didn't want to ask him.

JAMES Dad—

WEEBJOB Does this concern you? *(*SWEET POTATO *gets up and exits.)*

PICK UP Weebjob, father of Sweet Potato, holy man, prophet of Salazar Canyon, may I have permission to marry your daughter?

WEEBJOB I know you're serious about Sweet Potato. I wondered when my next trial was coming from God. Now I know. Whom he loves he chastens. It doesn't seem I have any choice. Yes, Pick Up, you have my permission to marry Sweet Potato. I wish it could be some other way . . . *(Pause)* But I've already given her my blessing.

PICK UP Thank you, Weebjob.

JAMES Thank you, father. *(*PICK UP *leaves stage to find* SWEET POTATO.*)*

WEEBJOB Now maybe he'll stay home.

JAMES I have to leave now. Hersah will have supper waiting by the time I get there . . . *(They say goodbye and* JAMES *walks past* PICK UP *and* SWEET POTATO.*)* I'll talk to you later. *(He exits.)*

PICK UP Weebjob has consented, and I didn't injure him before he did.

SWEET POTATO You have shown patience.

PICK UP Now, when we can get married?

SWEET POTATO As soon as you like. But I won't wear a dress.

PICK UP And I will NOT be married on "Canaan." *(He holds her in his arms.)* See that bright spot in the desert where the sun comes through the clouds and makes a ring of light?

SWEET POTATO When I'm standing on the road with my thumb up, the heat trying to take my breath, the fear of passing cars pounding in my chest, I feel one with the land. The shrubs speak to me like children. The dry river beds maybe without a trickle of water. I wash in the heat and feel alive on Interstate 40 West. Not straining for existence any longer, but filled with meaning.

PICK UP But what's in Gallup?

SWEET POTATO Nothing, I guess, but getting there. I forget I'm a reject of this world. When I'm on my way to Gallup, I'm INDIAN. I like these worn hills with wrinkles like an old man's face, and with sand as brown as our skin. The divided highway is not like 380 through the canyon. Wind plays with my hair and the heat laughs . . . The terrible heat that pulls one into itself, and windows of the skin are open and we are running with the heat. Not hardly anyone knows but us. I like the morning sun on my back and the long fingers of the evening shadow across the highway. I want to go again across the Cibolo County line to Gallup.

PICK UP I believe you do, Suzanne.

SWEET POTATO Palomino rocks. Mountains and plateaus. Sometimes I sit in the shade of a bush and listen to the cars pass. *(*PICK UP *looks away from her a moment. It's hard for him to listen to part of what she says, especially when he realizes there is danger in what she does.)* I don't ride with anyone who stops. I look them over first. There are white men who would use me . . .

PICK UP *(Turns away from her)* Indians too.

SWEET POTATO That's why they can't see and feel the life of the desert, and can't hear the Great Spirit walking in the heat – in the midst of the fiery furnace. See, I know some of the Book too. *(*PICK UP *walks away from her.)* What's the matter, Pick Up?

PICK UP Go to Gallup. Maybe you have more there on the road than I can give you.

SWEET POTATO When I get as far as Mesita I know I'll make it. Rock slides where the highway cuts through the plateaus. Payute. Cubero. James goes up into the Pinos Mountains, but I have to go farther.

PICK UP All the way to Gallup!

SWEET POTATO What's wrong with hitch-hiking to Gallup?

PICK UP It isn't for a woman.

SWEET POTATO It's exactly for me. Every place speaks my name and I know what to call them in return. The cactus and hills and arroyos.

PICK UP I don't want you on the highway for another man to see. I don't want you misused, Sweet Potato. You can under-stand that. I want to protect you – *(He looks at the ground.)* I want to consume you myself.

SWEET POTATO Last week before I left I kept thinking of El Morro. San Rafael. Quemado. I don't ride with anyone. Sometimes it's like they're dead already when I look at their eyes. They look like a lava rock to me. *(She touches* PICK UP.*)* I'm glad you worry about me. It's always been me who saw others look at you. I remember the women who wanted you – Why didn't you ever marry after the first time?

PICK UP I never found anyone I really wanted to marry. But you've caught me, Suzanne. You have a sweetness too, like your mother. You get a little rusty sometimes, like the desert water in my well – but you're not so tough, Miss Long Chalk. I won't tell anyone, though.

SWEET POTATO Sometimes the jackrabbits hop right in front of me. *(She ignores him.)* Pick Up, I'm alive on the road to Gallup.

PICK UP It's suicide for you to hitchhike, Sweet Potato.

SWEET POTATO I've run into the bad ones before . . . *(She looks at* PICK UP.*)* There was a man who tried to pick me up once. He followed me along the highway for a while, but I wouldn't get into his car.

PICK UP *(Angry with her)* God, Sweet Potato.

SWEET POTATO I always got away from any trouble.

PICK UP But you might not always . . . How can I let you go? I remember when you had to sit on books to reach the supper table. And now you're hitchhiking? Why do you want to go to Gallup?

SWEET POTATO For the thrill of passing Ozanbito. The army depot and cathedral. The Outpost Restaurant where I worked that summer on my own. I used to cross the street and eat in the cemetery. The hand-made grave markers. A picket fence like a play-pen. The little weeds that jumped at my feet.

PICK UP The street-corner crowd at Indian capital? The "No Loitering" sign at the cemetery?

SWEET POTATO On Sundays I walked up the Cathedral.

PICK UP You could teach, Sweet Potato. You aren't too old to go back to school. The children at Indian missions need teachers . . .

SWEET POTATO I don't know—

PICK UP I remember you in a little pinafore with the straps crossed on your bare back. They made a big white X and I knew then you were one I could probably wait for— *(SWEET POTATO pushes Pick Up away when he tries to kiss her.)* I have to go – I might have some calls for my tow truck . . . *(He kisses her.)*

Scene 2

WEEBJOB *sits by* SWEET GRASS *at her loom.*

WEEBJOB Mutton. All the kissing I see them doing! To be around someone in love is like being in a mountain storm when the sky comes down upon you. The young are restless as the pines. But what's his excuse?

SWEET GRASS You are muttering against what will make Sweet Potato happy?

WEEBJOB A man serves God, but his reward does not always come at first.

SWEET GRASS Your problem is that you've never had a problem. God has blessed your life from the beginning.

WEEBJOB Not so, wife – Sweet Potato running to Gallup. William's unrelenting pursuit of the legal profession, forgetting his spiritual nature. James looking for visions in peyote and drugs.

SWEET GRASS Just peyote in the Indian church.

WEEBJOB In the reservation and boarding schools as a boy, I first saw the Thunder Hawk vision. I didn't need peyote for it to come.

SWEET GRASS Weebjob, you don't bend.

WEEBJOB No, wife. It's by faith we see these things.

SWEET GRASS We don't all see as you do, Weebjob.

WEEBJOB *(He looks at her as she weaves.)* You never used to contradict me, Sweet Grass.

SWEET GRASS Because I express my opinion, you call it contradiction? Haven't I always been free to say what I think?

WEEBJOB Yes, because what you've said always agreed with what I thought you should say.

SWEET GRASS But if I should want to say something that didn't agree with what you think I should say, then I should be quiet?

WEEBJOB You're not going back to visit your sister.

SWEET GRASS *(Laughs)* It isn't her.

SWEET POTATO *(She joins her parents after* PICK UP *leaves.)* Is he threatening to return you to the Female Seminary?

SWEET GRASS Nearly.

WEEBJOB I can't. It's closed down.

SWEET POTATO It should have never been opened.

SWEET GRASS It wasn't that bad, Sweet Potato. There was such upheaval in our lives . . . It was probably the best place for us. *(Pause)* Why are you always against school?

SWEET POTATO Why do you ask such stupid questions? *(Angrily)* Because I couldn't do it! You ought to know that! *(Impatiently)* I got tired of bad grades . . . Not knowing anything . . . *(Pause)* I don't mean to snap at you. But I always failed. Why do you want me to say it?

SWEET GRASS I'm sorry I brought it up. Yes, I remember your struggle. I don't think you stuck with it, Sweet Potato.

SWEET POTATO How long does it take to find out you can't do something?

SWEET GRASS It's not easy for anyone. I remember how hard it was to learn. The days were long . . . And the nights . . . Memories were frightening as the booger dancers. Those wooden masks with their horrid faces jumped into my dreams. *(She looks at* WEEBJOB.*)* There were puzzling

times too. I remember the heat under my nightdress where I had not felt a man . . .

SWEET POTATO *(Embarrassed by her mother's sudden frankness)* I never knew you felt anything like that, mother. *(*SWEET POTATO *has always been in awe of her mother, and felt she could never equal her. Now she realizes her mother is human, and they have similar feelings.)*

SWEET GRASS I guess it's the thought of you wanting to marry Pick Up . . . I remember how I felt when I saw Weebjob. I didn't have time to love him. He just decided I would be his wife. But later . . . Those feelings always stayed unspoken.

SWEET POTATO How could you marry like that?

SWEET GRASS We didn't know any other way.

SWEET POTATO You're quiet for once, Weebjob.

WEEBJOB Ah! Yes, I am. I was listening to Sweet Grass, and didn't know what to say. I remembered when I went to the Female Seminary for a wife. I had a friend who I went to see, and all the girls out on the lawn made me think it was a place to get a wife. I was thinking of the boarding school for Indian boys . . . *(Pause)* I like this time of evening. I remember the fingers of the sun across the yard of the boarding school from the canyons and arroyos as evening reached from the parched desert. We couldn't ignore it. We woke up in the morning sweating with the heat. It only intensified during the day. We couldn't ignore the poverty of the school. The dreariness of the land. Our heritage was rich with tradition, and it was taken from us. We had to learn a new way, dry and dull, against our reasoning. I longed for Indian ways just as the others. Christianity wasn't enough. And nothing came to fill the particular hunger we felt. Others grew bitter, later drank and wasted their lives. But I have always felt the closeness of the Great Spirit, and that he would manifest himself to me. Why would I have the hunger if there was nothing to fill it? And in the desolation of the nights, when I could hear other boys cry or moan with nightmares, the vision of the Thunder Hawk came, not the vision, for it was the Thunder Hawk himself. A magnificent bird from the spirit world full of light like a blue, stained-glass window in a cathedral. The vine at the window in the winter also reminded me of him. When the land was even deader than it was in summer. The dry vine rattling at the window was like the wings of the Thunder Hawk coming to me right through the walls of the boarding school for Indian boys. It was like the sweat lodge I heard about from the old Indian men before we were taken to school. It seemed to me to be "Canaan" that was talked about in the Book. And this place too, here where I've lived all these years, where I can do what I want without fear or interference. It is "Canaan." I see the Thunder Hawk to this day. He has never left me. Great Spirit, how can you merge with us, who are mortal in our flesh and bound with error and filled with weakness? I must go to the squash patch for a while. I feel the wind over me like the presence of the Great Spirit . . . like the hot shower in the motel in Roswell when William got married and I stayed until the water ran cold and Sweet Grass called for me to get out. (SWEET GRASS *laughs.* . WEEBJOB *goes to the squash patch.*)

Scene 3

WEEBJOB *prays in his squash patch. The Thunder Hawk comes to him in a vision again, twirling with colored lights something like a moving stained-glass window in a cathedral. But this is a new-age vision. While the Thunder Hawk hovers, the characters rise and dance a Genesis/Turtle-Island creation myth: they pull dry land out of Cayos. It spreads on the ground of the squash patch. The characters dance with signs from* WEEBJOB's *fence. One sign reads: Salazar Canyon. But Cayos rises again and covers the land. There's a "civil war" of sorts. The sound of a tow truck is heard. Slowly it pulls Cayos away. Dry land is established again. Now the characters continue the "Sign Dance." The sign: "Canaan" has a field day. Another sign "Weebjob has a map" dances with it. The whole scene is a rush of movement, a preliminary to the wedding scene which follows. What happens in the spirit world will be acted out in the physical. This scene is the story of how we come from Cayos into maybe as much light as we can stand. And how struggle to stay there.*

Scene 4

SWEET GRASS *(She is dressed for the wedding.)* It's a lovely day in Salazar Canyon. Just the day for Weebjob's daughter to marry Pick Up. Already the guests arrive. Come in. Come in. *(Several people enter carrying bowls of food.* SWEET GRASS *motions them to the house.)* Would you carry the table off the porch? *(Two men carry the table from the porch and set it in the yard. The women set the bowls of food on the table. Others arrive.)* Clement Thousandsticks. How nice to see you. Did you have a pleasant drive here? Hersah. James is still in the house. I think he's helping Weebjob get himself ready for the wedding.

(SWEET GRASS goes into the house. Others stand in clumps talking and greeting one another. There are two new signs on the fence: "By the thunder of his power who can understand? Job 26:14" and "Miserable comforters are ye all, Job 16:1.")

CLEMENT *(He speaks to WARHALL.)* Well, I wonder how the holy war was fought in "Canaan" when Pick Up asked Weebjob to marry his daughter. Bah! Bah!

WARHALL Hua! *(Laughter)*

CLEMENT You've got pen stains in your shirt pocket again, Warhall. I see you're still working crosswords in the Roswell Gazette.

(There is the sound of talking among the WEDDING GUESTS. At times some conversations are heard above others:)

WEDDING GUESTS *(Severally)* Been hunting lately?

Jack Rabbits run like deer. You shoot when they stop and look back. Though you could almost shoot them at a run, they move so steady.

A cotton tail keeps going until he's gone. He won't look back to see if you're still there.

If they're not careful, Old Lincoln will be under a foot of honeysuckle by next summer.

At least it'll cover those old buildings they painted turquoise.

The Gallup rodeo's big as Albuquerque's.

SWEET GRASS *(She comes from the house.)* William. Reesah. Hello. Thank you for bringing Mary Jane. *(They embrace.)* Such a lovely day for the wedding.

WEEBJOB Uuuuah! *(He moans from the house.)*

SWEET GRASS *(When everyone looks toward the house)* Weebjob is still getting ready. Don't worry about him. Come. *(SWEET GRASS takes MARY JANE's arm.)* I need your help for a moment. *(SWEET GRASS goes into the house and gets a roll of crepe paper, returns to the yard where they wait.)* Wrap this around the fence-posts in the squash patch. We didn't have time to get ready for the wedding. I hadn't seen you in such a long time before I came to Hobbs. Now we've seen each other twice in such a short time.

CLEMENT Sarah Long Chalk and Mary Jane Collar. I can remember you two dazzling young sisters.

MARY JANE And Clement, I can remember running from you when I came to visit Sarah.

WARHALL That's probably the wisest thing you ever did.

CLEMENT Let's rodeo!

SWEET GRASS Here now, Clement, the musicians and minister have arrived. Show them the squash patch. When will Weebjob be ready?

MARY JANE How lovely the squash patch looks with its yellow blossoms! *(She and REESAH go to the squash patch and wrap the fence-posts with crepe paper. The little girl stands with them.)*

CLEMENT *(He takes the MINISTER and the two Indian MUSICIANS with flute and drum to the squash patch.)* This is where the show-down will take place.

MARY JANE I've never heard of a wedding in a squash patch, but Weebjob was never typical. *(The flute plays, which is the traditional instrument for love songs.)*

REESAH It was Sweet Potato's idea.

MARY JANE That figures. *(JAMES and HERSAH come from the house. They talk to WILLIAM and the other GUESTS. A few more people arrive. Some bring bowls of food which they set on the table. Some bring presents. SWEET GRASS greets everyone.)*

SWEET GRASS Weebjob *(She goes to the house.)* Our guests are here. James, where is he?

JAMES He's taking his time. *(JAMES turns and looks at the door of the house.)* I thought he was behind us. I'll go see what's holding him up now. *(JAMES goes back into the house.)*

SWEET GRASS It would be nice to gather for your wedding too, Hersah.

HERSAH Not yet.
(PICK UP arrives and they all make a clamor over him.)

CLEMENT Pick Up!

PICK UP Clement Thousandsticks.

WARHALL Pick Up! You've come to your wedding in "Canaan." The old stick is going to make it. He's looking a little pale.

CLEMENT Ba-aah! *(PICK UP ignores the men.)* Are you going to Gallup on your honeymoon?

WILLIAM Gentlemen. We're gathered here for a solemn and joyous occasion. Let us respect Pick Up and his new bride.

WARHALL Hear! Hear! *(Both MUSICIANS play and the WEDDING GUESTS start to gather around the squash patch.)*

JAMES *(He coaxes WEEBJOB from the house.)* Come, father, you must greet the wedding guests.

WEEBJOB *(He appears dressed for the wedding.)* For once, I wish Mighty Warrior would bark and scatter this "assemblage." *(Pause)* I cannot believe Pick Up is going to become my son-in-law in my own squash patch on "Canaan." Never in all my imagination . . . *(He lifts his fist to heaven.)* I'm at a crossroads in my life.

CLEMENT Ah, Weebjob! How grand you look!

WEEBJOB *(He comes into the yard.)* Mutton!

WARHALL Weebjob! Father of the Spud who is going to become wife of Pick Up.

WEEBJOB *(He swats into the air.)* As many flies as there used to be arrows.

SWEET GRASS Weebjob. Where have you been?

WEEBJOB I'm not late. I don't see Tuber yet.

SWEET GRASS She'll be the last one here, Weebjob. She's the bride. I have spoken to the minister about where to stand. Come, greet the guests. They've brought a lot of food.

WEEBJOB *(He greets the GUESTS and seems to feel better.)* Ofred. Warhall. Kutchell. Clement Thousands of Ticks. *(He shakes many of their hands.)* Reesah. Little One. William. *(He hugs them.)* Mary Jane Collar who takes my wife away. Hersah. All. *(He shakes the MINISTER's hand.)* My Father in heaven. *(He lifts his arm to the sky again.)* Squash patch. *(He greets his beloved plot of land.)* With crepe-paper— *(He looks at SWEET GRASS)* —on holy ground?

SWEET GRASS It needed decoration for the wedding. *(Pause)* Weebjob, there is someone you haven't spoken to—

WEEBJOB I will see enough of him until my name is called from beyond the mountain. Pick Up, my son. *(They embrace.)* WILLIAM *stands with* REESAH, *the child and* MARY JANE COLLAR. JAMES *and* HERSAH *and* SWEET GRASS *stand in front of the* MINISTER *who has his back to the audience, and the others draw close to the squash patch, leaving a middle aisle for* WEEBJOB *and* SWEET POTATO. *They all turn when she enters from the back.* PICK UP *smiles.)*

SWEET POTATO Yes, father. The desert is white with harvest. I see it now like you always said it was . . .
(The MUSICIANS *play background flute and drum.* WEEBJOB *and* SWEET POTATO *walk to the front of the people gathered for the wedding.* SWEET POTATO *wears a dress.)*

WEEBJOB *(Moans)* How can all this be?
(The flute plays a wedding song. WEEBJOB *moans again several times during the ceremony.)*

MINISTER Relatives and Friends. I want this couple, whose hearts are about to be joined as one, to bless themselves with holy cedar smoke, to cleanse and clear their minds of any bad or negative thoughts for their walk through life. Ah-ho wah-kon-tah. Bless the use of this cedar for which it is intended.
(The MINISTER *passes the bowl of cedar in front of* SWEET POTATO *and* PICK UP, *then the* WEDDING PARTY. *They wash the thin trail of smoke over them.)* I want to wish you well, you whose hearts have joined hands to walk the road of life, may your walk be soft and long, always be kind and courteous to each other and may you see many grandchildren and maybe even great-grandchildren. Any way you want it. It will be that way. Ah-ho. *(The* MINISTER *hands the two-necked wedding vase to* SWEET POTATO *and* PICK UP. *They drink from it.)* The union of husband and wife in heart, body, and mind is intended by the Great Spirit for their mutual joy. Into this holy union, Percy Willingdeer and Suzanne Long Chalk are come to be joined. If any of you can show just cause why they may not lawfully be married, speak now; or forever hold your peace. (JAMES looks at WEEBJOB, who remains quiet.) Aho.

WEDDING GUESTS Aho.

MINISTER Percy, will you take this woman to be your wife; to live together in the covenant of marriage? Will you love her, comfort her, honor and keep her, in sickness and in health; and, forsaking all others, be faithful to her as long as you both shall live?

PICK UP I will.

MINISTER Suzanne, will you have this man to be your husband; to live together in the covenant of marriage? Will you love him, comfort him, honor and keep him, in sickness and in health; and, forsaking all others, be faithful to him as long as you both shall live?

SWEET POTATO I will.

MINISTER Will all of you witnessing these promises do all in your power to uphold these two persons in their marriage?
(SWEET GRASS looks at WEEBJOB. *They both speak with the* WEDDING GUESTS.)*

WEDDING GUESTS We will.

MINISTER Let us pray. O gracious and everliving God, you have created us male and female in your image. Look mercifully upon this man and this woman who come to you seeking your blessing, and assist them with your grace, that they may honor and keep the vows they make; through Jesus Christ our Savior, who lives and reigns with you in the unity of the Holy Spirit, one God, forever and ever. Amen.
(WILLIAM's wife REESAH wipes her eyes, and WILLIAM puts his arm around her.)

PICK UP *(He faces* SWEET POTATO, *takes her right hand and repeats after the* MINISTER.) In the Name of God, I, Percy, take you, Suzanne, to be my wife, to have and to hold from this day forward, for better, for worse, for richer, for poorer, in sickness and in health, to love and to cherish, until we are parted by death.

SWEET POTATO *(She takes* PICK UP's *right hand in hers and repeats after the* MINISTER *also.)* In the name of God, I, Suzanne, take you, Percy, to be my husband, to have and to hold from this day forward, for better, for worse, for richer, for poorer, in sickness and in health, to love and to cherish, until we are parted by death.

MINISTER Bless, O Lord, this ring to be a
sign of the vows by which this man and
this woman have bound themselves to
each other.
(WEEBJOB moans again.)

WEDDING GUESTS Hua! Hua!

MINISTER Now that Percy and Suzanne
have given themselves to each other by
solemn vows, with the joining of hands
and the giving and receiving of a ring, I
pronounce that they are husband and
wife in the name of the Father, and of the
Son, and of the Holy Spirit.

PICK UP *(Enthusiastically)* And in the name
of the sun and wind and mountains and
streams . . . *(He kisses his new wife.)*
*(The MUSICIANS play. The WEDDING
GUESTS hug the Long Chalk family. Even
WEEBJOB. They congratulate PICK UP and
SWEET POTATO. The women, MARY JANE
COLLAR and REESAH, go to the table and
arrange the bowls of food.)*

SWEET GRASS Do you remember when we
were married, Weebjob, and they—

WEEBJOB *(He interrupts her.)* Yes, and we
got away anyway.

SWEET GRASS But not everyone knew it.

SWEET POTATO They can speak in half-
sentences and know what the other is
going to say . . .

PICK UP May we be married that long.

WEEBJOB You'd be Methuselah by then.

CLEMENT Ah, Pick Up and his young wife
*(Acts like he is going to congratulate SWEET
POTATO with a kiss)*

PICK UP *(Holds his arm up to CLEMENT)*
None of you horned toads are going to
kiss my wife. *(The WEDDING GUESTS
begin to form a train and make an Indian
dance around "Canaan." The MUSICIANS
continue to play.)*

WEEBJOB *(He swats himself.)* Barking
flies!

CLEMENT How does it feel to have a son-
in-law like Pick Up?

WEEBJOB Go dance with youself, Clement.

CLEMENT At least he has Sweet Potato
now. She's not your worry any longer.

WEEBJOB She was never that much of a
worry.

CLEMENT Hoa! A female child who runs
off? Tut, tut, Weebjob.
*(While the GUESTS are in the circle dance,
these conversations are heard:)*

WEDDING GUESTS *(Severally)*
I thought you wanted to dance.

No, I'll sit and talk.
Fine wedding.
Strange though.
Chua. Chua. Whssp. Yah, a cottontail
keeps going until he's gone.
The Long Chalks always did things their
own way.
Good fry bread.
I'll give you my recipe for judenedo.
Yah, there's nothing like cactus jelly.
You voting for Chief?
Not for you, Ofred.

WEEBJOB *(To WILLIAM)* Belief is a matter
of will. I choose to believe. Yet I have
seen also in the squash patch when the
Thunder Hawk comes to me. You don't
believe because you don't choose to.

WILLIAM I see no evidence of it.

WEEBJOB Because you don't take time. You
fill your days with law. But your rational
mind will never explain enough to satisfy
you. You have to admit that God
descended into flesh.

WILLIAM I don't see what that's got to do
with anything.

JAMES Why don't you say those things to
me?

WEEBJOB I guess I didn't think you wanted
to hear them.

JAMES You always talk like that to William
and he doesn't want to hear.

WEEBJOB Another crossroads in my life.

WILLIAM I have to see how Reesah is
doing.

WEEBJOB I have felt Sweet Potato's anger
too. I gave her life and made it bitter for
her. But now I want things healed
between us. I was always too serious. And
with you, James, I've not been serious
enough. *(Pause)* I'll make a a new sign for
the fence at Highway 380: "I have heard
by hearing, but now I see with my eyes,
Job 42:5."

CLEMENT *(Overhearing)* Another wooden
smoke signal? You've got your fence by
the highway nearly covered. What are
you going to say about having Pick Up as
a son-in-law? Tut, tut.

WEEBJOB I welcome him to the family.

CLEMENT *(He moves to PICK UP and SWEET
POTATO to tease them again.)* The old war
horse and his bride. Where are you going
to take her on your honeymoon?

PICK UP What the shit, Clement. We're
going to hitchhike to Gallup!

Marga Gomez

Biography

Harlem born and San Francisco based, Marga Gomez has earned a living in theater and comedy venues since 1980. Her stand-up has been featured on public television, A & E, VH-1, Comedy Central and HBO's Comic Relief V1, as well as "The Best of Comic Relief." Her stage background includes performances with the Tony Award-winning San Francisco Mime Troupe, Lilith Feminist Theatre and the ground-breaking Latino Ensemble Culture Clash. Her theatrical monologue *Memory Tricks* has been optioned by American Playhouse, as a feature film, and she is currently writing the screenplay.

Artistic Statement

I was the only child of the marriage of a Cuban comedian–impresario to a Puerto Rican dancer and aspiring actress. I grew up in the sixties believing that my parents were big time stars . . . and in the Latino community of Manhattan, they were. There was nothing more fun than tagging along with my parents to the Teatros on the weekend and being a fly on the wall backstage while my parents and their show biz colleagues (some very talented, others just well endowed) entertained the familias, from the grandparents to the babies, all dressed in their best. It looked like church with a beat.

As I got older and saw my parents' grandeur dissipate into failure, I spent hours and hours reliving their heyday in my mind. I will always be a nostalgia queen even though I realize the present and future offer more for someone of my ethnic background and sexual orientation.

I do what I do because of my parents. Solo performance feels natural to me because I grew up as an only child and I was weird. As a stand-up comedian for eight years I used my personal experiences as material fodder but too often I had to simplify my ideas to get laughs. Since I was wanting to explore the complexities of assimilation and sexual identity, comedy clubs were becoming less appropriate venues.

In 1990 I got a call from someone who was involved in presenting a multicultural theater festival at the University of

Photo: Irene Young

California at San Diego (UCSD). Her committee had been informed that I was a solo performance artist and they wanted to include my work in their festival. I said I would love to perform but I was in the process of changing the title of my piece and I would call her tomorrow with the new title. That's how I switched careers from stand-up comic to solo performance artist in one phone call.

For years I harbored the secret desire to write a play about my parents and make them famous for real and forever. After that was done I'd be free to create my own dramas. Unfortunately I had no idea how to write a play. I was already doing it in my stand-up act on a smaller scale.

Accepting the UCSD gig put a fire under me to quit procrastinating. Because my mother had been diagnosed the year before with Alzheimer's there was no question that my first theatrical monologue *Memory Tricks* would be about her life and our relationship. Writing and performing the piece and playing my mother has helped me discover the love that was there between us, and the resentment I had for her ceased to exist.

Five months after the UCSD festival I premiered a two-act version of *Memory Tricks* at San Francisco's The Marsh. The audiences were enthusiastic, the houses were full, but the piece needed something. After two years of touring, rewriting and almost killing it, I learned that what *Memory Tricks* needed was less. Thirty minutes were cut which included some very funny but unnecessary jokes, and my father's presence in the piece was greatly reduced. Since its premiere at the New York Shakespeare Festival it has been performed straight through without intermission and I'm always thirsty at the end.

When *Memory Tricks* first played in my home base of San Francisco, my stock rose. I went from being a starving undervalued artist to a starving valued artist. But there were detractors in town saying it wasn't gay enough and accusing me of going mainstream – like that was easy. At the same time a couple of my coolest friends were opening Josie's Cabaret and Juice Joint, a queer performance space in the Castro. I wanted to be involved right away so I booked four weeks in October of 1991 for *Marga Gomez Is Pretty Witty & Gay*. I wrote this second performance monologue to flaunt my queer credentials, and at the same time say "fuck you" to those members of the mainstream, and my own community, who gave me grief. But the main reason I wrote *MGisPW&G* so soon after *Memory Tricks* was because I wanted to remind everyone that I can be very funny, and nothing but funny, from beginning to end. And then I asked myself, why is my self-worth dependent on making people laugh?

In October of 1993 I was invited by the Latino Ensemble Culture Clash to work in a show they were developing for the Mark Taper Forum which focused, among other things, on the heritage of Latino performers. I began to write about my father. The short vignette called *The Thirteen Minutos* was well received. I was commissioned by the New WORLD Theater and the Mark Taper Forum to write a full monologue about my father which is now titled *A Line Around the Block*.

My father died in 1983 but he has appeared in my dreams regularly since then. I think he would want a piece written about him more than my mother would. If he were alive and healthy now he would probably do a one-man show about himself. He appeared in spectacular variety shows and later in half-empty dives but he always tried to maintain complete control over the productions. He was a very funny and charming man on stage, but moody and melancholy in private. Although a major theme of *Memory Tricks* is the fear and inevitability of becoming my mother, I still believe that I inherited more traits from my father. As I continue to remember and record his life I find good and bad parallels to my own experiences in relationships and as a performer. With these insights I can hopefully avoid making the same mistakes.

The three monologues have been referred to as a family trilogy, but I'm not so sure that *MGisPW&G* is as revelatory as its companion pieces. It's a topical comedy I'm proud of, but my deeper truths are in between the lines of my parents' stories. Maybe I need to write a fourth piece about the real me. And I'll run my quartet indefinitely in rep Off-Broadway, Monday through Thursday, with a three-day weekend until I have a baby who will write my fifth monologue about me and add it to my pentagoria.

Production History

Memory Tricks was produced as a work in progress by the University of California at San Diego Multicultural Festival in November of 1990. It was produced as a two-act workshop performance at The Marsh Performance Space, San Francisco, and the Solo Mio Festival at the Life on the Water Theatre, San Francisco. It was workshopped as a one-act at Josie's Cabaret, San Francisco, and subsequently previewed at both the Festival of New Voices at the New York Shakespeare Festival, Public Theatre, New York City and at the New WORLD Theater, Amherst, Massachusetts. It was premiered as a one-act at the New York Shakespeare Festival, Public Theatre, New York City in April of 1993 and has received numerous subsequent productions at venues including the International Theatre Festival of Chicago, Wellington Theatre; the Just for Laughs Comedy Festival, Gesu Theatre, Montreal; and in Scotland at the Edinburgh Fringe Festival.

Marga Gomez is Pretty Witty & Gay premiered at Josie's Cabaret, San Francisco, in October of 1991 and has been produced at numerous venues including P.S. 122, New

York City; the Whitney Museum's Biennial Performance Series, New York City; Highways Performance Space, Santa Monica, California; the New WORLD Theater; the International Theatre Festival of Chicago; the Wellington Theatre; and the Edinburgh Fringe Festival.

A Line Around the Block was read at the Mark Taper Forum, Music Center, Los Angeles, in May of 1994 and was workshopped at Josie's Cabaret, San Francisco, in June 1994 and at the New WORLD Theater, in September of 1994.

10 *Excerpts from* Memory Tricks, Marga Gomez Is Pretty Witty & Gay *and* A Line Around the Block

Marga Gomez

Memory Tricks

MARGA (MARGITA) tells the following story on a stage that is bare except for a park bench.

MARGITA

My mother complained whenever she made a deal with me so I wouldn't know that she got the better end. Like on the night of my seventh birthday. We were living on 169th Street in Manhattan. You could call that Harlem. We called it Washington Heights. We had the only house in the neighborhood. It was squiched in by three big apartment buildings. And some of our neighbors would occasionally throw beer bottles and bags of trash into our yard. But my parents acted like we lived on a country estate and they would throw these high-class patio parties for their friends in Spanish show business and never invite those neighbors.

(As WILLY, *her father*)

I want to make a toast. Whiskey, please. Para todos aquí – Bienvenidos y Salud.

(*Sound of beer bottle crashing*)

MARGITA

But for my birthday they made an exception. I could invite kids from the neighborhood, although none of them could go because my party didn't start until ten on a school night.

(*Music and tiki lights come up.*)

So it was all adults. The first guest to arrive was Daisy the crazy dancer.

(As DAISY)

Margo, mi amor. Besito. Pues, I been workin'. Miami, Chicago, Union City. 'Cause who's better than us tu sabes negra. Donde sta Margita? No. That's your daughter? I didn't recognize her, she got so chubby. Que gordita sta la nena. God bless her. How do you do it, Margo?

MARGITA

And my mother bragged like she always bragged.

(As MARGO)

My daughter eats like a man.

(MARGO *and* DAISY *laugh.*)

(As DAISY)

Margita, I'm thirsty. Make me a cuba libre.

MARGITA

And I said "How do you make a cuba libre?"

(As DAISY)

Well, first you KILL CASTRO.

MARGITA

My parents had a lot of fascist friends like that and they were all there that night. Singers, actors, dancers, and they all had that grown-up Latino thing for pinching chubby children.

(As RIVERA)

So. This is Margita. Look at that face. Look at those cheeks. I have to pinch them. Ben aqua. Pero nena ven aqua. (*Chases* MARGITA, *huffing and puffing and wiping his brow.*) Margo, I don't think your daughter likes me.

(As MARGO)

Margita, be nice to Rivera. He's going to do a story about me for El Diario.

(As RIVERA)

Si. Seguro. Margo is the number one dancer in New York. Don't you agree, princess? Is your mother not a fantastic creature. Claro que sí! And you, little one. Monkey. Ratoncito. I got you a present but you have to guess which hand. Ahh. Ah. Got you. (*He pinches* MARGITA'S *cheek.*)

MARGITA

After that my mother took me to her room for some deal making.

(*Music and tiki lights fade out.*)

(As MARGO)

Margita, look at what Rivera gave you. An old torn twenty dollar bill with Scotch tape.

He must be drunk. What kind of present is that for a child. It looks like it was in the gutter. This is what he should have given you. Do you see how clean and crisp this five dollar bill is? It's brand new. I hate to do this but because it's your birthday, I'm going to trade my beautiful five dollar bill for your disgusting twenty. Margita, it doesn't matter if it's twenty or one hundred dollars, when it's ripped no one will take it. It's no good. Okay, it's a deal. I don't know what I'm going to do with his old twenty. *(Stuffs it delicately into her cleavage)* You know, you are the most intelligent girl in the whole world. You're going to be just like me when you grow up.

Marga Gomez is Pretty Witty & Gay

The action takes place in MARGA's *bedroom the night before she is to appear on a national television talk show. There is a bed; a bedside table with a lamp; a radio; a clock and some books.*

MARGA

... What are Sam Nunn and General Colin Powell and all the other colons so worried about? Why can't they lift the ban on gay men and lesbians in the military? Are they afraid that millions of us will enlist? I doubt it. Don't you have to get up early there? I'll do that one day a year – for the parade. We just want the right to enlist. Like my girlfriend and I want the right to have a legal wedding. But we don't want to get married. We're queer, not crazy. Are they afraid that if we could be out in the military we wouldn't obey orders? "Company halt!" "No. We have to dance first." Or maybe they're afraid we won't salute anymore – just snap, "Yes, girl!"
Not that I'm pro-military, I'm anti-war. I just want to wear a sailor suit once in my life. Put a sailor suit on and go dancing for one night. White bell-bottoms are hard to find. But this will be denied me because I'm considered a deviant.

My love is deeper than the ocean, wider than the sky and too complex to be narrowly defined. But if you must apply a label – call me a dyke, maricona, queer, ac-dc, or an ice-pick wielding lesbian ... But not deviant. Because that implies I'm a super-freak in bed and I was raised Catholic. And

I make love like a Catholic. Not good. With a lot of guilt. 'Cause we feel with enough guilt there's no sin. We're still pure in the eyes of the Lord. That's what I have to tell them tomorrow ... The couch potatoes. The millions of Americans who will be watching me on television with that expression on their faces, the one they use to look at queers. *(Assumes homophobic expression)* This way no one will think that they're queer. "I'm normal, look at my face. This expression tells you that I have never met a homosexual and if I did meet one I would run because I am sure they would try to have sex with me."

I tried to get out of this. But there are so many of these homosexual talk shows. You dodge one and then there's: LESBIANS WITH LONG HAIR TOMORROW ON OPRAH. LESBIANS WHO HAVE NEVER BEEN ON OPRAH TOMORROW ON DONAHUE. GAY MEN WITH ORDINARY APARTMENTS ... BISEXUAL, MONOGAMOUS GRANDPARENTS ... How would ... you know? And why are we being so unfair to straight people? Straight people can't get on talk shows anymore. No room! Straight people still have problems don't they? HETEROSEXUAL MARRIAGES, WHY? AND WHAT ABOUT THE CHILDREN? It would be nice to share the limelight, because the demand for homosexual talk show guests is exceeding our supply. Let's face it. We breed minimally, carefully, only after much thought and couples counseling. Contrary to popular belief we do not recruit. We can only impress.

And according to the Kinsey Report we are only ten percent of the population. Maybe it's a higher percentage in this room. But we're being used up by these talk shows. Squeezed ... spent. I didn't ask to do this. This was not a choice for me. It was mandatory. They had my social security number. This is my lesbian jury duty. I'll serve my time to the best of my ability and who knows I might make a difference. To just one person. Just one. That's not enough people for me to do this. I want BIG results. I want to be a role model to many lesbians, bisexuals, some gay men and even progressive heterosexuals of Latino descent. I can do it. I just need to change my personality.

I need to be more positive and perky. "Hello America, I love a woman, yes! A wonderful, wonderous, one of a kind woman. Yes, I love a sister, a sensational, sensitive, sensuous sister. Not my sister America! Just some woman, okay. We have a marriage just like your marriage, although ours is not legally recognized. No priest performed a ceremony. We received no avocado fondue sets from our relatives. Nobody tied tin cans to the back of our car and painted 'Just Lesbians' on our windshield. But in every other way it's just like your marriage. We vowed to be together till death do us part. And we have been together for five years. Five years is a long time for any marriage. We live together. We sleep in the same bed. This bed America. *(Writhes on bed)* And you know this bed has seen a lot of action – until about four years ago. Just like your marriage . . ."

After MARGA *has a confrontation with the cute young dykes who live upstairs and is left humiliated:*

When did I go from positive and perky to bitter and pathetic? I'm just like the first lesbians I ever saw. I was ten. I saw them on David Susskind's "Open End," one of the first television talk shows. We were there. I never watched David Susskind back then, it was too dry, but my mom had it on that night. She turned down the volume very low. But I could hear David Susskind say "Tonight's program might be offensive to people with certain religious beliefs and not suitable for children. I will be interviewing lady homosexuals." I could hear this upstairs, with my bedroom door closed and my radio blasting because by ten I had already developed HOMOSEXUAL HEARING. I followed David Susskind's voice down the stairs into the living room and sat next to my mother on the sofa.

I made sure to put that homophobic expression on my face. So my mother wouldn't think I was mesmerized by the lady homosexuals and riveted to every word that came from their lesbian lips. They were very depressed, very gloomy. You don't get that blue unless you've broken up with Martina.

There were three of them. All disguised in raincoats, dark glasses, wigs. It was the wigs that made me want to be one. *(Puffing on cigar, sitting with legs wide apart)*

"Mr. Susskind, I want to thank you for having the courage to present Cherene and Millie and Me on your program. Cherene and Millie and me, those aren't our real names. She's not Cherene, she's not Millie, I'm not me. Those are just our, you know, our synonyms. We must cloak ourselves in a veil of secrecy or risk losing our employment as truck drivers."
(Change to SUSSKIND, *who is also smoking)*

"I only hope that everyone watching will realize that you are human beings who deserve to love whomever you choose. It's really nobody's business is it. Yes, Cherene?"
(As CHERENE, *smoking)*

"It's just that when you live in a small, anytown, USA then you better get used to people staring and whispering behind your back. Everybody from the bag boy at the A & P, to the Avon lady, she knows, to every neighbor in the neighborhood 'cause the Avon lady told them. Mr. Susskind. When you are in *THE LIFE*, such as we, it's better to live in Greenwich Village or not to live at all! *(Breaks down and snaps out of it)*

"At this time we want to say 'hello' to a new friend who is watching this at home with her mom on WNEW-TV in Massapequa, Long Island. Marga Gomez, Marga Gomez, welcome to the club Cara Mia." *(Flicks her tongue lasciviously)*

My mother was in such denial she didn't pick up on Cherene's clue. Mr. Susskind and the lady homosexuals chain-smoked through the entire program. I think it was relaxing for them. I don't think they could have done it without the smokes. It was like they were in a smokey bar just before last call. And all that smoke curling up made *THE LIFE* seem more mysterious.

THE LIFE, that's what they called it back then when you were one of us. You were in *THE LIFE*! It was short for The Hard and Painful *LIFE*. It sounded so dramatic. I loved drama. I was in the drama club in high school. I wanted to be in *THE LIFE*, too. But I was too young. I asked my mother to buy me *LIFE* Cereal and *LIFE* Magazines. And for Christmas I got the game of *LIFE*. *(Smoking)*

And as I moved the lonely game pieces around the board I pretended I was smoking *LIFE* cigarettes and living *THE LIFE* life. But by the time I was old enough nobody called it *THE LIFE* anymore. Because it sounded too isolating and politically incorrect. Now we say *THE COMMUNITY. THE COMMUNITY* is made up of all of us who twenty years ago would have been in *THE LIFE.* And in *THE COMMUNITY* there is no smoking. *(Stamps out imaginary cigarette)*

Marga's incessant worrying leads her to her ex-Catholic schoolgirl's fear of eternal damnation for going on the talk show.

. . . God. God. God, this is Marga Gomez, a sinner . . . God please don't punish me. I've suffered enough. I'll do whatever you want. What do you want? Talk to me God, talk to me. I'll be born again. I'll tell my girlfriend, "I cannot lay with you unless you're born again too." . . . Okay, no girlfriend. I'll take unto me a husband. We'll have a Christian wedding. We'll never use birth control and I'll bear many Christian babies and they'll hate me and I'll hate them too. We'll be a typical Christian family God, okay? And we'll leave San Francisco. We'll go someplace you like God. What do you like? . . . Annaheim, Virginia. Just give me a sign God.

The upstairs neighbor's stereo is heard loudly through the ceiling.

Excuse me I'm talking to God. The nerve. And you know what? They're gay girls up there. They should have some consideration for me. But they're cute, young dykes and they don't care what I think. They are very happy about their lives. They don't know what I know! Why do they have to have fun in the building. I don't. Why can't they go out to one of their trendy, hip, au courant clubs. They have so many clubs why don't they use them? I know where they go. They go to the G Spot, Uranus, Club Snatch, Club Clit, Club Pussy! They go to all the body parts. When I was their age I went out every night. I was a regular at Club Rumors, The Hideaway, Don't Tell Mama's, The Incognito – places you could feel proud to be a lesbian. Sounds like they're starting their own club upstairs. Club Work My Nerves!

Oh the dykes today, who can understand them? They buy expensive Italian, black leather motorcycle jackets. You know, they're at least five hundred dollars a pop. Then they go and plaster political bumper stickers all over the back of these jackets.

LABIA VISIBILITY. U.S. OUT OF NORTH AMERICA. PETE WILSON IS AN ASSHOLE. Because our Governor Pete Wilson vetoed the gay rights bill and also because he's an asshole. When we were twenty-one, we put bumper stickers on our cars, not on our jackets because we wore down vests. Bumper stickers would pull out the feathers and then you'd have an asymetrical down vest. Which was a fashion faux pas in the seventies. The only fashion faux pas there was in the seventies. But we expressed ourselves. We wore political buttons, lots of them, we looked like refrigerators covered with magnets.

That's where they got the bumper sticker idea from, from our confrontational, in your face, buttons: HOW DARE YOU PRESUME I'M HETEROSEXUAL? Step back! And we thought this one was so funny, remember FESBIAN LEMINIST? Get it? Don't tell me we weren't cutting edge. We paved the way for you. Tell me we didn't pave the way for you. We wore the Frye boots so you could pierce your noses today! Oh the dykes today with their piercings! So many earrings they wear! How can they hear with all those earrings? And the ones upstairs pierced their eyebrows. Ow. Oww! I can't even pluck my eyebrows. My girlfriend wanted us to pierce our noses so we can wear matching nose rings like all the other couples. But I couldn't take the pain. I said, "How about a clip on, honey?" And now they're piercing nipples. Who started that? *(Fondling tits)*

OOooo this feels great . . . Think I'll drive a spike through it! These girls are full of holes. They whistle while they work.

A *Line Around the Block*

3:00 A.M. Closing time at Blanco's Spanish Restaurant, Greenwich Village, 1979.

WILLY

Goodnight my friends. Come and see us next week we're gonna have Eneida, the lady contortionist. You won't believe your eyes. And two for one paella.
(He turns the "closed" sign over and staggers to the juke box. He stands with his back to the audience acting drunk.)
Hey, the cigarette machine is broken. I put in ten quarters already and all it does is play music.

(Laughing at his jokes, he goes over to the lobster tank. We hear "Que se yo" on the juke box and the lobster tank bubbling.)

My dear lobstercitos, whadyaknow we made it through another night in this dump. I'm gonna find something better than this. Don't worry. You know when it's slow here I don't waste my time. I take out a guest check and my pen. I write a song. Boleros, tangos and a rock number just like my daughter listens to. I know I got some hits here. This one's called "What Do I Know?"

"What do I know if she loved me?
What do I know if she lied?
All I know is I adored her
But it's all over now
I will see her ruined
In this life and the next
It was the hypocrisy of her lips
What do I know it made me happy."

I have in mind to send a Bolero to Bobby Sylvio. He's a good friend of mine, he'll have a sensation with this one because no one knows how to write about a man and a woman any more.

Blanco, let's go, I'm waiting! First he say to me, "Willy, you are just here to do a show." Then with a little time, "Willy, bring that table menus we're short tonight." Now, it's, "Coming with me to the warehouse and help me carry the meat to the car." Ay, mama, why wasn't I born rich instead of beautiful?

(He takes out a tin of cocaine.)

I never pay for this. I get it free from the boys at the bar. And I don't take too much, just a little for my heart.

(WILLY walks over to the juke box and plays the song again. Lights fade out.)

Terry Gomez

Biography

Terry Gomez was born in San Francisco, California. She is from the Comanche Nation of Oklahoma, Pena-tuka band, descendant of Comanche Chief Wild Horse. She attended public school in Oklahoma and attended the University of New Mexico for three years, majoring in Sociology. She gratuated from the Institute of American Indian Arts, in Santa Fe, New Mexico, where she majored in two-dimensional arts and creative writing. She is married to Donovan Gomez and they have two children, Autumn and Matthew. This is Terry's first full-length play. She is currently living in Santa Fe, New Mexico.

Artistic Statement

It is not possible to deal with all of the issues affecting Native Americans today within the boundaries of one play. The negative side to that is that everything needs to be addressed *now*. On the positive side, there is no lack of inspiration for future works. This play began in a workshop class at the Institute of American Indian Arts in Santa Fe, New Mexico. I was determined to state all the wrongs ever done to the Indian people. Fortunately, my peers were quick to let me know that too much anger, thrown too soon at someone, isn't going to be very interesting.

Although I do not want to make any generalizations, stereotyping of Native people is one problem that is still hounding our race. *Inter-Tribal* is not autobiographical and none of the characters are anyone that I've ever known; I took some experiences from the past and characteristics from certain people and combined them.

There was also the decision of whether or not to bring alcoholism into the arena of the play. This issue is so delicate to Indian people because of the massive stereotype of the "drunk Indian." This still affects us today. Actually, it is a simple distinction. There are many Indian families that don't allow any alcohol in their families. Then there are those individuals that do drink and have a problem with it. Just as there are such in every culture. Economic disadvantage has made us more visible and vulnerable in some aspects. Yet, that doesn't

Photo: Donovan Gomez

mean we are a helpless people. Struggling, yes; but not defeated.

When someone puts his boot on your head to hold you down, fight like hell to get it off! That's my philosophy and belief when describing the treatment of Native women. We've been treated as if we were of no significance to present-day society. Somehow we have survived this as well as women of other races have. I write about the present. This play is not a pageant, although it contains scenes from a pow-wow, and one actor is wearing his Indian clothes. This play is not mythology. It is more about symbolism and finding humor in tragedy. I've heard it said that this element of humor is what pulls Indian people through. It's true from what I've seen in my family and others. Sometimes it's the only way to cope when one realizes the absurd turn that life has given Indian people.

Indian people have a wealth that no others can destroy. Our heritage and spirituality will pull us through if we let them. Going to the bottom and then coming back up again has convinced me that if *I* can believe in myself and pull myself up to where I want to be, anyone can.

Discrimination has played a large role in

my perception of what non-Indians think of Indians. In my first year in school in Oklahoma, only the Indian children (two of us) would get paddled every day. In junior high school, the Indian kids wanted to fight because I hung out with white friends. In high school, the effects of the American Indian Movement and Wounded Knee were still fresh in our minds; we had nothing to do with white students. There was such a small Indian population at the public school that we clung together in a small, tough group; proud of who we were but not really encouraged to pursue any type of academic career. There were few Indian students that the school seemed to look upon as "college material." The rest of us were given directions to the vo-tech. This was how even the Native faculty handled the students at this time.

After a reading, I was asked who this play was written for. It was written for my grandmother and great-aunts, my mother, sisters, nieces and daughter. Indian women are here, all over the country, right now. The past is important, we'll never forget or let our children forget the wars, torture, disease, and murders. What I want to write and know about are the Indian people from the 1920s and into the future. This is our children's history – the people who seemed invisible and obsolete but who held firmly to their way of life, those that tried and/or tried not to assimilate. Someone else asked me what "traditional" people would think of this play. I feel that most Indian people think of themselves as traditional. Love for your family, knowledge of your religion, ceremonies, history, dances and songs, love

of the earth, your tribe and knowing your language (if you are fortunate) is tradition. Tradition is in your soul. Sexism and racism against me have made me a stronger person. I know that I can help my children accomplish their goals by teaching them to love who they are and to hold up their heads in any situation.

This play, *Inter-Tribal*, is about tradition, generations and choices. When I go home to Oklahoma it seems that things have changed. There are now gangs roaming around at pow-wows and in the small towns that I grew up in. That just really blows my mind, that with all that we have, our younger generations are turning to gang activity. Through my writing and painting, I want to bring problems like this into the light and help find solutions.

This is dedicated with love and hope to all the Native American women, my family and friends (past, present and future). "Uda" (Thank you) Bill Yellow Robe and Jon Davis.

Production History

A staged reading of *Inter-Tribal* was given at the Institute of American Indian Arts Museum, Sante Fe, New Mexico, on 16 April, 1994. The reading was directed by William Yellow Robe and featured cast members Kathleen Gonzales, Edith Mora, Alan Emarthele, Bunky Echo-Hawk, Jack Sabon, and Terry Gomez. It subsequently was produced at the Institute of American Indian Arts Museum, Santa Fe, November 1994. It was read at The Public Theater, New York City, New York, May 1995.

11 Inter-Tribal

Terry Gomez

Characters

BABY

HATTIE

JOYCE

TWO-STEP

EDDIE

HARLEY

MAN

DELIVERY MAN

MC ANNOUNCER

Act 1

Scene 1

*The scene takes place in a dimly lit pool hall.
Three Indian men are standing around,
playing pool, looking for women. There is
grungy shag carpeting on the floor, a pool
table and two sets of tables and chairs around
the room. There is a cigarette machine and
jukebox. The door to the manager's office and
the door to the restroom are on either side.
Neon paint on black paper signs advertising
cheap beer hang on a dingy wall.*

HATTIE *is an old Indian woman, about 70.
She is small with long gray braids, round
eyeglasses. She is wearing a homemade faded
dress, generic sneakers with short white socks,
no jewelry. She has a big purse with her full
of gum, coins, coin purse, candy, brush, etc.*

HATTIE *puts her purse on the table and
slowly empties the contents trying to find
change for the phone. Her back is turned in
the direction where* BABY *enters.* BABY *is a
young Indian female, around 18 years old,
with long dark brown hair, wearing faded
jeans, tee-shirt, sneakers. Homemade tattoo on
her hand, gold hoop earrings. She rushes onto
the stage and goes directly through the door
marked restroom. Enter* JOYCE, BABY's
roommate, 22 years old. JOYCE *is a real
urban Indian, doesn't know much about
Indian ways. She is tall and thin. Her hair is
long and frizzy. She has on tight jeans and a
low-cut blouse and some black high heels.
Heavy make-up, lots of jewelry. Graduated
from high school same time as* BABY.
*Receptionist at Goodyear Auto Supply.
Surprised,* JOYCE *sees* HATTIE *but steers clear
of her and sits down at one of the two tables.*
HATTIE *sees* JOYCE.

HATTIE   Say there! Say there! I see you
Joyce Lamebull!
(*The men in the corner laugh*)

MAN   Aaaye, Joyce, answer your grandma!
You're busted!
(HATTIE *ignores this and goes up to*
JOYCE.)

JOYCE   Hi, Grandma! Why are you here?
Come to play pool? Bet you could beat Jr.
over there!

HATTIE   Joyce! Where is Baby? I haven't
seen her in a week! What have you girls
been doing?
(BABY *enters again from restroom.*)

BABY   Grandma, what are you doing here?

HATTIE   Looking all over town for you –
where have you been? You're never
home!
(*One of the three men comes and puts three
beers on the table. He backs away, smiling.*)

HATTIE   Get that away from me!

BABY   Grandma! (JOYCE *scoots all the beers
towards herself, relaxes, leans back into the
booth with her feet up. listening.*) This is
not a place for you to be!

HATTIE   Why not? It's good enough for you
and your "friends," isn't it?

BABY   You don't belong here. This is not a
"old" people place. Why can't you just let
me alone for a little while.

HATTIE   So this is what it has come to,
Baby? You really like this kind of place?
It's really dirty in here. Look, there's a
roach just sitting on the wall. Look at
these men. Low-down and don't work.
You know what they're probably saying
about you.

BABY   Grandma, I'm not sorry. Christ,
what's so wrong with coming in to see a
friend. It's just a place to relax . . .

JOYCE   Grandma, they're saying the same
damn thing about you! Yeah, just look at
that great lookin' old babe sitting' over
there. Hell, nobody ever buys just me and
Baby beers! (*Pats* HATTIE *on the back*)

HATTIE   (*Shocked*) What! How is it you talk
to me like that, Joyce Lambull? I didn't
come here to hear your dirty talk. If I
wasn't concerned about my granddaughter
I would never step my foot into this kind
of place. You two need to get some self-
respect.

JOYCE   That's right Grandma – pull your
skirt up – unbutton a button or two on
the top. Get some lipstick on. We'll all go
out dancin'. Pick out one of these guys,
pick one, any one!

BABY   Joyce! Shut up. Man, everywhere I
go I catch sh . . . uh, trouble from everybody. You don't need to get nasty, Joyce.

HATTIE   (*Upset*) Baby! I'm leaving. I'm
going home. I want to see you later, do
you hear?

BABY   Yeah, Grandma. Go home! I'll see
you there. (*Opens door for her*) Bye!

HATTIE   Well, you don't have to throw me
out.

JOYCE   Bye Grandma!

BABY   Shit, Joyce – lighten up, will you?
(*Grabs beer*)

JOYCE Lighten up? What do you mean? She was likin' it! Seriously, don't you get sick of her putting you through a guilt trip every time she sees you? How can you stand it?

BABY Leave her alone, Joyce. And don't call her Grandma. I don't like it when you call her that. It sounds mean when you say it.

JOYCE Fine. I'll try to come up with something else. How about . . . *(She gets up, goes and gets another beer.)* Don't you think that that old woman walks all over you? She always wants you to drive her to some pow-wow, take her to a hand-game, go help her clean. Doesn't she think that you have your own life?

BABY She just gets lonely. And you know she's almost my mother. I have an uncle and cousins somewhere up in Kansas, but it's been so long since we've seen them. Their mother is white and you know, they don't seem like they're from around here anymore. Then we have relations from around here and . . .

JOYCE Yea, well, I don't have a family, thank God! Look how good I got it! *(JOYCE is starting to get drunk. An old man, the DELIVERY MAN, comes in the place delivering a load of beer. He enters stage and puts down the box, keeping his back towards the audience.)*

JOYCE *(Bored)* Hey honey!

BABY Joyce!

JOYCE *(Bored)* Oh, he's just some old drunk! Hey, sweetie! *(Kisses loudly at him. She lays back in her seat, closes eyes.)* *(DELIVERY MAN exits, looking at Joyce, unsure.)*

BABY I think he works here, Joyce. *(Looking down at table)* You know, Grandma is OK. She really cares about me. She's taken care of me since mom died. Then that time I got pregnant. She didn't even get mad. Didn't say nothin' mean. The only time I ever see her cry is when people die. *(JOYCE, who has heard this story many times, pretends to sleep. She leans her head back and snores loudly.)* Oh, forget it. I need some fresh air. *(She starts to get up.)*

JOYCE Hey, sit down. C'mon, I was just kidding. Baby, you know I know that story . . . don't leave me . . . *(Loudly)* . . . I love you, Baby! *(Choked up)* Baby, don't go! *(Laughs loudly)*

(Men in pool hall laugh.)

MAN Hey you two – this isn't that kind of place!

BABY Joyce, you're no shame! Dammit, cut it out! *(Sits back down)* I don't even know why I hang around with you. Well, with what all I know about you . . . let's see. Let's talk about that time we were at that party and you disappeared for awhile and then that guy came out of the room wearing your pants. Let me see, if I remember right, you went home wearing his. Weren't they like four inches too long on you . . . *(laughs)* You remember that?

JOYCE Oh hell, you know that happened when I was just a kid. In fact that's the same night . . . Never mind. That ass Stan was mad, at work today. I only took a twenty-minute lunch break, so I left a little early. He was pissed because I didn't finish processing a work order for the tribe, but that's too bad – he's gotta wait until Monday. He wanted those Indians' money, probably do shoddy work and they'd never know.

BABY Uh-huh. Hey, I saw Two-Step today. He was driving the tribal work truck. He said he's working over there now. He said that there's a pow-wow over at the culture center.

JOYCE Really. *(Smiling)* How is he? Is his hair still long? Damn, I bet he looks good in that new truck!

BABY Yeah, he looked cute, but I didn't notice his hair. You know, when you talk to him all you notice are his crooked teeth! Aaa, I joke. No, I just notice his eyes. *(Dramatic)* They're like two shining stars on a cold winter night!

BABY and JOYCE Aaaa! *(They laugh)*

JOYCE Damn, is he still livin' with his girlfriend, that ol' ugly thing!

BABY He was really tryin' to make me feel sorry for him. He was sayin' how boring monogamy is, but you know men. They all talk like that, especially him!

JOYCE What else did he say?

BABY You mean, did he mention you?

JOYCE Well, yeah!

BABY *(Teasing JOYCE)* No. Oh yeah, wait a minute!! Maybe he did!

JOYCE Well, c'mon!

BABY Asked me if he would see you at the pow-wow tonight. Actually it seemed as if he wanted me to be sure to tell you he would be there tonight. I wonder why . . .? Could it be he wants to see you again? But I said no, that after that last time you wouldn't want to see him again. No, not you . . .

JOYCE   Damn it Baby, you'd better not have! Did you? I wish he'd come here, right now. We'd have our own pow-wow right here.

BABY   The time he did he didn't have a very good time. Those white guys that came in her were trying to start something with him.

JOYCE   Damn, Baby, why wouldn't he leave that old bag of bones? I just never could understand why he won't.

BABY   I could count some of the reasons and they all had on blue jeans and cowboy boots and worked for old man McDuffy's ranch. But I won't rub it in . . .

JOYCE   Oh, come on. I was just a kid. He was just a kid. It was all in fun. I mean how you gonna know what life's all about if you don't try it out.

BABY   Oh, so that's what life's all about, huh? All you want to do is to see Two-Step. I told him that my family is still in mourning for the baby. It has been over a year, but grandma doesn't even act like it.

JOYCE   Like I told you, life goes on, put the past behind you. She could learn a thing or two from you anyway. When bad things happen to you, you keep going. That's why I like you, you're tough! And if you don't dance at the pow-wow, you can still go . . . Eddie might be there!

BABY   Eddie who?

JOYCE   Eddie – that guy you thought was cute at that last Indian rodeo. That cowboy I introduced you to.

BABY   I don't know if I like cowboys. Is he rugged? And I can't stand country music. Yeah, he is pretty cute. When I was looking at him, I notice that he's got a nice throat . . .

JOYCE   A nice throat? Damn, what are you, a vampire?

BABY   No. but from the angle we were sitting at in the rodeo all I could see of him was the side of his head and his neck.

JOYCE   I suppose you were thinking of all those hickeys you could be giving him! (Laughs)

BABY   You are one sick, sick woman. But sometimes that thought does cross my mind . . .

JOYCE   You are a vampire! I heard you Indian girls were like that! So what are the plans for tonight? Are you going to Grandma's house?

BABY   Can you believe that she was really in here? I might go by and see her, see what she says about the pow-wow and get chewed out, at the same time! I don't want to embarrass my family. These people around here sure can talk . . . you'd think they don't have anything else to do besides talk about what we do. They act like there's nothing wrong with their families.

JOYCE   Ah, who cares? Go on then – I'll stay here and get a sandwich or something. (Looks at one of the men) What if I come over later and see if you want to go? I'm wiped out and just wanna relax. Sellin' tires all day took a lot out of me. Aaa. Hey you got a couple dollars for a poor Indian girl?

BABY   I gotta go listen to Grandma give me hell. Yeah, come by and rescue me, we'll go do something later. I don't know about the pow-wow, maybe a movie? Here, here's some money. Let's see that's about fifty bucks you owe me now . . .

JOYCE   OK, OK, I know. You know one of these days I'll pay you back big time. We're gonna get out of here and we'll be shoppin' in damn Los Angeles, California. Rodeo Drive. We'll be buying those long, tight, sequined dresses and hanging all over those rich white men and then we'll take all their money and go to the biggest country and western bar . . .

BABY   You had me hooked for a minute there, sister. I'm not in the mood for hanging on no white guy, rich or not. Not after the way the white guys here treat us. Talking to me and grandma like we can't understand English. Not waiting on us when we go to eat . . . uh-uh, no. They're all the same, if you ask me. Calling us squaws . . . that's full of . . . ah, never mind. Don't stay too long in here.

JOYCE   Not all people treat each other like shit. There must be somewhere that they'd treat us the same.

BABY   Nowhere I've been, lately. See you later. (Exits)

JOYCE   Yeah, nowhere I've been lately, either.

(Lights fade out.)

Scene 2

HATTIE's *living room. Old couch covered with bedspread. Table with beads, threads, fringes, and old sewing machine. Small TV on table, old calendar and portrait of JFK on the wall.* HATTIE *comes on stage with bowls and spoons.* BABY *is seated at table.*

HATTIE Eat these beans. You want fry-bread?

BABY Yeah. *(She eats.)*

HATTIE I don't like that you were at that place. Is that why you moved with her, to drink? Why is it that you like that place? I know young girls need friends and all. In my time young women wouldn't be caught dead in a beer joint. My brothers would have beat me themselves if I set foot in one, I'll tell you that!

BABY It's not a beer joint. I don't drink a lot and I'm not doing anything wrong! You probaby think I'm going to get pregnant again. Is that it? *Is it?*

HATTIE What? I didn't say anything about that!

BABY That is it, isn't it? Why don't you come right out and call me a . . . *whore!*

HATTIE I said I didn't say that! What I mean to say is that you young people have no regard for what is right. No respect for the president, your families, God. Last time I went to the pow-wow I noticed that the kids weren't even standing during the honor song for the veterans. *(She goes over and points to JFK's picture.)* Look, here's a good man right here! This is the kind of honest man young people should look up to.

BABY Grandma, you know that picture is stolen government property.

HATTIE Well, your uncle gave it to me, and I didn't know then that he stole it when those AIMS broke into the White House.

BABY Grandma, it wasn't the White House, it was the BIA building!

HATTIE So, you're correcting me. I guess you young ones know everything. *(BABY throws spoon down roughly on the table.)*

BABY Why don't you take that picture down? It's ugly and who cares about the damn president. I sure as hell don't. When are you going to hang an Indian face on that wall?

(HATTIE gets up angrily. Takes JFK off the wall. Goes and gets photo from bedroom and hangs on wall, really hard.)

HATTIE How's that?

BABY Oh brother, now why did you have to do that?

HATTIE You said you wanted an Indian face on that wall. There it is! My great-granddad.

BABY Yeah, yeah, I know who it is. You know that's the reason I wanted to move out.

HATTIE Because of this picture?

BABY No! Because you are always telling me what is the right way to run my life. I want to control my own life without anybody always telling me what to do and how to do it.

HATTIE You're in for a big surprise. There's always going to be someone telling you what to do, be it teachers, boss, husband . . .

BABY Husband? I'm sorry but I'm not going to spend my life having some man telling me what to do!

HATTIE Are you saying that is what I did?

BABY No.

HATTIE Indian women have come a long way from being treated as cruelly as some of the old ways were. You know if a woman left her husband took a lover, her husband could cut off the end of her nose.

BABY The first cosmetic surgery. Grandma?

HATTIE What?

BABY Do you think it's OK if I go pow-wow?

HATTIE That's up to you. Grieving after someone has died is different for every-one. Our tradition is to wait for a year, at least, out of respect. Nowadays, people don't seem to remember or care. But, like I said, each person has to decide for themselves.

BABY Well, it's been over a year and some of my friends are going.

HATTIE Who? Joyce? She don't dance. I don't know why she . . .

BABY Joyce, Two-Step . . . some other people . . .

HATTIE Two-Step? Did he quit his wife?

BABY It's not his wife, it's just his girl-friend.

HATTIE See how you are! She's his wife, Indian way. They've been together a long time. He might as well be married.

BABY   I don't think he's very happy.

HATTIE   That's what he gets! Well, you girls shouldn't be after married men. There are plenty of nice young men around. What about that Herman Big Arm's son, Harley? He's kind of decent looking.

BABY   Grandma, all the girls are scared of him. You know, about the pow-wow . . . I still don't feel like dancing at all.

HATTIE   You lost a child. When we lost your mother, then your granddad, I had my mourning time. But this time was so different. There's not a day goes by I still think of that beautiful baby. I'm not ready to go to a dance. Will I ever be? But if you want to go . . .

BABY   I guess I can stay for awhile. Me and Joyce can find something to do (Looking at picture on wall) Who did you say that this is? Is this a real war bonnet he's wearing in this picture, or is it a fake?

HATTIE   What do you mean?

BABY   You know, the kind you can get from any old store . . .

HATTIE   No, those are Eagle feathers all the way down to the ground. The feathers are surely a sign of a good and honest man. How's that for an Indian face on my wall?

BABY   Just asking. Was he a chief or one of those Indians who, you know, did the Pocahontas thing? Did he help roll out the red carpet for all the whites?

HATTIE   What are you talking about? What do you know about this man on the wall? I know I'm getting old, but I know a heck of a lot more than you. You still have a lot to learn, Baby. You think you're so smart. All you know so far is what white people have taught you in school . . . you don't seem to remember anything I have tried to teach you. When are you going to take time and learn about your own people? And watching "Billy Jack" movies doesn't show me anything!

BABY   I do know about our own people. Our people are still here. All the younger ones that you have no respect for are our people, too. I know that we still have to depend on the PHS Hospital, and the BIA still tells us what to do. We're still eating commodities, still get followed around by the clerks and security guards in the stores in town. And now I know that I'm going with my friends. At least they think I have sense.

(There is a knock on the door. HATTIE opens it. Enter JOYCE. BABY is clearing her dishes.)

HATTIE   Joyce, what are you doing here?

JOYCE   (Slurred, drunken) Grandma! You took my partner away! Hey, sis! Let's go pow-wow!

BABY   I don't know Joyce, you look like you could use some rest.

(HATTIE goes off stage.)

JOYCE   Baby, are you out of your mind? I thought you said that you would like to snag Eddie. Him and Two-Step are in the truck! I went to the pow-wow to get them.

BABY   What? Wait! I don't know about this! (Noise at the door, EDDIE and TWO-STEP enter. Eddie is about 23 years old. He wears jeans, tee-shirt, baseball cap. TWO-STEP is about 25, long braids, ribbon shirt, jeans.)

TWO-STEP   Let's go! There's a '49 at Moonlight Mile after the pow-wow tonight. (He dances around a little.) (BABY and EDDIE have been checking each other out.)

EDDIE   Hi, Baby. There's a '49 tonight. You should come.

BABY   What are you doing here, Two-Step? Did you escape? Are you dancin' tonight? (HATTIE comes out on stage.)

HATTIE   Since you're going to the pow-wow, I wonder if you can drive me, Baby?

JOYCE   Well, let's all go then. I found these two hangin' around by the door.

BABY   I have to drive Grandma.

JOYCE   Maybe someone will drive her home for you. (Looks at BABY, shakes her head as if disgusted and exits) (Off stage) Baby! Damn you! AAAA, I joke!

EDDIE   Bye, see you there?

BABY   Yeah, cool, see you there. Don't let Joyce drive.

TWO-STEP   Let's go! I have to get my costume on – have to contest! Prize money!

(Exit TWO-STEP and EDDIE)

BABY   Grandma, why did you say that?

HATTIE   Say what?

BABY   That you wanted to go pow-wow. You haven't been in over a year. You know that I wanted to spend time with my friends. Aren't you still in mourning?

HATTIE   I just wanted to get rid of them. That woman was drinking. And who was that guy?

BABY   That's Two-Step's friend, Eddie. He's

northern. Lives with his folks in the city. I'm gonna go. I think we would both enjoy our evening more.

HATTIE You're an adult.

BABY Thanks for the food. I'll see you later. (HATTIE *turns away.*) Grandma? Oh, never mind.

(BABY *exits, sound of slamming door.*)

Scene 3

A pow-wow. Soft drumming and singing is heard off stage. The stage is dimly lit. Occasionally music gets louder as if people open and close door to go in and out. Only EDDIE and JOYCE are standing on a vacant stage. They are outside of the dance.

EDDIE Look, I'm, going to go. She's not coming. Let's just go on in for awhile.

JOYCE Oh, come on Ed. Two-Step is already dancing. Besides he won't even talk to me in public. He has to wait until after dark so nobody will tell his girl-friend. Can you believe it? He is always telling me what a pain she is and how boring their life is . . .

EDDIE Yeah, but he really loves those kids of his. You should see him with his boys. They both look just like him.

JOYCE Kids? Yeah. Boys, did you say? How old are they anyways?

EDDIE Don't know. Two or three, some-thing like that . . .

JOYCE Two and three. Oh, hell. Let's forget about them and why don't you and me go sit in the truck and have a drink or two? I don't think Baby will be here tonight and you and I could maybe talk and then go for a little drive somewhere quiet . . .

EDDIE You mean drive on over and look for Baby? Sure. Well, let's go on in and give it a few minutes more. If she's not here in about half an hour we'll see.

JOYCE That's no fun.

EDDIE Say, why don't you go on in and see if Two-Step's planning to dance all night. I need to go on over here and take a . . .

JOYCE And see a man about a horse? Go ahead. Need any help?

EDDIE No, go on in.

JOYCE Tell you what. I'll wait in the truck. I need a drink.

EDDIE Suit yourself. (He *walks off stage.* JOYCE *shrugs, walks off in opposite*

direction. EDDIE *comes right back on, looks around.*) Man, I hope she stays in the truck. That woman is kinda pushy. Hey, Baby, where are you?

(TWO-STEP *enters, full fancy dance outfit.*)

TWO-STEP Ed! Got a smoke? Where's Joyce? Damn, it's hotter than hell in there! Those old folks like to crank up the heat. Say, where's Baby? Did you scare her away? I told you to lay off that Thunderbird or is it Boone's Farm you're drinkin' these days?

EDDIE Hell, I don't know. You're the expert on cheap alcohol. Heard about you layin' in the alley with a can of hair spray!

TWO-STEP With your sister . . . Aaaye! And then your momma made you all a big pot of dog stomach for breakfast!

EDDIE At least it wasn't the dog's balls. She said you already ate those.

TWO-STEP Ah, I'll tell you what to go do with that dog, you dog eater . . .

EDDIE Hey, here come some cars! Maybe she's in one of them.

TWO-STEP You really like her, huh? Maybe you should find a job over this way.

EDDIE I had a hard enough time finding the work I have now, there's just not that much call for us poor Indian boys. I don't know if I like her well enough to start makin' plans. You know, maybe it might be just a one-nighter. If she shows up . . .

TWO-STEP I know what you mean. Hey, I'm gonna go dance. You guys come in when she gets here. Can you get me a Coke out of the car? I don't want Joyce to come in without Baby. Some of Sheila's aunts are here and they've moved their chairs near where I'm sitting. I think they're watching me. I don't want them to know we're with Joyce.

EDDIE Do you really like this Joyce? She's a wild one. Boy, she's really gettin' liquored up out in your truck. Hey, how do you know Sheila won't show up here?

TWO-STEP She don't pow-wow no more. She's like an old woman. Those kids make her tired. She don't ever want to go to the '49 any more. She won't even go out and have a drink or anything. Well, we're not married anyway. And you know, Joyce, old flames and all.

EDDIE Old flames?

TWO-STEP Yeah, you just can't put 'em behind you. I tried but every time I see her we just kinda gravitate towards each other. Never lasts though. Joyce likes to party too much. I'm kinda gettin too old for all of that myself. Too hard to make it to work the next day. Gettin' old. But she's pretty. Damn, I even lose my breath when I dance too hard. *(Laughs)*

EDDIE   That's just all those damn dog sandwiches you ate. Your gut is gonna get so big you're gonna have to kill about three more turkeys and add their feathers on to your bustle. Your new Indian name will be Big Chunk!

TWO-STEP   Damn, brother, tear me up!

EDDIE   You need to hear the truth once in awhile. What about Sheila? She know you're here?

TWO-STEP   Sheila. She knows about Joyce. She don't want to raise them two kids by herself. So she gives me hell for a few days and then eventually she forgets about it . . . until the next time. *(Laughs and exits)*

(BABY enters, walking onto the stage very fast.)

EDDIE   Hey there, Baby.

BABY   Eddie? Where's Joyce and Two-Step? Inside? I'm gonna go find them.

EDDIE   What's the hurry? Are you dancing, too?

BABY   No. But you know. Just come to see what Joyce was gonna do. Where is she?

EDDIE   How come you're not dancing? You didn't even bring your shawl?

BABY   Because, actually, I'm not even supposed to be here.

EDDIE   You're not! Are you under house arrest or what?

BABY   House what? No, ah, no. My family has been in mourning. It's been over a year. I guess you know I had a baby that died. She had been sick for awhile. I have to try to go on with my life. I haven't been to a pow-wow since that time, and I kinda thought . . . *(Stops, gazes off)*

EDDIE   No shit. Well, I'm, sorry about that. Two-Step said something about that. Do you want to leave? If you really don't belong here . . . maybe I'll catch a ride home with you.

BABY   Where're you staying? Hey, there's Joyce. She's getting out of the truck. *(Yelling)* Joyce! Here she comes . . .

EDDIE   Hide!

JOYCE   *(Drunkly)* Baby! Baby doll!

BABY   oh-oh!

JOYCE   Where have you been! It's time to party! Go get Two-Step. Let's go!

BABY   Joyce. Take it easy, woman. I want to at least see who's here. You're the one who wanted to come here so badly, so here we are. Let's go on in.

EDDIE   Hey, I'm willing to leave if you don't want to be here.

JOYCE   PARTY! PART-TAY!

BABY   Let's go on in!
(Lights fade out as they go off stage. Lights come back up right away. Pow-wow contest song is heard Fast war dance. JOYCE, BABY and EDDIE are on stage. They stand as if looking on at the dance. TWO-STEP enters at one side of the stage, spinning in a fast war dance, dances off the other side of stage.)

JOYCE   *(Very loudly)* Did you see those legs? GO Two-Step! C'mon you guys! Cheer him on!
(BABY and EDDIE move a few inches away from her.)

EDDIE   Look. I don't think this is a good idea. You're not supposed to be here. Joyce isn't supposed to be here either. Look at her. She's bombed. You know it looks bad already and you need to . . .

BABY   Just a second. I don't even know you and you seem to know what's best for me all of a sudden. I have enough people telling me what to do without you . . .

EDDIE   Hey, if I insulted you . . . I see some people I know over there, think I'll go say hello . . . *(Exits)*

BABY   Joyce, hey, get over here!

JOYCE   Baby, why didn't you cheer for my man to win? He's the best one out there. Look at all those old guys out there. Gee, it looks like a damn burial exhibit! *(Laughs loudly)* Two-Step! You're the best one out there!

BABY   Hey, be cool! Get a hold of yourself, Joyce! Damn, you're acting like you did when you first discovered him!

JOYCE   Well, you can call me Columbus. If I discovered Two-Step then I'm ready to claim and explore him!

BABY   Or do you mean *steal* him? How much have you had to drink anyway? You're not supposed to be drinking at a pow-wow. That's disrespectful to the singers and the dancers and everyone else here!

JOYCE   What are you talking about? I'm not drunk! Disrespectful? Look at that drummer. Take a good look at his shirt.

Got a picture of two dogs doing it right there on the back of his shirt. Now that offends even me! And that girl, see, the one in the real tight buckskin dress. She was out in back just a few minutes ago with that other woman's husband. Doesn't sound respectful to me. How about that man over there? He's really nasty and . . .

BABY Be quiet. You're making stuff up now. Be quiet, someone's gonna hear you and they'll . . .

JOYCE And just look at these kids roaming around without their parents watching them, the little hoods . . . And they'll do what? Hey, I'll take on anyone who thinks they can tell me . . .

(EDDIE comes back over to where they are standing.)

EDDIE Two-Step said he was gonna change clothes and he'll be ready to take you girls to the '49 in a little while. I think I'm gonna catch a ride with some of these people over here. So, see you girls later . . .

JOYCE Eddie, where in the hell do you think you're runnin' off to?

EDDIE Look, Baby doesn't want me around. I understand, I mean you more or less pushed us together, pushed me off on her.

JOYCE You're just breakin' my heart!

BABY Hey Eddie. I'm sorry about what I said a minute ago. I was just coming from my grandma's and well, she was on my butt pretty bad and I just felt that everyone was pushing and pulling at me, and not letting me do what I needed to do!

EDDIE Which is?

JOYCE To get down with you, Eddie!

BABY *(To JOYCE)* I've just about had it with you! *(To EDDIE)* Don't pay any attention . . .

EDDIE I won't. This is something that I would never normally say to a woman but Joyce, anyone ever tell you that you got a big mouth?

JOYCE Never! Anybody ever tell you that you got a big . . . *(She looks at the front of his pants)* well now, no . . . I guess they never would say that it's big exactly! *(Laughs)* That's a joke, Eddie, c'mon! Don't you two ever laugh! (BABY *and* EDDIE *just stare at her with no expression.)* Man, it's like standing around with two sticks-in-the-mud. You two were made for each

other! HEY! TWO-STEP! TWO-STEP! GET OVER HERE AND LET'S PARTY! When we go, when we, oh-oh! I think I need some fresh air! I kinda feel like I'm spinnin'! *(She goes off stage.)*

EDDIE Listen, hurry, go on out there with her, we'll figure out what to do when we get out of here. I'll go talk to Two-Step. Did you see how white his face went when she called him? Any other time it would be kinda funny . . . poor guy!

BABY I think she can handle herself out there. She just needed some air. It's hot in here.

EDDIE Could you please go out there and keep her out of here? I wouldn't want to hear her yelling at Two-Step again!

BABY Well then, maybe you should go on out with her and I'll go talk to Two-Step.

EDDIE Hey, she's not my friend!

BABY I told you, she's OK!

EDDIE Baby, she seems like she doesn't even know where she is! I don't want to be seen with drunk women at a pow-wow!

BABY *(Coldly)* Drunk . . . women?

EDDIE I mean a drunk woman, I didn't mean the both of you!

BABY Listen, Eddie. I don't know you very well but I know that you have some kind of weird attitude. No one tells me what to do. I look after myself, I don't do what some guy tells me to do . . .

EDDIE Wait a minute! I'm not telling you what you should do! It's just that I been brought up thinkin' that women, well, not just women, all people really, don't drink alocohol at pow-wows. You know it makes me uneasy to be around all this. People talk and this will get back to my family and my relatives will all be givin' me hell!

BABY I know how that is. All right. *(Looks off stage)* OH NO! Look at her! Where did she get that shawl?

(The sound of a fast war dance comes up.)

EDDIE Oh no! Does she know how to dance? Lookit how she's movin' around out there!

(JOYCE *goes swirling across the stage with a shawl on. It is obvious that she doesn't know how to dance, she's just hopping around crazily. She goes off the stage.)*

BABY Oh my god! No she doesn't dance, doesn't know how to . . . see? Look how she's got her shawl on!

EDDIE Hey, she's slammin' into people . . . OH. She stepped on some little kid!

BABY Now what?

EDDIE Now look!

(JOYCE goes swirling across the stage again, this time with shawl and wearing a big cowboy hat on her head, goes all the way across the stage and exits.)

(Music stops, lights dim, spotlight on EDDIE and BABY; they stand frozen.)

MC ANNOUNCER Let me ask everyone to clear the arena. We all like having our non-Indian friends here along with all our wonderful dancers but . . . if you can't observe the procedures of this dance then you are to remain on the outer edge of the circle. Someone hopped on this little girl's moccasin and her beads busted off! Also we've had complaints of intoxicated people being in the arena. Where's the arena director? Also, Monkey Little Creek said someone took off with his hat . . . please return it! All right let's hear from the Red Snake singers! How about a round dance . . . Oh, how I used to round dance all night long!

(Lights come back up, and a round dance song is heard. JOYCE comes on stage and takes the hat and shawl and thows them off stage.)

EDDIE Real good dancin' there. Looks like you got yourself kicked out of the arena.

JOYCE He said your non-Indian friends were drinking. Last time I checked I was still an Indian. My skin looks brown to me . . . or is it supposed to be red? Maybe a nice toasty brown? Eddie. Are you red or brown . . . or yellow?

BABY Joyce you ripped that little girl's moccasin! This means something to people! They want to dance, to listen to songs. They don't need people jumping, spinning, running, tripping out! If anyone is gonna do that they have no business out there! Indian or non-Indian!

JOYCE How did I know that! Leave me along! Where's the keys! I'm going out to the truck!

EDDIE You had them.

MC ANNOUNCER We have found some keys up here. The keychain says Geneva's Gas-n-Go. Please come up here and get your keys. You kids! Clear the arena . . . Where is our arena director!

BABY I'll go up and get them. *(Exits)*

JOYCE And you'll hurry up about it!

EDDIE Then you should hurry up and get out!

JOYCE What's that? Get out? You're such a funny guy Eddie! *(BABY comes back.)* Hey, Baby, isn't he the funniest guy you know? And so good looking! The only thing that bugs me is that big bump on your face, in the center, right above your mouth

EDDIE I'll be outside.

JOYCE Oh, I'll be right there!

(Lights dim to black, come back up. JOYCE and BABY are now center stage. EDDIE and TWO-STEP are on stage but far enough away to appear outside while the women are inside.)

JOYCE You know, that Eddie's a creep!

BABY You're being a creep. I think it's about time we should be getting out of here.

JOYCE Don't you want to see me dance again?

BABY Real funny.

JOYCE I'm serious. I've never been more serious in my life. Now you know I'm not the pow-wow type of girl, but you know I think I could really get into this. *(She starts dancing in place, really exaggerated.)* I felt free! Kind of like a wild deer moving with grace, gently touching the earth, becoming one with the heartbeat!

BABY Joyce, I hate to burst your bubble but you looked more like a wild goose trying to flap her wings. Plus that shawl you were wearing was on wrong.

JOYCE A wild bird trying to what? A wild goose in heat? When did you ever see a wild goose in heat? Do birds go into heat or do they just mate? Do you know? Do they?

BABY Yes, no . . . I don't know! What in the heck are you talking about? You know, you're really losing it Joyce! That beer is taking its toll on your brain. I didn't say anything about a bird in heat.

JOYCE *(Cheerful)* Anyway, I think I'll dance!

BABY No. The crowd is really thinned out now. You would be way too noticeable.

JOYCE Oh, OK. Where's Two-Step?

BABY He went to go change clothes a while ago. Maybe he went on outside. Want to go see?

(They go a few steps toward EDDIE and TWO-STEP, and the men come towards them almost to center stage.)

JOYCE Say, why didn't you tell us you were out here? Baby was moaning because she thought she would never see Eddie again!

TWO-STEP She was moaning? She was moaning in the morning . . .

(BABY is embarrassed, EDDIE sees this and takes her hand.)

JOYCE Aaaye, Eddie's ready to moan, too! *(TWO-STEP laughs loudly.)*

BABY Cut it out you two. Well, what do you think? Shall we make it to the '49 or shall we call it a night . . .

TWO-STEP Hell no, let's go, I want to dance 'till sun up! *(The start of a '49 song is heard in the background.)* Hear that! They're over in the pasture about a mile back. Hurry, jump in the truck, let's go! *(He and JOYCE run off stage.)*

EDDIE Baby, wait!

BABY What is it?

EDDIE I . . . oh, nothing! Let's go! *(Music comes up louder as lights dim.)*

Act II

Scene 1

The scene takes place on a vacant stage except for the '49 songs fading in and out in the background. TWO-STEP enters first, walking very fast. BABY and EDDIE follow.

BABY Wait Two-Step . . .

EDDIE I can't believe you left Joyce talking to that guy.

TWO-STEP I told her we were going on ahead. What were you guys pouring into her anyhow? Hey, I'll be right back, there's my buddy over there . . . *(He exits.)*

BABY We'll be right here. I don't see anyone I know out here. Hey, some of these kids must be only 12 or 13. They seem kinda young to be out here.

EDDIE There's some real old guys over there . . .

BABY You're right, they're really crusty . . . You want a beer?

EDDIE I heard that at '49's in the old days all that happened was dancing and singin all night long. Probably people snagging and stuff like that but no alcohol. Nobody drinking. If drunks were around they were run off from the place. It wasn't allowed in the circle even there. Drunks were the outcasts . . .

BABY Times change things I guess. But people don't come to 49's just to drink.

Sometimes you just have to get away from the older people, you know?

EDDIE What do you mean get away from older people, there they are . . .

The thing that I don't like that goes on here is the violence. There was a shooting and a guy was killed at the Indian fair last year. Some kid got his leg cut off after someone accidentally ran him over and dragged him. Do things like that have to happen?

BABY You make it sound like that's all that happens. It feels good to come out here and dance, sing and listen to some good songs. See people you haven't seen in awhile. Laugh and joke and forget everyday problems for awhile. *(A boy and girl walk by hugging and laughing, having fun)* Not to mention what the moonlight and the cool night air can do to you . . .

EDDIE Now that you do mention it . . . *(He turns and kisses BABY.)*

(JOYCE enters.)

JOYCE Oh my god, well what have we here!

EDDIE When did you get here? Where's that guy you were talkin to, what's his name, Harley?

JOYCE Yea, that's right, Harley . . . why'd you guys leave me with him? I've been trying to get away from him all this time. He hurt my wrist!

BABY We told you to come but you wouldn't listen.

JOYCE Where in the hell is Two-Step?

EDDIE He's right over . . .

(HARLEY enters. He's a big chubby guy, long bushy hair. He says all his lines really loud. Pushy and sleazy.)

HARLEY Joyce . . . there you are. Me and my buddies are going to go dance. Bring your ass and let's go over there.

JOYCE Leave me alone. I'm waiting for Two-Step.

HARLEY Me and you need to get to some serious hugging! Two-Step is Sheila's old man. Isn't he? *ISN'T HE?* Hey, Baby . . .

BABY Don't be talkin' to her like that. What do you want? Go dance!

HARLEY I could just sing right here . . . *(Breaks into a '49 song)*

EDDIE Damn guy, you're really hitting all those high notes.

HARLEY Shall I sing some more? Joyce is getting doe eyes over my voice . . .

JOYCE Why don't you go help those guys

down the road start singing. They sound like they're havin' trouble getting started.

HARLEY Only if you'll go with me you long beautiful creature. No, no, not you Joyce, I was talkin' to that old woman over there! aaaaye! Oh, now, don't get jealous, you're some kind of creature, too.

JOYCE Hey, if anyone is a creature, it's you. Your momma calls you Swamp Thing.

HARLEY Yeah boy, I'll go to a swamp anytime and see those lovely Seminole women. Yeah, Eddie. You ever snagged any of those beautiful women?

BABY Yeah, Eddie, why don't you tell us.

EDDIE No, no, I can't say I have.

JOYCE Neither have you, Harley!

HARLEY How would you know about that? I did see some of them on a TV special on the Everglades. Those are some fine . . . (Off stage, some man calls for HARLEY to come and join them.) Hey, I gotta go over here . . . (He exits.)

JOYCE That guy scares me!! He tried to kiss me and really jerked my wrist when I told him to go to hell . . .

BABY He scares everybody . . . How long has he been after you now, about twelve years? You better watch out . . .

JOYCE Then he tried to tear my shirt! Damn, big jerk! Some people came by and I got away. Where the hell is Two-Step?

BABY Right over there with those people.

JOYCE Two-Step! over here!

TWO-STEP What! I was just over here with my buddies. Stop yelling at me Joyce! Let's go on up to the dance.

JOYCE When in the hell are you going to leave that other woman?

TWO-STEP C'mon woman, let's go. (He tries to pull her away but she jerks away.) Never said I was going to leave her.

JOYCE You son of a . . .

BABY OK you guys . . .

TWO-STEP That's OK., maybe that's what I am. But Joyce, I never promised you anything.

JOYCE You said you loved me.

TWO-STEP The last time I ever said anything like that was years ago. But I do like you.

JOYCE And Sheila? Do you love her?

TWO-STEP I don't owe you an explanation about Sheila.

EDDIE I thought that we were going to go dance?

JOYCE You know what, Two-Step?

TWO-STEP Say what you have to say, Joyce.

JOYCE I've waited for you for too long. All these years. Waiting for you. I never got involved with any other guy because of you.

TWO-STEP Ah, hell, Joyce. Every time I seen you around town you're wrapped all over different dudes . . .

JOYCE When have you ever seen me?

TWO-STEP All the time. Driving through town. At restaurants. Ah shit, you're just talkin' drunk!

JOYCE I don't know what you mean!

TWO-STEP I know. If you would take the time to sober up, Joyce. I can't live my life with a drunk. Sure, it's fun, you're funny and we have a lot of laughs. But day after day, it gets old. Every time I've been with you, you've been drunk. I'm sorry, but maybe I shouldn't see you no more.

JOYCE Do you think I care? Harley wants me. If you don't want me, fine. There are other men that do. To hell with you Two-Step! Do you hear me? To hell with you. You're no longer my friend!

TWO-STEP Eddie – think you guys can catch a ride to town? Or you wanna leave now?

JOYCE To hell with you all! Me and Baby are staying!

BABY Joyce, it's all right. Let's go get my car. You'll feel better if we walk on over.

EDDIE Baby – I can go with you guys, can't I?

TWO-STEP It's up to you, man.

JOYCE That's all you ever have to say. Always the easy way out, isn't that right?

TWO-STEP Listen, I never said I would leave Sheila. Hell, OK, the only reason I am with her is because of the kids – I'm your friend, Joyce – I'll always be your friend.

JOYCE I don't need just another friend. I need someone that needs me. And I'm not a drunk – I'm not! If I am, it's because of you. You gave me that first drink when I was 16.

TWO-STEP Yeah, but we were kids. How did I know you'd love it so much. Is that what you are, just another drunk Indian?

EDDIE A drunk Indian! How can you talk to her like that. I would never talk to my woman like that, even if she was drinking. Man she needs some help not a damn kick in the head. I'd never treat my woman like that!

JOYCE   Shut up, Eddie!

TWO-STEP   Fuck you, you don't even have a woman, Eddie.

EDDIE   Sometime I will, and when I do I will try my best not to be the pig you are!!

BABY   Why don't we . . .

JOYCE   Why don't we what? Take me to the re-hab center? You're all ganging up on me! First Eddie, then Two-Step, go ahead Baby, next!

BABY   Joyce, Eddie was just sayin' Two-Step needs to treat you better. Calm down. Let it go. Let Two-Step go. You don't need . . .

EDDIE   How about we get out of here? I'll take you girls somewhere to eat.

BABY   OK! How about it? Let's go!

JOYCE   I don't want to be a part of your little tea party. I hate you all! (She takes off, running off the stage.)

BABY   Joyce! Shit, come back here! Eddie, Two-Step, let's go get her! I have a bad feeling about this!

TWO-STEP   No. I meant what I said. I can't deal with her anymore. I'm getting the hell out of here!

BABY   She was right. You used her, now you won't bother to help her. You're not her friend.

TWO-STEP   Sorry you feel that way. I loved her once. I really did. (He exits.) What I do just doesn't matter. Never has, never will.

EDDIE   I've had a bad feeling about this all night.

Scene 2

JOYCE is standing alone on the stage, crying. HARLEY comes up and tries to hold her.

JOYCE   I knew you would come looking for me! Harley! I thought you were Two-Step. Don't touch me like that! (HARLEY holds her in an embrace.)

HARLEY   It took a long time, but now I finally get my chance to be with you, Joyce. I could really tell you wanted to get rid of Two-Step and come with me. He's an asshole, Joyce . . . you should hear some of the things he's said about you . . . I know how to treat a woman like you, I seen it on "Billy Jack".

JOYCE   You're crazy! I don't want to be

with you, let go of me! Two-Step! Help! Let go! (She struggles to get away.)
(HARLEY is slowly lowering her to the ground.)

Scene 3

HATTIE's house. HATTIE and BABY are sitting and talking, drinking coffee.

BABY   And then she tried to get away from him. But he had her by the hair and kept telling her that she was going to get into the truck. Some woman and her husband were going by and they saw all this happening. Thank God, they went and got some big guys to help them and those guys beat the crap out of Harley, that son of a . . . Anyway, Joyce had been so scraped up they thought she wasn't going to make it. Grandma, if anything would happen to her I don't know what would happen to me.

HATTIE   But something did happen to her. I tell you and tell you but you won't listen to me. I could never imagine why you wanted to run around with her. After you had the baby, I thought you would be responsible and grow up. You did pretty good with that child. But after she died, you ran around with Joyce again. I know better to say that she asked for it but . . .

BABY   Where is your compassion? You always tell me about the old ways, about Christian ways. Yet you turn your back on people that really need your understanding.

HATTIE   That's not true. I do the best I can. I'm not perfect. I'm not the wise old medicine woman who can give you the meaning of life while we sit and beadwork. That's the movies, Baby. I'm a woman that has been brought up learning about the woman's lib, the civil rights movement, why, we were allowed the vote just after I was born. I was raised by boarding school idiots, people that took me away from my beloved grandparents. I do the best I can. I was taught that the white way was the best way to live, it took me years to figure out that who I really am is all of these things. The main thing I realized is that Indians survive. We have so many things against us, and we are alive! Every generation knows more of the white way, but we old folk have to hurry and teach you all we can. Show you how to be proud of yourselves. We are beautiful people. We don't deserve all that we have been though!

BABY But it's so hard, Grandma. There are things like what happened to Joyce, unemployment, drugs and alcohol abuse, even when our own people make it they forget where they come from.

HATTIE It is hard. But Indian women are *strong.*

(There is a knock on the door; BABY *goes to open the door.)*

BABY Joyce! Eddie! What are you guys doing here?

EDDIE Joyce called you, but you weren't here. Then I called over here and your grandma asked me to go and pick up Joyce from the hospital and bring her on here.

BABY You did?

HATTIE Yes, I knew you girls didn't have any food in your place and she's going to be hurting for a few days. Baby, you and Joyce can stay in my room until she's better. Start some dough for some fry-bread and go get a blanket for our girl. She's cold. Let's go Eddie. Get my purse and you must drive me to the store. We'll be back in a little while.

EDDIE Let's go, Grandma.

JOYCE Thanks, Grandma.

BABY *(As* HATTIE *leaves the stage)* Yes, thanks Grandma.

(Lights fade.)

Lisa Jones

Biography

Lisa Jones is a playwright, journalist, and author. Her plays include works for radio, *Stained, Aunt Aida's Hand*, and *Ethnic Cleansing*, commissioned by the series New American Radio for National Public Radio. She is a recipient of a Van Lier Playwriting Fellowship at the Manhattan Theatre Club, a New York Foundation for the Arts Fellowship in Playwriting, and a Jerome Foundation Fellowship for Emerging Playwrights from the Minneapolis Playwrights' Center.

Lisa is a staff writer for *The Village Voice*. A collection of her essays, *Bulletproof Diva: Tales of Race, Sex, and Hair*, was published by Doubleday. She received a BA from Yale University and an MFA in filmmaking from New York University. She lives in Brooklyn.

Photo: Barron Clairbourne

Artistic Statement

I grew up in New York City's East Village back when it was still called the Lower East Side. My mother, a writer, raised my older sister and me. Summers and weekends I spent in Newark, New Jersey with my father, a writer, and my grandparents, a social worker and a post office supervisor.

In many ways I had a magical childhood, though my parents were divorced and I grew up, literally, a block away from the Bowery. Summers not spent in Jersey, I was shipped various places – Greece, Trinidad, a horse farm, drama camp, upstate New York. We had little money, but my mother always wheeled and dealed us away from the concrete.

Newark of the late sixties (known as "New Ark") was a capital of the Black Nationalist movement. It was a time of rallies, poetry readings, African dance classes, and "nation building." The high point of every weekend was Sunday night "Soul Session," a gathering where my father and other poet/activists preached the gospel of blackness. In between speeches, we'd dance to soul music. The summer I turned 11 I worked for Jihad Press, stocking volumes of Black Arts poetry and political manifestos.

I won creative writing awards in high school, but made up my mind to be a lawyer and eventually sit on the Supreme Court with Thurgood Marshall. Following my freshman year in college, I took a typing test to qualify for work as a paralegal. I flunked. Instead of a law office, I spent that summer in the mail order division of a book store, writing blurbs for book catalogs. Law school never had the same allure.

At Yale in the early eighties I took Hazel Carby's landmark course, "Black Women and their Fictions," and studied the passing novels. It fascinated me that there was a whole school of literature about "mulattos" (a new word for me) and other "light-bright" Negroes who jumped the color line. An obsession was born. If I have a literary project of sorts, it's to contribute to this body of writing; to borrow the genre to interrogate America's contemporary constructions of race.

After college, I headed to London, where I worked as a waitress and freelance writer. London back then was a vibrant place with its own fledgling black arts movement. Through Scottish author Jackie Kaye I met other young black women writers. Yale during my day had been a corporate breeding farm, a lonely place for a young woman coming out as an artist. Meeting Jackie and her friends gave me a community.

Back in New York I took a gig at the *Village Voice* as an assistant editor. This began my day-job odyssey as a journalist. Also at this time I hooked up with more young black women who were doing the art thing. Like me, these performers, photographers, and writers were grappling for a voice as artists; one that could chronicle our experience as African American women coming of age in the latter part of the twentieth century – both our privileges and burdens. We formed a collective, Rodeo Caldonia High Fidelity Performance Theater, and mounted theater pieces around town, among them my first play, *Carmella & King Kong*.

Rodeo Caldonia produced a staged reading of *Combination Skin*, my second play, at St. Marks Church in the fall of 1986. It was an exciting time for young artists of color. What I like to call the Newest Negro Renaissance, in full bloom now, was just beginning. The energy from the largely young black audience assembled in the St. Marks sanctuary that night gave me such a rush; a sense of being connected to, all at once, history and the future. It stays with me still.

Combination Skin is an exploration of the tragic mulatto archetype, as brought to us by fiction and film. It's also a send-up of assimilation and the sugar plums of "crossover" success offered to black artists in the eighties. The play began to take shape for me with one vivid image. After I left London, I traveled in France for a bit. In a little town near Nice, I came across a bookshop selling a collection of photographs of Michael Jackson. The cover photo showed Michael in closeup, his eyes airbrushed blue. For 1984 this was a new image, disturbing and provocative.

The play reads to me, in retrospect, like an exorcism. I felt I had to do battle with the mighty caricature of the tragic mulatto before I could clear a space in the world for myself as a black woman of mixed-parentage – quite a normal human being I think, and not an anomaly. The characters aren't meant to be flesh-and-blood people, they're symbols, ideas. The real drama is in the language. There's a war of representations happening on stage, and though one person gets the booty, no one really wins.

My interest in playwriting begins with a love for pageantry and spectacle. Naturalism doesn't interest me much. And naturalistic theater is certainly not the only theater that can address politics and history. Theater should be engaged in the world, at the same time it takes you places you can't go on earth.

Production history

Combination Skin was first produced in workshop by the Rodeo Caldonia High-Fidelity Performance Theater at St. Mark's Church in New York City in December 1986, with the following cast:

Vendetta Goldwoman	Pamala Tyson
Teen Bomb	Amber Villenueva
Specimen Number One	Raye Dowell
Specimen Number Two	Sandye Wilson
Specimen Number Three	Alva Rogers
Queen Mama King, Material Girl	Candace Hamilton
Guard, Material Boy	Donny Webster
Bob Pardu	Vernon Reid

The production was directed by Lisa Jones; set by Alice Norris and Anne Loving-Cortes; costumes by Donna Berwick; sound design by Derin Young; slide research by Kelley Tice; Celina Davis was assistant director.

A second workshop of *Combination Skin* was produced in 1991 by the New Faces, New Voices, New Visions series at Aaron Davis Hall, City College, in New York City. Laura Greer was series producer.

It premiered at the Company One Theatre in Hartford, Connecticut, in October 1992, with the following cast: Hazelle Goodman, Sherri Pullum, Sandye Wilson, Peggy Johnson, Sean Sharp, and Wayne Pretlow. The production was directed by Valerie Curtis-Newton.

Combination Skin won the 1991 East Central Theater Conference Award. It has also been staged by the San Diego Repertory Theatre, Yale University's Heritage Theatre Ensemble, The Frank Silvera's Writers' Workshop, and the Pillsbury House Theater in Minneapolis.

12 Combination Skin

Lisa Jones

In memory of Mark Brown

Characters

VENDETTA GOLDWOMAN: television personality in her late thirties; self-important, opportunistic, but a little resentful of the younger generation that pursues the crossover dream so unabashedly

BOB PARDU: offstage announcer; a wicked Howdy Doody

TEEN BOMB: the game show "boy"; mute for the most part, but lots of eye language

Three women in their twenties:
SPECIMEN NUMBER ONE: the "multi-culti"; worldly, but defensive

SPECIMEN NUMBER TWO: the "mixed-child"; tough, but insecure

SPECIMEN NUMBER THREE: a brown-skinned Diana Ross clone from Detroit; seemingly spacey, but calculating

QUEEN MAMA KING: of Specimen One's mulatto nightmare

GUARD: Queen Mama's boy

THE RARE COGNAC WOMAN: actress in commercials

THE RARE COGNAC MAN: actor in commercials

(The roles of QUEEN MAMA KING and the RARE COGNAC WOMAN may be played by the same actor; same with the GUARD and RARE COGNAC MAN.)

A note about casting

This is a play about color and race. It uses skin color, without apology, to make its point. Hence, why the character breakdown calls for SPECIMEN NUMBER THREE to be played by a brown-skinned actress; a woman who, according to stereotype, would not be physically recognizable as "mixed-race." This is a choice integral to the climax and theme of the play

Time

The 1990s, heading toward the millennium

Set

Furnishings suggest a television studio. The stage is bare except for three gold-draped cushions, a glittering "X" on the stage floor, and a billboard on which words and images are projected. Some of these words and symbols are familiar to game show viewers. Others are more elliptical references to the content of the play. Periodically we hear piped-in sound-effects that underscore the vaudevillian mood of a game show.

The Scene:

House lights go black. In the dark, we hear the first notes of an old back-road blues, just a guitar and a lonely hum. The first image appears on the billboard: JESUS CHRIST NEGRO BLOOD IN HIS VEINS/THE WONDER OF THE 20TH CENTURY *(a headline from a Reconstruction-era black newspaper).*

The music segues to a medley of slow jam "talkies" from the history of Afro-America to the present: we hear spirituals, the blues, doo-wop, and contemporary pop. The billboard follows the music with images of mulattos and race mixing. We see family photographs, entertainers, magazine headlines, skin-lightening products, movie posters, and book sleeves from the turn of the century to the present.

The preamble's final image is HOW BLACK IS BLACK? *(a headline from* Ebony *magazine), which fades as the music finishes. Lights come up on* VENDETTA GOLDWOMAN, *who stands center stage with her back to the audience.*

VENDETTA *(Fussing with her hair, turning head to face audience)* Bob, are my roots showing?

BOB (OS) They don't read from here, Vendetta. Please stand by for your cue.
*(*VENDETTA *exits through audience. Lights dim.)*

BOB (OS) Five, four, three, two, one . . .
(Game show theme music, reminiscent of the Shaft *film score, comes up over* BOB's *lines. Lights rise.)*
Ladies and gentlemen welcome to television's most talked about game show, the $100,000 Tragic Mulatto, where you have everything to win, and everything to lose – even the skin on your chinny chin chin! Yes, here we are on the $100,000 Tragic Mulatto!
(The show's logo, $100,000 TRAGIC MULATTO, flashes on the billboard.)
And ladies and gentlemen, live from Baldwin Hills, California, your hostess of the mostest, that debonair crossover act, prime-time debauchee herself . . . *(Drum roll)* Vendetta Goldwoman!
(Clap track)
*(*VENDETTA *enters from the audience with career-woman confidence; shakes hands, blows kisses.)*

VENDETTA Wow, it's won-der-ful to be here . . . Just heavenly . . . It's a great day, isn't it? . . . You look very mix and match this afternoon . . . You brought your better half along, huh? . . . That's nice . . . Thank you very much . . . Thank you all . . . And you know something? . . . I love each and every one of you. Because without you, I couldn't pull the salary I do today. That's right. Without you, I wouldn't have enough greenbacks to count on one hand, or enough wetbacks to prepare my morning meal. Yes indeed. I wouldn't be weekending in Port au Prince, sipping Zombies from a coconut shell. Without you, I couldn't ask my Peti Negra to fetch me a silk outfit . . . Peti Negra, I'm feeling very Morocco today. Let's try the harem duo with the crème de menthe polka dots. Yes, lovely. Just the simple pleasures of life, and I owe them all to you. Because without you, I'm not me. The wealth, the good looks, the relentless lip . . . oh, and by all means, the weave! *(Drum roll)* I'd be just any ordinary Negro woman who doesn't like her nose. Yes, life's simple pleasures. Let me introduce you to one: my assistant Teen Bomb.
*(*TEEN BOMB *enters.)*

VENDETTA A lovely creature, isn't he. He's what might be referred to in some circles as a Def Freak. Yes, yes, young and tender. You can buy a fillet mignon, but you can't buy firm flesh, and the lord knows I've tried. That's enough, young man. Yes, the simple pleasures. Just a roll in the hay. A sale at Cartier. A gram of white girl . . . Oops, Bob can you delete that for me?

BOB (OS) We're on top of it, Vendetta.

VENDETTA Yes, yes. A sale at Hammacher Schlemmer. A good chase around the briar patch. A cup of fresh brewed coffee, and . . . *(To the audience)* Did I leave something out?

TEEN BOMB A rent-control apartment on the Upper West Side?

VENDETTA No, no, no, social realism is such a bore. If we didn't have better homes and gardens, we wouldn't be here, n'est-ce pas? No, I'm thinking of something a bit more caustic. Anything *else*, Teen Bomb?

TEEN BOMB A college education?

VENDETTA What a throwback! Booker T. Hello. Booker T? Where's Booker T when you need him? Stop asking for handouts and get some hands-on! Why hanker after financial aid when you have Live-Aid at your fingertips.

VENDETTA and TEEN BOMB *(Singing)* Reach out and touch a starving Biafran child's hand, make any place but America a better place, if you can . . .

VENDETTA *(To TEEN BOMB)* And by the way honey, this may be colored TV, but it's prime time, not nation time, okay? None of this educate to liberate stuff. Don't give candy to strangers, and don't lift anybody up by the bootstraps but yo'self. Now act your bank balance, not your color!

No, ladies and gentlemen, we're searching for the last simple pleasure in life. Not social realism, not fornication, not affirmative action. It's something a bit more . . . give and take. You know, a bit more on the self-hatred and ambiguity side of life . . . why, yes . . . it's that big barrel of monkeys, the color question! *(Billboard:* THE COLOR?*)*

(Ominous horns are heard in the distance.)

Thanks to fluctuations in the economic cycle and that tumultuous wave of social history *(cough)*, we have in the 1990s a wide, open market on the color question. In fact, it's a free enterprise at last. Not Huey, not Angela, not Mandela. But thank God almighty, it's a free enterprise at last.

(Billboard: FREE ENTERPRISE*)*

(We hear electronic instrumental version of "We Shall Overcome." VENDETTA *and* TEEN BOMB *do church rock to music.)*

VENDETTA *(As in church)* I mean finally, ladies and gentlemen, finally we have reached the glory days of color is a state of mind. And like any state of mind worth having, it can be bought and sold. Yes, it's a new day on the black market. *(Turns into sleazy flasher)* What you need, baby? A race lift? Got just the thang for ya, a nose lift! You uptight? Just relax baby, relax it, just let it ride in the wind. Got some bluest eyes here. Good stuff. Contact me at your earliest convenience. Yes ladies and gentlemen, no need to go chasing after some back-alley colored magician, the caucasoid epidermis is right at your fingertips!

(Billboard: SKIN PEELS*)*

Just consult your White Pages. It's legal, and honey, perfectly okay. Don't let anybody tell you different. After all, who says it's the black man's burden to be black? Just send them to me, okay. Forget about the sixties: our bricks through store windows, our povertycrats, our African afterbirth. Make peace with it fair souls. Reap the benefits, but don't sow the bitterness. Goddamn it already, no more wake-up calls to the sleeping underclass. Let them sleep. You may have walked through some open doors in your life, but now it's time to close them behind you.

(Door slams)

(Billboard: BLACK CONSCIOUSNESS*)*

But don't let me rattle on, we've got a show to do, a buck to pass. You know, we've got to run a tight ship here 'cause the color question could take us any-where, couldn't it? Where you want to go? Capetown? The Cosby Show? Or you could just walk on by. Because behind every question there's a mirror. That's the risk, isn't it? And risks are our business. So listen, right now we're gonna get specific, I mean, small, and personal. As you know, our schtick is the tragic mulatto.

(Billboard: photo of actress Freddie Washington)

And let me tell you, she's a hot item these days. From the slave quarters to the big house, from Convent Avenue to Hollywood, she's on everyone's lips. She used to be a family skeleton, a dark secret.

(Billboard: FAMILY SKELETON*)*

But now she's a box-office thorough-bred. She used to be Plantation Drama's leading lady. Ooooh, what that poor child had to go through: black blood cursed, red blood shed. Back in those days, when black met white, semen was bound to splatter, not to mention the guilt and squandered lives. Yes, she was our case for the Negro race, our paperback martyr; just an innocent byproduct, a victim of miscegenation . . .

(Billboard: MISCEGENATION*)*

Bestiality, whatever you choose to call it. But it's not the act that matters to us, it's those tragic figures caught in between. So today, I'd like to ask . . .

VENDETTA and TEEN BOMB *(Singing like Sade)* Is it a crime? Is it crime? To be born privileged, yet powerless; destined for madness or death?

VENDETTA Heavens no! It's a wonderful moment to be young, gifted, and half and half, or better yet, young, buxom, and white at heart. The best time yet! None of this one drop of black blood stuff!
(Billboard: JUST ONE DROP)

Pour it on. But don't forget the cream! None of this fear of passing bizness! You don't even have to be light or bright these days, just shed your skin, state your claim, your piece of the great white of way. And get your beep on down to the crossroads! So without further ado, ladies and gentlemen, let's play the hottest game show this side of Paradise Island, The $100,000 Tragic Mulatto!
(Theme music rises.)
(Billboard: $100,000 TRAGIC MULATTO)

And here's how. We bring out three gorgeous girls . . .
(Billboard: 1, 2, 3)

Oh, they're young and tender alright, like a proper mulatto should. But this is the good part, they're wallowing in self-hatred and ambiguity. And that's not right, is it? Not in this modern age, when they could have it all. Well, guess what? Tonight we're actually gonna give it all to one lucky lady. But before we do, we're gonna push, we're gonna pry, we're gonna get those shadows of a doubt, those darker selves, on the table . . . yes, yes.
(Like a revival meeting; TEEN BOMB *assists)*
Then we'll decide who'll wear the crown, who'll get the contract, just who will carry the cross of our black image as we trudge into the light. Yes, we'll breed ourselves a $100,000 Tragic Mulatto!
(Billboard: $100,000 TRAGIC MULATTO)

Teen Bomb, bring out Specimen Number One, please.
(Billboard: photo of SPECIMEN NUMBER ONE)
*(*SPECIMEN NUMBER ONE *enters to entry theme music.)*

BOB (OS) Specimen Number One hails from Old Boy, Connecticut, where she spent her formative years in a split-level, colonial-style home in a predominately Caucasian neighborhood, where the daddies head for power street in the morning, and the mommies head for the Valium bottle. But now this lovely lady is a young novelist and a world traveler, can you believe it? Yes. When she's not toiling over her IBM PC, Specimen One is in Haiti buying primitive artifacts to decorate her Manhattan pied-à-terre. Specimen One's also an avid collector of coon art, and she's fond of pointing out that she owns more tubes of darkie toothpaste than anyone outside of the Philippines.
(Billboard: $100,000 TRAGIC MULATTO)

VENDETTA Shalom, Specimen One, it's just so nice to have you on the show.

SPECIMEN NUMBER ONE Thanks, Vendetta. You know, I almost didn't make it? First, I nearly missed my flight in from Rio – you know, I've been in Bahia for two months researching my new novel. Then I had the most absolutely gruesome lay-over in the San Juan airport. After six hours of screaming niños and overweight señoras, I just about pulled my hair out.

VENDETTA Don't ever do that, honey! Fate worse than death. Tell us about the weave, my pet.

SPECIMEN NUMBER ONE Weave? *(Amused)* Oh no, it's natural. Wash and wear, that's it.

VENDETTA Natural? You know we don't use those terms anymore, my little toasted bialy. The FDA won't stand for it. I mean, really, let's just give thanks to modern technology for making nappy hair a proverbial no man's land.

SPECIMEN NUMBER ONE Yes, it's a shame what certain people do to their hair. I've never understood it, personally.

VENDETTA Not much to understand, sugar. Either you're born with it or you buy it. And prices are going up, girl. Whenever I'm in Taiwan I try to pick up as much as I can get my hands on. Those Korean middle men in Brooklyn just charge too damn much. Speaking of supply and demand, humor us, if you will, with a taste of what it means to be you. Just what are you, my love? Or, shall I say, how do you see yourself? Because that's what's important, right?

SPECIMEN NUMBER ONE You know, Vendetta, I decided a long time ago that I'm strictly a member of the human family.

VENDETTA Don't give me that humanity b.s., girlfriend, what box do you check? Black or white?

SPECIMEN NUMBER ONE Vendetta, we all know, I mean I think we all should know, that race isn't that important anymore. I mean, it's even kinda passé.

VENDETTA Shoot! It better not be passé. I gotta make a living off of som'thin, chile. Whoa! whoa! Better stop spreading those falsehoods. Now 'fess up, black or white? And don't say *other*.

SPECIMEN NUMBER ONE *(Offended)* What's wrong with other? It's going to be a verifiable category on the United States Census in the year 2000.

VENDETTA Yes, yes, wonderful news. Oh, don't be offended, sweetmeat. I was just pinching your racial nerve. You know me, child, give me an inch, and I'll drag you for a mile. Hee, hee, hee. No, no, really, really, some of my best friends are *others.* *(Tenderly)* What kind of *other* are you?

SPECIMEN NUMBER ONE Well, my mother's French, German, and Caribbean, and my father's Venezuelan from the coast. Actually, you know, I don't think I have much American Negro in me at all.

VENDETTA Is that right? Well, what kind of Negro *do* you have in you?

SPECIMEN NUMBER ONE It's kinda funny you should say that because with all the traveling I do – let's see, I was in Papua, New Guinea last year, Brussels, Tibet, Iceland; a month in Berlin catching up with some expatriate friends of mine – And in all these places, everywhere I go, I run into dibs and dabs of Africa . . .

VENDETTA Yes, drop them off anywhere, and they'll take seed. I get it, yes, the Trans-Atlantic slave trade was just an act of divine pollination. Manifest destiny, no problem. My dear, I must ask you this, how is that you know so much about the colored cultures of the world, and write so eloquently about colored people, but not have a single black friend?

SPECIMEN NUMBER ONE I guess I just haven't had much contact with them, except in my novels, I guess.

VENDETTA Well, it's nice to keep in touch, whatever way you can. Yes, tell us about your first novel. It hasn't wound up in the remainder bins yet, has it? What's it called again?

SPECIMEN NUMBER ONE *Combination Skin.*

VENDETTA Oh yes, I remember now. Rivaling Creole families in New Orleans 'round the turn of the century. That's right, incest is best if you keep it in the family. Didn't one family kill the children who were too dark and use their bones for soap?

SPECIMEN NUMBER ONE Yes . . . I don't know where that came from . . . my mind . . . but thanks for remembering.

VENDETTA No, honey, I remember too much, that's my problem. Let me ask you this, 'cause I just couldn't make heads or tails of it: Why were all the fair-skinned, wavy-haired young heroines in the book always being forcibly deflowered by blue-black casanova kings of hoodoo?

SPECIMEN NUMBER ONE *(With nervous laughter)* You know, honestly, Vendetta, I like to leave that kind of thing to our friends the critics . . .

VENDETTA The critics! You did write the book, didn't you? I mean, just why does Antoine Jones, the coal-black sailor with the chest of steel, tie the young octoroon Colette Lefant to her canopied bed and suck her bush dry? Were you trying to make some point about race relations?

SPECIMEN NUMBER ONE No, I was just giving life to characters as they appear in my head.

VENDETTA Don't be coy with me, Madame Bovary. Your parents are from New Orleans, aren't they? *Combination Skin* is your life story, isn't it? You're an incest victim, aren't you? And every night you dream of being ravaged by a runaway buck from way down Bama, don't you?

SPECIMEN NUMBER ONE Look, *Combination Skin* is not my life story, okay, and for the last time, dammit, I'm not from New Orleans, I'm from Connecticut, two miles from Darien, okay? Why do you people take everything so literally? What's her face from BET asked me the same stupid questions. Do I have to explain this on every black talk show? You know, I'm really getting to think American blacks don't know a damn thing about art or commerce.

VENDETTA What ever do you mean? We dance, we buy more electrical appliances than anyone in this country. That's what the new Mohnihan report says. But honey, let's not split hairs, we've got a show to tell.

(Theme music rises.)

VENDETTA Now, playing the $100,000 Tragic Mulatto is quite simple. We don't tax your technical aptitude or challenge your knowledge of celebrity crossbreeding, we just let you hang yourself, isn't that right, Teen Bomb?

TEEN BOMB You've got it, Vendetta.

VENDETTA So step right up to the cross-roads, my pet, and let's begin.
(VENDETTA, TEEN BOMB, and SPECIMEN NUMBER ONE move down stage to the flashing 'X' on the stage floor.)

VENDETTA Yes, it's quite simple. The most ghoulish voyage over the racial mountain, the most muckraking mulatto tragedy, wins the booty. Just share with us your deepest, darkest secrets, and if we're moved, we'll send you on your merry way to fame and fortune. How do we do it, you ask? Aha ... We take you back in time ... *(We hear a loud ticking clock.)* But a special sort of time – Colored People's Time. *(The clock slows down.)* No sense of the linear, just the circular rhythms of the heart, of the good black earth. Yes. we put you in a trance, you speak to us in tongues, and then we bring you back from the black void, safe and sound. So, Specimen One, prepare for blast-off. Close your eyes, click your heels together, and repeat after me: There's no place like the black unconscious, there's no place like the black unconscious ...

SPECIMEN NUMBER ONE *(Fading out slowly)* There's no place like the black unconscious, there's no place like the black unconscious ...
(VENDETTA and TEEN BOMB move upstage, where they are lit in silhouette like dream figures, while downstage, stage lights blink, strobe, and change colors rapidly, suggesting time travel. We hear time warp music, then very polite chamber music.)
(Billboard: A BLACK EXPERIENCE)

BOB (OS) *(Clears his throat, interrupting chamber music. In Queen's English:)* Ladies and Gentlemen. On behalf of the American National Book Award Committee it is my pleasure to announce this year's finalist in the fiction category – *Combination Skin* by Specimen Number One.
(We hear gasps, murmurs of approval, canned applause.)
(VENDETTA and TEEN BOMB mime applause.)

BOB (OS) *Combination Skin* is a moving document of *THE* black experience. The novel brings the many of us who aren't familiar with *THE* black experience closer

to knowing what it means to be part of *THE* black experience. And by illuminating *THE* black experience in such painstaking detail, Specimen Number One has somehow managed to create a work that is – yes, it's been said before, but we'll say it again, and again, and again – UNIVERSAL!

VENDETTA Oh, universal!

TEEN BOMB Such univer-si-a-lity, chile!

BOB (OS) And here to accept this year's American National Book Award for fiction is the author herself, Specimen One.
(Clap track)
(SPECIMEN NUMBER ONE moves down stage to imaginary dais.)

SPECIMEN NUMBER ONE Thank you, thank you. Thank you all. This means so much to me in so many different ways. All my life, I've just wanted to write. I wanted to be Emily Brontë and write about the things that wealthy British women who live alone in castles write about – love affairs with servants, how the moss on the moors changes colors at dawn. But I couldn't, because that was not *THE* black experience. And some little birdie told me it was important to write about *THE* black experience or I wouldn't get published. So I did a little research. And I had a few BLACK experiences of my own ...

BOB (OS) *(As the author's unconscious)* "He little imagined how my heart warmed toward him when I beheld his black skin – I mean – eyes as they withdrew so suspiciously under their brows, when I rode toward him on my silver stallion ..."

SPECIMEN NUMBER ONE ... yes! And sure enough, I learned to write about *THE* black experience. And now, though I am not Emily Brontë, the Emily Brontës of the world do buy my books.
(We hear loud static, a beep tone, then a recorded message: "This is a test of the emergency broadcasting system." *African drumming segues in at high volume.)*
(Billboard: BLACK ON BLACK CRIME)
(The armed GUARD marches in from the audience, followed by QUEEN MAMA KING.)

GUARD *(Reading from a scroll)* Greeting from the Muthaland. Cooperate and no one will be harmed. We come in search of one sacrificial lamb to lay on the pyre of righteousness.

QUEEN MAMA KING *(Grabs scroll)* Let me do this myself, boy. *(Reading)* Greeting from the diaspora, I hereby relay a sworn proclamation from her terribleness, the blackest of all, Queen Mama King . . . wait a minute, would you read this please?

GUARD Yes Mama. I hereby relay a sworn proclamation from the one and only matron of black honor and tried and true tour guide emeritus of the black psyche, Queen Mama King . . .

QUEEN MAMA KING Available for lectures, walk-ons, and sit-ins. My service number is 777 – Ninety-Three – Eleven.

GUARD The Queen Mama finds Specimen One's novel *Combination Skin* to be the most unscientific, negative-imaged work of fiction ever conceived of by a so-called black.

SPECIMEN NUMBER ONE But I'm half French, German, Caribbean, Venezuelan, and half, 100 percent Irish . . .·

GUARD Not only does the novel masquerade as a work of art, but it does absolutely nothing to advance the struggle of the race. It's completely nonfunctional and doesn't even approach the realm of the revolutionary . . .

QUEEN MAMA KING Imagine, naming a black male character King Kong. Do you hear me? She turned one of our precious black males – a species already dangerous close to extinction because of yellow menaces like you – into a gorilla!

SPECIMEN NUMBER ONE Wait a minute now, I really do not have a black male character named King Kong. You're confusing me with another writer.

QUEEN MAMA KING An ape, do you hear me? Then had the nerve to talk about it on the radio . . .

(VENDETTA *and* TEEN BOMB *move down stage and interrupt the action.)*

VENDETTA Enough! When will your people learn that time is money? Can you wrap up your bag of tricks Miss Mama, so I can call this a day? (QUEEN MAMA *shoots* VENDETTA *a vicious look.)* My most humble apologies. Sorry if I offended your blackness, King Mama Queenie . . . ah, ah . . . Can I call you a cab, or will you be traveling by the Black Star tonight? *(She gets another knock-out-drag-out look from* QUEEN MAMA.) The underground railroad stops across the street.

QUEEN MAMA KING No thank you, nothing so common. I'm a descendent of free blacks, I'll have you know. Our caravan is

hitched out back. But we're going nowhere until we have a little human sacrifice.

(GUARD *moves to snatch* SPECIMEN NUMBER ONE.)

VENDETTA Now wait Queen Mama, this is getting a little out of hand. This is my show, after all. And she's such a harmless little thing, just a shade lighter than the dark side of the moon.

QUEEN MAMA KING It's you or her . . .

VENDETTA Her! With my blessings!

(VENDETTA *and* TEEN BOMB *exit in a hurry.)*

SPECIMEN NUMBER ONE You can't let them do this. This is my dream, I made all of you.

(GUARD *grabs* SPECIMEN NUMBER ONE.)

QUEEN MAMA KING You're public domain now, my sister. Talk about haints, girl, I'm gonna haunt you forever. You'll be mumbling to yourself on Second Avenue, screaming at the top of your lungs in supermarkets, a permanent fixture in front of the Gem Spa, reciting Nikki Giovanni for your breakfast money . . . NIGGER CAN YOU KILL, NIGGER, NIGGER, NIGGER, CAN YOU KILL?

SPECIMEN NUMBER ONE Your ghetto scare tactics won't work on me, Miss Mama. I'm not really black, I'm from the suburbs.

QUEEN MAMA KING And she's uppity! Must've got caught up with that women's movement in New York. Don't worry, traitor, we're removing your name from the black list post haste! Walk!

(GUARD *starts to haul away* SPECIMEN NUMBER ONE.)

SPECIMEN NUMBER ONE Wait, wait . . . this could ruin my career. I'm only twenty-five. Who's gonna write my memoirs? *(We hear time warp music. The stage lights blink and the dream dissolves.* QUEEN MAMA *and* GUARD *exit before lights come up.* VENDETTA *and* TEEN BOMB *enter.)*

VENDETTA There's no place like the black unconscious . . . There's no place like the black unconscious . . .

SPECIMEN NUMBER ONE There's no place like the black unconscious . . . There's no place like the black . . .

(VENDETTA *snaps her fingers.)*

SPECIMEN NUMBER ONE . . . what happened?

(VENDETTA *sits* SPECIMEN NUMBER ONE

down on one of the gold draped cushions.)

VENDETTA Not much, unfortunately, but thank you for sharing. These literate types, not much of a fantasy life, eh? I must say, I'm a bit disappointed. I was expecting a lot more sex. Rape scenes with lower primates; chimpanzees that leave you stranded in the banana tree once they discover you ain't really white meat. But don't worry your pretty head about it, there's a lot of fun to come. But first, we got to pause for the commercial cause. Bob . . .

BOB *(OS)* Yes, Vendetta, this portion of our program has been brought to you by Sister Fate, Dial a Miracle.

(Billboard: Advertisement for SISTER FATE, READER AND ADVISOR)

Are you hard in luck? Is your husband or wife spending the money on someone else? Call Sister Fate now for help. Are you having trouble with your legs, stomach, or head? Have you lost your nature? Is your hair falling out? The sister will remove bad luck and evil from your body. Tell you how to be lucky at horses, cards, bingo, and the numbers. Reunites the separated. Call 1–900–777–8181 and be healed. Call Sister Fate today, tomorrow may be too late.

(Billboard: $100,000 TRAGIC MULATTO)

VENDETTA Sho', sho', sho', showtime! Sho' is. But first I'd like to pass on a good word to the aspiring few in our studio audience.

All the major networks are now casting black soul brothers and sisters in high-visibility supporting roles. So if you've got some soul to spare a white leading man – you know, let him beat you at basketball or dance circles around you, or jackoff with his blues guitar in your holy roller church – do, soul brothers and sisters, send in your eight-by-ten's asap. Bob . . .

BOB *(OS)* Hotter than a Gucci watch, the $100,000 Tragic Mulatto! *(Theme music rises.)*

VENDETTA We're back, we're back . . . I wasn't gonna leave you baby, not you, sugar lumps. *(Laughs)* Let's get workin'! Teen Bomb, bring out Specimen Number Two, please!

(Billboard: photo of SPECIMEN NUMBER TWO)

(Entry theme music is cut short.)

BOB *(OS)* *(Clears throat)* Excuse me,

Vendetta, Specimen Two has a special request: She wants to read her own bio.

VENDETTA What?

BOB *(OS)* Yes, something about linguistic appropriation and taking back the night . . .

VENDETTA Well, let's have it, Miss Two. *(SPECIMEN NUMBER TWO enters and walks solemnly down stage.)*

SPECIMEN NUMBER TWO *(Painfully genuine)* This bio is dedicated to Kathleen Cleaver and Queen Mother Moore, my black sisters in the struggle . . . Some say I'm just a misbegotten voodoo chile of the Aquarian age, with the lion spirit of Judy Mowatt, and Billie Holliday's victim beauty. But I know one thing, I'm a strong black woman. I've moved mountains. And my foremothers, also strong black women, have moved them too. Let me tell you their names, Sojourner Truth, Phyllis Wheatley, Rosa Parks . . .

VENDETTA Enough! Save it for black history month, my sister. Now, give up some real data. Just where are you from, again?

SPECIMEN NUMBER TWO Well, the last two years I've been playing the chitlin' circuit with my band, Black Freud. We play roots, rock, agit-prop music based on the teachings of LKJ and the Bad Brains . . .

VENDETTA No child, where were you born, and don't tell me Little Rock.

SPECIMEN NUMBER TWO I and I black brethren from Ethiopia . . .

VENDETTA What does your birth certificate say?

SPECIMEN NUMBER TWO *(Reluctant)* Palo Alto.

VENDETTA Now we're making progress. Yes, Palo Alto, let's see, you must be a faculty brat. What does your daddy teach?

SPECIMEN NUMBER TWO My father is a jazz musician.

VENDETTA Whoopi! *(Sings)* I've got rhythm, who could ask for anything more! So your mother's the academic, right? And what does she teach . . . no, let me guess . . . Hebrew languages and literature?

SPECIMEN NUMBER TWO How did you know?

VENDETTA It's the nose, my little schvartze! Oh, Ladies and Gentlemen, what a treat. We've got a honest to goodness young hybrid on the show tonight. Take a bow.

(Clap track)

VENDETTA Let us in on your beauty secrets, will ya babe? Do you use QT or Sudden Tan to get that fresh-out-the-oven cornbread crust?

(SPECIMEN NUMBER TWO is offended.)

VENDETTA And is that a Toni Home permanent or a Loreal Body Wave?

SPECIMEN NUMBER TWO Nature is my hairdresser.

VENDETTA Hmm, I need to go. How much does she charge? *(Laughs)* Let me stop!

SPECIMEN NUMBER TWO I'm proud of my *natural* black hair . . .

VENDETTA With your ethnic ambitions, you just ought to be.

SPECIMEN NUMBER TWO I don't have to listen to this mess. I only came on this show to let you know that some honkie capitalist media running dogs are in the next room cashing in on this bogus mulatto stuff. I ain't a mule.

VENDETTA Hold on now, our sponsors are sensitive people, and you know, I am more than willing to put my job before your life.

SPECIMEN NUMBER TWO And I am more than willing to die for my people. 'Cause, hey, all you need to get your shit stamped colored in this country is one-sixteenth a drop of black blood. What does it mean anyway if you've got one-eighth or one-tenth of a drop? Is it possible to have one-seventy-fifth?

SPECIMEN NUMBER ONE Actually there is a word for it . . . ah, sentaroon, or sen . . .

SPECIMEN NUMBER TWO My sister, my sister, we're all part of the African rainbow . . .

SPECIMEN NUMBER ONE The human family . . .

SPECIMEN NUMBER TWO It's the whites that impose the blood question. Don't you understand, my fallen black queen? It's up to us, the African people, the chosen, to combat their propaganda. Which is why I agreed to do this show. And if I win the money, I'm gonna open a soup kitchen/African free school/Reggae music warehouse in Oakland, California.

VENDETTA Check with Ericka Huggins first. She and the sisters in the Party could tell you a thing or two about running the revolution outta your home. But Specimen Two, we've dawdled long enough. To the crossroads, please! And give us your deepest, darkest fears. Sin,

ladies and gentlemen, uncut and funky.

(VENDETTA, TEEN BOMB, and SPECIMEN NUMBER TWO move to the X.)

VENDETTA No sense of the linear, just the circular rhythms of the heart, of the good black earth. Repeat after me, There's no place like the black unconscious . . .

SPECIMEN NUMBER TWO There's no place like the black unconscious. There's no place like the black unconscious. There's no place like the black unconscious . . .

(VENDETTA and TEEN BOMB move up stage. The lights blink. Time warp music cuts abruptly to sensuous, but foreboding East Indian music.)

(Billboard: RACE WARS*)*

SPECIMEN NUMBER TWO You're in somebody's foreign country. You've traveled hundreds of miles in search of your father, the famous jazz musician, in exile. You want to live with him, dedicate your life to the upkeep of his blackness, his muse, his mask. You finally corner him in the Tandoori Palace off of Seven Sisters. His breath smells of wine-soaked olives. A hand pulls at his beard, the other tends a cigarette, and a foot keeps time – eighth notes – under the table. This could be Bombay. Low ceilings. The waiters' sweat mingling with the curry. They bring out the relishes, the pickles. It's been so long. You sway in your chair. There is so much silence to clear.

But the silence doesn't move. He doesn't look you in the eye until he's had enough to drink. Then he asks why you've come this far for nothing. The oil spill starts in your throat. There's bile, thick black streams of it, on the table-cloth, on your chin. You stand on the table, your moccasins in the Vegetable Bhuna, and pull up your shirt to show him what is left of your umbilical cord. I'm not Pilate – you say, calling on the only black godmomma you know – You will have me, like you had me. Like you fucked my mother, all deep and steady.

Oh, I don't expect you to understand, he says, so cool, so collected, tucking his saxophone into its tapestry case. You're too young, but you'll know soon. You belong to the devils. That wicked witch of the west, your mother, claimed you years ago. I gave my seed, there's no more I can do. You'll never be black. And you'll never know what it's like. Stop reading the books. Your blood's too thin. That's why you're on top of the table screaming like a white girl wet with the blood of the banshee. Wet with the blood of the banshee.

On the boat back to civilization, there's a little blonde doll on the deck, sitting next to a big blonde doll, her mother. She smiles at you, then tugs at her mother's coat. "Look mother," she says staring between your eyes, "It's a gorilla . . ."
(We hear time warp music. The lights blink as the dream dissolves.)

VENDETTA There's no place like the black unconscious. There's no place like the black unconscious . . .

SPECIMEN NUMBER TWO There's no place like the black unconscious. There's no place like the black . . . *(VENDETTA snaps her fingers.)* . . . Damn . . . leave me alone. *(VENDETTA escorts the shaken SPECIMEN NUMBER TWO to a cushion.)*

VENDETTA You'll be okay, honey, we almost went a bit too far there. Bob, can you make sure we don't go overtime again, reality can be such a drawback . . . That's okay, sugar, put your head on Aunt Jemima's bosom. Suckle. Crawl up my black womb, do whatever you want, but stop crying. Hey, hey, where's your chutzbah? Bob, let's break.
(VENDETTA and TEEN BOMB exit.)

BOB (OS) That's right, Vendetta, we'll be right back to you after this message from our sponsor.
(Billboard: RARE COGNAC advertisement)
(RARE COGNAC MAN, in smoking jacket and slacks, and RARE COGNAC WOMAN, in shimmering evening dress, enter and strike poses on stage borrowed from a magazine ad for Hennessey Cognac. RARE COGNAC WOMAN jerks her neck to look at RARE COGNAC MAN.)

RARE COGNAC WOMAN I assume you eat pussy.
(RARE COGNAC WOMAN and RARE COGNAC MAN strut off stage.)
(Billboard: $100,000 TRAGIC MULATTO)
(Theme music rises.)

BOB (OS) It's the $100,000 Tragic Mulatto with your hostess of the mostest, Vendetta Goldwoman!
(VENDETTA and TEEN BOMB enter.)

VENDETTA It's good to be back. Yes it is. I missed you. I really did. You know,

sometimes I lay awake at night in one of my 100 percent silk negligees with the powder-blue mohair trim and I think. Yes, I do. I think about your full-bodied laughter and your thunderous applause, and I get this warm glow all over my body. So all I'm asking you to do for me, ladies and gentlemen, is to give it to me before you get home . . .
(Clap track)
(TEEN BOMB prompts the audience to clap along.)

VENDETTA Yes . . . oh yes . . . right there . . . *(The clap track fades.)* Ah shucks! Don't tell me you're all a bunch of three-minute heroes? What am I supposed to do now, make breakfast? I don't break bread with just anyone, you know. So get out. All of you, that's right. Pack it up, outta here .. . You think I'm kiddin'? . . . You think I'm kiddin'? . . . Well, I am! *(Belly laughs)* Yes, we're back, ladies and gentlemen, and we gave you a dose of melodrama with Specimen Two, didn't we? And you liked it, didn't you? Well, you lookeded like you likeded it! Shall we see what Teen Bomb has in the wings for us? Let's. Teen Bomb, get Specimen Three out here, pp-leease.
(Billboard: photo of SPECIMEN NUMBER THREE)
(SPECIMEN NUMBER THREE walks on stage to entry theme music.)

BOB (OS) Lovely Specimen Three is from the Motor City, Detroit, Michigan's Scutter Homes Projects. But because she's on the fast-track to stardom, touring with the Step-and-Fetch Revue, she hasn't been back to that hellhole in eight months. Yes, Miss Three can sing, she can dance, she can bring tears of I'm-so-glad-they're-them-and-I'm-me to your eyes. Yes, here she is, the lovely Specimen Three!
(Billboard: $100,000 TRAGIC MULATTO)

VENDETTA Why Specimen Three, it's a pleasure. And girlfriend, the doo is looking too correct!

SPECIMEN NUMBER THREE I press it myself.

VENDETTA Yes, it's been said before, but I think it's time to say it again, shall we? *(Recording (OS): "It's so hard to find good hair these days.")*

VENDETTA I keep plenty of irons in the fire myself. But you know, I've been meaning to get down to one of those relaxation tanks. They're supposed to slay the hair all over your body. I mean, you wants to go down on the Bermuda Triangle and run into the dark continent? And honey, the outfit. I know it's not a Chanel, but it's a . . . *(Walks over to check tag)* Halston for J.C. Penney! The babe has class! Integration got some of us better wardrobes, huh? Yes, Specimen Three, Bob tells us you sing, you dance, you move white folks to tears. What don't you do?

SPECIMEN NUMBER THREE Oh, I forgot to mention, I also do Sensorama analysis by appointment.

VENDETTA Oh, you're a smart cookie. And just twenty-five years old. If you were one year older, you know, we couldn't have you on the show, the mulatto shelf life being what it is. Yes, yes, but fill me in now, just what is Sensorama analysis consultant work by appointment only?

SPECIMEN THREE I visit clients in the privacy of their own homes and tell them how different aromas can change their lives. I'm really into how things smell.

VENDETTA Let me ask you this. Is it true that all Negroes smell alike?

SPECIMEN NUMBER THREE Well, it is, but it's also true that they don't have to! In fact, my line of fragrances includes a full range of sense-si-bilities. Let's see, there's Bap-and-Blue Blood – a favorite with my Ivy League clients. And there's Chicken Lickin' – some blacks do buy this, but mainly I sell it to my white neo-primitive friends downtown. And of course, there's Black Rage . . . Specimen Two, you might enjoy this one.

(SPECIMEN NUMBER TWO rolls her eyes.)

VENDETTA Specimen Three, you must be wearing Mulatto.

SPECIMEN NUMBER THREE Isn't it divine? So sheer, yet complex.

VENDETTA Bundles of talent, yes indeed, Specimen Three. You know, you make me happy. You fit in. You do. And I can see that you're really trying to get some-where.

SPECIMEN NUMBER THREE Yes, I love networking.

VENDETTA That's refreshing. So many of us want to stay in the dark ages. You know, quotas, guaranteed minimum wage. Don't get started, it's about that time. Specimen Three, please join me at the crossroads.

(VENDETTA and TEEN BOMB walk SPECIMEN NUMBER THREE to the X.)

VENDETTA Yes, share with us your deepest, darkest secrets. Repeat after me . . . There's no place like the black unconscious, there's no place like the black unconscious . . .

SPECIMEN NUMBER THREE There's no place like the black unconscious, there's no place like the black unconscious, there's no place like the black unconscious . . .

(VENDETTA and TEEN BOMB move up stage. We hear time warp music, then the opening chords of a familiar Christmas song. SPECIMEN NUMBER THREE hums a few bars.)

(Billboard: WHITER WHITES*)*

SPECIMEN NUMBER THREE I was in the White House dreaming of a White Christmas, my white slave, Patricia Nixon, blowing kisses from the white rose garden. The white heat of summertime – oh the living is easy, fish are jumping – down on my white shoulders, white elephant contraband from black Afrique. While my white-collar hubby is at his white-walled office down on White Street in White Plains, white America, whiting out what's left of black America, I'm gonna go shop at a white sale. But before I do that, I'm gonna get my po' white trash to hook up my white carriage to my white stallions and we're gonna go for a ride through the new White South. We'll pass huge white mansions on our way to see my lover, the white knight in his white castle. And I'll drink some white wine with him as he whispers little white lies into my lily white ears, and the whites of my eyes will shine all the way to Whitehall. Then we'll drink some White Russians, and he'll tell me how the white man's burden has been taking him out of the country lately. As we talk, white-throated sparrows and white-tailed deer will pass by the castle's white picket fence. What a panorama! And a white hunter will knock on the door and ask humbly for some white sauce to put on his white sea bass, a special meal for his fair white lady who has just returned from a whites-only hospital where she was being treated for the white plague.

In the afternoon, the white trash and I will leave the castle, go up the road a spell, and check into the White Hotel near White Fish Bay, where my second lover, the white supremacist, will be waiting in his white robe. We'll chat for a while about the woes of the white race, white-blood cells, and the white power movement. We'll have a little white powder, then he'll pull down the white blinds, and I'll take off my white lace panties and stretch out on the white satin comforter, and say, come and get me killer! And the white bed will rock and he'll fulfill my great white hopes with his big white whipping stick, and my white teeth will shine as the dark falls over us like a white sheet . . . *(Singing)* I was living in the White House, dreaming of a White Christmas.

(Time warp music segues in. The lights blink as the dream dissolves.)

VENDETTA There's no place like the black unconscious . . .

SPECIMEN NUMBER THREE There's no place like the black unconscious. There's no place like the black . . .

(VENDETTA snaps her fingers. SPECIMEN NUMBER THREE edges back to her cushion, embarrassed, as if caught in a very personal act.)

SPECIMEN NUMBER THREE . . . Toto, are we black?

VENDETTA *(Teary-eyed)* Yes dear, we're still black. What a gifted child, a carte-blanche to her race.

(Billboard: CREDIT TO YOUR RACE)

Ladies and Gentlemen, it's time for that moment of truth and no there's no doubt in my mind that there's only one young and tender little lady out there worthy of the booty, the $100,000 Tragic Mulatto. Bob . . .

BOB (OS) Yes, Vendetta, it's time now to ask our studio audience for their two cents. Ladies and gentlemen, we present to you these three lovely ladies: Specimen One, Two and Three. And *you* tell us – with your applause – who has the brazen ambition and the marketing savvy to be this week's $100,000 Tragic Mulatto. Are you ready folks? Specimen One, give us what you got!

(SPECIMEN NUMBER ONE stands. We hear a clap track.)

BOB (OS) How 'bout it for Specimen Two!

(SPECIMEN NUMBER TWO stands. The clap track plays.)

BOB (OS) And what about little Miss Specimen Three!

(SPECIMEN NUMBER THREE stands. Extra-loud clap track blares in.)

VENDETTA Bob, can we have the verdict, Bob?

(Drum roll)

BOB (OS) Specimen Two, will you please stand? Yes, Miss Two, as our third prize winner, you have the choice, in this land of opportunity, of walking away with two hundred, that's right $200, or whatever lies behind door number one.

(Ticking clock)

(Billboard: DOOR NUMBER ONE)

SPECIMEN NUMBER TWO I'll take door number one.

(Billboard: photo of a newborn baby)

BOB (OS) Yes, Specimen Two, you've been chosen to have Philip Michael Thomas's fourth child out of wedlock.

(Clap track)

SPECIMEN TWO You uncle tom, assistant chauffeur to the capitalist media running dog's gofer . . .

VENDETTA Cut her mike please.

(SPECIMEN NUMBER TWO continues to mouth words but isn't heard.)

BOB (OS) And Specimen One, will you stand. As our second-place gal you have the chance of walking away with five hundred, yes, $500, or taking home whatever's behind door number two.

(Ticking clock)

(Billboard: DOOR NUMBER TWO)

SPECIMEN NUMBER ONE Bob, I'll take the money!

(Billboard: $$$)

BOB (OS) The check is in the mail, honey! *(Coon laugh)* Now, Specimen Three, *(Thunderous drum roll)*

BOB (OS) Isn't she a beauty? Specimen Three is this week's $100,000 Tragic Mulatto!

(Billboard: $100,000 TRAGIC MULATTO)

(Clap track)

(TEEN BOMB puts a sash that reads "$100,000 Tragic Mulatto" on SPECIMEN NUMBER THREE. She parades down stage. The other two specimens take beauty-queen poses on stage as BOB speaks. VENDETTA and TEEN BOMB join them in stiff poses.)

BOB (OS) And here's what's in store: First . . . a one-year modeling contract for Crossover Dreams Fade Cream. You'll travel from Freedom, Pennsylvania to

Backwater, Mississippi with Crossover Dreams Fade Cream – the cream that keeps lasting even when your dream has deferred. Then there's the . . . Talented Tenth scholarship to Harvard University in Cambridge, Massachusetts, where you'll get to renew your vows with the Negro race, without ever having to step foot in a black community. And let's not forget, Specimen Three, we're giving you honorary white status in twenty-four foreign countries including Brazil!
(Theme music rises.)
*(*VENDETTA *reanimates, but the group remains stationary.)*

VENDETTA   Time to call it a show, ladies and gentlemen. Thanks for coming out. Remember, I love you, I love you all, I love you more than her . . .
*(*SPECIMEN NUMBER THREE *waves one hand like a beauty queen on a float.)*
     In fact, I love you more than anyone on the face of this earth . . . Thank you . . . thank you all.
BOB *(OS)*   Live from Baldwin Hills, California, Vendetta Goldwoman, give her a hand, and that's the $100,000 Tragic Mulatto!
(All remain in place with frozen smiles. Blackout.)

229

Cherríe Moraga

Biography

Cherríe Moraga is a playwright, poet and essayist whose plays and publications have received national recognition, including the NEA's Theatre Playwrights' Fellowship in 1993. A San Francisco-based writer, Cherríe has premiered her work at The Theatre Rhinoceros, the Eureka Theatre, and Brava! For Women in the Arts. Her play *Shadow of a Man* won the Fund for New American Plays Award in 1990. Brava's production of *Heroes and Saints* in 1992 received numerous awards for best original script, including the Will Glickman Prize, the Drama-logue and Critic Circles Awards and the Pen West Award. The play has been presented throughout the Southwest, in Chicago and at The Working Theatre in New York. Both *Shadow of a Man* and *Heroes and Saints* were collected, along with Cherríe's first play, *Giving Up the Ghost* in a volume entitled *Heroes and Saints and Other Plays*, published by West End Press in 1994.

Cherríe has also published as an essayist and poet. She is the co-editor of *This Bridge Called My Back: Writings by Radical Women of Color* which won the Before Columbus American Book Award in 1986. She is the author of *Loving in the War Years: Lo Que Nunca Pasó Por Sus Labios* (1983) and *The Last Generation* (1993), published by South End Press in Boston. She has edited numerous publications including *Cuentos: Stories by Latinas* and *Third Woman: the Sexuality of Latinas*.

As the playwright in residence at Brava! For Women in the Arts, Cherríe teaches Writing for Performance to gay and lesbian youth and Creative Writing to Latinas and Native American women. She is presently working on a new play, *Watsonville*, to be produced by Brava in its 1995–96 season. In addition to her teaching at Brava, Cherríe has also taught theater, creative writing, Chicano Studies and Women's Studies at various Bay Area institutions, including Stanford University and UC Berkeley.

In 1994, Cherríe was commissioned by the Berkeley Repertory Theatre for a new work, entitled *Mexican Medea* and she is presently working on a commission from the Committee on Black Performing Arts at Stanford University to write a play about the black and immigrant community that

Photo: Jean Weisinger

neighbors the affluent Stanford campus.

In the meantime, Cherríe tries to thoroughly raise her two-year-old son.

Artistic statement

My first acquaintance with theater began in the early seventies when I was an undergrad at a private-progressive-gone-bankrupt-in-the-Reagan-years-now-defunct-college in the Hollywood Hills. For some reason, I enrolled in a literature class entitled "The Theater of the Absurd" and was introduced to the writings of Ionesco, Beckett, Camus, Sartre, and others. The college also had a very vital experimental theater program and although I signed up several times for its intro course, "Theater Games," I never actually attended. Invariably, by the first week of school, my "cold feet" syndrome would return and I'd drop out before ever stepping one frozen foot into the rehearsal room. Theater on the page fascinated me, especially the existentialists. But theater off the page terrified me. As a scholarship student, I viewed acting and theater, as I did art in general, as restricted to the privileged classes – those kids whose fathers were movie-makers, doctors, lawyers, professors or artists themselves.

Somewhere in my mind I equated confidence, self-expression, the capacity for self-indulgence required of being an artist as the prerogative of the wealthy. They were the students who could afford to live on campus, (not commute as I did), who didn't have to do work-study (I had three jobs), and who had the *leisure* to "act out" in the dining hall with no apparent shame or embarrassment.

Writing, on the other hand, was a private act. Like reading, one could write in secret without fear of ridicule. One could indulge oneself in the realm of ideas, just as the theater absurdists had. And so, I became a writer, first a poet, then an essayist, and finally a playwright.

Now, twenty years later, I write for actors as "locos" as those college students back in 1972, but these have brown faces and Spanish surnames and backgrounds and backyards similar to mine; and I make them speak a language in which my mother and aunts can hear themselves. In other words, I've made theater my own: my own class and race, my own culture and voice. Mainstream theater didn't show me how to do this, Chicano theater did. Black women's literature did. Lesbian poetry did. James Baldwin, Luis Valdez, Toni Cade Bambara, Judy Grahn, Audre Lorde. They were my family of writers and visionaries.

I was privileged to come of age as a writer in a time when people of color, lesbians, feminists were writing in the context of a social change movement. Art and cultural affirmation were critical aspects of that movement and allowed me to find place and voice as a Chicana lesbian. I learned early on that trying to write like white people (if you weren't white) would simply make you a cheap imitation thereof; that my best shot as a writer was to speak with a Chicana voice that had never found its way to the page or the stage. Luis Valdez didn't do it, although his Teatro Campesino in the late sixties and early seventies broke open the rich terrain of the Chicano *male* worker, student, rebel and dreamer.

I did not come to the theater quickly. My plays grew out of that place where my poetry and autobiographical essays left off, a place where having told my own story as honestly as I was able (*Loving in the War Years*, 1983), a space opened up inside me

inviting entrance for the first time for fictional characters to speak their own stories. *Giving Up the Ghost* was my first play, begun in 1984, and reflects my transition from poetry to theater. A kind of *teatropoesía*, *Ghost* is a Chicana lesbian love story. In 1985, I worked with María Irene Fornes for one year in her Latino Playwrights Lab at Intar Theater in New York City. In 1990, Fornes directed the play which I had developed in the lab, *Shadow of a Man*, in a San Francisco Eureka Theater/ Brava! For Women in the Arts production. *Shadow* was my "family" play, in which I tried to expose the secrets and silences affecting both men and women in the traditional Chicano household. Moving from the intimate relationship of lovers (*Ghost*), to the familial place from which lovers are created (*Shadow*), to the community that houses them both (*Heroes and Saints*), I feel that my plays have always occurred in dialogue with the Chicano/Latino community. They provide an intra-cultural critique and celebration. They are not written with the Anglo audience in mind because to do so would mean writing in translation. As any writer of any culture should, I try to write as specifically as possible of the complexities in our lives. In that the universality of the Chicano experience is found and the work becomes "cross cultural" in the deepest sense.

Since 1990 and the co-production of *Shadow*, I have continued my relationship with Brava! For Women in the Arts. In 1992, Brava produced *Heroes and Saints*, and in 1996 the company will produce my next play, *Watsonville*. Being the playwright-in-residence at Brava has been the greatest blessing for me and my work. Without a stage, the writing remains on the page and playwrights eventually return to their poems and unfinished novels and may despair of ever seeing their drama take flesh. I know this could have easily been my scenario. Brava changed that for me. As a multi-cultural women's theater organization especially interested in premiering works by lesbians and women of color, Brava became a home, bringing together my concerns as an artist and cultural activist. Through Brava, my plays have been shown to audiences as diverse as the city of San Francisco itself. In addition, the teaching aspect of my residency has provided me with the opportunity to help produce a new generation of American theater artists and writers, including gay and lesbian youth, Chicanas, Latinas and Native American women.

This is where my road comes full circle (not as an end, but a continuance). It's been nearly a quarter of a century since those early college days when I believed one had to be wealthy to be an artist. I no longer believe that and I am here to prove the same to my students and to my audiences. The plays which I have written and are yet to be written are drawn from people I have known, people I have imagined, and people I have interviewed for the express purpose of writing a play. They are, for the most part, people I have never read a line by in a book or have never seen not wearing a maid's uniform in a film, TV show, or play. They are my people. My subject. My heart.

Production history

Heroes and Saints was initially commissioned through Jose Luis Valenzuela's Latino Lab of the Los Angeles Theatre Center and was performed there as a staged reading under the direction of Jose Guadalupe Saucedo. The play was also presented in the Latin American Theatre Artist Staged Reading Series under the direction of the author.

Heroes and Saints had its world premiere on April 4, 1992 at El Teatro Misión of San Francisco, produced by Brava! For Women in the Arts under the Artistic Direction of Ellen Gavin. It included the following cast: Jaime Lujan, Juanita Estrada, Charo Toledo, Viola Lucero, Anna Marina Bensaud, Jennifer Proctor, Angelo Pagan, Hector Correa, and Gary Martinez. The production was directed by Albert Takazauckas.

13 Heroes and Saints

Cherríe Moraga

Before day breaks we shall
set out from these yards and
reach their city . . . in the dawn
showing in public places the full extent of
  our misery

appealing to anything with a human look.
What will come after, I don't know.

St. Joan of the Stockyards

Aztlán belongs to those who plant the seeds,
water the fields, and gather the crops . . .

For Aztlán's Children

Characters

CEREZITA VALLE: the head

AMPARO: the comadre and activista

ANA PEREZ: the news reporter

DOLORES: the mother

BONNIE: a neighbor's child "adopted" by
AMPARO and DON GILBERTO

YOLANDA: the hairdresser sister

MARIO: the sometimes-student brother

FATHER JUAN: the "half-breed" leftist priest

DON GILBERTO: the compadre, AMPARO's
husband

POLICEMAN

EL PUEBLO: the children and mothers of
McLaughlin; THE PEOPLE/PROTESTORS/
AUDIENCE participating in the struggle
(ideally, EL PUEBLO should be made up of
an ensemble of people from the local Latino
community)

Notes on CEREZITA

CEREZITA is a head of human dimension,
but one who possesses such dignity of
bearing and classical Indian beauty she can,
at times, assume nearly religious propor-
tions. (The huge head figures of the pre-
Columbian Olmecas are an apt comparison.)
This image, however, should be contrasted
with the very real "humanness" she exhibits
on a daily functioning level. Her mobility
and its limits are critical aspects of her
character. For most of the play, CEREZITA is
positioned on a rolling, tablelike platform,
which will be referred to as her "raite"
(ride). It is automated by a button she
operates with her chin. The low hum of its
motor always anticipates her entrance. The
raite can be disengaged at any time by
flipping the hold on each wheel and
pushing the chin piece out of her reach. At
such times, CEREZITA has no control and
can only be moved by someone manually.

Setting

The play takes place in McLaughlin,
California, a fictional town in the San
Joaquin Valley. The year is 1988.
  McLaughlin is a one-exit town off
Highway 99. On the east side of the
highway sits the old part of town, consisting
primarily of a main street of three blocks of
small businesses – the auto supply store, a
small supermarket, the post office, a
laundromat, an old central bank with a
recently added automatic teller machine, a
storefront Iglesia de Dios and, of course, a
video movie rental shop. Crossing the two-
lane bridge over Highway 99, a new
McLaughlin has emerged. From the highest
point of the overpass, a large island of
single-family stucco houses and apartments
can be seen. The tracts were built in the
late 1970s and reflect a manicured unifor-
mity in appearance, each house with its
obligatory crew-cut lawn and one-step front
porch. Surrounding the island is an endless
sea of agricultural fields which, like the
houses, have been perfectly arranged into
neatly juxtaposed rectangles.
  The hundreds of miles of soil that
surround the lives of Valley dwellers should
not be confused with land. What was once
land has become dirt, overworked dirt, over-
irrigated dirt, injected with deadly doses of
chemicals and violated by every manner of
ground- and back-breaking machinery. The
people that work the dirt do not call what
was once the land their enemy. They
remember what land used to be and await
its second coming.

To that end, the grape vineyards, pecan tree orchards and the endless expanse of the Valley's agricultural life should be constant presences in the play and visibly press upon the intimate life of the Valle family home. The relentless fog and sudden dramatic sunbreaks in the Valley sky physically alter the mood of each scene. The Valle family home is modest in furnishing but always neat, and looks onto EL PUEBLO through a downstage window. Scenes outside the family home can be represented by simple, movable set pieces, e.g., a park bench for the street scenes, a wheelchair for the hospital, a set of steps for the church, etc.

Act I

Scene 1

At sunrise in the distance, a group of children wearing calavera masks enters the grape vineyard. They carry a small, child-size cross which they erect quickly and exit, leaving its stark silhouetted image against the dawn's light. The barely distinguishable figure of a small child hangs from it. The child's hair and thin clothing flap in the wind. Moments pass. The wind subsides. The sound of squeaking wheels and a low, mechanical hum interrupt the silence. CEREZITA *enters in shadow. She is transfixed by the image of the crucifixion. The sun suddenly explodes out of the horizon, bathing both the child and* CEREZITA. CEREZITA *is awesome and striking in the light. The crucified child glows, Christlike. The sound of a low-flying helicopter invades the silence. Its shadow passes over the field. Blackout.*

Scene 2

Mexican rancheras can be heard coming from a small radio in the Valle home. ANA PEREZ *is on the street in front of the house. She holds a microphone and is expertly made up.* AMPARO, *a stocky woman in her fifties, is digging holes in the yard next door. She wears heavy-duty rubber gloves.*

ANNA PEREZ *(To the "cameraman")* Bob, is my hair okay? What? . . . I have lipstick? Where? Here? *(She wets her finger with her tongue, rubs the corner of her lip.)* Okay? . . . Good. *(Addressing the "camera")* Hello, I'm Ana Pérez and this is another edition of our Channel Five news special: "Hispanic California." Today I am speaking to you from the town of McLaughlin in the San Joaquin Valley. McLaughlin is commonly believed to be a cancer cluster area, where a disproportionate number of children have been diagnosed with cancer in the last few years. The town has seen the sudden death of numerous children, as well as a high incidence of birth defects. One of the most alarming recent events which has brought sudden public attention to the McLaughlin situation has been a series of . . . crucifixions, performed in what seems to be a kind of ritualized protest against the dying of

McLaughlin children. *(DOLORES, a slender woman nearing fifty, enters. She carries groceries.)* The last three children to die were each found with his corpse hanging from a cross in the middle of a grape vineyard. The Union of Campesinos, an outspoken advocate for pesticide control, is presently under investigation for the crime. *(Spying DOLORES.)* We now are approaching the house of Dolores Valle. Her daughter Cerezita is one of McLaughlin's most tragic cases.

(Upon sight of ANA PEREZ coming toward her with her microphone, DOLORES hurries into the house. AMPARO intervenes.)

AMPARO You should maybe leave her alone; she don' like the telebision cameras too much no more. .

ANA PEREZ *(To the "camera")* Possibly this neighbor can provide us with some sense of the emotional climate prevalent in this small, largely Hispanic farm worker town.

AMPARO She said es como un circo—

ANA PEREZ *(To the camera)* A circus.

AMPARO Que la gente . . . the peepo like tha' kina t'ing, to look at somebody else's life like that t'ing coont never happen to them. But Cerezita's big now. She got a lot to say if they give her the chance. It's important for the peepo to reelize what los rancheros—

ANA PEREZ *(Overlapping)* The growers.

AMPARO Are doing to us.

ANA PEREZ Cerezita. That's an unusual name. Es una fruta ¿qué no?

AMPARO That's what they call her because she look like tha' . . . a red little round cherry face. I think maybe all the blood tha' was apose to go to the resta her body got squeezed up into her head. I think tha's why she's so smart, too. Mario, her brother, el doctor-to-be, says the blood gots oxygen. Tha's gottu help with the brains. So pink pink pink she turn out.

ANA PEREZ And how old is Cerezita now?

AMPARO: A big teenager already. Cerezita come out like this before anybody think too much about it. Now there's lotza nuevas because lotza kids are turning out all chuecos and with ugly things growing inside them. So our pueblito, pues it's on the map now. The gabachos, s'cuze me, los americanos are always coming through McLaughlin nowdays. Pero, not too much change. We still can' prove it's those chemicals they put on the plantas. But we know Cere turn out this way because Dolores pick en los files cuando tenía panza.

ANA PEREZ Uh . . . pregnant, I think.

AMPARO Dolores tells me que no le importa a la gente and maybe she's right. She says all the publeesty gives peepo somet'ing to do. Peepo que got a lotta free time. It gives them a purpose, she says – like God.

ANA PEREZ Señora, what about the boy?

AMPARO ¿Qué boy?

ANA PEREZ The boy on the cross . . . in the field.

AMPARO Memo?

ANA PEREZ Yes. Memo Delgado.

AMPARO He died a little santito, son angelitos todos.

ANA PEREZ That's the third one.

AMPARO Yes.

ANA PEREZ Why would someone be so cruel, to hang a child up like that? To steal him from his deathbed?

AMPARO No, he was dead already. Already dead from the poison.

ANA PEREZ But ma'am—

AMPARO They always dead first. If you put the children in the ground, the world forgets about them. Who's gointu see them, buried in the dirt?

ANA PEREZ A publicity stunt? But who's—

AMPARO Señorita, I don' know who. But I know they not my enemy. *(Beat)* Con su permiso. *(AMPARO walks away.)*

ANA PEREZ *(With false bravado)* That concludes our Hispanic hour for the week, but watch for next week's show where we will take a five-hour drive north to the heart of San Francisco's Latino Mission District, for an insider's observation of the Day of the Dead, the Mexican Halloween. *(She holds a television smile for three full seconds. To the "cameraman")* Cut! We'll edit her out later.

(BONNIE and a group of small CHILDREN enter wearing calavera masks. They startle her.)

THE CHILDREN Trick or treat!

ANA PEREZ No. I mean . . . I don't . . . have anything to give you. *(She exits nervously.)*

Scene 3

Crossfade to the Valle kitchen. It is late afternoon. YOLANDA *is breastfeeding her baby,* CEREZITA *observes.*

CEREZITA I remember the first time I tasted fear, I smelled it in her sweat. It ran like a tiny river down her breast and mixed with her milk. I tasted it on my tongue. It was bitter. Very bitter.

YOLANDA That's why I try to keep calm. Lina knows when I'm upset.

CEREZITA I stopped drinking. I refused to nurse from her again, bit at her breasts when she tried to force me.

YOLANDA Formula is expensive. Breastfeeding is free. Healthier, too. I'll do it until Lina doesn't want it no more. *(She buttons her blouse, puts the infant into her crib, sings to her softly.)* "Duerme, duerme, negrito" . . . *(Continues singing)*

CEREZITA But imagine my sadness, my longing for the once-sweetness of her nipple.

*(*YOLANDA *positions* CEREZITA *for her weekly beauty treatment. She takes out various beauty supplies from a bag.* MARIO *enters, towel wrapped around his hips. He is well built, endearingly macho in his manner. He is drying himself briskly.)*

MARIO ¡Hijo! It's freezing! These cold showers suck, man! We should all just get the fuck outta here. I'm gonna move us all the fuck outta here!

CEREZITA Where to, Mario?

YOLANDA Go 'head, chulo. You keep taking those showers purty boy and your skin's gonna fall off in sheets. Then who's gonna want you?

MARIO The water was cold, man. Ice cold.

YOLANDA I turned the water heater off.

MARIO Great. My skin's gonna freeze off from the cold sooner than any chemicals. How can you stand it?

CEREZITA Where you gonna move us to, Mario?

MARIO *(Looking out the window)* What?

CEREZITA Where we going?

MARIO: I dunno. Just away.

YOLANDA *(Has filled up a glass of water from the faucet)* Here.

MARIO Chale. The shit stinks.

YOLANDA C'mon, chulo, Tómalo. Why don't you just throw it down your throat better? It's the same thing. You suck enough of it up through your skin taking those hot baths three times a day.

MARIO Two.

*(*YOLANDA *starts to spread the beauty mask onto* CEREZITA's *face.* DOLORES *can be seen coming up the porch steps after her day's work.)*

YOLANDA You wanna see Lina's nalguitas? They're fried, man. The hot water opens your pores and just sucks up the stuff. She cried all night last night. This shit's getting outta hand! Doña Amparo told me—

DOLORES *(Entering)* Es una metiche, Amparo.

YOLANDA They shot through her windows the last night.

CEREZITA Who?

YOLANDA Who knows? The guys in the helicopters . . . God.

DOLORES Por eso, te digo she better learn to keep her damn mouth shut. Ella siempre gottu be putting la cuchara en la olla. I saw her talking to the TV peepo last week right in front of the house. It scare me.

YOLANDA What are you scared of?

DOLORES They come to talk to Amparo on the job yesterday.

MARIO Who?

DOLORES The patrones.

MARIO The owners?

DOLORES Not the owners, pero their peepo. They give her a warning que they don' like her talking about the rancheros.

YOLANDA Cabrones.

DOLORES She gointu lose her job.

MARIO Got to hand it to Nina Amparo. She's got huevos, man.

DOLORES She got a husband, not huevos. Who's gointu support Cere if I stop working?

(The room falls silent. CEREZITA's *face is now covered in a facial mask.)*

MARIO Well, I better get ready. *(He starts to exit upstage,* DOLORES *stops him.)*

DOLORES I better see you back el lunes temprano ¿m'oyes? I got the plaster falling down from the front of the house.

MARIO Okay.

CEREZITA Where you going, Mario?

*(*DOLORES *goes to the stove, puts a pot of beans to boil.)*

YOLANDA Don't talk. Cere. You're gonna crack your face.

MARIO ¡San Pancho, 'manita!

YOLANDA (*Running a slab of facial down his cheek, softly*) Better stay away from the jotos, you don't wanna catch nothing.

MARIO (*"Slabbing" it back, teasing*) I got it covered, hermana.

DOLORES What are you two whispering about?

MARIO Nothing, 'amá.

DOLORES You know, secrets kill sometimes.

YOLANDA It was nothing, 'amá.

DOLORES You don' believe it, pero tha' place, it's crazy. They got all those crazy peepo que sleep on the street nowdays. You never know one could come up and shoot you right in the head.

YOLANDA They're shooting us here anyway.

DOLORES ¿Crees que soy una exgerada? We'll see.

MARIO (*Mimicking*) "We'll see." ¡Hijo! I hate when she says that like she knows something we don't.

YOLANDA I know.

DOLORES Pues, maybe I do.

MARIO (*Coming up behind DOLORES and wrapping his arms around her*) I'm fine, 'amá.

DOLORES (*Softening*) "I'm fine, 'amá." ¿Qué sabes tú about "fine"?

(AMPARO *can be seen coming up onto the porch.* JUAN *trails behind her carrying a five-gallon tank of spring water. He wears jeans and a flannel shirt.*)

AMPARO ¡Halo! Anybody home? I got a sorprise for you!

DOLORES Abra la puerta, hijo.

AMPARO (*Calling out behind her*) Right here! This is the house!

MARIO (*Going to the door*) What's up, Nina?

AMPARO ¡Ay! Te vez bien sexy.

DOLORES (*Spying JUAN at the porch*) ¡Ay, Dios! (*She quickly pushes CEREZITA out of sight, drawing a curtain around her.*)

YOLANDA (*Whispering*) Why do you do that to her?

DOLORES Cállete tú.

MARIO (*To JUAN, with interest*) Hello.

JUAN Hello.

AMPARO This is my godson, MARIO. (*MARIO takes the bottle from JUAN.*)

JUAN Thanks.

MARIO No problem.

AMPARO That's Yolanda y su baby, Evalina.

YOLANDA Hi.

AMPARO And this is my comadre, Dolores Valle.

DOLORES Halo.

JUAN Mucho gusto.

DOLORES ¿Habla español?

JUAN Soy mexicano.

DOLORES ¿Verdad?

AMPARO (*Aside*) Half y half.

MARIO (*Suggestively*) Like the cream?

AMPARO And a priest. Father Juan Cunningham.

DOLORES Mario, why you standing around sin ropa? Go put some clothes on.

MARIO All right. I was just helping the man. I mean, the priest.
(*He puts the water onto the dispenser, then exits.* JUAN's *eyes follow him.*)

DOLORES Siéntese, Father.

YOLANDA So, where'd you get the water, Doña Amparo?

AMPARO The Arrowhead donated it.

JUAN Thanks to Doña Amparo. Last week's newscast stirred up everyone!

AMPARO It wasn' me. It was la crucifixión. That's what brought the newspeepo here.

DOLORES ¡Es una barbaridad!

AMPARO The newspeepo, they wanted to talk to Cereza, comadre.

DOLORES Y ¿por qué?

YOLANDA Cere knows, 'amá.

DOLORES Cerezita don' know nothing.

YOLANDA She sees.

DOLORES She sees nothing (*To JUAN*) She looks out the window all day, nomás. What can she see?
(*The lights crossfade to CEREZITA at the window.* BONNIE *sits near her, playing with a doll. She prepares bandages for it, tearing a flour-sack cloth into strips and wrapping it around the doll's head.*)

CEREZITA The sheep drink the same water we do from troughs outside my window. Today it is an orange-yellow color. The mothers dip their heads into the long rusty buckets and drink and drink while their babies deform inside them. Innocent, they sleep inside the same poison water and are born broken like me, their lamb limbs curling under them.

BONNIE (*Takes out a thermometer and puts it into her doll's mouth*) ¿Estás malita, mija? (*Checking the temperature*) Yes. I think you got "it." (*She rubs the top of its head, chanting.*)
Sana sana colita de rana, si no sanas hoy sanarás mañana.

Sana sana colita de rana, si no sanas hoy
sanarás mañana.
Sana sana colita de rana, si no sanas hoy
sanarás mañana.
*(She puts the doll into a small box and
covers it tenderly with the remains of the
cloth.)*
CEREZITA I watch them from my window
and weep.
(Fade out.)

Scene 4

DOLORES *and* JUAN *are at the kitchen table.
He is eating a taco of chorizo. She embroiders
a dishcloth.*

DOLORES And then I started working in
the packing houses and the same thing
was happening. The poison they put on
the almonds, it would make you sick. The
women would run out of the place coz
they had to throw up. Sure, I dint wannu
go back in there, pero after awhile you
start to accept it because you gottu have a
job.
JUAN Where do you work now?
DOLORES Otro packing house. *(Pause)* ¿Le
gusta la comida, Father?
JUAN Sí está muy sabrosa.
DOLORES Pues, I'm glad you came. Most a
the priests, they not like you, they don'
come to the house no more unless you
got money. It's not right, Padre.
JUAN No, no es justo, Señora Valle.
DOLORES But the priests should be worried
because a lot of peepo they leaving la
iglesia. ¿Sabe qué? A buncha my vecinos
already turn into the "Holy Rollie."
JUAN Holy Rollie?
DOLORES Tha's what my Yolie calls them.
They turn from the Catholic god. They
"Chrishins" now.
JUAN Oh, you mean Pentecostals.
DOLORES One time I was feeling so tire,
so lonely, just dragging myself home from
work and I hear a tamborín coming out
of the panadería. Now it's a church, but it
usetu be la panadería de la familia
Hernández. It still smell like pandulce un
poco when you go by. An' it was like the
tamborín me 'staba llamando, telling me
to come inside, if only para quitarme el
cansancio a little. So I go in and sit in the
back. And they were all jumping up and
down and shaking their hands in the air.

Pura raza, singing songs like children. It
scare me, Father. Their faces look kina
dopey-like, kina like their eyes had
turned to hard glass por las lágrimas que
tienen all lock up inside them. Se llama
"Iglesia de Dios," but there wasn' no God
there. And too much noise. How can your
soul even find God con tanto ruído?
JUAN I guess they feel they find him with
one another.
DOLORES No es posible, God es una cosa
privada, un secreto que guardas and
nobody can touch that part of you. Even
the priest has to forget every secret you
tell him. *(She observes* JUAN *as he finishes
the dripping taco. He licks his fingers.)* ¡Ay,
qué pena! *(She brings him a clean dish-
towel.)* You been a father a long time,
Father?
JUAN About ten years.
DOLORES You still have the eyes of a man.
JUAN ¿Perdón?
DOLORES No importa. It's good you
experience the world a little. Some of
these priests, you confess to them your
sins y que consejo te pueden ofrecer? A
little life doesn' hurt nobody. *(Pause)*
Come see my Cerezita. She'll like you. It's
been years since a priest come to see her.
JUAN Would you like me to hear her
confession?
DOLORES What sins could a girl like her
have, Padre? She was born this way. Es
una santa. We should pray to her, I think.
(They both rise.)

Scene 5

Crossfade to CEREZITA *speaking into a tape
recorder.*

CEREZITA It is so, he came to meet her
seeking the purity of nature he'd lost. He
sought baptism in the fire of her original
desire.
JUAN *(Entering timidly)* Hello . . . *(CEREZITA
turns the tape recorder off with her chin.)*
Am I . . . interrupting? *(She doesn't
respond.)* Your mother asked me to come
by. I hope it's . . . all right with you?
CEREZITA She must like you. Few people
get past her inspection.
JUAN Can you turn around? I'd like to talk
to you face to face.
CEREZITA You're wasting your time, Padre.
I have no use for God.

JUAN   You don't believe?

CEREZITA   I don't care.

JUAN   I see. *(Pause)* Can I read you something? Your mother says you are quite a reader.

CEREZITA   *(Reluctantly)* What is it?

JUAN   Just something I'm reading. It struck me.

CEREZITA   I got ears.

JUAN   *(Reading from a small paperback)* "Then, they named rich the man of God, and poor the man of flesh. And they determined that the rich would care for and protect the poor in as much that through them, the rich had received such benefits."

CEREZITA   "Entonces llamaron rico al hombre de oro y pobre al hombre de carne. Y dispusieron que el rico cuidara y amparara al pobre por cuanto que de él había recibido beneficios." . . .

JUAN   *(Impressed)* "And they ordered that the poor would respond on behalf of the rich before the face of truth."

CEREZITA   "Y ordenaron que el pobre respondería por el rico ante la cara de la verdad." . . .

JUAN   "For this—"

CEREZITA   *(Slowly turning to him)* "For this reason our law states that no rich person can enter heaven without the poor taking him by the hand."
(Seeing her fully for the first time, JUAN's *face registers both awe and tenderness.)*

JUAN   Balun Canan. Rosario Castellanos.

CEREZITA   First, the Maya. *(Pause)* Am I your pobre, Father?
(Fade out)

Scene 6

Early morning. AMPARO *and* DOLORES *come out of the house, wearing work clothes.*
DOLORES *carries a small bucket of plaster and a trowel.* AMPARO *carries a shovel and heavy gloves.*

DOLORES   This house is falling apart. ¡Ayúdanos, Dios!

AMPARO   You think God is gointu take care of it? Working is what changes things, not oraciones.

DOLORES   Ya te dije, I'm not going to your protesta.
*(*AMPARO *puts on the gloves, begins digging in the yard.* DOLORES *goes over to the side of the house and starts applying plaster to it.)*

AMPARO   ¿Sabes qué? I don' even go to church no more, ni recibir comunión . . . coz I'm tire of swallowing what they want to shove down my throat. Body of Christ . . . pedo.

DOLORES   I hate when you talk like this. It makes me sick to my stomach.

AMPARO   *(Digging more vigorously)* Pues, the truth aint so purty sometimes.

DOLORES   I'm not going. *(To herself)* You'd think I could get the only son I got to do this for me, pero no. He's always gallivanting around con sus secretos.

AMPARO   *(Hitting upon something on the ground)* Mira. Hay algo aquí. Ayúdame.

DOLORES   Wha' chu find?

AMPARO   No sé. Help me.
(They both get down on their hands and knees and dig. They pull out an old, thick rubber hose.)

DOLORES   No es nada.

AMPARO   You don' believe me, but they bury all their poison under our houses. Wha' chu think that crack comes from? An earthquake? The house is sinking, te digo como quicksand.

DOLORES   It's the only house I got.

AMPARO   They lied to us, Lola. They thought we was too stupid to know the difernce. They throw some dirt over a dump, put some casas de cartón on top of it y dicen que it's the "American Dream." Pues, this dream has turned to pesadilla.

DOLORES   Where we apose to go? Every three houses got a For Sale sign. Nobody's gointu buy from us now.

AMPARO   The gov'ment owes us the money.

DOLORES   Oh sí, and they're gointu drop it de los cielos. *(She sits on the porch step.)*

AMPARO   No, pero not'ing gointu change if you don' do not'ing. How can you jus' sit with your hands folded? You see Yolie's baby, ya 'stá malita.

DOLORES   She got a little rash, nomás. Anyway, I do somet'ing before and what good did it do me? Somos mas pobres que antes. A'least before I open my big mouth, Cerezita had a father.

AMPARO   What kina father? A father who wouldn' let his own child feel the sun on her face, who kept her hidden como algo cochino. And now you do the same thing to her. It's not right, Lola. You think hiding her is gointu bring Arturo back?

DOLORES No. *(Pause)* It wasn' fair what I did to him. I humiliate him.

AMPARO Tha's an old tune, comadre. He never humiliate you?

DOLORES The men are weaker. They can't take what a woman takes.

AMPARO Adió. You did it to educate the peepo.

DOLORES I did it to make him ashame, I tole him, ¿Ves? "Half a father make half a baby." *(Pause)* He believe it.

AMPARO That was a long time ago. Wha' chu got to stop you now?

DOLORES *(Returning to plastering)* Vete. Go to your marcha. No tiene nada que ver eso conmigo.

(DOLORES slaps some more plaster onto the wall. AMPARO tosses the hose into the junk heap and exits. The sound of a low-flying crop duster fills the stage. DOLORES stares up at it as its shadow passes over her. Fade out.)

Scene 7

The wheels to CEREZITA's raite can be heard in the darkness. At rise, MARIO is on his back, tightening a bolt under the wheelchair. CEREZITA is reading a medical book, periodically turning the pages with her mouth. The infant sleeps in her crib.

CEREZITA So, what kind of cancer did Memo have?

MARIO He had a neuroblastoma. Hand me that screwdriver, will you, Cere? *(She picks it up with her mouth, drops it down to him.)* Watch it. You almost hit me.

CEREZITA I can't see you from up here.

MARIO Pues, wátchale. *(He rolls the raite back and forth, it squeaks loudly.)* How's that feel?

CEREZITA Fine, but can you do something about the squeak?

MARIO Where's the oil?

CEREZITA Check under the sink. *(He does.)* What's a neuroblastoma?

MARIO *(Coming back with the oil)* A tumor. They usually arise in the adrenal gland or any place in the sympathetic chain. *(Pointing out a reference in the book)* See.

CEREZITA Like in the chest.

MARIO Well, they can appear there. Memo's started in the abdomen.

CEREZITA It says that the prognosis is worse than most leukemia.

MARIO *(Applying the oil)* Usually even surgery can't cure it. *(He puts her chin piece back in place. CEREZITA gives the raite a little test drive.)* There, a smooth ride. Memo didn't have a chance, Cere. Kids' bodies are so vulnerable. They pick up stuff way before adults. They got no buffer zone. "The canary in the mine shaft" . . . that's exactly what they are. *(He puts the tools away, washes his hands, then runs a comb through his hair.)*

CEREZITA You going out, Mario?

MARIO Yeah.

CEREZITA Tell me the story about the Mayan god before you go.

MARIO Ah, Cere, my ride's coming.

CEREZITA Please, don't go just yet.

MARIO Okay, but the short version. *(Sitting down next to her)* Cousin Freddie—

CEREZITA Hadn't been in the states too long, maybe a few months and he liked everything American . . .

MARIO *(Amused)* I guess even me. God, Freddie was beautiful. Dark. He had cheekbones to die for, like they were sculpted outta some holy Mayan rock. And he had this little twitch in the side of his jaw that would pulse whenever he got excited or upset or something. The party was still going on and I was supposed to be sleeping in the next room. But Nino Gilberto started singing and letting out those famous gritos of his . . . *(Imitates "los gritos")* So, no way, man, was I gonna get any sleep. I could hear Freddie laughing in the patio and I started following his voice around. I'd think about his smile, I'd imagine him waving his hands in people's faces while he talked, getting a little pálido from all the pisto. The next thing I know he's standing—

CEREZITA No, you forgot the boleros.

MARIO Right. When the boleros came on, I could hear him singing along with them and I'd think about those veined hands around Yolie's back while they danced, wishing I was there inside those hands. The next thing I know, my young god is standing at the foot of my bed. His shirt's open to his waist . . . more Mayan rock. It's kinda sticking to him from the sweat he's worked up on the dance floor. My little heart is pounding as he tells me

how he just came in to check on me.
"Mijo," he calls me.

CEREZITA Mijo.

MARIO That little twitch pulsing. (A car
horn sounds from the street. He gives
CEREZITA a peck on the cheek.) That's it.

CEREZITA Ah, Mario.

MARIO (Spotting YOLANDA through the
window). Look-it, Yolie's coming home.
Have her take you out back. It's nice out
right now. Ay te watcho. (He grabs a
leather jacket, goes out the door.)

YOLANDA Your "friend" is waiting for you,
ése. (MARIO gives her a kiss and exits;
YOLANDA comes indoors.) That was one
sleazy-looking gringo in that car.

CEREZITA Mario doesn't like him.

YOLANDA Well, for not liking him, he sure
sees him a lot.

CEREZITA He gives him things.

YOLANDA That I believe.

CEREZITA Take me outside, Yolie.

YOLANDA (Checking the baby in its crib) Did
Lina wake up?

CEREZITA No. Take me outside, Yolie.
Mom's gonna be home soon.

YOLANDA Okay, let's go. Your hair's lookin'
raggedy. I'm gonna give you a good
conditioning later. (Pushing the raite) Hey!
What happened to the squeak?

CEREZITA (With pride) Mario fixed it.
(Fade out.)

Scene 8

That evening, CEREZITA is reading a book.
YOLANDA passes by with a diaper over her
shoulder and a small stack of them in her
hands.

CEREZITA It recommends making a tea
from flor de muerto. It's good for indiges-
tion.

YOLANDA I'm not giving my baby anything
called "flower of the dead."

CEREZITA It worked for the Aztecs,
Zempasuchitl, the yellow marigold.

YOLANDA Forget it.
(YOLANDA exits. CEREZITA shuts the book
just as she spots JUAN coming up the front
steps.)

CEREZITA Come in.

JUAN (Entering) Hello. You alone?

CEREZITA No, Yolie's in back with the
baby. Lina's been throwing up her milk.

JUAN Oh.

CEREZITA If you came to see my mom,
she's next door.

JUAN No. I came to see you.

CEREZITA She's trying to get Don Gilberto
to stop Amparo from leading the protest
at the school tomorrow. Can you hear
them?

JUAN No.

CEREZITA Sure, my mom's going, "What
kina man are you, you can't control your
own wife?" And Don Gilberto answers, "I
don't gotta control her, I love her."

JUAN I can't hear them.

CEREZITA Yeah, but that's what they're
saying. Are you going to the demonstration, Father?

JUAN Yes. I was hoping your mother would
bring you.

CEREZITA No, I don't go out.

JUAN Never?

CEREZITA Never. (She observes JUAN for a
moment.)

JUAN I . . .

CEREZITA Touch my hair, Father.

JUAN What?

CEREZITA Touch my hair. (He hesitates) Go
'head. It's not gonna hurt you. I'm normal
from the neck up. (He touches a strand
very gingerly.)

CEREZITA Well?

JUAN It's very . . . smooth.

CEREZITA Like silk, huh?

JUAN Yes.

CEREZITA Oughtabe. Yolie just gave it the
works. She studies all these beauty
magazines and tries out every new item
that hits the market. She's into "natural"
these days, which I'm very grateful for.
Over the last five years, Yolie experi-
mented in every fashion from beehives to
buzzcuts. It was fun for a while, until my
hair started falling out. And if my hair
doesn't look decent, I don't have much
going for me now, do I, Father?

JUAN (Pause) No, I guess . . . not.

CEREZITA So now my hair tends to smell
more like an overripe tropical garden
than anything else. You know, coconut
and mango juice shampoo, avocado
conditioners, et cetera.

JUAN I wouldn't know.

CEREZITA Now it just grows long and thick
like a beautiful dark curtain. Nice huh?

JUAN (Touching it again) Yes.

CEREZITA I like it, too . . . sometimes I just
spin my head around and around so I can

feel it brush past my cheeks. I imagine it's what those Arab women with the veils must feel like . . . all those soft cloths secretly caressing their bodies.

JUAN You think about that?

CEREZITA What, the Arab women? Give me a break, Padre. All I've got is this imagination.

JUAN Yes . . .

CEREZITA And a tongue.

JUAN A tongue?

CEREZITA Yeah, and mine's got the best definition I bet in the world, unless there's some other vegetable heads like me who survived this valley. Think about it, Padre. Imagine if your tongue and teeth and chin had to do the job of your hands . . . you know, *(She demonstrates)* turning pages, picking up stuff, scratching an itch, pointing. I mean your tongue alone would have to have some very serious definition. For me . . . well, it's my most faithful organ. Look it up. *(She sticks out her tongue, "pointing" to the dictionary on the shelf.)*

JUAN What?

CEREZITA Get the dictionary. *(Pointing)* Look up the word *tongue*.

JUAN But why?

CEREZITA You'll see. Check it out. *(JUAN gets the dictionary.)*

JUAN *(Reading)* "Ton. Tonality. Tone. Tongue. Latin: Lingua."

CEREZITA Spanish: Lengua.

JUAN "1 a: a fleshy movable process of the floor of the mouths of most vertebrates that bears sensory end organs and functions especially in taking and swallowing food."

CEREZITA *(Reciting from memory)* "2: The power of communication through speech." Your turn, Padre. *(He hesitates.)* Go on.

JUAN "3: The flesh of the tongue used as food."

CEREZITA *(With JUAN)* "4 a: Language, especially a spoken language."

JUAN "b: ecstatic usually unintelligible utterance accompanying religious excitation. c: the charismatic gift—"

CEREZITA *(Overlapping)* "Of ecstatic speech."

JUAN The gift of tongues!

CEREZITA "d: the cry of a hound in sight of game–used especially in the phrase," italicized . . . *(suggestively)* "to give tongue" *(She pants like the hound.)*

JUAN C'mon now.

CEREZITA Be a sport, Padre.

JUAN "Verb, 1 *archaic*: scold."

CEREZITA "2: to touch or lick with; to protect in a tongue."

JUAN "3: to articulate," parenthetically, "notes by" . . . *(He hesitates.)*

CEREZITA Yes? . . .

JUAN "By tonguing."

CEREZITA My brother Mario brought me a trumpet once, the old medieval kind. No fingering needed . . . just a good, strong tongue. "Tongue in cheek."

JUAN "Characterized by insincerity, irony, or whimsical exaggeration."

CEREZITA *(Provocatively)* "Tongue-lash."

JUAN "To chide or—"

CEREZITA Regañar.

JUAN "Tongueless."

CEREZITA "Lacking the power of speech."

JUAN "Mute. Tongue-tied—disinclined or" . . . *(He looks up at her.)*

CEREZITA "Unable to speak freely." *(Fade out.)*

Scene 9

The school grounds, McLaughlin Elementary. BONNIE enters carrying a lunch box. DON GILBERTO is pushing a broom. He wears a janitor's uniform which reads McLaughlin School District on back. BONNIE sits, opens her lunch box and takes out an apple. She watches him sweep for a moment.

BONNIE Don Gilberto, I dreamed Memo before he died.

DON GILBERTO You did?

BONNIE Yeah. I dreamed Memo alive playing on the merry-go-round like we used to before he got sick. He's in the middle of it, holding on real tight and I'm pushing the merry-go-round faster and faster. And then I see his face starts to get scared, so I try to stop the merry-go-round but I can't. I can't grab the bars. They just keep hitting my hands harder and harder and he's spinning around so fast that finally his face just turns into a blur. And then he disappears.

DON GILBERTO Just like that?

BONNIE Well, then I woke up. *(Pause)* Now when I go to sleep, I make a prayer so I don't dream about nobody.

DON GILBERTO What kind of prayer?

BONNIE Just one that asks God that . . .

when I'm sleeping, that he'll keep all the kids outta me. Maybe you make your dreams come true. Maybe you kill people that way.

DON GILBERTO *(Taking out a handkerchief from his back pocket and polishing the apple)* Sometimes when you're worried or scared about something, hija, your dreams draw pictures in your sleep to show you what the feelings look like.

BONNIE Like Memo blurring?

DON GILBERTO Sí. *(He hands her back the polished apple.)*

BONNIE I have to think about that, Don Gilberto.

DON GILBERTO That's all right. You think about it. *(He kisses the top of her head, goes back to sweeping.)*

BONNIE Look, Don Gilberto! It's the news lady!

(ANA PEREZ appears in front of the "cameras." AMPARO and a group of PROTES-TORS are approaching, including MARIO, JUAN, and YOLANDA. They are carrying placards reading "The School Board Lies!" "Save Our Children!" "Sin Agua No Tenemos Vida," etc. ANA PEREZ straightens her jacket, lightly brushes back her hair. She addresses the "camera.")

ANA PEREZ A crowd is beginning to form out here in front of the town of McLaughlin's elementary school. Mostly mothers and other neighbors have shown up this morning. There is no sign of school officials as of yet. Local residents are outraged by the school board's decision to refuse Arrowhead's offer of free drinking water for the schoolchildren. They believe local tap water, contaminated by pesticides, to be the chief cause of the high incidence of cancer among children in the area. They claim that the extensive spraying, especially aerial spraying, causes the toxic chemicals to seep into the public water system. The majority of residents are from a nearby housing tract of federally subsidized housing. It has been alleged that the housing was built on what was once a dump site for pesticides with the full knowledge of contractors. What we have here, Jack, appears to be a kind of 1980s Hispanic Love Canal.

(The PROTESTORS have arrived at the school grounds, led by AMPARO.)

DON GILBERTO *(With affection)* She's gonna get me fired, mi vieja.

AMPARO *(Under her breath, to* DON GILBERTO*)* I think I got the cold feet, Berto.

DON GILBERTO Pues, warm 'em up quick. You got all this gente here esperándote. *(She hesitates.)* ¡Adelante, mujer!

ANA PEREZ It looks like a local resident will be addressing the crowd.

(DON GILBERTO helps AMPARO up onto a bench. The crowd goes quiet. As the speech progresses, the PROTESTORS become more and more receptive, calling out in response.)

AMPARO *(Tentatively)* Our homes are no longer our homes. They have become prisons. When the water that pours from the sink gots to be boiled three times before it can pass your children's lips, what good is the faucet, the indoor plumbing, the toilet that flushes pink with disease? *(Gaining confidence)* We were better off when our padres hang some blankets from a tree and we slept under the pertection de las estrellas, because our roofs don' pertect us. A'least then, even if you had to dig a hole in the ground to do your biznis and wipe yourself with newspaper, you could still look up hasta los cielos and see God. But where is God now, amigos? ¿Y el diablo? El diablo hides between the pages of the papeles we sign that makes us afraid. The papeles they have no weight. ¡Ay! They could fly way en la brisa, they could burn hasta una ceniza with a simple household mecha. But our children are flesh and bone. They weigh mucho. You put them all together and they make hunerds and hunerds a pounds of Razita. *(Pause)* Yesterday, the school board refuse the gift of clean water for our chil'ren's already poisoned thoats. The board says, No, there's not'ing wrong with our water. We don' know for sure, it hasn' been prove. How much prove you need? How many babies' bodies pile all up on top of each other in the grave? *(Pause, coming down-stage)* Comadres, compadres. ¿Qué significa que the three things in life – el aire, el agua, y la tierra – que we always had enough of, even in our pueblitos en México, ya no tenemos? Sí, parece que tenemos all that we need. In the morning the air is cool y fresco, the ground stretches for miles, and all that the ranchero puts into it grows big and bright and the water pours from our faucets sin término. Pero, todo es mentira. Look into your children's faces. They tell you the truth. They are our future. Pero no tendremos ningún futuro si seguimos siendo víctimas.

(The PROTESTORS *come down into the audience, passing out pamphlets of information about the pesticide problem.* CEREZITA *has been looking out the window at the demonstration.* DOLORES *is sweeping, trying to ignore the sounds of the protest invading her house.)*

CEREZITA Mira, 'amá. They're all going house to house, giving out pamphlets. Father Juanito's there and Don Gilberto. They even got the news cameras.

DOLORES Get your face out of the window.

CEREZITA Nobody's looking over here.

DOLORES Quítate de allí, te digo. *(She disengages* CEREZITA's *raite and moves her away from the window.)*

CEREZITA Ah, 'amá!

DOLORES Pues, you don't know who could be out there. All this protesta is bringing the guns down from the sky.

CEREZITA I just wanted to see.

DOLORES You don't need to see. *(She gets down on her hands and knees and begins picking up various books and newspapers that* CEREZITA *has left around the floor.)* Mira todos los libros que tienes. One a these days your brain's gointu explode por tantas palabras.

CEREZITA Wha' else am I supposed to do?

DOLORES You're suppose to do nothing. I'm suppose to do everything.

CEREZITA Martyrs don't survive, 'amá.

DOLORES Your brother teaches you tha' kina talk. Don' get smart with me.

CEREZITA I am smart.

DOLORES Maybe you read a lot, but tha' doesn' mean you know about life. You think you find life in a book?

CEREZITA No, I don't think I find life in a book. *(She tosses her hair around, trying to feel it against her cheeks.)*

DOLORES It's a pig's pen around here, you leave all your junk laying around . . . candy wrappers, the little crumbs from the erasers. *(On her hands and knees, picking at the rug)* What do you do with them? Chew them?

CEREZITA Erase.

DOLORES Mentirosa. I seen you chew them.

CEREZITA Well, sometimes . . . when I'm thinking.

DOLORES Well, stop it. It makes a big mess. I can' get those tiny pieces out of l'alfombra. *(*CEREZITA *lays her face down on the raite, rubs it back and forth, trying to feel her hair against her face.* DOLORES *finds an open book on the floor)* ¿Qué's esto? Cere?

CEREZITA Huh? . . . Nothing. It's just one of Mario's old anatomy books.

DOLORES Es cochino. Tha's what it is? I thought he give you the books to study about the sick peepo. This is not the sick peepo.

CEREZITA God, Mom, it's just the body.

DOLORES So, what bizniz you got with the body? This jus' puts thoughts in your head. *(She flips through the book.)* ¿Qué tiene que ver una señorita with this kind of pictures? *(Slams it shut)* I should call in the father.

CEREZITA Father Juan?

DOLORES Jus' cuz you don' got a body doesn' mean you can't sin. The biggest sins are in the mind.

CEREZITA Oh God.

DOLORES Tu eres una inocente. That's how God wanted it. There's a reason he made you like this. You're old enough now . . .

CEREZITA I'm old enough now to go out!

DOLORES Pues vete. *(She engages* CEREZITA's *wheels, puts the chin piece in place.)* You think you're so tough, go on. But we'll see how you feel the first time some stranger looks at you with cruel eyes.

*(*DOLORES *goes to the table. After a pause,* CEREZITA *crosses to her.)*

CEREZITA Give me a chance, 'amá. If nobody ever sees me, how will I know how I look? How will I know if I scare them or make them mad or . . . move them? If people could see me, 'amá, things would change.

DOLORES No, hija. Dios es mi testigo. I'll never let nobody look at my baby that way.

*(*DOLORES *caresses her,* CEREZITA's *face is rigid as the lights crossfade to* MARIO *and* JUAN *sitting on a park bench.)*

JUAN Why didn't you bring Cerezita out to this?

MARIO My mom. She protects her.

JUAN From, what?

MARIO Ridicule. The world.

JUAN She wanted to be here.

MARIO You bring her out, then. Maybe Lola would let you. You're God on earth, after all. You're all the protection she'd ever need.

JUAN She needs you.

MARIO Oh, Padre, they all need me, but I got other plans.

JUAN Like what?

MARIO Getting out. Finishing school. Having a life, One, life, not two.

JUAN Two?

MARIO You don't know what it's like gowing up in this valley.

JUAN I was born in Sanger, Mario.

MARIO Yeah? Don't show.

JUAN My family left when I was about twelve.

MARIO To LA, right?

JUAN Right.

MARIO At least you got out. *(Pause)* When I was in high school, I used to sit out there in those fields, smoking, watching the cars go by on 99. I'd think about the driver, having somewhere to go. His foot pressed to the floorboard, cruisin'. He was always a gringo. And he'd have one arm draped over the steering wheel and the other around the back of the seat and it'd never occur to him that anybody lived there between those big checkerboard plots of tomatoes, strawberries, artichokes, brussels sprouts, and . . .

JUAN Grapes.

MARIO Hundreds of miles of grapes. He'd be headed home to his woman and TV set and sleeping kids tucked into clean sheets and he'd have a wad of bills in his pocket and he'd think he'd live forever. But I'm twenty-five and stuck here in this valley and I know I won't.

JUAN But twenty-five's so young, Mario.

MARIO I get high, Padre. I smoke and snort and suck up anything and anyone that will have me. Those are the facts. *(A car horn sounds from the street.* MARIO *jumps to his feet. He motions to the driver.)* Why did you come back, Father? All you'd need is a nice Buick, a full tank of gas and you'd be indistinguishable on that highway. Just don't stop to pick me up. Your type can destroy me.

(MARIO runs off. JUAN watches the car drive away. The lights fade to black.)

Scene 10

JUAN *fills up a glass of water from the dispenser.*

JUAN Some of the union people were at the rally. They were trying to enlist people to join in the fast with them. I agreed.

CEREZITA That's good. People like to see priests and celebrities sacrificing. I'd do it, too, if anyone would notice me. The trick is to be noticed.

JUAN Six months ago, that's the very thing that brought me here . . . to the Valley.

CEREZITA What?

JUAN The union's fast. I saw this newspaper photo of Cesar Chávez. He had just finished a thirty-three-day fast. He looked like a damn saint, a veritable Ghandi. Even the number was holy. Thirty-three.

CEREZITA The age of Christ's death.

JUAN So I came home. I came home to the valley that gave birth to me. Maybe as a priest it's vanity to believe you can have a home. The whole church is supposed to be your family, your community, but I can't pretend I don't get lonely.

CEREZITA Why did you become a priest, Father Juan?

JUAN Too many years as an altar boy. *(He takes a drink of water.)* And because of the fabric.

CEREZITA The fabric?

JUAN Yes. Literally, the cloth itself drew me to be a "man of the cloth." The vestments, the priest's body aleep underneath that cloth, the heavy weight of it tranquilizing him.

CEREZITA Will you always be a priest, Father Juan?

JUAN Yes. There's no choice in the matter. Once ordained, you've given up volition in that sense. The priesthood is an indelible mark. You are bruised by it, not violently, but its presence is always felt. A slow dull ache, a slight discoloration in the skin . . .

CEREZITA A purple-red spot between the eyes, the size of a small stone.

JUAN I wish I had a third eye, Cere.

CEREZITA But that's your job, isn't it, Father, to make people see? The "theology of liberation." It's a beautiful term. The spiritual practice of freedom. On earth. Do you practice what you preach, Father?

JUAN It's the people that are to be liberated, not the priests. We're still caught in the Middle Ages somewhere, battling our internal doubts Spanish Inquisition-style. *(Pause)* I always wanted that kind of sixteenth-century martyr's death. To die nobly and misunderstood, to be exonerated centuries later by a world that was finally ready for me.

CEREZITA *(Smiling)* You've been reading too much Lorca.

JUAN He's my hero.

(Fade out.)

Scene 11

AMPARO *and* DOLORES *return home from work, wearing white uniforms. They are a little tipsy, having stopped off at the local bar for a few beers first. They are singing a ranchera. They come into the house and pull out a few chairs onto the porch.* BONNIE *rides up on a bicycle. Nueva canción music can be heard coming from the radio indoors.*

AMPARO I dunno how much longer I could aguantar working in tha' place anyway. I dunno wha's worser, the bending to pick en los files or standing on your feet all day in the same damn spot. Me 'stoy poniendo vieja. *(They sit down in front of the house, take off their shoes.)* Mira los bunions. *(BONNIE joins them, AMPARO shows her her feet.)* You see how the toes all bunch up there on top of each other? . . . Mi viejo usetu tell me I had beautiful feet. Beautiful. Like a movie star. Ya no.

BONNIE You want me to rub 'em, Doña Amparo?

AMPARO ¿Qué, mija?

BONNIE Your feet. You want me to rub 'em for you?

AMPARO Pues, okay!

DOLORES ¡Ay! The royal treament. *(BONNIE massages AMPARO's feet.)*

AMPARO Your feet get crooked when you gottu squeeze 'em into zapatos que take all the blood from you. They don' tell you cuando eras una chamaca tha' you suffer the rest a your life for the chooz you wear at sixteen. ¿Qué no?

DOLORES Tha's for darn chure.

AMPARO Tha's nice, hija. La verdad es que siempre he sido pura ranchera. If I had my way, I'd go barefoot. Ahora these

patas don' fit into not'ing but the tenny shoes.

DOLORES *(Rolling down her stockings)* What I got is the varicose venas. It's from the cement floors. They squeeze you from the soles up and then el cansancio press you from the neck down. In between, your venas jus' pop out.

BONNIE Ouch!

AMPARO Pinche jale. Who needs it? *(YOLANDA comes out onto the porch. She wears rubber gloves, stained with black hair dye.)*

YOLANDA I thought I heard you out here.

DOLORES You got a customer, mija?

YOLANDA Señora Reyes. She's under the dryer.

AMPARO What color she want this time?

YOLANDA Midnight blue.

AMPARO Ya no quiere ser güera.

YOLANDA I think she's given up . . . tired of fighting the roots.

DOLORES Bonnie, go get us a coupla beers from the refrigerador, eh?

BONNIE Okay, Doña, Lola. *(She goes to get the beer.)*

DOLORES ¿Quieres una, mija?

YOLANDA No. Looks like you two have already had a few.

DOLORES Una, nomás.

AMPARO 'Stamos celebrando.

YOLANDA What?

DOLORES The varicose venas y los bunions.

AMPARO They kicked me from the job. hija. *(DOLORES gestures to YOLANDA not to ask.)*

YOLANDA But . . . why?

AMPARO They heard about the protesta. It affect "the workers' morale," me dijeron, que I set a bad example.

YOLANDA They fired you for speaking at a rally?

AMPARO Pues, también I was giving out los panfletos from the union.

DOLORES I tole her not to.

YOLANDA I can't believe they fired you.

AMPARO Good thing I got the green card or right now I be on the bus back to Coahuila. *(BONNIE comes out with the beers, passes them to DOLORES and AMPARO.)*

DOLORES Gracias, mija.

BONNIE Here you go, Doña Amparo.

AMPARO Thank you, chula.

(The radio music is suddenly interrupted by a news break.)

RADIO VOICE This is KKCF in Fresno. News brief. San Salvador. UPI reports that at 6 a.m. this morning six Jesuit priests, along with their housekeeper and her daughter, were found brutally murdered. The priests, from the Central American University, were outspoken opponents to the ruling rightist ARENA party.

DOLORES Cere! ¡Baja la radio! *(To the women)* We got enough bad news today without hearing about the rest a the world también. *(The volume lowers, then fades out.)* If she can't be in the world, she brings it into the house and we all gottu know about it. First, it's her brother and now it's the priest. He got her all metida en cosas she got no biznis knowing about.

AMPARO How long you think you can shelter her from the suffering of the world, Lola? *(DOLORES doesn't respond, puts her shoes back on.)*

DOLORES *(To YOLANDA)* Did your brother come home?

YOLANDA No. What're you gonna do now without a job, Doña Amparo?

AMPARO Pues, first thing I put that husband of mine on a diet. *(DOLORES gets up, looks down the street.)* He still got a job, mija. We'll make it all right. But if they wannu shut me up, they thinking of a purty good way to do it.

DOLORES *(To YOLANDA)* Did he call?

YOLANDA Who?

DOLORES Tu hermano.

YOLANDA Yeah, he said he's leaving on Saturday. He's already packed, 'amá.

DOLORES Fine. I'm tired of worrying for him. This way, if you don' know nothing, you got nothing to worry about.

YOLANDA He said if you wanted he'd come by Friday night.

DOLORES Díle que no thank you. I don' wan' no good-byes. I had enough good-byes already in my life.

AMPARO Pues, you tell mi querido ahijado he better not move nowhere without saying good-bye to his padrinos. It would break his Nino's heart.

YOLANDA I'll tell him, Doña Amparo. *(YOLANDA goes back inside to check on Señora Reyes. Crossfade to JUAN, who is walking to the Valle home, books stuffed under one arm. He reads from a newspaper article.)*

JUAN They blasted their brains out in their sleep! Just like that! *(DON GILBERTO enters carrying a lunch pail, returning home from work.)*

DON GILBERTO ¿Qué le pasa, Padre? It looks like you saw one of those holy ghosts of yours.

JUAN 'Scuze me?

DON GILBERTO Read some bad news, Father?

JUAN Yes. *(He shows DON GILBERTO the article.)*

DON GILBERTO Did you know the guys?

JUAN No, but they were Jesuits, my order.

DON GILBERTO You'd think a priest in a Catholic country couldn't get shot up in his pajamas.

JUAN But they were intellectuals.

DON GILBERTO That didn't seem to matter too much to the bullets, Padre. *(He pats JUAN on the shoulder, continues on home. YOLANDA comes out onto the porch.)*

DOLORES ¿Y la Señora Reyes?

YOLANDA She fell asleep under the dryer.

CEREZITA I hope she like el cabello frito.

BONNIE Fried hair?

AMPARO Un estilo nuevo, mija. *(The laughter of the women calls JUAN's attention. He crosses to them.)*

DOLORES Oh, hello, Father.

JUAN Buenas tardes.

YOLANDA Visiting the sick again, Padre?

JUAN No. Yes . . . I mean I have some books for Cerezita. *(To DOLORES)* If that's all right with you, señora?

DOLORES Go 'head. What else she gottu do, la pobre. *(He starts to go inside)* Oh, Father . . . *(He stops at the door.)* Can you come over to the house Friday night? Mi hijo is moving to San Francisco and we gointu have a little get-together, nothing fancy, just some enchiladas rojas. Son Mario's fav'rit.

JUAN Of course, I'd love to . . . ¿Con su permiso?

DOLORES Pásale. Pásale. *(He goes inside. To AMPARO)* And bring tu viejo. This way he gets some food in his estómago antes que you start to starve him to death.

YOLANDA ¡Orale! ¡Una pachanga!

DOLORES I dint say nothing about una pachanga.

YOLANDA You know what happens when Don Gilberto comes – it's party time!

DON GILBERTO Pues, it'll be nice to have some men in the house for a change.

AMPARO   And tha' priest, he's plenty a
man.

YOLANDA   Yeah, I don't trust him.

DOLORES   He means well, hija.

AMPARO   Pero you know wha' they say,
Lola. A man is a man first, no matter
wha' he is. If he's a priest or an uncle or
a brother, no importa.

THE WOMEN   *(To* BONNIE*)* ¡Un hombre es
un hombre!
(They laugh. The lights fade out.)

Scene 12

*Música Norteña. At rise, a pachanga in full
swing. The records are spinning, the beer and
tequila are flowing.* JUAN *sits at the kitchen
table watching* MARIO *and* AMPARO *dance.*
CEREZITA *is just finishing a game of Lotería
with* BONNIE. DON GILBERTO *is playing la
guitarra, while* DOLORES *sits on the couch,
embroidering a dishcloth.* YOLANDA *sits next
to her, holding the baby. After a few minutes,*
DON GILBERTO, *who's pretty well plastered,
puts his guitar down and pours himself
another beer.*

DON GILBERTO   ¿Sabe qué, Padre? I love
that muchacho. He's lo máximo. You
wanna know the truth, Padre? That boy's
not just my godson, he's my real son.
That's right, mi propio hijo cuz I love him
that much. Right, hijo?

MARIO   That's right, Nino.

DON GILBERTO   An' he's getting outta this
pinche valle.

DOLORES   Compadre!

DON GILBERTO   I can talk like that with
you. ¿No, Padre? You're off duty right
now.

JUAN   Sure you can.

DON GILBERTO   That's right. God's back
there in the church. The only men we
got at this table are hombres de carne y
hueso. Vieja!

AMPARO   ¿Qué?

DOLORES   *(Intervening)* Wha' chu handsome
men wan' here?

DON GILBERTO   Tenemos sed, comadre.

DOLORES   Coming right up.
*(*AMPARO *helps* DOLORES *with the drinks,
preparing the tequila, salt and lemon. They
take a few shots themselves.* MARIO *joins
the men at the table.)*

DON GILBERTO   She's got a heart of gold,
that woman. And she loves her kids,

¿sabe? There aint nothin' she wouldn't do
for her kids. Look-it Cerezita over there.
*(*CEREZITA *is radiant.)* 'Sta contenta
because she knows she got a family, a
mother, that loves her. It's hard, Padre . . .
You listenin' to me, Padre?

JUAN   *(Pulling his gaze from* CEREZITA*)* . . .
Yes.

DON GILBERTO   You can imagine how hard
it's been for Dolores, but she did it, and
alone. My compadre . . . bueno, it's hard
to even call him that now after leaving
his family like he did. When a man
leaves his wife alone to raise his kids,
well to me that no longer qualifies him to
be a man. A big macho, maybe. Maybe
he can fool las viejas, act like que tiene
huevos. But that's the easy part, jumping
in and out of the sack. A real man tiene
brazos. Nos llaman braceros because we
work and love with our arms. Because we
ain't afraid to lift a sack of potatoes, to
defend our children, to put our arms
around la waifa at night. This family,
they've suffered a lot, Padre. When a
father leaves, it's like cutting off the arms
of the family. *(Hugging* MARIO*)* Even this
guy. He had a lot on his shoulders.
¡Chihuahua! I usetu remember this little
mocoso coming home from school all the
time with his nose all bloody. He wasn' a
fighter. But after so many times, finally,
Dolores tells me, "Compadre, tienes que
hacer algo." *(He brings* MARIO *to his feet,
starts to box with him.)* So, I put the gloves
on him and showed him my famous
"apricot." *(*DON GILBERTO *winds up, lets
out a wild "uppercut" in the air and ends up
on his butt. They all rush to him.)* And
they never messed with him again. Right,
hijo?

MARIO   Right.

DON GILBERTO   ¡Eso!

JUAN   So, all your kids are grown, Don
Gilberto?

DON GILBERTO   Well, I guess that's why la
vieja and me, we kina adopt these guys.
We couldn't have no children. Amparo's a
good woman, she wanted kids bad! But it
was me. She never tells nobody cuz she
thinks I get ashamed. But it's biology,
right, Padre? Mi madre, she had two of
us, see. And my cuate, well it seems he
just hogged up all the jugo, if you know
what I mean. He got a pile of kids, nietos
too. *(He takes another shot.)* ¿Y tú, Padre?

What's your excuse?

JUAN ... I'm a priest.

DON GILBERTO That's no excuse! *(Busting up)* When los conquistadores come to America with their priests, half the Mexican population got fathers for fathers! *(Busting up again)*

JUAN *(Embarrassed)* I don't know. You just make choices, ... I guess.

DON GILBERTO Pues, sometimes you don't get to choose. But that just teaches you que you gotta make familia any way you can.

CEREZITA Ya, viejo. You gointu put the father to sleep con tanta plática. Mira, the father's glass is almost empty.

DON GILBERTO Pues, fill it up then.

DOLORES Aquí lo tengo ya. *(She carries a tray with drinks.)*

DON GILBERTO ¡Tequila! ¡Sí! ¡Celebremos! You watch, mi ahijado's gointu go to the big university. He's gointu be a doctor someday and cure all the sickness que tiene nuestra raza. Right, mijo?

MARIO That's right, Nino.

DON GILBERTO Pues, lez drink to that. *(Toasting)* ¡Salud! *(They all raise their glasses.)*

JUAN Amor, dinero.

MARIO Y tiempo para gozarlos.

DON GILBERTO ¡Eso! *(He picks up the guitar again and the family joins in singing "Volver".)*
"Y volver, volver, volver
a tus brazos otra vez.
Llegaré hasta donde 'stés.
Yo sé perder, yo sé perder.
Quiero volver, volver, volver."
(MARIO rises, lights a cigarette, and steps out onto the porch. DOLORES' eyes follow him.)

JUAN *(To DOLORES)* May I have this dance?

DOLORES You don' dance to "Volver," Padre. You cry.

JUAN May I have this cry?

DOLORES Bueno, I think this one, pues ... it's all mine.
(Crossfade to MARIO smoking on the porch. He watches the sky as the fog begins to roll in. Sound of crop duster overhead. He waves back at it sarcastically. DOLORES comes out onto the porch.)

DOLORES Why they spraying at night now?

MARIO Nobody sees them that way. Nobody that matters anyway.

DOLORES I'm tired of it. I wish we were all going away.

MARIO I'm sorry.

DOLORES Really?

MARIO Yes.

DOLORES But it doesn't stop you from leaving us.

MARIO I want a future, 'amá.

DOLORES The school is not why you're going. It's something else.

MARIO What?

DOLORES Your leaving with a secret.

MARIO It's no secret, 'amá. You're the only one that doesn't want to see it.

DOLORES I'm not talking about that. I know already for a long time. You think I dint know since the time you was little? How you want to do everthing like Yolie. Play with her dolls, put on her dresses. "Jus' pertend," you say, "jus' pertend, mami." Pertend, nada. Me chocó the first time I seen your hands digging into Yolie's purse like they belong there. *(Grabbing his hands)* Look at your hands, hijo. Son las manos de tu padre, las manos de un obrero. Why you wannu make yourself como una mujer? Why you wannu do this to the peepo who love you?

MARIO *(Pulling his hands away.)* Who loves me, 'amá?

DOLORES Tienes familia.

MARIO Family you don't take to bed.

DOLORES You think those men who put their arms around you in the night are gointu be there to take care of you in the morning?

MARIO No.

DOLORES Necesitas familia, hijo. What you do fuera del matrimonio is your own biznis. You could have familia. Eres hombre. You don' gottu be alone, not like Yolie. Who's gointu want her con una niña already?

MARIO I can't do that, 'amá. I can't put my body one place and my heart another. I'm not my father.

DOLORES He loved us, hijo.

MARIO He loved his women, too.

DOLORES Can't you forget that? You hold that in your heart, it's gointu poison you.

MARIO Can you? We've always been lonely, 'amá. You and me waiting for someone to come along and just talk to us with a little bit of kindness, to tell us how fine and pretty we are, to lie to our face.

DOLORES Me das asco.

MARIO Why? Because I remind you of you. What love did you ever get from my dad? He had a sweet mouth, that's all. A syrupy tongue that every time he dragged himself home, could always talk you back into loving him. That's not the kind of man I want to be.

DOLORES You'd rather suffer like a woman instead?

MARIO No.

DOLORES God made you a man and you throw it away. You lower yourself into half a man.

MARIO I don't want to fight, 'amá. I'm leaving in the morning. Give me your blessing. Send me on my way with the sign of the cross and a mother's love.

DOLORES No puedo.

MARIO You don't have to approve of it, 'amá.

DOLORES No puedo. Peepo like you are dying. They got tha' sickness. How can I give mi bendición para una vida que te va a matar. God makes this sickness to show peepo it's wrong what they do. Díme que te vas a cambiar y te doy mi bendición. Tu eres el único macho. I want you to live.

MARIO I want to live, too. I can't make you see that. Your god's doing all the seeing for you. (He takes off down the street.)

Scene 13

The party is over. CEREZITA *is looking out the window.* DON GILBERTO *is asleep in the chair.* AMPARO *and* JUAN *are just finishing the dishes.* YOLANDA *has retired with the baby.* BONNIE *is asleep on the couch.*

CEREZITA Mario won't return to us. He will grow ill like his brother and we will ignore this brother, this son, this child of ours who failed in his manly destiny.

(JUAN puts the last of the dishes away.)

AMPARO Gracias, Father. But don't tell Dolores I let you help me. She kill me. ¡Imagínese! A priest doing the dishes!

JUAN I enjoyed it.

AMPARO That's coz you don't haftu do it every day. (She goes over to BONNIE, awakens her.) C'mon, mija. Ya nos vamos.

BONNIE Okay.

AMPARO Bueno, I guess I better try to get this old man out of here.

JUAN You need help?

AMPARO No, I'm usetu it. (She goes to DON GILBERTO and nudges him awake.)

DON GILBERTO (Startled) Soñé contigo, vieja. You had un montón de chamacos mamando tu pecho.

AMPARO (Helping him to his feet) The only baby I got is right here.

DON GILBERTO I was so proud!

AMPARO You tell Dolores I talk to her in the morning.

JUAN Sure.

AMPARO (To CEREZITA) Good night, mija.

CEREZITA Good night, Doña Amparo . . . Don Gilberto. (DON GILBERTO throws her a kiss.)

BONNIE 'Night, Cere.

CEREZITA 'Night, mija.

(They exit. JUAN comes up behind CEREZITA. He stares out the window.)

JUAN There's nothing to see. The fog's barely a foot from the window.

CEREZITA Sometimes I wish it would swallow the whole house up. I don't blame Mario for leaving. I'd leave if I could.

JUAN You're gonna miss him, aren't you?

CEREZITA There's nothing for him here. No Mayan gods. Nothing.

JUAN (Awkwardly) Well, I guess I better go, too. Do you . . . need something before I leave?

CEREZITA Yeah, just put a towel over my cage like the canaries. Martyrs don't survive.

JUAN Cere, I . . .

CEREZITA I want out, Father! Out into that street! And I will not have time for anybody who can't help me.

(She turns her face away. JUAN hesitates for a moment, then leaves.)

JUAN (Passing DOLORES coming back into the yard). Buenas noches, señora. Gracias.

DOLORES Buenas noches, Padre.

(JUAN starts to say more, but she has already started toward the house. He exits. Moments later, the sound of the crop duster passes overhead again. DOLORES follows the sound.)

Why don't you just drop a bomb, cabrones! It'd be faster that way!

(The lights fade to black.)

Act II

Scene 1

Several months later, DOLORES *is sneaking around the outside of the front of the house. Crouching down behind a bush, she peeks into the windows, trying not to be seen.* JUAN *is passing by. He is saying prayers from his breviary, his lips moving silently.*

JUAN *(Nearly bumping into her)* Señora Valle.

DOLORES ¡Ay, Padre! Me asustó.

JUAN ¿Qué hace, señora?

DOLORES *(Conspiratorially)* I'm looking through the windows.

JUAN But . . . why?

DOLORES To know, Father.

JUAN To know what?

DOLORES To know what you can see inside the house at night. The peepo going by can see through the windows. ¿Qué vió, Padre, when you were coming up the street?

JUAN No sé. I wasn't paying attention.

DOLORES Next time, Father, you pay attention, eh? So you can tell me from how far away you can see wha's going on inside the house.

JUAN Certainly, I . . .

DOLORES Cere don' wan' the shades down. She wants to look at the street lamps, she say.

JUAN Es todo lo que tiene, Señora Valle.

DOLORES Sí, pero anybody que pasa por aquí can see we don' got no men in the house. Mire, Father. *(Indicates the window.* JUAN *crouches down next to her.)* Can you tell Cere is sick from here?

JUAN What do you mean?

DOLORES ¡Que no tiene cuerpo!

JUAN No, no se ve.

DOLORES It looks like she could just be sentada, no?

JUAN Sí, sentada or stooping behind something.

DOLORES Bueno, tha's all I needed to know. Gracias, Padre.

JUAN Buenas noches.

DOLORES Buenas noches.

*(*JUAN *continues on with his prayers,* DOLORES *goes inside.* YOLANDA *sits near the baby's crib.* CEREZITA *is reading.)*

YOLANDA I can't get her to feed. She keeps pulling her face away.

DOLORES Pues, no tiene hambre.

YOLANDA Yesterday was the same. Look. She just sleeps. I have to wake her up to feed her.

DOLORES ¿Tiene calentura?

YOLANDA A little. I took her temperature about an hour ago.

DOLORES ¿Y que te dijeron en la clínica?

YOLANDA Nothing much. They say maybe there's something wrong with my milk. They gave me formula. She doesn't want that either.

DOLORES A ver . . . *(Goes over to the baby, checks for a temperature)* Todavía tiene un poco de calentura. Get some cold toallitas y pónselas en la frente. Tal vez that'll bring her fiebre down.

YOLANDA I'm scared she's really sick, 'amá.

DOLORES No pienses así. Traele la toallita. *(*YOLANDA *goes to get the wet cloth, applies it to the baby's forehead.* DOLORES *serves up sopa from the stove for* CEREZITA, *puts a napkin under her chin, begins spooning the food into her mouth.)* Así me rechazabas when you was a baby. All of a sudden, you dint wan' the chichi no more.

CEREZITA That was a long time ago, 'amá.

DOLORES But a mother never forgets those things . . . cuando su bebé turns her face away like that.

(She continues feeding CEREZITA, *periodically wiping her mouth.* AMPARO *enters carrying a large, rolled-up chart.)*

AMPARO I'm jus' in time for dinner, eh?

DOLORES Sí, comadre. Ya 'stá caliente la cena.

AMPARO No, no. I'm just kidding. Ya comí. *(Going to the baby)* Ahora ¿cómo está?

YOLANDA Igual.

AMPARO I'm sorry, hija. *(Beat)* Vente. Quiero enseñarles algo.

YOLANDA ¿Qué?

AMPARO Hice un mapa. *(She unrolls the chart onto the table.)* A chart of all the houses en la vecindad que tiene gente con the health problems.

YOLANDA Let me see.

AMPARO Miren, the red dots mean those houses got someone with cancer. Estos puntos azules donde tienen tumores. Los green ones son para birth defects y los amarillos, the miscarriages.

YOLANDA What are all these orange dots?

AMPARO Bueno, smaller problems como

problems del estómago, las ronchas, cosas así.

YOLANDA Cheezus, it's the whole damn neighborhood.

CEREZITA Where's our house?

AMPARO Aquí donde están the orange dot and the green dot.

CEREZITA That's me, the green dot.

YOLANDA (Lightly) You put us on the map, Cere.

CEREZITA That's right. (They laugh)

DOLORES Go 'head, make the jokes. (To AMPARO) ¿Por qué traes estas cosas a mi casa?

AMPARO Bueno, I—

DOLORES I got one baby que eighteen years later I still got to feed and clean and wipe, que no tiene ni la capacidad to put a spoon a food in her mouth. I got a grandchild si no 'stá llorando por las ronchas, she sleeps all day sin ganas de comer, and I got a son that might as well be dead coz almost a year go by and I don' know nothing about him. So, I don' need a chart to tell me que tengo problemas.

AMPARO I'm not trying to tell you about your problems, comadre. I'm trying to tell you que no 'stás sola.

DOLORES I am alone and I'm not gointu hold out my hand como una mendiga a nadie.

AMPARO No one's going begging. It's not begging to make the government pay for what we got coming to us.

YOLANDA We need help, 'amá.

DOLORES Vete. Take tu comunismo someplace else.

AMPARO Ay, Lola, me das vergüenza. Soy tu comadre. Don' make me into a stranger.

DOLORES Pues ya no te reconozco. You change since they put your picture in the papers and on the TV. I think you like it.

YOLANDA That's not fair, 'amá.

AMPARO No, tiene razón tu madre. It does give me somet'ing. It makes me feel good to watch peepo que no tiene ni educación ni sus papeles, show the guts to fight para sus niños.

DOLORES ¿Qué sabes tú? No tienes niños.

YOLANDA 'Amá. (The baby cries. YOLANDA starts toward it, but DOLORES intercepts.)

DOLORES This is my work. (Patting the infant. The cries subside.) When you got a baby, when you feel that baby come out entre las piernas, nothing is the same after that. You are chain to that baby. It doesn' matter how old they get or how far away they go, son tus hijos and they always take a piece of you with them. So you walk around full of holes from all the places they take from you. All the times you worry for them – where they are, who they with, what they doing. All the times you see them suffer on their faces and your hands are tied down from helping them. Como se puede sentir una mujer whole and strong como quieres tú with so many empty places in her body? El Dios es el único que nos llena. Not you and not your gov'ment. (She goes to AMPARO, grabs the chart from her.) This is the las' time I'm gointu say it, I don' wan' this biznis in my house.

(DOLORES throws the chart out the door and goes back to feeding CEREZITA, shoving the food into her mouth. AMPARO leaves in silence. Fade out.)

Scene 2

Lights rise on front room. CEREZITA is watching BONNIE play. She is constructing a coffin out of a small shoe box. DOLORES sits on the sofa, softly murmuring the rosary.

BONNIE We knew she wouldn't make it. The cancer got her.

CEREZITA How did you know?

BONNIE She bled through all her openings: her mouth, her ears, her nose . . . even through her pee hole, she bled. It was outta control.

CEREZITA What are you doing now?

BONNIE I gotta bury her. I'm making her coffin.

CEREZITA The shoe box is her coffin?

BONNIE Yeah, but I'm making it real purty inside. I got some valentine cards in there and some of Yolie's ribbon for her hair. See, look. (She shows CEREZITA the box.)

CEREZITA Yeah, Rosie will be nice and cozy in there.

(YOLANDA enters with an overnight bag. She stops at the door, riveted by BONNIE's words.)

BONNIE Lina's gonna die too, just like this. When they send the children to the hospital, they never come back. They keep 'em in the hospital bed until they put 'em in a box. Then they'll put dirt

over her face. When she wakes up, she won't be able to breathe cuz the dirt will be in her nose and her mouth. (BONNIE *shows the box to* YOLANDA *as a kind of offering.*) Look, Yolie.
(Horrified, YOLANDA *goes into the kitchen, pours herself a shot of tequila and sits at the table.* DOLORES *goes to her.)*

DOLORES I know what you're feeling. I know what it feels like to have a sick baby. When Cerezita come out of me, I dint even wannu look at her, I tole the doctors to put a blanket over her head to suffocate her, but she scream and scream so loud, the doctors couldn' do it. They tole me un grito así means the baby wants to live with all its heart and soul.

YOLANDA Evalina's dying, 'amá. My baby's dying.

DOLORES No hables así. You don' know tha'!

YOLANDA I know it's a tumor. I know it's malignant. I know what that means.

DOLORES It means you gottu pray to God. Fíjate. Cerezita es un milagro. Every day that she lives, it's prove que el Dios does not forget us.

YOLANDA He's forgotten you and me and everybody else in this goddamn valley. *(Sound of low-flying helicopter suddenly fills the air. Searchlights flood the kitchen windows.* YOLANDA *rushes to the front door, swings it open, runs outside.)* Take me! You mutherfuckers!

DOLORES *(Going after her)* Yolie! No, they'll see you! Mija! *(*YOLANDA *is ablaze with light. Chopper sounds grow nearer.)*

YOLANDA *(Shouting into the sky)* C'mon, you sonavabitches! Take me! C'mon! Here I am! Look it! Shoot me you mutherfuckers! Kill me!

DOLORES *(Grabbing her)* No, mija! Come back in. (DOLORES *and* YOLANDA *fall to the ground together weeping as the chopper retreats.)*

YOLANDA Don't you see, 'amá? I gotta find her killer. Put a face to him, a name, track him down and make him suffer the way we suffer. I want to kill him, 'amá. I want to kill some . . . goddamn body!

DOLORES *(Stroking her)* Sí, mija. Sí. Ya lo sé, hija. I know.
*(*DOLORES *helps her daughter to her feet and brings her back into the house. The lights fade to black.)*

Scene 3

Lights rise to reveal a political demonstration. ANA PEREZ, *in an overcoat and scarf, standing before the "cameras" with a microphone. In the distance, the* PROTESTORS *are approaching, the* MOTHERS *wearing white bandanas. Their expressions are heavy with the faces of the dying and the memory of the already dead. The* PROTESTORS *carry signs reading "Boycott Grapes," "No Compre Uvas," etc. One child holds up a sign saying "Quiero Vivir!" and another, "I Want to Live!" The red-and-black Union of Campesino flags can be seen above their heads.* DON GILBERTO *and* JUAN *are among the protestors, as are* BONNIE *and the* CHILDREN. *A drum beats slowly.*

ANA PEREZ It's a frostbitten morning here in Sacramento, Jack, but that hasn't discouraged the Mothers and Friends of McLaughlin from making the long trek up here from their home at the southern-most end of the San Joaquin Valley.

PROTESTORS *(Chanting)* "¡El pueblo unido jamás será vencido!" *(They continue to the beat of the drum.)*

ANA PEREZ The mothers' demands are quite concrete. They believe that the federal government should pay for their families' relocation to an environmentally safe community, since federal moneys subsidized the building of their housing tract. They further demand that the well which provides tap water for the area be shut down and never again be used for drinking water. And finally they urge the governor to see to the establishment of a free health clinic for affected families and to monitor the growing incidence of cancer in the region. *(The* PROTESTORS *begin to move downstage. They stand shoulder to shoulder.)* Amparo Manríquez, the founder of Mothers for McLaughlin, has approached the capitol steps. I understand they have prepared some kind of statement.
(As AMPARO *steps forward, she holds up a picture of a dead child. Each of the* MOTHERS *follows in the same manner.)*

AMPARO Sandy Pérez. Died August 15, 1982. Ailment: acute leukemia. Age 9.

MOTHER Frankie Gonzales. Died March 16, 1986. Ailment: bone cancer. Age 10.

MOTHER Johnny Rodríguez. Died July 10,

1987. Ailment: adrenal gland tumor. Age 5.

MOTHER Rosalinda Lorta. Died June 5, 1980. Ailment: chest muscle tumor. Age 5.

MOTHER Maira Sánchez. Died August 30, 1987. Ailment: pituitary tumor. Age 6.

MOTHER Mario Bravo. Died November 26, 1987. Ailment: cancer of the liver. Age 14.

MOTHER Memo Delgado. Died October 24, 1988. Ailment: adrenal gland tumor. Age 6.

YOLANDA Evalina Valle. Died November 2, 1989. Ailment . . . ailment . . . era mi jiha . . . era . . . ¡mi hija!

(She collapses in AMPARO's *arms. The* PROTESTORS *advance, forming a line of resistance. A* POLICEMAN *in riot gear holds back the crowd. They continue to press forward.)*

PROTESTORS ¡Asesinos! ¡Asesinos! ¡Asesinos! . . .

*(*BONNIE *slips.* AMPARO *steps out of the line to retrieve her. The* POLICEMAN *knocks* AMPARO *down with his nightstick.)*

ANA PEREZ She's been struck! Amparo Manríquez . . . oh my god! The police-man! . . . *(He continues to beat her in slow, methodical blows.)* Stop him! Jesus! Somebody stop him! No! No! Stop him! *(*DON GILBERTO *breaks through the line and throws his body over* AMPARO *to shield her. The* PROTESTORS *scatter. Blackout.)*

Scene 4

JUAN *has brought* CEREZITA *outdoors. The sun is setting. Black silhouettes of pecan trees on the horizon, grave vineyards in the foreground.* CEREZITA *is transfixed by the view.* JUAN *paces back and forth nervously.* BONNIE *is on the porch, softly singing a lullaby. She ties two twigs together in the shape of a cross, then hangs her doll onto it, wrapping string around its wrists and ankles.*

BONNIE

"Duerme, duerme, negrito,
  que tu mama está en el campo, negrito.
  Te va a traer rica fruta para tí.
  Te va a traer muchas cosas para tí . . ."

JUAN I got scared. I don't know why. I . . . I could have done something. They beat her so bad, Cere.

CEREZITA Heroes and saints.

JUAN What?

CEREZITA That's all we can really have for

now. That's all people want.

JUAN They want blood?

*(*CEREZITA *glances at him, presses her mouth to the* raite *button, and comes downstage.* JUAN *looks over to* BONNIE. *She waves back with the crucified doll.)*

CEREZITA Look, Juan, it looks like a thousand mini-crucifixions out there.

JUAN What?

CEREZITA The vineyards. See all the crosses? It's a regular cemetery. *(*JUAN *comes up behind her, his eyes scan the horizon.)* The trunk of each of the plants is a little gnarled body of Christ writhing in agony. Don't you see it?

JUAN Sort of.

CEREZITA See how the branches look like arms with the bulging veins of suffering. Each arm intertwined with the other little crucified Christs next to it. Thousand of them in neat orderly rows of despair. Syphilitic sacks of grapes hanging from their loins.

JUAN How do you see these things, Cere?

CEREZITA I see it all. A chain gang of Mexican Christs. Their grey wintered skin, their feet taking root into the trenches the machines have made.

JUAN They *are* lifelike, aren't they?

CEREZITA They're dead. *(Suddenly the sun bursts through a cloud. It bathes* CEREZITA's *face. She basks in it for a moment.)*
The living dead of winter.
Dead to the warmth of sun on my face melting into the horizon.
Pecan trees like rigid skeletons black against the sky.
Dead to the deep red and maroon the grapevines bleed.
Dead to the smell of earth,
  split moist and open
to embrace the seed.
*(*BONNIE *approaches. She carries two small two-by-fours.)*

BONNIE I got the wood, Cere.

CEREZITA Bring it here, mija.

JUAN *(Stopping her)* No! Give it to me.

*(*BONNIE *hesitates, looks to* CEREZITA.*)*

CEREZITA Dásela.

BONNIE *(Handing the wood over to him)* Are you gonna make the cross, Father Juan? *(He raises up the two pieces of wood, forming them into the shape of a small, child-sized cross. His eyes are fixed on* CEREZITA's.*)*

JUAN Yes.

(Sudden flute and tambor. Fade out.)

Scene 5

The hospital. DON GILBERTO *brings* AMPARO
*out in a wheelchair. She has a black eye and
wears a hospital gown and carries a small
purse on her lap.* JUAN *is with them.* DON
GILBERTO *sits, takes out the Racing Form.*

AMPARO   They cut out my spleen, Father.
It was completely smash.

DON GILBERTO   El Doctor Fong . . . es un
Chino ¿sabes? He says que the spleen is
the part of the body que 'stá conectado
con el coraje.

JUAN   It's the place of emotion, of human
passions.

AMPARO   Pues, that policia got another
thing coming if he think he could take
away mi pasión. ¿No, viejo?

DON GILBERTO   Yeah, she already been
trying to pull me on top of her in the
wheelchair. She gonna bust her stitches I
tell her.

AMPARO   No seas exagerado. *(To* JUAN) The
doctor dice que me parezco a su madre,
que I'm tough like his mother con el
dolor.

DON GILBERTO   *(Teasing)*   Mi Chinita.

AMPARO   Cállete el hocico tú. El padre
came to visit me. I'm the sick one. *(DON
GILBERTO smiles, starts reading the Racing
Form. As the conversation ensues, he begins
to nod off, then finally falls asleep. The
newspaper lies draped across his chest.)* Y
Dolores . . . ¿cómo 'stá?

JUAN   Yolanda seems to be handling the
baby's death better than Señora Valle. I
had to pull her out of the bushes last
night.

AMPARO   ¿Otra vez?

JUAN   This was worse. It was already past
midnight, and she wouldn't budge. She
said she had seen Mario's ghost . . .

AMPARO   ¿Cómo?

JUAN   That Mario's ghost was trying to get
back into the house.

AMPARO   ¡Qué raro!

JUAN   She was shaking . . . and as white as
a ghost herself.

AMPARO   Pero ¿por qué dijo eso?

JUAN   I don't know. Nobody can reach
Mario.

AMPARO   My comadre is a very scared
woman, Father. *(Pause)* Mira.
*(AMPARO takes a news clipping out of her
purse, unfolds it, hands it to JUAN.)*

JUAN   It's Cerezita.

AMPARO   Barely two years old and in the
New York Times. Fifteen years ago, Cere's
face was in all the newspapers, then
Dolores just shut up.

JUAN   Why?

AMPARO   She lost her husband on account
of it.

JUAN   On account of what?

AMPARO   Advertising his sins. She believe
Cere was a sign from God to make her
husband change his ways. But he dint
change, he left.

JUAN   But it was pesticides.

AMPARO   In her heart, Dolores feels difernt.
Nobody wants to be a víctima, Father.
Better to believe that it's the will of God
than have to face up to the real sinners.
They're purty powerful, those sinners.
You start to take them on, pues you could
lose. This way, por lo menos, you always
get to win in heaven. Isn' that what the
Church teaches, Father?

JUAN   Well, the Church counsels that—

AMPARO   You gointu do the rosary tonight,
Father?

JUAN   Yes. At seven, then the vigil will go
on all night.

AMPARO   And Cerezita will be there?

JUAN   Yes, it's at the house.

AMPARO   *(Looking over to make sure DON
GILBERTO is asleep)* Cuídala, Father. Don'
let her go out tonight.

JUAN   But Cere . . . never goes out.

AMPARO   The men in the helicopters,
they're hired by the growers. Anybody out
en los files tonight, they'll shoot them.
They don' wan' no more publeesty about
the crucifixions.

JUAN   Then you think Cere—

AMPARO   I don' think not'ing. I'm jus'
asking you not to let your eyes leave her
tonight. Hazme el favor.

JUAN   Of . . . course.

AMPARO   Bueno. Now give me one of those
priest's prayers of yours. A ver si me
ayuda.

JUAN   You want me to pray for you?

AMPARO   Insurance, Padre.
(He smiles. AMPARO *closes her eyes as*
JUAN *blesses her. The lights fade to
black.)*

Scene 6

Later that night. CEREZITA *is sleeping.*
DOLORES *is standing by the small coffin. It is
surrounded by candles and flowers. Trancelike,
she takes one of the candles and places it on*
CEREZITA's *raite. She kneels before her.*

DOLORES I can't pray no more to a God
que no tiene oídos. Where is my Dios,
mija? I turn to you coz I got nobody left
now. Give me a sign mi querida virgencita. Enséñame como aliviarnos del
dolor que nos persigue en este valle de
lágrimas.
*(*CEREZITA *slowly opens her eyes, sees her
mother praying to her.)*
CEREZITA Go to sleep now, 'amá. I'll watch
over Evalina.
DOLORES Gracias, virgencita. *(She rises,
carrying the candle, goes to the window.)*
Mario carried death with him. I saw it in
his cansancio, in the way his head fell
down, tan pesada entre los hombros. In
the way he put one foot onto the porch
and then the other . . . and then he
change his mind. *(She blows out the candle,
as she does the others by the coffin. With
each one, she names her progeny.)* I miss
my babies, mi Evalina, mi Mario, mi
Cerezita . . .
CEREZITA I'm still here, 'amá.
DOLORES *(Staring at her daughter, momen-
tarily confused)* Arturo, do you remember
when I was big with Cere and the whole
house was full of babies?
(She exits, quietly muttering to herself.
CEREZITA *presses her mouth to the raite
button and goes over to the small open
coffin.)*
CEREZITA Before the grown ones come to
put you in the ground, they'll untie the
ropes around your wrists and ankles. By
then you are no longer in your body. The
child's flesh hanging from that wood
makes no difference to you. It is . . . you
are a symbol. Nada más.
*(*JUAN *appears at the window, taps it
lightly.)*
CEREZITA *(Whispering)* Juan?
JUAN Yes, its me.
CEREZITA Come in.
JUAN *(Entering with a duffel bag)* Is every-
one asleep?
CEREZITA Yes.
(Trying to contain his excitement, JUAN *gets
down on his knees and starts pulling things
out of the bag.)*
CEREZITA You hardly look like a grave
digger.
JUAN Shovel. Flashlight. Rope. Did I forget
anything?
CEREZITA Do you know how beautiful you
are?
JUAN What?
CEREZITA I've never seen you like this.
You're almost glowing.
JUAN I am?
CEREZITA Glowing.
JUAN Are the children waiting? *(He repacks
the duffel bag.)*
CEREZITA They'll meet us in front of the
church. There's time yet.
JUAN I saw Amparo today. She knows,
Cere.
CEREZITA She wouldn't stop us.
JUAN No, but . . .
CEREZITA What?
JUAN She says it's dangerous. She says
they'll shoot anything that moves out
there in the field tonight.
CEREZITA Then we'll have to leave the
kids behind. I don't need them now. I
have you. You're not afraid are you,
Juan?
JUAN No. Yes, I'm scared, but it's exciting.
CEREZITA Things are gonna change now,
Juan. You'll see.
JUAN *(Walks over to the coffin, blesses it)* She
looks peaceful.
CEREZITA She is. What we do to her body
won't disturb her peace.
JUAN Yes, I'm supposed to know that.
CEREZITA Nobody's dying should be
invisible, Juan. Nobody's.
(There is a pause. JUAN *prays by the coffin.*
CEREZITA *observes.)*
CEREZITA Juan? . . .
JUAN Hmm? . . .
CEREZITA You know when they killed
those priests in El Salvador?
JUAN The Jesuits.
CEREZITA Did you know they killed the
housekeeper and her daughter, too?
JUAN Yes.
CEREZITA If the Jesuits died as priests,
does that make them saints?
JUAN I don't know. They're martyrs,
heroes. They spoke out against the
government.
CEREZITA Did the housekeeper and her
daughter?

JUAN What?

CEREZITA Speak out against the government?

JUAN I don't think so.

CEREZITA I don't either. It wasn't their job. I imagine they just changed the priests' beds, kept a pot of beans going, hung out the sábanas to dry. At least, the housekeeper did and the girl, she helped her mother. She did the tasks that young girls do . . . girls still living under the roof of their mother. And maybe sometimes one of the priests read to the girl, maybe . . . he taught her to read and she . . . fell in love with him, the teacher. *(Pause)* Touch my hair, Juan.

(Coming up from behind her, he touches her hair very tenderly, brings a strand to his face. He smells it, puts his hand to her cheek, caresses her. She moves her cheek deeper into the palm of his hand, moans softly. She lifts her face to his. He hesitates, then kisses her at first awkwardly, trying to find her mouth at the right angle. CEREZITA *moans. Suddenly,* JUAN's *face takes on a distanced look. He grabs* CEREZITA's *cheeks between his hands.)*

CEREZITA I want to taste you, Juan.

(He hesitates, then kisses her again. CEREZITA's *moaning increases, intensifies. He comes around behind her, presses his pelvis up against the backside of the raite. He brings her head against him, his fingers tangled in her hair.)*

CEREZITA I want the ocean in my mouth.

(She pulls at his shirt with her teeth, trying to bring him back around.)

CEREZITA Juan, help me. I need your hands.

(JUAN closes his eyes.)

CEREZITA Juan, look at me.

(He digs his pelvis into the raite, pulling her head deeper into him.)

CEREZITA Juan, where are you?

(He pushes against her harder, deeper.)

CEREZITA Open your eyes. Juan.

(He comes to orgasm.)

CEREZITA Juan.

(He grabs the duffel bag and runs out.)

CEREZITA Juan!

(After a few moments, the sound of an approaching helicopter, then gunshots are heard. Blackout.)

Scene 7

Dawn. MARIO *is lying on a park bench, wearing a jacket, the collar turned up, a knapsack at his feet. He has a constant cough.* JUAN *walks by. Still in his priest's clothes, he appears somewhat disheveled.*

MARIO Got a cigarette?

JUAN Mario.

MARIO Hello, Father.

JUAN We'd almost given you up for lost.

MARIO You're out pretty early.

JUAN I . . . couldn't sleep.

MARIO I've forgotten what sleep is.

JUAN Why didn't you answer my messages?

MARIO Wasn't even sure I was coming until I found myself hitching out on the interstate.

JUAN You been to the house?

MARIO Yes. Well . . . almost.

JUAN *(Indicating the bench)* May I?

MARIO For a cigarette.

JUAN Oh, right.

(MARIO gets up, JUAN sits beside him, lights up a cigarette for each of them.)

JUAN You shouldn't be smoking, Mario . . . with that cough.

MARIO Lung cancer's the least of my worries, Padre. *(They sit in silence for a few moments. Sounds of the highway can be heard in the distance.)* This place is strange. Just one hundred yards off that highway, and you're already right smack back into the heart of the Valley. In minutes, it feels like you never left, like it won't ever let you leave again, . . . like a Chicano Bunuel movie. *(JUAN smiles.)*

JUAN Except it's too real.

MARIO The city's no different. Raza's dying everywhere. Doesn't matter if it's crack or . . . pesticides, AIDS, it's all the same shit.

JUAN Do you regret going, Mario?

MARIO No. *(Pause)* I've always loved sex, Father, always felt that whatever I had crippled or bent up inside me that somehow sex could cure it, that sex could straighten twisted limbs, like . . . the laying on of hands.

JUAN Like tongues of fire.

MARIO Yeah. Even holy like that . . . with the right person. *(Pause)* And when you love your own sex, and they got your own hungry dark eyes staring back at you, well you're convinced that you could even cure death. And so you jus' keep

257

kissing that same purple mouth, deeper and harder, and you keep whispering, "I'm gonna wipe all that sickness outta you, cousin." And then weeks and months and maybe even a year or two go by, and suddenly you realize you didn't cure nothing and that your family's dissolving right there inside of your hands.

JUAN *(Pause)* And your blood family, Mario? . . .

MARIO I've had to choose, Father. I can't come home. I'm not strong enough, I'm not a woman. I'm not suited for despair. I'm not suited to carry a burden greater than the weight of my own balls. *(He picks up his knapsack.)*

JUAN You're leaving?

MARIO I'm sick, Father. Tell my family in whatever way you can. *(He starts to exit.)*

JUAN Mario.

(He hands him the pack of cigarettes. MARIO smiles and walks off. Fade out.)

Scene 8

A few hours later. YOLANDA *wears a black slip and is ironing a black blouse.* CEREZITA *watches her.*

YOLANDA My mom hasn't said one word to me about Lina. She just keeps asking what time mi 'apá's coming. What are we gonna do? We barely got a family left. *(She puts on the blouse, starts to button it.)*

CEREZITA You gotta leave this place.

YOLANDA *(Grabbing her breasts)* ¡Carajo! I can't stop them. I can't stop them from running.

CEREZITA What?

YOLANDA My breasts. They're so heavy, Cere. They're killing me. Nothing takes the pain away. They want a mouth and there's no mouth to relieve them. They feel like they're gonna burst open. I wish they would, I wish they would spill onto everything, turn everything to milk. Sweet milk. My baby's sweet mouth, I miss my baby. *(Her breasts run.)* Look at me. I'm a mess. They're dripping all over me. *(She grabs a bunch of tissues, continues stuffing them into her bra, taking them out and stuffing more in.)* Every time I think of her, they run. Nobody told my body my baby is dead. I still hear her crying and my breasts bleed fucking milk. I remember

the smell of her skin and they bleed again. My body got used to being a mother, Cere. And then it's cut off . . . like that! A child's not supposed to die before her mother. It's not natural. It's not right. That's why you hear about women throwing themselves in front of speeding cars, blocking bullets to save their kid. I get it now. It's not about sacrifice. It's instinct. *(She pulls at her breasts.)* I want to rip them off of me. They feel like tombstones on my chest!

CEREZITA *(Presses the button on her raite, crosses to* YOLANDA*)* Sister! I wish I had arms to hold you.

YOLANDA Cere . . .

CEREZITA It's almost over now, 'mana. You gotta get outta here, start a new family.

YOLANDA I'm afraid, Cere. I think my womb is poisoned.

CEREZITA No. Let me take the pain away. Your breasts, they're so heavy.

*(*YOLANDA *goes to her, opens her blouse and brings* CEREZITA's *face to her breast. The lights fade to black.)*

Scene 9

BONNIE *holds her doll in one hand and a large pair of scissors in the other.* CEREZITA *watches her as she begins to cut the doll's hair.*

BONNIE This isn't going to hurt you, hija. It's for your own good.

CEREZITA Bonnie, vente.

*(*BONNIE *goes to her. They huddle together, speaking in whispers.)*

CEREZITA *(Aloud)* After this there will be no more sacrificial lambs. Not here in this valley. No more.

*(*BONNIE *nods and exits as* JUAN *enters,* CEREZITA *will not look at him.)*

JUAN I came to see if you were all right. *(Pause)* Cere, turn around. Please . . . I heard there were gunshots. The children—

CEREZITA The children were waiting for you. They were waiting for you with their little flashlights, their children's shovels, their children's hearts.

JUAN I lost heart.

CEREZITA Yes, you lost heart.

JUAN *(Pause)* After I left here, I just started driving north. I didn't know where I was going, I was going nowhere. The fog was so thick. I could barely see the front end of the car. *(Pause)* And it suddenly hit me, how this had happened once before, that I had done this before, somewhere else with some other—

CEREZITA Pobre?

JUAN Yes. *(Pause)* I turned the car around.

CEREZITA Why?

JUAN I had to come back. See you.

CEREZITA We had a plan, Juan, a plan of action. But your small fear stopped you.

JUAN I couldn't after that. I—

CEREZITA After what?

JUAN It shouldn't have happened.

CEREZITA Stop, Juan.

JUAN I'm a priest, Cere. I'm not free. My body's not my own.

CEREZITA It wasn't your body I wanted. It was mine. All I wanted was for you to make me feel like I had a body because, the fact is, I don't. I was denied one. But for a few minutes, a few minutes before you started *thinking*, I felt myself full of fine flesh filled to the bones in my toes . . . I miss myself. Is that so hard to understand?

JUAN No.

CEREZITA And I'm sick of all this goddamn dying. If I had your arms and legs, if I had your dick for chrissake, you know what I'd do? I'd burn this motherless town down and all the·poisoned fields around it. I'd give healthy babies to each and every childless woman who wanted one and I'd even stick around to watch those babies grow up! . . . You're a waste of a body.

JUAN Cere . . .

(BONNIE re-enters, carrying the small cross. The CHILDREN stand behind her.)

CEREZITA I'm not gonna let you stop me. Juan. Nobody's going to stop me.

(The lights fade to black.)

Scene 10

JUAN *has exited. In the half-darkness, the CHILDREN surround CEREZITA and begin to transform her as BONNIE cuts away at CEREZITA's hair. Moments later, they scatter. The lights rise to reveal DOLORES standing in the doorway. A brilliant beam of light has entered the room and washed over CEREZITA. She is draped in the blue-starred veil of La Virgen de Guadalupe. Her head is tilted slightly toward the right, her eyes downcast in the Virgin's classic expression. DOLORES is riveted by the sight. The raite is covered in a white altar cross with the roses of Tepeyac imprinted upon it. The cross rests at the base of the raite. The light, brighter now, completely illuminates CEREZITA's saintlike expression and the small cross. DOLORES drops to her knees.*

DOLORES Mi virgen.

(Blackout.)

Scene 11

The baby's coffin has been brought out, draped in a funeral cloth of white. DOLORES stands by it, praying softly, then crosses to la virgen. She lifts up the veil slightly and touches CEREZITA's face. DOLORES exhibits a calm not previously witnessed in the play.

DOLORES And you usetu have such beautiful beautiful hair. But it was you, mi virgencita, that made this sacrificio para nosotros. *(Crossing herself with the rosary, she kneels before the image of la virgen.)* "El quinto misterio doloroso, la crucifixión." Querida virgen santísima, watch over nuestra baby Evalina. *(She begins to pray the rosary. YOLANDA enters, wearing a black chapel veil.)*

YOLANDA ¿Está lista, 'amá? . . . Cheezus! What's wrong with her? Why are you praying to her?

DOLORES It was a sign from God.

YOLANDA What sign? Cere-girl. Answer me!

DOLORES Ya no 'stá.

YOLANDA Whadayou mean, she's not there? Cere?

DOLORES She went already to another place.

YOLANDA What place?

DOLORES A place inside herself. She said she was going on a long jornada. She tole me with her eyes.

YOLANDA No, 'amá.

DOLORES She gave me a sign, a sign of the cross. Esta mañana I found it, just like this. *(She takes the cross, holds it up to her.)* The sun was coming in por la ventana y la cruz estaba iluminada en luz. We've had no pertection, hija. La virgencita will protect us now.

YOLANDA Cere. Talk to me.

DOLORES ¡Imagínate! Un milagro en nuestra propia casa.

YOLANDA 'Amá, what did you do to her?

259

DOLORES *(Pause)* I pray, hija.
(In the distance the sound of singing and the slow beat of a tambor)
EL PUEBLO *(Singing)*
"Oh María, madre mía! Oh consuelo, del mortal!
Amparame y guiame a la patria celestial!"
(BONNIE comes into the house and approaches DOLORES.)
DOLORES ¿Qué quieres?
BONNIE La cruz, Doña Lola. It's the funeral.
DOLORES *(As if realizing for the first time)* The funeral.
(DOLORES reluctantly hands the cross over to her. YOLANDA goes to the coffin, hesitates for a brief moment, then tenderly lifts it up and carries it out to meet the procession, following BONNIE. Hearing the voices approaching, DOLORES pulls the curtain around CEREZITA. Outside, ANA PEREZ addresses the "camera.")
ANA PEREZ This is Ana Pérez coming to you live from McLaughlin, California. Today is the funeral of Evalina Valle, the tenth child to die of cancer in this small Valley town.
(JUAN, dressed in full vestments, accompanied by altar boys and EL PUEBLO, passes before the Valle house. They crane their necks to get a glimpse of CEREZITA, but DOLORES stands resolute before the window, shielding her from view. YOLANDA gives the altar boys the coffin. They all continue in procession, BONNIE leading with the cross.)
ANA PEREZ Although funerals are becoming commonplace here in McLaughlin, rumors of a miracle occurrence in the family of the deceased have spread rapidly and have already attracted a huge following. Just before nine this morning, it was reported that Dolores Valle, the mother of Cerezita Valle, found a wooden cross in the disabled girl's sleeping chamber. The cross was illuminated in a wondrous glow and from that moment the young virgin has ceased to speak and has assumed an appearance and affect strikingly similar to the Virgin of Guadalupe ... *(She spies YOLANDA as the procession passes.)* This ... virgin, this saint is your sister?
YOLANDA I don't want to talk to you.
ANA PEREZ The priest asked me to be here.

YOLANDA Father Juan?
ANA PEREZ He said there was to be a crucifixion.
YOLANDA My god! ¡Mi hija! *(She rushes off to catch up with the procession.)*
(EL PUEBLO have arrived at the church steps. JUAN prays over the coffin, blessing it with holy water. YOLANDA hovers near the coffin. DON GILBERTO arrives with AMPARO in the wheelchair. ANA PEREZ stand on the sidelines, observing. The church bells toll.)
JUAN Señor, hazme un instrumento de tu paz. Donde hay odio ...
EL PUEBLO Que siembre yo amor;
JUAN Donde hay injuria ...
EL PUEBLO Perdón;
JUAN Donde hay duda ...
EL PUEBLO Fe;
JUAN Donde hay desperación ...
EL PUEBLO Esperanza;
(They continue praying. In the Valle home, DOLORES has covered her head with a black rebozo. She starts to exit.)
CEREZITA Let me go, 'amá.
DOLORES Hija?
CEREZITA I know about death. I know how to stop death.
DOLORES ¿Has visto la cara de Dios?
CEREZITA Sí, 'amá. I've seen the face of God. But I'm not free.
DOLORES No entiendo.
CEREZITA You tie my tongue, 'amá. How can I heal without my tongue? Do I have arms or legs?
DOLORES I cut them from you.
CEREZITA No. 'amá. You gave birth to me. Eres mi madre.
DOLORES Sí ...
CEREZITA Now, let ... me ... go.
(Church bells resonate throughout the town. They call her to action. She turns back the curtain. DOLORES is stunned by the resolve in CEREZITA's eyes. There is no need for more words, DOLORES pushes the raite with la virgen out the door.)
JUAN Pues es dando ...
EL PUEBLO Que recibimos;
JUAN Es perdonando ...
EL PUEBLO Que somos perdonados;
JUAN Y es muriendo ...
EL PUEBLO Que nacemos a la vida eter—
(Upon the sight of la virgen, the prayer is interrupted. A hush falls over the crowd.)
JUAN *(To himself)* My God, Cere, what have they done to you?

(They arrive at the church steps. DOLORES *calls out to* ANA PEREZ.*)*

DOLORES Come, señorita. Come see how my baby se vuelve a santita. Come show the peepo.

*(*ANA PEREZ *is noticeably shaken by the image of* CEREZITA. *She signals to the "cameraman" to begin filming. In procession,* EL PUEBLO *bring forth pictures of their dead and deformed children in offering to la virgen.)*

EL PUEBLO *(Singing)*

"Oh María, madre mía! Oh consuelo, del mortal!

Amparame y guiame a la patria celestial!"

(The singing continues as they pin milagros to the white cloth of CEREZITA's *raite.* DOLORES *raises her hand to quiet the crowd.* CEREZITA's *eyes scan the faces of the people. There is a pause.)*

CEREZITA Put your hand inside my wound. Inside the valley of my wound, there is a people. A miracle people. In this pueblito where the valley people live, the river runs red with blood; but they are not afraid because they are used to the color red. It is the same color as the river that runs through their veins, the same color as the sun setting into the sierras, the same color of the pool of liquid they were born into. They remember this in order to understand why their fields, like the rags of the wounded, have soaked up the color and still bear no fruit. No lovely red fruit that el pueblo could point to and say yes, for this we bleed, for this our eyes go red with rage and sadness. They tell themselves red is as necessary as bread. They tell themselves this in a land where bread is a tortilla without maize, where the frijol cannot be cultivated. *(Pause)* But we, we live in a land of plenty. The fruits that pass through your fingers are too many to count – luscious red in their strawberry wonder, the deep purple of the grape inviting, the tomatoes perfectly shaped and translucent. And yet, you suffer at the same hands. *(Pause)* You are Guatemala, El Salvador. You are the Kuna y Tarahumara. You are the miracle people too, for like them the same blood runs through your veins. The same memory of a time when your deaths were cause for reverence and celebration, not shock and mourning. You are the miracle people because today, this day, that red memory will spill out from inside you and flood this valley con coraje. And you will be free. Free to name this land *Madre*. Madre Tierra. Madre Sagrada. Madre . . . Libertad. The radiant red mother . . . rising.

*(*JUAN *moves to the center of the crowd to give a final bendición.* MARIO *appears upstage. He goes to* DOLORES. *They embrace.* EL PUEBLO *kneel as* JUAN *blesses them and all those witnessing the play.* BONNIE *approaches* JUAN *with the cross.)*

BONNIE Now is it time, Father?

*(*JUAN *nods, then takes the cross from her. Another child brings* JUAN *some rope. He goes to* CEREZITA, *touches her cheek, and releases the locks on the raite. Her eyes do not leave him. He puts her mouthpiece attachment in place. They both turn to* YOLANDA. YOLANDA *now understands that she is to offer up her dead infant. She goes to the coffin, takes it from the altar boys, kisses it, then hands it over to* JUAN. CEREZITA *presses her mouth to the button of her raite and slowly turns toward the vineyard. The tambor begins to beat slowly, while* EL PUEBLO *watch in silence.* JUAN *and* CEREZITA *head out to the vineyard.* CEREZITA *pauses briefly as she passes her mother.)*

CEREZITA Mamá.

*(*DOLORES *blesses her.* CEREZITA *and* JUAN *proceed offstage into the vineyards. Moments later, the shadow and sound of a helicopter pass overhead.* EL PUEBLO *watch the sky. Then there is the sudden sound of machine gun fire.* EL PUEBLO *let out a scream and drop to the ground, covering their heads in terror.* MARIO *suddenly rises, raises his fist into the air.)*

MARIO Burn the fields!

EL PUEBLO *(Rising with him)* ¡Enciendan los files! *(They all, including* ANA PEREZ, *rush out to the vineyards, shouting as they exit.)* ¡Asesinos! ¡Asesinos! ¡Asesinos! *(Moments later, there is the crackling of fire as a sharp red-orange glow spreads over the vineyard and the Valle home. The lights slowly fade to black.)*

Bina Sharif

Biography

Bina Sharif, a playwright, actress and director, has had eight plays including *My Ancestor's House* produced at Theater for the New City in New York, and four one-acts produced by Lower Levels of Society also based in New York. She is a Joseph Jefferson Award Nominee actress from Chicago's Goodman Theatre. She is currently working on the second part of a trilogy of plays entitled *One Thousand Hours of Love*, which is a metaphoric love story between an Indian woman and an English man dealing with the colonization of India by Britain. The second part of the trilogy is called *Sleeping with Horses*. She is a recipient of the New York Council of the Arts grant for her plays *Fire* and *Stars of War*. Bina is an MD and has a Masters degree in Public Health from Johns Hopkins University. She does not practice medicine, ". . . a mistake . . . like many others made innocently."

Photo: Ann Mermet

Artistic statement

As a woman playwright who was born in Pakistan and has lived in America for the last fifteen years, I explore the issues of socioeconomic decline in Western society: merciless violence, homelessness, racism, sexism and the enormous pressure to be successful, youthful and perfect. These elements versus the evils of oppression against women in poverty amidst the narrow-minded, religious beliefs of Eastern society constitute a cultural collision course in my life.

I came to America to be an artist. And my parents knew it. Especially my father. He was afraid for me. Not because he didn't believe in me . . . he did. He was the only man in my life who gave me total freedom, and for a Muslim man that's a heroic act. He knew that I would like to pursue a theater career and was worried that I would suffer (he foresaw what I couldn't), and made me promise him that I would finish my education in America, which I did. I got my master's degree in public health from Johns Hopkins University and then ended my medical career and started furiously pursuing my writing and theater career. I always wanted to write because one of my sisters who died when I was very young wrote, and my father was a man of letters.

And thus the beginning of my very costly and precious dream began. The most important reason for me to leave my country to come to America was to pursue not only my artistic tendencies and abilities but to pursue liberty, freedom, equality, and justice.

As a woman in Pakistan I felt confined and I fought for equality. Rulers of Pakistan were almost all men who manipulated the customs, rules and religion in their own favor. Even if women were getting higher education, such as law and medical degrees, still there were things which were expected of them, which were confining – small things like not being able to ride a bicycle, or smoke a cigarette. At that time those little things used to bother me – if I only knew what lay ahead for me in America.

I am considered more Muslim in this country by some who are prejudiced against Islamic religion in America. Because my name, Sharif, is the most prominent Muslim name, I get labeled as a Muslim playwright. Not that I mind; I am actually very proud of it. It amuses me sometimes that I had to leave my Muslim homeland and come to America to be labeled a "Muslim woman playwright." I am sure it's making my mother smile in her grave. Finally her daughter who wanted to run away to get away from all kinds of labels and groupings is being confined into a very narrow inch of a corner without many exits.

Thinking about *My Ancestor's House*, I get drowned in the most painful sea of emotions because it is so personal and evokes very complex and powerful memories of my childhood and the good days gone forever. I particularly loved my family and didn't realize that if I separated myself physically and emotionally from them I would disintegrate in the deepest sphere of my psyche. It was like taking the center out of the nucleus of the cell of my very existence. My emotional strength and my structure weakened when I crossed the ocean and separated myself from my homeland, from my loved ones, from my parents, my brothers and sisters, from my seasons, my spice, my language, from the fallen leaves in autumn and long narrow mud paths lined with daffodils and roses.

My Ancestor's House was written for Deedi. I don't know if I did justice to her but in reality nobody did her justice. No one, neither her family, nor her husband, nor society, nor her Kismet, nor her God.

She had an unhappy life and then she died. Deedi was my own sister. She had grace, beauty, talent and more courage than all of us combined. She took a rebellious step in her own country . . . chose a husband for herself and got punished for that, by everyone, by the gods and by herself.

My artistic concern is to reach a wide audience from all spheres of life, to make people aware of the fragility of human feelings, emotional conflicts, and the difficulty of just surviving. My writing expresses the horrifying alienation and loneliness which come with the pursuit of freedom in the West. The darker side of my characters elicit the universality of emotions and the lack of understanding between Eastern and Western values. Themes of shared humanity remain of utmost importance in my work in the theater.

Production History

My Ancestor's House premiered at Theater for the New City, New York, directed by Francisco G. Rivela, 3–20 December, 1992. The cast included Gleen Athaide, Rasjhree Daryanani, Madhur Jaffrey, Sunita Mukhi, Karim Panjwani, Sol, and Tamir.

14 My Ancestor's House _____

Bina Sharif

This play is dedicated to my sister: Deedi.

> Being crazy this way wouldn't be so bad if
> only ... if only ... if only when you put
> your foot forward to take a step, the ground
> wouldn't come up to meet your foot the
> way it does.
>
> E.B. White

Characters

BEGUM HAJIRA: mother, age 50–70

SAHID: eldest son, age 45–50; a brigadier in
the Pakistani army

NAZO: eldest daughter, age late
thirties/early forties

BINDIA: daughter, a year or two younger

ROONA: daughter, in her early thirties

DEEDI: youngest daughter, in her late
twenties

ALI BUKSH: a family servant, age 40–50

MOAZZAN: a Muslim man, knows how to
recite Azan (a call to prayer in Arabic),
any age

MUSICIANS (ON STAGE): three men or
women:

TABLA PLAYER

SITAR PLAYER

HARMONIUM PLAYER

The play is set in Pakistan

Author's production notes

This is a memory play and must be treated
as such. The actors can be already in place
when the audience walks in. Tabla, sitar
and harmonium are heard. The garden, or
at least a very believable impression of it, is
a must. The grave must be of fresh real
earth and stays lit by candles; it should be
placed downstage left.

The MUSICIANS are on stage. Their music
is the reminder of the lost good old days.
DEEDI is more or less seen as an apparition
or a dream figure or a memory. DEEDI
must always be dimly lit.

BEGUM's scene can also be staged less
conventionally. For example, she can be in
bed lying still downstage right through the
whole play, seemingly watching the demise
of her family. However, the actors should be
unaware of her presence on stage. As far as
they are concerned she is in the hospital.
BEGUM should be completely covered by
white sheets. Only her face should be seen.

Costumes

The climate of Pakistan is extremely hot in
July. The element of heat is a very important aspect of the play. The costumes must
be of thin cottons and linens of very light
colors. The only bright colors in the play
are worn by DEEDI. She must dress as a
Pakistani bride in red and gold and wear
expensive-looking jewelry, her head covered
by a red and gold dupatta, a Pakistani long
scarf. The other daughters' heads must also
be covered in Act II with dupattas, and they
wear shalwar kameez, a traditional Pakistani
dress.

At the funeral all actors wear white
clothes, everyone's heads covered by white.
The men wear white caps. ALI BUKSH, the
servant, should be included in the funeral.
All actors must be barefoot at the grave.

Songs

The ghazals (folkloric songs) of Begum
Akhtar, a legendary Indian singer, are
suggested for DEEDI's songs, but if that is
not possible any sad folkloric Pakistani
songs will do.

The play can be performed without an
intermission.

Act I

Scene 1

The voice of MOAZZAN *is heard. He recites Azan in Arabic (a call to prayer).* DEEDI *sings. Cemetery, evening, July 9, 1984. A newly dug grave (already lit with candles). No gravestone. Some flowers on the grave.* SAHID, NAZO, BINDIA, ROONA *and* ALI BUKSH *standing, dressed in Pakistani tunics and pants. Heads covered, holding flowers.* MOAZ-ZAN *joins the funeral and he recites a prayer for the dead. They are saying their prayers. Prayers are said individually and then in unison. Prayers sound like a tragic Greek chant . . . Silence after the prayers for a few seconds.*

ROONA (*Sobs . . . has difficulty with the following words*) This is the one who got cheated the most! She never . . . never hurt anyone but herself!
   (*An outburst of crying and wailing . . . Music – Blackout –* DEEDI *sings, her lament is overlapped by* MOAZZAN's *prayer. As these sounds fade, music of tabla and sitar and harmonium comes up.*)

Scene 2

A day earlier, July 8, 1984. Early morning. NAZO's *dining room. Just finished having breakfast. Dining table, chairs. Freshly cut roses in a vase on the table.* ALI BUKSH *clearing the dining table.* NAZO *helping him with the dishes.* ROONA *and* NAZO *dressed in Pakistani clothes.* BINDIA *in jeans and a t-shirt. She smokes.* ROONA *is glancing through a Vogue magazine.*

NAZO (*To* ROONA) Would you like some tea?
ROONA Yes, please, could I have it strong? The last one wasn't strong, wasn't even hot.
NAZO (*To* BINDIA) What about you?
BINDIA I would love another cup! Darjeeling tea never tastes the same in New York.
ROONA Do you know why it doesn't taste good? Because the water in New York City doesn't taste the same as in Rawalpindi. When you go back why don't you take some water from here so your tea will taste better.

NAZO (*To* ALI BUKSH) Babaji, make more tea. Strong and hot. Begum Bindia likes it strong and hot. (*He looks at* BINDIA; *she nods, and smiles.*)
ALI BUKSH Yes, Begum Sahib. Right away! Anything for Begum Bindia. You know Bindia I always make very good tea – when you were this little you were playing on my shoulder – everyday I taking you outside in the garden. You are like my daughter – why would I not make excellent tea for you? But you promise never go to America – promise my daughter Bindia, wild country, kafir country. (*The actor now summarizes these lines in Urdu.*)
   (ALI BUKSH *looks at* BINDIA *and exits.* BINDIA *smiles and reaches for a cigarette from a pack of Marlboros. This is her fourth since breakfast. Lights the cigarette, smokes. A little nervous trying to hide it.*)
NAZO You have started smoking a lot.
BINDIA Yup!
ROONA Now you know you are in Pakistan. Here even the servants tell you what to do and what not to do. When he comes back, he will ask you, why are you wearing jeans and why are you smoking.
NAZO You smoke a lot!
BINDIA Yes . . . I know.
NAZO Why?
ROONA Leave her alone.
NAZO Smoking is not good for you.
BINDIA Yes . . . I know.
   (ALI BUKSH *enters with a fresh pot of tea and cups in a tray. The tray is lined with white lace. Puts the tray in front of* NAZO, *clears the other empty cups from the table ready to exit while* BINDIA *speaks.*)
BINDIA Babaji! How is your family?
ALI BUKSH (*Very happy*) Good, good, Begum Sahib. Fine, Begum Bindia, fine, my wife, she fevers ten days . . . and child, the young one . . . (*he gestures with his hands*) vomiting . . . and the other son cough. Does not matter Begum Bindia, it's our fate, God has given us everything and we have to thank our God for that – we are Muslim people – we believe in our God – in our Kismet – little things like cough and fever does not matter – everything is fine – (*Summarizes in Urdu*)
ROONA Yes it's our Kismet, look what Kismet – our destiny – did to us. Did Kismet do anything for you in America?

BINDIA My Kismet gave me chakkar. I run around in circles.

ROONA Do you think I do any better here?

BINDIA So everything is not fine then, Babaji?

ALI BUKSH No, no, Begum Bindia – do not say that – everything is fine – we must pray and thank God – it's our fate, Kismet, one can't change our Kismet. Why are you smoking cigarettes? You smoke cigarettes? *(Summarizes in Urdu)*

ROONA *(Laughs)* See what I told you?

BINDIA Yes, Babaji.

ALI BUKSH You smoke . . . in America also?

(ROONA laughs.)

BINDIA Yes, Babaji.

ALI BUKSH It's not good Begum Bindia – not good, in Pakistan – it is not good for a woman to smoke you are Muslim woman – not good – Muslim country woman smoking is not good. You lose• your health and wealth. *(Summarizes these lines in Urdu)*

NAZO *(To ALI BUKSH)* Go and water the plants.

ROONA Bindia, in this country, everyone is going to talk to you about the value of wealth, and the importance of holding on to it.

BINDIA *(Looks towards the tall windows with a little sigh)* You have a lovely garden. The jasmines, the daffodils, the beautiful birch trees. They remind me of Chekhov's estate. The air is so fresh and the grass is so clean and green – and the roses, oh! the lovely roses. *(Looks at the roses on the table)* These must be from your own garden?

ROONA Of course. Nazo will only have the best rosebuds from the English garden on Shakar Parian Nursery. Bindia, do you know that Nazo's garden was designed by her husband? You know, he is now considered the best and the wealthiest architect in Pakistan.

NAZO Yes.

BINDIA Roses from your own garden. I can never dream of anything like this . . . like this in New York City. There is a lot of cement there and steel and concrete and glass . . . the dampness, the fog, the darkness, the dogs . . . and it rains all the time.

(She sits back, takes another cigarette from the pack, ready to light it.)

NAZO It might not be a good idea to smoke in public in Pakistan . . . People are not quite that liberated here yet. You know what I mean!!!

(BINDIA stares at the unlit cigarette and lets it stay unlit.)

BINDIA I know . . .

ROONA *(Tries to change the subject)* How was your flight?

BINDIA Exhausting.

ROONA How long did it take?

BINDIA Almost twenty-two hours.

NAZO No!

BINDIA Yes. Almost twenty-two hours.

NAZO That long?

BINDIA Actual flying time is eighteen hours but the plane stopped in Paris, Frankfurt, Cairo and Dubai before landing at Islamabad. I feel as if I have not slept in years!

NAZO It all sounds so exotic. Paris and New York and London and Cairo. I only read about those places in the story books. I wish I could go there someday! *(Pause)* But I know it will never happen. I am the eldest daughter. I have responsibilities.

ROONA You can take time off and go. You can afford the trip.

BINDIA It is not as exotic as it sounds. And especially when you live there. *(Looks around. Looks at the garden.)* You have a wonderful life here, a good husband! A good job! Beautiful children! Servants! And that . . . that lovely garden . . . You could never have a garden in New York.

NAZO *(Interrupts)* If I was a doctor I could.

ROONA Nazo, please don't start this medicine business again. *(To BINDIA)* I think you should take a cool bath and get into something more comfortable. I'll put a pair of shalwar kameez for you in the bathroom. You look awfully hot and sweaty in those jeans.

BINDIA That sounds like a good idea. *(Trying to get up from the chair)* I will take a bath, rest for a while and then visit mother this afternoon.

NAZO Why don't you take a bath and visit her now?

BINDIA I do not think I have the strength to see her right away.

ROONA I think she should sleep for some time before she goes to the hospital. *(To NAZO)* For heaven's sake give her a chance to rest a bit, compose herself.

NAZO *(Ignoring* ROONA*)* Mother must be waiting for her!

BINDIA Is she conscious?

ROONA Not fully.

NAZO But she understands.

BINDIA *(Sits)* Does she?

NAZO Oh yes!

ROONA Nazo, what are you talking about?

BINDIA Does she know I am coming?

NAZO Yes. I told her yesterday.

BINDIA What did she say?

NAZO Nothing. She just nodded her head.

ROONA She cannot speak. She's . . . *(Pause)* Are Asad and Zali coming from Denmark?

BINDIA Yes, I think so. When I got the phone call from Nazo *(looks at* NAZO*)* I telephoned right away. It might take them a day or so. Zali never has any money.

NAZO *(Speaks to herself sarcastically)* I wonder why people live wherever they live. If they cannot afford the money to buy a ticket to come where they belong. *(*ROONA *and* BINDIA *look at each other.)*

ROONA Money, money, money . . .

BINDIA Did Sahid come?

ROONA Yes.

BINDIA Where is he? Is he at the hospital?

NAZO No, he went to attend a conference at Islamabad. He will be back for dinner.

BINDIA Did his wife come to visit mother?

ROONA Yes! She came for a few hours.

BINDIA For a few hours. I hear mother's condition is critical.

ROONA Bindia, have you forgotten his wife? Have you forgotten how she is? Did she ever care for us? She couldn't care less. She was worried about the children, being alone with the servants.

BINDIA I heard her mother was living at our brother's house. Why couldn't she take care of the children?

ROONA She is vacationing at Sahid's country home. Cities are too hot for her.

BINDIA Cities were never too hot for mother! Did mother ever go to his country home to rest?

ROONA No! Never. You know how hot it gets in Faisalabad in June/July. Last year she wasn't feeling well and the doctor suggested that she should be in the country. Doctor thought that the fresh air will do her a lot of good. And I think mother wanted to go but you know how proud Ammi always was. But he never came around to it. And his mother-in-law

for the last ten years has been breathing the fresh country air.

BINDIA Did he not invite her?

ROONA Never. But he always said he would.

BINDIA Did he ever visit mother?

NAZO Nobody ever visited mother except me!

BINDIA Mother wrote to me that nobody visited her or sent her any money since father died.

NAZO *(Interrupts)* I did! I always visited mother.

BINDIA Yes, she said no one except you.

NAZO Roona never visited mother.

ROONA I did go, but you know I don't have as much time as you.

NAZO Once – in two years!

BINDIA Mother said that Sahid never even came for father's first death anniversary either.

ROONA Do you think they would leave their country gardens and come to the hot city for the anniversary? You know how they are. No one really cares in this family anymore. We just claim to be caring.

NAZO I care!

ROONA *(Angrily)* Yes! You do! No one else except you!

NAZO *(Angrily)* Yes, no one except me. I went on many weekends. I would take a bus early in the mornings and be with her in seven hours, I have my life to live too you know. I have a job and children but I did manage to spend time with her.

BINDIA You were fortunate that you were able to spend more time with her. You won't have to live with the remorse, for the rest of your life. I wish it was possible for me . . .

NAZO *(Interrupts)* And why wasn't it possible for you?

ROONA Stop it.

NAZO Why wasn't it possible?

BINDIA *(Silent for a few seconds)* I live so far away and . . . it . . . costs so much money to come here . . .

NAZO *(Interrupts again)* But you must make a lot of money? You live in America. Don't you make a lot of money? Last time you came you told us you had a great job.

BINDIA No! I don't!

NAZO You must make more money than us . . . one dollar is equal to fifteen rupees . . . so . . . whatever you make . . . you make fifteen times more money than me!

(BINDIA *and* ROONA *look at each other surprised at* NAZO's *hidden anger.*)

ROONA Is that all you can talk about at a time like this?

NAZO If you don't make a lot of money, which is not believable, why do you live there?

(BINDIA *does not answer . . . she smokes again.*)

NAZO Why do you?

BINDIA *(Quietly)* I do not know. I simply do not know. I ask myself the same question.

NAZO Are you happy in America? *(*BINDIA *doesn't answer.)* Are you?

BINDIA What do you think?

NAZO So, if you are not happy there and you don't make much money, why don't you think of coming back and living with mother? Why not at least make mother happy? I don't really care where you may live, but you were unhappy there and mother was unhappy here without you, why didn't you give a thought of coming back to your own country?

ROONA *(To* NAZO*)* Why are you getting into this now? This is not the time to get into stuff like that. It is the same thing over and over again. We never solve anything. Do we? The last time she came and the time before. The moment she arrives, we get started. We stay – indoors – and we quietly tear each other apart. Mother is ill now. Bindia has just arrived and we've already put her on trial. *(Looks at* BINDIA*)* I did not go to visit mother – all right – isn't it a bit too late for us to ask her why she didn't come to live with mother and why should she? *(Looks at* BINDIA *again)* We ask her to make choices, extremely important decisions the moment she lands in this country, without ever having any idea what she would do if she ever decides to live here.

NAZO *(Calmly)* Whatever we do here! This is not that bad a country and it's your own country. People who have lived abroad and now settled here are perfectly happy. She can practice here. In a year's time she will have a car and in a couple of years she will have her own house, with a garden. Mother always wanted this for her. *(To* ROONA*)* You have no idea how much mother missed her. You never went to visit mother but I did. She always talked about her, and wanted to see her. Whatever I did for her was nothing. She always wanted to be with her . . . she waited for her until the last minute . . . when I was taking her to the hospital, I asked her who would she like to see the most and she said Bindia.

(BINDIA *is crying quietly.*)

ROONA See what you did? I knew this would happen. Don't let her get to you. This is what she wants. Nazo, isn't this what you want?

NAZO I am sorry. I don't want her to feel bad. We are all feeling bad. It is quite unfortunate what has happened to this family. We haven't recovered from our father's death yet. I am not against her living in America. Or in any other country. All I am trying to say is why live some place feeling alienated . . . with remorse and guilt while you can live as a perfectly decent human being in your own country? I am your older sister. I am at your mother's place now. I love you. I love you all. I worry about you. She doesn't seem very happy in New York. I just want the best for her. She is an educated woman. She doesn't have to feel this bewildered. Mother always wanted her to come back and live with her. She could get a job here tomorrow. If she had come back, mother would not have felt so left out and Bindia would have been more comfortable. Does she seem happy to you? *(Asks* ROONA*)* Does she? *(*ROONA *doesn't answer.)* People who graduated with her have their own private practice, they have houses, gardens, plots, property, cars, jewelry. They live in their own country, visit their parents once in a while like normal people. What is wrong with that? People go abroad to achieve something. What did she achieve? Abandoned a highly respectable profession, left her home, a loving home, made herself isolated for no reason.

BINDIA You are doing a great job . . . making me feel guilty . . . you people have done a great job . . . for the last ten years blaming me for deserting mother and father, for abandoning the family, for not taking care of them in their old age. For not being a practicing doctor in this country, for not practicing medicine in

America, for not buying all of you bungalows, and cars, for not sending your children gifts, for not bringing VCRs and diamond rings, for not living here as a spinster . . . as a good, obedient daughter, a Muslim spinster . . .

ROONA Victims of traditions like Deedi, our forgotten sister . . . who is never a part of this loving family anymore. It is a sin to love ourselves in our beloved society but when one destroys oneself by its demands and taboos – they are the first ones to blame you for your own self-destruction – like they have been blaming her for so long that she finally let the exhaustion set in – the willingness to let anything be done to her.

BINDIA I was stronger than Deedi. I . . . left . . . but wasn't strong enough to survive in another jungle. In a massive jungle of loneliness, of poverty, of disillusionment, with the shame. . .with the shame of leaving my own . . . with the shame of not – returning, with the shame of abandonment, with the shame of being abandoned . . . with the shame of being dark . . . I was not strong enough.

ROONA Our religion, our parents, our Qur'an, our men, had weakened our soul.

BINDIA Even before I left I felt weak. But I left . . . from one brilliant country to another . . . from one brilliant job to another . . . from one brilliant nervous breakdown to another . . . I crossed the ocean . . . I wanted to cut the cord . . . the cord . . . stretched, and stretched across the Atlantic like a strong nylon that never breaks . . . distance was so long . . . it stretched . . . and stretched . . . soon it will get tangled . . . soon it will suffocate me.

ROONA Soon it will suffocate Deedi . . . soon the uncut cord will choke us . . . suffocation is creeping all over us . . . over our brains . . . over our eyes.

BINDIA Over my face, over my chest, in my heart. My heart is being torn . . . You are killing me, mother's approaching death is killing me, Deedi's disintegration is killing me . . . I want to ignore my history altogether.

But even if I do . . . where do I go from there? Everything I do takes me right back into the womb, my womb, my mother's womb . . . I am on an exiled land.

ROONA I feel like I have always been on an exiled land.

BINDIA I feel as if I have no right to take any space anywhere . . . (Sobs) (Everyone is shook up. Nobody moves. Complete silence. NAZO gets up, comes slowly to BINDIA, holds her.)

NAZO I am sorry. I did not mean . . . I did not mean to hurt you. I am terribly sorry. You are exhausted. It is wrong of me to talk about things which . . . are so sensitive to you . . . I was only trying to help . . . believe me . . . I will run a cool bath for you . . . you should rest for a while. (Exits)
(ROONA and BINDIA sit very quietly – BINDIA lights a cigarette. Lights fade on them. And lights up on DEEDI – she sings a plaintive lament. After her song, BINDIA starts to speak.)

BINDIA How come Deedi is not here?

ROONA They don't want her here.

BINDIA Who?

ROONA Sahid . . .

BINDIA But it is not his house.

ROONA Nazo and Sahid are very tight these days. She will do anything to please him, and you know he never cared for Deedi.

BINDIA But this is entirely different, mother being so ill. They managed to get me here from the United States. Did they never tell her about mother?

ROONA They casually mentioned it a few days ago over the phone that mother is not feeling well.

BINDIA You mean Deedi doesn't know mother is in the hospital?

ROONA No.

BINDIA This is awful.

ROONA They are afraid she will come with her husband and they hate his guts.

BINDIA I hate his guts, too. He has ruined Deedi's life . . . if this kind of situation happened in America . . . to an American woman, man she would kick his ass in one minute. Deedi should have left him a long time ago. That devil skunk of a husband. What does he do for a living?

ROONA Nothing . . . he has no job.

BINDIA He hasn't worked for a long time, has he?

ROONA As long as I can remember.

BINDIA How does he feed the kids?

ROONA Sells Deedi's gold.

BINDIA Oh, What a mess we have been in all our lives.

ROONA I hate the sight of that man but believe it or not Nazo's husband is more dangerous and manipulative than any man I have ever known. They have exploited mother against everyone – you, me, Deedi. You know, right after father's death, I became pregnant. Throughout my pregnancy I had rough times. Ashoo was still very young. I was working. It was hard for me to drive twelve hours to go visit mother. My husband had a pretty bad relationship with his boss. He could never get leave for an extended period of time, and Nazo . . . who claims to be such a loving, compassionate elder sister never sat down with me and asked me, if . . . I needed something . . . She made mother her exclusive property . . . you know why? They wanted her house. They know two of the brothers live in foreign countries, you live away . . . Deedi . . . doesn't know what's going on. She, poor thing, is so completely lost and she is sick a lot . . . I worry about her . . . I worry about her children . . . I worry about you . . . Nazo and Sahid are more worried about mother's house than her illness . . . I am only very close to you and Deedi . . . and . . . you left, and Deedi . . . she is here . . . but her mind is so shattered . . . I wish I could do something for her.

BINDIA I wish I could do something too. I miss Deedi a lot. And I missed you in America. I miss all the children. I pass in front of a toy store in New York, one of the big ones on Fifth Avenue, and I never go in . . . It breaks my heart . . . I would love to send so many toys and gifts to them. They are so fond of me, and I am so fond of them . . . they imagine me as their wonderful Aunt living in America. I am so totally unhappy there . . . Roona, I am not a doctor. I never could pass that exam. Those medical books I can't go through them anymore. They remind me of Deedi's enlarged heart, which flickers a million beats per minute. They remind me of the ultimate impotence of doctors in the face of death. Death has frightened me from such an early age that I cannot deal with sick people. I cannot face death. Every time I saw a person dying it reminded me of the uselessness of life, the absurdity of life . . . and the truth of being no more. I know the unbearable story of watching people's last breath stuck in their throats. I know the story of watching that last breath vanishing forever. I became too old and too sad when I was too young. I could not go back to the medical books. Sometimes I even forced myself but I thought I would lose my sanity. But I never established myself in America. And all the pressure from back home . . . the pull . . . "come home". . . "come back." The more I suffered there, the less I wanted to come back . . . I felt exactly like Deedi. My dilemma was exactly like Deedi's . . . the difference was only the obvious distance. I left, she didn't. I had no one to turn to in a foreign country. I have been so frightened. I felt like a lost child – looking for other lost children. I ran in circles . . . hoped . . . maybe one day . . . something will happen . . . something good will happen . . . I will be able to get Deedi in America . . . Away from that husband of hers. Maybe one day I will be able to get everybody in America and we will all be together like the old days. The good days. Remember our jasmine-filled courtyard . . . father with his hookah pipe . . . the tea . . . us laughing all night . . . father getting upset at us . . . "Turn off those lights, the electricity costs too much." But we would just giggle and giggle and talk all night and tell each other stories.

ROONA Remember we used to sit by the fire and tell each other about our princes. I would say to you, who are you going to marry? And you would say . . .

BINDIA Who are you going to marry?

ROONA And I would say, my prince will be taller than your prince.

BINDIA And my prince will be as tall as father. We had hopes and dreams, we had no sorrow, we had no pain, we had no . . . shame . . . and then father died without me ever being able to take him there, to New York, to the Plaza Hotel . . . the afternoon tea . . . I always fantasized . . . father . . . with me and you and all of us. We taking him to this elegant hotel, him being dressed in his white, starched native clothes . . . with his turban. Everyone . . . everyone will look at him . . . so tall, and so handsome, and then we will all have tea. And then the bill will come and of course I will pay and father will ask me, "How much?" and I will smile and say, "Not much." And he will say, "How much?" And I will say, "This much!" And he will say, "That much, for tea only?" But that was just a fantasy, and the desire to get Deedi to America and have her go through heart surgery, another fantasy . . . If I were only a practicing doctor in America. Just for Deedi's sake.

ROONA Her husband never cared.

BINDIA I lived through this anguish for so long that I . . . felt exactly like Deedi: helpless, bewildered, alone.

ROONA I feel the same and I live right here in my own country. I work so hard to get my life going. I want . . . for my children . . . what we never had . . . and I have to bring up three daughters. In a few years, I will have to worry about their marriages and dowry . . . you beg or borrow. You have to give them jahez, dowry, expensive things. Otherwise, no man or no man's family will ever marry them, no matter how pretty, no matter how educated, If they cannot bring cars, frigidaire, VCRs, sofa sets, cutlery, jewelry, furniture with them as part of being brides . . . men in this country have never changed their attitude . . . they want more and more every day, their mothers want more and more every day and if my daughters marry on their own – our society and religion will never forgive them like they never forgave Deedi. Even if I never care . . . even if I become liberated enough . . . society will never be liberated . . . then they will have to live with the guilt of choosing their own husbands and hurting us for the rest of their lives. And God forbid . . . if they choose the wrong men, like Deedi did, then we, the parents, will never forgive them. So I have to find husbands for them, I have to work hard to provide trousseaus for them. I work so hard . . . I get up every morning at six o'clock, make breakfast for my husband, get children ready . . . take them to school, take the little girl to the babysitter's. Work in the office the whole day, with the men who treat us all like slaves – slaves, yes, now they call us "educated slaves." Then, I come home, cook dinner . . . by nine o'clock in the evening I am so exhausted I can hardly keep my eyes open, and my husband sits and watches TV and reads the newspapers. He thinks he is the last intellectual left in the world, and then he yells that one button on his shirt was missing and he felt embarrassed in the office because other men's wives sew the broken buttons on their husbands' shirts. He forgets that I bring three thousand rupees home every month, more than he makes. He forgets that, but he never forgets the broken button on his shirt. And still I cannot leave him. Where am I going to stand in this society if I leave him? A divorced or unmarried woman has still no place in this damn country. The men only seem modern, but they are modern for themselves. Not for us. There is no one I can communicate with. I have no social life. I am an intelligent woman. I am struggling to find out why my spirit and my mind are failing. I had an absolute belief in myself . . . that was, and is, to some extent the only thing that keeps me going . . . I had belief in my father . . . and my brothers and my homeland, but I did not depend on them. I depended and trusted my belief in myself. That belief and trust I am losing. I feel as if I go down and down every day, there is a hollow, a space, a hole, inside me which keeps getting bigger and bigger. I want to look around and find somebody – who can hold me tight and tell me not to be afraid. You are better off in America. Even if it is hard there. Bindia, trust me it is much harder here. And American society . . . must be so free, and different. So open. Just to be able to breathe. You could do anything you want. Be anything you want.

BINDIA Yeah, it is different. Too many lights, too many avenues. I wanted to follow a straight path and could not handle the turns. I got lost somehow. I have a personal weakness. In my heart of hearts I wanted to destroy myself. People over there were different but they wanted me to be part of them. I kept feeling too small . . . too little . . . like nobody. I did not know better. Lights kept blinking in my eyes. I kept missing home. My heart kept shrinking with some kind of unknown fear of losing something. Not belonging anywhere. My heart was not there. It was here . . . in these courtyards . . . in the jasmine trees, in the sunshine.

My heart stayed with Deedi's heart. I missed my soil, my nieces, my nephews, my sunshine. I kept looking back – I could not go forward. I could not go back. My soul got weaker and weaker. I wandered around aimlessly in the gloomy streets of my new home, which I could not call home. Maybe I never wanted a home. Maybe I wanted to be the "civilized bum" of the family. *(She smiles. Pause. Phone rings off stage.)* An educated penniless, homeless woman like Deedi. I wanted to help Deedi by destroying myself. I wanted to tell her, "Deedi, you are not alone! I am going to go with you all the way – share the same fate oceans apart . . ."
(NAZO enters.)

NAZO Bindia, it's getting awfully late. I never leave mother alone for so long. We have to go to the hospital. I ran a cool bath for you. Go change. And Roona, your husband is on the phone long distance. *(ROONA gets up. Exits. BINDIA follows her. NAZO clears the table. Lights fade.)*

ACT II

Scene 1

Hospital, same afternoon. BEGUM *in hospital bed. An older woman, with grey hair: propped up by pillows, only the face of the lady is seen; the rest is covered with white sheets.*
BINDIA *and* NAZO *standing at the head of the bed.* BINDIA *dressed in Pakistani tunic and pants.* BEGUM *has a vacant look – keeps staring at* BINDIA *and sometimes stares at the ceiling. It is hard to tell if she recognized* BINDIA. *She just stares.* DEEDI *is also lit upstage.* NAZO *touches her mother's forehead – leans forward, starts to speak slowly.*

NAZO Mother . . . Mother . . . How do you feel? . . . Mother. Look who is here . . . You waited all those years, all those months . . . she is is here now. Bindia is here . . . your daughter Bindia is here from America . . . Don't you recognize her? You do recognize her, don't you? She flew all the way, right away . . .to be with you . . . your sons are also coming from Denmark. Don't worry about . . . anything . . . Bindia loves you. We all love you. You will be all right. Talk to her. Tell her you

love her. Tell us you love us, mother. *(She cries.* BINDIA *has been extremely quiet.* BEGUM *stares at* BINDIA. *It is such a vacant stare . . . that it is almost frightening.* BEGUM *tries to lift up her hand . . . tries hard . . . but she cannot . . . tries to speak . . . but cannot.* BINDIA *touches her mother's forehead . . . touches her hair.)*

BINDIA *(She has difficulty speaking)* Mother . . . Mother . . . I left the moment I heard about you . . . I have come from so far away, mother, please speak to me . . . You'll be all right. When you get better, we will sit in the kitchen and you will cook for us like the old times . . . and I will taste everything and we will laugh and do all the gup shup . . . I love you mother . . . I have always loved you. *(She kisses her forehead, touches her hair, kisses her again.)* Have you recognized me? *(BEGUM looks at her and nods her head.* MOAZZAN's *voice is heard reciting the prayer. Lights fade.* DEEDI *cries.)*

Scene 2

Same evening. NAZO's *garden with garden chairs and table, a telephone with a long wire.* ALI BUKSH *talks out loud to himself as he brings trolley with fruits, nuts, biscuits and samosa, and tea.*

ALI BUKSH Begum Bindia has come after such a long time, and I never have the chance to sit with her and talk, because there is so much work for me to do. Make tea, water the plants, wash the car. My salary is only 200 rupees, that's not enough to feed five children. I'm going to ask Begum Bindia to tell Nazo to raise my salary. I like Begum Bindia, she's the only one I like. I do not want her to go back. *(SAHID enters with his sisters, NAZO, ROONA and BINDIA. He is wearing a light pin-striped summer suit. All the sisters are dressed in Pakistani clothes.)*

ALI BUKSH *(To ROONA, as he pours the tea in cups)* Begum Roona, now Begum Bindia is here. Now is the time to take care of your mother's house, I think Begum Bindia should go and live there and never go back to America. *(Summarizes in Urdu)*

SAHID Babaji, you have started talking too much nonsense, go and wash my car. Go.

ALI BUKSH Yes Sahib, yes Sahib, right away, sorry Sahib, yes Sahib, right away sir. I will wash your car. *(Summarizes in Urdu. Exits.)*

SAHID *(Tries to change the subject. To* BINDIA:) Did you visit mother?

BINDIA Yes!

SAHID How is she?

NAZO The same!

SAHID Did she recognize you, Bindia?

BINDIA I want to believe that so much . . . I think she did.

SAHID What do you think of her condition? *(BINDIA does not answer.)* How did she look to you?

BINDIA Not good . . . she is very ill, I think mother is dying. *(Pause)*

SAHID *(Trying to console)* We are all grown-ups. We have to accept certain things . . . without being very emotional. Death is the other end of life . . . we have to accept death the same way as we accept life . . . She is old and one day she has to go . . . like father did . . . like all of us are going to!

BINDIA I just wish I came back a little bit earlier. A week earlier . . . or even just a day before she had this stroke. Then I would be able to speak to her . . . she might never be able to speak to me again.

SAHID Then why – didn't you?

BINDIA I have been trying to come for some time, but it just did not happen. I always lived with this strange kind of fear that I might never be able to see her again . . . one day the phone will ring early in the morning like it did . . . when father died . . . and it will be too late . . . I had been having nightmares. I kept dreaming about father saying, "Sacrifice, sacrifice." I didn't understand what he meant but now I think he was trying to tell me to sacrifice the whole lamb to uplift the evil which had befallen mother . . . but I didn't understand . . . Every time I got ready, something happened. I do not remember what, but every time something happened. I . . .

ROONA *(Interrupts her)* Listen, you have had a long rough day with your long flight and mother . . . and all that. Let's go in and try to get some sleep before we get into something else!

NAZO *(To* ROONA*)* Let her stay in the garden. It is so lovely out there.

BINDIA It is really lovely. That first stroke of fresh breeze against my face this morning when I arrived was so rejuve-

nating. You do have a lovely garden.

NAZO Wait till you see Sahid's garden. Huge. At the back of the house and in the front. *(Looks at* ROONA*)* Roona also has a garden, but a little smaller. But Sahid has a real big rose garden.

SAHID Big and hard to manage.

ROONA But you have servants . . . you can have as many servants from the army as you want . . . when you are that big an officer in the military in a military-ruled state, you can get away with anything . . . civilians . . . are the ones who suffer in this country. They cannot afford many servants because they do not make much money, and I do not make much money. So I do have a smaller garden. My husband is not in the army as you know, and we do have three little girls, so I have to have a smaller garden.

SAHID *(Surprised)* What's the matter with you today?

ROONA Nothing is the matter with me.

SAHID *(To* BINDIA*)* What kind of job do you have now?

BINDIA The same.

SAHID The same – what do you mean . . . the same with the United Nations?

BINDIA Yes!

SAHID How much money do you make? How many dollars a month?

BINDIA Just enough to survive.

SAHID I heard you got married!

BINDIA Yes.

SAHID When?

BINDIA Three months ago.

SAHID What does your husband do?

BINDIA He's an actor.

SAHID Oh! Anyone we know?

BINDIA He is not an established actor yet. *(Pause)*

SAHID American . . . I suppose?

BINDIA Yes.

SAHID Does mother know?

BINDIA I do not know.

SAHID *(Forcefully)* What do you mean, you don't know?

BINDIA *(Defensively)* I don't know.

SAHID *(Impatient)* Didn't you write to her?

BINDIA No.

SAHID So how would she know?

BINDIA I telephoned Roona and she promised that she would tell mother.

SAHID *(To* ROONA*)* Did you tell mother? *(ROONA doesn't answer.)* Did you tell mother?

ROONA No. I didn't tell her

SAHID Why not?

ROONA I was afraid to tell her.

SAHID (To BINDIA) Why didn't you tell mother?

BINDIA Because Roona promised me that she would tell her.

SAHID But it was not her responsibility . . . It was yours.

BINDIA I know. I asked Roona to do me a favour. I wanted Roona to prepare her first and then tell her. I did not want to shock her by a letter or a phone call.

SAHID (To ROONA, angrily) Why didn't you tell mother?

ROONA (Angrily) Because I was also afraid that it would shock her.

SAHID So both of you think it would have shocked her.

ROONA Yes, I think so. You know it would shock and upset her, and you know why it would shock and upset her. it's all the rules that have been bestowed upon us. (BINDIA does not answer.)

SAHID (To BINDIA) So you think you did something wrong.

BINDIA (Loses her patience) No, not at all! It is just that mother might had been disappointed! I was her last hope. She always hoped that one day I would come back and take care of her . . . especially after father's death . . . and none of you were of any help . . .

ROONA (Interrupts excitedly) I am so glad that you got married, and especially to an American man. You should have done this a long time ago. The moment you went to America you should have married an American man – maybe we should have all married American men, then nobody would be able to treat us like second-rate citizens right in our own country. (Laughs) Now they cannot pressure you to come back. Now they can't provoke mother against you. Now they can't tell her, "Oh, Bindia, she is not married, she has no purpose if she is not married, she has no life of her own if she is not married. She will come and live with you . . . and take care of you. She did it before. She will do it again, she is a sucker."

BINDIA No, I am sorry that I did not tell her. Maybe she would have loved the news. She always wanted me to get married.

SAHID (Interrupts) But not to an American. (ROONA and BINDIA look at each other, shocked. Complete silence for a few seconds.)

SAHID (Coughs – a nervous cough, a little embarrassed) I do not really care who you marry. You are pretty independent and have been for quite some time. It is just that mother is very religiously and rigidly Muslim and her relatives are religiously Muslim and her friends and her neighbors are religiously Muslim – maybe it would have been hard for her to break the news to her neighbors and relatives.

ROONA So it is good that she did not find out then.

BINDIA Roona is right. Once in my life I did the right thing.

SAHID I do not know, maybe she would have loved the news. Maybe she would die in peace, maybe she would have accepted it. (Pause) She loves you the most. You who detached yourself physically and emotionally from the family for the last ten years.

BINDIA I am not sure if she loved me the most. But I am sure she needed me the most. She got used to me doing things for her and father . . . when I lived here . . . I did all kinds of things for their comfort, for their health, for the household. No one else gave a damn. That's why she wanted me back. She didn't love me more than you or her. (Indicating NAZO. To SAHID:) I think she loved you the most. (SAHID laughs loud and cynical.)

ROONA Of course she loves you the most. You are her first born. The first son in a Muslim family.

BINDIA You were her eldest son. You know how it is . . . the eldest son, one of the highly ranked officers, in the up-and-coming Army, their real pride and joy. You are the real success, the obvious success with your chauffeur-driven limousine – which she never had the pleasure to ride in.

SAHID (Laughs again) I knew it! It was coming. It is nothing new, every time you come back you aggravate any and every kind of existing situation. Last time you were here you created a lot of confusion . . . and tension. You had fights with mother, fights with my wife, you are married now . . . you should be less frustrated.

ROONA It is awfully cruel of you to say

that and . . . you blame her for detaching herself physically and emotionally by moving to a foreign country but you who lived right here in the same country where your mother and father lived . . . and yet, with all your resources and posh living never visited them or never invited them to come rest in your servant-studded house! How come you abandoned her and us? How come you never ever invited mother to come live in your home with her grandchildren whom she loved so much? And how come Deedi is not here?

NAZO *(To* BINDIA *and* ROONA) Would you both just stop it. Show some respect for your eldest brother. He is in your father's place now.

BINDIA Oh, he is?

ROONA Well, he never treated us like a father.

SAHID *(Pointing towards* BINDIA, *to* ROONA) See what she does? She has not been here for more than twelve hours and she has already managed to provoke you against me.

ROONA Well, she hasn't done a thing. You think I am a child that can get provoked. You think I don't know what's going on.

SAHID *(To* ROONA) You and I always have a perfect relationship until she arrives.

BINDIA *(To* SAHID) You don't like me, do you?

SAHID I have nothing against you. I like you . . . I like all of you . . . I am always proud of you. I tell people, "Our sister is a medical doctor in America, in New York." How many Pakistani women go on their own and get themselves established in New York? I read about New York constantly. It is a hell of a city. The crime, the mafia, the drugs, the killings, the suicides, the high technology, the human loneliness, the television, the show business, the glamour, the isolation. You survived through it all. You are the real achiever, not me. You are the one who should be their real pride and joy. Not me. Not me.

BINDIA Yes, I should be the real pride and joy. Yes, I survived in New York City. I could not breathe but I survived. I could not scream but I survived. I could not eat but I survived. I could not tell anyone who I was and where I came from and what happened in between. An educated woman with nothing to do except go mad . . . but I survived . . . but none of you knew how I did it. You just kept telling people that you have a sister who is a doctor in America. You would not know how to survive on your own because you were always provided for. Father had to actually loan his house, the only property he had, to send you for the best education. You lived like a Pakistani prince, and spent like one . . . and we suffered, hoping that one day you would get him his house back. But you couldn't care less.

ROONA We moved to a smaller and dirtier house in a poorer neighborhood with no hot water so you could go to an elite college. So you could speak the perfect Queen's English.

BINDIA While father worked hard day after day and I assumed the duty of an eldest son. I promised myself that one day I would get father's house back for him.

ROONA And she did.

BINDIA Father had no money and Deedi was ill and every one of us was scared and you never knew . . . while I gave up my childhood and my youth and assumed the responsibility of looking after everyone. Deedi and I always slept in one bed because we could not afford another quilt. We always took baths, one after the other, because we couldn't afford more hot water.

ROONA Deedi and I were childhood friends but we lost our childhood.

BINDIA Somewhere – somewhere . . . with the misery and poverty, and when you got back . . . after all your education . . . you were too good for us. We could not speak English like you. You could not bring your friends home because the house was too ugly for you.

ROONA And then you moved out and started living with your uncle and aunt, because they had sofa sets, they spoke better English, they played cards at night and then you married their daughter.

BINDIA And I . . . I had to pay for it, I had to get the house back. I had to become a doctor to take care of your debts! Now all of you are so concerned about the house . . . I couldn't take all that . . . all those burdens thrown upon my young shoulders . . . I couldn't take it . . . none of it and that's why I left.

ROONA (*Interrupts*) She left but took her remorse with her. Deedi stayed. But made one mistake . . . she went out and picked a man for herself, but not the right one . . . and the parents never forgave her for that. And all of a sudden you were our big brother again. How dare she bring a bad name to the family? Her illiterate husband . . . drove her towards destruction. And we, all of us, had an equal share in it. She never forgave herself for hurting father and father never forgave her. She kept hurting herself and we kept hurting her. She wanted our love back.

BINDIA She hurt herself more to get our attention.

ROONA But we were too successful by then, we became cruel.

BINDIA And it is that cruelty which has destroyed us. What we are today is the result of that cruelty.

NAZO No. It's not that cruelty. It's the cruelty which Deedi inflicted on father. Imagine a Muslim woman marrying on her own. Where do you think we live? We live right here in an Islamic country. We have responsibilities toward our religion, our society, our parents. Our father became the laughing stock of the whole city. An Islamic man – who had never missed a single prayer in his life – could not face people in his mosque. He was a broken man – he died a broken man. He never recovered after that.

ROONA (*Interrupts*) He recovered . . . but he made sure she didn't. She suffered quietly but she never complained. She is as educated as you, and me and her, you think she didn't understand that mother and father favored us.

NAZO That is not true. They loved us equally.

ROONA No, they did not. We were their symbols of success. We were clever enough to make them believe that the husbands they chose for us were good men, good husbands who have made us happy. We played the game right because we were shrewd.

BINDIA She couldn't . . . because we wouldn't let her.

ROONA And then she drove herself towards – madness. She became totally lost. She lost her soul.

NAZO She is not mad. I think all of you think it is quite fashionable and romantic to assume mental illness these days. I am a perfectly happy, well-functioning human being. I have a good home, I have a social life. I work at it. I don't have the illusions of grandeur, I don't live in a dream world. I don't play your intellectual games. I constantly remind myself about the things which happened to the rest of you and ask Allah to give me strength to look after my family, my mother and my brothers and sisters.

SAHID (*Interrupts*) I wish I was a doctor. I would be able to do a lot more. It seems as if Bindia is ashamed of being a doctor.

ROONA If she insists not to be called a doctor why do we insist on calling her one? Why? So we can ridicule her? So we can say that she is a doctor in the United States of America but she never sent any money to her poor parents. She is rich but she has forgotten her roots. Is that what we are saying? We are punishing her for leaving . . . because we never left . . . we are punishing her for taking a chance . . . the chance we never took. We stayed right here. In this damned rotten sick country. Stayed right here . . . but never paid any attention towards the rest. Never took care of mother, abandoned Deedi, and kept telling ourselves that it is not our fault. It is the fault of those who left.

SAHID Who is blaming whom? And who is abandoning Deedi? She is having the best of all of us. She is living in mother's house, with her children and unemployed husband. The husband who never stood up to be a father to his own kids, never stood up to be man enough to take care of his wife. Deedi is my flesh and blood, she is part of me. I love her. Do you think seeing her this way doesn't hurt me? He has exploited us all . . . and most of all me. He wants us, he wants me, to bring up the children, he wants me to feed them. He is the one who has brought all this misery to the family, and all of you with all your brilliant brains are on his side. The man who never worked in his life wants us to provide him with a house . . . our mother's house . . . and he will get it, mark my words. Because you people do not understand his motives. You become too emotional about Deedi and the children and he knows that. He is exploiting us all and you are letting him do this to us . . . to me. He has to wake up and take responsibility. *(To* BINDIA*)* And stop blaming me and tell him to take care of her. We have our own lives to live. We have our own children to support. You live in another world. You do not know the politics of the people of this country anymore. You, who have no children of your own. You put too much pressure on us . . . too much . . . It is continuous from your side. We cannot bear the weight and . . . *(shouts)* stop blaming me for every catastrophe which happens to this family.

ROONA *(Shocked and very hurt for* BINDIA *but tries to calm her down)* Nobody is blaming you and we all know that Deedi's husband is a wretched man . . . he will never take responsibility for her and the kids, so should we just completely forget about her too? She needs help. We should not compete with that man. And you should help her kids like you helped Nazo's kids. And don't try to kick her out of her own mother's house.

NAZO They have been living there for the last year. Your own mother with her ailing health had to take care of all of them. Deedi had horrible fights with mother. And it was all your idea. *(Points to* BINDIA.*)*

BINDIA It was never my idea, not the way you are implying it, I never knew what the hell was going on. Deedi wrote me a letter that she wasn't feeling very well and needed a change away from her one-room apartment with no bathroom. I suggested that she should visit mother for a while. She went to mother's and you and your husband went to kick her out.

NAZO That is not true and you better leave my husband out of it. He has been better than all of you. Yes, all of you. It's my husband who became responsible for mother's needs after father's death. Needs which should have been met by our brothers. *(She is kind of nervous about what she just said.)* I mean brothers who live abroad, I understand Sahid's problem. He never can afford the time, with his immense responsibilities. But what about Asad, and Zali? What about them? Didn't they know they have a mother who needs their care and attention? Or have they completely forgotten who gave birth to them? Is buying diamonds for their European wives the only responsibility left for them? . . . Well . . . all of you are

too modern to take care of an old lady – your own mother . . . my husband was the only scapegoat we could find. A simple man, an Islamic man who fears God and knows that he will be rewarded by God in doing what he is doing, and besides, it was not my idea to go there. It was your brother's. *(Points towards* SAHID*)*

SAHID It was not my idea. It was your mother's.

BINDIA *(Angrily)* Why do you keep calling her "your mother"? Why can't all of us at least say "our mother"?

SAHID Well "our mother" then. She telephoned me and wanted me to come and get them all out so she could decide about the house. And breathe without that nuisance.

ROONA *(To* SAHID*)* So you appointed her husband as your envoy to kick your own sister from her own mother's house.

NAZO *(Very angry)* No one went to kick her out. We went to bring mother here. My husband should have never gone.

BINDIA Damn right. Who is he to kick her out of her own house? It is as much Deedi's house as yours, Roona's, and mine. Since Deedi is already living there let her stay there!

SAHID It is nobody's house. It is mother's.

BINDIA And after her, it is yours.

(Silence. Long pause.)

SAHID You are calling me a bastard.

BINDIA I am not.

SAHID You don't trust me. *(BINDIA doesn't answer.)* You don't trust me. You have never trusted me. None of you . . . it's no use . . . you don't give me a chance . . . you hate me. You won't let go. We all make mistakes in the past. But you won't let go. You would rather live with the contempt . . .

BINDIA That's not it.

SAHID Then what is it?

ROONA How many houses do we need to live in? We already have our own houses . . . we don't need mother's house, but Deedi does, so . . .

SAHID If she lives there, her husband will never work . . .

BINDIA He will not work even if she does not live there.

ROONA Who cares about him? But at least Deedi will have a comfortable life.

SAHID I have something else in mind . . . if all of you trust me that would be the best solution.

BINDIA What is it?

SAHID Well, if you all give me the power of attorney, then I will go ahead. The house is on such a central and commercial location that there are many Saudi Arabian banks who are offering me to build a bank . . . the property would still be in our names. They would still pay us rent; in ten or twenty years it will be worth lots of money.

BINDIA Who will get the rent?

NAZO All of us.

ROONA All of us?

BINDIA I will never see that money . . . neither would the brothers in Denmark. (Laughs) This family hasn't sent me a postcard in ten years . . . they are going to mail me money every month . . . regularly . . . every month. (Laughs)

SAHID It is because of you that nothing gets settled in this family.

ROONA And who will be taking care of the construction? It is a full-time job.

SAHID I have asked Nazo's husband to take six months' leave from his office and I will make sure that he gets the leave.

BINDIA Oh! So it is all planned already. Does your husband want to do it?

ROONA Of course he wants to do it.

NAZO He is not very keen on it, but he has agreed to do us a favour.

BINDIA This does not seem feasible to me.

ROONA Not to me either.

SAHID Why not?

BINDIA I think we should rather sell the house and give everybody their share – I can use the lump sum, so can Roona and Zali, and Deedi . . . us . . . we "who are not settled." We can use it for some kind of investment, and once we give the share to Deedi she and her husband can do whatever they want with it, they can buy a small house or start a business or gamble it away – then none of us would have to feel bad about her anymore.

SAHID But it is not good business to sell it now . . . the value of the property keeps going up . . . let's be practical and peaceful about it.

ROONA Who knows what will happen in ten years? I would like to do something now with the money, maybe invest for my little girls.

SAHID (Angrily) But I do not want to sell the house . . .

BINDIA (Interrupts) And I don't want the construction.

ROONA Neither do I.

SAHID Then there is no point discussing it anymore. Is there? You don't trust me and we never come to a peaceful solution.

BINDIA But you always want what is in your favour. Isn't it?

ROONA You always do.

SAHID (Angry. Pounds on the table.) I do not want to sell the house and it is not only in my favour. It is for Deedi also . . . I will protect her . . . and . . . mother, she never wanted to sell the house . . .

BINDIA (Interrupts) Since when . . . have you started to fulfill mother's wishes – your never showed any concern or warmth or love. We never had any peace and warmth amongst us.

ROONA What peace and warmth! It's nothing but an unending quarrel. Peace and warmth!

SAHID Yes, I know we never had any peace and warmth amongst us. We are empty souls, wandering around, trying to blame others for our vacuum. We somehow with all our education, creativity, and sensitivity have become emotionally crippled monsters incapable of having a healthy conversation without getting into a primal scream, which starts from nothing and turns into nothing! This exhausts us. We stay calm . . . "apparently calm" for some time and then repeat the same horrendous phenomenon again. I am trying to save our children . . . your children . . . my children . . . us . . . us . . . I am trying to save Deedi! And how it hurts me that you don't trust me. I hadn't recovered from our father's death. I promised myself to prevent further decay of my family. This fickle universe of summers and winters and autumns and springs . . . made me weep and tremble . . . and I woke up . . . from the intoxicating sleep . . . and I promised. I will help . . . Just give me a chance. Everything will be all right. I am going to get Deedi out of this mess. I promise you. Even if I have to kill that bloody bastard. She will come to live in my house. I don't want any of you to come back to this hell. You are the ones I admired the most . . . you had the courage to leave . . . not me . . . even my baby brothers left. You think having a garden and a job in the army is

enough? You left. All of you suffered.
What about me? I only sip tea all day
long, in a garden, in another garden, in
headquarters, in the barracks with the
bloody Generals. As long as they will rule
the country, I will be here ... doing
nothing but sipping tea. I am a slave of
my uniform. I will always remain a
bloody slave of my uniform. I feel like an
orphan of the barracks ... an orphan
with a uniform! An orphan of slavery. An
alien in a uniform, an immigrant in a
uniform ... I am in an exiled land. Land
which we can never call our own.
Someone else's colony. Someone else's
target, someone else's manipulative
grounds, someone else's country. I am
taking a journey in someone else's
country, with a uniform on. I am wide
awake and still walking through my
nightmare in someone else's country, in a
territory occupied by the uniform-clad
spies, the dirty, slimy spies are creeping
through my head, crawling through my
skin, digging holes in my brain, eating
me up alive and then spitting me out.
The world of monsters and beasts ... are
eating me alive ... and spitting me out –
all over me! ...
*(Phone rings. Everyone stares at it. No one
answers.* BINDIA *finally picks up the phone.
Everyone is completely still.* BINDIA *can't
believe what she hears. She is frozen. She
puts the phone down. She cannot speak. No
one can speak. Everyone looks at her.*
BINDIA *slowly starts to open her mouth.)*
BINDIA She is dead!
ROONA Oh no ... mother ... mother ...
ammijan, ammijan, Hai, Hai, Bindia,
Ammi is gone forever.
BINDIA It's ... It's ... It is Deedi. Deedi is
dead. Deedi is dead.
*(Everyone is stunned with the shocking
news. They stay still. Light starts to fade on
them and dim lights come up slowly on*
DEEDI, *who is walking from the upstage
area towards the grave. She stands still at
her own grave.*

Silence for a moment and slowly DEEDI
starts to speak.)

Epilogue

DEEDI
Now I will die
Now they will cry

My heart is enlarged
It pounds and flutters too much

My face is too swollen
Oh, but once it was carved

My ankles are too heavy
I cannot walk

Once we held hands
And ran across the golden fields

Once we talked to each other
Now I do not talk anymore

No one listened to me

Once we shared the same fate
Once we told each other stories

Once we shared the world

Once we had life in us
Once our eyes gleamed with hope
Now they are vacant
There is no way out

I am young
But I won't live
I will die

They will live
Their heart is not enlarged
It has shrunk

I was delicate
I was frail
I could not fight
My nerves got raw
My mind got pierced
My soul got damaged
Soon my soul will leave my body
Soon the wounds will never heal
Soon I will
Lose
My childhood friend
Soon I will have no more dreams

(Silence)

*(*DEEDI *sings a sorrowful lament in Urdu.
Towards the end of her song, lights slowly
start to fade on her. The last part of her
song is heard in total darkness.)*

Anna Deavere Smith

Biography

Actress, playwright and solo artist Anna Deavere Smith has acted on Broadway, Off-Broadway, regionally and in film and television. She has received an Obie Award, a Drama Desk Award, The Lucille Lortel Award, the George and Elisabeth Marton Award, and The Kesselring Prize, and was a runner-up for the Pulitzer Prize in Drama for *Fires in the Mirror: Crown Heights, Brooklyn and Other Identities*. She is the recipient of an honorary doctorate from her alma mater, Beaver College and from the University of North Carolina, Chapel Hill. In 1993 she was chosen as one of *Glamour* magazine's Women of the Year. *Twilight: Los Angeles, 1992* and *Fires in the Mirror* are a part of a series, of which Anna is the author and performer, called *On the Road: A Search for American Character*. *Fires in the Mirror* was first performed at the Joseph Papp Public Theatre. Recently, Anna has been on tour with *Fires in the Mirror*, including performances at the Arena Stage, the Long Wharf Theatre, the Royal Court Theatre in London, the Brooklyn Academy of Music, the American Repertory Theatre, the English Institute, the National Council on Foundations, the McCarter Theatre and Berkeley Repertory Theatre. The American Playhouse version of *Fires in the Mirror* ran on PBS stations across the country in April 1993 to wide critical acclaim.

For *Twilight*, Anna has received two Tony nominations, the Obie Award, Drama Desk Award, and an Outer Critics Circle Special Achievement Award for Documenting and Interpreting Events of Our Time in a Unique Theatrical Form. She also was honored by the Drama League of New York with a Distinguished Performance Award. Her play *Piano*, which was produced at the Los Angeles Theatre Center, received the 1991 Drama-Logue Award for Playwriting. She has appeared on the Arsenio Hall Show, and in the feature films *Dave* and Jonathan Demme's *Philadelphia*. *On the Road* includes pieces created for the Eureka Theatre of San Francisco (*From the Outside Looking In: San Francisco, 1990*); the Rockefeller Center, Bellagio, Italy (*Fragments: On Intercultural Performance*); Crossroads Theatre (*Black Identity and Black Theatre*); Princeton University (*Gender Bending*); the National

Photo: Mary Ann Halpin

Conference of Women and the Law; and Stanford University. Anna collaborated with Judith Jamison on a ballet called *Hymn*, for the thirty-fifth Anniversary Season of the Alvin Ailey American Dance Theatre, which was presented at the City Center in New York City in December 1993.

Artistic Statement

I see the work as a call. I played *Twilight* in Los Angeles as a call to the community. I performed it at a time when the community had not yet resolved the problems. I wanted to be a part of their examination of the problems. I believe that solutions to these problems will call for the participation of large and eclectic groups of people. I also believe that we are at a stage at which we must first break the silence about race and encourage many more people to participate in the dialogue.

One of the questions I was frequently asked when I was interviewed about *Twilight* was "Did you find any one voice that could speak for the entire city?" I think there is an expectation that in this diverse city, and in this diverse nation, a unifying voice would bring increased understanding and put us on the road to solutions. This expectation surprises me. There is little in culture or education that encourages the development of a unifying voice. In order to have real unity, all voices would have to first be heard or at least represented. Many of us who work in race relations do so from the point of view of our own ethnicity. This very fact inhibits our ability to hear more voices than those that are closest to us in proximity. Few people speak a language about race that is not their own. If more of us could actually speak from another point of view, like speaking another language, we could accelerate the flow of ideas.

The boundaries of ethnicity do yield brilliant work. In some cases these boundaries provide safer places that allow us to work in atmospheres where we are supported and can support the work of others. In some cases it's very exciting to work with like-minded people in similar fields of interest. In other cases these boundaries have been crucial to the development of identity and the only conceivable response to a popular culture and a mainstream that denied the possibility of the development of identity. On the other hand the price we pay is that few of us can really look at the story of race in its complexity and scope. If we were able to move more frequently beyond these boundaries, we would develop multi-faceted identities and we would develop a more complex language. After all, identity is in some ways a process toward character. It is not character itself. It is not fixed. Our race dialogue desperately needs this more complex language. The words of Twilight, the ex-gang member after whom I named the play, address this need:

Twilight is that time of day between day
  and night
limbo, I call it limbo,
and sometimes when I take my ideas to my
  homeboys

they say, well Twilight, that's something you
  can't do right now,
that's an idea before its time.
So sometimes I feel as thought I'm stuck in
  limbo
the way the sun is stuck between night and
  day
in the twilight hours.
Nighttime to me is like a lack of sun,
but I don't affiliate darkness with anything
  negative.
I affiliate darkness with what came first,
because it was first,
and relative to my complexion,
I am a dark individual
and with me being stuck in limbo
I see the darkness as myself.
And I see the light as the knowledge and
  the wisdom of the world, and the understanding of others.
And I know
that in order for me to be a full human
  being
I cannot forever dwell in darkness
I cannot forever dwell in idea
of identifying with those like me
and understanding only me and mine.

Twilight's recognition that we must reach across ethnic boundaries is simple but true.

Production history

Twilight: Los Angeles, 1992 was originally produced by the Center Theatre Group/Mark Taper Forum in Los Angeles in May 1993, directed by Emily Mann. *Twilight* had its New York premiere in March 1994 at the New York Shakespeare Festival Theatre, followed by an immediate move to the Cort Theatre on Broadway, both under the direction of George C. Wolfe. In 1995 it was remounted for touring at the Berkeley Repertory Theatre, directed by Sharon Ott.

15 *Excerpts from* Twilight: Los Angeles, 1992

Anna Deavere Smith

Indelible Substance

JOSIE MORALES: clerk-typist, City of Los Angeles uncalled witness to the Rodney King beating, Simi Valley trial

In a conference room at her workplace, downtown Los Angeles

We lived in Apartment A6
right next to A8,
which is where George Holliday lived.
And, um
the next thing we know is, um
ten or twelve officers made a circle around him
and they started to hit him.
I remember
that they just not only hit him with sticks,
they also kicked him,
and one guy,
one police officer, even pummeled his fist into his face,
and they were kicking him.
And then we were like "O, my goodness,"
and I was just watching.
I felt like "Oh my goodness"
'cause it was really like
he was in danger there,
it was such
an oppressive atmosphere.
I knew it was wrong –
whatever he did –
I knew it was wrong,
I just knew in my heart
this is wrong –
you know they can't do that.
And even my husband was petrified.
My husband said, "Let's go inside."
He was trying to get me to come inside
and away from the scene,
but I said, "No."
I said, "We have to stay here
and watch

because this is wrong."
And he was just petrified –
he grew up in another country where this is prevalent,
police abuse is prevalent in Mexico –
so we stayed and we watched the whole thing.
And
I was scheduled to testify
and I was kind of upset at the outcome,
because I had a lot to say
and I was just very upset
and I, um,
I had received a subpoena
and I told the prosecutor, "When do you want me to go?"
He says, "I'll call you later and I'll give you a time."
And the time came and went and he never called me,
so I started calling him.
I said, "Well, are you going to call me or not?"
And he says, "I can't really talk to you
and I don't think we're going to be using you because
it contradicts what Melanie Singer said."
And I faxed him a letter
and I told him that those officers were going to be acquitted
and one by one I explained these things to him in this letter
and I told him, "If you do not put witnesses,
if you don't put one resident and testify to say what they saw,"
And I told him in the letter
that those officers were going to be acquitted.
But I really believe that he was dead set on that video
and that the video would tell all,
but, you see, the video doesn't show you where those officers went

282

and assaulted Rodney King at the beginning.
You see that?
And I was so upset. I told my co-worker, I
    said, "I had a terrible dream
that those guys were acquitted."
And she goes "Oh no, they're not gonna be
    acquitted."
She goes, "You, you,
you know, don't think like that."
I said, "I wasn't thinking I had a dream!"
I said, "Look at this,
they were,
they were acquitted."
Yeah, I do have dreams
that come true,
but not as vivid as that one.
I just had this dream
and I saw the
men
and it was in the courtroom and I just
had it in my heart . . .
something is happening
and I heard they were acquitted
Because dreams are made of some kind of
    indelible substance.
And my co-worker said, "You shouldn't
    think like this,"
and I said, "I wasn't thinking
it was a dream."
And that's all,
and it came to pass.

To Look Like Girls from Little

ELVIRA EVERS: general worker and cashier,
Canteen Corporation
A Panamanian woman in a plaid shirt, in an
apartment in Compton. Late morning, early
afternoon. She has a baby on her lap. The
baby has earrings in her ears. ELVIRA *has a*
gold tooth. There is a four-year-old girl with
large braid on top of her head and a big smile
who is around throughout the interview. The
girl's name is NELLA

So
everybody was like with things they was
    takin'
like
a carnival
and I say
to my friend Frances,
"Frances, you see this?"
and she said, "Girl, you should see
that

it's getting worst."
And I say, "Girl, let me take my butt
up there before something happen."
And, um,
Then somebody throw a bottle
and I just . . .
then
I felt
like moist,
and it was like a tingling sensation – right?
and I did like this
and it was like itchin',
and I say, "Frances, I'm bleedin'."
And she walk with me to her house
And she say, "Lift up your gown, let me
    see."
She say, "Elvira, it's a bullet!"
I say, "What?"
I say, "I didn't heard nothin'."
She say, "Yes, but it's a bullet."
She say, "Lay down there. Let me call St.
    Francis and tell them that
you been shot
and to send an ambulance."
And she say,
"Why you?
You don't mess with none of those people.
Why they have to shot you?"
So Frances say the ambulance be here in
    fifteen minutes.
I say, "Frances,
I cannot wait that."
I say,
"I'm gone!"
So I told my oldest son, I say,
"Amant, take care of your brothers.
I be right back."
Well, by this time he was standing up there,
    he was crying,
all of them was crying.
What I did for them not to see the blood –
I took the gown and I cover it
and I didn't cry.
That way they didn't get nervous.
And I get in the car.
I was goin' to drive.
Frances say, "What you doin'?"
I said, "I'm drivin'."
"She say, "No you're not!"
And we take all the back streets
and she was so supportive,
because she say, "You all right?
You feel cold?
You feel dizzy?
The baby move?"
She say, "You nervous?"

I say, "No, I'm not nervous, I'm just worried
    about the baby."
I say, "I don't want to lose this baby."
She say, "Elvira, everything will be all
    right." She say, "Just pray."
So there was a lot of cars, we had to be
    blowing the horn.
So finally we get to St. Francis
and Frances told the front-desk office, she
    say,
"She been shot!"
And they say, "What she doin' walkin'?"
And I say, "I feel alright."
Everybody stop what they was doin'
and they took me to the room
and put the monitor to see if the baby was
    fine
and they find the baby heartbeat,
and as long as I heard the baby heartbeat I
    calmed down,
long as I knew whoever it is, boy or girl,
    it's all right,
and
matter of fact, my doctor, Dr. Thomas, he
    was there
at
the emergency room.
What a coincidence, right?
I was just lookin' for that familiar face,
and soon as I saw him
I say, "Well I'm all right now."
Right?
So he bring me this other doctor and then
    told me,
"Elvira, we don't know how deep is the
    bullet.
We don't know where it went. We gonna
    operate on you.
But since that we gonna operate we gonna
    take the baby out
and you don't have to
go through all of that."
They say, "Do you understand
what we're saying?"
I say, "Yeah!"
And they say, "Okay, sign here."
And I remember them preparing me
and I don't remember anything else.
Nella!
No.
(Turns to the side and admonishes the child)
She likes company
And in the background
I remember Dr. Thomas say, "You have a
    six-pound-twelve ounce little
girl."

He told me how much she weigh and her
    length
and he
say, "Um,
she born,
she had the bullet in her elbow
but when we remove . . .
when we clean her up
we find out that the bullet was still between
    two joints,
so
we did operate on her and your daughter is
    fine
and you are fine."
(Sound of a little child saying "Mommy")
Nella!
She want to show the baby.
Jessica,
bring the baby.
(She laughs)
We don't like to keep the girls without
    earrings. We like the little
girls
to look like girls from little.
I pierce hers.
When I get out on Monday,
by Wednesday I did it,
so by Monday she was five days,
she was seven days,
and I
pierced her ears
and the red band is just like for evil eye.
We really believe in Panama . . .
in English I can't explain too well.
And her doctor, he told . . .
he explain to me
that the bullet
destroyed the placenta
and went through
me
and she caught it in her arm.
(Here you can hear the baby making noises,
    and a bell rings.)
If she didn't caught it in her arm,
me and her would be dead.
See?
So it's like
open your eyes,
watch what is goin' on.
(Later in the interview, NELLA gave me a
    bandaid, as a gift.)

I Was Scared

ANONYMOUS YOUNG WOMAN: student,
University of Southern California
February. A rainstorm. Late afternoon, early
evening. Dark out. Just before dinner. A
sorority house at the University of Southern
California, which is a very affluent university
in the middle of South Central. We are in a
small room with Laura Ashley furnishings.
Lamplight. While we are talking, someone
comes by ringing a dinner bell which is a
xylophone.

I was scared to death.
I've never felt as scared, as frightened, in
  my life.
Um,
and it was a different fear than I've ever
  felt.
I mean, I was really afraid.
At a certain point
it dawned on us that they might try to
  attack the row,
the sororities and the fraternities.
Because they did do that during the Watts
  riots.
And, um, they . . .
they went
into the house,
where they smashed the windows.
I don't know how we got this information
  but somebody knew that,
so that
spread in the house real fast,
and once we realized that,
we started packing.
We all packed a bag and we all had put on
  our tennis shoes.
This was late in the evening, and we all sat
  in our hallways upstairs,
very small hallways,
and we all said,
"Oh, if they come to the front door, this is
  what we're gonna do."
Many things I can tell you.
First of all, my parents were on their way,
to drive to California,
to take part in a caravan
in which they bring old cars,
old forties cars,
and a whole bunch of 'em, all their friends,
  a huge club.
They all drive their cars around the
  country.
My dad has an old car.

It's a '41 Cadillac.
I told 'em, to turn around, go home.
I said, "Go home, Mom."
All I can think of . . . one bottle.
one shear from one bottle in my father's
  car,
he will die!
He will die.
He collects many cars,
he has about fifteen different kinds of cars.
This is his thing, this is what he does.
He's got Lincoln
Continentals
and different Town and Countries.
All forties.
His favorite is a '41 Cadillac.
And, um, so . . . he keeps them from five to
  ten years,
you know.
Depending on whether you can get a good
  value for 'em.
It's a business
as well as a hobby.
And so I don't specifically know what he
  came out in.
But one of 'em.
And those are his pride
and joys.
They are perfect.
They are polished.
They are run perfect.
They are perfect.
All I can think of is a bottle gettin' any-
  where near it.

Ask Saddam Hussein

ELAINE BROWN: former head of the Black
Panther Party, author of *A Taste of Power.*
A pretty black woman in her early fifties. She
is in a town outside Paris, France, on the
phone. It is five p.m. France time. Spring.

I think people do have, uh,
some other image
of the Black Panther Party than the guns.
The young men, of course, are attracted
to the guns,
but what I tell them is this:
Did you know Jonathan Jackson?
Because I did,
and Jonathan Jackson was seventeen years
  old.
He was probably one of the most brilliant
  young men
that you could meet.

He happened to be a science genius.
He was not a gang member, by the way,
but Jonathan Jackson
went to a courtroom by himself
and took over for that one glorious minute
in the name of
revolution and the freedom of his brother
and other people who were in prison
and died that day.
My question to you,
seventeen-year-old young brother with a
    gun in your hand,
tough and strong and beautiful as you are:
Do you think it would be better
if Jonathan Jackson were alive today
or that he died
that day in Marin County?
Me personally,
I'd rather know Jonathan Jackson.
That's what I'd rather do,
and I'd rather him be alive today,
to be among the leadership that we do not
    have,
than to be dead and in his grave at seven-
    teen years old.
I'm talking merely about strategy,
not swashbuckling.
I think that this idea of picking up the gun
    and going into the street
without a
plan and without
any more rhyme or reason than rage
is bizarre and so, uh . . .
And it's foolish
because it will, uh . . .
I think that
all one has to do
is ask, to ask the Vietnamese
or Saddam Hussein
about the power and weaponry
and the arsenal of the United States govern-
    ment and its willingness to
use it
to get to understanding what this is about.
You are not facing a,
you know, some little Nicaraguan clique
here.
You are not in Havana in 1950 something.
This is the United States of America.
There isn't another *country*,
there isn't another *community*
that is more organized and armed.
Uh,
not only is it naive,
it is foolish if one is talking
about jumping out into the street

and waving a gun, and doing that bad thing,
because you not that bad,
you see what I'm saying?
You just not that bad.
You *think* you bad,
but I say again,
ask Saddam Hussein
about who is bad
and you'll get the answer.
So what I am saying is:
Be conscious of what you are doing.
If you just want to die
and become a poster,
go ahead and do that –
we will all put you on the wall with all the
    rest of the people.
But if you want to effect change for your
    people
and you are serious about it,
that doesn't mean throw down your gun.
Matter of fact, I would def . . . definitely
    never tell anybody to do that,
not black and in America.
But if you want a gun,
I hope you can shoot
and I hope you know who to shoot
and I hope you know how to not go to jail
    for having done that
and then let that be the end of that.
But if you are talking about a war
against the United States government,
then you better talk to Saddam Hussein
and you better talk to the Vietnamese
    people
and the Nicaraguans
and El Salvadorans
and people in South Africa
and people in other countries in Southeast
    Asia
and ask those motherfuckers
what this country is capable of doing.
So all I am saying is:
if you are *committed*,
if you seriously make a *commitment*,
because . . .
and that commitment
must be based not on hate but on love.
And that's the other thing.
My theme is
that love of your people.
Then you gonna have to realize that this
    may have to be a lifetime
commitment
and that the longer you live,
the more you can do.
So don't get hung up

on your own ego
and your own image
and pumping your muscles
and putting on your black beret
or some kinda Malcolm X hat or whatever
    other
regalia
and symbolic vestment you can put on your
    body.
Think in terms of what
are you going to do
for black people.
I'm saying that these
are the long haul,
because then you might be talkin' about
bein' in a better position for a so-called
armed struggle.
At this point you might be talkin' about
    piss-poor,
ragtag, unorganized, poorly armed
and poorly, poorly,
uh-uhm,
poorly led
army
and we will be twenty more years
trying to figure out what happened to
    Martin, Malcolm,
and the Black Panther Party.

Swallowing the Bitterness

MRS. YOUNG-SOON HAN: former liquor
store owner
*A house on Sycamore Street in Los Angeles
just south of Beverly. A tree-lined street. A
quiet street. It's in an area where many
Hasidic Jews live as well as yuppie types.
MRS. YOUNG-SOON HAN's living room is
impeccable. Dark pink-and-apricot rug and
sofa and chairs. The sofa and chairs are made
of a velour. On the back of the sofa and chairs
is a Korean design. A kind of circle with lines
in it, a geometric design. There is a glass
coffee table in front of the sofa. There is
nothing on the coffee table. There is a mantel
with a bookcase, and a lot of books. The
mantel has about thirty trophies. These are
her nephew's. They may be for soccer. On the
wall behind the sofa area, a series of citations
and awards. These are her ex-husband's. They
are civic awards. There are a couple of
pictures of her husband shaking hands with
official-looking people and accepting awards. In
this area is also a large painting of Jesus
Christ. There is another religious painting over*
*the archway to the dining room. There are
some objects hanging on the side of the
archway. Long strips and oval shapes. It is
very quiet. When we first came in, the
television was on, but she turned it off.*
*   She is sitting on the floor and leaning on the
coffee table. When she hits her hand on the
table, it sounds very much like a drum. I am
accompanied by two Korean-American
graduate students from UCLA.*

Until last year
I believed America is the best.
I still believe it.
I don't deny that now
because I'm a victim,
but
as
the year ends in '92
and we were still in turmoil
and having all the financial problems
and mental problems.
Then a couple months ago
I really realized that
Korean immigrants were left out
from this
society and we were nothing.
What is our right?
Is it because we are Korean?
Is it because we have no politicians?
Is it because we don't
speak good English?
Why?
Why do we have to be left out?
(She is hitting her hand on the coffee table.)
We are not qualified to have medical
    treatment.
We are not qualified to get, uh,
food stamp,
(she hits the table once)
not GR,
(hits the table once)
no welfare.
(Hits the table once).
Anything.
Many Afro-Americans
(two quick hits)
who never worked,
(one hit)
they get
at least minimum amount
(one hit)
of money
(one hit)
to survive.
(one hit)

We don't get any!
(Large hit with full hand spread)
Because we have a car
(one hit)
and we have a house.
(Six-second pause)
And we are high taxpayers.
(One hit)
(Fourteen-second pause)
Where do I finda [*sic*] justice?
Okay, Black People
probably
believe they won
by the trial?
Even some complains only half right?
justice was done.
But I watched the television
that Sunday morning,
early morning as they started.
I started watch it all day.
They were having party and then they
   celebrated,
all of South Central,
all the churches.
They finally found that justice exists
in this society.
Then where is the victims' rights?
They got their rights.
By destroying innocent Korean merchants.
. . . .
They have a lot of respect,
as I do,
for
Dr. Martin King?
He is the only model for Black community.
I don't care Jesse Jackson.
But
he was the model
of nonviolence.
Nonviolence?
They like to have hiseh [*sic*] spirits.
What about last year?
They destroyed innocent people.
(Five-second pause)
And I wonder if that is really justice
*(and a very soft "uh" after "justice," like
   "jusitcah," but very quick)*
to get their rights
in this way.

(Thirteen-second pause)
I waseh swallowing the bitternesseh,
sitting here alone
and watching them.
They became all hilarious
(three-second pause)
and, uh,
in a way I was happy for them
and I felt glad for them.
At leasteh they got something back, you
   know.
Just let's forget Korean victims or other
   victims
who are destroyed by them.
They have fought
for their rights
(one hit simultaneous with the word "rights")
over two centuries
(one hit simultaneous with "centuries")
and I have a lot of sympathy and understanding for them.
Because of their effort and sacrificing,
other minorities, like Hispanic
or Asians,
maybe we would suffer more
by mainstream.
You know,
that's why I understand,
but
I would like to be part of their
'joyment.
But . . .
That's why I had mixed feelings
as soon as I heard the verdict.
I wish I could
live together
with eh [*sic*] Blacks,
but after the riots
there were too much differences.
The fire is still there –
how do you call it?
igni . . .
igniting fire.
*(She says a Korean phrase phonetically: "Dashi
   yun gi ga nuh")*
It's still dere.
It canuh
burst out anytime.

Diana Son

Biography

Diana Son is a playwright living and working in New York City. *Stealing Fire* was produced at Soho Rep. *The R.A.W. Plays: Short Plays for Raunchy Asian Women* was produced at HERE by HOME for Contemporary Theater. *2000 Miles* was produced by Ensemble Studio Theatre, the No Pants Theatre Company at Synchronicity Space and by Under One Roof. Diana is currently a member of the Playwright's Unit in residence at the Joseph Papp Public Theater. Her fiction has been published by *Asian Pacific American Journal* and she has read her short stories at City University of New York, the Queens Museum of New York, and Hunter College High School. She is currently working on a new full-length play, *Boy*. Diana is a 1993 Van Lier Fellow at New Dramatists. She has a BA in Dramatic Literature from New York University.

Photo: Pamela Jennings

Artistic statement

Living in New York City, I am relentlessly asked, *Where are you from? Where are you from?* Whether I'm sitting in a cab, waiting on a table, meeting someone new, or trying to get my plays produced. *Where are you from?* Because something about me – my face, my speech, my manners, my confusion as to whether to put butter or cream cheese on a bialy – sends up the red flag: NOT FROM HERE! SHE IS NOT FROM HERE! Which I'm not. I've lived in New York for eleven years but I know no matter how long I end up staying here, I'll never be *from* here.

The real reason that question convulses me like it does is not because I resent being noticed as a non-New Yorker but because I fear that my answer to *Where are you from?* will disappoint the person asking it. My face promises an exotic background, one with majestic mountains, spicy peasant food, primitive outdoor markets and colorful folk dresses. The place that I am truly *from* is Dover, Delaware. My actual background includes a shopping mall, jello wrestling at The Hub, a drive-thru church and Maypole dancing on May Day. Exotic, maybe, but not what people expect from me.

I was born in Philadelphia where my parents met in a Korean car pool. My mom was a nurse on an exchange from Korea and my dad was a sponsored student at the Philadelphia College of Pharmacy. They both worked at Lankenau Hospital and my dad drove other Koreans to and from work in his red striped Gran Torino. After my brother Grant was born, my parents had to leave the country for a year because of their visas. They went to Surinam because my dad had a job offer there. Being born in Surinam would put some spice in my bio but my parents beat it back to Philadelphia to make sure I would be American born. With a slight case of roseola, I was.

Growing up in Dover, I spent my childhood in a KMart – we lived behind one and there was reason to go to there almost every day. On the weekends, my friends and I would spend entire afternoons there: trying on wigs, having each other paged, chasing down the blue light special. My neighborhood and my school were made up of an almost equal proportion of blacks and whites and we mixed. I grew up ignorant of the tension between blacks and Koreans. To me, being biased against black people was something that white people did. It made me aware that I was neither.

By adolescence, I was a mall nymph. I had a perm. I swam backstroke on the swim team. I had an 8-track player which I jammed with tapes of AC/DC, Cheap Trick, and Pat Benatar. I was safely anonymous except for two things – I was the only one among my friends who knew what I wanted to be and I was the only one who got called "ching chong" when cruising through Sears.

In 1983, I came to the city to be a student at New York University. A friend from my dorm invited to me to see a production of the Experimental Theatre Wing at NYU. It was Anne Bogart's *South Pacific*. Bogart had staged it as a production being performed by patients in a Vietnam Vet Hospital. Stagehands dressed as orderlies walked in and out of the scenes. Actors dressed as patients disrupted the scenes. Action was taking place in four to five different parts of the playing area at a time. Actors repeated movements and lines over and over changing them slightly each time. I didn't know where to look. I didn't know whose lines to listen to. I didn't know who was who. I was confused. I was enthralled. I wanted to understand what was happening emotionally, psychologically, historically, theoretically, to understand what was going on in this careful mess.

I became a dramatic literature major, and under the auspices of Professor Una Chaudhuri I started to get some ideas about the theatre. Nine years after I saw *South Pacific* and a dozen more of her productions, I studied with Anne Bogart and I started to make some theatre.

As a playwright, I try to incorporate aural and visual elements into the text. How the text is arranged on the page, the sounds the words make, the rhythm between them are as important to me as their meaning. I like to use slides because I think words are aesthetically beautiful. Also, by letting the audience read for themselves, they are given the power of interpretation. An active audience is not a bored audience.

In 1993, dramaturg Chiori Miyagawa invited six playwrights to form the Asian American Playwrights Lab at the Public

Theater. We decided to write short pieces dealing with intercultural themes. Each of us – some trepidatiously, others naturally – chose one of the cultures represented to be Asian American. I was one of the quivering ones. To me, the stage is the size of a planet. Whereas fiction and movies are like microscopes through which you can view the minute movements of an amoeba, plays are telescopes through which you can see the grand action of massive beings. To be so specific and narrow as to say "this play will deal with what it is to be Asian American," seemed to me like pointing a telescope at an ant hill. But by describing what I saw through the lens, I realized that a lot of other people didn't know how ants lived. They were worth looking at closely after all.

In *R.A.W. ('Cause I'm a Woman)* I wanted the man's lines to be slides because I didn't want lines like "I've never been with an Oriental woman before" to be delivered with exaggeration or mockery. Slides are non-judgmental. I am not trying to condemn men who say lines like this. The words express themselves, no commentary is necessary. But I want people to know that Asian American women have to hear these comments all the time. At every performance of *R.A.W. ('Cause I'm a Woman)*, I have been gratified to have men and women from diverse cultures, sexual orientations, hair colors, ages and backgrounds come up and say, "That play includes me."

Production history

R.A.W. ('Cause I'm a Woman) premiered at the Ohio Theatre as part of the T.W.E.E.D. New Works Festival on May 19, 1993, directed by Lenora Champagne and performed by Kim Ima, Lisa Ann Li, Liana Pai and Elaine Tse. It was read at the Joseph Papp Public Theater and produced at Columbia University, and at HERE by HOME for Contemporary Theatre.

16 R.A.W. ('Cause I'm a Woman)

Diana Son

Characters

RAUNCHY ASIAN WOMAN 1

RAUNCHY ASIAN WOMAN 2

RAUNCHY ASIAN WOMAN 3

RAUNCHY ASIAN WOMAN 4

Slides

The slides represent men's voices. However, the slides should not be substituted with an actual man's voice. A live actor can be tempted to interpret the man's character, to give him an attitude. By using slides, the audience can give the man whatever voice they hear internally. The slides should be white text on a black background. The size of the letters should be big enough to be readable without being overwhelming. A plain sans serif font works best.

Music

"I'm a Woman," by Jerry Leiber and Mike Stoller, sung by Peggy Lee

Music: The first four measures of Peggy Lee's "I'm a Woman" repeated long enough to accompany the slides

Slide: Exotic.
Slide: Submissive.
Slide: Chic.
Slide: Obedient.
Slide: Mysterious.
Slide: Domestic.
Slide: Petite.
Slide: Oriental.
Slide: **R.A.W.**
Slide: **R**aunchy
Slide: **A**sian
Slide: **W**omen

ALL: Fuck!

Music: Intro.

1: In a crowded room,
3: in a smoky place,
2: in a bar with no light,
4: a man walks up to me and says:

Slide: I love your eyes.

1: And I ask him "What is there to love about—"
3: My eyes.
2: That they have given earnest love to men.
4: And complex love to women.
3: That through them he feels the grace that God has lent me.

1: That they're slanted.

3: Making me a geisha.
2: Who will walk on his back.
4: Who'll have dinner on the table and dessert between my legs.
1: Who will give him the blowjob of his life.

Music: 'Cause I'm a woman.

2: And he asks me:

Slide: Where are you from?

2: And I say:
1: From a place where I was neither black nor white.
3: Where I checked the box marked

"other."
4: Where I made myself. Where I changed.

2: He responds:

Slide: I mean what *country* are you from?

2: Because he wants to hear:
4: I'm from a fishing village off the Yangtze river.
3: Where my mother was a shaman who taught me shiatsu.
1: Where my father made musical instruments out of fish bones and moss.
2: Where I invented tai-chi.

Music: 'Cause I'm a woman. W-O-M-A-N.

3: He says:

Slide: I've never been with an Oriental woman before.

3: And I try to give him the benefit of the doubt.
4: I think "been with" that comes from "to be."
1: He wants to be with me.
2: He wants to know me.

3: He wants to fuck me.

4: He wants to see if my clit is sideways.
2: He wants to make me moan in ancient languages.
1: He wants me to bark like a Lhasa Apso.
3: He wants to wow me with the size of his non-Asian dick.

Music: 'Cause I'm a woman. W-O-M-A-N. I'll say it again.

4: Then he says:

Slide: I love Oriental women.

3: And I want to say.
4: So do I.

Music: 'Cause I'm a woman. W-O-M-A-N. I'll say it again. I got a 20 dollar gold piece that says

there ain't nothing I can't do
I can make a dress out of a feedbag
and I can make a man out of you.
'Cause I'm a—

Music: Intro.

1:   I will not give you a massage.
3:   I will not scrub your back.
2:   I will not cook exotic meals using
     animal parts that aren't normally
     eaten.
4:   I will not *not* get on top.
1:   I will not be your Soon Yi.
3:   I will not kill myself to save your
     son.
2:   I will not light your cigarette
     afterwards.
4:   I will not let you come without me.
1:   I will not be your china doll.
3:   I will not be a virgin.
2:   I will not call you papasan.
4:   I will not worship you.
1:   I will not be your fetish.

(Stop music.)

4:   But I will love.
3:   And be loved.
2:   Yes.
1:   I will.

4:   But not by a:

Slide: SWM
Slide: MBM
Slide: Bi-Curious F
Slide: Open-minded DJM
Slide: Separated HM with kids

(The slides and lines occur at the same time.)
Slide: East Asian scholar
1:       Geek.
Slide: Vietnam vet
3:       Psycho.
Slide: Ivy leaguer
2:       Jock.
Slide: New Age philosopher
4:       Pot head.
Slide: Long-haired musician.
1:       Slob.

Slide: Looking for

Slide: Oriental Beauty
3:       Slant-eyed slut.

Slide: Sexy Asian Gal
2:       Manicurist with a bad perm.
Slide: Bi-Oriental F
4:       Joan Chen look-a-like for him and
         his wife.
Slide: Import from the East
1:       Non-English speaking babe with
         bound feet.
Slide: Vegetarian SAF preferably from
         Nassau or Queens
3:       PC Chinese girl with a fast car.
Slide: of Inner Beauty
2:       Who won't talk too much.
Slide: And Spiritual Strength
4:       Has no ideas of her own.
Slide: Who is Graceful
1:       Easy to flip over.
Slide: And likes to be wined and dined
3:       Gets drunk on one glass of chardon-
         nay.

(The slides go quickly, the lines overlap.)
Slide: To show me exciting new horizons.
Slide: Give me a first-time cultural
         experience.
Slide: Exchange sensual customs with.
1:       To do what the white girls won't do.
3:       To act out his most exotic fantasies.
2:       To let him come in my mouth and
         say "thank you."
4:       To be his dominant–obedient,
         desirable–untouchable, autonomous–
         dependent, virgin–whore.
ALL: **It hath made me R.A.W.**

ALL: R.A.W.
3:       'Cause I'm from New Hampshire.
         How exotic is New Hampshire?
ALL: R.A.W.
2:       'Cause I'm not even that good in
         bed, OK?
ALL: R.A.W.
1:       'Cause these are the kinds of creeps
         I end up going out with. Why?
ALL: R.A.W.
4:       'Cause how am I supposed to be a
         virgin and a whore at the same
         fucking time?
ALL: R.A.W.
4:       Because I want to love.
3:       And be loved.
2:       Yes.
1:       I do.

3:       I had my first boyfriend when I was
         15 years old Paul Rossman.

293

4:     Built like a brick shithouse Paul Rossman.

3:     He lived in the old part of town in an old Colonial house with his divorcée mom. Once I caught them dancing. She was drunk, he was embarrassed. I was glad I came in when I did.

2:     Paul was six-feet two inches of purebred whiteboy.

3:     He had flaky chapped lips which he marinated in vaseline, kissing him was like licking a carburetor but we had a big love.

1:     Huge, it consumed me.

3:     I was just 15.

2:     It was early for love.

3:     I had feathered hair parted in the middle.

4:     It was early for sex.

3:     I wore pink oxford shirts tucked into wide-wale corduroys.

1:     I was the only Asian in town. I was a famous preppie.

3:     Paul used to drive me home after field hockey practice. "Don't bring him in the house!" Mom would say, "It stinks, I've been cooking daddy's food. It smells. It smells like kimchee." Mom fed me lasagna with Green Giant green beans as daddy's dinner reeked on the stove. "Don't eat the kimchee," Mom would say as she brought daddy's food to the table "You'll never have an American boyfriend." "I have Paul," I would say. "Kimchee smells terrible," Mom said. "It's not nice for Paul." But mom ate daddy's food. Mom ate kimchee. "How come you can eat kimchee?" She gave me green jello for dessert. "Because daddy eats it too. You can't smell it if you both eat it." Mom was Asian. Daddy was too. I ate green jello with little marshmallows in it and clean my breath was clean. My breath was clean for kissing Paul Rossman.

2:     A beautiful woman should never have to beg for the love of a man but I. Have begged because I. Am not beautiful outside no I know. They called me plateface when I was a child. Not just to tease me because I was Chinese because I was Japanese because I was KoreanThaiVietnamese all rolled up into one no I know. My face is flat and truly flat when I was a child. And company came we ate store bought desserts off of white china dishes. They measured seven inches across seven inches up and down and sneaking one into the bathroom I put one up to my face and seven inches all around it fit me. The plate fit my face like a glove. And my eyes are squinty. Small not almond shaped like the pretty geishas but slits like papercuts tiny. My hair is straight flat not shiny like the girl on the macadamia nut bottle but dry I got a perm it helps but I hate the smell. I have trouble finding men you're not surprised no I know. I took an ad out in the personal ads Single Asian Female looking for Single Man of any race to love to care for to share bountiful joy with. Will answer all replies. I got a jillion replies a bouquet of hopeful suitors. I answered them all I said I would. It took days I found some nice ones. I arranged to meet them at convenient times in attractive places. The men came but they wore disappointed faces. I said I never promised you I was pretty. They said you said you were Asian – I assumed. I forgave them these men who were not so cute themselves. I held no grudge I let them off the hook. Outside I am ugly no I know. But I am beautiful in my heart yes God knows my heart is the home of great love. These men weren't beautiful inside or out. I missed nothing. I don't feel bad. This beautiful woman will never beg.

4: No one ever suspects me of being queer so its hard to score *dates* they're so *innocent* these women I mean get a *clue*. A hand on her thigh when we're sitting next to each other, a finger down her back as I stand behind her, a kiss on her neck instead of her cheek and they think "She's so warm." I'm so warm I'm *hot* somebody *notice* me Jesus *Christ*! What's a girl gotta do to get some attention from the same *sex* these days, stick my tongue down her throat and say "and I don't just mean that as friends"? I mean a goodlooking girl should not have to spin her own bean as often as I do. And I know what it is I know what it is. No one thinks the nice little oriental girl likes to DIVE FOR TUNA. Likes to MUNCH MUFF. Likes to EAT HAIR PIE but I do I'm telling you I do. I've had plenty of guys as lovers and I can tell you that getting RAMMED that having someone's ROD IN MY FACE didn't really do it for me I like girls and as soon as I can get one TO LOOK AT ME like a woman I'll probably be . . . I don't know, maybe really happy. There was this woman at work, she wasn't even my type physically but she was really funny, I loved the way she used her hands the way she touched things. I wanted her hands to touch me I thought they would feel really good. So I flirted I asked her out I tried to kiss her she said wait. *Wait*. Are you saying you're gay? She was shocked she was embarrassed she said she had no idea. Why would a cute Asian girl have to be queer? I mean am I more cute than Asian? Am I more Asian than queer? And should I ask myself these questions if she wasn't willing to let me be all of them?

mother's house in Queens in your top of the line Hyundai. I did not kiss you on the cheek and tell you I had a nice time. In fact, we met in a dingy nightclub where you were dancing on the bar and I was shooting bourbon straight from the bottle. We took the subway to my apartment in Chelsea, fucked each other goodnight and I didn't have to tell you I had a nice time. I got involved with you *despite* the fact that you were a Korean man and I assumed that you made the same forgiveness of me. I grew to love your gentle wildness, your clumsy grace, your spirit your spirit. And I had leaned on the hope that there were similar things to love about me. I didn't want you to think of me as a Korean woman. Men who have been attracted to me for being Korean were interested in who I am only on the surface without knowing who I am not in the deepest part of my heart. I am not ashamed of the presence of my heritage on my face but I mourn shamefully for the absence of Korea in my heart. You and I had an unspoken pact – I wouldn't be Korean to you if you weren't Korean to me. We went to movies, we threw parties, we spent many sweaty hours in bed and then one otherwise nameless night while my breath was still heavy and your legs were still pressed against mine you looked at me and said *sarang hae*. I had never heard it before. *Sarang hae*. You were telling me you loved me and I didn't understand what you were saying. *Sarang hae*. You asked me to say it. I couldn't say it. How could I use words that had no meaning to me to say what I knew in my heart. *Sarang hae*. The next time I say it I'll mean it.

1: Looking back I'm surprised we managed to love each other at all when the whole relationship was based on what we were not, who we were never going to be, what we weren't going to ask of each other. We were not a classic Korean couple. You did not pick me up from my

3: I have had glimpses and tall moments of real love.

2: I can be recognized as a woman who has a beauty apart from good looks.

4: I can be cute Asian warm hot queer.

1: And I can love any man who can see what I am as clearly as what I am not.

295

3:     Because I am not bitter.

2:     I am not destructively angry.

4:     I do not hold a grudge.

1:     I am not jaded.

3:     I am not fed up.

2:     I am not without hope.

4:     I am not too hurt to feel victimized.

1:     I am not afraid to try again.

3:     And I will eat kimchee and kiss you right afterwards.

2:     And I will let you love me inside and out.

4:     And I will stick my tongue down your throat because we *are* more than friends.

1:     And I will spend sweaty hours speaking a language that we both understand.

3:     And I will give you the benefit of the doubt.

2:     And I will let you know me.

4:     And I will have ideas of my own.

1:     And I just may give you the blowjob of your life, I mean it depends on the ones you've had before.

3:     And I will love.

2:     And be loved.

4:     Yes by God—

1:     I will.

3:     'Cause I'm a—

2:     W.

4:     O.

1:     M.

3:     A.

2:     N.

Slide: That's all.

Music: That's all.

That's all.

Spiderwoman Theater

Biographies

Spiderwoman Theater takes its name from the Hopi goddess Spiderwoman who taught the people to weave and said, "you must make a mistake in every tapestry so that my spirit may come and go at will." Spiderwoman has prophetic insight into the future, speaks all languages, and by nature of being a spider is ever present to give and to guide. The women of Spiderwoman Theater call their technique of working "storyweaving," in which they create designs and weave stories with words and movement, creating an overlay of interlocking stories, where fantasy and power are comically intertwined.

Lisa Mayo (Kuna/Rappahannock) is a founding member of two Native American performing arts groups, Spiderwoman Theater and Off the Beaten Path, with whom she has toured worldwide. A performing member of Masterworks Laboratory Theatre of New York, she studies at the New York School of Music and is a classically trained mezzo-soprano. She has studied with Uta Hagen, Robert Lewis and Walter Witcover, as well as Charles Nelson Riley for musical comedy. In 1981, Lisa was the recipient of a CAPS Fellowship, and in 1985 she received a grant from the New York State Council on the Arts for the development of *The Pause That Refreshes*, a piece she created and directed. She performed and studied with Tina Packer and Kristin Linklater of Shakespeare and Company, and in 1990 she taught theater crafts and acting to young people as part of the Minnesota Native American AIDS Task Force. In 1991, Lisa directed the Native American Actor's Showcase at the American Indian Community House, New York, where she also serves on the board of directors. In January of 1994, she appeared in New York Theatre Workshop's production of *The Res Sisters*. Lisa and her sister Gloria are recipients of a 1994 Rockefeller grant for the development of a new piece tentatively entitled *The Kuna Project*. They have recently finished the first phase of this project – a three-week journey to the San Blas Islands to study and speak with the Kuna Indians.

Photo: © *The Advertiser/Sunday Mail, Adelaide*

Gloria Miguel (Kuna/Rappahannock) studied drama at Oberlin College, Ohio, and is a founding member of Spiderwoman Theater. She has worked extensively in film and television; toured the United States in *Grandma*, a one-woman show; toured Canada as Pelajia Patchnose in the original Native Earth production of Tomson Highway's *The Rez Sisters*; and performed in the Canadian play *Son of Ayash* in Toronto. She performed as Coyote/Vitiline in *Jessica*, a Northern Lights Production in Edmonton, Canada, for which she was nominated for a Sterling Award for outstanding supporting actress. She was a drama consultant for the Minnesota American Indian Youth AIDS Task Force to develop a play on AIDS. In January of 1994, Gloria reprised her performance as Pelajia Patchnose in *The Rez Sisters* at the New York Theatre Workshop. She and her sister Lisa are recipients of a 1994 Rockefeller grant for the development of a new piece tentatively entitled *The Kuna Project*. When not on tour she is a drama teacher at the Eastern District YMCA in Brooklyn, New York.

Muriel Miguel (Kuna/Rappahannock) is a founding member and artistic director of Spiderwoman Theater. She is also a founding member of Open Theater, Off the Beaten Path, Thunderbird American Indian

Dancers and The Native American Theater Ensemble. As a member of Spiderwoman Theater, Muriel has been instrumental in the development of over twenty shows in the last seventeen years. The most recent of these is *Power Pipes*, which premiered in the fall of 1992. She taught drama at Bard College for four years. She has worked extensively with Native American youth, developing and directing a project for the Minnesota American Indian AIDS Task Force in 1991 and also co-directing *Indian Givers*, a play created by the Native American Youth Council of New York City. She has also taught at the Native Theatre School in Northern Ontario for the last two summers. Muriel has a one-woman show, *Hot'n'Soft*, which she developed in 1991 and which has played to critical acclaim in the United States and Canada. Most recently, she co-directed and performed in the Off-Broadway production of *The Rez Sisters* at the New York Theatre Workshop.

Artistic statements

One time I found several postcards of very elegant white ladies. They were obviously rich. They were wearing long white lace dresses and had flowers in their hair. For fun, I cut up snapshots of my sisters and myself. I pasted our faces on those ladies' faces. It was difficult, I had to maneuver and squeeze the faces into place. The final image was funny, the postcards looked lopsided.

I thought this is what my family is like. Struggling to fit in, we look lopsided.

Where were our role models?

When you grow up in a hostile atmosphere where you are different, you try very hard to squeeze and push and smash yourself into some form that does not make waves.

Where were our role models?

Many years later after a performance of *Sun Moon and Feather*, three little Ojibway sisters came backstage. They announced that the eldest was Lisa and the middle Gloria and the youngest me. They were proud of us! They wanted to be us! We were their role models.

I write to tell my innermost stories and to reach out. To knock on the hearts of native people (young, old, women, men). To tell them yes I have been there and I'm still traveling.

Muriel Miguel

I write to capture my fantasies and to use those fantasies as building blocks for a story that is already with me.

I write because I want to leave my mark. Many voices inside of me have a need to be heard. For example, the "Fat Goddess" needs to be heard.

I write to keep a record of what the voices I hear have to say. Sometimes, if I am not fast enough, one may get away from me and I may not ever hear from that voice again.

Lisa Mayo

I'm an actress
I realize the words
    of others
These words are not enough
It leaves a hole in my
    belly
As a woman, a native
    woman
I survive by telling
    my stories

Gloria Miguel

Production history

Sun Moon and Feather premiered at the New Foundland Theater, New York in 1981. It has been toured extensively including performances at Theater for the New City, New York; New York Feminist Art Institute; Women's Theater Festival, Boston; Trent University, Ontario, Canada; Helsinki, Finland; Frankfurt, Germany; Harbor Front, Toronto, Canada; First Indigenous Women's Conference, Adelaide, Australia; Sister Fire, Washington, D.C.; Centro Culturo De La Raza, San Diego, California; the New WORLD Theater, Amherst, Massachusetts; The Onandaga Indian Reservation, Aspen Institute, Colorado; and At the Foot of the Mountain, Minneapolis, Minnesota.

17 Sun Moon and Feather

Spiderwoman Theater

Characters

LISA MAYO/ELIZABETH

GLORIA MIGUEL

MURIEL MIGUEL

The title *Sun Moon and Feather* is taken from parts of our native names.

The play is performed on three levels. A taped discussion on poverty and home movies filmed by our Uncle Joseph Henry accompany the staged performance.

Setting

A large patchwork backdrop, made of cloth pieces called molas, and including material from our tribe. Attached to the backdrop is a white bedsheet which serves as a movie screen. The projector is placed in the audience. It is an old projector, 16 mm, used for film without sound. What we hear is the sound of the projector.

The feeling is of being at home looking at home movies.

Pink gels wash the backdrop and stage.
There is a chair center stage facing SL.
Another chair SR midstage. Next to the chair is
a small basket; in it a small mola, a Kuna
rattle, a calabash and a rag doll. Also a pair
of shoes. Another chair is placed SL down-
stage, facing toward mid-stage.

Audience out, stage lights dim, Poverty tape
on. No one is on stage. Only the tape is heard.
Five beats. Mozart's K.546 Adagio and Fugue
in C minor on.

(Poverty tape:)
You were only 13
He didn't believe she was 13
I said she was 17
And he said look at the moon.
And she was only 13
I was 15
And you know
I looked at the moon
We were lost in Brooklyn
Remember the guys who left us off?
Way way in another part of town
Oh God
That was really terrible
That was really treading on thin ice
We ended up in the depths of some god
  awful neighborhood.

Hello pretty one you have 10 cents for me?
Oh my. I have everything except for 10
  cents
What do you need 10 cents for
For the machine
It's only 10 cents
No two quarters and a 10 cents I don't have
  10 cents
Oh yeah
What you oughta do is take another 60
  cents. Just in case your coat doesn't yet
  dry
I had a lotta change but I don't have 10
  cents. They didn't give me that.
I don't have 10 cents either I only have two
  nickels
Oh I probably have it.
Look in that bottle
There's 10 cents on the floor in that big
  bottle of money
How do you know that Gloria?
She's been looking at my bottle
Can I take a dime from there
Yeah I was going to see what I have in
  there
Have you another two quarters

I have no more dimes
She has lots of dimes
Here these are dimes
It's the same as 10 cents
Yes *(Laughter)*
Hurry up and wash your coat
What did you give her?
These are all hers she has lots of dimes
You have plenty of them.
I didn't know one dime was the same as 10
  cents that's all *(Laughter)*
A dime and 10 cents are the same
  (Poverty tape continues:)
LISA So we were talking about that layer of
  worthlessness, selflessness, coming out of
  being poor, being dirty, not having
  enough to eat.
GLORIA There wasn't much hope. When
  you came home after school to a cold
  house, no food, a drunken father, a
  depressed mother, a neighborhood that's
  very hostile to you.
LISA What is there? It's horrible. How did
  we make it?
GLORIA A dirty house with bedbugs.
LUCY We used to clean the house ourselves. When we tried to clean the house
  they would get so upset. Mama gave up.
  Mama gave up a long time ago.
MURIEL I used to wish that we had six
  o'clock dinner like everybody else. At six
  o'clock I would be sitting around and all
  the kids would be gone in to eat. I would
  still be sitting on the stoop.
LISA Where was our family? When did you
  eat?
MURIEL Anytime somebody made food I
  ate. It was strange because in a way that
  was good, you weren't programmed like
  everyone else was. That's how it is in
  Italy. Six o'clock dinner. You hear the
  sound of the knives and forks, clinking of
  dishes. It smells so good. Didn't it smell
  so good? I wished I could stay and have
  school lunch because it was so impossible, she would give me these meals. I
  would have tomato soup for a month.
  And the reason I hate oatmeal. I had
  oatmeal for breakfast and oatmeal for
  lunch, for I don't know, for months.
  Whenever I see oatmeal or smell it I get
  so angry, I hate oatmeal.

Halfway through the tape the film comes on.
The film is beautiful. It shows all of our
uncles and our father. Beautiful Indian

faces. Then shots of the lovely islands that they come from, The San Blas islands, home of the Kuna nation. The juxtaposition of that sad tape and the lovely islands where they come from. The worry about money in the city against a coconut culture. The wonderment: how did they get here? How did they survive?

(Poverty tape is on and film is on.)

LISA *enters wearing a light green, low-cut nightgown, hose to match and silver high heels. She sits on* CS *chair. There is a sad aura about her. She sits looking straight in front of her like she is looking out a window. Ten beats later* MURIEL *enters* SR *wearing a tea-dipped rayon dress over a many-tiered petticoat that shows through an opening in front of her skirt, ruffled sparkley blue socks over light pink hose and black med-high Baby Janes. She wears a pop bead necklace and has one side of her hair caught up in a ponytail with a bow. She sits in chair* SL *mostly out of the light. She is watchful.* GLORIA *enters from audience. She is wearing a tattered dark blue lace dress mended in places with red patches. Her hair is in ponytails on the sides of her head. She is barefoot, and is dragging a red net.*

(Mozart tape is on, simultaneous with poverty tape and film.)

GLORIA *is play-acting as if she is alone in a room. She is dragging the net with great effort as if it is a heavy burden, i.e. Jesus Christ with cross. It is a child's fantasy, and on another level a dance à la Isadora Duncan, and on another level transformations with one item. It is very, very, very dramatic.*

She climbs up on stage, drags the net SL *and* US *to* CS *where she trips. The film goes off. She lowers the net, unloading a heavy burden. She puts the net over her head and it becomes a bridal veil and she walks* DSC. *She becomes a Madonna, unveils one hand and begs for pity and mercy. With both hands she claws and searches the net for an escape then pushes the net as if under great pressure and fights until the pressure wins and bends her knees. She takes the net off. The net becomes a rope and she twists it around her body. She pulls both ends, squeezing the life out of her, then hangs*

herself. Next she throws it on the floor. The net becomes blood on the sand and she steps back in fear. She runs to it and pokes it with her toe. She lifts up the net with her toe. Then she carries the net in her arms like a dead child. The net becomes a majestic cape and she walks like a queen around in a circle. She walks DSC and puts the net across her right arm and raises her arm. The net becomes a curtain to hide behind. She pulls the curtain back and peeks out fast. She peeks out again and slowly pulls the curtain back and slowly looks out and gets scared by ELIZABETH (LISA).

While GLORIA *is pushing the net* ELIZABETH *starts to move. All the next action is performed simultaneously.*

ELIZABETH *gets up and goes* SR. *She pulls in a duffle bag that contains a sleeping bag, seven stuffed dolls and animals, and a long pink cloth. She pulls with great effort like it is laden with burdens and responsibilities and places it* CS. *She is very excited and busy. Then she gets a chair* SR *with a basket and places it* CS. *She takes her chair and places it* SL. *Both chairs are now facing* DS. *She gets a second duffle bag and places it next to her chair. She opens up the first duffle bag and takes out the sleeping bag and places it between the two chairs* DS. *She takes out the stuffed animals and dolls and places them on the sleeping bag. She places two stocking dolls near her chair. She takes out the pink cloth very quietly and sneaks up behind* GLORIA *and scares the shit out of her.* GLORIA *screams and* ELIZABETH *laughs uproariously. Both tapes go off and lights bump up.*

GLORIA Don't laugh! That's not funny. She always made fun of me. You're too slow, dummy. Here, let me do it. I'm much better than you are.

LISA Dummy. Here take this. *(Hands her the pink cloth)*

GLORIA What's the use? Who cares. Doesn't matter anyway. *(Takes pink cloth. From this point* GLORIA *tries to do everything opposite of what* LISA *wants. She twists the cloth, punches the dolls, throws the napkins and plates.)*

LISA *(Tries to get* GLORIA *to fold cloth)* Pull it out now. Hold it still. Gloria don't twist it. Now take this end. Fake it, hold it tight. Gloria do it nice. Now put all the dolls on here. Put them on nice. No

301

don't do that I said put them on nice.
(Crying) You can't do that. Now everybody
has to have a place. You hear me? Don't
throw them like that. It's not nice. *(Goes
to second duffle bag and pulls out brown
paper towels)* Gloria, do you see what we
have here? *(GLORIA, sitting on floor near
chair, has taken out her pony tails and put
on her shoes; she places the mola on the
floor and puts the doll in the calabash. She
undresses the doll, washes the doll, and the
doll pees. She spies the paper napkins that
LISA has, takes one and wipes the doll's
bottom.)* Gloria look pure damask linen
napkins. All hand rolled. Wonderful.
Everybody must have one of these. Do it
nice: I said nice. *(Takes out two empty
plastic plates)* Gloria, Gloria, look, do you
see? This plate has cream puffs all piled
high and filled with whipped cream and
all covered with chocolate. And this plate
has crumpets. These are crumpets. They
are warm and the butter is melting.
Gloria you must give everybody one. One
cream puff and one crumpet. Gloria, but
nice. Oh God! You're going to ruin this
party for me. I said do it nice, you hear?
(Takes plastic cups from duffle bag) Gloria.
Gloria look. Look at this – absolutely the
most delicate china that was made in the
world. So delicate. It's so fine you can see
straight through it. And it's all hand-
dipped. And we're the only family in
North America with hand-dipped china.
*(Gives them to GLORIA who throws cups at
dolls. LISA takes out a small plastic measuring cup.)* Gloria, look a cream pitcher and
it's blue and white, it's Delft and the cream
is so thick you can eat it with a spoon.
Gimme your hand. *(She gives GLORIA the
cup.)* Everybody must get cream. Don't
ruin my party. *(Takes out plastic double-end
measuring cup.)* Gloria look, do you see
what we have here? Gloria this teapot
comes all the way from China and it has
all sorts of writing on it in gold AND it's
from the Ming dynasty. Gloria look, it's a
magic teapot. This teapot is never empty
because if it's empty, you just turn it over
and it's full again. So wonderful! Now
everybody gets tea. *(She puts tea in the
cups on the floor.)* You must keep your
pinky up like this and talk fancy. *(Sits
down with a panda and a stocking doll, a
napkin and a teacup. Gives tea to her dollies
and whispers to them.)*

GLORIA *(Playing with doll)* Elizabeth, do
you remember when Aunt Ida and Uncle
George and Uncle Frank used to take you
out and leave me home? I used to sit at
the window for hours wondering, why
couldn't I go? There you were all dressed
up with a big bow in your hair, going out
and I had to stay home. I used to think
there was something terribly wrong with
me.

LISA *(Playing with her dolls)* I was sitting in
the back yard with my dolls and my baby
carriage and Aunt Lizzy came in to the
yard carrying a bundle. She went over to
the baby carriage and put the bundle in it
and said, "You're not the baby anymore." I
went over and I looked in and there was
a baby in there and I wanted to smash it.
That was the first time I ever saw my
sister Gloria. *(Throws doll at GLORIA then
waits five beats)*

My family lived in a big compound in
Brooklyn and they never went out of the
house. My grandfather bounced me on his
knee and my grandmother sang hymns
and folk songs and she said I was one of
them.

GLORIA *(Still playing with her doll.)*
Sunshine, bright sunshine. Morning
glories. Beautiful red and yellow morning
glories. They grew all along the backyard
fence and up the side of the house. My
mother and I would pick them and put
them in bowls of water and decorate the
house with them. I helped mama clean
the house. We had fun together. *(She sings
and splashes the doll in imaginary water in
calabash.)* Ramona wooshie wooshie
wooshie woo. On Sunday afternoon all
daddy's friends and relations from San
Blas would visit and I was allowed to play
with them. They would talk Kuna. I
didn't understand them. Ige benuga, be a
beni. E be nueti. They called me Tuli girl.
(Sings) Tage. Tage.[1] *(Film up: scenes of the
family in the backyard waving and playing
with baby MURIEL)*

LISA I am the granddaughter of Elizabeth
Ashton Mourn, a beautiful Rappahannock
Indian woman from West Moreland
county, Virginia. My great-grandmother
Felicia was a midwife and she taught my
grandmother how to deliver babies. My
grandmother delivered me and both my

---

1 Tage: Prounced ´tā-gay

sisters. (sings to herself)
Oh are-re-vy.
My mother gave me to the witch
Oh Why
Oh are-re-vy
(Continues softly under GLORIA)
The dust goes up in the sun
The sun shines on my hands
Oh Why
(MURIEL gets up, walks US, crosses SR and stands in front of film. She watches.)

GLORIA See here! That child belongs to me. She's no savage. She's a Spencer. She belongs here with me. She belongs here with me. (She cradles doll and taps heavily on doll's chest with rattle and sings Kuna lullaby.) Lay Lay Lay Lay Lay Lay Lay (sings as a young child) Lay Lay Lay Lay Lay Lay Lay (sings as a mother) Lay Lay Lay Lay Lay Lay Lay (sings as a grand-mother)
(MURIEL walks CS, sits on sleeping bag and pink cloth, grabs stuffed toys and bangs them on floor, crying like a hurt child.)

MURIEL I am the only child of my two sisters. I am covered with love and very lonely. I have two friends Paby and Kalleewiko. No one else can see them. I am the only child of my two sisters. My mother never talks to me. I live in a house with my mother and father. I'm covered with love and very lonely. I am the only child of my two sisters. (Covers her head with cloth)

LISA (Grabs MURIEL to her knee, removes cloth) I wanted her to be happy. (Takes tissue, cleans MURIEL's nose) I wanted her to be an Indian and carry on the tradi-tions of the family, so I could leave.
(GLORIA gestures that she wants MURIEL. LISA throws MURIEL to GLORIA; GLORIA cleans MURIEL's face, smooths her hair.)

GLORIA I wanted her to be happy. I wanted her to be clean. I wanted her to be educated. I wanted her to be cultured. (She and LISA fight over MURIEL. They pull her by her arms like she is a doll.) Let's take her for a walk. (Pull)

LISA Oh yeah? (Pull)

GLORIA I'll take her to the ballet. (Pull)

LISA I'll teach her folk dancing. (She swings MURIEL US. MURIEL stays there at backdrop, back to audience. LISA is USL back to audience.)

GLORIA (DSC) The day Muriel was born, I met my father coming down the steps.

He was carrying a large white basin. It contained blood. I helped my father bury the placenta under a tree in the backyard. (She sits CSR.)

LISA (Turns, walks DS) When I left my first husband, I went to live with my younger sister Muriel. She got me my first date. I came home all excited, "He wants to make love to me." She said, "So? . . . Do you like him?" I said, "I'm not sure." She said, "Well, if you like him, make love to him. If you don't, don't. Why do you have to make things so complicated." (To GLORIA) How does it make you feel when your baby sister steals the limelight? (Sits SL)

GLORIA I don't care. She can have the limelight. I'm really very proud of Muriel. But sometimes I feel lonely when I'm with her. I think my presence makes her face something she doesn't want to face. I fear I'm part of the burden she wants to drop. I don't know why but I'm afraid I'll lose her.
(Film off. MURIEL does a strange little dance rubbing her legs and crouching like she is in agony.)

MURIEL Jerry. Jerry. The car turned over and over. I felt his body shake against me. Elizabeth, Gloria, he's dead, he's dead!!! (Freezes)

GLORIA I wrote your name on the sand. Suddenly a wave came and washed it away. Your name isn't there anymore.
    Oh, why is there always such an air of sadness about me?
(MURIEL relaxes and stands behind GLORIA's chair. LISA sees how sad they are and tries to cheer them up. Again it is a transformation. Out of nowhere she starts to pluck an imaginary guitar.)

LISA (Sings) Plunky Plunky Plunky Plunk (GLORIA looks at MURIEL, cheers up, and plays an imaginary muted trumpet. MURIEL reluctantly gets pulled in, plays an imagi-nary bass.)

GLORIA (Sings) We three, were all alone

MURIEL (Talks) Were all alone

GLORIA (Sings) Living in a memory

MURIEL (Talks) Ah memories

GLORIA (Sings) My echo, my shadow and me

MURIEL (Gestures) My echo, my shadow and me

GLORIA (Sings) We three, we're not a crowd

MURIEL (Talks) Not four, but three

GLORIA   (*Sings*) We're not even company

MURIEL   (*Talks*) I love you baby

GLORIA   (*Sings*) My echo, my shadow and me

MURIEL   (*Gestures*) My echo, my shadow and little old me
(*All three sing and dance.*)
What good is the moonlight
The silvery moonlight, that shines above

LISA   Plunky Plunky Plunk

ALL   I walk with my shadow, talk with my echo.
But where is the one that I love.
(*ALL repeat chorus singing and humming in harmony. LISA and MURIEL continue to hum while they clear the stage of cloth sleeping bags, plastic cups etc. GLORIA does not participate, she just watches. LISA and MURIEL find plastic cups and toast each other. Everything is placed SL.*)

GLORIA   I'm leaving. (*She is ignored. A little louder, still ignored:*) I'm leaving! (*Shouting, startles MURIEL*) I'm leaving!!!

MURIEL   Why don't you just go? (*To LISA*) She always does that. (*GLORIA exits behind white sheet.*)
(*LISA discovers net and plays with it while she sings and hums Massenet's "Elegre." MURIEL is still clearing the stage. She watches LISA and is frustrated that LISA is not helping. MURIEL's and LISA's lines are from Chekov's* Three Sisters.)

MURIEL   I have a craving for work. Just as one has a craving for water on a hot summer day. I have a craving for work. If I don't get up early and go to work, give me up as a friend.

LISA   Father trained us to get up at seven. Now Muriel wakes at nine and lies in bed till twelve thinking and looking so serious.
(*MURIEL sets up three plastic bags SL next to her chair. She pulls out old-fashioned (circa 1950) purses, gloves, hats and one brocade jacket for LISA.*)

MURIEL   You still think of me as a little girl. That's why it seems so strange to see me serious.
(*LISA does a double take, realizes she hurt MURIEL's feelings. She trys to find a way to express her love. She sings, tweaking MURIEL's nose, pinching her cheeks, pokes her in the belly and finally kisses her.*)

LISA   For I love you truly, truly dear.
Life with its sorrows.
Life with its fears, fades into dawn:
When you do appear

For I love you truly, truly dear.

MURIEL   (*Excited*) Gloria's coming! Gloria's coming! (*Film on*) I can hardly wait to see her!
(*GLORIA punches sheet from behind. She makes a grand entrance. She is walking down a huge staircase. She hears applause, everybody loves her. She tap dances á la Fred Astaire. LISA and MURIEL compete for her attention.*)

LISA   I saw a bird of paradise and I thought of you.

MURIEL   I saw a red rose and I thought of you.

LISA   I saw Gloria coming down the stairs and I was so happy to see her.

GLORIA   (*Tap dancing*) Are you happy to see me? That makes me so happy to know that you're happy to see me.

MURIEL   I made a beautiful cake just for you.

GLORIA   (*Takes cake, dumps it, does a few ballroom turns*) A beautiful cake just for me?

LISA   Now that I've met you, I don't care if I die tomorrow for I will have fulfilled all my fondest hopes and desires.

GLORIA   (*Stops dancing*) Say it over and over. It's like diamonds in my ears.

MURIEL   I'll fight battles for you, stop bullets for you, lie for you, steal for you, die for you, all this I will do with the greatest of joy.

GLORIA   (*A la Katharine Hepburn with a few tango steps*) Love me but don't die for me or I'll be bereft of all feeling.

LISA   I trust you so implicitly, we don't have to be together.

GLORIA   I love you so much, I'd stay in a room forever and only go out for fresh air and water.

MURIEL   Of all my girls, I love you most, Gloria. That's my girl.

LISA   (*Pokes MURIEL in belly*) And she has a beautiful voice and don't you forget it.
(*LISA and MURIEL go US to backdrop, backs to audience.*)

GLORIA   I love you Mimi Mama. Never let me go. (*Moves CS*) He said "Goodbye, Desert Rose", and gave me a long lingering kiss. He walked down the street, out of sight and I never saw him again. I never get that kind of love anymore. Maybe I get that kind of love and don't recognize it. No! No! If I did get that kind of love I'd be happy. I wrote your name on the water and the sand washed it away. *(Crying)* Oh! I'm all mixed up. My life is a failure. What's the use, who cares, it doesn't matter anyway.

(LISA at first is laughing at GLORIA then becomes concerned at GLORIA's reaction. GLORIA is bawling. MURIEL thinks it is amusing, does not care, thinks GLORIA is silly.)

LISA   There. There. Calm down. *(To MURIEL)* Get her some water, she's crying. *(Gets a chair for GLORIA and one for herself, both sit SR. MURIEL still laughs.)*

GLORIA   You don't know how I suffer. I suffer. I really suffer. I suffer in my bones, my bowels, my kidneys, the ends of my hair, my fingernails.

LISA   I suffer much much more than you. You don't know what suffering is. My ears suffer, my eyelashes, my belly·button suffers.

(MURIEL reluctantly brings water.)

LISA   Here's your water.

GLORIA   *(Snarling, slaps MURIEL's hand)* I don't want your old water.

(MURIEL watches the two of them then walks downstage. She happily tells what she sees.)

MURIEL   She's crying. She's suffering. Great big balls of water are dripping down her cheeks. She's suffering. *(She giggles, walks back to them and watches. Then she realizes she has the space to herself and tells her own story. She walks SL and mimes opening a door.)* I opened the door. Oh! hi. Nice to meet. *(Ogles make-believe person)* Oh you're with her. I'm tired. I'm going to bed. *(Sits on floor, looks up surprised)* It's all right you can come in. I'm not very tired. *(Indicates SL)* You can sit over there. *(Follows with eyes from SR to SL, stares)* She is really very beautiful. *(Seductive)* A Leo. You know a lion. *(Growls, laughs)* An actress. Spiderwoman Theater. It's a feminist theater group. She's really very beautiful. If I look at you, will you look at me? If I touch you will you touch me? Does she like me? *(Follows with eyes SL to SR)* Hey, where are you going. It's all right. You can stay.

LISA   When I first saw them together, I felt sick to my stomach.

GLORIA   Whatever happened to the blonde fellow, the one with the long legs?

MURIEL   *(Following with eyes SR to SL)* Are you stoned or drunk? Oh both. Yeah I'll smoke. *(Lies down on back, throws leg up and wiggles)* I'll just lie here and we can talk. *(Sits up fast, follows with eyes SL to SR)* Hey where are you going? It's all right. You can stay.

LISA   When Gloria first found out, she cried all night.

GLORIA   What happened? What went wrong? I don't want her to be that way.

LISA   and GLORIA   Gay.

MURIEL   *(looking SL)* Look at me. Do you like me? *(Follows with eyes SL to SR)* Hey where are you going? It's all right you can stay.

GLORIA   It doesn't matter. I love her anyway.

LISA   I love her.

MURIEL   *(Follows with eyes SR to CS, on knees, arms up, moving DS)* You're leaving? *(Arms up for a hug, lips pursed for a kiss. Disappointed, drops arms and shakes hand.)* Good night.

LISA   *(To GLORIA, demanding)* You have to listen to me. I am sister number one. I am 20 months away from you. *(Measures with hands between her and GLORIA)* Like this. *(To MURIEL)* And you, you never listen to me. I am years away from you. *(Measures between her and MURIEL)* Like this. *(Fast transformation)* Oooo!! Let's have a tea party!

(ALL run SL to plastic bags, Elizabeth dons jacket, hat and gloves. She gets purse and plastic measuring cup, pours tea. GLORIA dons hat and string of beads. Gets purse and plastic cup. MURIEL dons hat and gloves, gets purse and plastic cup.)

LISA   *(With a make-believe English accent)* The Queen is coming to tea, and we must talk very fancy. Hold your pinky up like this. We must talk on lofty subjects. I was so cunning. My Aunt Ida had a little round box and in that box she kept my brown silky ringlets all tied up with a pink ribbon.

(MURIEL pays no attention, hums to herself, drinks tea.)

GLORIA   Yuck.

MURIEL   There she goes again.

GLORIA   Why bring her up?

LISA   Why not? She's my friend, isn't she?

GLORIA   That's not necessarily true.

LISA   I really don't agree with you.

GLORIA   I have to think my own thoughts.

LISA   That's the way you think. I don't.

GLORIA   That's my truth.

LISA I've got to get out of here. *(To* MURIEL, *startling her)* You never listen to me.

GLORIA *(To* MURIEL*)* You turned your back on me.

MURIEL *(To* GLORIA*)* What were you doing behind me?

GLORIA You walked in front of me.

MURIEL I really hate that about you.

GLORIA You didn't want to be with me.

MURIEL *(Jumps up, goes toward* GLORIA*)* Do you think I left you out on purpose?

GLORIA *(To* LISA*)* You didn't give me any tea.

LISA I did too.

MURIEL No you didn't.

GLORIA You always leave me out.

LISA Oh yeah?

GLORIA Yeah.

MURIEL Yeah.

LISA Why are you two so mean to me?

GLORIA Tell the truth.

LISA If I let you, you two would put me into the ground.

GLORIA You two don't understand me. You never understood me.

LISA Oh yeah?

GLORIA Yeah.

(GLORIA throws bag. Big fight. MURIEL *holds* LISA, GLORIA *kicks and scratches* LISA. MURIEL *yells.)*

MURIEL Leggo, leggo.

(LISA breaks away from MURIEL. *Throws her US. Throws* MURIEL's *chair USC and throws herself on floor yelling and crying.)*

LISA I hate you bitches. Hope you both die!

(GLORIA gloats. Takes gloves off, throws them on LISA.*)*

GLORIA Elizabeth. Elizabeth. Daddy's coming.

LISA *(Still crying)* Don't talk to me. Get away from me.

GLORIA *(Kicking* LISA*)* Is he drunk? Elizabeth is he drunk?

LISA He's drunk! He's drunk!

GLORIA Tell Mama not to fight.

LISA Don't fight Mama. Don't fight.

GLORIA Get the baby!

LISA Get the baby. Hide the baby.

(GLORIA gets MURIEL US *and places her on chair CS.* LISA *and* GLORIA *stand in front of* MURIEL *to hide her.)*

GLORIA Daddy came home drunk and he started to fight with Mama.

LISA Don't fight Mama. *(MURIEL makes fighting sounds.)*

GLORIA We were in the bedroom. There was a noise in the dining room. Daddy was drunk and Mama began to fight with him. Then Mama called, "Girls, girls, help me. Help me." We ran into the dining room. Daddy had one leg out the window, both legs out the window.

LISA and GLORIA Don't jump Daddy, Don't jump. *(MURIEL still making angry noises)*

GLORIA Mama jumped up and pulled the window down. Mama grabbed Daddy by the waist, we grabbed Mama and we pulled and pulled him down to the floor. *(LISA, GLORIA and* MURIEL *stay in tableau of pulling position for three beats then* MURIEL *pops up.)*

MURIEL *(Takes off gloves, clears space)* OK. Line up.

(They line up, LISA SL, GLORIA SR, MURIEL *goes into the middle).*

GLORIA Oh no! Muriel. I belong in the middle, that's my rightful place. *(She gets between* LISA *and* MURIEL, MURIEL *goes to the other side of* LISA.*)* Muriel, I belong in the middle. Mama always said Gloria is second born, she belongs in the middle. *(MURIEL steps out of line, looks at situation.)*

MURIEL Gloria it would look better if I were in the middle.

(LISA and MURIEL *line up together, they look smug.* GLORIA *looks enraged.* GLORIA *waits two beats then lines up with* MURIEL *in the middle.)*

MURIEL Every summer, my family went to the beach. We had a beautiful red and white bungalow on a beautiful beach by a beautiful bay.

(GLORIA gives MURIEL *an incredulous look.)*

GLORIA Cedar Beach. A dilapidated old bungalow in New Jersey on a dirty beach off a dirty polluted bay.

LISA There was a fish house and twice a day there was a god-awful odor.

MURIEL My father bought a great big red and white boat with a great big wind-shield and a great big motor.

LISA That boat was a little bigger than a row boat and it had a motor in it that never worked.

GLORIA And daddy and Uncle Joe set about to make that boat seaworthy.

MURIEL My father would stand at the helm of that boat with his brown safari hat and his wooden staff and he'd look out over the ocean. He was going to sail the seven seas.

LISA   The only trouble was'em

ALL   It never went into the water.

GLORIA   It just stayed in the backyard.

MURIEL   And every summer, my father would paint it, caulk it, pet it, hose it down; then all our friends and all our family would come. (ALL *push very hard* SL.) And we would—

ALL   Puuush it. To the other side of the yard.

GLORIA   Then we would pose by it, on it and under it. (ALL *strike poses like being photographed by boat.*) And Daddy and Uncle Joe wold stand at the helm and pretend.

LISA   And then next summer, my father would paint it, caulk it, pet it, hose it down; then all our friends and all our family would come. (ALL *push* SR.) And we would—

ALL   Puuush it. To the other side of the yard.

GLORIA   Then we would pose by it, on it and under it. (ALL *strike poses.*) And Daddy and Uncle Joe would stand at the helm and pretend. And the next summer, my father would paint it, caulk it, pet it, hose it down; then all our friends and all our family would come. (ALL *push* SC.) And we would—

ALL   Puuush it to the other side of the yard.

MURIEL   Then one summer, it was ready to go into the water.

LISA   My mother gave a party. She made potato salad, punch and sandwiches.

GLORIA   All our friends and family—(ALL *push* DSC.)

ALL   Puuushed it into the water—(ALL *stare at the same spot on stage.*)

MURIEL   It started to take on water—

LISA   It was like a sieve—

MURIEL   We had to bail out the water—

GLORIA   And then it sank.

(ALL *still staring at same spot*)

LISA   Then Daddy said, oh well. Next summer. (ALL *shrug.*)

(LISA *and* MURIEL *go* US, *clean up stage.* GLORIA *goes* CS. LISA *and* MURIEL *stand very close together* USC.)

GLORIA   To squeeze, squeeze o, squeeze as, squeeze a, squeeze amos, squeeze ais, squeeze at.

GLORIA *tries to squeeze in between* MURIEL *and* LISA. *She pries them apart, lets them go and they rebound off each*

other. *She finally squeezes in. She stares eye level* SL *which makes* LISA *and* MURIEL *look.*

The look: This is about a hostile environment. Having your antennae out if one sister feels threatened. They give the impression of being three cats using all their senses to smell out their enemy. Using only their eyes and slight turning of their heads, they spot five places out in the audience then a slow count SR *using only eyes then a quick return to center audience. They gather all their energy and walk as a unit towards the audience. They are strong but also menacing, invulnerable. The soft spot: The sisters are vulnerable, sometimes naive and innocent. The question here is, should you let your guard down? Do you take the risk? What happens when you do? This is all performed in sound, movement and words, simultaneously. They use questions that have previously got them into trouble or hurt.*

LISA   Why did you ask that question? What's the matter? You have a funny look on your face. (*Gets punched in stomach*)

MURIEL   Oh! You look funny. What's wrong? (*Gets pushed in chest*)

GLORIA   Is that true? How is that possible? My thoughts are— (*Gets hit on shoulder, hit in belly, spun around. This is repeated until* GLORIA *as catalyst starts next segment, picks up chair and sits·* CS.) Bored. Bored Bored Bored.

(LISA *and* MURIEL *place chairs on both sides of* GLORIA. *They crowd each other.* MURIEL *shakes her leg and disturbs* GLORIA *who tries to stop her.* LISA *places her hand on top of* GLORIA'*s.* GLORIA *places her hand on top of* LISA'*s. They get tangled up. They are pulling and pushing against each other.*)

GLORIA   When I grow up. I'm going to marry a man from far away, from way across the sea AND he's going to take me away from all this and I'll never come back again.

LISA   I'm going to marry a rich man and he's going to give me things like a fur coat and a refrigerator full of food.

MURIEL

I'm going to get me an apartment.
I'm going to get me an apartment.
(*They slowly relinquish their grip on each other and do a tap chair dance and sing.*)

ALL   (*Sing*)

Give my regards to Broadway
Remember me to Herald Square
Tell all the gang at 42nd Street
That I will soon be there
Tell them of how I am yearning
(They separate, LISA *takes chair* DSR,
GLORIA *takes chair* CSL, MURIEL *faces*
DSR.)
To mingle with the old time throng
Give my regards to old Broadway
And say that I'll be there ere long.
*(*MURIEL *is upside down in chair, kicking
her legs, singing, and continues to sing while*
LISA *decides to entertain audience with*
GLORIA.)
MURIEL Long long long long.
LISA Hey Gloria we have a captive audi-
ence – let's you and me play "Indian
Love Call."
GLORIA Oh yeah.
LISA OK? I'm Jeanette MacDonald and I've
got this long red hair and big green eyes.
GLORIA Elizabeth. Elizabeth? Let me be
Jeanette MacDonald?
LISA No!
GLORIA But you always take the biggest
part.
LISA No I don't.
GLORIA I want to be Jeanette MacDonald.
LISA You have some nerve. It's my game.
GLORIA I want to be Jeanette MacDonald.
LISA Harum Scarum Lady.
GLORIA I have a high voice.
LISA No!
GLORIA *(Begs)* Please.
LISA Oh all right, but I'm Nelson Eddy.
GLORIA I don't care who you are.
MURIEL I'll be the horse. *(They ignore her.)*
GLORIA *(simultaneously with* LISA*)* I'm
Jeanette MacDonald and I have great big
green eyes and long red hair that comes
down to there. And I have a low-cut
white dress that goes down to there and
goes in like this and out like that and
lace all around the bottom. And I'm
standing on a mountain *(stands on a
chair)* and I look down and there he is
on a big white horse and I go like
this.
LISA *(simultaneously with* GLORIA*)* I've got
a Royal Canadian Mounted Police uniform
on. A big red jacket. I'm wearing black
leather boots up to here. I have a big tan
hat with a leather thong under my chin.
I've a beautiful white horse and I'm
standing at the foot of a mountain.

GLORIA *(Sings)*
Oooo Oooo Oooo
(Plays make-believe piano)
tootle tootle doo
tootle tootle doo (twice)
So echoes of sweet love notes
gently falls
Through the forest stillness
are fond waiting
Indian lovers call
LISA *(Sings)*
When the lone lagoon
stirs in the spring
Welcoming home
Some swanny white wing
when the maiden moon
shines in the sky
Drawing her star-eyed
dream children nigh.
GLORIA *(Sings)*
That is the time of the moon and the
year.
When love dreams to Indian maidens
appear. And this is the song that they
hear.
LISA and GLORIA *(Sing)*
When I'm calling you oooo ooo
Will you answer too oooo oooo
GLORIA *(Sings)*
That means I offer my love to you
To be your own
LISA *(Sings)*
If you refuse me
I will be blue and waiting all alone.
GLORIA and LISA *(Sing)*
But if when you hear my love call
ringing clear
GLORIA *(Sings)*
And I hear your answering
echo so clear
LISA and GLORIA *(Sing)*
Then I will know
Our love will come true
*(*GLORIA *gets off chair.)*
You belong to me
I belong to you
*(They run to each other and dramatically
kiss three times.)*
LISA Oh how the music is playing so
gayly, so bravely and one wants to live.
GLORIA Oh how the music is playing.
They are leaving us, one is gone entirely,
entirely forever.
We'll be left alone to begin our lives
over.
(All three sit in chairs, MURIEL USC,

GLORIA CS, LISA DSR. *Transformation: the inside of a limousine coming from the cemetery.)*

MURIEL I guess there will be no more funerals for a while. I wonder who will die next.

LISA So much heaviness. So much responsibility. Mama's dead now. There will be even more responsibility. *(Pause)* Father died one year ago today the fifth of May.

GLORIA Mama. Mama. I'll never hear that voice again.

LISA It was cold then and snowing. I thought I'd never live through it. *(To* MURIEL*)* You were lying in a dead faint.

GLORIA *(Hums song "Trees" by Joyce Kilmer)* Mama would want me to sing that song. I don't remember the words *(Sings hesitatingly)* I think that I shall never see, a poem as lovely as a tree. *(Hums)*

LISA But now a year has passed and we can speak of it freely. You have a light dress on. Your face is beaming. The clock was striking then too.

MURIEL She's dead. She died a long time ago for me.

GLORIA *(Hums)* Poems are made by fools like me but only—*(hums)*

LISA I remember as though it were yesterday. They carried Father along. The band was playing but there were very few people following along behind. It was raining though then. Heavy rain and snow.

MURIEL I'm crying. I'm crying.

GLORIA Imagine. I'm already beginning to forget her face.

MURIEL God grant it will all work out.

GLORIA Just as we won't be remembered either.

MURIEL Weather is beautiful today.

GLORIA They'll forget us.

MURIEL I don't know why my heart is so light. This morning when I got up I remembered it was my birthday and I remembered when I was a little girl and Mama was still alive.

GLORIA No. She'll go on in us, in me and my family.

MURIEL Such wonderful thoughts thrilled through me. Such thoughts.

GLORIA I'm the only grandmother now, the only grandmother in the family.

LISA It's warm today.

(Film on. Lights dim. They sing "We Three" in the dark until film ends.)

Elizabeth Wong

Biography

Elizabeth Wong, a native of Los Angeles, writes for ABC's *All American Girl*, the first Asian-American family sitcom, and her plays *Kimchee and Chitlins*, and *Letters To A Student Revolutionary* have been produced in Los Angeles, Seattle, New York City and Chicago, among other places. She writes editorial columns for the *Los Angeles Times* and teaches playwriting at the University of California, Santa Barbara.

Artistic statement and Production history

We moved out of Chinatown after I got caught in the alley behind the Croatian church by a girl gang. I was in my early teens, walking home with my Big Stick popsicle, which was dripping in the summer heat, when I was surrounded by a taunting horde and their ringleader, a husky girl who was in junior high and a notorious bully. I got slapped around, my popsicle hit the asphalt, and I ran home the long way, trying to shake them.

And that was a pleasurable memory.

Life in Chinatown was harsh for a chubby, non-athletic, non-achiever like myself. I was the geeky four-eyed kid anxious for the arrival of the bookmobile. I'd monopolize all the best books, checking out the maximum ten, all the Nancy Drew, anything in the fantasy section, anything on talking cats or magical closets or time travel.

So I, like Anna May Wong, dreamed of the world outside the stifling reality of the ghetto. I escaped the hordes of cockroaches who lived under the appliances, the death of my father, the sorrow of my beautiful and overworked mother, the boredom of my overly-sheltered life; I escaped by keeping my nose in Narnia, and watching old movies on the black and white, dreaming of Fred Astaire and tuxes and ball gowns and spiraling staircases.

So years later, when browsing in a Greenwich Village card shop, I was struck by the image on a postcard of actress Anna May Wong, with her China doll geometric haircut and her glamorous mien. I knew instantly here was a soul sister, a ghetto girl like me. Anna May grew up on Flower

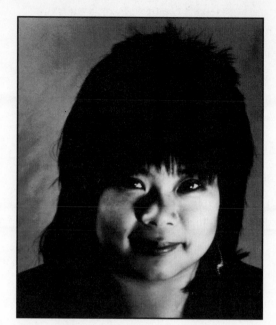

Photo: Self-portrait by Elizabeth Wong

Street, not far from my own stomping grounds on Bunker Hill. Anna May, like me, had gotten the hell out of Chinatown.

I tried doing research on Anna May to see if her own journey as an artist had lessons for me, now that I was certain I would be a playwright. I was new to the artist life, to its financial insecurities, its emotional vicissitudes, the loneliness of the empty room. I had been a newspaper reporter for ten years and was used to the daily give-and-take of the newsroom. Coverage of the Jesse Jackson presidential campaign, the whitewashing of racial issues engendered by his candidacy, had infuriated me and put the final nail on my journalism career. So, I looked towards Anna May for guidance.

But, zip nada zero, nothing substantive on Anna May, except for the occasional still photo, which usually featured a "real" star, the likes of Laurence Olivier, Douglas Fairbanks, Marlene Dietrich, George Raft. Plenty of information on them, but the story of America's first Chinese-American star was strangely elusive.

Frustrated, I put that postcard in a drawer and began instead the process of re-educating and re-creating myself. I was heartened by the Broadway success of

David Henry Hwang, a guy I knew from high school. Inspired, I moved to New Haven, where I snuck into Leon Katz's dramaturgical course and where I befriended Yale School of Drama graduate students who smuggled me into their classes, gave me comps to nearly everything theatrical, and encouraged me to write, write, write.

Thus encouraged, I moved to New York City to a sixth-floor walk-up on MacDougal Street, two blocks away from Washington Square Park and New York University. I had been accepted in the graduate program at NYU's Tisch School of the Arts. My mother was fond of telling people I was in law school. To pay her back, I put that sentiment into my first semester play, *Letters To A Student Revolutionary*.

The play, which is about rebellion and friendship, launched me on a path of no return. The play first won a contest sponsored by TheatreWorks in Colorado Springs, and not long after, the play was workshopped by Theatre In The Works, where I met Roberta Uno, artistic director of New WORLD Theater, whose boundless enthusiasm and support for work by artists of color gave me courage and encouragement.

Tisa Chang, artistic director of Pan Asian Repertory Theatre, gave the play its world premiere and I found myself visiting the twofer ticket booth in Times Square just to see the name of my play on the boards. My first Off-Broadway production was seen as a political as well as a theatrical event. Performances were followed by discussion panels. Opening night proceeds went to benefit Human Rights In China.

At about the same time, the play came to the attention of Chiori Miyagawa, then an assistant literary manager to Michael Bigelow Dixon at Actors Theatre of Louisville. Ms. Miyagawa asked me for a ten-minute play, and when I told her I had none to offer, she said, "So write something." So, I did and I called it *China Doll*.

This ten-minute playlet is the blueprint for a full-length play still in the works. *China Doll* was initially my response to the 1990–91 *Miss Saigon* controversy that swirled around the casting of an Anglo actor in a role originally meant for an Asian actor. Inspired by Roberta Uno's desire to archive works by artists of color, I wanted to do the same to reclaim a part of our American cultural past by reclaiming Anna May Wong, America's first Chinese-American actress.

I wrote a reasoned article for *American Theatre* on the *Miss Saigon* controversy, but the playlet, which was inspired by the brouhaha, is totally unreasonable. It telescopes a full life lived in a scant few pages, examining the changing images and stereotypes of Asian women as embodied by the career of Anna May, who played the gamut of the stereotypes, from malicious dragon lady to golden-hearted prostitute.

My work is about response. *Letters* was a response to the tragic events in China, and explored the way women seek political meaning in today's society. *Kimchee and Chitlins*, a satire that premiered at Victory Gardens Theatre in Chicago, was a response to the Black boycott of Korean stores in Brooklyn. It explored the dark demons haunting an upstart Chinese-American reporter covering that event. In the expanded version of *China Doll*, for example, Anna May's life is a barometer for the advances, or lack thereof, in the artistic expression of minority artists, particularly during the halcyon heyday of the Hollywood studio system. The play presented an opportunity for me to discuss various high points in American history and the responses to them by artists of color, such as the then-unrepealed miscegenation laws, the House of Representatives Un-American Activities Committee hearings, and World War II.

Most importantly, the playlet represents an exploration of the mysteries of love – the love of work, the love of artistic pursuit, the love of men, the love of movies. Anna May and I are women who impale ourselves on our loves. My biggest love is the theater, which in the words of Carol Joyce Oates is "the highest communal celebration of being." I love sitting in the dark. I love waiting for the curtain to rise. I love the magic that unfolds the mystery.

18 China Doll

Elizabeth Wong

Characters

ANNA MAY WONG: 33, an actress

Time
1940

Place
A movie soundstage

Production Notes

This play can be performed as a one-woman show or with a cast of an additional six silent characters, as follows:

MISS HARRINGTON, 20s, an actress

MR. WONG, 50s, ANNA's father

MR. IRVING THALBERG, a movie producer

MR. SAMUEL GOLDWYN, a movie producer

THE INTERPRETER

THE LIMOUSINE DRIVER

These characters are on stage throughout, frozen as if they were dolls on display. Their faces are white; the stage is white; the world is white.

A movie soundstage. The year is 1940. ANNA,
*a slender Chinese-American woman, 33, stands
in a spotlight. Her pose is ethereal, dreamy.
She speaks to an unseen actress.*

ANNA

Now, you see darling how it 'tis. My arms
like so. My legs like so. Then, you have the
suggestion of soft. The essence of feminin-
ity. And when your leading man sweeps
you up and gathers you in his arms, you
die a little. Like so. Just a small turn of the
head. That's all. Isn't it simple? This is how
they want to see a Chinese girl in the arms
of a white man. You die a little each time.
Now let's see you do it.
*(She retrieves a thermos, pours tea into a cup.
A pained expression comes over her face, as
the actress attempts an imitation.)*
No! No, no, no darling.
(ANNA steps back into the light.)
Well, it's interesting. But no. Look, this is
how you look.
(She takes an awkward pose.)
We don't want that. No self-respecting
Chinese girl thrusts out her breasts. And
your neck! It's like a chicken at the chop-
ping block.
(She slowly corrects the position.)
Bring your shoulders down. Your arms must
be aloft. If you persist as you do, your
yellow goop will rub off, your eye
prostheses will stick to your leading man's
nose, and the camera will see a white girl
in bad makeup. Now let's try it again.
(A pause. She watches.)
Look, Miss Harrington. Sit down. Any chair.
I know it's a difficult concept. Your New
England soul can't fathom it. But remember
darling, you are playing a Chinese.
Therefore, you are a fantasy. You are
sandalwood and jasmine. You are the
promise of faraway places. But you are
never real. You are not the mother. You are
never the wife. You do not perspire. You are
only a plaything – a China doll. *(Bitterly)*
China doll. Like me. But I never wanted to
be a China doll. Pretty China doll. And now,
my dear Miss Harrington, I'm teaching you
how to be one. That is what they call
ironic. Shall I tell you a secret? When I was
a little girl, I wanted to be blond just like
you.
(She pulls up chair, sits.)
I opened my eyes wide. I crimped my hair.
I squeezed and prayed for big breasts. Not

American enough, I said. So, I took my
Chinese name and threw it away. At the
age of 12, I gave myself a new name. Anna
May. Has a nice ring, doesn't it? I liked the
way it lifts like a soap bubble from my
tongue to the sky. Anna May. And where
did I get all my ideas? The movies. I
learned to be an all-American girl at the
movies!

A movie theatre. Lights dim.

I love the dark. The seats. The velvet
curtains that hide the inside from the out. I
love being naughty. When my parents
thought I was at Chinese school, I'd taken
the city bus on College Street heading . . .
out of Chinatown. Take me to Hollywood
Boulevard. Ever since I was 11 years old,
I've been sneaking to the movies. I knew,
even then, I was destined to be an actress.
Eleven years old!
(Lights flicker. A movie has commenced. ANNA
whispers.)
The Perils of Pauline. I just love this. Seen
it a million times.
(She addresses the screen.) Watch out Pauline!
Behind you! Oh gosh. Hurry, hurry. The
train is coming. *(She reacts. She shrieks,
covers her face with her hands.)* I can't stand
the suspense.
(Pause)
Seeing a movie is great. But being in the
movies? Is even better. Up there on the
silver screen. The camera moving in for a
closeup.
*(ANNA poses for a closeup. The light bright-
ens. She gets up, addresses the actress.)*
Yes, Let's take a look at your close-up, shall
we? All right . . . Scene 65. *(She refers to
manuscript.)* This is the garden scene. You
are betraying your mistress to her enemy.
No, use me as the camera. I'm the camera.
Turn slowly to me, as I move in closer. *(She
pretends to hold a camera.)* Oh please, don't.
Don't squint. Darling, look, darling, no.
Your eyes must look shifty – without being
shifty. Don't you know, we Chinese are a
devious underhanded race.
(Pause)
Don't agree with me, dear! That was a joke.
(Pours more tea from the Thermos)
By the way, darling, how old are you? *(Pause)*
Really? That young. *(Drinks tea)* I thought
you were a little older. Oh, me? I'm 33.
(Offers the unseen actress a cupful) Would you

care for some more tea? No?
(Pause)
Can I tell you my secret for staying young?
I drink seven cups of ginseng tea every day.
This tea makes women feel young and slim
and full of youthful beauty. It rids you of
bad breath, prevents high blood pressure,
prevents acne . . . and no wrinkles. Darling,
remember the camera never lies.
*(She holds a huge silk scarf against her body.
The fan blows softly.)*
In this scene, you will be clad in a
diaphanous . . . something. You may think
this restricts your movement. But it doesn't,
if you know the art. Let the fabric press
against your body. Don't be ashamed of
the hills and valleys. And move freely
about, as if you had nothing on. I learned
this gimmick in the *Thief of Baghdad*. I
wore little less than this piece of silk.
Naturally, that got me a lot of attention. Not
my father. He called me a courtesan. A
whore.

A new light. The fan stops. ANNA *is in her
parents' laundry. She folds the scarf slowly.
She is 17 years old.*

Please, BaBa, I am not a whore. I am an
actress.
(Pause)
It is not the same thing. I am not a dis-
grace. BaBa, why should I be ashamed? I
have a nice body. I'm pretty, BaBa. You
made me who I am. You and MaMa. You
should be proud of me. When I was 12, and
working as an extra, you didn't object. I'm a
big girl now. I'm 17. I'm getting famous. All
of America is getting to know Anna May
Wong.
(Pause)
No, BaBa, I don't want to marry. I don't
want to marry anyone I don't know. Let me
choose whom I will marry. Let me choose
my life. I don't want to sweat in the steam
of the laundry. I don't want to spend my
entire life folding underwear, ironing shirts.
(Pause)
Drape me in silk and jewels. Bring me men
in tuxedos. Regale me with laughter and
champagne and parties. Just get me the hell
out of Chinatown. *(Pause)* But don't, don't
ever call me a whore! I'm an actress.

Back to the soundstage. Normal light.

Well, maybe only a "B"-movie temptress to
the people of America. But, in Europe, they
hailed me a goddess – thousands of women
imitated my hair-do. At the backstage door,
I was greeted nightly by a legion of
Cleopatras chanting my name. Ah well,
that's all behind me now. Whereas you, you
are the bright light on the horizon. You will
be called a star.
(Picks up a script. Leafs through it.)
No Chinese was ever hailed a star. No
Chinese ever got a leading role, not even
me. It's true. After Baghdad, I got work.
Supporting ones though.
(Pause)
Oh God, the Crimson City? That was 1928.
Warner Brothers. No, no. You are mistaken.
I wasn't the lead. I supported Myrna Loy.
She was the lead. Made up to look Chinese.
(Pause)
Well, for your sake, I hope MakeUp will do
a better job on you than they did on Myrna.
(Finds the page. Holds the script.)
Now for your suicide scene. When it
comes to dying, I'm the expert. I've died a
thousand different movie deaths. You see an
Oriental woman can fall in love with a
white man, as long as she conveniently
dies. Hardly realistic, nonetheless a widely
accepted celluloid truth. Oh, we Orientals
have so much to live up to. Anyway, as I
read it, this scene of yours is fairly similar
to one I played with George Raft, *Limehouse
Blues*, 1934. We dance.
*(A la Fred Astaire, she uses the ghostlight as a
dance partner. Movie music swells.)*
Do you love me? Raft flings me to the floor.
I crawl back to him. We dance. He's half
Chinese. You are leaving me for a white
woman? No, say it's not true. Raft flings me
to the floor again. I crawl back to him. We
dance. I love you. He flings me to the floor.
I say to him: *(she clings onto the ghostlight)*
You are of the East. A white girl cannot
bring happiness to you.
(She moves away from the lightstand.)
Then I betray him to the police. And then,
I kill myself. I drink a strong poison. No,
that's not it. I walk into the heaving dark
and swirling waters of the Pacific. No . . .
wait. I think that was *The Toll of the Sea*.
Ah, I probably shot myself. Yes, I think
that's what it was.

*New light. She picks up her cigarette holder.
She fixes a cigarette to it, but doesn't light it.*

George Raft? No, I never got involved with him. The newspapers always linked me romantically with Philip, Philip Ahn. What a joke! I've known Philip since high school. He was more like my brother. The stories they cook up. After I did the Von Sternberg picture *Shanghai Express*, Hollywood thought I was a lesbian. That's what having your photograph taken with Marlene Dietrich will do to you. If you are not married, you must be Marlene's lover. Well, I'm not married. I would have married Mickie Nielan. But we couldn't. We just couldn't. It's just not done, you see. Inter-racial marriage is difficult. It's against the law. It would have ruined both our careers.

(She sits in chair.)

Life mirrors the movies, movies mirror life. In the movies, as in life, you are never the wife. As an Oriental, you will be lusted for, sought after, even kept. You gave him the biggest erection in his life. But no wedding bells for you and the white man, missy. Because you are bad. You are wily, possessive, vindictive, and manipulative. You are the dragon lady, don't you know? Do you think you can handle that? Do you think you have it in you to be that sexy AND that rotten? Well, I'm tired of playing those roles. You can have them. Have them. If only you had it in you to be as good as me. Let me tell you, you are nowhere near it. Because if you were, you wouldn't need to wear that stupid wig. Please take that damn thing off. I feel like I'm staring in a funhouse mirror at a sickly version of myself.

(Mutters to herself) Why doesn't he just give me the job? I'm sexy. I don't need to wear a wig. I don't need to put on a yellow face. I don't have to study sex manuals or take lessons in how to make love to the camera. Looking for a seductress? This is an Asian role, right? Excuse me, um, what about me? I'm Oriental through and through, isn't that enough?

(Pause)

Well . . . you my dear, you have to work so much harder. Sexiness for you is an acquired attribute. But for me, it is my definition.

(Pause)

I exaggerate of course. I'm sorry. It's a strain, sometimes, to lose roles one might otherwise play. Indeed, there were things I had to learn about being Chinese, just as you are learning. I went to China for that

very reason. To find out for myself first hand, if I am truly Chinese or just an American giving an interpretation.

New light. China. A banquet hall, the dais. ANNA *speaks first in Mandarin, then relies on her interpreter.*

"Sheh, sheh, sheh, sheh. Ne mon how." Tell them, I am happy to be here in Shanghai. I'm very excited about the opportunity to work here. I am sorry my Mandarin is limited. But just give me time, I promise I will soon be conversing with you in our mother tongue. I had no idea my films have been banned. I can understand why you see my portrayals of Chinese women as degrading, but that's all Hollywood will give me. That's all Hollywood wants to see of me. That's all Hollywood knows of Chinese women. Please tell them, I can't choose my parts. Jobs for Chinese are scarce in America, especially in the cinema. But I assure you, I am here in China to learn more about myself, and to bring a better interpretation to the rest of the world. *(Applause. She smiles.)*

New light, back to the soundstage. ANNA *addresses the actress.*

But they didn't know what to do with me. Over there, they thought I was too "white" to play Chinese, and back here, I'm just too "yellow." *(In Chinese:* You can't please either one.*)*

(Pause)

I stayed in China for nine months. I learned to speak Mandarin, just as I learned to speak German when I was in Germany. When I was in London, I acquired an Etonian accent, at considerable expense. I picked up French on my own. I was determined to conquer any barrier, to fight in any language for recognition as an actress.

(Pause)

Acting is my priority. I eat, drink, sleep, breathe acting. I don't know how to do anything else. I don't want to do anything else. I even gave up marriage for my career. I'm not telling you to give up marriage, all I'm saying, is if you have a dream, go after it. Fight for it.

New light. The office of Irving Thalberg. 1936. Long pause.

Mr. Thalberg, I've been waiting all my life for a role like this. This is 1936, not 1926. It's time for a truer portrayal of the Chinese. I know you agree with me, don't you?

(Pause)

Mr. Thalberg, I'm perfect for the role of O-Lan. Perfect. That role was made for me. Luise Rainer is a fine actress, of course, but she's German. She doesn't even look Chinese. *The Good Earth* is the most sympathetic movie on a Chinese subject and you are telling me NO?

(Pause)

Does this have something to do with the Doris Mackie interview? You can't possibly blackball me for that. That interview was three years ago. I won't deny what I said. Isn't it true, we Chinese always play the villains – murderous, treacherous, snakes in the grass. O-Lan is the first sympathetic role. That is why this role means so much to me.

(Pause)

Do you mean to tell me that a Chinese cannot play a Chinese? Are you saying, sir, that I do not know how to play myself? No, I won't calm down. Let me try to understand. In your opinion, Miss Rainer has as much right to this role as I do, and her interpretation would be just as valid as mine because this is acting after all. I strongly protest. It is not the same. It is not the same.

Back to the soundstage. Pause.

(To herself) The role of a lifetime to a German. I could start World War II myself.

(Pause)

What? Where were we? Sorry. Shall we try your swooning technique? Scenes 17, 78, 102. Now swoon.

(She watches impatiently.)

Stop! What was that you think you're doing? That's not swooning. You do not buckle your knees forward and lunge like a buffalo. That is the American way of dropping dead. We Asiatics are much more delicate. Pay attention, please.

(She gets up, demonstrates.)

First the knees wobble, then you shift your weight to the right side, and then . . . the head falls back gently and slightly to the left. Then you press, not clutch, at his chest wherein lies his beating heart. Do you see the difference. Yah? Now you try.

(She watches. Pause.)

Nein, nein, nein. *(Pause)* Absolutely, nyet! Think in oppositions. Oppositions! Try again. Swoon gracefully, please!

(A knock is heard.)

Yes, come in. I see. We're not through with the lesson yet, but I defer to duty. Miss Harrington, your limousine is here to take you to the location. Acting must come first. Well, we will continue our swooning tomorrow. Yes, same time. Goodbye.

(Pause. ANNA *lights her cigarette. Another pause. She picks up the receiver of a telephone, dials the office of Samuel Goldwyn. Pause)*

Hello? Mr. Goldwyn, please. This is Anna May Wong calling. Tell him it's urgent. It's regarding Miss Harrington.

(A short pause)

Hello, Sam? Sam, I can't work with this girl. Sam. I can't take any more of this. I can't teach this starlet anything. Her swooning technique is atrocious. She's too stiff. She's slow. She's not right for the part at all. I showed her how to cross her legs, the way a Chinese girl would do it. Emphasize the silky line of your calves, I said. But she's a cow. Her eyes twitch like marbles in a sack. She's a nervous Nelly. She's no good. Sam, I can do this role. Let me have it.

(A short pause)

Yes, yes. I know you need a scene coach first and foremost. Yes, but damn it, Mr. Goldwyn. This is killing me, Mr. Goldwyn. Please, don't discard me, put me on the shelf like a . . . China doll.

(Pause)

Yes. I understand. We discuss this in your office. Tomorrow? The next day then. Very well. At your convenience. *(She hangs up the phone.)*

(Long pause)

(To audience) Why won't they let me do what I . . . what I love most of all? I'm not a teacher. I'm an actress.

(Lights out)

Appendix

Published plays by American women of color

Selected works after 1940

Editor's Note: Plays marked * appear in more than one source.
We have listed either the most recent or the most available publication.

African American

ABRAMSON, DOLORES. *The Light. Three Hundred and Sixty Degrees of Blackness Comin' at You.* Ed. Sonia Sanchez. New York: 5X Publishing Co., 1971.

ADAMS, JANUS. *St. Stephen: A Passion Play. Confirmation.* Eds. Amiri and Amina Bakara. New York: William Morrow and Co., 1983.

AMIS, LOLA JONES. *Exploring the Black Experience in America.* New York: Franklin Square, 1976.

ANDERSON, T. DIANE. *The Unicorn Died at Dawn: Plays and Poems and Other Writings.* Luzt, Florida: Anderson Publishing, 1981.

BATSON, SUSAN. *Hoodoo Talkin. Three Hundred and Sixty Degrees of Blackness Comin at You.* Ed. Sonia Sanchez. New York: 5X Publishing Co., 1971.

BEALE, TITA. *A Just Piece. Liberator.* June 1970, 16.

BEASLEY, ELOIS. *The Fallen Angel. New Plays for the Black Theatre.* Ed. Woodie King, Jr. Chicago: Third World Press, 1989.

BOHANAN, MARY. *Find the Girl. A Galaxy of Black Writing.* Ed. R. Baird Shuman. Durham, North Carolina: Moore Publishing Co., 1970.

BROWN-GUILLORY, ELIZABETH. *Bayou Relics.* Colorado Springs, Colorado: Contemporary Drama Service, 1983.

——*Mam Phyliss. Wines in the Wilderness: Plays by African American Women from the Harlem Renaissance to the Present.* Ed. Elizabeth Brown-Guillory. New York: Greenwood Press, 1990.

——*Snapshots of Broken Dolls.* Colorado Springs, Colorado: Contemporary Drama Service, 1987.

CARLOS, LAURIE, JESSICA HAGEDORN and ROBBIE MCCAULEY. *Teenytown. Out From Under: Texts by Women Performance Artists.* Ed. Lenora Champagne. New York: Theatre Communications Group, Inc., 1990.

CHARLES, MARTIE. *Black Cycle. Black Drama Anthology.* Eds. Woodie King and Ron Milner. New York: Columbia University Press, 1972.

CHILDRESS, ALICE. *The African Garden. Black Scenes.* Ed. Alice Childress. New York: Doubleday, 1971.

——*Let's Hear It for the Queen.* New York: Coward, McCann, and Geohegan, 1975.

——*Mojo and String; Two Plays.* New York: Dramatists Play Service, 1971.

——**Trouble in Mind. Black Drama in America,* Ed. Darwin T. Turner. Washington, D.C.: Howard University Press, 1994.

——**Wedding Band: A Love/Hate Story in Black and White. 9 Plays by Black Women.* Ed. Margaret B. Wilkerson. New York: New American Library, 1986.

——*When the Rattlesnake Sounds.* New York: Coward, McCann and Geohegan, 1975.

——*Wine in the Wilderness. Wines in the Wilderness: Plays by African American Women from the Harlem Renaissance to the Present.* Ed. Elizabeth Brown-Guillory. New York: Greenwood Press, 1990.

CLARK, CHINA. *Perfection in Black. Scripts 7.* May 1972.

CLARKE, BREENA and GLENDA DICKERSON. *Re/membering Aunt Jemima: A Menstrual Show. Women & Performance: A Journal of Feminist Theory.* Vol. 6, No. 1, Issue 11, 1993, 95–130.

CLEAGE, PEARL. *Chains. Playwriting Women: 7 Plays from the Women's Project.* Ed. Julia Miles. Portsmouth, New Hampshire: Heinemann, 1993.

——*Flyin' West. Black Drama in America.* Ed. Darwin T. Turner. Washington, D.C.: Howard University Press, 1994.

——**Hospice**. *The Woman That I Am: The Literature and Culture of Contemporary Women of Color*. Ed. D. Soyini Madison. New York: St. Martin's Press, 1994.

——**Late Bus to Mecca**. *Playwriting Women: 7 Plays from the Women's Project*. Ed. Julia Miles. Portsmouth, New Hampshire: Heinemann, 1993.

COLLINS, KATHLEEN. **The Brothers**. *9 Plays by Black Women*. Ed. Margaret B. Wilkerson. New York: New American Library, 1986.

——**In the Midnight Hour**. *The Women's Project*. New York: An American Place Theatre Performing Arts Journal, 1981.

COOPER, JOAN "CALIFORNIA." **Loners**. *Center Stage: an Anthology of Twenty-one Contemporary Black-American Plays*. Ed. Eileen Joyce Ostrow. Urbana: The University of Illinois Press, 1991.

CORTHRON, KIA. **Cage Rhythm**. *Moon Marked and Touched by Sun*. Ed. Sydne Mahone. New York: Theatre Communications Group, Inc., 1994.

DAVIS, THULANI. **X**. *Moon Marked and Touched by Sun*. Ed. Sydne Mahone. New York: Theatre Communications Group, Inc., 1994.

DEVAUX, ALEXIS. **The Tapestry**. *9 Plays by Black* Women. Ed. Margaret B. Wilkerson. New York: New American Library, 1986.

DICKERSON, GLENDA · BREENA CLARKE. **Re/membering Aunt Jemima: A Menstrual Show**. *Women and Performance: A Journal of Feminist Theory*. Vol. 6, No. 1, Issue 11, 1993, 95–130.

FLANAGAN, BRENDA A. **When the Jumbie Bird Calls**. *Roots and Blossoms: African American Plays for Today*. Ed. Daphne Williams Ntri. Troy, Michigan: Bedford Publishers, 1991.

FRANKLIN, J.E. **Black Girl**. New York: Dramatist Play Service, 1971.

——**Miss Honey's Young'uns**. *Black Drama in America: An Anthology*. Ed. Darwin T. Turner. Washington, D. C.: Howard University Press, 1994.

GIBSON, P.J. **Brown Silk and Magenta Sunsets**. *9 Plays by Black Women*. Ed. Margaret B. Wilkerson. New York: The New American Library, 1986.

——**Long Time Since Yesterday**. New York: Samuel French, Inc., 1984.

HAMILTON, DENISE. **Parallax (In Honor of Daisy Bates)**. *Women Heroes: Six Short Plays from the Women's Project*. Ed. Julia Miles. New York: Applause Theatre Book Publishers, 1986.

HOUSTON, DIANNE. **The Fisherman**. *Center Stage: An Anthology of Twenty-one Contemporary Black-American Plays*. Ed. Eileen Joyce Ostrow. Urbana: The University of Illinois Press, 1991.

JACKSON, ANGELA. **Shango Diaspora: An African-American Myth of Womanhood and Love**. *The Woman That I Am*. Ed. D. Soyini Madison. New York: St. Martin's Press, 1994.

JACKSON, CHERRY. **In the Master's House There are Many Mansions**. *Center Stage: An Anthology of Twenty-one Contemporary Black-American Plays*. Ed. Eileen Joyce Ostrow. Urbana: The University of Illinois Press, 1991.

JACKSON, ELAINE. **Paper Dolls**. *9 Plays by Black Women*. Ed. Margaret B. Wilkerson. New York: New American Library, 1986.

——**Toe Jam**. *Black Drama Anthology*. Eds. Woodie King and Ron Milner. New York: New American Library, 1972.

JACKSON, JUDITH ALEXA. **WOMBman WARs**: *Moon Marked and Touched by Sun*. Ed. Sydne Mahone. New York: Theatre Communications Group, Inc., 1994.

JOHNSON, FRANCINE. **The Right Reason**. *Roots and Blossoms: African American Plays for Today*. Ed. Daphne Williams Ntri. Troy, Michigan: Bedford Publishers, 1991.

KENNEDY, ADRIENNE. **Adrienne Kennedy in One Act**. Minneapolis: University of Minnesota Press, 1988.

——**The Alexander Plays**. Minneapolis: University of Minnesota Press, 1992.

——**The Dramatic Circle**. *Moon Marked and Touched by Sun*. Ed. Sydne Mahone. New York: Theatre Communications Group, Inc., 1994.

——**The Lennon Play: In His Own Write**. New York: Simon and Schuster, 1972.

——**A Movie Star Has to Star in Black and White**. *Wordplay 3*. New York: Performing Arts Journal Publication, 1984.

——**She Talks to Beethoven**. *Plays in One Act*. Ed. Daniel Halpern. New York: The Ecco Press, 1991.

——*Sun: A Poem for Malcolm X Inspired by His Murder*. Scripts 1. May 1972, 5–28.

KIMBALL, KATHLEEN. *Meat Rack*. Scripts 7. May 1972.

KING, RAMONA. *Steal Away*. New York: Samuel French, 1982.

KLEIN, SYBIL. *Get Together*. Wines in the Wilderness: Plays by African American Women from the Harlem Renaissance to the Present. Ed. Elizabeth Brown-Guillory. New York: Greenwood Press, 1990.

MARTIN, SHARON STOCKARD. *Cannned Soul*. Callaloo. Spring 1975.

——*The Moving Violation*. Center Stage: An Anthology of Twenty-one Contemporary Black-American Plays. Ed. Eileen Joyce Ostrow. Urbana: The University of Illinois Press, 1991.

——*Proper and Fine*. The Search. New York: Scholastic Book Services, 1972.

MASON, JUDI ANN. *Livin' Fat*. New York: Samuel French, 1976.

MCCAULEY, ROBBIE, LAURIE CARLOS, and JESSICA HAGEDORN. *Sally's Rape*. Moon Marked and Touched by Sun. Ed. Sydne Mahone. New York: Theatre Communications Group, Inc., 1994.

——*Teenytown*. Out from Under Texts by Women Performance Artists. Ed. Lenora Champagne. New York: Theatre Communications Group, Inc., 1990.

MEDLEY, CASSANDRA. *Ma Rose*. WomensWork: Five New Plays from the Women's Project. Ed. Julia Miles. New York: Applause Theatre Book Publishers, 1989.

——*Waking Women*. Plays in One Act. Ed. Daniel Halpern. New York: The Ecco Press, 1991.

MOLETTE, BARBARA and CARLTON. *Dr. B. S. Black*. SADSA Encore. Nashville: SADSA, 1970.

——*Noah's Ark*. Center Stage: An Anthology of Twenty-one Contemporary Black-American Plays. Ed. Eileen Joyce Ostrow. Urbana: The University of Illinois Press, 1991.

——*Rosalee Pritchett*. Black Writers of America. Eds. Richard K. Barksdale and Kenneth Kinnamon. New York: Macmillan, 1972.

NSABE, NIA. *Mama Don't Know What Love Is*. Three Hundred and Sixty Degrees of Blackness Comin' at You. Ed. Sonia Sanchez. New York: 5X Publishing Co., 1971.

NUBIA, KAI. *The Last of the Reapers*. Roots and Blossoms: African American Plays for Today. Ed. Daphne Williams Ntri. Troy, Michigan: Bedford Publishers, 1991.

PARKS, SUZAN-LORI. *The American Play*. American Theatre. March 1994, 25–39.

——*Betting on the Dust Commander* (Practice Makes Practice Makes), New York: The Playwrights' Press, 1987.

——*Death of the Last Black Man in the Whole Entire World*. Women on the Verge: 7 Avant-Garde American Plays. Ed. Rosette C. Lamont. New York: Applause Theatre Book Publishers, 1993.

——*Imperceptible Mutabilities in the Third Kingdom*. The Best of Off-Broadway: Eight Contemporary Obie-Winning Plays. Ed. Ross Wetzstoen. New York: Mentor Original, 1994.

——*Snails*. The Best American Short Plays, 1990–1992. Eds. Howard Stein and Glenn Young. Garden City, New Jersey: The Fireside Theatre, 1992.

PARRIS-BAILEY, LINDA. *Dark Cowgirls and Prairie Queens*. Alternate Roots Plays from the Southern Theatre. Eds. Kathie deNobriga and Valetta Anderson. Portsmouth, New Hampshire, Heinemann, 1994.

RAHMAN, AISHA. *The Mojo and the Sayso*. Moon Marked and Touched by Sun. Ed. Sydne Mahone. New York: Theatre Communications Group, Inc., 1994.

——*Unfinished Women Cry in No Man's Land While A Bird Dies in a Gilded Cage*. 9 Plays by Black Women. Ed. Margaret B. Wilkerson. New York: New American Library, 1986.

RHODES, CRYSTAL. *The Trip*. Center Stage: An Anthology of Twenty-one Contemporary Black-American Plays. Ed. Eileen Joyce Ostrow. Urbana: The University of Illinois Press, 1991.

RICHARDS, BEAH. *A Black Woman Speaks*. 9 Plays by Black Women. Ed. Margaret B. Wilkerson. New York: New American Library, 1986.

SANCHEZ, SONIA. *Dirty Hearts*. Scripts 1. November 1971.

——*Malcolm/Man Don't Live Here No Mo*. Black Theatre 6. 1972.

——*Sister Son/ji*. Wines in the Wilderness: Plays by African American Women from the Harlem Renaissance to the Present. Ed. Elizabeth Brown-Guillory. New York: Greenwood Press, 1990.

——*"Uh Huh, But How do It Free Us?"* The New Lafayette Theatre Presents. Ed. Ed Bullins. New York: Anchor Press, Doubleday, 1974.

SHANGE, NTOZAKE. *Daddy Says*. New Plays for the Black Theatre. Ed. Woodie King, Jr.

Chicago: Third World Press, 1989.

——*A Daughter's Geography*. New York: St. Martin's Press, 1983.

——*for colored girls who have considered suicide/when the rainbow is enuf*. New York: Macmillan, 1977.

——*From Okra to Greens*. St. Louis: CoffeeHouse Press, 1984.

——*The Resurrection of the Daughter: Liliane*. (excerpts) *Moon Marked and Touched by Sun*. Ed. Sydne Mahone. New York: Theatre Communications Group, Inc., 1994.

——*Spell #7: A Theatre Piece in Two Acts*. New York: Samuel French, 1981.

——*Three Pieces*. New York: St. Martins Press, 1981.

SHARP, SAUNDRA. *the sistuhs*. Los Angeles: Poets Pay Rent, Too, 1990.

SMITH, ANNA DEAVERE. *Fires in the Mirror: Crown Heights, Brooklyn, and Other Identities*. New York: Doubleday, 1993.

——*Fires in the Mirror: Crown Heights, Brooklyn, and Other Identities* (excerpts). *Moon Marked and Touched by Sun*. Ed. Sydne Mahone. New York: Theatre Communications Group, Inc., 1994.

——*Piano*. New York: Theatre Communications Group Plays-in-Progress. Vol. 9, No. 10, 1989.

——*Twilight: Los Angeles, 1992*. New York: Doubleday, 1994.

STILES, THELMA JACKSON. *No One Man Show*. *Center Stage: An Anthology of Twenty-one Contemporary Black-American Plays*. Ed. Eileen Joyce Ostrow. Urbana: The University of Illinois Press, 1991.

TAYLOR, REGINA. *The Ties That Bind*. Woodstock, Illinois: Dramatic Publishing, 1995.

——*Watermelon Rinds*. *Best American Short Plays. 1992–1993*. Eds. Howard Stein and Glenn Young. New York: Applause Theatre Book Publishers, 1993.

VANCE, DANITRA. *Live and in Color*. *Moon Marked and Touched by Sun*. Ed. Sydne Mahone. New York: Theatre Communications Group, Inc., 1994.

WELCH, LEONA NICHOLAS. *Hands in the Mirror*. *Center Stage: An Anthology of Twenty-one Contemporary Black-American Plays*. Ed. Eileen Joyce Ostrow. Urbana: The University of Illinois Press, 1991.

WEST, CHERYL, L. *Jar the Floor*. *Women Playwrights: The Best Plays of 1992*. Eds. Robyn Goodman and Marisa Smith. Newbury, Vermont: Smith and Kraus Books, 1992.

WIDEMAN, ANGELA. *Hard to Serve*. *Roots and Blossoms: African American Plays for Today*. Ed. Daphne Williams Ntri. Troy, Michigan: Bedford Publishers, 1991.

WILLIAMS, ANITA JAMES. *A Christmas Story*. *Center Stage: An Anthology of Twenty-one Contemporary Black-American Plays*. Ed. Eileen Joyce Ostrow. Urbana: The University of Illinois Press, 1991.

YOUNGBLOOD, SHAY. *Shakin' The Mess Outta Misery*. Woodstock, Illinois: The Dramatic Publishing Company, 1994.

——*Talking Bones*. Woodstock, Illinois: The Dramatic Publishing Company, 1994.

Asian American

AMANO, LYNETTE. *Ashes*. *Kumu Kahua Plays*. Ed. Dennis Carroll. Honolulu: University of Hawaii Press, 1983.

BARROGA, JEANNIE. *Two Plays by Jeannie Barroga*. San Francisco: CrossCurrent Press, 1993.

——*Walls*. *Unbroken Thread: An Anthology of Plays by Asian American Women*. Ed. Roberta Uno. Amherst: University of Massachusetts Press, 1993.

CHOW, DIANA. *An Asian Man of a Different Color*. *Kumu Kahua Plays*. Ed. Dennis Carroll. Honolulu: University of Hawaii Press, 1983.

CHUN (now YEE), WAI CHEE. *For You a Lei*. *Paké: Writings by Chinese in Hawaii*, Ed. Eric Chock. Honolulu: Bamboo Ridge Press, 1989.

HAGEDORN, JESSICA (with LAURIE CARLOS and ROBBIE MCCAULEY). *Teenytown*. *Out From Under: Texts by Women Performance Artists*. Ed. Lenora Champagne. New York: Theatre Communications Group,. Inc., 1990.

——*Tenement Lover: no palm trees/in new york city*. *Between Worlds*: Contemporary Asian-American Plays. Ed. Misha Berson. New York: Theatre Communications Group, Inc., 1990.

HOUSTON, VELINA HASU. **Asa Ga Kimashita**. *The Politics of Life: Four Plays by Asian American Women*. Ed. Velina Hasu Houston. Philadelphia: Temple University Press, 1993.

——*Tea*. *Unbroken Threads: An Anthology of Plays by Asian American Women*. Ed. Roberta Uno. Amherst: University of Massachusetts Press, 1993.

IKO, MOMOKO. **The Gold Watch**. *Unbroken Thread: An Anthology of Plays by Asian American Women*. Ed. Roberta Uno. Amherst: University of Massachusetts Press, 1993.

INOUYE, BESSIE TOISHIGAWA. **Reunion**. *Kumu Kahua Plays*. Ed. Dennis Carroll. Honolulu: University of Hawaii Press, 1983.

KUBOJIRI, CLARA. **Country Pie**. *Talk Story: Big Island Anthology*. Eds. Steven Sumida and Martha Webb. Honolulu: University of Hawaii Press, 1979.

LEE, G.M. **One in Sisterhood: Asian Women.** *Asian Women's Journal*. Ed. Emma Gee. Berkeley: University of California at Berkeley, 1971.

LIM, GENNY. **Bitter Cane**. *Bitter Cane and Paper Angels: Two Plays by Genny Lim*. Honolulu: Kalamaku Press, 1991.

——**Bitter Cane**. *The Politics of Life: Four Plays by Asian American Women*. Ed. Velina Hasu Houston. Philadelphia: Temple University Press, 1993.

——*Paper Angels*. *Unbroken Thread: An Anthology of Plays by Asian American Women*. Ed. Roberta Uno. Amherst: University of Massachusetts Press, 1993.

LIM-HING, SHARON. **Superdyke, the Banana Metaphor and the Triply Oppressed Object**. *Piece of My Heart*. Cambridge: Sister Vision Press, 1992.

LUM, CHARLOTTE. **These Unsaid Things**. *Paké: Writings by Chinese in Hawaii*. Ed. Eric Chock. Honolulu: Bamboo Ridge Press, 1989.

NODA, BARBARA. Excerpts from **Aw, Shucks**. *Vortex*. Vol. 1, No. 4, Fall 1981, San Francisco, 1989.

SANBO, AMY. **Sukiyaki Mama**. *Western Edge*. Seattle: publisher unknown, 1978.

TOISHIGAWA (INOUYE), BESSE. **Reunion**. *Kumu Kahua Plays*. Ed. Dennis Carroll. Honolulu: University of Hawaii Press, 1983.

WONG, ELIZABETH. **Assume the Position**. *Script Magazine*. New York: New York University, 1990, 42–84.

——**Letters to a Student Revolutionary**. *Unbroken Thread: An Anthology of Plays by Asian American Women*. Ed. Roberta Uno. Amherst: University of Massachusetts Press, 1993.

YAMAUCHI, WAKAKO. **12-1-A**. *The Politics of Life: Four Plays by Asian American Women*. Ed. Velina Hasu Houston. Philadelphia: Temple University Press, 1993.

——*And the Soul Shall Dance*. *Between Worlds: Contemporary Asian-American Plays*. Ed. Misha Berson. New York: Theatre Communications Group, Inc., 1990.

——**The Chairman's Wife**. *The Politics of Life: Four Plays by Asian American Women*. Ed. Velina Hasu Houston. Philadelphia: Temple University Press, 1993.

——**The Music Lessons**. *Unbroken Thread: An Anthology of Plays by Asian American Women*. Ed. Roberta Uno. Amherst: University of Massachusetts Press, 1993.

Latina

ALVAREZ, LYNNE. **Don Juan of Seville**. New York: Theatre Communications Group Plays-in-Progress. Vol. 10, 1989–90.

——**The Guitarrón**. *On New Ground: Contemporary Hispanic-American Plays*. Ed. M. Elizabeth Osborn. New York: Theatre Communications Group, Inc., 1987.

——**Tirso de Molina's Don Juan of Seville**. New York: New Dramatists Playwrights' Press, 1990.

CHAVEZ, DENISE. **Novena Narrativas**. *The Woman That I Am: The Literature and Culture of Contemporary Women of Color*. New York: St. Martin's Press, 1994.

CRUZ, MIGDALIA. **Dreams of Home**. *The Best American Short Plays 1990–92*. Eds. Howard Stein and Glenn Young. Garden City, New Jersey: The Fireside Theatre, 1992.

——**Miriam's Flowers**. *Shattering the Myth: Plays by Hispanic Women*. Ed. Linda Feyder. Houston: Arte Publico Press, 1992.

FORNES, MARÍA IRENE. **Abingdon Square**. *WomensWork: Five New Plays from the Women's Project*. Ed. Julia Miles. New York: Applause Theatre Book Publishers, 1989.

——(trans./adapt.) **Cold Air**, by Virgilio Pinera. New York: Theatre Communications Group Plays-in-Progress. Vol. 6, No. 10, 1985.

——**The Conduct of Life**. *On New Ground: Contemporary Hispanic-American Plays*. Ed. M. Elizabeth Osborn. New York: Theatre Communications Group, Inc., 1987.

——**The Danube**. *María Irene Fornes Plays*. Preface by Susan Sontag. New York: PAJ Publications (a division of Performing Arts Journal, Inc.), 1986.

——**Dr. Kheal**. *Promenade and Other Plays*. New York: Winter House, 1971.

——**Lovers and Keepers**. New York: Theatre Communications Group Plays-in-Progress, Vol. 7, No. 10, 1986.

——**Molly's Dream**. *Promenade and Other Plays*. New York: Winter House, 1971.

——**Mud**. *María Irene Fornes Plays*. Preface by Susan Sontag. New York: PAJ Publications (a division of Performing Arts Journal, Inc.), 1986.

——**Promenade**. *Promenade and Other Plays*. New York: Winter House, 1971.

——**Sarita**. *Maria Irene Fornes Plays*. Preface by Susan Sontag. New York: PAJ Publications (a division of Performing Arts Journal, Inc.), 1986.

——**The Successful Life of Three: A Skit for Vaudeville**. *Promenade and Other Plays*. New York: Winter House, 1971.

——**Tango Palace**. *Promenade and Other Plays*. New York: Winter House, 1971.

——**A Vietnamese Wedding**. *Promenade and Other Plays*. New York: Winter House, 1971.

——**What of the Nights**. *Women on the Verge: 7 Avant-Garde American Plays*. Ed. Rosette C. Lamont. New York: Applause Theatre Book Publishers, 1993.

LÓPEZ, EVA. **Marlene**. *Nuestro New York*. Ed. John V. Antush. New York: Mentor, 1994.

LÓPEZ, JOSEFINA. **Simply Maria, or The American Dream**. *Shattering the Myth: Plays by Hispanic Women*. Ed. Linda Feyder. Houston: Arte Publica Press, 1992.

MORAGA, CHERRÍE. **Giving up the Ghost: Teatro in Two Acts**. Los Angeles: West End Press, 1986.

——**Heroes and Saints and Other Plays**. Alberquerque: West End Press, 1994.

——**Shadow of a Man**. *Shattering the Myth: Plays by Hispanic Women*. Ed. Linda Feyder. Houston: Arte Publico Press, 1992.

PORTILLO, ESTELA. **The Day of the Swallows: A Drama in Three Acts**. *The Woman That I Am: The Literature and Culture of Contemporary Women of Color*. Ed. D. Soyini Madison. New York: St. Martin's Press, 1994.

PRIDA, DELORES. **Beautiful Senoritas and Other Plays**. Ed. Judith Weiss. Houston: Arte Publico Press, 1992.

RAMIREZ, IVETTE M. **Family Scenes**. *Recent Puerto Rican Theatre: Five Plays from New York*. Ed. John Antush. Houston: Arte Publico Press, 1991.

RODRIGUEZ, YOLANDA. **Rising Sun, Falling Star**. *Nuestro New York*. Ed. John V. Antush. New York: Mentor, 1994.

SÁENZ, DIANA. **A Dream of Canaries**. *Shattering the Myth: Plays by Hispanic Women*. Ed. Linda Feyder. Houston: Arte Publico Press, 1992.

SANCHEZ-SCOTT, MILCHA. **The Cuban Swimmer**. *Plays in One Act*. Ed. Daniel Halpern. New York: The Ecco Press, 1991.

——***Dog Lady and The Cuban Swimmer: Two Related Short Plays**. New York: Theatre Communications Group Plays-in-Progress, Vol. 5, No. 12.

——**Evening Star**. New York: Dramatists Play Service, Inc., 1989.

——**Roosters**. *On New Ground: Contemporary Hispanic-American Plays*. Ed. M. Elizabeth Osborn. New York: Theatre Communications Group, Inc., 1987.

SIMO, ANNA MARIA. **Going to New England**. New York: Theatre Communications Group Plays-in-Progress, Vol. 11, No. 12, 1991.

SVICH, CARIDAD. **Gleaning/Rebusca**. *Shattering the Myth: Plays by Hispanic Women*. Ed. Linda Feyder. Houston: Arte Publico Press, 1992.

VILLARREAL, EDIT. **My Visits with MGM**. *Shattering the Myth: Plays by Hispanic Women*. Ed. Linda Feyder. Houston: Arte Publico Press, 1992.

Native American

GLANCY, DIANE. *War Cries: A Collection of Plays*. Duluth, Minnesota: Holy Cow! Press, 1995.

KEAMS, GERALDINE. *The Flight of the Army Worm*. The Remembered Earth: An Anthology of Contemporary Native American Literature. Ed. Geary Hobson. Albuquerque: University of New Mexico Press, 1981.

MOJICA, MONIQUE. *Princess Pocahontas and the Blue Spots*. Toronto: Women's Press, 1991.

SPIDERWOMAN. *Winnetou's Snake Oil Show from Wigwam City*. Canadian Review. Fall, 1991, 54–63.